New Directions in the Study of Foreign Policy

New Directions in the Study of Foreign Policy

EDITED BY

Charles F. Hermann
Ohio State University

Charles W. Kegley, Jr.
University of South Carolina

James N. Rosenau
University of Southern California

HarperCollins *Academic*
An imprint of HarperCollins*Publishers*

Published by
HarperCollinsAcademic
77-85 Fulham Palace Road
Hammersmith
London W6 8JB, UK

First published in 1987
Fourth impression 1989
Fifth impression 1991

British Library Cataloguing in Publication Data

New directions in the study of foreign policy.
Bibliography: p.
Includes index.
1. International relations – Research. I. Hermann, Charles F.,
1938–   II. Kegley, Charles W.   III. Rosenau, James N.
JX1291.N49   1986   327'.072   86-17282
ISBN 0-04-327093-X (alk. paper)
ISBN 0-04-327094-8 (pbk.: alk. paper)

Library of Congress Cataloging in Publication Data

New directions in the study of foreign policy.
1. International relations – Research
2. International relations – Methodology
I. Hermann, Charles F.   II. Kegley, Charles W.
III. Rosenau, James N.
327.1'01'8   JX1291
ISBN 0-04-327093-X
ISBN 0-04-327094-8 Pbk

Typeset in 10 on 12 point Palatino by Phoenix Photosetting, Chatham
and printed in Great Britain by Biddles Ltd, Guildford, Surrey

Contents

Acknowledgements   xi

1 *Introduction: New Directions and Recurrent Questions in
   the Comparative Study of Foreign Policy,*
   JAMES N. ROSENAU   1

PART I

Assessments and Proposals
for the Field

2 *The Evolution and Future of Theoretical Research in the
   Comparative Study of Foreign Policy,*
   CHARLES F. HERMANN and GREGORY PEACOCK   13

3 *Political Economy Approaches to the Comparative Study of
   Foreign Policy,* BRUCE E. MOON   33

4 *Toward Single-Country Theories of Foreign Policy: The
   Case of the USSR,* JAMES N. ROSENAU   53

PART II

Foreign Policy Patterns, Performances and Evaluations

5 *A Lag Sequential Approach to the Analysis of Foreign Policy
   Behavior,* WILLIAM J. DIXON   77

6 *Evaluation: A Neglected Task for the Comparative Study of
   Foreign Policy,* GREGORY A. RAYMOND   96

7 *Understanding Anomalous Success: Japan, Taiwan and
   South Korea,* DAVIS B. BOBROW and STEVE CHAN   111

8 *Substituting Arms and Alliances, 1870–1914: An
   Exploration in Comparative Foreign Policy,*
   BENJAMIN A. MOST AND RANDOLPH M. SIVERSON   131

Contents

PART III

Foreign Policy as an Interactive Process

9   *Dyadic Case Studies in the Comparative Study of Foreign Policy Behavior,* NEIL R. RICHARDSON   161

10   *Structure and Action in Militarized Disputes,* RUSSELL J. LENG   178

PART IV

Cognitive Processes in Foreign Policy Decisions

11   *Opening the Black Box: Cognitive Processing and Optimal Choice in Foreign Policy Decision Making,* CHARLES A. POWELL, HELEN E. PURKITT and JAMES W. DYSON   203

12   *Analogical Reasoning and the Definition of the Situation: Back to Snyder for Concepts and Forward to Artificial Intelligence for Method,* DWAIN MEFFORD   221

PART V

The Collective Process of Foreign Policy Decision Making

13   *Decision Regimes and the Comparative Study of Foreign Policy,* CHARLES W. KEGLEY, JR.   247

14   *Role Theory and the Origins of Foreign Policy,* STEPHEN G. WALKER   269

15   *What Do Decision Makers Do When They Make a Foreign Policy Decision? The Implications for the Comparative Study of Foreign Policy,* PAUL A. ANDERSON   285

16   *How Decision Units Shape Foreign Policy Behavior,* MARGARET G. HERMANN, CHARLES F. HERMANN and JOE D. HAGAN   309

PART VI

Domestic Influences on Foreign Policy

17   *Regimes, Political Oppositions, and the Comparative Analysis of Foreign Policy,* JOE D. HAGAN   339

Contents

18 Foreign Policy, Learning, and War, JOHN A. VASQUEZ   366

19 Cultural Influences on Foreign Policy,
    MARTIN W. SAMPSON III   384

PART VII

International Influences on Foreign Policy

20 Opportunity, Willingness, and Small States: The
    Relationship Between Environment and Foreign Policy,
    MARIA PAPADAKIS and HARVEY STARR   409

21 Soviet Behavior, Presidential Popularity, and the
    Penetration of Open Political Systems: A Diachronic
    Analysis, EUGENE R. WITTKOPF and MARK J. DEHAVEN   433

22 International Organizations and Foreign Policy: Influence
    and Instrumentality, MARGARET P. KARNS and
    KAREN A. MINGST   454

References   475

About the Authors   525

Index   530

*Dedicated to the
memory of
BENJAMIN A. MOST,
respected colleague and valued
contributor to this volume.*

Acknowledgements

Before offering words of acknowledgement, some mention of the context that led to this book's production may add to the understanding of the kind of assistance we have received from many people. In preparing this collection of original studies our efforts have been animated by the conviction that the appropriate time has arrived to assess the state of the field of cross-national and longitudinal studies of foreign policy and to stimulate new theoretical and empirical developments. Accordingly, a major conference, co-sponsored by the Mershon Center at The Ohio State University, the Department of Government and International Studies at the University of South Carolina, and the Institute of Transnational Studies at the University of Southern California, was organized and held May 9–11, 1985, at The Ohio State University in Columbus.

The premise behind the conference and this resulting book was that new initiatives could be fostered by presenting recent research and proposals for new departures by both young and senior scholars, subjecting them to careful review, and by assessing trends in the field. We believed that many scholars working in this field were only minimally aware of the recent developments of others who were taking somewhat different approaches from their own. Thus, this conference was seen as an occasion for an exchange and dialogue on current developments and on the trends and needs for future research.

We issued a broad call for candidate papers for the conference. The response to our invitation to submit proposals for papers was extremely gratifying. After a careful screening of submitted paper proposals, we selected authors whose proposals best advanced the purposes of the conference. Our great regret remains that funding was not available to bring scholars from outside of North America to the session. We recognize that much valuable research in the field is going on elsewhere and that the increased interaction among this larger community of scholars must be encouraged.

With hindsight after the conference, it became apparent to us that the foundation had been created for a volume that would capture in a more permanent form many of the exciting papers presented. All selected authors for this book were admonished to revise their papers to take into account the extensive exchanges that had taken place at the conference over each paper and to relate their own work whenever possible to other studies selected for inclusion. As editors, we appreciate the responsiveness of our contributors to these requests.

The book's central mission is to serve as a sourcebook, to characterize the scope of current research in the United States in this field and to serve as a catalyst for future inquiries. In pursuing this objective we have been assisted by many people.

At the outset, we would like to extend out appreciation to our respective institutions for their financial assistance and faith in the vision that has motivated the undertaking of this project, and for the belief in the intellectual value of this venture that their support expresses. We are, of course, indebted greatly to our colleagues who so capably responded to our calls for papers and our requests for revision. All the conference participants as well as the contributors to this volume have provided insightful suggestions to each other and to us. In particular, the two conference commentators—Dina A. Zinnes of the University of Illinois and James A. Caporaso of the University of Denver—provided extremely perspicacious evaluations of the entire field of research and the specific contributions that each author made to it.

The editorial and research assistance of Mary Burns, William A. Clark, Donald Hottell, Cheryl Fischer, Lori Joye, Lucia Wren Rawls, and Barry Rich of the University of South Carolina proved invaluable, as did the vigorous aid of Diane Chapman, Rabbi Mendoza, Annie Santos, and Conrad Trible at the University of Southern California. The herculean tasks of compiling the conference transcripts, the list of references, and the index performed by Lorene Allio and Cecilia Cicchinelli at the University of Southern California merit special commendation. At the Ohio State University's Mershon Center, the administrative support provided by Carole Dale in so effectively managing the conference in Columbus also is deserving of our enthusiastic acknowledgement. Josephine Cohagen proved invaluable not only in working on the conference but in assisting with the final copy-editing. She was ably assisted in the latter task by Margaret Hermann and Teri Lloyd. We wish also to thank Gordon Smith, John Whitehead and Lisa Freeman-Miller, our attentive task-masters at Allen and Unwin, for the guidance, support, care, and concern they provided in bringing this project to published completion.

Finally, we wish to underscore our belief that the scientific study of foreign policy is, and is destined to remain, a truly collective, collaborative enterprise. The field is no more or less than the sum of the activities of those venturesome scholars who together have contributed to its development and increasing sophistication. Accordingly, we are greatly indebted to our colleagues and students for sharing with us a commitment to the rigorous analysis of foreign policy.

Charles F. Hermann
Charles W. Kegley, Jr.
James N. Rosenau
August, 1986

1

Introduction: New Directions and Recurrent Questions in the Comparative Study of Foreign Policy

JAMES N. ROSENAU

The contributors to this volume are venturesome scholars. They dare to seek comprehension across an extraordinary array of human phenomena. From the calculations of officials to the demands of publics, from the norms of culture to the limits of geography, from the conflicts of bureaucratic agencies to the pressures of recalcitrant allies, from the careful mobilization of resources to the selective application of force, from the behavior of small groups to the dynamics of large collectivities, students of foreign policy seek to fit together the pieces of endlessly challenging puzzles. The whole gamut of human experience falls within their purview. No facet can be safely ignored, or easily held constant. Where students of local politics tend to hold the national scene constant, where students of national politics tend to do the same for the international scene, and where students of world politics tend to treat subnational variables as constants, those who study foreign policy must, perforce, concern themselves with politics at every level. For the sources of foreign policy span all the levels as the collective energies, hopes, and fears of people converge around their state's efforts to ward off threats from abroad and procure the wherewithal from the global community necessary to the realization of goals.

Like biochemistry and social psychology, in other words, foreign policy analysis is a bridging discipline. It takes as its focus of study the bridges that whole systems called nation-states build to link themselves and their subsystems to the even more encompassing international systems of which they are a part. It is in some profound sense a discipline with limitless boundaries: the discipline is imposed by the need to organize inquiry around the external behavior of nation-states (i.e., the foreign policies of governments); but insofar as its independent variables are concerned, the scope of the field is boundless. Whatever may bear upon the activities of a state abroad is grist for the mill, whether it be the productivity of farm lands, the propensities of new generations, the perplexities of science, or any of the myriad resources, processes, and institutions through which collectivities cohere and cope. For certain purposes relating to the building of knowledge and the training of specialists, even this collection of essays can be seen as embraced by the field.

Still another way of grasping the boundless scope of the field is to ponder the multiple meanings and explanations that underlie even the simplest of foreign policy actions, say the announcement of a chief-of-state that he or she will be traveling abroad. One can peel off a wide range of causal layers to lay bare the sources of such an event: at one and the same time it reflects the decision of an individual, the deliberations of a committee, the outcome of a policy-making process, the sum of clashing interest groups, the values of a dominant elite, the product of a society's aspirations, the reinforcement of a historical tradition, the response to an opportunity or challenge elsewhere in the world—to mention only a few of the explanatory layers that students of foreign policy must consider to achieve a comprehensive analysis.

And to all of these complexities inherent in the processes of foreign policy must be added the historical dimension wherein dynamic technologies have greatly reduced social and geographical distances in the waning years of the twentieth century. In earlier centuries, when change was slower and societies less complex, foreign policy could be—and was—the sport of kings. That is, the heads of collectivities were not restrained by active publics, constrained by large bureaucracies, or dependent on elaborate socioeconomic processes. They could act with relative autonomy and the explanation for their actions could be found in the perceptual and experiential dynamics of individual behavior rather than in multiple layers of causation. Today, however, the sport of kings has become the deadly serious business of everyone's life.

Accordingly, as the world has become ever more interdependent, so has the study of foreign policy become ever more challenging and intriguing. This is so not only because the danger of conflict and violence grows with the growing overlap of groups and nations, but also because the sources and consequences of foreign policy have become inextricably woven into the patterns of interdependence, thus requiring those who study the subject to expand their horizons, enlarge their kit of analytic tools, and probe for meaning in heretofore unexplored areas of social, economic, and political life. With the passage of time, in short, foreign policy has come to encompass nothing less than the full range of individual and collective processes whereby people seek to give meaning and hope to their lives.

As in any field whose frontiers are rapidly expanding, students of foreign policy have had to confront a number of new problems as the pace of interdependence and change quickens. One of these is to avoid becoming so preoccupied with the new problems as to obscure the old ones that remain unsettled and require attention. While recent decades have witnessed much progress in the study of foreign policy, a number of longstanding theoretical, methodological, and epistemological challenges still resist clear-cut solution. How to trace the decisional processes through which foreign policies are framed, how to measure their direction and intensity, how to conceptualize the interplay of forces that impinge upon those who make the policy decisions—these are old issues that, as will be seen in many of the ensuing chapters, continue to engage the energies of creative analysts dedicated to uncovering the dynamics of state behavior in world politics.

As for the new theoretical and methodological problems posed by the advent of an ever more interdependent world, two are particularly noteworthy. One involves the increasing relevance of economics to the conduct of foreign policy. With the advent of nuclear stalemate and the emergence of Third World demands for a greater share of the world's wealth, issues of economic productivity and distribution have been elevated from low on the global agenda to the realm of high politics, and this shift has required a corresponding expansion of the skills and concerns of foreign policy analysts. Similarly, with issues of political economy now occupying a central place on the global agenda, the role of the state, its limits, scope, and autonomy, has emerged as a prime consideration in the conduct of foreign affairs. For students of foreign policy this development presents a challenge because for several decades they have not been inclined to treat the state as a substantive concept, preferring instead to equate it with the actions of governmental decision makers and thus to bypass the questions of its role, competence, and autonomy. For better or worse, such an inclination is no longer tenable if foreign policy analysts are to bring their work into harmony with the many observers for whom the state's place in the processes of political economy has become pivotal.

But perhaps the most challenging consequence of growing interdependence concerns the continuing erosion of the distinction between domestic and foreign issues, between the sociopolitical and economic processes that unfold at home and those that transpire abroad. It is not clear that this distinction could ever be drawn with

3

much clarity (though many a study in the past purported to do so); but surely the line dividing internal from external phenomena has been greatly obfuscated, possibly even erased in some respects, by the advent of issues and dynamics that are global in scope. Consider, for example, the large extent to which domestic economies and the politics to which they give rise are conditioned and shaped by the international political economy. It is no longer meaningful to speak of rates of inflation, interest, employment, or currency exchange as exclusively matters of domestic economic policy. The level and direction of such rates at any moment in time can be as much a response to developments abroad as they are to governmental practices at home. Much the same is the case for labor, immigration, capital investment and re-industrialization policies, and the dependence of crop prices within countries on what happens to crops in other countries is hardly less conspicuous. And to this list of "standard" domestic issues can be added the new ones fostered by interdependence, such as environmental pollution, the utilization of outer space, and terrorism, all of which have wide internal consequences within a number of countries even though they unfold on a transnational scale.

In short, the origins and dynamics of many public issues have extended beyond the competence of national actors. The latter have authority over some issue dimensions, but increasingly their jurisdiction is out of phase with the problems for which national governments feel and are held responsible, a discrepancy which has so fully rendered domestic and foreign policies functions of each other as to make them virtually indistinguishable.

All of this is not to imply that the field lacks structure, focus, or discipline. As can be seen in the account of the next chapter by Hermann and Peacock, it does have a structure, one that includes a rich, if sometimes skewed, history as well as a tradition of self-corrective criticism that bodes well for future comparative inquiries into foreign policy. Equally conspicuous, the field does have a central focus—the plans and actions of national governments oriented toward the external world—and it does have a storehouse of conceptual and methodological equipment that can be used to probe the plans and actions that may be of interest. To infuse order within this context and to account for the dynamics it encompasses, however, is to require roaming far afield, to all those domains of human activity from which the necessity, direction, and quality of government action springs. It is little wonder, then, that the essays assembled here represent the work of venturesome analysts.

New Directions and an Old Commitment

The confluence of new dynamics and old problems occasioned this collection of essays. Despite several decades in which the boundaries, concepts, variables, and methods of foreign policy analysis were progressively delineated and elaborated, the contributors to this volume, all of them deeply committed to employing comparative methods in the study of foreign policy, share the view that the time has come to take stock and chart new directions. More than a decade has passed since collective efforts at stock taking and direction charting were last undertaken (Rosenau, 1974, 1976a; Kegley *et al.*, 1975), and during this time so many new developments evolved in world politics and so many old forms eluded full comprehension that the need for a balanced reassessment of where the field has been and where it ought to be going seemed especially compelling.

In short, the task loomed as twofold. On the one hand, there was the challenge of new issues and the new emphasis on economics, along with the emergence of new international regimes and newly invigorated institutions such as the IMF to cope with the dynamics of interdependence, all of which need to be incorporated into the analytic foci of the field. If national governments are confronted with a wide range of different international circumstances, it seemed clear, so are those who employ comparative methods to study foreign policy. On the other hand, there was the challenge posed by the criticisms of analysts who perceived the field's progress as faltering (e.g., Faurby, 1976a, 1976b; Korany, 1983), with some even suggesting that it had become barren, its methodologies unproductive and its theories insufficient (Smith, 1981; Kagan, 1985). This tension between the old and the new, between continuing to focus on methodological, epistemological, and theoretical issues that have long been troublesome and veering off to acknowledge the implications of changing dynamics in global life, is manifest throughout the ensuing chapters.

To meet the twofold challenge a call for papers was issued in November, 1983, by the editors. Subsequently, in May of 1985, twenty-seven papers were subjected to intensive discussion at a conference convened in Columbus, Ohio, and sponsored by the Mershon Center of the Ohio State University, the Department of Government and International Studies of the University of South Carolina, and the Institute for Transnational Studies of the University of Southern California. Most of the papers were then revised for inclusion in this volume.

It is perhaps a measure of movement into a new, more mature era of inquiry that philosophical and methodological argumentation is conspicuously absent from these essays. Where earlier works were pervaded with efforts to clarify the epistemological foundations and methodological premises on which the analysis rested, here such matters are largely taken for granted. Gone are the triumphant paragraphs extolling science, the holier-than-thou espousals of quantification, and the elaborate claims as to the virtues of one method over another. No longer do researchers need to parade their commitment to scientific methods. Now, instead, they just practice them, noting the problems they seek to clarify and then proceeding quickly to the analysis itself, eschewing unqualified conclusions and yet suggesting questions for further exploration.

But while research has been freed of the warp and woof of a scientific élan, the centerpiece of the field, its commitment to comparative analysis, remains intact across the several generations who have sustained the field. What distinguishes the chapters of this volume, as it does the prior work of the field, is the notion that comprehension can best be advanced by a rigorous readiness to compare and a studious avoidance of observations and/or conclusions in which contrasts are not drawn.

This goal is not easily served and we may not always have achieved it in the essays that follow. Whatever the results, however, throughout the commitment to comparative inquiry drives the analysis. Only in this way, it is felt, can the vagaries of intuitive analysis and the pitfalls of unverifiable impressions be avoided. Only in this way can findings be differentiated and cumulated. In our original call for papers, therefore, it was made clear that we sought to chart new directions in the context of reaffirmed principles:

> The search is for papers that advance a framework, model, or conceptual orientation for the comparative study of foreign policy; for papers that offer empirical assessments of one or more existing frameworks; or for papers that concern modes of analysis which are specifically tailored to the needs of foreign policy research. Proposals for such papers will be welcomed so long as they share the following precepts:
>
> (1) Understanding of the policies and actions of international actors can be enhanced by perspectives that for a defined set of actors assumes a comparative orientation involving either the comparison of different actors at one point in time and/or the same actor compared with itself through time.
> (2) Understanding is to be fostered by explicit theory development that permits empirical investigation and comparisons to alternative theories intended to account for similar aspects of foreign policy.
> (3) Understanding of theories about foreign policy and their evaluation depends upon the development and application of appropriate modes of analysis; accordingly, research methods and data sources must be vigorously pursued in support of theoretical efforts.

It is the commitment to comparison, of course, that underlies the longstanding readiness of analysts in the field to quantify their data. Quantification has never been a goal in itself. It is, rather, a derivative of comparative inquiry in the sense that one undertakes comparison in order to identify central tendencies, those patterns that recur with sufficient frequency to be reflective of underlying regularities rather than unique or exceptional circumstances. But the analyst can never be sure whether a single observation depicts the regularities or the exception. So a second comparison is made, and then a third, and so on through as many more as may be needed to provide confidence that, for a given population, either the central patterns have been uncovered or that no such patterns exist.

But what to compare? What analytic units are so central to the conduct of foreign policy as to warrant tracing their patterns through quantitative inquiry? An answer to these questions came early in the surge toward the comparative study of foreign policy. It derived from a conception of all foreign policy behaviors as having a common structure: whatever their content and purpose, every behavior was seen to consist of a discrete action initiated by one state and directed toward one or more targets in the world arena. This structure came to be called an event and the classification of events by their quality and targets yielded vast data bases that could be used for a variety of analytic purposes. Indeed, precisely because events were so fundamental and simple in structure the use of them as a basic analytic unit intensified as well as reflected the surge toward comparative inquiry as more and more analysts discerned in the quantification of events a basis for probing the particular patterns that concerned them. Stated differently, the early years of the field were marked by the compilation of several extensive data bases that were both responses to and stimuli of corresponding efforts to construct viable theories of foreign policy.

Even as events data have allowed for rich comparative inquiries into the external behavior of states (e.g., East, Salmore and Hermann, 1978), however, so did the initial enthusiasm for them yield to a recognition that they represented a methodology ill-suited to a number of important foreign policy questions. Decisions not to undertake action are an obvious case in point. More subtle is the impact of shifting trade patterns, the influence of the balance of power or any global structure, the consequences of new weapons—these are but a few of the many complex dynamics relevant to foreign policy that do not lend themselves to investigation through events data as usually defined. Such dynamics are, in effect, long-term trends or contextual structures that may have become patterned through endless repetition (i.e., events), but it is the existence of the predispositions and belief systems underlying the patterns and not their repetition at any moment in time that accounts for their dynamism. Accordingly, it is hardly surprising that in recent years the comparative study of foreign policy has been less and less preoccupied by the events data methodology. Such data are still valuable for particular kinds of problems, but increasingly analysts have ventured beyond them to the generation and use of different empirical materials and methodologies more suitable to the challenges of a changing, increasingly interdependent world.

Diverse Foci

This very same readiness to be venturesome and think afresh is also evident in the diversity of the foci spanned by the various chapters. They cluster into no less than seven main parts, each of which explores an important aspect of the field. The three comprising Part I share a broad, comprehensive approach that seeks to demonstrate how a number of variables can be brought together into a coherent context. In Chapter 2 Hermann and Peacock do so by reviewing and assessing the development of the field, while in Chapter 3 Moon undertakes to demonstrate how the foreign policy and the political economy approaches can be synthesized, and in Chapter 4 Rosenau outlines procedures whereby comparative and systematic methods can be employed to theorize about the foreign policy of a single country.

Part II consists of four chapters that share a focus on foreign policy, its contents and patterns. The particular expression of this concern differs considerably among the four, but an effort to trace and assess the substance of what states do abroad is a common thread among them. In Chapter 5 Dixon suggests a method for connecting discrete events into larger patterns. In Chapter 6 Raymond stresses the need to develop methods for evaluating policy contents, while in Chapter 7 Bobrow and Chan actually do evaluate the policies of three countries and seek to assess why these particular systems have been successful in their foreign policy endeavors. In Chapter 8 Most and Siverson take a narrower approach and seek to explore empirically the ways in which governments substitute arms and alliances as instruments of their foreign policies.

The same concern with policy content marks the two chapters of Part III, but they do so in a different fashion by stressing policy outcomes as interactive phenomena. While Richardson calls for a dyadic focus to capture the interactive character of foreign policy in Chapter 9, Leng examines in Chapter 10 the structure of one type of interaction (disputes) to determine its effect on the subsequent behavior of the parties.

In Part IV the focus shifts to the cognitive processes whereby foreign policy decisions are considered and choices made. In Chapter 11 Powell, Dyson and Purkitt provide a succinct overview of various cognitive approaches and in Chapter 12 Mefford offers an application of one of these approaches, artificial intelligence, to a specific historical situation.

Of course, the making of foreign policy involves more than processes that unfold within individuals. Those that unfold among officials are no less important, since the ways in which cognitions get formed and expressed are responsive to the social and organizational dynamics at work in the interactions among policy makers. This collective dimension of foreign policy decision making serves as the focus of the four chapters that comprise Part V. Kegley probes how shared norms and rules can integrate the policy-making process in Chapter 13. Walker looks at the way role phenomena may affect the process in Chapter 14. Anderson treats policy making as a social process and in Chapter 15 offers a fascinating comparison of how US officials framed goals, generated alternatives, employed bureaucratic expertise, and reached closure in thirteen high-level crisis meetings between 1950 and 1962. In Chapter 16 Hermann, Hermann and Hagan assess the links between the structure of decision units and the policies they formulate.

But policy makers do not operate in a vacuum. Quite to the contrary, in many respects they can be viewed as vehicles for, or instruments of, larger forces at work in their society or externally in the global arena. Their choices do get shaped by the intellectual and organizational dynamics at work prior to the point of decision, but these dynamics are in turn a product of—or at least conditioned by—the aspirations, fears, opportunities, and limitations operative in the domestic and international environments. Indeed, policy-environmental links are often considered for analytic purposes to be sufficiently strong as to justify examining them directly, with the decision-making processes through which they pass being assumed to have limited effect and thus held constant.

Such links—and the accompanying presumption that governmental decision making accommodates to their formation and maintenance—are the prime focus of the six remaining chapters. Three of these are concerned mainly with domestic links and the last three concentrate on international links. The former constitute Part VI and consists of Hagan's effort in Chapter 17 to explore the interaction between domestic regimes and their oppositions, Vasquez's examination in Chapter 18 of the same dynamics in the context of decisions to

9

go to war, and Sampson's search in Chapter 19 for a way of studying how cultural factors may influence the formulation and conduct of foreign policy.

The diversity of international links that can have a significant impact on foreign policy are demonstrated by the three chapters clustered together in Part VII. In Chapter 20 Papadakis and Starr focus on the various sources that can shape the behavior of small states and, in so doing, they suggest how both domestic and international influences can, interactively, affect policy content. In Chapter 21 Wittkopf and DeHaven approach the interaction of internal and external factors in another way, through an empirical analysis of the extent to which the political climate—and thus foreign policy decision making—in the United States is affected by the actions of the Soviet Union. Finally, in Chapter 22 Karns and Mingst review the ways in which international nongovernmental organizations may serve as external sources of foreign policy.

There are, of course, a number of issues, concepts, and methods that the ensuing chapters do not explore. A coherent volume does not necessarily imply a coherence in the field it probes. Our essays fit together well and they cover a variety of important dimensions. But there is still much to be done and many gaps to fill before the field acquires a comparable coherence. As noted at the outset, its scope is broad and its expansion has been rapid.

So it is unreasonable to expect that a full range of the field's concerns could be captured in a single volume. What follows, however, is a good sample of the venturesomeness and satisfactions that can be enjoyed when one undertakes to compare and comprehend the external behavior of states in an ever more complex world.

PART I

Assessments and Proposals for the Field

2

The Evolution and Future of Theoretical Research in the Comparative Study of Foreign Policy

CHARLES F. HERMANN and GREGORY PEACOCK

What has been accomplished through the comparative study of foreign policy? Is there a future for the field? Researches engaged today in the comparative study of foreign policy (hereafter CFP)[1] must confront serious questions about past intellectual products of this field as well as engage in serious examination concerning reasonable expectations for its likely future. It is no longer sufficient to advance rosy predictions about the field, about the scientific approach to CFP, or about the payoffs of comparative methodology. As an area of inquiry moves from infancy to adolescence, people begin to form judgments about its present and future based on the performances, not the promises, of those involved. Profound and diverse challenges must be met, if desired CFP performances are to be realized. In the spirit of self-reflection, this essay provides an interpretation of the past and present in the comparative study of foreign policy with an emphasis on the central problems to be confronted.

Assessments of the Field

The comparative study of foreign policy as a field of inquiry was given an early definition in Rosenau's now well-known "fad, fantasy, or field?" article (1968a). Voicing dissatisfaction with previous work in the area of foreign policy analysis (particularly reliance on noncomparable,

13

noncumulative case studies), Rosenau argued for adoption of a more rigorous comparative method producing relevant generalizations and for a more explicit focus on foreign policy phenomena as the object of study. The CFP field, he claimed, could be shown to have a coherent subject matter, a particular viewpoint and potential for a unique set of theoretical propositions, thus qualifying it as an identifiable field of independent inquiry. Implicit in this description, and explicitly stated in an article he published the same year (1968b), was a commitment to a scientific approach to the study of foreign policy phenomena. At this relatively early stage, Rosenau's vision of the future potential of CFP was very optimistic. Of course, this vision was not Rosenau's alone, but was shared by a growing community of scholars.

Subsequent research and writing in the field frequently led to similarly upbeat assessments of the future intellectual potential of the CFP research program. In an article describing the formation and development of the Inter-University Comparative Foreign Policy (ICFP) Project,[2] a cautious, yet still positive assessment of the field was delivered (Rosenau, Burgess and Hermann, 1973). In a reprinting of the "fads" article seven years after the original publication, Rosenau's evaluation of work in CFP, in a new introduction to the essay, is unabashedly positive: "The comparative study of foreign policy, in short, is a serious enterprise, one that seems likely to be around for a long time and to entice an ever larger number of students to its ranks" (1975, p. 33). He added: "In sum, there is still much to be done, but if progress in the next few years is anything like that which has marked the past eight, there is reason to believe that the dynamics of foreign policy will begin to yield rapidly to greater understanding" (pp. 37–8). Finally, at a conference of ICFP participants convened in 1973, Rosenau (1976b) characterized CFP as a Kuhnian normal science whose primary activities could be described as mopping-up operations. Lest it be thought that Rosenau stood alone in these views, note the generally positive evaluations by other conference participants (especially Kegley and Skinner, and Powell *et al.* in Rosenau, 1976a) and by McGowan and Shapiro (1973) in the introduction to their survey of empirical CFP research.

These optimistic pronouncements, however, were not the only positions on the development of CFP research. At the same time that Rosenau and others offered glowing views of the future of the field, other scholars were beginning to have doubts about major components of this research tradition. At the 1973 ICFP conference, gentle, though consequential, criticisms of CFP research were aired (see contributions by McGowan, Harf *et al.*, and Wittkopf, in Rosenau, 1976a). Such perspectives were generally supportive of the goals of

14

CFP as previously defined, although critical of efforts which had to that point attempted to make good on earlier promises. These were not calls for dismantling of the CFP research orientation, but rather suggestions for reorienting its efforts.

Much more profound criticisms also began to be heard. Ashley's review of the CFP field described it as a "static or degenerating research nucleus" with some potentially useful spinoffs (Ashley, 1976, p. 155). In his thoroughgoing critique of eight "orthodoxies" in the comparative study of foreign policy, Munton cut much deeper by criticizing central assumptions in the field, even going so far as to suggest that "a distinct comparative study of foreign policy ought to disappear . . . by merging with a scientific study of international politics" (Munton, 1976, p. 268). Later, and from the other side of the Atlantic, Smith (1979, 1983) argued that the North American approach to comparative foreign policy studies was only one version of a larger intellectual enterprise and that it was not as appropriately grounded as was commonly believed by its practitioners. Although sympathetic to the comparativist and scientific commitments of CFP, Faurby (1976a), another European, advanced similar criticisms in a careful review of published CFP research (1976b). He argued that the CFP conceptions of comparative method and of science were not the only ones available and appropriate for this type of research. As an alternative, he suggested incorporating broader perspectives on these matters into the research agenda in order to increase the likelihood of a more comprehensive understanding of foreign policy phenomena. Each of these critiques of the prevailing CFP program went beyond earlier assessments in suggesting radically different or entirely new directions in the study of foreign policy. In his recent description of a theory of cascading interdependence, Rosenau (1984c, p. 252) appears also to make party with such critiques by denigrating his earlier "narrow preoccupation with foreign policy as the phenomenon to be explained".

This brief march through varying assessments of the development of the comparative study of foreign policy has of necessity emphasized overall judgments. The evaluations referred to above engage arguments at many levels and address problems of theory, methodology, and substantive content. However, our purpose is not to review all these controversies; we have attempted rather to give a sense of the boom and bust quality of writing about comparative foreign policy research in the last two decades. Kegley's (1980) excellent overview of the field provides a useful historical sense of developments and a more detailed listing of perceived problems than is included here. These assessments serve as a backdrop for our interpretation of the past in CFP as well as for our prescriptions for the future of this field.

15

Charles F. Hermann and *Gregory Peacock*
The Growth of Knowledge
in the Comparative Study of Foreign Policy

Unquestionably, one of the greatest disappointments experienced by early CFP proponents has been their perceived failure to generate intellectual products even roughly commensurate with early expectations. This failure has been particularly debilitating because of the heady epistemological claims made early in the development of the field. It was widely believed that adoption of more rigorous methodological techniques in the context of more explicitly comparative research would yield large quantities of reliable, readily comprehensible information about foreign policy phenomena. This information would both stimulate and substantiate generalizations relating variations in foreign policy outputs to variations in factors relevant to foreign policy undertakings. Accumulation of such generalizations would in turn lead to theories about foreign policy that would be both general and verifiable. Many thought that in this fashion demonstrable growth in knowledge (cumulation) would be assured. Having internalized these expectations early on, the subsequent failure of the program to reach such lofty goals produced a gap between expectation and reality that led to disillusionment among CFP adherents.

Though many explanations of these shortcoming have been offered, suggesting a wide range of problems (see Kegley, 1980), at the heart of most of these accounts have been concerns about the lack of objectively identifiable and focused growth of knowledge in the field. Failure to deliver on this central feature of the research enterprise is an issue that must be addressed by any proposal for new major initiatives in the comparative study of foreign policy.

The central core of this essay consists of a proposal for reconceptualizing the basis for the growth of knowledge in CFP. We believe the two prevailing logics of inquiry that have been applied in evaluating CFP are inappropriate. We argue that by providing a more defensible view of the acquisition of knowledge and the nature of cumulation, past efforts in CFP research can be more appropriately interpreted and evaluated. Further, such a reconceptualization has implications for the direction of current research and for orientations of future work in the field.

In order to establish this reorientation it is necessary to examine more closely the central assumptions of CFP research as commonly defined. Previously we indicated that Rosenau's early definition of the field included two central features: (1) a commitment to foreign policy phenomena as the object of inquiry and (2) a commitment to the comparative method. These have been widely accepted and deserve elaboration.

16

The study of foreign policy phenomena resulted in a commitment to the concept of foreign policy and the external behavior of international actors (Hermann, 1972b, 1978b). Foreign policy had to be considered not only as a concept but as a variable or set of variables that could assume different discernible values in covariation with other variables. Such requirements opened the way for the exploration of different kinds, types, or scales of policy whose condition at various times and places could be reliably assessed. This need led to considerable fascination with events data as a measurable indicator of policy. Although some CFP investigators experimented enthusiastically with the collection and use of these relatively new forms of data, many scholars attracted to the field (e.g., Brecher, 1972, 1975) recognized alternative ways of measuring foreign policy.

Theoretically the emphasis on foreign policy as a variable resulted in various conceptualizations of its relationship with other variables. The most pervasive orientation envisioned foreign policy as a dependent variable the patterns of which are to be understood by examining various explanatory sources (e.g. see the contributions to Rosenau, 1974; and Wilkenfeld *et al.*, 1980). Other theoretical orientations viewed certain kinds of foreign policy as the source or independent variable for explaining domestic policies of government and other internal features of societies, as envisioned, for example, in linkage politics (e.g., Deutsch, 1966; Rosenau, 1969a) or dependency theories (e.g., Galtung, 1971; Gobalet and Diamond, 1979). Rosenau's (1970) interest in political system adaptation illustrates still another perspective in which foreign policy is represented as one type of mediating variable for regulating among political, economic, and social structures. Action-reaction models (e.g., Holsti, Brody and North, 1964) conceptualized foreign policy as produced in an endless cycle where one actor's policy triggers another's which in turn precipitates new policy by the first actor or perhaps a third party. Despite the prevalence in early CFP research of conceptualizations emphasizing foreign policy as the phenomena to be explained (i.e., the dependent variable), numerous other perspectives emerged from heightened attention to the concept of foreign policy (see Hermann, 1983a).

The second commitment in CFP—to comparative method—though seemingly straightforward, involves at least three related subcommitments. First, it includes a commitment to multi-nation comparisons.[3] This sense of comparative study is, of course, part of the traditional meaning employed by students of comparative politics. In much of the comparative foreign policy research under consideration here, the emphasis is on extensive cross-national comparisons involving a substantial number of nations. Because this differed from prior practice, the scope of comparison envisioned by CFP researchers is much broader than that assumed in more traditional foreign policy case studies. Through the use of aggregate and events data, an enlarged sense of the comparativist commitment appeared.

A second, more consequential, commitment inherent in the adoption of comparative methodology is explicit, systematic comparison of similar features (variables) in each of the entities under study. Thus, various influences on foreign policy outcomes are conceptualized to exist in greater or lesser degree in all political systems. Variations in the presence or absence of these influences is systematically related to features of the external behavior of each state. Comparison is therefore explicit and grounded in prior conceptualizations of variables and relationships. This view of comparative method can be contrasted to the less-focused comparisons found in some traditional case and country studies.

The final commitment in the adoption of the comparative method entails the use of scientific methods. Scientific methods play an important part in the definition of CFP because of the epistemological claims associated with scientific activities. To proponents of the new field, the prospect of reliable empirical data, verifiable generalizations, and explanatory theory all pointed to the greater promise of expanding bases of knowledge concerning foreign policy phenomena. As Kegley (1980, p. 5) has observed, in adopting scientific methodology, expectations for the growth of knowledge looked exceedingly promising while the risks appeared small. To suggest a commitment to scientific methodology does not, of course, imply the use of any single methodology or technique.

Given this picture of the central commitments of CFP, the overall history of successes and failures in the field might be interpreted in any number of ways. Two conceptualizations of scientific inquiry that seemed particularly prominent in the first years of CFP research were neopositivist inductionism and Kuhnian normal science.

Neopositivism and Normal Science

The neopositivist vision of science partially adopted by some CFP proponents was rooted in the behavioral orientation of the period. Although few scholars viewed themselves as holding a strict neopositivist view of science (e.g., fact/value distinctions, objectification of human action, empirical commitments, methodological unity of science, and reliance on inductive methods of inference), many of their products reflected some of these characteristics. One result of these neopositivist beliefs was adoption of a "building block" view of science in which successive layers of empirical findings (i.e., tests of hypotheses) would lead through an inductive process to ever more general theories of foreign policy behavior and hence to a growing body of verifiable knowledge. (See, for example, the propositional inventory of McGowan and Shapiro, 1973.) This neopositivist perspective on scientific inquiry might be characterized as the inductivist approach to the study of foreign policy—hypothesis creation and testing occurring across a wide variety of domains in search of generalized relationships on which to construct theories. Zinnes (1976a) has characterized this approach as *ad hoc* hypothesis testing, and indeed, much early empirical research in CFP reflected this model.

Another common approach viewed CFP as a Kuhnian normal science, with the paradigm for such a science being the set of central assumptions described earlier. Rosenau (1976b) came to favor this conception of the development of the CFP program, as did McGowan (1976) and more recently Kegley (1980).

Each of these interpretations of the development of the CFP field is organized around a logic of inquiry (or meta-methodology) that includes not only a particular perspective on scientific activities (rules, prescriptions, etc.), but also a defence of epistemological claims associated with each approach. Thus claims about the growth of knowledge in any scientific endeavor are ineluctably tied to the logic of inquiry adopted. This connection is important for understanding the widespread discontent with CFP research products. As suggested earlier, at the heart of this dissatisfaction lies the perception that exceedingly little growth in knowledge concerning foreign policy problems has occurred to date. This perceived deficiency, we argue, is due in part to inappropriate conceptualizations of the logic of inquiry relevant to CFP research. Such a thesis may appear trivially true to some and unrealistic to others. A word of clarification is therefore in order.

The linkage between accepted logic of inquiry and judgments about the cumulativeness of research products can be argued at two levels: (1) the impact on day-to-day research practices and (2) the evaluation of the research program as a whole. First, it is unquestionably the case that the intellectual products generated by social science research reflect the structure and content of the logic of inquiry held by the researcher. This may not be an explicitly conscious emphasis of the research process, but for the most part, logic of inquiry concerns are mirrored in the choice of problems, the selection and measurement of variables, and the inference-drawing procedures. More importantly, logic of inquiry commitments are influential in structuring and justifying the conclusions that are drawn and in defending the knowledge claims advanced by the researcher. Thus although the researcher does not stop at every step in the research process to ask whether he/she is following good falsificationist or positivist or Marxist methodological prescriptions, such considerations do significantly shape the research process.

At a more general level, when evaluating a body of research, logic of inquiry questions always comprise the core of the evaluation. This is so because the logic of inquiry provides the basis for making claims about the acquisition of knowledge. Such claims traditionally propound a view of the rationality of science in which the particular logic of inquiry is shown to provide a rational basis for the practice of science. Thus, logic of inquiry concerns emerge as particularly consequential for *ex post facto* evaluations of a series of research products. The implications of this discussion for the evaluation of comparative foreign policy research can be summarized in the following question: Relative to the professed goal of growth in knowledge concerning foreign policy, what are the consequences of viewing CFP as a particular type of inquiry (i.e. representing a particular logic of inquiry)? The two conceptualizations of the logic of inquiry frequently applied to the comparative study of foreign policy—the neopositivist view and Kuhn's notion of normal science—each establish different criteria for evaluation.

As noted, the early neopositivist view of research in CFP emphasized discrete empirical findings. Much empirical research has been undertaken in the last two decades, yielding a few fairly well grounded generalizations (e.g., the importance of a nation's size in differentiating the volume of foreign policy behavior; the tendency of decision-making activities to cluster among a small group of top officials in a foreign policy crisis; the prevalence of "maintenance" or "participation" activities in the overall volume of foreign actions of states; the distinction between dyadic behavior and behaviors in which multiple recipients are addressed; the absence of an unmediated relationship between a country's domestic conflict and international conflict). These findings, however, have not been integrated into broader theoretical formulations. Using the model of cumulation inherent in this methodology, precious little has actually occurred. A largely negative assessment of progress in the field has followed. Further, skepticism about the account of science offered by neopositivism is now so profound and widespread as to suggest that this view of cumulation will never guide research in meaningful directions (Popper, 1963; Lakatos, 1970; Fay, 1975; Bernstein, 1978).

The Kuhnian view of CFP would seem to lead to similar negative assessments. As interpreted by Kegley (1980), selected aspects of foreign policy research do appear similar to some portions of Kuhnian normal science. For example, until recently a fairly coherent community of CFP scholars could readily be identified. Likewise, CFP adherents share deeply-held commitments to comparative methodology. Unfortunately, what is lacking in this description is any mention of a set of shared theoretical commitments. As described by Kuhn, the theoretical component of a paradigm for normal science is absolutely *essential* (Kuhn, 1970: especially ch. 1 and postscript). Unless investigators share a theoretical perspective, Kuhn's argument is largely hollow. Absence of a common framework undermines any knowledge claims based on reference to his position. Cumulation in Kuhn's normal science model can be seen as an integrated set of solved puzzles that serve as exemplars for new generations of scholars. Because CFP is primarily a set of methodological commitments—as Kegley (1980, pp. 10–16) ably documents—conceptualization of CFP as a normal science misrepresents the past and provides no meaningful guideposts for present and future research. That CFP lacks a shared theoretical paradigm argues against Kegley's paradigmatic criteria and prevents an optimistic view of the field's overall progress from the Kuhnian perspective.

These two approaches to the logic of inquiry, however, do not exhaust the alternatives available for evaluating CFP research. They do highlight how a conceptualization of knowledge growth—particularly if inappropriate—can lead to discouragement and reduction of effort. Against the viewpoints just described, we would argue that the critical focus in evaluations of CFP should be upon efforts at gradually building more adequate theory. The growth of scientific knowledge is the growth of theoretical knowledge. Consequently, assessments of cumulation must first of all consider efforts at providing theoretical statements about foreign policy phenomena. To the extent that past evaluative efforts have focused on cumulating empirical findings or building upon an alleged paradigm, they have misrepresented the significance of past efforts.

In reorienting the focus of CFP assessments, we will provide a new evaluation concerning the achievements of scholars engaging in comparative foreign policy studies. The logic of inquiry described by Lakatos's (1970) methodology of scientific research programs is more hospitable to our proposed reassessment of CFP research than either of the previously described approaches. This methodology emphasizes the interplay of continuity and change in science through the juxtaposition of competing theories within the larger structure of a research program. Growth in knowledge occurs as the empirical content of theories increases. The important referent for cumulation, then, consists of series of theories that compete among themselves on the basis of

21

their empirical content and the results of empirical tests. Our conviction that growth in theoretical knowledge is essential to progress in explaining foreign policy phenomena prompts adoption of Lakatos's position.

Theoretical Developments
in the Comparative Study of Foreign Policy

We have made the argument for a theoretically based assessment that is also attuned to the necessity for empirical research. Now it is time to re-examine efforts at theorizing in the comparative study of foreign policy. Some observers might argue that in turning towards theory evaluations rather than assessments that are more explicitly based on completed, small-scale empirical research, we have guaranteed a negative assessment of the field (see McGowan, 1976; Kegley, 1980). We would not argue against the relative paucity of comprehensive theories in the study of foreign policy. There have been, however, a small but continuous number of serious attempts at theory building from which much has been learned and which could, we argue, form the basis for more comprehensive theories in the future. Our optimism about the future of CFP rests more on our faith in the ability of scholars to build on this theoretical base than in the adequacy of any of the theories currently known to the CFP community. Hence, we too believe that ours is a theoretically undernourished discipline, but one with a tradition of persistent, if uneven and incomplete, theory building. We would also maintain that the development of the field demonstrates an evolving consensus about the substance of an adequate theory of comparative foreign policy phenomena. To substantiate these claims, we turn to an interpretive overview of six past theoretical efforts and conclude with a review of current CREON work in this continuing stream.[4]

Richard Snyder and Associates

The first major effort to theorize in a scientific mode about foreign policy predates the self-conscious emergence of CFP scholars, although its influence on subsequent efforts cannot be ignored. This approach is the decision-making framework of Snyder, Bruck and Sapin (1954). As a reaction to the dominance of *realpolitik* analyses of foreign policy based on power and national interest, Snyder and his colleagues argued that human decision making was central to the interpretation of foreign policy actions. Against the prevailing view, they suggested the importance of decision makers operating in an organizational context and affected by various elements of the internal and external setting and by the process through which they reach foreign policy decisions. Their very creative analysis suggested a richly differentiated view of foreign policy decision making.

The Snyder framework, at a concrete level, consisted of an extensive listing of potentially relevant factors. It offered few indications of expected linkages or temporal orderings among the variables, nor did it treat foreign policy as a variable having different values or properties that might be expected to change with the identified factors. Even without describing variability in foreign policy action, the framework seemed extremely complex. To apply it empirically required detailed data on numerous variables that the social sciences in the late 1950s had only begun to develop. It is little wonder that the major direct application of the Snyder framework used the case study technique (i.e., Paige, 1968). As an attempt to conceptualize how foreign policy is made, the decision-making framework provided many more potential referents than did previous efforts and thus, together with its emphasis on explicit assumptions and definitions, constituted an important conceptual orientation for scholars disposed to a scientific approach to the study of foreign policy.

The Snyder framework posed a fundamental question: Why do foreign policy officials (not nations) make the choices that they do? The impact of phenomenology emerges in the way this question is treated. Snyder suggested that answers to the central question require the introduction of the entire panoply of theory and research on human behav or from the psychology of perception to organizational behavior, from the analysis of communication networks to the examination of societal norms and values.

James N. Rosenau

More than a decade after the original appearance of the Snyder decision-making monograph, Rosenau (1966) presented his "pre-theories" essay. If Snyder's framework invited scientific inquiry, Rosenau insisted upon it. He called for the generation of testable "if-then" propositions and the casting of foreign policy research in a manner that encouraged the location of specific observations of foreign policy activity in general explanatory frameworks. Although a thorough review of the intellectual origins of CFP would properly trace many roots, it is beyond question that Rosenau's pre-theories essay and subsequent writing and organizing activity resulted in the self-conscious emergence of CFP as an area of inquiry. Numerous research articles, doctoral dissertations, and several textbooks drew upon

23

Rosenau's framework. Although he continued to extend and modify his contribution to the comparative study of foreign policy—linkage politics (1969a), domestic sources (1967a), and most notably his adaptation framework (1970)—Rosenau's initial essay arguably has had the most far-reaching effect on his colleagues.

Rosenau proposed a manageable typology for differentiating among nations. He contended the variables that would be most important in accounting for a country's foreign policy would depend on its nation type. Significantly, the three variables Rosenau selected to construct his typology (size, development, and political accountability) bore a marked resemblance to the underlying factors Rummel (1979a) and others independently discovered through factor analysis. Rosenau also advanced a classification system for explanatory variables that had intuitive appeal. Less successful was the attempt in the pre-theories essay to create a fourfold classification of issue areas, but their inclusion served as a marker for future researchers as an area in need of further conceptualization.

Many of Rosenau's concepts remained quite ambiguous and the external domain of explanatory variables was conceptualized as a single "systemic" category. Although he developed the explanatory variables considerably, what they were supposed to explain (i.e., foreign policy) remained remarkably undifferentiated. Without greater specification of the behavior or policy variables, it is not surprising that, like Snyder before him, Rosenau offered few statements of relationship among variables. Nevertheless, his typology of nations with its postulated implications for the relative importance of different sets of explanatory variables provided a real and manageable agenda to match his call for hypothesis-testing comparative research. Rosenau sharpened Snyder's original question of why do policy makers choose by framing the question: Which kinds of explanatory variables are most potent in accounting for decision makers' choices? That question has structured much empirical inquiry in the field to the present.

Michael Brecher

In his original theoretical essay with associates (Brecher *et al.*, 1969), and in his subsequent work, Brecher (1972, 1975) picked up on another theme present in the Snyder work and developed more generally in international relations by the Sprouts (1965). This concerned the relationship between the environment and the decision makers' perception of that environment or what Brecher called the operational environment (external influences) and the psychological environment (the interpretation of those influences by decision makers). Using an

24

input-process-output perspective, Brecher advanced a more comprehensive classification of the variables that might be expected to come into play in a foreign policy decision-making system. Far more than either Snyder or Rosenau, Brecher classified the potential sources of influence in a country's external environment including its global system, its regional subsystem, and its dominant bilateral subsystem.

He introduced a descriptive set of policy issue areas (military-security, political-diplomatic, economic-developmental, cultural-status), but like his predecessors, Brecher did not offer hypotheses specifically relating the variables in his system. Instead, Brecher demonstrated by example how one might discover discrete propositions from comparative case studies (another useful innovation also being explored by George (1979a) and others including Richardson in Chapter 9). His fuller explication of the network of explanatory and behavior variables and his use of multiple case studies stand as important contributions. Brecher also reinforced the interest in the discovery of if-then, empirically investigable propositions. His introduction of the concepts of the decision makers' image structures and attitudinal prisms lacked the refinement to reveal how these features would act as the interface between the operational and psychological environments. Brecher, nevertheless, highlighted the possibility of using selected decision-making variables as the master elements for combining multiple sources of influence. He can be interpreted as asking the question: How do decision makers interpret and integrate the various potential sources of outside influence? The question introduces the assumption that if we can understand those dynamics, decision making can serve as the integrating mechanism for multi-source explanations of foreign policy. As shall be indicated below, we believe this perspective continues to be at the cutting edge of theory-building efforts in the field.

Rudolph J. Rummel

Few social scientists have devoted their professional careers with more singularity of purpose than R. J. Rummel. Yet relatively few foreign policy scholars appear to have more than a passing familiarity with his Dimensionality of Nations (DON) project (Rummel, 1972, 1977, 1979a). It may be that they are intimidated by its axiomatic and formal presentation or that they fail to see the applicability of the research to CFP. We believe, however, that Rummel has made several valuable contributions. He has examined how the difference in the characteristics of pairs of nations influences their likelihood of conflict. This inquiry parallels the interest of a number of those in CFP with the

25

relationship between national attributes and foreign policy behavior.

From the beginning, Rummel carefully specified conflict behavior as the kind of foreign policy activity whose variability he sought to interpret. Moreover, he formulated explicit hypotheses relating explanatory variables to conflict behavior. Initially his investigation of hypotheses appeared to fall in the tradition which both Rosenau and Brecher advocated and which Zinnes (1976a) characterized as *ad hoc* hypothesis testing. The construction of theory through the testing and cumulation of discrete hypotheses, we have noted, has roots in the neopositivist approach to science. In his further development of field theory and his subsequent grafting to it of a nation's status or rank discrepancy, Rummel abandoned the examination of discrete hypotheses for a more comprehensive set of logically connected axioms as the framework for theory.

In contrast to the other theorists we review, Rummel has confined himself to a narrow domain. He has opted to attend only to explanatory variables that can be constructed from national attributes data and has applied them exclusively to conflict behavior. He ignores the question that concerned Snyder and Brecher about how such environmental variables are perceived or misperceived by decision makers. His critics contend that the resulting theory is largely devoid of substantive content; that is, what can be said about conflict from the theory is very limited. But in the evolution of the theory-building enterprise, Rummel's contribution remains substantial. He designated the kind of foreign policy to be explained and implicitly suggested that what might account for one kind of behavior might not do for another. He moved beyond discrete hypothesis testing and consciously developed networks of relationships among variables entering into his theory—a task that escaped many earlier contributors. Although the early interest of CFP in events data owes much to Charles McClelland (e.g. McClelland and Hoggard, 1969) and Edward Azar (e.g., Azar and Ben-Dak, 1975), clearly Rummel was one of the pioneers in its use and one of the strongest advocates of quality control with such data.

PRINCE

William D. Coplin and Michael K. O'Leary designed and developed the Programmed International Computer Environment (PRINCE) as a heuristic device for the analysis of public policy (Coplin and O'Leary, 1972) and extended its application to the study of foreign policy (Coplin *et al.*, 1973; O'Leary, 1976). Their framework focused on issue areas and the different actors (at any level, not just the state) involved with a given issue. For a particular issue all the pertinent actors must be identified and then each must be assigned values specifying their position on the issue (degree of support or opposition to the issue), power (capabilities to resolve the issue), salience (importance of issue to the actor) and affect (friendship–hostility between actors). They address the question: How likely is a given issue to be resolved and in what direction? Weighting issue position, power, and salience equally, the PRINCE designers combine the scores for each actor on the three variables, add the resulting product for all actors, and then convert the result to a probability estimate. Affect scores are used to determine movement among actors to form coalitions and, with other variables, it indicates the likelihood of change in an actor's issue position.

PRINCE provides no insight into the impact of subjective estimates of power or position and ignores the possible effects and dynamics that shape issue positions that had concerned Snyder, Rosenau, and Brecher. Whether the relationship among variables as they actually operate can be adequately captured by simple arithmetical procedures involves an assumption whose validity invites inspection. Yet, in the development of foreign policy theory building, PRINCE addresses a previously badly neglected component—the specification of a robust dependent variable. Rummel's work on conflict provided conceptual and empirical work on one kind of policy, but neglected everything else. Brecher offered a fourfold classification of issue areas, as did Rosenau, but neither devoted much attention to their conceptualization or component elements. Coplin, O'Leary and their associates also pose the question whether actors aggregated at the level of national governments or ruling political parties constitute the most appropriate level for determining foreign policy outcomes.

Interstate Behavior Analysis (IBA)

This project headed by Jonathan Wilkenfeld and involving a number of his colleagues entailed one of the most ambitious theoretical models yet designed for empirical investigation (see Wilkenfeld *et al.*, 1980). Wilkenfeld and his associates included a broad array of explanatory variables at multiple levels of explanation (i.e., psychological, political, societal, interstate, and global). Similarly, they incorporated a diversity of foreign policy behaviors reduced to several underlying dimensions through factor analysis. Nation types—following the vision of Rosenau of his pre-theories essay—served as mediating elements between the explanatory variables and the dimensions of behavior. A statistical technique, partial least squares (modified with a regression to permit the introduction of the mediating variables) not only constituted the empirical procedure to test the model, but also provided the logic by which the relationships among variables were established.

Permitting the statistical procedure to determine the nature of the relationships linking the model's variables raises serious questions. Unless the researchers can demonstrate that the method of combining variables in the statistical technique approximates that found in the actual world of foreign policy making, then the validity of the operation appears open to major challenge. Also, the slippage between the conceptualization of the model's variables and the empirical indicators of those variables frequently seems substantial. It demonstrates the continuing difficulty of establishing cross-national data sets on a number of variables judged to be important sources of foreign policy.

Whatever the disappointment with some aspects of the Interstate Behavior Analysis project, it undeniably "pushed the edge of the envelope." In some important respects, Wilkenfeld and his associates substantially elaborated the Rosenau pre-theories model and subjected it to an empirical investigation. They adopted his orienting research question about the relative potency of explanatory variables. But they did more than that. They recognized that the multiple sources of foreign policy explanation must somehow be combined or integrated in a fashion permitting empirical inquiry. They recognized that the diversity in foreign policy outputs must be accounted for in a comprehensive model. They share the belief of several earlier theorists that the fashion in which explanatory variables operated might vary considerably in different types of nations.

CREON

The reader will instantly recognize that the authors cannot review the contribution of the theoretical enterprise of which we are a part in the same manner as we have assessed previous efforts. Acknowledging that our presentation of the Comparative Research on the Events of Nations (CREON) project will not be identical in composition to our account of other efforts, we include it because we view it as building on the previous theoretical efforts and as continuing the development process to which they all have contributed. Although the CREON Project began some years ago (e.g., see Hermann *et al.*, 1973; East *et al.*, 1978), the project continues to evolve as one of the current inheritors of the tradition we trace back to Snyder.

The CREON investigators share a concern with the fundamental question: When faced with a given type of problem in a specified set of circumstances, what kind of behavior (if any)—out of the repertory of possible actions—is a national government most likely to initiate and why? Thus, the focus is on estimating the likelihood of a particular kind of behavior viewed as one of a series of discrete actions. This can be contrasted with the frequent interests of foreign policy researchers in accounting for general patterns of a nation's policy that emerge across time. The members of the CREON project also have devoted considerable energy to the conceptualization and measurement of the behavior that comprises these discrete actions. Concluding that behaviors are the element of foreign policies most observable on a cross-national basis, we have elected to disaggregate foreign policy behaviors into universal constituent properties. Among these are level of commitment, degree of affect, kind of instrument, and nature of recipient. When combined in specific ways these properties produce the behaviors of various types with which we all are familiar (Callahan *et al.*, 1982; Hermann and Dixon, 1984).

A second fundamental question of primary interest among those in the CREON project is what combination of explanatory variables best accounts for or forecasts the observable behavior? Rather than ask which class of explanatory variables contribute the most to foreign policy (i.e., the relative potency question), we have an ultimate desire to combine variables in a multi-level design. It is our expectation that some integration of source variables—using a substantively based explanation or logic—will yield accuracies in characterizing expected behaviors beyond that obtainable from any source variables used in isolation. We intend to subject this expectation to empirical investigation.

CREON consists of a series of components each of which introduces a set of explanatory variables that are expected to be an important contributor to estimating the most likely behavior. Each component set of variables contains its own set of theoretical expectations that enable us to isolate its effect on foreign policy behavior. The components are: (1) foreign policy problem, (2) external or situational predisposition, (3) domestic attributes and conditions (i.e., political economy), (4) domestic opposition, and (5) decision unit and political choice. Another chapter in this volume describes the decision unit and political choice component (Chapter 16). The chapter (17) by Hagan describes work related to the political opposition component. In the future our intention is to construct one or more integrative or overarching decision-making frameworks that will take into account each of these components as the relevant decision makers would be expected to perceive and synthesize them. Thus, decision making is seen as the integrative control mechanism which, of course, is capable of distorting or misrepresenting some of the component effects as well as, on occasion, producing their accurate integration (Hermann and Hermann, 1985).

Conclusions

How should we assess the theory-building enterprise in the comparative study of foreign policy over the past several decades? If, in the spirit of neopositivists, we expect continuously growing stockpiles of confirmed hypotheses that ever more adequately describe the world of foreign policy, then the record of achievement may seem disappointing. It is not only the lack of empirically investigated hypotheses that is disappointing (as noted, some do exist); but also the widely shared impression that the collective set of propositions reveals to us no more about foreign policy than each of the individual findings.

If we expected a normal science with a widely accepted paradigm in the Kuhnian sense, then we again must acknowledge disappointment. Kegley (1980) is most likely correct in suggesting that Rosenau's pretheory came somewhat closer than anything to date in that it organized for a brief period the research agenda of a number of independent scholars. Yet it takes nothing away from Rosenau's achievement to recognize that it lacked the fundamental characteristics of a Kuhnian paradigm.

And yet a well-read and thoughtful scholar starting to work today on theory development in CFP has a significant theory-building heritage that his or her early predecessors lacked. Of course Snyder had important intellectual foundations for his work in 1954, as did Rosenau somewhat more than a decade later. But with respect to theoretical insight into foreign policy, they did not have the advantage of the cumulative theoretical efforts which they and others have gradually compiled for us today. It may be stretching too far to call these various contributions (as well as others we have not discussed) a research program in the spirit of Lakatos (1970). We do not yet have much in the way of competing theories accounting for the same substantive content. Nevertheless, we find evidence in the collective work reviewed, as well as that found in some other contributors, of cumulation in theoretical comprehension and in the conceptual development of foreign policy. Adopting a Lakatos perspective, we believe we can identify in past theory efforts the foundations of a collective research program. We are able to specify some of the building blocks that have been assembled.

Now more than before, there is a broader recognition of the need to specify explicitly the nature of foreign policy behavior to be examined thanks to the progressive efforts of Rosenau, Brecher, and particularly the PRINCE associates. Likewise it has become clear that fuller explanations of foreign policy phenomena require multi-level and multi-variable explanatory frameworks. We have had a series of efforts trying to address this integrative task more adequately from the early lists of Snyder and Rosenau to the statistical models of Wilkenfeld and his colleagues. Furthermore, there is a greater sensitivity to the temporal/spatial constraints inherent in any social theory, whether this is partially achieved by use of types of nation-states as Rosenau and Wilkenfeld have done or in terms of issue-areas as proposed by Coplin and O'Leary. Both internal and external sources of foreign policy behavior are increasingly recognized as mutually essential parts of any theoretical framework as a result of the efforts of scholars like Brecher. (Of course the particular mix of factors is still the subject of considerable disagreement). An adequate theory of foreign policy, as the progressive efforts of Rummel among others has shown, must have explicit substantive content. This means that the logic linking various components of a framework cannot be simply represented as statistical decision rules. Finally, some attention has been directed to the dynamic properties of the phenomenon to be modeled (e.g., Brecher's systems perspective; and Rummel's changing status discrepancies).

Expectations about theory development in the comparative study of foreign policy certainly shape our evaluations of what has been achieved. From our point of view, however, the situation is not unlike that facing Tom Sawyer on attending his own funeral and concluding that reports of his demise seemed rather premature. So also it seems to us are some judgments about the comparative study of foreign policy. Future theory builders in the area can start from a base that did not exist 20 years ago. Given that achievement, some optimism about the prospects in the years ahead is reasonable.

Notes

1 The frequent use of the acronym CFP and of phrases such as "the comparative study of foreign policy" may lead to misunderstanding if not properly clarified. The use of such terms to characterize the activities of a collection of scholars may create the impression of a tightly knit group, all of whom interact continuously with one another and share a common set of beliefs about their intellectual enterprise. While some scholars did engage in frequent exchanges, many who have contributed to the comparative study of foreign policy were part of no organized group nor would all agree upon a narrow conceptualization of the field. The reader should therefore not allow our shorthand references to CFP and our summary statements to create the image of a monolithic group of scholars which in fact never existed. Our statements should suggest broader perspectives, perhaps akin to the notion of central tendencies in the field.
2 The ICFP should not be confused with CFP. The former was a coherent group of scholars working on some shared programs while the latter is a shorthand way of making reference to efforts in the field.

31

3 Some have stressed that the comparative study of foreign policy also includes comparisons of a system through time as well as comparisons across units. To date, however, no careful specification of the requirement for longitudinal comparison of different states of the same foreign policy system have been developed by anyone in the field. Similarly underdeveloped is the comparison of foreign policy among non-nation units despite such initial efforts as those of Mansbach, Ferguson and Lampert (1976).

4 The contributions to CFP theory development reviewed in this essay should be regarded as representative of what we regard as major trends and developments. Those included illustrate theory building by researchers who would appear to share a commitment to (a) more comprehensive theories involving multiple sources of explanation, (b) a consciously cross-national orientation, that is, theory applicable to more than one country or actor, and (c) an intent to fashion theories that can be subjected to empirical investigation by scientific methods. Our review is not intended to be exhaustive. In a more comprehensive review a strong case could be made for the inclusion of the innovative work of Choucri and North (1975) who relate select national attributes to conflict behavior according to an explicit interpretive theory or the efforts of McGowan (1974) to formalize a theory of foreign policy adaptation. A similar argument could be made for the examination of national elite beliefs by Bobrow *et al.* (1979), of individual beliefs by George (1979a) and others, and of role by Walker (see Chapter 14). If we relaxed the commitment to the scientific mode of inquiry, then certainly the studies of the effects of bureaucratic politics on foreign policy (e.g., Allison, 1971) deserve attention. Except for reference to our own work on the CREON project, we have excluded consideration of still emerging developments such as applications of artificial intelligence to foreign policy or international political economy as reviewed by Moon in Chapter 3.

3

Political Economy Approaches to the Comparative Study of Foreign Policy

BRUCE E. MOON

As witnessed by the existence of this volume and the conference which spawned it, there is little doubt that the current state of comparative foreign policy theory mandates the exploration of "new directions". Against that backdrop, this chapter offers a brief diagnosis of the existing literature's shortcomings and a sketch of an alternative approach built upon political economy conceptions that have generated considerable interest in related areas. In particular, the theoretical treatment of the state and the sources of its behavior are considered and key elements of that behavior are identified. A broad framework for understanding linkages between various aspects of foreign policy behavior illustrates the potential of political economy approaches.

Contemporary Comparative Foreign Policy Research

Many have lamented the continuing absence of theoretical integration in contemporary comparative foreign policy research (Rosenau, 1976a: Rosati, 1985; Kegley, Chapter 13; Powell, Dyson and Purkitt, Chapter 11). Despite a body of *ad hoc* middle-range propositions held together by methodological orthodoxy, there is no sense of a cumulative enterprise centered around a coherent and widely shared set of assumptions. Indeed, there is little common currency of concepts, no consistently applied theoretical perspectives, and few agreements about the important issues to be addressed.

The problems are not merely ones of convergence, however. Individual research efforts have seldom been adequately grounded in compelling general theory. Such influential frameworks as the decision-making approach of Snyder (1958) or the pre-theory of Rosenau (1966) encourage *ad hoc* hypothesis testing, while the promising bureaucratic politics approach yields highly indeterminate outcomes that frustrate nomothetic analysis (Allison, 1971; Halperin, 1974; Powell, Dyson and Purkitt, Chapter 11; Anderson, Chapter 15). With little guidance from the indirect and ambiguous connections between general theory and specific propositions found in these frameworks, empirical studies have relied too much on inductivist empiricism. The result is relatively few significant findings and fewer still with the potential to go beyond "islands of theory" (East and Hermann, 1974; Rummel, 1968; Kean and McGowan, 1973; Hermann and Peacock, Chapter 2 above).[1]

If there were no alternatives to the present course, it would be hard to fault those who despair of a nomothetic comparative analysis of foreign policy. (I. Anderson, 1985; P. Anderson, Chapter 15). I agree with those who argue that we would have seen more vivid signs of progress by now if success were possible by continuing along this vein (Rosenau, 1976a; Powell, Dyson and Purkitt, Chapter 11). Of course, it may well be that foreign policy will remain the exclusive province of idiographic analysis while the sphere of generalization can include only such descriptive curiosities as what types of nations have been most conflictual (Small and Singer, 1976; Rosenau, 1974).

Before conceding defeat, however, we must consider new directions for achieving a genuinely nomothetic and causal theory of foreign policy. The preferred alternative is an approach which contains a strong and explicit theoretical formulation as a focus for research which will no doubt continue to be significantly inductive and empirical. While relatively unconfining frameworks which avoid rigidity and premature closure were appropriate at an early stage, we must now enter a phase in which we take some chances.

The approach proposed here recognizes recent substantive changes in international relations and responds to theoretical developments in the social sciences by adopting a political economy perspective. The suggestions are admittedly preliminary and the theory is more crudely sketched than finely honed; but a political economy perspective offers a particularly attractive alternative since it invites merger with existing approaches. Ironically, political economy and events-data-based approaches are quite compatible because their greatly different conceptual foundations incline each to explain what the other accepts as a given.

Political Economy Approaches to
Politics and Policy

Political economy approaches have grown rapidly in recent years across a number of areas within the social sciences, including international relations (Lindblom, 1977; Weaver and Jameson, 1981; Moon, 1983a; Blake and Walters, 1983; Petras, 1978).[2] Some components of political economy theorizing have already entered the literature in the comparative study of foreign policy.[3] For example, modern theories of foreign policy behavior are sensitive to the economic bases of national power and many empirical studies have examined the circumstances under which economic instruments of influence can be used successfully (Hirschmann, 1945; Richardson and Kegley, 1980).[4] World-systems analysis emphasizes cyclical changes in the global economy and related changes in the power balances and political and economic structures between nations (Wallerstein, 1974, 1979, 1980; Chase-Dunn, 1978). Since the foreign policy of states must take these into account, the current state of the system is a major determinant of foreign policy behavior in both a direct and an indirect way (Keohane, 1979; Cohen, 1983).

Potentially important political economy contributions remain to be applied, however. While this chapter cannot do justice to the range of political economy theories, the discussion synthesizes several of them. The neo-Marxist analysis of social and economic structures, for example, has contributed to understanding certain constraints of policy making (Best and Connolly, 1982; Hicks *et al.*, 1978; Hicks and Swank, 1984). While most of this analysis is explicitly addressed to economic policy in advanced industrial societies (especially the United States), the insights offered by such theorists as O'Connor (1973) and Offe (1975) are more broadly applicable than has been realized. For example, the motivation for foreign policy behavior may derive from certain functional requisites of system maintenance (especially as self-interestedly divined by economic elites) rather than from the imperatives of national interest defined as power. From the point of view of poor countries, the class analysis of imperialism theory and dependencia is also a promising addition to more traditional approaches (Chilcote and Johnson, 1983). And the hypothesized linkage between economic structure and the political order transforms dependencia into a theory of public policy formation with potential implications for the analysis of foreign policy (Cardoso and Faletto, 1979; Moon, 1983b, 1985a).[5]

From these and other bodies of literature, the principles of an inchoate political economy framework of comparative foreign policy are drawn together and treated in greater depth below. First, policies

35

arise from states which are lodged within a political economy that shapes their behavior (McGowan and Walker, 1981; Gold *et al.*, 1975). Thus, an explicit theory of the state must consider structural constraints on behavior and recognize state interests in relation to its own society as well as relative to other international actors (Caporaso, 1982; Becker, 1982).

Second, the environment which shapes the character and behavior of states must also be understood in global terms and with respect to both economic and political phenomena. The relevant international system, for example, is as much a Wallersteinian structure of core, periphery and semi-periphery production and exchange relations as it is a Kaplanesque structure of polarity and military power (Snyder and Kick, 1979; Chase-Dunn, 1981; Rapkin, 1983).

Third, the heart of many nations' foreign policy lies in the sphere of economic relations which bear upon the balance of class forces and the distribution of economic surplus within the nation. Thus, domestic economic groups are as much the target of foreign policy actions as are external actors.

In the sections below, we especially consider the political economy challenge of two assumptions frequently made in the current literature: (1) the conception of the state as either autonomous from or irregularly constrained by social forces, and (2) the primacy of target-directed events data in foreign policy behavior.

Conceptions of the State in Comparative Foreign Policy Research

Contemporary comparative foreign policy research has attempted to explain the behavior of states without any coherent conception of the nature of the modern state nor any general theory of policy determination (Lentner, 1985). The lack of a consistent viewpoint on the nature of the state and the bases for its behavior can be traced to the absence of a theoretical paradigm. In its place, the Rosenau (1966) pre-theory has served as a guiding light for nearly two decades, but by simply organizing classes of explanatory factors by levels of analysis it has encouraged *ad hoc* and atheoretical analysis.

Thus, theoretical inconsistencies and ambiguities abound. On the one hand, nations are often assumed to act in a relatively undifferentiated manner.[6] They will pursue interests, especially power accumulation, and react to the behavior of others, exhibiting inertia and reciprocity, in ways that are not unlike other states. Indeed, the use of stimulus-response models without a mediating organism are common

(Richardson, 1960; Dixon, Chapter 5 below). Such universalist assumptions appear to be rooted in the *realpolitik* perspective while similar reliance upon an implicit *raison d'état* rationality seems to underlie the justifications offered for a wide range of empirical generalizations (Zinnes *et al.*, 1961; Russett, 1968; Singer and Small, 1968; Midlarsky, 1974; Wallace, 1972; Bueno de Mesquita, 1981).[7]

On the other hand, however, the search for domestic determinants of cross-national differences in foreign policy behavior goes on. *Ad hoc* propositions have been advanced which center on levels of domestic conflict, form of government, the size of the nation, leadership types, and many more (Sullivan, 1976; Wilkenfeld *et al.*, 1980; Rummel, 1979a). Thus, state-centric analyses which posit autonomous behavior for states disjoined from their social context exist side by side with conceptions of the state as societally constrained through some vague, perhaps pluralistic, mechanism (Krasner, 1978).

An approach rooted in the more general theory of state policy determination, of which comparative foreign policy research should be a branch, would provide a more coherent foundation. The political economy family of approaches centers upon theoretical conceptions of the state and its structural relations with the economy within which it is embedded (O'Connor, 1973; Gold *et al.*, 1975). This perspective on the state differs from more traditional notions in at least two significant respects. First, the defining mission of the state and the issue locus of its behavior lie in the economic sphere, not in the security or collective welfare areas (McGowan and Walker, 1981). Second, the criteria for policy success—and consequently goal orientation—concern a relatively small minority of the population rather than the entire community.

Structuralist theorists (represented by O'Connor, Offe, Poulantzas and others) emphasize that the relative autonomy of the state from political-economic forces in society is sharply limited. Indeed, the broad outlines of the behavior of the state are given by the twin necessities of fostering capital accumulation and maintaining its own legitimacy.

The assumption that the state in capitalist society is mandated to sustain the conditions necessary for the maintenance of capital accumulation differs from conventional views of state economic involvement in two ways. First, satisfactory economic performance is explicitly defined in terms relevant to the capitalist class rather than by the mass-oriented indicators found in the political-business cycle literature, namely unemployment and inflation (Frey, 1978). This is so simply because the pluralist assumptions of democratic control are rejected in favor of the view that the state represents the balance of class forces, which in capitalist society always favors, to some degree, the interests of the dominant economic class (Martin, 1975). Second, the continued existence of the state itself—not merely the electoral prospect of an individual office-holder—is at stake if accumulation should be threatened. Consequently, this fundamental dependency on accumulation functions as a boundary condition on state policy, or what Wright (1978) calls "structural limitation". While the necessity of accumulation may not unambiguously require *particular* policies, it will surely narrow considerably the range of choice (Offe, 1975). In this respect, the requirement of accumulation is equivalent in function to the "national security" assumption of more traditional foreign policy analysis, though it seems to have a rather more clear empirical referent.

The requirement of *legitimation* involves the state in the ideological task of "conveying the image of an organization of power that pursues common and general interests of society as a whole." This requires that "the capitalist state appeal to symbols and sources of support that *conceal* its nature as a capitalist state" (Offe, 1972, p. 127). The treatment of the concept of "national interest" is thus an enormously important difference between a political economy conception and a realist conception of foreign policy. For the latter, the state pursues the "national interest," though why this occurs is never seriously defended from pluralist challenges (Krasner, 1978). For the former, however, the state *appears* to pursue the national interest, while the actual motivation is to retain the stability of capital accumulation both through direct policy action and more indirectly through the maintenance of the legitimacy required to sustain more direct efforts. In fact, structural views characteristically regard the concept of "national interest" as nothing but an ideological invention designed to obfuscate the actual purposes and consequences of state action.

The economic essence of the state flows from the materialist assumptions of Marxism and thus stands in sharp contrast to the security basis of the Hobbesian state and the heroic character of Rousseau's social contract state (Lentner, 1985). Indeed, the institution of the state is not insulated from the competition to control the distribution of economic surplus which motivates most political behavior (Poulantzas, 1973). In fact, the state is a tool used by social classes to appropriate as large a share of the surplus as their political power will permit (Miliband, 1969). And, while such goals as maximizing the standard of living of the population or furthering broad ethical goals are not irrelevant to the state, they command little more centrality than that provided by their instrumental leverage on the economic surplus (O'Connor, 1973). Further, there is no reason to presume that these considerations are any different in foreign policy than they are in domestic policy.

Quite obviously, this is a markedly different perspective on foreign policy than that provided by a nation- or state-centered view which postulates nationalism, collective welfare, ideology or even a drive for power/security as a central motivation for state action (Krasner, 1978). Consider, for example, the common assumption that all states have an interest in maximizing economic growth and prosperity. A class-analytic perspective, by contrast, suggests that the pattern of economic and political power in Third World nations dictates that states may frequently pursue the systematic *frustration* of that goal. Since much economic development creates the foundations for new economic classes while undermining the relative position of current dominant classes, it may be *blocked*, not facilitated, by the state (Weaver and Jameson, 1981; Tullis, 1985). Further, foreign policy may well be employed to that end.

It is not surprising that this conception of the state is seldom found in theories emanating from contemporary foreign policy research. Some would explain this as a product of the state's success in obfuscating its true nature; thus, bourgeois social science theory is both a reflection of that success and a factor in its perpetuation. While there is no doubt some truth to this, a more compelling explanation points the way toward a potential synthesis.

To begin, the class character of the state and the economic component of its function, motivations and consequences captures only one facet of its nature. First, both the appearance and the reality of the state's economic and class character varies across types of nations. Since most comparative analyses of foreign policy emphasize developed nations, they systematically oversample democratic nations in which the balance of class forces most approximates a pluralistic compromise. The resulting institutional setting, ideological identifications, and currents in public debate encourage an emphasis upon "national interest" arguments and require behavior easily justified on such grounds. By contrast, the influence of class-based power inequities on foreign policy are greater and more evident in Third World nations less frequently examined in comparative foreign policy research. Stated differently, the behavioral consequences of alternative theories of the state are least divergent in those nations most studied.

Second, the visible face of the state varies across issue-areas and facets of state activity. As we see below, the emphasis of most comparatively-based theories of foreign policy is on the interactions of states—where psychological dynamics and "national interest" considerations loom especially large—while the emphasis of political economy is on economic policy—where distributional questions and class interests are much more prominent. For this reason, we turn to a second major difficulty with contemporary comparative foreign policy research, an over-reliance upon an events data conception of foreign policy behavior.

Conceptualizing the Dependent Variable in Comparative Foreign Policy Studies

Beginning with the WEIS project's attempts to quantify and compare the vast array of foreign policy actions, "who, does what, to whom, how" events data conceptual schemes have become increasingly sophisticated (East *et al.*, 1978). In making events amenable to statistical analysis, however, a great deal of information about coded events is lost while other elements of foreign policy have been largely ignored.

The requirement of comparability prohibits events data from incorporating the details of policy initiatives and their intended consequences, and instead forces reliance upon measures such as affect levels, degrees of commitment, and event targets. Missing these vital components, the foreign policy *measured* by events data analysts lacks the coherence of the foreign policy *formulated* by governments. This, in turn, seriously constrains the explanations which can be pursued. For example, a realist theory cannot explain preferences for outcomes—and therefore behaviors in pursuit of those outcomes—unless those outcomes are defined in interest terms. Clearly, events data descriptions do not allow that. Instead, emphasis is placed upon theoretical ideas which *can* be made operational in this context: inertia, reciprocity, affect, escalation, and so on. This directs attentions toward the actor-conflict aspects of foreign policy and away from the issue-outcome dimensions.

Together with the implicit conceptions of the state discussed above, these limitations account for the peculiar theoretical groundings of much comparative foreign policy work. Frequently the unstated premises are an eclectic combination of realist concerns (a "high politics" orientation and a nation-state focus) and idealist perspectives (an emphasis upon affect and interaction effects and an implicit normative concern with conflict prevention).

A more satisfactory treatment must incorporate both events data and additional dimensions of foreign policy. Emphasizing the headline-making interactions represented by events data, for example, seriously neglects the most important elements in the foreign policies of *small* states whose activities in global "high politics" are constrained by their limited resources and aspirations (see Papadakis and Starr in Chapter 20 below).[8]

Let us consider four elements of foreign policy and the means available to measure comparatively the behavior of nations with respect to each. Following this we consider the likely determinants of certain of these behaviors.

First, in order to regulate the macroeconomy and other domestic systems, a broad range of policy actions are undertaken to control transactions across national boundaries. These transactions are important for developed nations but vital in small and poor countries. It is not unusual, for example, for half of domestic production to be consumed abroad and a like percentage of aggregate consumption to be produced elsewhere. Financial transactions tend to be even more international with a large percentage of investment funds as well as capital equipment coming from abroad. These transactions have tremendous leverage on domestic variables central to the political program of any regime: employment levels, standard of living, inflation rates, distribution of wealth and income, and interest rates (Todaro, 1981). Inevitably, levels of violence and the political fortunes of political actors follow from them. Thus, though often not recognized as "foreign" policy, capital controls, exchange rate valuation, commercial policies and barriers to trade can dwarf in importance most of what states do in traditional "high politics" foreign policy areas (short of war).

Concern with foreign economic policy flows naturally from a political economy perspective which emphasizes capital accumulation and sees economic interests and issues as the main stage of political activity. Not only are such policies important in and of themselves, but they also represent the substantive heart of the issues at stake in international interactions. Yet they have been given little attention by comparative foreign policy research. With the exception of foreign aid, only recently have analysts begun to consider most aspects of foreign economic policy: nationalization (Kobrin, 1980), foreign investment restrictions (Jodice, 1980; O'Leary, 1983), tariffs and commercial policy (Conybeare, 1983; Dessler *et al.*, 1983; Cupitt, 1985); exchange rates (Moon, 1982), and stances toward the New International Economic Order (NIEO) (Hart, 1981).

A second element of a nation's foreign policy is its official public stance on major global issues. Generally represented operationally by UN voting patterns, issue stances reveal the application of such fundamental principles of foreign policy viewpoint as right/left, East/West, and North/South orientations. The positions taken on individual issues are highly patterned and generally sum to a visible, coherent and stable outlook on the interests, values and perspectives which dominate—though not so publicly—other aspects of state policy (Moon, 1985a).[9] Despite UN voting data's long history in international

41

relations research, some still contend that position taking is without importance unless resources are expended in pursuit of the positions advocated (Tomlin, 1985). This impression is mistaken, however, since for most nations the predominant goal of position taking is not resolution of the issue itself but rather expression of the stance of the nation. These positions communicate alignment to external actors—which can be of great significance in a variety of ways—and can also be an extremely important element of the legitimation function. It has long been accepted, for example, that the anti-imperialist rhetoric of the NIEO has insulated many Third World governments from domestic criticism of poor economic performance.

A third dimension of foreign policy is the set of actions undertaken in response to specific external "problems" which may or may not involve broader global issues or regulatory efforts. Most often they are dyadic. The actions are usually directed at identifiable actors, but focused upon the resolution of the specific problem. The barriers to making comparable and quantifiable the diverse issues arising in dyadic relations are virtually insurmountable and events data, while aspiring to measure these elements, actually focuses more effectively upon the closely related fourth dimension of foreign policy—affective relations with external actors.

This fourth element consists of both the level of hostility manifested in daily event interactions and the institutionalized cooperation measured by diplomatic representation, alliance status, long-term aid relationships and the like. The first of these is best measured by events data. While the substance of a precise policy proposal or issue position may be difficult to capture in any simple or comparable way, the level of affect—whether interpreted as the general state of relations or as a referendum on the position taken by other actors in this particular case—can be scaled with reasonable simplicity and aggregated over time. It is surely clear, however, that this measure is severely limited as a general description of the foreign policy behavior of a nation. It can capture only indirectly most of the key components of foreign policy because it can reflect the *form* of policy so much better than its *content*.

While any comprehensive understanding of foreign policy requires attention to all four elements, most current studies have considered only the single facet for which their theoretical explanation is best suited. Psychological process models, for example, use events data to focus on affective relations, national attribute approaches have used UN voting data to study position taking, while case studies in decision making and bureacratic politics, less bound by the requirements of comparability, have focused on politico-military "strategic" policy. Of course, a fusion among them is eventually desirable—and a small step toward that goal is taken in a later section—because these components interact such that explanations for elements exogenous to one analysis may be found in another. Substantive policy choices affect relations with other actors, for example, while actor relations affect substantive policy. However, we must enter the circle of causation somewhere and it is prudent to apply political economy approaches first in those areas in which they are likely to be most effective. Consequently, the following section illustrates some key lines of causation in the context of foreign economic policy.

The Determinants of Foreign Economic Policy

If political economy approaches to the comparative study of foreign policy are to have value, they must be capable of generating plausible and testable empirical propositions. This requires a precise enough statement of the constraints imposed by the requirements of system reproduction—accumulation and legitimation—to produce predictions of state behavior. That is, how are we—or, for that matter, actual decision makers—to determine what behaviors will reproduce the system? Moreover, given that more than one avenue for reproduction probably exists—or will be seen to exist—what choices will be made between plausible competing policies?

These questions clearly cannot be answered in the abstract or in any generalized way. Behavior designed to maintain a system must surely respond to the policy environment of the individual state and thus vary from nation to nation. But what "national attributes" determine state behavior? Political economy approaches postulate the structure of the economy as a significant predictor of behavior through its interrelationships with key factors such as the relative political strength of various classes and fractions of classes, the ideological orientation and institutional make-up of the state, and the linkages of domestic actors to external ones. Because theories of political economy assume these relationships are both strong and nonrecursive, it is difficult to sort out the key causal factors without making distinctions which are theoretically artificial. At the same time, neither the interactions among these structural attributes nor the postulated linkages with foreign policy behavior have been subjected to systematic empirical test. Consequently, the formulation of five related independent variable clusters presented below is quite rough and the illustrative hypotheses concerning foreign economic policy are necessarily extremely preliminary.

Such dimensions of economic structure as the degree of industrialization, the nature of factor and final goods markets for leading products,

43

the unevenness of sectoral development, and interactions with the global economy will strongly influence the reproduction requirements of the system through several mechanisms. We begin by considering the structure of the economy and the resultant pattern of class formation.

First, the structure of the economy and the make-up of the dominant economic class or fraction are sufficiently interrelated that we may crudely measure the latter through the former. The make-up of economic elites—their interests, values, and perspectives—will influence policies designed to provide for capital accumulation because accumulation takes place largely among elites whose interests are thus adopted as a guidepost for state policy. The embracing of elite interests as the goals of the state is further encouraged by the pattern of personnel recruitment in the state apparatus. Economic wealth translates to political power which, in turn, inclines the state toward choices among plausible policies which coincide with the interests of the elite.[10]

We may roughly identify three potentially dominant classes or fractions which correspond to different structures of the macroeconomy—a traditional agrarian elite, a national bourgeoisie, and an international bourgeoisie. The division between the latter two concerns both ownership of industry and the market destination of the industrial output, each of which affects the interests, values, and perspectives of domestic actors. Alliances between various fractions are likely but too complex for the constraints of this chapter (see Evans, 1979).

The characteristic interests of these groups suggest the following expectations:

H1: The greater the power of the internationalist fraction of capital, the more likely the adoption and continuance of an export-oriented development policy, the greater the encouragement of foreign direct investment and the fewer the restrictions on multinational corporations.

H2: The greater the power of the nationalist fraction of capital, the more likely the adoption of an import-substitution development policy and the greater the restrictions on multinational corporations.

H3: The greater the power of the traditional agrarian sector, the more likely the adoption of a *laissez-faire* development policy.

These hypotheses follow straightforwardly from the interests of the dominant fraction of capital, but they are neither tautologically true nor unchallenged by alternative theoretical formulations. It has been argued, for example, that restrictions on investments of multinational corporations increase as their penetrative capacity exceeds a threshold which threatens national autonomy (Rothgeb, 1985). Similarly, export and import patterns can lead to an external reliance which generates negative side effects and social and political tensions. The above hypotheses, by contrast, postulate a positive feedback unaffected by national interest or popular protest considerations as elites actively resist policies which would threaten their power.[11]

The second major variable cluster involves an aspect of class relations whose political expression is found in governmental forms, the relative strength of the working class and peasantry. Arguably, their interests may be represented by the state directly in state socialist systems where significant nonstate bases of economic power—personal wealth, ownership of the means of production, and an effective franchise—are abolished. Democratic states represent a very different structure, but one of considerable, albeit quite variable, power for the working class and peasantry.

A closely related third variable cluster consists of the ideological precepts which dominate both state policy and mass perceptions. These precepts, which summarize the political program of the ruling coalition as well as the economic and political theories and rhetoric which support it, are strongly related to the balance of class forces, since constraints on policy choice can be considerable in those systems in which the working class has achieved some measure of political power. While the requirement of capital accumulation can never be displaced as the pre-eminent goal of state action in a capitalist system, class power can force a different pattern of trade-offs between accumulation and legitimation. O'Connor (1973) argues, for example, that the policy instruments of the welfare state are requisite for the survival of the system in advanced industrial nations marked by strong class consciousness. On the other hand, the balance of class forces in Somoza's Nicaragua forced no such concessions—at least for a long time—while the balance of forces in Mexico led to a pattern of legitimation which involves the rhetoric of state ideology more than the real effects of state policy.

In general, these elements covary along a simple right-left scale (Stephens, 1979). Social democratic parties and powerful labor unions mark one end of the democratic continuum with rightist democracies (manifesting the ascendency of economic elites) occupying the other. Conservative regimes in which traditional elites dominate without the balancing mechanism of democratic processes lie still further along the scale, which is finally anchored on the far right by political economies which are not marked by strong self-conscious class formations (Blondel, 1969). In addition to working-class power muting the strength of the relationships in H1–H3, the following hypotheses derive from these conceptions:

H4: The greater the political power of the working class and peasantry, the further left the ideology of the state and the more likely the adoption of a basic needs development policy.

H5: The less developed the class formation, the more likely the adoption of a *laissez-faire* development policy.

H6: The further left the ideology, the greater the restrictions on multinational corporations and the greater the efforts to achieve partner diversity in international transactions.

Fourth, the location of the economy in the global division of labor is strongly related to the structure of the economy itself (Wallerstein, 1979; Moon, 1985b). The links between the economy and the global system condition the historical development of the former and modify the effects of contemporary policies. Crucial dimensions of these linkages include the extent of reliance on foreign trade, aid and investment as well as the specific character of that reliance (e.g., the elasticity of supply and demand for certain products and factors). The independent effect of global structural position is difficult to ascertain, of course, since it is intertwined with economic structure and class formation (Moon, 1985b). Its influence on development choice occurs through these latter two in addition to the following direct impacts:

H7: The more exclusive the external dependence, the more likely economic policy will be in accord with the preferences of the dominant partner.

H8: The greater the external reliance and the weaker the state with respect to external actors, the more likely economic policy will be in accord with international norms (i.e. liberal).

Fifth, particular short-term economic conditions will impel nations toward particular policy behaviors. Some conditions will exacerbate reliance on external actors or liberate the nation, accentuate or ameliorate the legitimation crisis, and, of course, alter the strategy which must be pursued in order to maximize capital accumulation.[12] For example:

H9: The greater the decline in economic growth—and, interactively, the greater the instability or the democratic processes of the political system—the more pronounced will be the tendencies in development policy to conform to expectations based upon economic structure and ideology.

H10: The greater the decline in net factor inflows—and, interactively, the greater the instability or the democratic processes of the political system—the more pronounced will be the tendencies in MNC policy to conform to expectations based upon economic structure and ideology.

This last cluster illustrates the difficulty of general theory since the variable impact of short-term economic forces across cases mandates hypotheses which are conditional in form.

The above formulation contains an alternative to Rosenau's identification of classes of explanatory variables for comparative foreign policy analysis. However, it is important to note that the theoretical nature of the cluster scheme introduced here contrasts sharply with the levels of analysis categorization of Rosenau. However, the sketch is meant to be illustrative of a political economy orientation rather than a definitive theoretical edifice. Moreover, the focus on economic policy highlights an area in which political economy approaches can be expected to have the greatest utility. It remains to consider both other elements of a nation's foreign policy and the integration of political economy with more traditional approaches. It is to these tasks that we now turn.

Toward a Comprehensive Framework for the Comparative Study of Foreign Policy

Any comprehensive understanding of foreign policy must eventually consider all four dimensions of behavior: affective relations, position taking on global issues, problem-oriented behavior, and economic policy. The latter was the special focus of the last section, but the relevance of political economy approaches to other elements must also be demonstrated. While length constraints prohibit any detailed discussion, three brief notes will point the way toward potential applications to the former two.

First, because the four elements interact, we can expect that explanations of global issue position-taking and patterns in affective relations will be improved by including foreign economic policy as an *independent* variable along with the other five clusters. While the elements are interrelated, political economy conceptions of the state and its primary objectives suggest economic policy as the centerpiece from which the remaining elements of foreign policy flow. Certainly, national economic policies often bear directly on the issues now dominant on the agendas of international institutions. Also, economic policy differences cast a heavy shadow on the affective relations of many nation dyads.

Second, political economy approaches offer more theoretically compelling explanations for some patterns already observed. Previous efforts at explaining UN voting, for example, have generally followed one of two paths. The national attribute approach of Vincent (1971) identified size, level of economic development, and degree of political "openness" as explaining the bulk of cross-national variance. The political compliance approach of Richardson and Kegley (1980) attributes

47

position taking to the influence of external actors who control key economic flows. The former approach is highly atheoretical while the latter is an economic corollary to power politics theory resting at best on weak empirical support (Moon, 1983b, 1985a).

More persuasive explanations can be generated by political economy approaches which attribute issue positions to state ideologies rather than the degree of "political openness" with which it is partially correlated (Moon and Dixon, 1985). Further, explanations centered on those elite interests and perspectives which derive from economic structure and global position more clearly identify causal mechanisms than national attribute approaches which simply cite partial correlates like size and level of development.

Of course, the effects of international economic transactions on foreign policy need not be confined to the elementary application of economic compellance or deterrence since political economy orientations stress the effects of transactions on the social/political/economic structures which give rise to the policy preferences of elites (Moon, 1982). Moreover, the influencing agents need not be other nation-states; they may be such international institutions as the World Bank, such subnational actors as international banks, or such impersonal agents as markets for goods or currencies (see Karns and Mingst in Chapter 22 below).

Third, political economy approaches also have the intriguing capacity to be integrated with more traditional approaches to the explanation of affective relations. This integration is especially desirable since neither approach is individually capable of offering a comprehensive explanation without recourse to key variables which are themselves exogenous. For example, most interaction models are either implicitly or explicitly dominated by the processes of inertia and reciprocity. They have produced some important implications for our understanding of escalation processes and conflict resolution, but they require the stipulation of initial conditions—often in the form of the history of affective relations—to transform them from descriptive or predictive estimation models to properly explanatory causal models. Arms race models, for example, assume an exogenously determined "grievance" factor (Richardson, 1960); CREON assumes prior affect in defining various elements of its "external predisposition" (Hudson et al., 1982); stimulus-response models require a triggering event (Dixon, Chapter 5 below); and many others are so narrowly defined that such assumptions are hidden in the selection of the sample (Gamson and Modigliani, 1972; Wilkenfeld et al., 1972; Zinnes et al., 1961).

Moreover, the inability of events-data-based theoretical developments to account for these factors is probably fundamental; such approaches must rely upon another component of a comprehensive theory to supply explanations for them. A broader model might identify affective relations as the twin products of a "predisposition" toward a given level of affect and a precise history of interactions whose dynamic forces may incline nations away from that predisposition.[13] Previous efforts to establish such "baseline" expectations at time "$t-1$" have been neither theoretically compelling nor empirically successful. Among the most comprehensive efforts, for example, is the "field theory" of Rummel (1977) which translates various national attributes into a "social distance" between the actors in any given dyad. The underlying mechanism for these conflict determinants remains unclear, however, and the attributes which make up the *relevant* difference between nations is determined *mathematically*, not *theoretically*. A political economy approach would define the expected affect between pairs of nations to be a function of (1) the ideological distance between them; (2) the strains imposed by different, especially competing, foreign economic policies; (3) the class make-up of the ruling elites; (4) the structural relations between them and their respective locations in the global division of labor, and so on.

Thus, because political economy approaches are oriented toward explaining the substantive policies and perspectives which constitute the background conditions while other models are more oriented toward short-term perturbations from a given background predisposition, the potential bridges between them are quite obvious. Unfortunately, this topic cannot be pursued further within the confines of this chapter though it is the hope of this author that the ideas will be explored by others.

Conclusion

This chapter has presented only the broad outlines of a political economy approach to the comparative study of foreign policy. Length considerations prevent a more extensive presentation of hypotheses or a more detailed theoretical sketch. It nonetheless has suggested some major benefits from pursuing further this option.

Previous theories of comparative foreign policy have been built upon conceptions more accurately applied to a few relatively large and developed global powers than to the broad universe of contemporary states. Emphasis upon high politics is characteristic of the foreign policies of NATO and WTO nations, but not of UNCTAD member nations. The class character of the state in advanced industrial societies is less obvious—and less important—than in societies without an institutionalized class compromise of the welfare state type. Ideology is more easily seen as a significant determinant of policy in nations whose ideological spectrum spans fascism, liberalism, and communism than in an American political culture of Tweedledum/Tweedledee centrist parties. For all these reasons, political economy approaches are likely to be rather more broadly applicable than the current alternatives.

Political economy approaches are also more likely to be integrated with other social science research thrusts. Because political economy is a growing theoretical perspective in public policy, comparative politics, and international relations research, the cross-fertilization possibilities are far greater than in the insular world of *raison d'état*.

Finally, political economy perspectives have the advantage of having seldom been tried. Whether they represent a major new beginning for foreign policy analysis or just another dead end is very much an open question. We would not be inclined to think of novelty as an asset were it not true that *by contrast*, it appears that for current theories, the jury of peers is already in.

Some interpretive caution is warranted, however, because the framework sketched in this chapter is highly speculative. It is built upon some *particular* political economy conceptions and theories; by no means does it exhaust all of them. Further, its presentation is sufficiently sparse that the implications of major splits in political economy orientations are concealed. I thus close with a plea: if the infant theory proposed here is found wanting, let us not on that basis condemn the future generations of its family.

Notes

1 From the standpoint of general theory, even relatively successful forecasting approaches fall short. The fine work of the most recent CREON generation (Hermann, 1983b; Hudson *et al.*, 1982), for example, must be considered a forecasting and not a causal model since key explanatory elements—prior affect levels and the triggering event—are themselves exogenously determined.

2 Political economy approaches are so diverse that it is easier to roughly characterize their shared core than to define them. These approaches assume that economic and political/social/cultural processes are intertwined through mechanisms so difficult to disentangle that studies must cut across boundaries of traditional fields to grasp the strands of causality (Gilpin, 1975b). In practice, most political economists tend to ascribe causal priority to economic phenomena, though this is by no means universal and in any case never complete (Cardoso and Faletto, 1979). The political bases of economic forms, institutions, behaviors and outcomes are never neglected (Herring, 1980).

3 The analysis of the foreign economic policy of advanced industrial societies is

a well-developed tradition, but it is not generally integrated with other aspects of a nation's foreign policy (Krasner, 1976, 1978; McGowan and Walker, 1981; Keohane, 1979; Katzenstein, 1978; Helleiner, 1979; Cohen, 1982).

4 For a complete guide to this literature and a reanalysis of the quantitative findings, see Moon (1983a, 1985a).

5 Of course, through its treatment of the returns to various factors of production much orthodox economic analysis (e.g. the modern trade theory of Heckscher-Ohlin) also offers insight into the questions of distribution which dominate Marxist class-based political economic analysis.

6 The clearest example is the widespread use of game-theoretic and other formal approaches which explicitly accept the essential similarity of nations and their decision-making processes. Empirical analyses also use such assumptions, though not always willingly. The fine analysis of Leng and Wheeler (1979), for example, requires treating all nations in order to arrive at a large enough sample of situations.

7 This is unfortunate because methodological incompatibilities make it difficult to accurately translate such venerable principles as "national interest" into operational variables in cross-national research.

8 This is far more than the commonly cited source bias problem in which the event interactions of small and poor countries are not as faithfully reported as those of more "important" nations. Rather, events data do not measure other policy elements which are more important than event interactions for the former group.

9 Critiques of UN voting data based upon the absence of correlation with events data aggregates miss the point (Tomlin, 1985). First, given the notorious reliability problems of events data, it is strange that events data should be used as a standard. Second, and more significantly, these two measures are actually measures of quite different dimensions of foreign policy. There is no inconsistency in two nations having similar global issue positions, but either strikingly antagonistic dyadic relations (e.g., India–Pakistan) or few dyadic interactions (e.g., Mali–Nicaragua).

10 In simple terms, the choice between these two paths of causation—one emphasizing the structural necessity of state policy and the other the reality of self-interested state personnel—is the difference between the structuralist views of Poulantzas and the instrumentalist views of Miliband. Poulantzas emphasizes the relative autonomy of the state from the various fractions of capital so as to enable the state to operate in the interests of capital as a whole. Miliband emphasizes the state as a tool of class domination through the mechanism of domination of the state apparatus. This discussion attempts to steer a middle course between the two and consider both branches of the causal linkage between economic elites and state policy.

11 The intent is not to assert that the "national interest" is not served by elite actions. The ambiguity of the term itself and the complexities in calculating utilities prevent any serious defense of that proposition. Rather, the thrust of this style of analysis is to ignore "national interest" arguments and to search for the motives of state behavior elsewhere.

12 Over the longer term persistent economic conditions can transform the nature of class relations, the structure of the economy and even location within the global division of labor. Such long-term effects are beyond the

bounds of this chapter, however, and are noted here only to serve as a reminder of the dynamic analysis which is required to fill out the framework completely. Indeed, it is this very emphasis upon the dynamic interactions between structure and process which is the single most marked methodological characteristic of political economy approaches.

13 Elsewhere (Moon, 1985a) I have compared this "baseline" behavior and movements away from it to the "normal vote" approach of voting behavior theorists in distinguishing relatively enduring versus short-term influences on voting decisions (Converse *et al.*, 1969).

4

Toward Single-Country Theories of Foreign Policy: the Case of the USSR

JAMES N. ROSENAU

The study of foreign policy cries out for developmental theory, for formulations which anticipate how the major determinants of a country's external behavior interact across time. In recent decades sociologists have evolved a subfield of life-cycle sociology, psychologists have accorded subfield status to developmental psychology, economists have done the same for developmental economics, and political scientists have used various labels to identify a subfield of political development. Comparable tendencies in the foreign policy field, however, have yet to stir. Indeed, for very different reasons, both area specialists and comparative foreign policy analysts tend to reject the very idea of a developmental subfield that is committed to scientific methods and that aspires to building viable and testable theory. Committed to accounting for the unique details and cultural nuances that differentiate their region or country of concern, area specialists do not see themselves as engaged in a scientific enterprise. For them, historical narrative and idiographic inquiry are the preferred modes of analysis and any attempt to frame testable theory about their region or country tends to be viewed as a violation of the very diversity that renders it distinctive. Comparativists, on the other hand, resist the idea of a developmental subfield because they do regard their endeavors as scientific and fear that a focus on development across time will confine them, perforce, to a single case and accounting for the impact of specific events, foci they see as the very antithesis of science with its stress on identifying and explaining central tendencies among many cases.

To be sure, comparativists occasionally pay lip service to the legitimacy of using the premises of science to compare a single country's policies across different time periods. But the prime thrust of their theoretical efforts has been to compare different actors at the same time or under similar circumstances. To my knowledge, in fact, no comparativist honors the idea of single-country theory in practice; or at least one is hard pressed to identify any theory of any country's foreign policy that is grounded in the epistemology and methods of science. Single-country theories do exist in abundance—those of the Soviet Union are perhaps especially numerous—but they are the products of either diplomatic historians or area specialists who rely on historical examples to demonstrate how the pieces fit together and, in so doing, conspicuously avoid explicit hypotheses as to how specified variables will interact under specified conditions.

This gap in the comparative literature is all the more glaring when viewed in the context of current affairs. Perhaps a preponderance of the problems that arise in world politics concern the behavior of a single country. What will the Soviets do in Afghanistan? Will Peru be able to follow a new course in handling its international debts? How will the United States respond to terrorism? Is East Germany likely to seek further accommodations with the Federal Republic? These are just current examples of the myriad single-country problems that are on the world's agenda at any moment in time. But somehow students of comparative foreign policy have yet to develop a systematic approach to such questions. The commitment to comparative analysis has focused attention so thoroughly on types of actors—such as bureaucracies, developed countries or African states—that can be contrasted as to obscure the need to be similarly systematic about the single actor. Also, since the analysis of a single actor is bound to require accounting for its unique history and culture, the idea of using scientific methods to probe its conduct is likely to seem impossible to those who conceive of science as suited only to the investigation of generic types.

Persuaded that the core of scientific theory involves expectations as to what happens when specified variables interact under specified circumstances, the ensuing discussion suggests that it may be possible to construct developmental or single-country theories of foreign policy without forgoing the basic commitments of science. Indeed, I would argue that efforts along this line are mandatory if the comparative study of foreign policy is to evolve a full storehouse of equipment for exploring the wide range of phenomena encompassed by the field. Furthermore, single-country theories may also prove valuable as components of broader formulations about the interactions of two or more states. Conceivably they may even facilitate the construction of more general models about the class of actors in which the country subjected to this form of theorizing is located.

In short, broad theoretical development and the analysis of specific foreign policy problems are not incompatible enterprises. To argue for single-country theory is neither to reject a nomothetic orientation nor to abandon the search for generalizable knowledge that spans a single sequence of events. The commitment to "anti-case study" approaches (Rosenau, Burgess and Hermann, 1973) is not diminished, or in any way undermined, by focusing on the foreign policy processes and actions of a single country. As a number of scholars have noted (Russett, 1970a; Lijphart, 1971, 1975; Eckstein, 1975; George, 1979a), the specific case can be used for theory development if care is exercised in the identification of its wider relevance and the specification of its key variables.

The Soviet Union as a Theoretical Case

In order to explore the potentials of single-country theory, the analysis that follows focuses on the USSR as a concrete example. The Soviet Union is especially challenging in this regard not only because of its importance on the world scene, but also because information about its policy-making processes is relatively scarce. If viable single-country theory about the Soviet system can be developed, I would contend, then it ought to be possible to do at least as well in theorizing about any country.

In a sense political scientists are fortunate that information about Soviet policy-making processes is scarce and access to its officials minimal, that—as Churchill once commented—the USSR is a riddle wrapped in a mystery inside an enigma. Under these conditions we need not fear being overwhelmed by data, relying too heavily on skewed samples, or succumbing to the fallacy of letting the facts speak for themselves. Nor need we feel inundated by the extensive information that can flow from press conferences, legislative hearings, inter-agency rivalries, or any of the other channels through which important voices are sorted out from a multiplicity of sources. Stated differently, in seeking to comprehend the USSR we have the advantage of not being able to peek into the black box and thus are free to be imaginative about the ways in which the inputs from abroad and the domestic scene get converted into policies and actions.

Put in another way, we can luxuriate in being forced to theorize. The scarcity of facts, samples, and data leaves us no choice but to concept-ualize the dynamics operative upon and within the black box that has long enveloped the Soviet policy-making organization. And, having been compelled to explicate our expectations as to how these dynamics function, we are then in the happy position of needing to look only at outcomes to test our theorizing. Just as the experimental psychologist can test hypotheses about learning by varying rewards and punishments to observe the effects on behavior rather than by exploring the workings of the psyche, so can we extend our knowledge of the Soviets by assessing the fit between stimuli and responses without having to trace or measure any intervening effects.

To some extent, of course, my euphoria over the prospects of solving Soviet riddles is forced. A plenitude of information, facts, and data is, plainly, preferable to a scarcity. Clearly, the capacity to interview officials and ponder hearing transcripts is preferable to not being able to do so. Yet it is more than sarcasm to discern opportunities in the black box that encases Soviet policy making. The riddle-mystery-enigma conception of the USSR has hindered scholarship by providing a rationale to cling to, rather than test, preconceptions about its dynamics. Instead of aggressively framing testable hypotheses about how Soviet behavior may vary in response to different stimuli, the dominant tendency is to be intimidated by the paucity and unavailability of information and thus either to refrain from theorizing explicitly or to be so inhibited in developing rigorous propositions as to settle for untestable speculation that is bound to confine and curb inquiry. These inclinations can be overcome, however, if the scarcity of data is treated as opportunity rather than obstacle.

And, outrageous as it may seem, there are good reasons to reverse our perspective in this way. Parading methodological horribles and empirical obstacles is no route to creative theory and sound knowledge. Einstein did not shrink from theorizing about the physical universe because the capacity to observe and measure it from deep in space did not exist. Rather he played the game of "as if," proceeding as if the capacity to test his theories was, or would eventually become, available. Equally important, the propounding of his relativity theory was an incentive to the development of the methodology and technology necessary to test it. Much the same can be said about the Soviet universe. If we play down the closedness of the Soviet system and proceed as if it was open to observation, we are likely to be more incisive and creative in our theorizing about it and, subsequently, more innovative in the development of techniques for generating relevant data with which to test and perfect our understanding.[1]

A second reason not to be overly sensitive to the closedness of the Soviet system is the ever-present possibility of new openings, or at least new peepholes, in the black box. In the 1950s, for example, no one foresaw that Stalin's daughter would flee to the West and write about her father (Alliluyeva, 1967), that Khrushchev's memoirs would be published (Talbott, 1970), or that the highest ranking Soviet official in the United Nations would defect and publish an account of how foreign policy is formulated in the USSR (Shevchenko, 1985). Just as science fiction thrived by highlighting the theoretical possibility of deep probes in outer space, in other words, so must we allow for the theoretically possible advent of changes in the Soviet system that permit more direct observation of its policy-making processes. Indeed, even in the absence of such changes, the passage of time is bound to reveal more and more about these processes as their outcomes cumulate across decades. The recent spate of leadership successions is a case in point. The enlargement of these outcomes from three to six since 1980 has greatly facilitated comprehension of institutionalization in the Soviet system and how its structures handle the recruitment and consolidation of top officials.

Besides, we are not averse to asserting conclusions about what occurs in the black box. Rare is the student of the Soviet Union who does not have a position on its foreign policy goals, its openness to long-term change and influence, its capacity for policy reversals, or the relative importance of its internal and external commitments. Many analysts, to be sure, are quick to note the limits of their informational base, but these limits are no bar to the holding of perspectives which posit the Soviets as aggressive, or cautious, or pragmatic in world affairs and rigid, or inefficient, or innovative in the domestic arena. Indeed, the informational limits often seem to relieve analysts of a felt need to be skeptical about their interpretations and to permit them to adhere to uncomplicated and unqualified, if not ideological and polemical, conceptions of Soviet motives and actions.[2] More importantly for present purposes, the sturdiness of the black box encourages the conviction that the only way to know anything about the Soviets is through a familiarity with Russian history and culture—that is, area studies—that can at least yield projections of past patterns. Scientific theorizing, many Russian specialists seem to say, is fruitless in such a research setting, albeit they do not shrink from using historical experience to justify assertions, perspectives, and positions on what the USSR is up to at any moment in time.

In short, the fact is that the paucity of information does not prevent theorizing about Soviet dynamics; it only inhibits thorough, rigorous, and systematic theorizing. Persuaded that they are dealing with riddles, mysteries and enigmas, many analysts tend to downplay the utility of established standards of social scientific inquiry, tending instead to interpret whatever happens in the Soviet Union as reaffirming their notions of what drives that system. The first law of social dynamics— that we see what we want to see—thus rarely gets subjected to thorough, rigorous and systematic challenges in the field of Soviet studies. The idea of manipulating variables, holding some constant and treating others as interactive, appears to be viewed as hopeless, given the lack of access to data, and this sense of futility in turn fosters a resistance to framing theory and hypotheses that can be tested and falsified.[3] It is as if analysts believe that falsifiable theory should be developed only if the capacity to falsify it is immediately available. The possibility that such theory might be clarifying even in the absence of a falsification capacity, or that it might fruitfully be explored through synthetic, less comprehensive research methodologies, is apparently overlooked in the face of seemingly insurmountable obstacles to direct observation.

An instructive example of these atheoretical tendencies to cling to preconceptions and not to frame propositions that can be systematically tested is provided by the many analysts who, perhaps unknowingly, posit the Soviet system as impervious to change. One could cite, for instance, a number of studies in which the Russians are seen as never wavering in their foreign policy goals.[4] Undoubtedly the continuities of Soviet life are more powerful than the impulses to innovate and change, but it violates everything we know about social systems to presume that they can adhere to a never-ending constancy in foreign affairs, that goals and priorities are not altered across generations, and that the emergence of new technologies, institutions, and social structures have no consequences for the values that underlie policy making. Or at least we know enough along these lines to warrant pausing frequently to assess the presumption of constancy. Unfortunately, however, all too often such pauses are conspicuous by their absence. All too often analysts seem to treat the Kremlin as so capable of converting every dynamic of change into yet another instance of prior practice that they—the analysts—do not question the possible rigidities of their own premises.

In sum, in trying to fathom modern-day Russia, analysts need to come to terms at the outset with an overriding question: namely, how willing are they to treat the Soviet Union as a case among many and to what extent are they inclined, on the other hand, to treat it is a unique polity, with a unique history, culture, and circumstances? Virtually all of the literature on the USSR is crucially shaped by the answer to this question. And since it involves the proper route to understanding, it is a question that divides analysts in harsh ways, leading often to fruitless disputes that intensify the divisiveness without clarifying the question. My own view, as will be seen, is that both the single- and multiple-case perspectives can be creatively employed in theorizing about Soviet politics and that the theory-building enterprise is set back by the tendency not to be explicit as to the relative strength one attributes to dynamics derived from unique circumstances and those derived from more encompassing factors. Moreover, as will also be noted, the assertion that both the idiographic and nomothetic approaches are relevant stems from substantive premises and not from a wishy-washy impulse to find a middle ground between two extremes. Nor is the stress on synthesis a way of avoiding hard analytic choices. Rather, it is rooted in the assumption that any country is a composite of both unique and general factors, that there are dimensions of Soviet experience common to all industrialized and industrializing societies even as there are dimensions rooted in Russian history.[5] The task is to recognize these disparate elements and then synthesize them into coherent theory. And a large step in the direction of such theory is acknowledging that such a synthesis is both viable and legitimate.[6]

And there is a powerful urgency in the need to develop synthesized theories of the Soviet Union. Life-and-death questions are being decided by top officials in the West on the basis of crude and impressionistic expectations that are neither systematic nor testable, but that are nonetheless presumed to have empirical validity. Recently, for example, supporters of tests of antisatellite weapons in space argued for the testing program on the grounds that it "would create pressure on the Soviet Union to negotiate more seriously at arms control talks in Geneva" (*New York Times*, 1985). Whatever their truth or falsity, theoretical conclusions of this order are too crucial to be left to epistemologically naive politicians and bureaucrats. They desperately need to be made aware of themselves as participants in the theoretical enterprise, and such a sensitivity is going to develop only if scholars lead the way, demonstrating through their competing constructs both the dangers and rewards of explicit theorizing.

The Nature of Single-Country Theory

Given a euphoric orientation that stresses the fertility rather than the futility of the USSR as a research focus, how does one proceed? How to develop thorough, rigorous and systematic theory about the Soviet Union that identifies key variables and specifies how they can be expected to vary under different conditions? The answer lies, first, in acquiring the confidence that such theory can be framed and, second, in achieving syntheses between specific knowledge of Russian culture and history and general knowledge of the dynamics of industrialized and multi-ethnic societies with vast resources and longstanding international commitments. Such syntheses amount to what might be called single-country theory, a form of theorizing that appears to involve a contradiction in terms and thus may seem flawed to both the area specialist and the empirical comparativist. To overcome skepticism about the viability of such theory, and to build confidence in its feasibility, an explanation of its nature and construction is in order.

The objections of area specialists to single-country theory are likely to focus on the idea of deriving propositions about the Soviet Union from generalized models and findings relevant to how politics and economics unfold in certain classes of countries or under certain kinds of conditions. Such propositions are bound to be too broad, they argue, to allow for the historical experiences and cultural premises that are unique to the Soviets: yes, the USSR is industrialized and, yes, it is a superpower; but any propositions derived from these realities have only the most general relevance to the Soviet Union, its location in both Europe and Asia, its longstanding patterns of authoritarian rule, its communist revolution, its unending aspirations to a warm-water port, its suffering in the Second World War, and all the other characteristics which set it apart from any other country, even those that have also undergone industrialization and achieved great-power status. Only through intensive probings of its distinguishing characteristics, the area specialists conclude, can a grasp of the Soviet system be developed. And even then, what is grasped is not so much theoretical as it is sound understanding, since the personality of leaders and situational dynamics can vary so much as to nullify any theory.

Comparativists, on the other hand, are likely to doubt the utility of single-country theory on the grounds that knowledge is developed only by comparing across units and not by allowing for the operation of unique cultural and historical circumstances in a single unit. For them sound theory that is explanatory and predictive can never be rooted in the particularistic dimensions of a system. It must involve generalizations that apply to more than one case and, accordingly, that ignore the specific characteristics that differentiate one country from another. Yes, the USSR is uniquely astride Eurasia and, yes, it has never had adequate access to a warm-water port or been free of authoritarian regimes; but such realities of its history and culture only have theoretical import if they are cast, interactively, in a larger context. To know that tsarist and communist leaders alike aspired to a warm-water port, for example, is not to anticipate how Soviet officials are likely to respond today to a confrontation with the United States over Turkey, Iran or Iraq. Only propositions derived from, say, deterrence theory or findings relevant to how countries react in crisis situations, the comparativists conclude, can be of use in this regard.

In short, the comparativists contend that the area specialists lack a more encompassing, nomothetic context, and the latter see the former as woefully inattentive to idiographic detail. And this gap often seems so wide that rarely do either the generalists or the specialists attempt to bridge it, much less incorporate each others' findings and insights into their own formulations.[7] Yet, despite their differences, achieving a theoretical synthesis between the two perspectives is not nearly as difficult as it may seem. All that is required is a concession on the part of the generalists that comparing shifts in the key variables that sustain the same system across time is as much a form of scientific inquiry as comparing their operation across different systems, while all the specialists need to concede is that the functioning of any system at any moment in time can derive from generalized dynamics that condition many systems as well as from its unique cultural and historical experiences. Making these concessions may not be easy for an analyst long accustomed to reasoning otherwise, but their logic strikes me as impeccable.

Consider the case for within-system, across-time comparisons. Scientific inquiry involves the anticipation, identification, measurement and interpretation of patterns embedded in a number of data points. The investigator compares the patterns in different units as they might vary and/or break in response to specified stimuli or the emergence of different conditions. What renders these procedures scientific is not the nature of the units, but the availability of enough data points to form patterns and enough evidence of stimuli and/or conditions that are sufficiently different to justify before-and-after comparisons. If the data are sufficient and the breakpoints separating the before-and-after patterns clear-cut,[8] therefore, it does not matter whether the comparisons are made across several units or within one. The latter offers a laboratory for scientific inquiry in the sense that its structures, processes and policy outcomes at different moments in time constitute different system states and outcomes—and thus different data points—that can be analyzed for patterns and fitted (or not) to theory. If the unit is the Soviet Union, the patterns are those of a single country and an explanation of them can thus be viewed as a single-country theory.

Viewed in this way, generalists need not fear compromising a core value. Their commitment to uncovering recurring patterns would not be jeopardized because a single country need not be construed as a case history. They would be treating the Soviet Union not as a single data point, but as a series of cases no less subject to comparative analysis than any sample drawn from a larger population. Indeed, it can be readily argued that such comparisons have considerable advantages over those made in a multi-unit format inasmuch as the continuities and differences across time all occur within the same unit, thus enabling single-country comparativists to hold a great many more variables—such as those linked to culture and history—constant than can their across-country counterparts.

An obvious example of how within-unit comparison can underlie theorizing about the USSR is the extensive hypothesizing in which analysts engage when successions bring a new leader to the very top. Will Gorbachev prove to be a self-serving party bureaucrat like Brezhnev? Or a maverick like Khrushchev? Will Gorbachev's generation, which did not fight in the Second World War, prove to be more pragmatic and less ideological than its predecessors?[9] Such questions involve different values for key variables at different time points and, as such, they compel comparative analysis. For Khrushchev, Brezhnev, and Gorbachev are differentiated not only by their personalities; each is also expressive of what the Soviet system did and did not permit in their era—through, say, the values underlying the party's recruitment and advancement policies as well as the prevailing state of the Soviet economy—and thus juxtaposing them analytically need not be cast simply in historical and chronological terms. An interrupted time series design can also be employed by treating the regimes of successive leaders as separate data points susceptible to disaggregation into variables and constants, with the end of each regime being regarded as a breakpoint and the interactive outcomes among the variables then contrasted for continuities and changes.[10]

This is not to imply, however, that breakpoints in Soviet history only occur when new leaders come to power or that the advent of new leaders necessarily constitutes a breakpoint. Such may not be the case if one's theory highlights variables other than those associated with leadership changes. The acquisition of nuclear capabilities, a major defection in Eastern Europe, or a decision to promote the use of personal computers are illustrative of developments that might also be worthy of delineating as breakpoints for analytic purposes. Whether individual leaders or macro dynamics are delineated, however, the point is that diverse breakpoints can be identified and that therefore single-country theory does not necessarily amount to single-case analysis. It can be comparative analysis if it involves contrasting outcomes.

The concession required of area specialists may also loom as hazardous and compromising. Acknowledging the relevance of generalized dynamics runs exactly counter to their premise that understanding is to be found in the particular and the unique, in those qualities and experiences that set the Soviets apart from any other people or country. Furthermore, it follows from such an acknowledgement that area specialists can no longer confine their attention to the USSR. They must, in addition, branch out to grasp the underpinnings of processes such as industrialization, bureaucratization, socialization, legitimization, foreign policy formulation, and the many other general dynamics that sustain human collectivities in the post-industrial era. Hence, reluctant to divert their energy away from their prime concerns in order to develop a broader but questionable theoretical perspective, and perhaps for other reasons as well, many area specialists are blinded by the idea of uniqueness; and the more they insist that the Soviet Union is unique under all circumstances, the more do they deprive themselves of access to rich theory about processes that are surely, in some respects, operative in the USSR.

It is as if area specialists often fear conceding that the operation of common stimuli across systems can result in comparable outcomes on the grounds that doing so is to deny that any cultural and historical factors are relevant and influential. Such, of course, is not the case and, in fact, often the specialists themselves rely on comparative insights in the course of focusing on the particulars of Soviet experience. Ponder, for example, how most specialists shared in the expectation held by generalists that the Soviets would eventually return to the arms-control bargaining table even though they adamantly insisted when they left in December, 1983, that they would resume negotiations only if the newly deployed US missiles in Western Europe were withdrawn. How did the specialists derive this expectation? Through an extrapolation from past practices in Soviet diplomacy or an understanding of how unique features of the Russian character lead to temporary face-saving rituals prior to the acceptance of political setbacks? Probably not. The greater likelihood is that they expected the Soviets to reverse the refusal because of a generalized dynamic operative upon and in any nation-state, namely, that it does not refrain from abandoning prior pledges when the external environment becomes increasingly threatening to its physical security. And this is especially true of superpowers with nuclear capabilities, irrespective of historical and cultural factors that may lead in a contrary direction. There are, in short, certain constraints and/or requirements of economic, political, and social life to which the leadership of any polity is compelled to be sensitive, and acknowledging as much in no way negates the relevance of the constraints and requirements embedded in the unique circumstances of every polity.

Herein, of course, lies the core of single-country theory. The conclusion that leaders and publics in any society at any moment in time are responsive to both their own pasts and the dynamics of prevailing domestic and international structures can serve as the basis for deriving explicit, elaborate, integrated and testable hypotheses which, when measured and assessed on either side of diverse historical junctures, will constitute a synthesis that meets all the standards of viable scientific theory while not ignoring the relevance of idiographic detail. More importantly in the case of the Soviet Union, such theory can enjoy the confidence of both specialists and generalists and thus facilitate their cooperation in confronting the challenges and opportunities posed by all those riddles wrapped in all those mysteries inside all those enigmas.

Let us be more specific. A theory of a single country is founded on the premise that at any moment in time that country's behavior is a product of two convergent sets of dynamics. One is all the distinctive features of its political structure, economic organization and cultural history. The second embraces all those processes that are common to countries with the same characteristics. Indeed, viewed as social processes, these two sets of dynamics are not so much independent of each other as they are interactive and locked into reinforcing tensions: "As techniques of communication and physical mobility develop, it is becoming more difficult to conceive of uniquely distinctive or autonomous societies . . . Yet divergent lines of historical development and the effects of different physical environments do not vanish in a few decades, however rapidly contemporary technology is diffused and however extensive the network of communications" (Hollander, 1978, p. 10).

In other words, any country is both different from all others and similar to some of them, the differences stemming from its unique circumstances and the similarities being the result either of structural requirements inherent in polities, economies and societies at comparable stages of development or of forces at work on a transnational scale in a particular era. Hence any single-country theory must synthesize idiographic and nomothetic knowledge, that is, the most salient aspects of a country's uniqueness as well as the dynamics it shares with other countries. Enough is known about the processes of industrialization, for example, to expect them to foster the evolution of large-scale organizations in any society which industrializes and, in so doing, to give rise to the processes of bureaucratic politics *even* as the bureaucratic politics of any one country are shaped by its particular cultural norms. Bureaucratic politics in the Soviet Union and the United States, to carry the example one step further, are thus presumed to have in common those qualities—such as the tendency of subordinates to report what they think their superiors want to hear— which attach to any large-scale organization, but at the same time to differ to the extent that the norms that Americans and Russians bring to organizational life differ.

Possible Approaches to Single-Country Theory

There are a number of precedents to which one could turn for guidance in blending the work of area specialists and comparative generalists. In medicine, for example, such a blend amounts to routine practice. Consider the response to a diseased kidney. On any patient the doctor focuses a broad understanding of how kidneys function and how they interact differently with different blood pressures and heart problems on the one hand, and what is known about the patient's medical history on the other. Hence the diagnosis is, in effect, a single-person theory of the kidney, blending both general and particular knowledge. Many of the same blending procedures are used with respect to comprehending political parties and the dissident wing, legislatures and the legislator, terrorism and the terrorist, crowds and the agitator, traffic jams and the motorist, markets and the consumer, and, indeed, any situation where the focus of inquiry embraces both macro and micro dynamics.

But how to proceed in foreign affairs? How to combine the unique and the general with respect to international systems and the nation-state? Around what issues, or through what procedures, should the foundations of a single-country theory be organized and the cooperation of area specialists and empirical comparativists facilitated? Several sets of issues and procedures come to mind here. One involves focusing the dialogue between generalists and specialists on those questions about Soviet dynamics where their respective forms of inquiry lead them to discrepant and conflicting interpretations. To concentrate on those dynamics where both converge around the same understanding is not to subject the methods and findings of either to a test, but confronting each with contrary findings about the same dynamics is to compel both to reconsider the premises, conceptual equipment, and observations on which their analyses rest and, no less important, to face directly alternative lines of reasoning. It would be instructive, for example, if specialists who explained Russian actions in Afghanistan in terms of a longstanding aspiration to surround the USSR with supportive buffer zones could enter into a challenging dialogue with generalists who discerned an alternative interpretation of the same behavior in bureaucratic rivalries. At the very least such a dialogue would force both groups to acknowledge those aspects of Soviet life they hold constant and those for which they allow variance in the process of articulating their perspectives, an acknowledgement which will surely serve as a useful and vivid reminder of how their perspectives on the Soviet Union are rooted in their intellectual processes rather than in those of reality.

More often than not, admittedly, such confrontations may affirm for each group the soundness of the procedures they employ, but at the same time there may be crucial ways in which the process of confrontation leads to an orientational revision in which some of the assumptions and methods of the other are seen to be useful and adaptable. And the more generalists and specialists engage in such dialogues and thus begin to accommodate each others' perspectives and materials, the more will the resulting incremental syntheses contribute to the development of a single-country theory of the USSR.

Instead of breaking off their dialogue when they come upon disagreements, in other words, it is precisely at those points where generalists and specialists get agitated over each others' statements about the Soviet Union that their dialogue should begin. An air of harmony and accomplishment may not follow, but at least both will have confronted the toughest theoretical question of all: under what circumstances, and to what extent, do unique aspects of Soviet life modify and/or override the dynamics inherent in economic development and superpower responsibilities, and vice versa? Given a clash between the specific and the general, which prevails and which yields? the traditional work ethic or the industrial requirement? the expansionist impulse or the nuclear restraint? the power of the party or the potential of home computers? the controls of the apparatus or the extension of global interdependence? the fading memories of the Second World War or the emergent challenges of a microelectronic revolution? the ideological commitment or the need to adapt? Or, put in terms of a research agenda, when, where, and to what extent does one look to Russian culture and history for guidance and when does one rely on models of societal, economic and international systems?

One basis for answering this last question is provided in Table 4.1, the two columns of which list, respectively, some of the idiographic and nomothetic factors that are cited in the literature on the Soviet Union as central to its development and conduct. Although the literature search used to compile Table 4.1 was limited in scope,[11] the results seem sufficient to highlight the tasks involved in constructing a single-country theory. Presumably a thoroughgoing theory of the USSR would at least have to consider, if not to synthesize, all or most of the dynamics set forth in both columns of the table. Another basis for integrating the specific and generalized aspects of Soviet experience is suggested below in the context of my theory of national adaptation. Whatever means are used to achieve a confrontation between idiographic and nomothetic factors, however, the point here is that theoretical progress is bound to ensue if the clash between the two can be kept as the focus of any dialogue between empirical theorists and Soviet specialists.

Table 4.1 Factors Central to a Theory of the USSR

Idiographic Factors	Nomothetic Factors
• History of political stability (156) • A nationality problem: domestic pressures for rectification of national grievances (149) • Soviet citizens expect to be governed, not left free to pursue any path; hence publics tend to be "undemanding" (167) and docile (156, 162) • Food prices kept artificially low to minimize discontent (162) • Inefficient agriculture (262) • Bureaucratic habit of intruding intermediaries into economic relationships (261) • Traditional Russian-Soviet nationalism is both defensive and aggressive (5, 16) • Sense of encirclement by adversaries and intense memories of suffering in Second World War (4) • Satisfaction over increased power and status since Second World War (24) • An explicit but flexible ideology that allows for sectarian, activist, and reformative interpretations (41, 77) • Common experiences and career patterns among leaders (76) • Serious energy crunch pending for a variety of reasons (238–9) • Tensions in relations with Eastern Europe (247 ff.) • Supportive communist parties throughout the world (433) • Traditional Soviet fear of being used by its clients (e.g., Cuba) (337–8) • Longstanding left–right cleavage within the leadership (344) • Memories of Stalin's excesses (89) • Foreign policy successes are principal means whereby elites legitimate their policy system; hence diminished "free hand" in foreign affairs (13) • A one-party dictatorship (363) • Relative weight of individual at apex of the political structure remains far greater in the USSR than in the USA (381)	• Reliance of rulers on large national armed forces and the production of large range of goods to keep populations satisfied (155) • Industrialization renders domestic conditions more relevant to foreign policy (155) and fosters less compartmentalization of foreign and domestic issues (109, 414) • Growing access to the decision-making process in foreign policy (109) • Increased social mobility and an occupational structure shifting toward more prestigeful jobs, thus resulting in more people with some stake in the system (163–4) • Increased intelligentsia, diminished peasantry (165) • A wiser, more alert public in foreign affairs (353) • A fluctuating economy, with periods of slowdown reducing the regime's maneuverability and making military preparedness more costly (413) • Complexity fostering a "need-to-know" explosion, an erosion of autocratic rule, and a politics of argumentation rather than of "label-sticking" (104) • Profound demographic changes involving reduced fertility, severe labor shortages, pending crisis of productivity, and marked slowdown in economic growth (203–25, 246) • Dependence on external resources (grain, technology, etc.) unless growth in consumption severely cut (168) • Dynamics of collective decision making (363, 366) generating a more structured policy-making process based on compromise (110) • "Rallying around the flag" consensus readily occurs in international crises (49) • Internationalization of nationality problem (148) • Hard-currency problems in managing trade with the West (193, 301, 413) • Inexorable process of functional differentiation since Stalin (349) • Relative weight of traditional political culture diminishing (356) • Learning process that emancipates top elites from doctrinal stereotypes (359)

Source: The parenthetic numbers after each entry refer to the pages in Bialer, 1981, from which the entries were derived.

Perhaps it is useful to note that in some respects such dialogues occur frequently in Western policy-making organizations. Whenever, say, responses to Soviet actions in Afghanistan need to be framed, doubtless advocates of various alternatives clash over Moscow's goal in the situation. These dialogues, however, are much briefer and less far-ranging than those suggested here. Transcripts of them might be of benefit to the scholar, but their purpose is to make sound policy and thus the implications of the various interpretations are pursued only to the point where consensus around a policy choice is achieved. The dialogues designed to develop single-country theory, on the other hand, cannot be so attenuated. To evolve a blend of the general and the particular they cannot rely simply on verbal interchange and compelling argumentation. Rather the challenges must take the form of demonstration through empirical proof, of assessing the fit of data to hypotheses through rigorous standards of acceptable evidence.

A second procedure for building a synthesized theory of the USSR would be that of focusing the dialogues of generalists and specialists on the values and decision rules at work when the Soviets engage in those behaviors that are most discrepant with Western orientations. We have become so accustomed to these discrepancies that they no longer seem baffling and, instead, we take them for granted, as if their sources are self-evident and immune to change. And, in so doing, we tend to cloak them in simplistic labels and categorize them in descriptive rather than explanatory terms, thus closing off what may be obscure but valuable openings in the black box.

Consider, for example, Soviet reactions to the shooting down of the Korean airliner or to the charge that they have cheated on prior arms control agreements. Their denials and countercharges often seem so contrived that scholars as well as journalists and politicians in the West readily dismiss them as "propaganda" and unrelated to whatever may empirically be the case. Our own perception of such events is rooted in such different values—that under no circumstances is the murder of innocent travelers justifiable or the violation of authoritative diplomatic agreements warranted—that we are inclined, at best, to forgo our usual research impulses to frame alternative explanations and probe for the dynamics underlying the denials and countercharges. At worst, it is all too easy to treat such unfathomable reactions to evidence, proof, and assertions as founded on "warped" decision rules. In either event, the result is that we retain our unquestioning assumptions and bypass the important question of what constitutes the decision rules on which the Soviet "propagandistic" denials and countercharges are grounded.[12]

Precisely because such behaviors provoke us to resort quickly and unthinkingly to ready-made interpretations, they can usefully serve as a spur to our theory-building efforts. We could, for instance, try to imagine the offices in which the Soviet propagandists work and to which word first comes of the downing of the Korean airliner or charges of cheating on arms control agreements. If our imagination then attempts to reconstruct what the relevant officials do with the information—who they consult, what kind of deliberations they engage in, what values they fall back on to give meaning to the information—the pictures that come to mind are likely to be far more complex than is implied by the notion of mere "propaganda" (see Chapters 11 and 12 in this volume). To presume that the reactions of such officials are only propaganda is, usually, to assume that decisions are made by rote, without hesitation, as if the calculation of ploys was simple. And in so doing we may easily overlook a very complex process that rests on a series of decision rules pertaining to when the officials treat the information as accurate, when Western claims about it are accepted, when they are accepted but seen as too damaging to acknowledge, when the claims give enough pause to check out the information through the intelligence system, when the feedback from the intelligence system is murky and therefore a clear-cut propaganda line is not evident, and when a whole range of other possible responses might be undertaken by those who, at each stage, are responsible for framing and issuing the "propaganda."

In other words, it seems inconceivable, if our understanding of human behavior is in any way reliable, that Soviet reactions spring exclusively from a rote set of decision rules which say, in effect, "deny everything." Presumably the decision rules and processes for those situations in which the USA and USSR assert discrepant perceptions, evaluations and interpretations are elaborate and not totally removed from the information reported by the Soviet intelligence network. Soviet interpretations may be far removed from American "truths," but they do have their own system of "truths" that is, presumably, embedded in the value and decisional framework through which their reactions are processed. It is a framework, moreover, that is embedded in the orientations of those who gather intelligence, in the minds of Soviet foreign service officers who interpret it, in the perceptual screens of top officials, and in the conventions of committee procedures and interagency rivalries.

"Propaganda" reactions, in short, spring from larger contexts, and it is a focus on these contexts which might serve the task of theory building. If we can avoid taking them for granted and instead recognize them as complex as well as discrepant from our own value systems, such decision rules can provoke us to search ever more deeply for the systems of values that sustain the Soviet policy-making organization (see Chapter 13).

A third procedure for fashioning a viable model of the Soviets involves seizing upon traces of change in their behavior and reconstructing alternative scenarios as to what promoted the occurence of change and what constraints may lie in any precedents it may set. Involved here are less changes of policy content and more changes of procedure. The former may be merely tactical and situational, but the latter could reflect the beginning of enduring responses to altered balances and/or new perceptions of needs and challenges. It seems a minor matter, for example, but there may be theoretical mileage in seizing on the recent tendency of top Soviet officials to hold open press conferences. This was done by Marshal Ogarkov after the shooting down of the Korean airliner and again by Foreign Secretary Gromyko several months later after the resumption of arms control talks. These are, indeed, the slimmest of traces, mere hints at the surface of underlying change. And they may also be expressive of the most superficial kinds of change, momentary adjustments to a public relations problem. On the other hand, being close together in time, the two press conferences suggest an emergent pattern which, given an aggressive theoretical impulse, at least ought to trigger the imagination and lead to posing and probing a series of questions: What transformations are occurring in the world that lead the Soviet policy-making organization to break with a longstanding policy of merely proclaiming reactions rather than exposing top officials to the hazards of press conferences? Is the emergent pattern reflective of what one observer perceives as the emergence of "a sense of quasi-accountability" to domestic elites by the makers of Soviet foreign policy (Dallin, 1981, 315)? What kind of exchange might have occurred among the Soviet policy makers who decided upon this new procedure for coping with potential setbacks? Did they view the idea of an open press conference as shocking at first or was it widely perceived as a useful innovation? Did their deliberations include a recognition that in initiating the new procedure they might foster expectations in future situations that could constrain and limit their options? Did they discuss with Ogarkov or Gromyko how he should respond to certain questions, warn him against pitfalls, discuss his goals, suggest a casual style? Or was there no prior briefing? Did Ogarkov and Gromyko simply decide on their own that the situation called for a Western-style press conference?

Such questions may seem trivial in some respects. But one never knows where they might lead and the builder of single-country theory cannot afford to ignore any signs of structures undergoing change. And especially where the black box is so heavily guarded, of course, such signs must be seized upon and fully mined for their theoretical ore.[13]

A fourth focus for single-country theory is that realm of politics wherein domestic and foreign dynamics converge. As technology renders the world smaller and increasingly interdependent, this convergence becomes ever more salient to the welfare, integrity, and survival of nation-states. Indeed, if states are to adapt to a fast-changing world, increasingly they will have to devote resources and energies to balancing the complex external and internal demands to which growing interdependence has given rise. This adaptive problem has become universal, and in its universality lies the core around which single-country theory can be constructed. That is, being a crucial and all-encompassing problem faced by all countries, both the area specialist and the comparative generalist can usefully focus and synthesize their respective skills and epistemologies upon it. The specialist has a contribution to make to the theory because the leadership of any country derives its orientations toward the domestic-foreign convergence partly from the country's particular historical, cultural, and geographic experiences. At the same time the comparativist has a lot to contribute theoretically because, even as they draw on their unique circumstances, the leaders of all countries must confront a number of general dynamics inherent in the requirements of industrialization, the state of the world economy, and the structure of world politics as they seek to cope with the convergence.

Stated differently, any leadership is faced with the necessity of evolving priorities in the relative importance it attaches to internal and external demands. Leaderships may differ greatly in the priorities they maintain, but maintaining some kind of balance between coping with problems at home and meeting challenges from abroad is a necessity. Why? Because, to repeat, not to maintain an effective internal-external balance is to run the risk of failing to adapt to a world that is undergoing rapid transformation.

Elsewhere I have developed a theoretical perspective which, whatever its shortcomings, does focus on the processes through which countries do or do not cope with the convergence of challenges from at home and abroad. I call it a theory of the adaptation of whole systems— either national societies (Rosenau, 1981) or national states (Rosenau, 1985b)—and at first glance it would seem especially easy to theorize about the Soviet Union as an adaptive system.[14] The USSR is, after all, a superpower deeply involved in a nuclear arms race during a period of mushrooming economic constraints, circumstances that thrust guns-or-butter issues to the fore and highlight the tensions between internal needs and external requirements, between stimulating the domestic

71

economy and contesting foreign adversaries. Indeed, precisely because their commitments are global in scope, superpowers today are compelled to monitor their self-environment orientations continuously. Each proposed new weapons system points to the possibility of a comparable diminution in consumer goods, just as every proposal for new investments at home hints at the likelihood of a corresponding contraction abroad. There is, of course, more to national adaptation than coping with guns-vs-butter conflicts, but for analytic purposes they can usefully serve to illustrate how a theory of the USSR might be developed.

Conclusion

Doubtless there are many more strategies that could be employed to evolve a single-country theory of the Soviet Union or, indeed, of any system. The point here has not been to indicate a preferred strategy, but rather to stress that such theory can be constructed in the context of a commitment to comparative and scientific inquiry.

Whatever strategy may be employed, moreover, it should be clear from the foregoing suggestions for probing the riddles, mysteries and enigmas of the USSR that the goal of single-country theory is *not* that of anticipating or explaining a specific action or event. No scientific theory aspires to such precision and it would be erroneous to conceive of single-country theory as an exception in this regard. To extrapolate from the idea of a single-country theory to a single-event prediction would be to misunderstand and exaggerate the kind of specialist-generalist synthesis being advocated. The goal is, rather, to develop a theory of the Soviet Union that explains and anticipates the likely developments and/or choices at crucial junctures, at those moments in the life of the USSR when emergent structures clash with persistent patterns, when continuities may seem increasingly counterproductive relative to the possibilities of change, when domestic needs and foreign challenges are in conflict. The persistence of crop failures, the recurrent underproduction of a stagnant economy, the currency crisis or oil embargo abroad, the guns-or-butter problem posed by new rounds in the arms race—these are the kind of critical turning points in which the making of choices seems inescapable and to which a single-country theory can be meaningfully addressed. As a life-course sociologist might put it, single-country theory focuses on the conjunction of economic time, political time and social time on the one hand, and historical time and cultural time on the other, during those eras when the dynamism of new technologies and the renewal of collective aspirations are stirring upheaval in the course of world affairs.

Notes

I am grateful to the Institute on Global Conflict and Cooperation of the University of California, Los Angeles, for permission to use the parts of this paper which were previously presented at the Conference on Domestic Sources of Soviet Foreign and Defense Policies, sponsored jointly by the Institute and the Carter Center at Emory University, Los Angeles, CA, October 11–12, 1985.

1 For a cogent example of how the assumption that the Soviet system is open to investigation led to a "remarkable" finding about Soviet defense spending, see Zimmerman, 1982. Indeed, Zimmerman is "convinced" that the closedness of the USSR to systematic observation can be readily reduced, that the defense-expenditure finding "is but one instance where surprising knowledge about issues or topics in Soviet foreign policy can be obtained from open sources through basic research" (p. 219). For a full presentation of this particular finding, see Zimmerman and Palmer, 1983. Another example of research in open sources yielding valuable and unexpected results can be found in Hauslohner, 1981.

2 One study (Hermann, 1983) found that most analysts adhere to any one of three theories organized around three different (and competing) assessments of the motives of Soviet officials—labeled the communist expansionism model, the *realpolitik* expansionism model, and the *realpolitik* defense model—all of which are long on assertions and short on falsifiable propositions and systematic evidence.

3 For an exception in which an expression of hopelessness over the problem of framing systematic hypotheses about Soviet politics is followed by a playfulness with the saliency of the relevant variables, see Dallin (1981, especially pp. 380–1).

4 For a recent illustration of the assumption that constancy marks Soviet conduct, see virtually all the essays in the symposium edited by Stremlau, 1985.

5 For a clear articulation of this assumption, see Dallin (1981), who notes that, "of all political systems, the Soviet seems most likely and most able to override, ignore, or distort what might otherwise or elsewhere be identified as natural or secular trends" (p. 343), even as he also attributes importance to three tendencies "identifiable in the Soviet system" that have marked other states undergoing industrialization:

(1) All developing systems tend to bring an increasing part of the population into passive or active political participation.

(2) Such systems eventually tend to produce integration at the level of the nation-state, at the expense of both parochial and internationalist preoccupations.

(3) Over time, developing systems tend to focus priority of attention, resources, and operationally relevant objectives on the domestic, rather than the foreign, arena.

(p. 348)

6 At some point in the process of theory development, of course, the proportion of unique to generalized dynamics that obtain in the USSR, or any country, poses empirical questions that need to be explored. Possible

procedures for combining the theoretical and empirical tasks are suggested below in conjunction with the presentation in Table 4.1.

7 For a cogent exception that explicitly takes note of the nomothetic-idiographic distinction, see Dallin, 1981, p. 343.

8 For a discussion of the problem of differentiating historical breakpoints, see Rosenau, 1983b.

9 An interesting discussion of the emerging generation of Soviet leaders is provided by Simis, 1985.

10 A compelling analysis along these lines, replete with derived hypotheses based on explicit comparisons of the Khrushchev and Brezhnev eras, can be found in Hodnett, 1981.

11 Designed only to be illustrative of what the components of a single-country theory might consist, the entries in Table 4.1 were drawn exclusively from the compilation of essays edited by Bialer, 1981. Even as such, however, they are by no means an exhaustive list of the factors cited by the various contributors to Bialer's stimulating volume.

12 Moreover, even in those rare instances when a Western scholar or journalist is inclined to attach credence to Soviet claims, the result is more a refutation of US contentions and evidence than an effort to reconstruct the decision rules underlying Moscow's pronouncement. Serious questions have lately been raised, for example, about the integrity of the US reaction to the downing of the Korean airliner, but at the same time the bases of Soviet decision making in the situation has not been seriously probed (Sayle, 1985; Wicker, 1985). On the other hand, again the work of Dallin, 1985, is an exception.

13 It should be noted, moreover, that by refining our theoretical sensitivities to the point where our questions may seem trivial, we will be in a position to enlist the assistance of diplomats, journalists, and others with routine Soviet contacts as data gatherers. It would have been relatively easy, for example, for a journalist to ask naively at the press conferences about how the decision to hold them was made. Conceivably the query would have generated a straightforward answer. What is trivial or commonplace to political actors, in other words, can have considerable import for the analyst who has been theoretically and explicitly creative.

14 For other applications of the theory, see Rosenau, 1982, 1983a, 1985a. At the same time it should also be noted that at least one able comparativist who specializes in the Soviet Union is dubious as to the ability of the adaptation model to "help significantly in understanding" the problem of how internal and external demands get synthesized in Moscow (Dallin, 1981, p. 388).

PART II

Foreign Policy Patterns, Performances and Evaluations

5

A Lag Sequential Approach
to the Analysis of
Foreign Policy Behavior

WILLIAM J. DIXON

Most of the chapters in this volume proceed from the premise that something is amiss in the comparative study of foreign policy. More often than not the ensuing brief highlights sins of omission, arguing that our collective enterprise has systematically ignored or diverted attention from some particular phenomenon or analytical task of great import to our eventual understanding of foreign policy activities. In this, the present effort is no exception. My complaint is that the models and methods of contemporary foreign policy analysis typically fail to take account of process at the level of discrete foreign policy actions. To borrow the analogy proposed by Hudson, Hermann and Singer (1985), a single frame of motion-picture film may manage to capture a single foreign policy behavior, but the picture is frozen in time just as if it were nothing more than a simple snapshot. It is only when several frames are strung together in sequence that we obtain a true motion picture. But not just any random motion will do. The motion in a motion picture appeals because it consists of patterned movement, the pattern being determined solely by the proper sequencing of individual frames.

The key here is sequence, for, as I will argue below, in sequence lies information. Sequence is preserved only by the systematic observation of discrete behaviors sampled from a naturally evolving behavioral stream, a data-gathering technique common to a wide range of social science disciplines. This mode of observation may be distinguished from other behavioral methods which rely on some prior structure or constraint to limit the variety of potential behaviors. Typically, but not always, this structure is imposed by the investigator, as when social psychologists employ laboratory techniques or standardized questionnaires to elicit a uniform set of behavioral responses. Foreign policy researchers follow a roughly analogous practice by using governmental responses to naturally structured stimuli, such as the annual budget cycle (e.g., military expenditures, foreign aid allocations) or a roll-call vote in an intergovernmental assembly. In contrast to these techniques, observational methods permit behaviors to unfold naturally over time without reference to some fixed structure or stimulus.

Despite the wide variation found among particular observational strategies and the social settings to which they are routinely applied, the end products of these methods often share a remarkable similarity. The end product is an encoded representation of discrete behaviors recorded so as to maintain the sequential continuity of an ongoing stream of behavior. Observational psychologists and ethologists have long recognized the importance of sequence in defining contingent relationships and patterns among the discrete behaviors of individuals involved in social interaction. In foreign policy studies observational data have been in common use for about two decades under the rubric of events data research, yet attention to sequential properties of behavior remains a rare exception (e.g., Schrodt, 1984). Statistical tools for categorical sequential analysis do exist, although not within the econometric tradition that now dominates foreign policy research. The purpose of this essay is to describe some of these techniques and to illustrate their use with applications to recent US–Soviet behavior. I begin this task in the following section by discussing some of the theoretical underpinnings of sequential analysis.

Sequence in Foreign Policy Behavior

Foreign policy behavior is comprised of discrete purposeful actions that flow from political-level decisions to attempt to influence the attitudes or behavior of other international actors. This definition makes it possible to conceive of foreign policy behavior as a kind of communicative activity, one in which the transmission of a signal from actor to recipient represents an influence attempt.[1] Notice the emphasis is on the actor's expectations and not on the fidelity with which the message is received or the signal's success in bringing about an intended outcome. Foreign policy behavior can also have communicative value apart from the content of explicit messages conveyed through written or spoken language. Some time ago Schelling (1960) pointed out that many types of foreign policy actions carry implicit messages that are communicated indirectly through the actions themselves. To formalize this idea at a somewhat more general level, the behavior of a social actor will be said to contain implicit communicative value, or what Gottman and Bakeman (1979, p. 31) term "communicative value in a social sense," when it reduces uncertainty in the behavior of another actor.

Viewing foreign policy behavior as a form of implicit social communication leads directly to the importance of pattern or sequence in a series of discrete observations. Communication, after all, is the transmission of information and information consists of patterned relationships. From this perspective, information can exist in a sequence of behaviors but not in any single behavior; in Deutsch's (1966, p. 84) apt phrasing, "it is not events as such, but a patterned relationship between events."

For purposes of illustration, suppose we have reduced the actions directed back and forth between nations X and Y into a very simple behavioral repertoire consisting of only cooperation and conflict. Suppose also that we have discovered that the probability of nation Y cooperating with X is rather low, that it cooperates only 20 times in 100 observed behaviors. Now, because we assume that these actors take explicit account of one another's behavior (Richardson, Chapter 9 below), we might consider the number of times that nation Y cooperates immediately after X has acted in a cooperative manner. If X were found to cooperate a total of 50 times and only 10 of these were followed by Y cooperating, then the conditional probability of Y's cooperation given X's cooperation would be 0.2 (10/50), which is exactly equal to the unconditional probability of Y's cooperation (20/100). In this example we acquire no new information—no reduction of uncertainty—about Y's behavior by examining X's prior behavior. Alternatively, suppose we had observed that all 20 of Y's cooperative actions followed cooperation by X. Under these circumstances, the conditional probability is 0.4 (20/50), twice the unconditional probability and a substantial reduction in our uncertainty about Y's behavior. The simple calculations used in these examples demonstrate a fundamental principle of sequential analysis: "Reduction of uncertainty is assessed by the difference between conditional and unconditional probabilities" (Gottman and Bakeman, 1979, p. 31).

Although a communications perspective is a useful device for developing the logic of sequential analysis, the advantages of this approach extend beyond any single theoretical orientation.[2] Surely one of the most appealing features of the sequential model—apart from its utter simplicity—is to be found in its treatment of time. Most contemporary analyses of dynamic foreign policy behavior incorporate time as a strictly defined metric imposed on the natural flow of events. This approach invariably directs the analyst's attention to properties of multiple behaviors (e.g., number of acts, average hostility level) occurring within some uniform but ultimately arbitrary interval of calendar time (e.g., weeks, months, quarters). Obviously, foreign policy decision makers do not really operate within this sort of strict temporal framework, yet it is only recently that researchers have begun to take explicit account of the irregular time durations separating individual behaviors. Although elaborate attempts have been made to model these durations under special conditions (Allan, 1983; Zinnes, 1983), empirical results so far have been inconclusive.

Time may be elastic in international politics, but it is not altogether irrelevant. Foreign policy events unfold in continuous succession, one after another, ordered in time but otherwise little affected by temporal imperatives. It is nevertheless of some importance to know the temporal order of events, to know, for instance, that a public denunciation followed an adversary's peace initiative rather than preceded it. In this example, the precise time span between the two events is (within some limit) considerably less relevant than their sequence of occurrence. There is, of course, nothing profound or even vaguely controversial in the claim that diplomatic events are only weakly ordered in time; this fact is so empirically obvious and intuitively reasonable that it hardly seems worthy of discussion. The problem is not with our thinking about dynamic international behavior, but rather with the assumptions of statistical and econometric time series techniques that we typically use in analyzing it. Schrodt (1984) identifies the most troubling of these assumptions to be the existence of a strict time metric whereby observations must be separated from one another by equal intervals. By relaxing the strict metric assumptions of conventional time series techniques, sequential analysis more closely approximates the loose temporal properties of real-world behavior. "Sequences," writes Schrodt (1984, p. 7), "preserve the notion of causality and are dynamic in a loose sense, but do not impose a greater temporal regularity on events than justified by common sense."

The preceding emphasis on weak temporal assumptions should not be construed to mean that sequential analysis is somehow inappropriate for behavioral data encoded from uniformly spaced observations. In fact, the sequential techniques to be described shortly are flexible and robust in the extreme; about the only restrictive assumption of any importance is the requirement that the data base maintain the sequential continuity of discrete behaviors. Exactly how that continuity is maintained—whether by a strict time metric or by ordinal sequences—will be a matter to be decided within the substantive context of each research problem. (One of the examples presented below is based on a standard metric to illustrate just this point.) Other issues of data collection and measurement (e.g., source validity, event definition, coding reliability, etc.), while of obvious importance in sequential analysis, are treated extensively elsewhere and will not be considered here (e.g., Munton, 1978).

Examples of Sequential Analysis

The several examples of sequential analysis offered here should be regarded as no more than illustrative of the kinds of applications available to foreign policy researchers. All of the examples focus on United States–Soviet behavior from 1966 through 1978 as represented in the well-known WEIS event file.[3] The United States and the Soviet Union were selected for this provisional examination because they comprise a highly interactive dyad whose mutual relations are likely to be familiar to most readers.[4]

As noted repeatedly in the preceding section, sequential analysis is designed for application to data representing precisely ordered discrete behaviors. Unfortunately, a precise ordering that is exhaustive of all observed behaviors is not possible with the WEIS set nor with most other international event collections because the public sources reporting events ordinarily do not provide sequencing distinctions finer than a single day. Although sequential methods are available to deal with cases in which two or more encoded behaviors occur simultaneously (Bakeman, 1978), for this initial inquiry I adopt a simpler approach based on the idea of "event sets" (Zinnes 1983). Because instances of multiple events initiated on a single day are relatively rare, at least for the US–Soviet dyad, these occurrences are lumped together into sets and treated as if they comprised but a single foreign policy action.[5] This means that some of the instances of behavior in the following examples will in fact be occurrences of two or more discrete actions that could not be ordered in relation to one another. This consolidation of behavior into events sets of one day's duration is common to all of the examples presented below; other operations on the data will be discussed in relation to specific sequential techniques.

State Transitions

The communicative nature of foreign policy behavior suggests that dyadic foreign policy interaction might be conceived in a metaphorical way as a kind of "behavioral dialogue" between two actors (Bakeman and Brown, 1977). Stripped to barest essentials, a dialogue consists of an exchange of utterances or, in this case, communicative acts. By considering just the simplest of behavioral attributes—a behavior either is present or it is not—a dialogic model may reveal underlying structures or patterns of interaction that could be obscured by conventional content-based descriptions. In the US–Soviet case, the dialogic model reduces interaction to a sequence of observed time intervals (days) coded to represent one of four mutually exclusive and exhaustive "dyadic states": (1) both nations act toward the other; (2) only the United States acts; (3) only the Soviet Union acts; (4) neither nation acts. The last dyadic state (4) is of particular interest because by including it we have restructured the natural sequencing of behavior to fit a uniformly spaced time metric consisting of one-day intervals. From a dialogic point of view, a strict metric is desirable because it focuses attention on the intervals between behavior, and the transitions into and out of them, patterns that may in some ways be comparable to lapses of conversation in interpersonal interaction.

The WEIS data cover the period from January 1, 1966, to December 31, 1978, a span of 4748 successive days. Treating each day as an observation yields the following raw freqencies for the four dyadic states:

(1)	(2)	(3)	(4)
673	511	558	3006

Obviously, the total absence of behavior, state 4, dominates even the highly interactive US–Soviet relationship, hardly a novel finding in international events research (e.g., Kegley, 1976). Raw frequencies provide only a static picture of US–Soviet interaction; a more dynamic view requires shifting our attention to state transitions, that is, to sequences of states. The frequency of transition from state to state can be displayed in matrix form such that the rows refer to the state at each time t and the columns mark the immediately succeeding state at time t^{+1}. Entries in the matrix (Table 5.1) register the number of times the row state was followed by the column state; for example, state 2 (USA

Table 5.1 *Frequency Transition Matrix*

		time t^{+1}		
	(1)	(2)	(3)	(4)
(1)	165	76	74	358
time t (2)	108	72	63	268
(3)	79	70	83	326
(4)	321	293	337	2054

acts) is followed by state 3 (USSR acts) a total of 63 times. Because there can be no transition from the dyadic state occurring on the last day of observation, the number of transitions will always be one less than the number of observed states.

Probabilities are usually a more convenient and informative way to characterize state transitions than raw frequencies. Transition probabilities are obtained by dividing each row entry in a frequency matrix by the sum of the frequencies in each row (i.e., the frequency of each state). For example, the 63 times that the dyad moved from state 2 to state 3 is now represented by a transition probability, written $p(3|2)$, equal to 0.123 (63/511). Naturally, transition probabilities in each row must sum to 1. See Table 5.2.

Table 5.2   *Probability Transition Matrix*

		time t^{+1}			
		(1)	(2)	(3)	(4)
	(1)	0.245	0.113	0.110	0.532
time t	(2)	0.211	0.141	0.123	0.524
	(3)	0.142	0.125	0.149	0.584
	(4)	0.107	0.098	0.112	0.684

Transition matrices such as the one presented here are not unknown in foreign policy studies, though usually they are associated with Markov chain models (e.g., Duncan and Siverson, 1975). Indeed, Markov models can be regarded as an important class of sequential techniques, but the use of transition probabilities is in no way limited to Markovian analysis. Transition probabilities are a versatile tool for *describing* data while Markov models "are used as a data reduction technique for *fitting* the observed lag sequential probabilities with a simpler mathematical assumption" (Gottman and Bakeman, 1979, p. 191; also see Gottman and Notarius, 1978).

The probability transition matrix is a rich source of descriptive information about the day-to-day interactions that comprise the US–Soviet "dialogue." Once again we see the dominance of dyadic state 4: no matter what happens on any given day, there is a better than 50/50 chance that both nations will be inactive on the succeeding day. US–Soviet behavior thus appears to be highly segmented or sporadic, broken up on virtually a daily basis by periods of inaction. But segmentation is not the whole story; the matrix also reveals a tendency for each .

dyadic state to continue into the next period in a kind of self-reproducing pattern. Let us put the question this way: Which state has the greatest impact on its succeeding state in the sense of changing its probability of occurrence? (This is not the same as asking which state is most likely to precede any given state; the answer to this question is very clearly the inactive state already identified as the most prevalent of the four.) Notice that the highest probability value in each column falls along the main diagonal of the matrix. This pattern indicates that the conditional probability of each state at time t^{+1} departs most significantly from its base probability when preceded by itself. In other words, the probability of, say, a US action (state 2) at time t^{+1} is greatest relative to its base rate when it is preceded by another US action at time t.

State transition probabilities can also be used to compare behavior patterns of individual nations. For example, the United States and Soviet Union exhibit a marked symmetry on several counts. Both nations are equally likely to initiate behavior (or remain inactive) following days when both are active [$p(2|1) = 0.113$ versus ($p(3|1) = 0.110$], and both have about the same probabilities of acting immediately on the heels of the other [$p(3|2) = 0.123$ versus $p(2|3) = 0.125$]. The Soviet Union does appear somewhat more likely than the USA to initiate behavior following periods of inactivity, though the difference is hardly a substantial one [$p(4|2) = 0.098$ versus ($p(4|3) = 0.112$]. Perhaps the most notable difference between the two nations is in their relative influence on the co-acting state (1); a US action is far more likely to produce subsequent activity by both nations than is a behavior initiated by the Soviet Union [$p(1|2) = 0.211$ versus $p(1|3) = 0.142$].

Before moving on to other sequential techniques, it should be noted that examination of state transitions is by no means limited to the simple dialogic representation used here for illustrative purposes. The versatility of this approach is bounded only by our ability to conceptualize the world as a dynamic sequence of states. For instance, we might augment the notion of dyadic states given above by further differentiating words from deeds, or friendly acts from hostile ones. We might even reject a strictly *dyadic* conception of "states" altogether. Hudson, Hermann and Singer (1985), for example, propose a general typology of international situations based on configurations of multiple roles and role occupants relevant to some immediate foreign policy problem. Their intriguing interpretation of foreign affairs "as a continuous stream of sequential situations" suggests that it may be of considerable importance to learn how these situations evolve over time by investigating the dynamics of situational (i.e., state) transitions.

Lagged Probability Profiles

The transitional probabilities examined thus far are simply conditional probabilities lagged one observation period. Sackett (1979, 1980) has shown how the descriptive power of transitional probabilities can be extended to more complex patterns, cycles, and contingencies merely by taking account of lags greater than one. Sackett's approach is especially effective for cases in which sequential relationships are sought among many different types of encoded behaviors. For this example and those to follow, the rather stark dyadic states representation of US–Soviet interaction used above will be reconfigured to incorporate some modest distinctions of behavioral content. Although any number of discrete content categories could be used for this purpose, for the sake of simplicity I have reorganized the standard WEIS codes to reflect the basic categories of positive, negative and neutral affect (Dixon, 1983).[6] This simple repertoire extends the scope of our inquiry from questions about the mere presence or absence of behavior to the more interesting realm of cross-actor contingencies described at the beginning of this essay. Because contingencies between behaviors are likely to be obscured by the strict time metric used earlier, the data are returned to normal event sequence form (i.e., observations are events with days of mutual inaction removed).

Sackett's analytic procedure begins by designating one behavior code to serve as a criterion behavior; every other behavior represented in the stream of codes is then examined for its frequency of occurrence immediately following the criterion (lag 1) and a conditional probability is calculated. This operation is then extended to behaviors positioned two lags away from the criterion, then three lags, and so on for as many lags as necessary to adequately describe the sequential pattern of interest. Finally, the whole process is repeated for each criterion behavior under study. Lags in Sackett's analysis can be specified as successive units of time in the conventional way or in terms of sequential event positions if the data are not uniformly spaced along a strict time metric.

For purposes of illustration, let us begin by examining patterns of Soviet affect toward the United States using US negative affect as the criterion behavior. As described above, every instance of US negative affect must be identified in order to examine the event immediately succeeding it in ordinal sequence. Most of these subsequent events will represent a Soviet behavior to be counted toward the occurrences of positive, negative, or neutral affect as appropriate. Some subsequent events, however, will turn out to be other US behaviors, which simply illustrates once again that international politics is not a tennis match even though we sometimes treat it as such. For now, instances of two or more succeeding events by a single actor will be omitted from explicit consideration. Carrying out the requisite calculations up to eight lags produces the conditional probabilities in Table 5.3.

The first row of the table is labeled "Overall" to indicate the overall or unconditional probability of each Soviet affect category in the total behavioral stream; the remaining rows give conditional probabilities at the designated lag following each occurrence of US negative affect. (The probabilities in Table 5.3 do not sum to 1 across the rows because instances of two or more consecutive US events have been removed.) A reasonable starting point in interpreting these probability values is to ask whether the individual categories occur more or less frequently after the criterion than we would expect based on their simple overall probabilities. Not surprisingly, the probability values at lag 1 indicate

Table 5.3 *Lag Sequential Probabilities of Soviet Affect*

	Positive	Neutral	Negative
	Criterion: US Negative Affect		
Overall	0.163	0.197	0.351
Lag 1	0.142	0.180	0.393
2	0.136	0.180	0.346
3	0.130	0.166	0.343
4	0.127	0.154	0.391
5	0.118	0.183	0.376
6	0.127	0.178	0.367
7	0.133	0.180	0.361
8	0.136	0.178	0.382

that Soviet positive and neutral affect occur somewhat less frequently and negative affect somewhat more frequently than can be expected by chance alone. As we move further away from the criterion it becomes increasingly difficult to keep track of the necessary probability values even for only three types of behavior. The usual solution to this problem, which obviously can get much worse with more sophisticated coding distinctions, is to present the numerical probabilities in a graphic display called a lagged probability profile.

Lagged probability profiles of Soviet affect following occurrences of US negative affect are presented in Figure 5.1. Each profile graphs conditional probability values along the vertical axis for the successive event lags listed horizontally: unconditional base probabilities are indicated by a broken line. This format represents sequential patterns by the relative positions of peaks and valleys in the lag profile of each

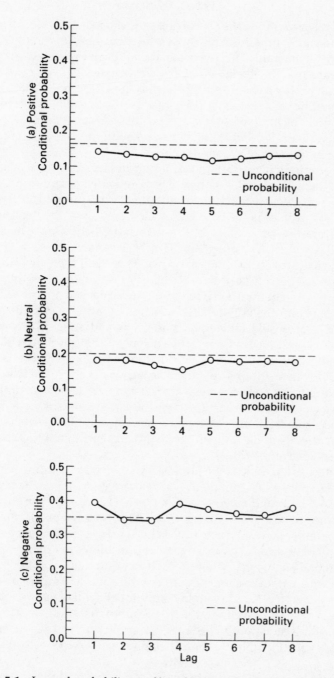

Figure 5.1 Lagged probability profiles of Soviet affect following US negative affect

behavior. For example, the probability of Soviet negative affect appears to peak at lags 1 and 4, marking those sequential positions following the criterion at which this affective evaluation is especially likely to occur. This means that the likelihood of a Soviet negative behavior increases immediately after a US negative behavior, then it tends to settle back to its unconditional rate for two lags before once again increasing in probability. The probability of Soviet positive affect, on the other hand, remains at steady levels just under the unconditional base rate, suggesting little in the way of sequential impact.

The patterns in Figure 5.1 are not strong and we should not make too much of them, though this is obviously more a function of our set of data than the profiling technique. One particularly appealing feature of probability profiles is the ease with which they allow the detection of recurrent chains or sequences of two or more behaviors. The actual probability values presented in Figure 5.1 contain no such chains. Nevertheless we can imagine what a plausible chain of behaviors might look like. Let us suppose that we had found a different probability profile for Soviet neutral behavior, a profile that peaked noticeably at the second lag from the criterion. This imaginary profile, in conjunction with the real profile for negative affect, would suggest a common sequence consisting of a US negative behavior (the criterion), followed by Soviet negative behavior at lag 1, followed by Soviet neutral behavior. Should such patterns be found the lag profile approach to pattern identification should be regarded as an exploratory tool. To confirm the pattern it would be necessary to search the complete event sequence for actual occurrences of this three-step chain, calculate its probability, and compare the resulting value to the chance expectation of this chain of behaviors (Sackett, 1979).

Lag profiles also hold some promise as a means for isolating patterns of "foreign policy substitutability" and "alternative triggers" (Most and Starr, 1984; Most and Siverson in Chapter 8). For present purposes we can define substitutability to be occasions in which a single stimulus behavior (i.e., criterion) is able to elicit two or more different responses. Substitutability thus acknowledges the possibility that foreign policy decision makers may choose to respond in different ways when confronted with what appear to be similar problems. A comparison of lag profiles generated from a single criterion behavior would appear to provide a way of detecting at least the more discernible patterns of foreign policy substitution. The notion of alternative triggers can be viewed as substitutability in reverse—rather than one behavior eliciting many responses, the concern now is with the possibility of many different behaviors all leading to one response. To construct a lag profile sensitive to alternative triggers we need merely reverse the direction of the lags. In this case the criterion becomes the response behavior and the lag probabilities (or, more accurately, "lead" probabilities) are calculated for behaviors occurring *prior* to the criterion.

All of the techniques discussed thus far depend in a critical way on comparisons of conditional and unconditional probabilities. Although probability profiles (and state transitions) can be descriptively interesting by themselves, we will usually want to know if a suspected pattern in the data actually does appear more often than expected by chance. One simple way to answer this question is to examine conditional probabilities in relation to a 95 percent confidence band around the expected (unconditional) probability values at each lag. Confidence bands are calculated in the usual way from the standard deviation of the expected probability (i.e., the square root of $(P_e[1-P_e])/N$ where P_e is the unconditional probability and N is the number of times the behavior follows the criterion). Confidence bands must be calculated anew for each lagged probability profile and the bands themselves are not comparable across profiles. This means that every combination of criterion and target behavior must occupy a separate graph (e.g., a total of 18 would be needed for a complete analysis of US–Soviet affect). Another method for gauging differences between conditional and unconditional probabilities is based on the binomial z statistic calculated by $(P_o-P_e)/SD$ where P_o is the observed probability, P_e is the expected probability as before, and SD is the standard deviation as calculated above (Sackett, 1979; 1980; Bakeman, 1983; see Allison and Liker [1982] for a somewhat different formula). As we will see below, z statistics provide a particularly convenient and compact method for expressing departure from chance occurrence.

Crosslag z Score Profiles

The z score procedure described in the preceding paragraph is open to at least two different interpretations. Bakeman (1978) regards the z as merely an index of the difference between conditional and unconditional probabilities because of the strong likelihood of nonindependence between successive points of observation. Sackett (1980, p. 315), on the other hand, takes pains to show that the z statistic probabilities closely approximate true binomial probabilities and therefore can be used in their usual hypothesis testing sense "as long as conservative alpha levels and interpretations are employed." Sackett does not ignore the potential problem of correlated observations, though he tends to view it more as an empirical question to be sorted out by comparisons of crosslag and autolag (i.e., probability of a criterion following itself) probabilities. Sackett's approach to the issue of nonindependence is a compelling one and we shall come back to it shortly; nevertheless, in the absence of randomization or some probability sampling procedure it seems imprudent to interpret the z score as anything more than an informal index.

For the US–Soviet exchange of affective evaluations, z score profiles are displayed in Figure 5.2.[7] Because the z indices are standardized to comparable values it is now possible to consolidate graphic profiles of multiple target behaviors under a single criterion. Thus, all three of the Soviet behaviors examined earlier in relation to the criterion of US negative affect are now contained in the lower right quadrant of Figure 5.2. The shaded segment of each graph corresponds to a z value of plus or minus 2, roughly the area of a 95 per cent confidence band around

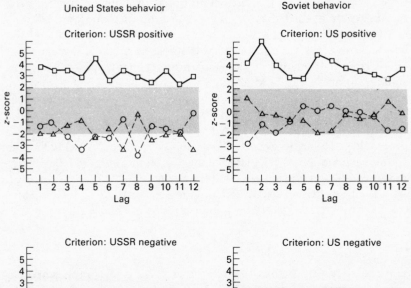

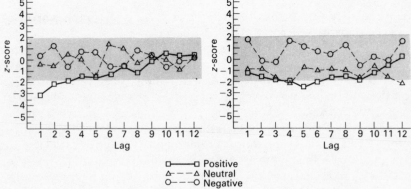

Figure 5.2 Crosslag z-score profiles for US–Soviet affect

90

the expected probability values (which are represented by a z score of 0). It is now evident that what had appeared to be a possible pattern in the lagged probability profile of Figure 5.1 (i.e., an increase in Soviet negative affect at lags 1 and 4) fails at either lag to exceed the threshold z value of ±2.

The most striking pattern that does emerge from the z score profiles is the strong positive-positive linkage displayed in the top two quadrants. Put simply, a positive behavior by one actor substantially increases the probability of a positive behavior by the other over a fairly long string of successive observations. What is perhaps most unusual about this finding is not that positive affect begets positive affect for the US–Soviet dyad—this relationship or something like it has been reported by others (e.g., Ward, 1982)—rather it is that the relationship remains so strong for so many successive event lags. One possible explanation lies in the time frame of the WEIS observational data base. It may be that the long chains of positive behaviors that form the basis for these patterns are not spread throughout the entire twelve-year period but are instead clustered together in a shorter interval that corresponds to the Nixon-Kissinger period of détente. This speculation is consistent with previous descriptive findings (Dixon, 1983), though it still needs to be tested by separate sequential analyses of detente and nondetente periods.

Also interesting is the fact that nothing even remotely approaching the sustained positive-positive linkages appears to follow instances of negative affect. If there are patterns involving negative affect they are both more subtle and shorter-lived. Rather than stimulating future negative behavior in a tit-for-tat fashion, negative affect seems to inhibit the incidence of future positive actions, though it does so differently for the two actors. For the United States this effect begins abruptly at the first lag and then quickly tapers off in a lag or two while for the Soviet Union the pattern develops several lags later and assumes a more gradual form.

The extreme subtlety of these patterns raises an issue of considerable importance for sequential analysis: are these patterns real in the sense of registering meaningful behavioral responses or are they merely chance occurrences? This issue is more generally known as the problem of Type I error, that is, of rejecting the null hypothesis when it is true. Unfortunately, the problem is even more vexing in sequential analysis than in the usual hypothesis-testing context because, first, so many separate measurements are calculated from the data that some extreme values will almost certainly be found and, second, because lag techniques are typically used in an exploratory fashion to identify patterns rather than to test preconceived hypotheses. Although we cannot hope to eliminate this problem altogether, Sackett (1979) argues that we can minimize its effects by always checking that more than about 5 per cent of the probabilities in any profile (the number typically expected by chance) are significant before interpreting results and by making sure that lag patterns make substantive sense in the context of a particular study.

Autolag z Score Profiles

Another issue of interpretation touched on in the preceding section has to do with the assumption of independence in sequential observations of behavior. Although the full implications of this issue cannot be considered here, one aspect of it deserves at least brief attention. Interaction studies are ordinarily undertaken with the aim of showing that the behavior of one actor is somehow dependent on the behavior of another or that the two of them are mutually dependent. This notion of mutual cross-actor dependence clearly underlies the previous discussion of the strong positive-positive patterns observed in Figure 5.2. At the same time, however, it seems reasonable to assume at least the possibility that the behavior of a single actor is related to itself over time, that is, the behavior is sequentially autodependent. Autodependence implies a kind of self-stimulation that is all too easily confounded with cross-actor effects. Of course, autodependent patterns can also be of interest in their own right, as well. For these reasons it would seem advisable to examine the degree of autodependence existing in any set of sequential data using the profiling methods outlined above.

Autolagged z score profiles for two categories of US and Soviet affect are presented in Figure 5.3. It is immediately evident from these lag profiles that a substantial degree of positive autodependence does exist in these data. The top figure plots positive affect with the solid line representing US behavior and the broken line Soviet behavior. Both nations' positive profiles are somewhat erratic, although both evidence a dampening effect over the full set of lags, suggesting that a positive behavior tends to excite the probability of subsequent positive behaviors as a declining function of its relative position from the criterion. This same general form is also found in the bottom figure for negative affect.

A comparison of the US and Soviet profiles across these two figures reveals some interesting observations. Notice, first, that the relative strength of autodependence functions is reversed in the top and bottom figures; Soviet autodependence is stronger for positive affect while US autodependence is generally stronger for negative behavior. The one exception to this statement occurs at the first two lags of

Sequential autodependency

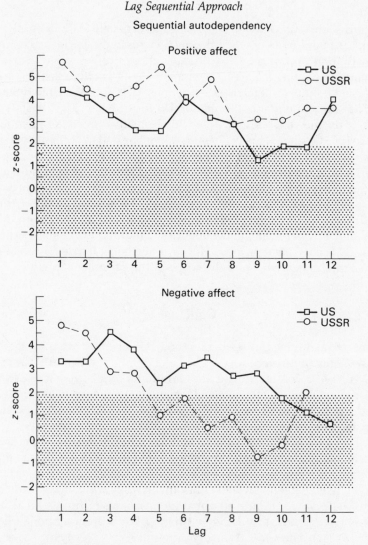

Figure 5.3 Autolag z-score profiles for US and Soviet affect

negative affect where it is the Soviets that exhibit the stronger auto-dependency. There is also a difference in how quickly the autodependence functions descend into the shaded region of chance occurrence. For the United States the positive and negative functions are similar, with both falling below the threshold value by the ninth or tenth lag (the rise at lag 12 for US positive affect appears to be an aberration when the function is plotted for additional lags). Two rather different patterns are found for the Soviet Union; negative autodependence drops off very quickly while the positive function declines even more slowly than that of the USA. In sum, these profiles suggest that the Soviet Union has a longer "memory" of its positive actions and a shorter "memory" of its negative actions than does the United States.

The autodependence found for US and Soviet affect casts some doubt on the reliability of the mutual positive-positive dependency discovered earlier. This problem is a familiar one to students of dynamic social interaction and is in no way unique to the categorical sequential techniques presented here. Sackett (1980) has shown how auto- and crosslag dependencies can be sorted out under the special conditions of strong cyclicity, and more recently logit-linear models (Allison and Liker, 1982; Dixon, 1985), latent structure analysis (Dillon, Madden and Kumar, 1983), and categorical weighted least squares (Budescu, 1984) have been proposed for the more general case. The details of these methods are beyond the scope of the present chapter.

Conclusion

Interest in the lagged sequential analysis of observational data has grown steadily in recent years as behavioral scientists in a variety of fields have given increasing attention to dynamic processes of social interaction. The lag techniques reviewed here by no means exhaust all of the possible ways that conditional and unconditional probabilities can be assembled to describe discrete behavioral sequences. These methods are extremely flexible and are easily tailored to specialized research questions or data representations (although not all data representations are appropriate for sequential analysis). For example, it seems reasonable to suppose that the investigation of lag sequential patterns may contribute to our understanding of how international crises (as discussed by Leng in Chapter 10) or interventions (Sloan, 1985) evolve over time. At a very different level of analysis, sequential methods might be applied to the sort of decision-making data collected by Anderson (see Chapter 15) to illuminate the dynamic character of group decision-making processes or to help in the identification of what Kegley has termed (in Chapter 13) decision regimes. Although the necessary computations range from tedious to downright overwhelming whatever the application, the basic statistics are nevertheless relatively easy to comprehend and computer programs are available in the public domain to ease the computational task (Sackett *et al.*, 1979; Bakeman, 1983).

Like the phenomenon it was designed to study, sequential

methodology is a dynamic affair. Recent developments point to an increasing concern for the testing of explicit hypotheses and interaction models in contrast to an earlier emphasis on searching for sequential dependencies (e.g., Budescu, 1984; Wampold, 1984; Dillon, Madden and Kumar, 1983). The position advanced in this chapter is that sequential approaches, whether purely descriptive or of the hypothesis-testing variety, will provide new and valuable insights in the study of foreign policy behavior.

Notes

Preparation of this paper was supported by a grant from the Emory University Research Fund. I am indebted to Charles Kegley and Neil Richardson for their comments on an earlier draft.

1 Other contributions explicitly emphasizing the communicative nature of foreign policy behavior include those by Hermann and Peacock (Chapter 2 above) and Hudson, Hermann and Singer (1985). For a more thorough statement of this definition and discussion of its implications, see Hermann and Dixon (1984).
2 Schrodt (1984), for example, develops a similar case for sequential analysis using methods from artificial intelligence research.
3 The WEIS data were supplied by the Inter-University Consortium for Political and Social Research. Naturally, neither the Consortium nor the original collectors are responsible for uses made of these data by others.
4 To be clear, the US–Soviet dyad is assumed to be only salient and illustrative: I do not claim it is either "typical" or "atypical" in Richardson's sense (see Chapter 9).
5 The WEIS file records the United States as initiating some behavior to the Soviet Union on 1184 separate days with 171 of these containing more than one identifiable action. For the Soviet Union the comparable figures are 1231 total days of activity with 140 having multiple behaviors.
6 For days encompassing multiple events by a single actor it was necessary to calculate a summary of the day's affect expressions. This was accomplished by assuming positive or negative affect had priority over neutral affect; thus, a day with both a positive and a neutral behavior was counted as positive, two neutral and a positive as positive, and so forth. On those rare occasions (16 for USA, 15 for USSR) when both positive and negative affect were expressed in a single day, affect was recorded as positive, negative, or neutral depending on the number of events in each category; thus, one positive and one negative was counted as neutral, two positives and one negative as positive, and so forth.
7 All z scores in this and the remaining examples are calculated according to Allison and Liker (1982) using algorithms devised by Bakeman (1983).

6

Evaluation: A Neglected Task for the Comparative Study of Foreign Policy

GREGORY A. RAYMOND

In recent years, there has been a growing emphasis on using social science methods to evaluate public policy. Revenue shortfalls and heightened public concern over accountability have led legislators, administrative officials, and members of the media to demand hard evidence on the effectiveness of government programs. As a result, evaluation research has been described as "one of the liveliest frontiers in American social science" (Cronbach *et al.*, 1980, pp. 12–13). Its rapid development can be seen by comparing the findings from two surveys of US federal government evaluations: whereas just over a decade ago the Urban Institute concluded that evaluations of federal programs were "almost nonexistent" (Wholey *et al.*, 1971, p. 5), only a few years later the General Accounting Office (1978, p. 8) reported that expenditures for program evaluations had risen to $146 million—a 500 percent increase since the period covered by the Urban Institute study. In short, what began almost half a century ago as a plea for scientifically studying the effects of the New Deal (see Stephan, 1935) has matured into a "robust and continuing endeavor" (Freeman, 1977, p. 20).

Unfortunately, despite a deluge of literature throughout the 1970s on designing and implementing social action evaluations,[1] there has been little spillover into the field of foreign policy analysis. Virtually all of the scientific research on foreign policy has focused on explaining state behavior; therefore, greater attention has been given to the sources of policy than to its consequences, and more emphasis has been placed on policy outputs than on their outcomes. Thus, at the very time when we are beginning to see some cumulation in our empirical findings on the determinants of foreign policy, most evaluations continue to be based on impressionistic appeals to that nebulous standard called the 'national interest.'

The purpose of this chapter is to present a general analytical framework that hopefully will facilitate the important but neglected task of foreign policy evaluation. It is offered out of a conviction that we can learn from experience and improve our ability to solve foreign policy problems if we scientifically study the reasons for our past successes and failures. As such, it is based on the same proposition advanced in Chapter 7 by Bobrow and Chan: a fruitful, new direction for the comparative study of foreign policy lies in assessing policy performance.

Underlying Assumptions

In his epic novel *Don Quixote*, Cervantes (1964, p. 763) describes a conversation between his protagonist and the owners of a large estate near Pedrola. One of the topics they discuss is the ability of Don Quixote's squire, Sancho Panza, to govern Barataria, a small island conferred upon him by a generous duke. Despite being "one of the drollest squires that ever served a knight-errant," Don Quixote predicts Sancho will be a good governor, for the main thing "is to mean well and desire to do right . . ." Embodied in this prediction is a distinction between judging government actions good or bad on the basis of their intentions, versus judging them according to their effectiveness in achieving intended results. The former is an aretaic judgment; the latter, an instrumental judgment. Because the grounds for aretaic judgments lie in normative theories of moral value, they are not subjects of social scientific evaluation. On the other hand, since the grounds for instrumental judgments lie in empirical claims about causal connections between policy actions and observed outcomes, they can be evaluated scientifically.[2]

Few people would quarrel with the assertion that we can learn from experience by evaluating the effectiveness of policy actions. As Levitan and Wurzburg (1979) have suggested, evaluation is much like sex: everyone is for it; everyone claims to understand it; and everyone thinks they can do it well simply by following their natural inclinations. Given the diversity of research inclinations among those who evaluate public policies, it is not surprising that there are numerous approaches to evaluation, each derived from different assumptions on how to gauge policy success. Some evaluators ransack history for parallel cases they can use in appeals to analogy when arguing for or against a policy; others hold hearings where they can gather testimony to employ in arguments based on appeals to authority; and still others interview members of certain target populations so their policy arguments can be anchored in appeals to popular sentiments. Evaluation, in other words, is an elastic term that program funders, managers, staffers and consultants have stretched to include a wide variety of practices.

The approach to evaluation taken here rests on three underlying assumptions: (1) foreign policy behavior entails a series of purposeful acts aimed at achieving desired goals; (2) it is possible to devise performance indicators that measure the extent to which a given goal has been achieved; and (3) the comparative method can be used to acquire reproducible evidence on whether the acts under investigation did, indeed, produce observed changes in the performance indicators. By approaching evaluation in this way, both the "chain of circumstance" conception of foreign policy behavior and the "goal-free" model of its assessment are rejected.

The chain of circumstance conception of foreign policy behavior downplays the roles of problem identification and goal setting in policy formulation. According to this view, most decisions "are like Topsy—they just grow" (Millar, 1969, p. 61). To quote Nicolson (1946, pp. 19–20):

> Few indeed are the occasions on which any statesman sees his objective clearly before him and marches toward it with undeviating stride; numerous indeed are the occasions when a decision or an event, which at the time seemed wholly unimportant, leads almost fortuitously to another decision which is no less incidental, until, little by little link, the chain of circumstances is forged.

Similarly, Seabury (1963, p. 5) contends:

> All too often policy is the product of random, haphazard, or even irrational forces . . . It may be no policy at all but simply a drift with events.

For these observers, then, foreign policy rarely emerges from deliberate plans; it unfolds incrementally, owing more to impulse than design. Certainly, many policies are ruled by a tyranny of small decisions; however, this does not mean they are aimless. Even when "muddling through" a problem, we strive to achieve some goal, if only survival. To be sure, our goals may be shortsighted or imprudent, but behavior initiated to attain them is nonetheless purposeful (Rosenau, 1971a, p. 89; Sprout and Sprout, 1971, pp. 95–7).[3]

If foreign policy officials act purposefully, then one way to evaluate their policies is in terms of how effective they are in attaining enunciated goals.[4] Of course, this is not the only way to evaluate effectiveness. Scriven (1972), for instance, maintains that ignorance of a policy's goals forces evaluators to widen their search for its impacts, thus increasing the likelihood they will discover positive and negative side effects. While it is important to document unintended consequences, the question of whether a policy achieved its prespecified ends cannot be avoided. Funds were appropriated and resources committed for a purpose. So-called goal-free evaluators, operating without knowledge of that purpose, tend to rely on their own preferences about what results are appropriate when assessing effectiveness (Patton, 1978, p. 111). Not only does this amount to replacing one set of goals with another, but it may give officials scant information on the policy's success at fulfilling its formally stated purpose. Therefore, a useful analytical framework for evaluating foreign policy should be built on a foundation of clearly specified goals, but still encourage research into possible unanticipated side effects.

Methodological Challenges

Having adopted a goal attainment approach to foreign policy evaluations, we now must address three methodological challenges. The first challenge is to *identify policy goals*. A perusal of government documents and the transcripts of public speeches on foreign policy undertakings will quickly show the magnitude of this challenge. Consider, for example, Prime Minister Winston Churchill's speech of May 13, 1940, to the House of Commons:

> You ask, what is our policy? I can say: It is to wage war, by sea, land and air, with all our might and with all the strength that God can give us; to wage war against a monstrous tyranny, never surpassed in the dark, lamentable catalogue of human crime. That is our policy.   (James, 1974, p. 6220)

Obviously the Prime Minister was more concerned with raising British morale than clearly delineating a set of immediate and long-range goals. Nevertheless, his speech illustrates a serious problem for evaluation researchers, namely, specific goals frequently are buried by the avalanche of rhetoric national leaders use to justify their policies.

This problem is compounded by the use of buzzwords and euphemisms in foreign policy discourse. Munich is synonymous with appeasement, Afghanistan with aggression, and Vietnam with humiliation. Like somber figures discussing the fate of an ailing friend, we speak in hushed tones about pacification, protective reaction strikes, and peacekeeper missiles. Yet these words explain little. They are the stuff of cocktail parties, consumed without a thought along with the paté and stuffed mushrooms.

Another problem in identifying policy goals comes from the nature of the political process. In order to appeal to a broad constituency and gain support from different factions, legislation often contains vague goals. Moreover, as Rutman (1980, p. 54) points out, poorly defined goals are attractive to program directors because they give them flexibility to tailor activities according to agency priorities. Taken together, legislative and bureaucratic politics may engender goal displacement, a tendency to substitute internal, procedural goals for nebulous policy goals.[5]

Finally, identifying policy goals is also difficult because policies are not static. In the first place, new purposes may be grafted onto old policies, as shown by the US decision in the fall of 1950 to add "roll back" to its original policy of repelling North Korea's attack on the South. In the second place, various actors within a government may have different perceptions of the policy's real purpose, as exemplified by differences between civilian and military officials in the Johnson Administration over whether the bombing campaign against the North Vietnamese was aimed at eroding their will or their capability to continue fighting. In the third place, a government may be uncertain about its goals, as in the case of the French intervention in Chad during the late 1970s (Farrands, 1985, p. 84). To sum up, for rhetorical, linguistic, political and programmatic reasons, identifying clear, specific goals is perhaps the greatest challenge in evaluating foreign policy. However, it is not the only challenge. Once goals have been identified, performance indicators must be devised to measure the extent to which they have been attained.

The second methodological challenge in evaluating foreign policy is to *link each goal to one or more concrete, measurable objectives*. These objectives operationalize the desired outcome; they are the standards of success we invoke when making instrumental judgments about a policy. To illustrate the relationship between goals and objectives, let us briefly look at Canadian foreign policy under Prime Minister Trudeau. When Pierre Trudeau first moved into 24 Sussex Drive, he initiated a comprehensive review of his country's foreign policies. A key recommendation from the review was that Canada should reduce its vulnerability to the United States (see Canada, Department of External Affairs, 1970; Sharp, 1972). Based on the premise that US economic penetration was one source of vulnerability, Parliament passed the 1974 Foreign Investment Review Act, which established a board to regulate new foreign investments and foreign attempts to take over Canadian firms. Was this action effective in reducing vulnerability? In order to answer on empirical grounds, an evaluation would have to link the goal in question to a set of performance indicators.

Taking the Foreign Investment Review Board as an example, board members could use data on direct American investment to construct indicators of economic penetration, then define some level of reduction in the values of these indicators as their objective. Given valid indicators, the effectiveness of their actions could be estimated by the extent to which the objectives were reached. Needless to say, findings from a Review Board study of the impact its regulations had on US economic penetration would constitute only one small piece of evidence on the larger question of Canadian vulnerability. Furthermore, even if a statistically significant decrease was found in the level of economic penetration, an evaluator could not simply infer it was caused by Review Board actions. Plausible rival explanations would have to be eliminated.

The third methodological challenge in evaluating foreign policy is to *obtain unbiased estimates of the net effects from policy actions*. Returning to the example above, the total reduction in economic penetration constitutes a gross outcome. In other words, it includes the impact of the policy actions, as well as the impact of factors such as market conditions, which also might have contributed to the decrease of US investments in Canada. Rival explanations of the reasons for the reduction cannot be eliminated without an estimate of net effect, the impact attributable solely to policy actions (Rossi and Freeman, 1982, p. 169).

Many evaluations of social amelioration programs use the experimental method to rule out rival explanations (see Boruch, McSweeney and Soderstrom, 1978). More than any other type of research design, the randomized experiment reveals whether a policy action or some extraneous factor brought about a particular result. Foreign policy, however, is rarely amenable to field experimentation; fortunately designs based on the comparative method offer evaluators an alternative way to estimate the net effects of policy actions.

Classification is a prerequisite for comparison. In order for evaluators to use comparative research designs, the programs under investigation must possess "substantially similar aims but clearly differentiated strategies for attaining them" (Weiss, 1972, p. 83). That is, their goals must be comparable; they must be of the same class for us to assess the relative effectiveness of different policy actions.

Ordinarily, foreign policy analysts attempt to classify goals on a substantive basis. Table 6.1 lists those categories frequently used for this purpose. Most analysts incorporate security and welfare categories into their typologies; many include prestige; and a few append additional categories. While all of their typologies are parsimonious, some contain categories which are not exhaustive, mutually exclusive, or operationally defined. Another drawback is their tendency to disregard the nonsubstantive properties of goals, an oversight which could

Table 6.1 *An inventory of common foreign policy goals*

Category	Components	Inventory sources
Security	Physical survival, territorial integrity, political independence	Osgood, 1953, p. 5; Organski, 1958, p. 63; Wolfers, 1962, p. 82; Aron, 1966, p. 72; Puchala, 1971, pp. 74–9; Yost, 1972, p. 21; Crabb, 1972, p. 5; Rosecrance, 1973, pp. 202–6; Finlay and Hovet, 1975, p. 87; Rainey, 1975, p. 5; Holsti, 1977, p. 145; Frankel, 1979, p. 98; Lerche and Said, p. 30; Reynolds, 1980, p. 49; Wendzel, 1981, pp. 75–8; Stremlau, 1982, p. 1; Hartmann, 1983, p. 75; Pearson and Rochester, 1984, p. 147; Spanier, 1984, p. 57.
Welfare	Prosperity, economic development, well-being	Organski, 1958, p. 63; Puchala, 1971, pp. 79–84; Yost, 1972, p. 23; Finlay and Hovet, 1975, p. 87; Rainey, 1975, p. 6; Thompson and Macridis, 1976, p. 16; Holsti, 1977, p. 148; Lerche and Said, 1979, p. 30; Reynolds, 1980, p. 49; Wendzel, 1981, p. 79; Stremlau, 1982, p. 1; Pearson and Rochester, 1984, p. 147; Spanier, 1984, p. 61.
Prestige	Recognition, status, respect, honor	Osgood, 1953, p. 6; Morgenthau, 1960, pp. 72–85; Aron, 1966, p. 73; Puchala, 1971, pp. 84–8; Yost, 1972, p. 22; Rosecrance, 1973, p. 201; Rainey, 1975, p. 6; Holsti, 1977, p. 149; Lerche and Said, 1979, p. 30; Wendzel, 1981, p. 80; Hartmann, 1983, p. 76; Pearson and Rochester, 1984, p. 148; Spanier, 1984, p. 59.
Ideological self-extension	Promotion of values, conversion	Organski, 1958, p. 63; Morgenthau, 1960, pp. 60–3; Wolfers, 1962, p. 92; Rosecrance, 1973, p. 201; Finlay and Hovet, 1975, p. 87; Holsti, 1977, p. 150; Lerche and Said, 1979, p. 31; Reynolds, 1980, p. 49; Wendzel, 1981, p. 80; Spanier, 1984, p. 62.
Material self-extension	Power, territorial expansion, exclusive access	Osgood, 1953, p. 6; Morgenthau, 1960, pp. 55–8; Wolfers, 1962, p. 91; Aron, 1966, p. 73; Rosecrance, 1973, p. 201; Thompson and Macridis, 1976, p. 15; Holsti, 1977, p. 150; Lerche and Said, 1979, p. 31; Spanier, 1984, p. 63.

Table 6.1   *continued*

Category	Components	Inventory sources
Self-abnegation	Peace, rectitude, international solidarity	Organski, 1958, p. 63; Wolfers, 1962, p. 93; Puchala, 1971, pp. 88–90; Finlay and Hovet, 1975, p. 87; Thompson and Macridis, 1976, p. 15; Spanier, 1984, p. 63.

lead two programs to be classified together based on a substantive interpretation of their goals, yet not be comparable because of differences in such nonsubstantive properties as their beneficiaries (Organski, 1958, pp. 76–81; Gross, 1969, pp. 282–6; Perrow, 1970, pp. 133–74; Mohr, 1973, pp. 475–6; Brady, 1982, p. 147), their importance (Morgenthau, 1962, p. 291; Crabb, 1972, pp. 4–5; Wendzel, 1981, pp. 75–81; Hartmann, 1983, p. 75–6), or their time frame for realization (Organski, 1958, p. 81; Wendzel, 1981, pp. 78–82; Brady, 1982, pp. 142–3). In summary, the methodological challenge of estimating net effects can be overcome by using the comparative method to determine whether a policy's benefits derived from program actions or extraneous outside factors. But meaningful comparisons hinge on an evaluator's ability to classify, and that ability is hampered if our typologies cannot clearly discriminate between the substantive properties of goals and continue to ignore their nonsubstantive properties.

A Framework for Foreign Policy Evaluation

With the presentation of the underlying assumptions and methodological challenges of foreign policy evaluation behind us, we can now turn our attention to the general analytical framework shown in Figure 6.1. What follows is neither a theory about organizational effectiveness, nor a model of the causes of policy failure. Rather, it is a scheme for organizing the welter of variables that affect foreign policy outcomes.

In Figure 6.1, the symbols G, O and A represent respectively policy goals, objectives and actions. Although foreign policies may have multiple goals, each goal must be linked to one or more measurable objectives in order to evaluate effectiveness. Furthermore, each objective should be tied to one or more actions, the sum of which constitutes a program. As stated earlier, the aim of evaluation research is to ascertain empirically whether program actions produced certain observed outcomes. This can be done by comparing programs in terms of the four sets of variables shown in the framework.

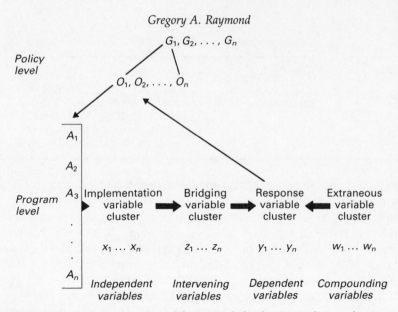

Figure 6.1 A general analytical framework for foreign policy evaluation

The first set consists of *implementation variables*. Simply put, they are factors that affect the integrity of program actions. Consider, as an illustration, Yeaton and Redner's (1981, p. 63) analogy from medical practice: although a given drug may help cure patients, failure to adhere to its recommended dosage, using it after the shelf life has expired, or taking it during meals diminishes treatment integrity. To put it another way, implementation variables account for the degree of congruence between intended and observed actions.

Incongruity between intended and observed action is a common theme in the literature of foreign policy. As former Secretary of State Henry Kissinger (quoted in Halperin, 1974, p. 245) once remarked:

> The outsider believes a presidential order is consistently followed. Nonsense. I have to spend considerable time seeing that it is carried out in the spirit the president intended. . .[6]

No doubt similar thoughts were on President Truman's mind when he commented that Dwight Eisenhower would find giving orders from the White House quite frustrating in comparison to his experience in the Army. Indeed, frustration with bureaucratic resistance and sabotage is so great that commentaries on foreign policy making teem with uncomplementary, junk-food similes. Career bureaucrats, for example, are likened to "cookie pushers" who work in a "foreign affairs fudge factory"; and getting them to carry out directives is likened to "pushing on a marshmallow" or shaking a "bowl of jelly" (Schoultz, 1981, p. 119).

Goal dissolution, the slippage between what is supposed to be done and what is actually done, can occur at any administrative level. Senior officials may fail to follow through on their own decisions, as in November 1964 when President Johnson failed to retaliate for a Vietcong attack on the Bien Hoa air base, even though he had recently approved a reprisal policy for just such occasions (Thies, 1980, p. 56). Subordinate officials may ignore commands they dislike, as State Department personnel did in 1961 when President Kennedy ordered the removal of Jupiter missiles from Turkey. Or, as in the ill-fated attempt during the spring of 1980 to rescue the American hostages held in Tehran, responsibility may be so fragmented that personal and organizational conflicts undercut the proposed actions (Smith, 1985, p. 28).

Discrepancies between intent and action appear to be a function of two types of implementation variables. The first type contains variables related to the tractability of the problem being addressed, such as technical complexity, the diversity of proscribed behavior, and the degree of change required. The second type contains variables related to the political context of the program, such as the amount of resources allocated, the depth of administrative commitment, and the amount of integration between implementing agencies (Mazmanian and Sabatier, 1983, pp. 21–35). Given that these types of implementation variables affect the integrity of program actions, they should be included as independent variables when evaluating foreign policy.

The second cluster of variables in the analytical framework consists of *bridging variables*. Strictly speaking, program actions attempt to reach a desired outcome by setting in motion some specific causal process. To use another medical example, when a foreign antigen enters the body through vaccination, it sets in motion a causal process which evokes the specific antibody that gives immunity to the disease in question. Hence, behind preventive immunization programs is a theory of how inoculation will set in motion those intervening variables which bridge the gap between action and outcome.

Another example can be seen in Henry Kissinger's rationale for détente. During the spring and summer of 1976, when Ronald Reagan became a serious threat to take the Republican nomination away from the incumbent President of his own party, the American public was given two different interpretations of détente. The view articulated by Reagan warned détente was merely an expedient used by the Soviet Union to put the United States off guard. Like the efforts of Foreign Minister von Ribbentrop and Ambassador Schulenberg which led to the Nazi-Soviet pact of 1939, Soviet diplomats were said to be promoting détente for tactical purposes. Just as Hitler wanted to divide Germany's opponents and acquire much-needed resources from his greatest ideological adversary, so too did the Soviet leadership seek to weaken the Atlantic Alliance, isolate the People's Republic of China, and obtain technological assistance from the United States.

In contrast to this interpretation of détente, the view which Gerald Ford inherited from the Nixon Administration had its roots in classical diplomacy. Throughout the nineteenth century, statesmen generally understood détente to imply a relaxation of tensions between countries. To a lesser extent, they also believed that in some situations détente could lead to the establishment of long-term cooperation. For instance, following the Fashoda incident of 1898, Foreign Minister Delcassé and Ambassador Cambon were able to lessen tension with their British rivals and therein lay the groundwork for future Anglo-French cooperation. According to Ford's Secretary of State, Henry Kissinger, future cooperation was also possible with the Soviet Union because it was no longer a revolutionary power pursuing unlimited, ideologically grounded aims. In order to draw Moscow into a new, collaborative relationship, Kissinger recommended using economic rewards and sanctions to modify Soviet behavior, and linking cooperation in one policy area to further cooperation in related areas. While many détentes had lapsed throughout history, he believed one based on a web of vested material interests and linkages would dampen competition and forestall crises.

In essence, Kissinger's recommendation rested on an implicit theory: incentives and linkages would set in motion a causal process, one which would give rise to the norms of reciprocity and restraint needed for a crisis-prevention regime. Thus, if we were to evaluate Kissinger's détente policy, we would want evidence on whether incentives and linkages gave rise to norms of reciprocity and restraint. Stated formally, we would want to test the program operation hypothesis that the actions implemented had the presumed effect on the bridging variables. Falsification of this hypothesis would imply program failure; support would lead us to another test.

The framework's remaining variable clusters consist of *response* and *extraneous variables*. The former encompasses the performance indicators contained in the objectives, as well as any possible side effects. The latter include contextual factors like the characteristics of the target, the behavior of other actors, and so on. Successful programs set in motion a causal process that leads to the desired outcome. Once we have evidence that the implemented actions affected the bridging variables, we need to test the causal impact hypothesis that the bridging variables (not some extraneous factors) produced the desired outcome. Falsification of the causal impact hypothesis would imply theory failure. That is to say, the implicit theory behind the program would be the source of the problem, either because no relationship was found between the bridging and response variables, or because the covariation between them was spurious. If, however, we have found support for the causal impact hypothesis, then our final task is to assess the program's effectiveness in terms of the extent to which the net outcome attained the objectives.

As an example, let us briefly look at the Caribbean Basin Initiative. On February 24, 1982, President Reagan proposed a new foreign economic policy for the Caribbean region. Founded on ideas he had previously voiced at the Cancún summit, the policy proposal had three components: (1) concessional aid; (2) a 12-year commitment to allow duty-free entry of Caribbean Basin products into the United States; and (3) a 5-year tax credit for US investments in the region. Eighteen months later (after the Congress had placed restrictions on the aid and trade components, and had eliminated the investment tax credit) the President signed the Caribbean Basic Recovery Act, which created the Caribbean Basin Initiative.

By promoting those conditions under which private entrepreneurship could flourish, the Caribbean Basin Initiative was expected to set a causal process in motion, one that ultimately would bring greater stability to the region. More specifically, it was anticipated that the initiative would provide incentives for increased production, savings, and investment. Innovation would be encouraged, and the position of the commercial middle class strengthened. When taken together, the actions initiated under the auspices of the Caribbean Basin Initiative were supposed to stimulate economic growth which, in turn, would provide a foundation for building stable democracies. Embodied in the initiative, then, is a causal impact hypothesis: the greater the economic growth, the greater the political stability. Following tests to ascertain if the program actions set in motion the economic bridging variables, an evaluation of the Caribbean Basin Initiative would proceed to test the causal impact hypothesis that linked economic growth to political stability. To be policy-relevant, evaluations must not only determine whether a program failed, they must also determine the reasons why it failed.

Policy Relevance Revisited

Years ago, when Rosenau (1971c, p. 87) first traced the outlines of the field we now know as the comparative study of foreign policy, he proposed that the responsive stage of state behavior should be at the center of our research concerns. Though admitting enormous methodological obstacles existed, he still maintained "a concern for foreign policy" could not be "sustained without the question of its effectiveness and consequences arising." The obstacles would just have to be confronted and overcome.

But few researchers used the comparative method to evaluate foreign policy undertakings. The methodological obstacles were not confronted, let alone overcome. This general neglect is surprising given the lamentations over policy relevance that reverberate throughout the academic community. Reseachers have been advised to study problems that rank high on the public agenda, focus on variables decision makers can manipulate, and seek out intermediaries who can communicate their findings to appropriate government agencies. It has been the thesis of this chapter that a new, policy-relevant direction for our field lies elsewhere, namely, in evaluating policy performance. The potential of evaluation research for improving performance can be seen when we examine literature on the sources of foreign policy. Within this volume, for example, Anderson, Kegley, and Hermann, Hermann and Hagan identify various social, psychological, and organizational factors in the policy-making process that often lead to serious miscalculations. By providing timely feedback on policy impact, evaluation research can help mitigate errors born of these miscalculations.

Admittedly, evaluations may be initiated for purposes which have little to do with improving performance. Partisan attacks on a program could be disguised as sincere calls for outside evaluation. Changes unwelcome by program personnel could be delayed if they claimed they had not completed their own in-house evaluation. But these ulterior motives notwithstanding, our learning from experience will remain haphazard until we scientifically study the responsive stage of foreign policy behavior. As suggested in the chapter by Papadakis and Starr, we need to overcome our fixation on output and give more attention to outcome and effect.

The analytical framework presented here has been intended as a preliminary step toward surmounting the obstacles that block foreign policy evaluation. Given the strong interest today in determining the impact of economic sanctions and other policy instruments (see Wallensteen, 1983), and given the applicability of the comparative method for determining the impact of behavior by nonstate actors (Mingst and Schechter, 1985; Hoole, 1977), foreign policy evaluation would seem to be a promising area for future research. Indeed, as Aristotle (1963, p. 300) once put it, praising involves comparison:

"Everything that is praiseworthy appears to be praised because it has a certain quality and stands in a certain relation to something else." By harnessing the comparative method to appraise foreign policy effectiveness, we shall be able to make better judgments on whether specific programs should be continued, modified, or terminated.

Notes

1 It is far beyond the scope of this paper to review the massive body of evaluation literature. For those interested in such a review, Dynes (1983) has assembled an annotated bibliography of the major works, while House (1980) and Hyde (1984) trace their historical development and interrelationships.
2 An example of these two types of judgments can be seen in the following statements by Morgenthau (1960, p. 6): "Neville Chamberlain's policies of appeasement were . . . inspired by good motives . . . Yet his policies helped to make the Second World War inevitable, and to bring untold miseries to millions of men." By drawing this distinction, I am not suggesting we should abdicate our responsibility to analyze the grounds for aretaic judgments. However, when someone says "Chamberlain's motives were good," the method we use in analyzing moral propositions of this sort is different from that used to evaluate the instrumental claim "Chamberlain's appeasement policy was ineffective in preserving peace." For a discussion of the difficulties in establishing normative criteria for evaluating foreign policy, see Kratochwil (1981).
3 Hermann (1978b, p. 30) raises an important question about the characterization of foreign policy as goal-directed behavior: "In what sense is it meaningful to suggest that a complex collective entity such as a government has goals?" Because of questions like this, the traditional view of organizational goals (see Weber, 1947; Parsons, 1956) has come under attack (e.g., Etzioni, 1960; Simon, 1964; and Yuchtman and Seashore, 1967). The approach taken here is to interpret program goals as entailing a consensus of intent, or what Kegley in Chapter 13 below terms a "decision regime." As Mohr (1973, p. 473) has put it: "Consensus means explicit or tacit agreement among those concerned that a certain behavior will under the circumstances be followed, notwithstanding the possibility that some might prefer other available alternatives." Stated differently, consensus implies a certain unanimity, but not necessarily enthusiasm or exclusive preoccupation. See also Gross (1969) and Perrow (1961).
4 Although I have chosen the criterion of *effectiveness* (i.e., the extent to which a policy attains its goals), Nagel (1982) demonstrates how goal-directed performance can also be evaluated in terms of *efficiency* (the ratio of benefits to costs) and *equity* (the distribution of benefits and costs in proportion to need). While no agreement exists on the meta-political standards for determining the relative merits of these three criteria (Anderson, 1979), most researchers have concentrated their attention on policy effectiveness. For a summary and critique of various ways these researchers have conceptualized and measured effectiveness, see Price (1968), Steers (1975), and Scott (1977).

109

5 The phenomenon of goal displacement was originally studied by Michels (1962; first published in 1915). More recent studies include Selznick (1949), Lipset (1950), Merton (1957), Downs (1967, p. 19), and Wildavsky (1979, p. 49).
6 Claims of personal vigilance notwithstanding, Kissinger admits even he did not always follow presidential instructions fully, as apparently was the case during his secret trip to Moscow in the spring of 1972 (cited in George, 1983, pp. 108–9).

7

Understanding Anomalous Successes: Japan, Taiwan and South Korea

DAVIS B. BOBROW AND STEVE CHAN

The recent experiences of Japan, Taiwan and South Korea suggest perspectives on some basic matters in the comparative study of foreign policy. How can we identify and measure successful and unsuccessful policy performance? How can we explain exceptional performance and thus better anticipate it? Our three Asian cases present anomalies in several ways. They have performed far better than Westerners expected and well beyond other similarly situated countries—without conforming to any single Western theory of political and economic development or national security. Their policies have helped arrange foreign relations to promote domestic stability and prosperity, as well as national security and autonomy. The cases then offer an intriguing springboard for thinking about modes of empirical assessment and about explanatory concepts for analyzing cross-national differences in foreign policy performance. Disappointment in realizing previous knowledge claims (see Hermann and Peacock in Chapter 2) seems to warrant some fresh thinking. We share the view that attention to a variety of exemplary, atypical cases should be emphasized (see Richardson in Chapter 9) and that research on foreign policy in the evaluative mode is warranted (see Raymond in Chapter 6).

Comprehensive treatment of our topic would include: (1) strategies to identify and measure anomalous policy performance (high and low); (2) concepts to explain the causes of exceptional performance; (3) case materials to test how well the concepts account for anomalous performance; and (4) attempts to replicate empirically the test results for other cases or time periods. We leave most of this agenda for other occasions and address only the first two elements. This essay will, at best, stimulate and not demonstrate.

Davis B. Bobrow and *Steve Chan*

Anomalous Policy Performance

Anomalies are surprises that clash with prevailing conventional wisdom. For theorists, they provide an impetus to revise, improve or even abandon existing conceptions (Kuhn, 1970). Anomalies provide comparative analysts of foreign policy with possibly eye-opening ways to think about policy performance, that is, relative national success and failure. Their very deviance demands explanation and poses puzzles. To illustrate for our cases, the occurrence of the unexpected leads us to ask why some small and poorly endowed countries have achieved upward mobility in the international system while large and better endowed countries have failed to do so (and failed in domestic development as well). The nonoccurrence of the expected raises the question of why some countries have managed to attain and sustain rapid economic growth without substantial sociopolitical instability and others have not. Of course, we cannot explain anomalous performance until we identify it.

We suggest that surprising foreign policy performances can be identified through several forms of hindsight. Several of these involve comparison of actual performance with expected performance. The expectations can be drawn from several sources. One is the prevailing conventional wisdom in communities of foreign affairs experts and officials. Another is more or less formal theory(ies). A third involves patterns based on quantitative cross-national historical analyses that yield probabilistic predictions. Other approaches work less with expectations than with behaviorally revealed phenomena that show some cases to be outliers from central tendencies in the performance of a larger set of countries. The empirical method used to do that can range from the simple to the complex. Examples include the use of regression analysis to find countries that deviate markedly from the regression slope for the set of countries examined (e.g., Russett, 1978, p. 916) and factor- and cluster-analytic approaches that show failure to fit with generally operative profiles as measured by low commonality scores (e.g., Banks and Gregg, 1963; Russett, 1967). Such tools can be applied at several points in time to determine to what extent the outlier performance amounts to a fluke or instead to a successful national effort to create special niches or roles in the international system (e.g., Chan, 1982; Park and Teng, 1983).

Whatever means are used, identifying anomalies involves relative judgments of three kinds. We are interested in the performance increment or decrement supplied by policy content and process. To get at that increment it does not suffice to throw all nations in our statistical hopper. The needed judgments involve, first, the choice of a peer

112

group with which performance can be compared. The second involves recognition of the assets and liabilities which policy has had to accept as givens. For example, attempts to assess relative policy performance in the face of the oil shocks of the 1970s should take into account whether countries are oil exporters or importers and, among the latter, differences of degree in import dependence. The third involves goals—what policy seeks to accomplish. Those ends may call for sustaining rather than changing policies and courses of national evolution in the face of externally administered shocks. One would then not treat behavioral departures as the sole indicators of superior or inferior performance (Rosenau, 1981; Raymond, in Chapter 6). Policy performance appraisals must then be made in relation to discernible national goals, assets, and liabilities—not in a vacuum. The menu of policy choices available to a country and the nature of policy payoffs it can realistically hope to attain are constrained by its objective conditions (Sprout and Sprout, 1957). It hardly seems sensible to argue that rich, strong countries that maintain their international status have equal policy performance to poor, weak countries that improve their international standing despite obvious handicaps.

This perspective differs from many evaluation research proposals (see Raymond's discussion in Chapter 6). First, it is less concerned with differing degrees of success on some policy outcome measure than it is with success relative to difficulty. Second, the primary objective is not to determine "what works" but rather to use knowledge of what has and has not worked to develop an explanatory theory of why some countries do what works. Third, it avoids neatly assigning particular operational objectives to particular goals, and particular policies to particular objectives. Reality presents fuzzy, fluid sets and overspecificity can be the enemy of understanding. Finally, it pays more attention to the choice and modification of targets for policy activity than to the impact of particular policy instruments.

The goals, capabilities, and policy outcomes we focus on are not those of superpower architects of a world order, would-be hegemons, or ideological zealots who propagate a particular mode of political and economic organization globally. They are more modest and more relevant to most nations at most times. Foreign policy goals obviously include national influence and power relative to those of external actors, with emphasis on physical security and national autonomy. They also include arranging external relations to support domestic prosperity and stability. The performance indicators for this last set very much include measures of such internal conditions as economic growth per capita, supporting advances in physical and human capital, equal opportunity within generational cohorts, provision of social

113

services and public goods, and economic and political stability. These "domestic" indicators reflect foreign policy performance as they are affected by "the geographical position, resource endowment and purchasing power of important actual or potential trading partners, the existence and proximity of political or military rivals, protectors, or clients and the systems in operation in each of these" (Koopmans and Montias, 1971, p. 30).

Expectations and Performance

Before proceeding to what we can learn from our cases, it seems appropriate to firmly establish their status as successful anomalies. We begin with expectations.

In the early 1950s, John Foster Dulles reportedly remarked that "those concerned with the future of Japan might well contemplate suicide, and understandably so." Japan had lost not only a war but also access to its major prewar trading partner (China). Its homeland had been devastated and occupied by a foreign army, and its political system subjected to radical changes imposed by an external power. Except for the lift provided by US Korean War expenditures, its economy seemed destined to flounder. There was neither the apparent will nor the means for self-defense. The image of South Koreans was that of a people economically backward, politically unsophisticated, and culturally unsuited for industrial society. Recently devastated, artificially divided, and militarily exposed, the future of the Republic of Korea (ROK) seemed unrelievedly bleak. The Republic of China (ROC) leadership seemed old, rigid, a demonstrable failure on the mainland, and incapable of developing a constructive *modus vivendi* with the predominant population of its territorial remnant. Whatever prospects these entities might have seemed to depend on US paternalism and Cold War ideology. Their future would be that of protectorates eking out a living on exports to a generous US market of cheap, low-technology consumer goods of inferior quality.

These images surely had faded by the 1970s, but were only to be replaced by ones of extreme vulnerability to external shocks. Some shocks were economic: oil prices and supply unreliability; dollar devaluations; global recession; and the rise of trade protectionism. Others were political-military: US–Soviet détente; US loss of zeal for military involvement in Asia; and rapprochement with the People's Republic of China (PRC) by major Western nations. These shocks revived prior perceptions of the international positions for which our three cases were destined. The gloomy portraits featured: massive

114

asymmetry in foreign economic dependence; loss of autonomy to the USA as a condition for military protection and economic support; diversion of scarce resources from economic development to defense spending (especially for the ROK and the ROC); international isolation and pariah status (the ROK and the ROC); and internal instability so severe as to undercut effective foreign relations (the ROK and the ROC).

In retrospect these expectations were unfounded or exaggerated. With respect to their external political and military situations after the events mentioned, all three countries have pursued active policies toward the Middle Eastern oil exporters. Japan and the ROK have made their own openings to the PRC as a counterbalance against the Soviet Union and as a hedge against US demands or withdrawal. Both have tried to construct durable elements of normalization in their relations with the Soviet Union while maintaining their alliance ties with Washington. As for the ROC, US recognition of the PRC and the withdrawal from the United Nations presaged *de jure* more than *de facto* change in its international status. It adjusted quickly to these setbacks and successfully prevented them from jeopardizing the far more important considerations of maintaining the regime's domestic authority, continuing its unofficial political representation abroad, securing minimum necessary military technology, and preserving Taiwan's active trade ties and attractions for foreign investors.

What about expectations based on existing theories and historical patterns? The cases do not conform to the predictions of Cardoso's (1973) theory of associated-dependent growth that a large underclass will form and economic inequity grossly increase. They pose enigmas for Olson's (1963) view that rapid economic growth reaps political instability. Taiwan and South Korea are notable for sustaining rapid industrial transformation while avoiding the civil strife and violence that prior studies suggest should follow given their regime characteristics and social frustration (e.g., Bobrow, 1968; Feierabend and Feierabend, 1966). Nor does the economic development literature of the 1950s and 1960s (e.g., Adelman and Morris, 1965) raise optimism about the prospects of our cases. Their only notable advantage would have seemed to be stocks of human capital, a plus swamped by a plethora of disadvantages including severe trade dependency, a lack of natural resources, and a small domestic market (except for Japan). Finally, despite frequent warnings about their military vulnerability, these countries have not experienced a significant military attack for the last quarter-century.

More quantitative comparisons conform equally poorly with expectations. Military performance can be assessed by the demonstrated ability to deter or avoid foreign attack, but most countries have met that test for the last 25 years. We can differentiate military security performance in terms of relative economic cost. Table 7.1 examines the efficiency of military security performance in terms of relative burden on national resources (wealth and people). For Japan, an appropriate comparison group is the OECD (Organization for Economic Cooperation and Development) countries. All ostensibly were facing a threat from the Soviet Union (and it is difficult to allocate Soviet forces solely to potential conflict with Japan). For the ROK and the ROC, primary threats have been regional ones, the Democratic People's Republic of Korea (DPRK) and the PRC respectively. In this perspective, both Japan and the ROK seem to have been very efficient. That is true with respect to military expenditures as a share of GNP and to

Table 7.1   *Military Security Efficiency*

| | A   *Military expenditures (% GNP)* | | | | | |
	Japan	OECD	PRC	Taiwan	DPRK	ROK	World
1972	0.9	4.3	13.7	8.8	21.0	4.8	6.0
1973	0.8	4.0	12.2	8.1	18.7	3.9	5.8
1974	0.8	4.0	12.0	6.8	19.4	4.4	5.8
1975	0.9	4.0	11.6	7.3	10.7	4.8	6.0
1976	0.9	3.7	11.2	6.8	12.8	5.8	5.8
1977	0.9	3.7	10.3	7.5	11.6	5.9	5.7
1978	0.9	3.6	9.6	7.6	10.6	6.3	5.6
1979	1.0	3.6	9.6	NA	9.4	5.5	5.5
1980	0.9	3.8	8.0	NA	18.9	6.6	5.6
1981	1.0	3.9	7.8	6.7	NA	6.7	5.7
1982	1.0	3.2	7.1	7.2	21.6	6.9	6.0

| | B   *Armed forces per 1000 people* | | | | | |
	Japan	OECD	PRC	Taiwan	DPRK	ROK	World
1972	2.2	9.1	3.4	36.2	31.3	18.4	6.6
1973	2.1	8.8	3.6	32.5	31.1	18.0	6.5
1974	2.2	8.6	4.6	31.2	30.3	17.6	6.7
1975	2.1	8.2	4.6	31.3	29.6	17.2	6.4
1976	2.1	7.8	4.5	28.8	30.7	16.4	6.2
1977	2.1	7.6	4.4	27.4	31.1	15.8	6.1
1978	2.1	7.5	4.6	27.5	37.0	15.6	6.1
1979	2.1	7.4	4.5	26.7	39.5	16.3	6.0
1980	2.1	7.3	4.4	28.3	39.1	15.1	5.9
1981	2.0	7.3	4.3	27.8	38.8	15.0	5.9
1982	2.0	7.4	4.3	27.2	38.0	14.7	6.0

Source: US Arms Control and Disarmament Agency, 1984.

allocation of manpower to the military. Taiwan relative to the PRC has not performed as well. Nonetheless, its record is still impressive on the financial side, given its objective situation. Only in the last year of the period examined (1972–82) did it match or exceed the percentage allocation of the PRC, although its military forces consistently imposed a much greater burden on the manpower pool.[1]

Other aspects of the performance of our three cases have been exceptional by almost any standard, given the stresses at work. For political stability, studies have shown Japan and Taiwan to rank very high, with South Korea considerably lower (e.g., Feierabend and Feierabend, 1966; Gurr and Ruttenberg, 1971). Japan stands out among advanced industrialized countries for ruling-party continuity. The ROK and the ROC have passed with relative ease through occasional flurries of active dissent. It is hard to think of many other examples where a ruling party or elite was decisively defeated in a civil war (albeit with international aspects), given a second chance, and achieved a sustained political comeback.

Economic and social performance are more readily captured by the standard indicators in Table 7.2. Once again relative performance is what matters. The appropriate comparison group for Japan is the industrial market economies. For the ROK and the ROC, we use the upper middle income developing countries. On the economic measures, Japan outperformed its comparison group substantially across the board in the period since 1970 and overcame some areas of underperformance (rate of inflation and rate of import growth) in the sixties. The outstanding record of export-led growth and domestic investment was accompanied by better equity performance than the USA, and life expectancy performance equal to or superior to the industrial market economies. Human capital formation was already advanced in 1960 and improved substantially afterward. Many of the same judgments apply with even greater force to the ROK and the ROC compared to the group of upper middle income developing countries. The general edge in economic performance was sustained. Over the years, the ROK's areas of underperformance narrowed relative to the group norm.

These countries thus pose anomalous successes. Thirty years ago, few would have proposed them as sources of positive learning about how countries can make their way in the world. Their policy performance is surprising in view of prior expectations, expectations that the elites of these countries have cultivated. Indeed, all three seem to have purposely abetted exaggerated attributions of national vulnerability and helplessness to mold foreign and domestic opinion. As a policy ploy, these attempts have helped to extract foreign concessions and

117

Table 7.2   *Economic and Social Performance in Perspective*

	Japan	Industrial market economies (average)	ROK	ROC	Upper middle income developing countries
Growth of production: average annual growth rate					
1960–70	10.4	5.1	8.6	9.1	6.4
1970–82	4.6	2.8	8.6	9.5^c	5.4
Industry 1960–70	13.0	5.9	17.2	16.4	9.1
Industry 1970–82	5.6	2.3	13.6	14.0^c	5.4
Manufacturing 1960–70	13.6	5.9	17.6	17.3	8.4
Manufacturing 1970–82	6.6	2.4	14.5	14.2^c	5.8
Gross domestic investment					
%GDP, 1960	33.0	21.0	11.0	20.0	22.0
%GDP, 1982	30.0	20.0	26.0	31.0^d	24.0
Merchandise trade: average annual growth rate					
Exports 1960–70	17.2	8.5	34.7		5.4
Exports 1970–82	8.5	5.6	20.2	22.9^e	7.1
Imports 1960–70	13.7	9.5	19.7		5.5
Imports 1970–82	3.5	4.3	9.8		7.4
Education (% age group enrolled in school)^a					
Primary school, 1960	103	114	94		88
Primary school, 1981	100	101	107	100^f	104
Secondary school, 1960	74	64	27		20
Secondary school, 1981	92	90	85	90/52^{b,f}	51
Higher education, 1960	10	16	5		4
Higher education, 1981	30	37	18	11^f	14
Life expectancy (at birth)					
Males, 1960	65	68	52	All:	55
Males, 1982	74	71	64	71^f	63
Females, 1960	70	73	56	All:	58
Females, 1982	79	78	71	71^f	67
Infant mortality (under 1)					
1960	30	29	78		101
1982	7	10	32	25^f	58
Child death rate (1–4)					
1960	2	2	9		15
1982	(.)	(.)	2		6
Inflation: average annual rate					
1960–70	5.1	4.3	17.5		3.0
1970–82	6.9	9.9	19.3		16.4

Income equity	*Japan (1979)*	*ROK (1976)*	*ROC (1971)*	*USA (1978)*
Share poorest 20%	8.7	5.7	8.7	4.6
Share richest 10%	21.2	27.5	24.7	33.4

Notes: ^{a} = numbers over 100 reflect double counting, ^{b} = junior high/senior high and vocational schools, ^{c} = 1970–1980, ^{d} = 1980, ^{e} = 1971–79, ^{f} = 1978.

Sources: ACDA, 1983; Lin, 1983; Sivard, 1981; World Bank, 1984; and Japan Economic Research Center, 1983.

forge domestic consensus, even though the gap between self-ascribed weaknesses and actual strengths has increasingly widened over time (especially for Japan).

Conceptual Departures

The lack of anticipation also followed from the conceptualization of the determinants of successful foreign policy adaptation in much of the West. Too much emphasis has gone to tangible military and economic assets and to recent historical experience. Too little importance has been given to political and social factors—especially policy management skills, human capital, effort mobilization, and learning from historical setbacks and difficulties. Too much emphasis has gone to a country's proprietary assets relative to those of other countries as if each country were operating on its own. Too little importance has been given to ways in which the countries could secure the transfer of assets to them from others with more, and to ways in which they could in effect help each other. In short, too much attention has gone to stocks of tangibles and to the model of international affairs in which most nations are linked directly only to one or the other superpower (i.e., the USA or the USSR). Too little attention has gone to stocks of intangibles, flows, and the role of linkages between non-superpowers in regional subsystems. Our cases show that success in foreign affairs depends as much on the exploitation of foreign assets and motives as on one's own resources and will.

These relatively ignored factors bring us to the heart of adaptive foreign relations—making creative use of what is at hand very much includes efforts to shape, abet and rely on other's proclivities. Treating countries as if they were "solitary" actors misleads. Policy circles are not indifferent to managing others' interpretations and actions, especially when the countries are tightly coupled in political, economic, or military ways (see Richardson's discussion of dyadic relations in Chapter 9). Countries that are long on liabilities and short on assets never finish adapting their foreign policy. For them, attention to policy planning analysis and implementation is essential to improve a weak hand dealt to them by nature and history (Reynolds, 1983, pp. 975–6). As an official of the Japanese Ministry of International Trade and Industry said to one of us, "we must ride the bicycle faster and faster, pedal harder and harder, forever—or it will fall over."

To understand these policy efforts, we need orientations that can accommodate the variety of practices, doctrines and priorities our three examples have pursued at different times. We are attracted to

119

conceptual approaches that are sensitive to the complexities of reality, as opposed to approaches that would force us to defend one artificial simplification versus another. For example, we do not want to have to justify the individual empirical or policy merits of the sovereignty-at-bay model, the dependencia model, or the mercantilist model (Gilpin, 1975a), when we know that the behavior of our cases has followed all three. Nor do we wish to be forced to choose between interpretations that stress centralized state direction and those that stress vigorous private-sector market competition, when both have been operating.

Koopmans and Montias (1971) provide a useful starting point when they formulate national performance as a function of a national system, external factors and policies. The particulars of policies and external factors for our three cases will be dealt with later. For now we focus on the system properties that determine what a country can do, including the way its key institutions relate to external factors. Adaptive performance works with two sets of key ideas. The first deals with policy capacity, that is, the internal characteristics that allow a country to make the most of available possibilities for attaining desired national outcomes. Dissecting policy functioning involves a level of detail made feasible by case studies (see Chapters 9, 13 and 15). The second deals with a country's world position; that is, a country's characteristics that create policy challenges for it and limit the range of policy responses available to it. Along the classic lines of political economy, countries possess different assets or stocks of values and are involved in a variety of exchanges current or potential across their borders (see Moon's discussion in Chapter 3).

Policy Capacity

The importance of policy capacity follows directly from the unexpected success of our three cases in relation to structural orientations. The most promising framework is the cybernetic steering model of Deutsch (1966) and Simon (1981). The steering metaphor treats the state of the external environment in relation to policy goals (that is, desired or undesired foreign relations situations) as the central dependent variable. The focus is dynamic and ongoing like foreign policy adaptation. A wide range of domestic actors and factors are represented in the control, implementation, and information units and their relations. The model does not limit domestic players to the public sector or even to elites. Players can be driven by different motives and be engaged in different games. Successful steering benefits from an ability to forge domestic consensus about policy ends and means, and by an ability to grasp and take advantage of the diversity of interests and actors operating in other countries. The model does not assume universal success or omniscient policy judgment. It does focus attention on recognizing and adjusting to policy disappointments, including creative learning from failures and disciplined acceptance of adverse changes beyond indigenous control. Since time, capabilities, goodwill, patience and policy attention always seem in short supply, a central challenge to policy steering is the efficient allocation of these scarce resources—that is, to adjust and trade off goals, work with others who cannot be worked around, live with recurrent problems that defy once-and-for-all solutions, nurse assets and pool them with like-minded others, decide carefully what conditions are unsatisfactory but tolerable and what conditions are clearly unacceptable, and select judiciously which fights to take part in and which to abstain from.

The general analytic categories of the cybernetic model apply to all countries, but their content in terms of actors, issues and procedures can vary enormously. This model does not provide a precise battery of instruments for measuring policy capacity. It does provide some *ceteris paribus* expectations for success and prescriptive heuristics for policy management in a complex environment. A country is likely to have great policy capacity, and thus more adaptive foreign policy, when:

(1) Its policy participants are wary of ignoring feedback about the external or internal environment, clinging to unrealistic goals, and treating the world as if it were static.

(2) Its policy participants regard the choice of goals and objectives as of the utmost importance, and recognize the need to avoid extreme specificity in order to provide latitude in their implementation.

(3) Its policy participants devote substantial effort to building national consensus about ends and means (to forging what Kegley terms a "decision regime"), so that policy debates do not get bogged down in arguments about vague principles and bureaucratic prerogatives.

(4) Its policy participants do not compartmentalize problems according to artificial divisions of agency missions, bureaucratic turfs, or domestic-foreign jurisdictions. Instead, the emphasis is on "whole-system" analysis in formulating policies.

(5) Its policy implementors share a common general understanding of the reasons for the goals and objectives, their importance, and the legitimacy of working to achieve them. Implementation is reliable and timely rather than a matter of foot-dragging and back-biting.

(6) Its choice of goals and implementation means is informed by realistic and wide-ranging information about assets that can be applied

121

to the external environment, likely effects on different domestic and foreign actors, and aspects of the external environment that are beyond one's influence.

(7) Its policy participants set goals and start implementation long before the time that the desired results are needed while recognizing that change is only imperfectly predictable.

(8) Its policy participants conceive of the external environment in cybernetic steering terms. Their image of this environment features diverse actors with different policy agendas engaged in multiple games. They do not see other nations as unitary actors, conduct foreign policy solely in bilateral terms, or ignore the impact of their conduct on important third parties.

(9) Its policy participants believe that improved policy capacity will be rewarded by success in foreign relations, and that success in foreign relations will increase the chances of their achieving private goals.

Clearly, these conditions are not entirely consistent or likely to be internalized by all policy participants. They leave much room for imperfection, stalemate and obsession. Yet, the very stress and tension created by an awareness of these elements can enhance policy capacity. The separate contributions of the individual elements will benefit policy capacity less than their joint effects. The whole is more than the sum of parts.

The cybernetic approach pays substantial attention to entropy as a threat to policy capacity. Two particularly pertinent conceptions of entropy are the muddling-through (Lindblom, 1959) and the garbage-can organized anarchy (Cohen *et al.*, 1972) models of decision making. The former features segmented attention, incremental adjustment and bureaucratic bargaining. Purposeful attempts to harness means to ends are stymied as the participants do not distinguish between them either conceptually or politically. The latter model emphasizes problematic preferences, unclear technology and fluid participation by relevant players. In its extreme form, policy products depend on so many interactions on so many issues among so many players that they resemble the haphazard result of a stochastic process. In both the muddling-through and garbage-can models, policy drift dominates policy steering. If either characterizes a nation's policy processes, its foreign policy will be inherently unadaptive.

The muddling-through and the garbage-can tendencies point to a set of avoidance maxims—pathologies to be resisted in order to be adaptive. Resistance often features social processes best noticed through systematic case studies (see Anderson Chapter 15 in this volume). Some familiar means use exclusion to impose some order on an otherwise chaotic situation. The number and variety of participants, problems and solutions can be restricted sharply to increase the homogeneity of participants' outlook and commitment, set parameters for "legitimate" policy debate, and establish the priority among competing claimants for resources and attention. The basis of exclusion can be formal or informal ideologies, shared experiences, or common membership in important reference groups (e.g., party, army, university). Policy obsessions can facilitate such consensus.

Exclusion can be counterproductive. Important issues can be ignored, unconventional views dismissed out of hand, and the collection and assimilation of information biased. Two measures can minimize these negatives. The first involves assigning different domains of policy responsibility to different specialized elites while encouraging frequent communication among them. The second involves informal conventions about policy formation and elite networks. Consensus building precedes rather than follows policy choice. Once established, it operates against constant revisions, interminable arguments, and attempts by outsiders to exploit internal differences. Webs of affiliation and personal connections facilitate extensive sharing of information and perspectives across specialist communities of profession and organization. These measures are time-consuming, and therefore must be seen as productive, legitimate undertakings rather than as nuisances.

Significant, but not incapacitating, stress helps bring the conducive factors to bear on foreign policy. Memories of foreign policy failures tend to hold complacency at bay. So, too, do convictions that the external world is volatile, unreliable, and yet manipulable at the margin. At the same time, viewing international interactions as a game with multiple innings cautions against impatience and recklessness.

The views and practices noted above help move the policy process closer to the ideal, unitary, rational-actor model of decision making, while harnessing the more rewarding aspects of the organizational process and bureaucratic politics models (Allison, 1971). They also avoid the worst effects of following any one of these models exclusively. All three models apply to most nations; none seems adequate to capture entirely the more crucial aspects of our problem. Bureaucratic politics interpretations are not useful for explaining aggregate national performance, as opposed to particular twists and turns in policies. Organizational tendencies seem less well-suited to explaining policy changes than policy stasis, and policy formation than policy implementation. Analyses based on a unitary conception of national interests are not illuminating about why different conceptions of national interest prevail at different times and places, why they change, and what strategies are deemed most fruitful for fulfilling the current conception. Nor do they explain sharp struggles over means and ends that occasionally occur within a country, or frequent attempts to manipulate particular actors and incentives in other countries.

World Position

Theories that try to explain how nations fare in terms of their position in the world have several common features. They stress some rather than other national attributes, posit a limited number of roles or niches that nations can occupy, focus on selective aspects of relationships between the occupants of particular niches, and treat the world in an undifferentiated fashion except for the selected attributes, niches and relationships. For example, they usually give little attention to regional subsystems. Despite their enormous variety, global models have common underlying themes of structural determinism and relationships of unequal leverage and dependence. The world has a particular structure, and countries are locked into it. Whatever their merits for other purposes, these characterizations may hinder rather than help an understanding of our three cases.

We know that the world position of countries needs to be assessed according to multiple dimensions of capabilities, issues and arenas. Hierarchical formulations that emphasize asymmetries on a single dimension cannot address the implications of varied positions on different dimensions. Even when these implications are addressed (e.g., in the status-inconsistency theory), conclusions tend to one-sidedly emphasize conflict rather than cooperation and difficulties rather than opportunities for upward mobility. Less attention has gone to peaceful ways of improving status and changing niches, including the possibilities of "graduation" and invention of desired niches. We need a framework that is sensitive to these possibilities, and that is as open to changes in world position as the cybernetic model is to changes in policy capacity. The complex interdependence perspective seems to fit our needs.

In this perspective (Keohane and Nye, 1977), the world is a forest of actors and a jungle of interconnections. These include trade, investment, technology transfer, as well as military, political and cultural linkages. Besides governments, relevant actors include private participants as well as international governmental and nongovernmental organizations. The possible number of niches and roles is very large as is the number of possible coalitions and relational networks. Since complete self-sufficiency is either impossible or appallingly unattractive, the world of complex interdependence offers a rich set of possible multiple-sum games. This view rejects a clear global hierarchy of issues or actors for one of multiple hierarchies and interwoven relationships. If we accept this view, the world position of nations often is far less clearly defined by discrete national assets than other conceptions assume. We do not contend that all countries have an equal opportunity in foreign relations. Nature and history surely have dealt out the cards in a highly biased way. Nevertheless, many countries do have many possibilities to improve their international position and carve out a desired niche for themselves.

One way to think about these possibilities considers what a country can get others to let it do and do for it. This conception includes restraint and omission as well as activity and commission, that is, what a country can get others to let it *not* do and *not* do to it. The bargaining power of a country at a point in time can usefully be thought of in terms of a supply-and-demand metaphor not limited to economic goods. The possibilities open to a country *vis-à-vis* others are then set in two stages. The first has to do with inherited features such as energy endowments and geographic location. The second has to do with far more contingent matters—the value of what it supplies to others and of what others supply to it. Those values and thus the strength of bargaining hands are in the final analysis set by internal politics. Internal politics in turn reflects domestic economics, social structure and cultural dispositions.

A particular country's position relative to another country is strongest when it is the only or an unusually attractive supplier of some value in great demand by politically influential groups in the other country, and when its own politically influential groups place little value on what the other country can supply, or can get that good on attractive terms elsewhere. It is only slightly less strong when the other country supplies something that is highly valued and unique *and* the internal politics of the other country provides overwhelming incentives for continuing to supply the good. Countries seek associations that promise valuable reward, and ignore each other when such incentives are absent.

Realism requires extending this view beyond bilateral relationships to bargaining involving third parties. These indirect considerations matter when a country enjoys an advantageous bargaining position *vis-à-vis* a third country whose fate is in turn important to the principal bargaining partner. A gains leverage over B when it has leverage over C, and when B cares about the political incentives operating in C. They also matter when the value of what B can supply to A depends in large measure on the pressures exerted by C on A. Should C ignore A, or have little influence over it, the demand for B's offering suffers.

Bargaining revolves around anticipations. History matters as it shapes relevant expectations about substitutability, supply reliability, and political values and costs. Relevant actors are not restricted to national governments. The importance of other actors depends on how they fit into prevailing domestic incentive structures and distributions of political influence.

This formulation suggests propositions about bargaining power associated with a country's position in the world. Whatever its position in terms of inheritance and objective assets, a country's bargaining power benefits when:

(1) It supplies something unavailable elsewhere, or only available at much greater cost and after a significant time lag. The good involved may be of economic, military, diplomatic or status value as may be the relevant costs.

(2) It supplies an important good to those politically influential in the other country, or to those who influence them.

(3) It refrains from actions that antagonize or create negative pressure on politically influential elements in the other country, or it undertakes actions that reduce this antagonism and cultivate goodwill.

(4) It fosters the conviction that the supply is reliable only if the other country avoids using certain means of leverage available to it.

(5) It works to head off developments that expand the supply of the good it provides to the other country, or that facilitate the recipient's switching to alternative suppliers.

(6) It adjusts its supply to compensate for increases in the availability of substitutes or declines in value.

(7) It changes the beneficiaries of its supply in line with changes in the distribution of political influence in the other country.

(8) It achieves and maintains the previous advantages *vis-à-vis* third parties, who in turn hold a similar position relative to the target country.

(9) It cultivates the belief in the other country that the exchange of values is equitable and mutually beneficial, and that disruption of this exchange will jeopardize the other's higher values.

(10) It generates the conviction in the other country that all these propositions will be equally or more fully manifest in the future.

(11) It does not rely on these expectations prevailing for the other country, and prepares to limit damage to itself should the other country suspend supply or raise the price of the good.

(12) It encourages developments that expand the available supply of the good sought, facilitate substitution for the good, increase the number of potential suppliers, and lower the costs for others to supply the good.

The ease with which a particular country can acquire and maintain bargaining power depends in important ways on the internal characteristics of the target country. A country benefits in its bargaining position *vis-à-vis* the target when:

(1) The target rejects measures to secure substitutes or reduce costs associated with their use.

(2) The target highly values the good it receives, so that continuing receipt is a criterion for judging the political performance of incumbent elites.

(3) The target attaches great value to providing the good it supplies, so that continuing provision is a criterion for judging the political performance of incumbent elites.

(4) The target manages its internal and external affairs to minimize the use of some means available for leverage and political incentives for using these means (e.g., to grant the good only as a matter of contingent concession or to threaten interruption in its supply).

(5) The target facilitates or at least does not hinder the other country developing a strong bargaining position *vis-à-vis* important third parties.

(6) The target avoids sudden, radical changes in its views on substitutability and value, distribution of domestic political influence, and orientation toward third parties.

Our formulation treats military security as a significant but not necessarily dominant concern on a nation's policy agenda. Military capability may or may not be used effectively as a bargaining asset on other issues. Accordingly, we addressed conditions for inducement and indirect deterrence more than those for compelling and outright coercion. International interactions are a mixed-motive game with cooperative and competitive elements. The policy challenge is to manipulate the other side's perceived self-interest so that it will behave as desired voluntarily, as opposed to being forced to act against its will. The conditions discussed are more pertinent to the weaker side in a bilateral relationship, as it tries to overcome its disadvantages. Emphasis lies on exploiting the other's domestic cleavages and third parties as points of leverage, on promoting the stronger country's positive attitudes toward the more intangible aspects of shared concerns and fears, and on ensuring its cooperation by providing enticements for that and disincentives for noncooperation. Due to varying distributions of assets, values and influences, a country will find it easier to improve and maintain a favorable bargaining position toward some countries than others. Thus we expect countries to have uneven records. We also expect countries to differ in the extent to which their bargaining positions are stronger or weaker than their inherited characteristics would imply.

This line of reasoning leads us back to policy capacity. A broad and deep comprehension of the external environment seems crucial. Only then will a country be able to identify different conducive partners on different issues and occasions, make the most of its relationships with unavoidable important others, align with or put pressure on third parties that can create additional leverage on principal suppliers, and adjust bargaining strategies according to changing circumstances. Successful adjustment calls attention to changes in substitutability, values, political influence and political incentives. A country with unusually great capacity in these respects has inherent advantages for recognizing current and future possibilities for improving its world position.

A premium also goes to policy integration that enables a country to override institutional divisions to assemble packages of offerings that fit foreign appetites, and modify them as the latter change. Furthermore, a premium goes to a country that diversifies the packages it purveys to foreigners at any one time. Uniform, general principles are useful as they abet diverse, context-specific practices. The world of complex interdependence is not a world of unilateral control or fixed advantages. A policy philosophy that recognizes the need for trade-offs and adjustment works better than one that attempts to settle problems once and for all. Together with the cybernetic notion of leadtime to hit moving targets, this philosophy encourages preparing for the future rather than focusing overwhelmingly on short-term considerations.

Recognition of the need to prepare for change and of the imperfectly predictable nature of change legitimates hedging, delaying immediate gratification, and developing an institutional capability for coping with setbacks. This policy climate fosters a belief that everything will not go as desired, *and* a belief that purposeful effort will on average make things turn out better than they would otherwise. Such beliefs discourage attempts at great leaps to improve a country's world position overnight (as among the elites of some oil-exporting countries during the 1970s). They direct energy to seemingly marginal gains that attention to policy capacity can make. Over time, these modest gains can accumulate to confer a significant advantage. That advantage will not continue automatically; it only provides the basis for further adaptation. Success then can be a threat as well as an advantage. The threat lies in the possibility that success will undermine the very traits that have led to it, including the perceptions of key external parties.

In sum, complex interdependence provides general heuristics for understanding and managing foreign affairs. Policy capacity furnishes the ingredients that acting wisely on these heuristics requires.

Conclusion

In a necessarily superficial and abbreviated way, we have tried to stimulate attention in the comparative study of foreign policy to identifying cases of anomalous policy performance, and to some concepts for understanding them. The first set of arguments is illustrated by the successes of Japan, South Korea and Taiwan compared with the expectations for them in policy circles, the anticipations based on existing theories and empirical patterns, and the performance of appropriate other countries and groups of countries. The second set of arguments emphasizes the key ideas of policy capacity and world position. We propose a set of conditions that tend to enhance a country's policy capacity and world position, and reason that those consequences are associated with anomalously successful policy performance. We expect the extreme absence of those conditions to be associated with unusually poor policy performance. The merit of these propositions remains a matter for conjecture until they are operationalized and tested on a set of countries with different revealed performance levels. We hope that the ideas in relation to our three cases are sufficiently intriguing to generate interest in those further steps.

The attractions of the approach we recommend and have begun rest on two more general principles with regard to the comparative analysis of foreign policy. These principles have set the direction of our work, and acceptance of them must take place for the directions we suggest to seem important. First, we believe that theory building and policy analysis must deliberately insure attention to the exceptional and abnormal and not become mesmerized by normal, well-understood behavior that fits a general pattern or central tendency for most countries. Theorists should give at least as much priority to explaining deviations from the norm as to maximizing the variance explained over a particular class of actors or phenomena. That posture is needed even more for policy analyses where it is the outliers that provide shocks and unprecedented challenges. This position is squarely at the center of the popular tradition of social measurement and explanation that focuses on the quintessential instances of the behaviors of interest.

Second, we reject an unwarranted separation between domestic and foreign policies and objectives. We believe that for our three cases—and probably for all countries including the superpowers—it is preponderantly the case that domestic and foreign policies and objectives are interwoven in terms of cause and effect and of means and ends. It is hard to imagine any major steps of foreign policy action and reaction not shaped by the institutional capabilities and interest alignments internal to the relevant countries. We are faced with a complex reality that cavalierly overrides simplifying distinctions along foreign-domestic lines. The linkages between matters of foreign and domestic politics and economics within countries and between interacting countries require systematic attention.

Notes

Off-the-record interviews and informal conversations with officials and experts in Japan, Taiwan and South Korea provided many of the ideas. Credit for perceptiveness goes to them: blame, to the authors. Generous support was provided for research in Japan by the Institute for Policy Science, Saitama University, and in Taiwan by the Graduate Institute of American Studies, Tamkang University.

1 Relative military inefficiencies may be offset by other benefits. The Taiwanese military draft alleviates undercapacity problems of institutions of higher learning, stabilizes the wage structure, limits unemployment, and slows down demographic increase.

8

Substituting Arms and Alliances, 1870–1914: an Exploration in Comparative Foreign Policy

BENJAMIN A. MOST and RANDOLPH M. SIVERSON

A sense of quiet desperation seems to beset those who describe themselves as students of comparative foreign policy (CFP). As virtually every contributor to this volume has observed, the study of CFP has not come as far as we would have liked.[1] While much has surely changed since the early part of 1967 when Rosenau first queried whether comparative foreign policy was a "fad, fantasy, or field" (1968a), foreign policy scholars seem frustrated and—if this volume is any indication—anxious to figure out what is going wrong.

Efforts to identify the factors which impede progress seem part and parcel of a developing tradition in quantitative international relations in general.[2] To some degree, such discussions reflect an exciting and healthy degree of intellectual ferment. There is surely considerable value in probing the lack of progress toward what Zinnes has called "integrative cumulation" (1976b). Nonetheless, it seems clear that many of the assessments of the impediments to cumulation which have appeared to date have failed to be particularly fruitful.[3] On the one hand, they have led us to discount—perhaps unfairly—those important things which have been learned.[4] On the other hand, whether it is because the critiques have been unheard entirely or simply ignored, analysts have generally failed to modify their procedures and build the new lessons into their research programs. As a consequence, many of those criticisms which were made a decade or more ago could simply be reiterated today. We could simply repeat an observation made in 1969:

First, we need to develop greater familiarity with the basic rules of scientific endeavor, as practiced in all those disciplines in which substantial theoretical

131

progress is discernible. Second, we need to pay much more attention to fundamental problems of epistemology in this field. As matters stand, we spend too much time entangled in the confusion caused by definitional inconsistencies and conceptual ambiguities. And third, there is emphatically *no substitute for good ideas* (Young, 1969).

That said, we hope that the reader will perhaps forgive a brief, somewhat prescriptive, digression while we focus on what we take to be a "good idea." There is a common, apparently rather seductive, tendency in situations such as this to equate "good ideas" with what we ourselves are doing; there is a predilection to presume that all of our problems would be solved if only all analysts would appreciate, understand, and presumably imitate the research which we (and, of course, our close friends and colleagues) are pursuing. For some, that will imply the recommendation of the particular method which they have spent time and energy learning; for others, it will mean urging that analysts consider yet another variable or class of variables which has been overlooked by others but which they themselves find interesting and already know a lot about. For some analysts, it will mean the assertion that progress will come once others join with them and embrace some entirely new approach; for still others, it will mean the touting of their own particular brand of theory.

If the truth were told, there is neither anything surprising—nor particularly wrong—about any of this. North's observation that, "the my-way-only approach is all too ubiquitous in all sectors of the profession," is hardly any less true today than when he offered it some time ago (1969, p. 241). If we have confidence in ourselves and believe in the quality of our work, then we will quite naturally tend to think that the whole enterprise would be further along if only everyone else thought, reasoned, and researched as we do.

The problem arises when everyone recommends *something—their* thing—as the critical innovation: a political economy approach; a focus on the situational imperative; a concern for decision regimes and rule-based decision making; an artificial intelligence approach; a concern for the state; a focus on microelectronics; a heightened concern for evaluation; more dyadic studies; more in-depth case studies; an even more elaborate rendition of the CREON theory; and so on. Each of us tends—again, quite naturally in our view—to want to protect the investments which we have sunk in our own work; thus, for each of us, the way of the future—the "new direction" for tomorrow—tends to be fairly close to what we are doing today.

While this may help to explain why so few of yesterday's criticisms have been incorporated into the ongoing research programs of other analysts, the more germane issue concerns the appropriate reaction to

132

assertions of this type. Given that each of us would be anxious to embrace the panacea, *even if* it meant abandoning the years we have spent on our own program, a difficulty arises in recognizing good ideas *in advance*. Just how do we begin to sort out the truly good ideas from those which only appear to be useful avenues of attack?

In our view, one answer is clear. Analysts have a right to expect or demand some sort of demonstration that a colleague is correct when he asserts that *his* way is—or should be—*the* way. It is not sufficient, in our opinion, to argue for example that a political-economic approach *must* be adopted simply because a plausible case can be made that it *might* be useful. It is not enough to assert that any one or any combination of several hundred variables have to be included simply because it is possible that somehow, somewhere, or under some conditions they all could be important. It simply does not suffice to assert that truth will out once analysts adopt this or that procedure, focus, framework or perspective.

The reason for this, we contend, is that there is almost no end to the possible new directions which one or another scholar might recommend. As academicians, we are extraordinarily creative. We will always be able to "complexify" our arguments by suggesting additional factors which should be considered. We will be able to think of a nearly endless string of design wrinkles, each of which may be touted as "the way." We will probably never fully exhaust that set of methods which proffer the solution to our problems.[5] If our only criterion for assessing those suggestions is their plausibility, therefore, it seems likely that we will be rather poorly positioned for sorting out the good ideas from those which might be better left aside.

That said, we should note that the work on which we report below is based on two types of demonstrations. The first flows from existing empirical work. Put simply, there are two hypotheses in the literature which concern how foreign policy decision makers adapt to insecurity-inducing changes in their environment. Empirical tests have failed to support either one. The argument we test below derives from a theoretical/logical effort to explain that result. Positing a simple model of decision making—what Kegley (Chapter 13) might describe as a decision regime—the argument logically demonstrates how the existing results could—and indeed, should—pertain. It shows how two apparently distinct foreign policy initiatives—changes in defense expenditures and alliance formations—can be conceptually integrated in a unified context.[6]

The second demonstration is sufficiently abstract that we can only outline it here. Suffice it to say that the work below is predicated on a logical *demonstration*—not simply an *assertion*—that foreign policy deci-

133

sion makers are a necessary element in any logically complete foreign policy model; failure to include decision makers and some sense(s) of how they decide will almost certainly assure that a model will fail to predict (or postdict) accurately.[7]

With all this in mind, we can say that our immediate purpose here is to conduct a preliminary empirical investigation of the interrelationship between arms and alliances. Specifically, the focus is on the extent to which decision makers in the six major European powers substituted alliance activity for increases in their arms (and vice versa) during the period 1870–1914.

The first section below briefly traces the outlines of the problem on which we will focus. Two concepts recently reviewed by Most and Starr (1984)—alternative triggers and substitution—are introduced: The rationale for basing this work on the behaviors of the major European powers during the pre-1914 period is then presented in the second section. The third section discusses the data. The analyses and results are presented in the fourth part. The conclusions and suggestions for further research are reviewed in a brief concluding section.

Alternative Triggers and Foreign Policy Substitution

Traditional power-centered analyses of international politics have usually posited the primacy of national security as a goal in the foreign policies of states. The need for security usually dominates other needs, it is often asserted, because of the inherently anarchical character of the international system. As Kaplan's (1957) conceptualization of the balance of power makes clear, the first rule that rational decision makers would follow in this state of anarchy would be to "act to increase capabilities." To fail to do so—to fail to place security at the apex—would leave a state prey to other nations.

The existing literature suggests that foreign policy decision makers may have at least two distinct strategies or options for adapting to their environments (Rosenau, 1981) and managing the national security problems which confront their states. On the one hand, leaders can opt to increase their own military capabilities by increasing defense spending and adding to their arms stocks; on the other hand, they can move to form alliances. By adding to their stock of weapons, decision makers may deter the leaders in potential opposing states which are about equal in power; leaders in weaker states may be intimidated. A difficulty commonly arises, however, when leaders in one state act to increase their capabilities in this fashion. Decision makers in other states may recognize what the first is doing; decision makers in those

134

second states may then calculate that, unless they act similarly, their own relative security will suffer. As a consequence of this recognition, arms races may become a frequent phenomenon in the international system.

As the literature also suggests, however, decision makers may be able to attend to their security problems and increase their capabilities by eschewing arms build-ups, *per se*, and hence, the prospect of arms races. They may instead move to enhance their security by forming alliances. While such a strategy might entail some significant loss of national autonomy, the formation of an alliance might offer several clear advantages over arms acquisitions as a method of pursuing security. First, an alliance might be entered into relatively quickly, whereas arms increases often require lengthy delays, particularly if complex weapons systems must be authorized, developed and deployed. Second, alliances do not typically require significant expenditures of funds. In fact, as we will explain below, it may be argued that alliances will often be chosen to allow budgetary savings. Third, military expenditures frequently create ongoing obligations, while an alliance, once it has served its purpose or run its stipulated length, may be discarded, broken or ignored.

As has been said, the traditional literature on security seeking in the anarchic international system generally recognizes the complementary character of arms expenditures and alliances. Any reading of the "realists" or diplomatic historians suggests a very close relationship between the two. Strangely enough, however, the contemporary theoretical and empirical literatures on alliances and arms races are relatively silent on their interrelationship. Little is known about whether or not decision makers recognize the potential substitutability of the two options. Little is known about the extent to which, or the conditions under which, leaders actually exploit the opportunities for complementing one type of option with another in the course of their efforts to manage their national security problems. Even less is known about whether or not decision makers in states which are differently configured react to similar threats in similar or different ways.

One recent effort to sort through some of the theoretical problems in this area is provided by Most and Starr (1984) who point to two phenomena which they describe as the difficulty of "alternative triggers" and the problem of foreign policy "substitutability." They argue that both phenomena can occur, in principle. To the extent that either phenomenon is common, they maintain further that the methods and procedures employed by many quantitatively oriented foreign policy analysts and international relations scholars will not lead to satisfactory explanations of nations' foreign policies.

135

As Most and Starr argue, the problem of alternative triggers arises because, through time and across space, *different* factors, cues, considerations or processes could lead decision makers to respond in *similar* ways or adopt identical policy options. The problem of foreign policy substitution was seen as the logical opposite: through time and across space, *similar* factors could plausibly be expected to lead foreign policy decision makers to adopt *different* foreign policy acts. Whereas alternative triggers constitute a many-to-one mapping, in mathematical terms, substitution can be seen as a one-to-many mapping.[8]

The nature of the two problems—and their relevance to the relationships between arms and alliances—can be readily understood by considering a hypothetical illustration (see Figure 8.1). Whether or not the leaders of some *i*th state intend it, they can, in principle, undertake any one (or any combination) of acts which might lead the decision makers in some second state *j* to perceive that their national security is low or decreasing. To the extent that leaders in *j* come to have that impression, they might attempt to redress their security problem by acting to increase their arms. Insofar as the decision makers of state *i* have a variety of means—arms increases, alliance formations, troop mobilizations, provocative raids, and so on—to create (or exacerbate) insecurities in the *j*th state which in turn lead the decision makers in *j* to increase their arms, the alternative triggers problem pertains. The different behaviors by *i* lead to similar reactions by the leaders of the *j*th state.

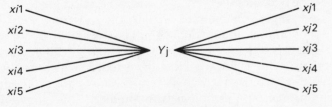

Acts of *i* at *t*   *j*'s perception of   Acts of *j* at *t*+1
                      low/decreasing/nonexistent
                      national security viability

KEY:
  *x*1: Increase in Arms
  *x*2: Effort to form an Alliance
  *x*3: Effort to obtain Arms Transfers
  *x*4: Mobilization/Repositioning of Existing Military Units
  *x*5: Attack or Raid

Note: A more complex form of the alternative triggers problem discussed by Most and Starr (1984) suggests that behaviors x_{j1}–x_{j5} need not necessarily be stimulated by national security concerns. An exploration of that aspect of alternative triggers, however, lies beyond the scope of this paper.

Figure 8.1 Alternative Triggers and Foreign Policy Substitution

If the notion of alternative triggers suggests the logical possibility that an increase in arms expenditures by j, for example, could be preceded by a similar increase by i in one instance, an alliance formation by i in a second case, or an attack by i in a third, substitution concerns the possible reactions of state j. *Given* that decision makers in j perceive a security problem, they could, in principle, respond in a variety of ways, x_{j1} to x_{j5}: increasing arms, moving to form alliances, seeking arms abroad, repositioning troops, launching attacks, and so on. Thus, an arms increase by the ith state could lead j to respond with its own increase at one time, while similar acts by i at other times could lead j to respond in different fashion. Put differently, the similar behaviors by i could lead to different reactions by the leaders of the jth state.

There is clearly no need to rehearse Most and Starr's argument much further. Nonetheless, the importance of these two problems should be emphasized. As they put it:

(1) If writers on the foreign policy behaviors of governments define "islands of theory" in terms of concrete phenomena, their work will not yield broad understanding. If governments behave differently to pursue their (perhaps heterogeneous) national goals and *under at least certain conditions* nations may *substitute* one means for another, then all of the behaviors which tend to be studied in fragmented fashion need to be conceived from the outset—*not* as separate and distinct phenomena, the understanding of which will eventually be integrated—but rather as commensurable behaviors or component parts of abstract conceptual puzzles.

(2) Applications of the standard approaches for testing models and hypotheses are likely to produce misleading results and lead analysts to reject theories and models that are "good," "nice," and "useful" even if they are not general or universally "true." If it is plausible to argue that states may pursue different goals, for different reasons and with different degrees of effectiveness, then it may be useful to reconsider the efforts to search for a "true," "general" or universally applicable explanation of what they do. It might instead be more sensible to search for models or theories that operate, hold, or are valid only under certain explicitly prescribed conditions.

(Most and Starr, 1984, pp. 383–4)

The relevance—and potential importance—of the alternative trigger and substitution problems can be seen in at least two other ways. First, even though analysts who focus on internation action-reaction processes have typically focused on tit-for-tat patterns (e.g., expenditure-to-expenditure relationships as in Richardson arms race models), alternative triggers and substitution suggest that states may have much more flexible response capabilities. To the extent that flexible response capabilities do pertain, moreover, we may begin to understand why so little progress has been made to date in identifying tit-for-tat patterns (see Zinnes, 1980).

The second point should be obvious. If the difficulties created by alternative triggers and substitution could arise in principle in the situations already outlined, then they might be even more likely to develop *across states*. As Rosenau (1966) seems to suggest in his original "pre-theory", different states are differently configured. Different factors might affect the foreign policy behaviors of those different states; because different states have different capabilities, face different environmental pressures, and so on, the precise nature of those behaviors may vary across states. Thus, different triggers may key behavior in different states while different states may have very different substitution patterns when they respond to similar triggers.

Even if one accepts all of this, however, an important question remains: Do the relationships between arms and alliances which are suggested by the traditional literature and which Most and Starr seem to help us to understand actually hold empirically? Are the alternative trigger and substitution problems—the trade-offs between arms and alliances—merely theoretical possibilities which hardly ever develop in the empirical world, or are they in fact sufficiently common that analysts must learn to take them into account when they undertake their empirical analyses?

The Empirical Domain

The remainder of this paper is an attempt to explore the dynamics of substitution in a specific context in which it has been widely, if not explicitly, recognized to operate. Again, the focus is on the extent to which arms and alliances were substituted for each other as the major European powers pursued their national security during the period 1870–1914.

At least three considerations prompt a focus on this period. The first is the existence of an anarchic international system in which leaders are thought to have perceived a major security problem. Second, the system that existed at that time contained a number of major powers which would, if we are correct, have been sufficient to promote substitution effects. Finally, a focus on the pre-1914 central European system is prompted by what may seem a counterintuitive rationale; put simply, it makes sense to look for substitution processes in that context because that is exactly where one might be most likely to find them.

Consider the first rationale. As has been said, scores of observers have argued that the major European states of the 1870–1914 period— the United Kingdom, Germany, France, Italy, Austria and Russia—did indeed exist in an anarchic world during the years leading up to 1914.

No set of central institutions existed to enforce rules (Waltz, 1979; Singer, 1981). Each state faced a security problem (Jervis, 1978). Each ultimately had to rely upon itself for security.

There are relatively few ways in which security can be achieved or maintained in such a state of anarchy. One, of course, is to pursue a policy of isolation or what is commonly called a strategy of "delinking." In an anarchic world which is dominated by only two major powers, a second option is to acquire arms. In lieu of a strategy of mutual cooperation between the two majors, each can attempt to promote its own security by adding to its own arms stockpiles.

Such a choice, over even a short period, can lead to an arms race between the two majors. The point to note, however, is that the two majors would probably not substitute alliances and arms in a bipolar world. Alliances might be formed in such a context if lesser states seek the protection (or fall under the domination) of one or another of the two great powers. Such alliances would not, however, contribute greatly to the security of either major for the very simple reason that the weapons of any small power(s) would be of little use in defending against the other superpower.

The situation might plausibly be expected to be quite different in the six-major/balance-of-power system which actually did exist prior to World War I, however. In that situation, the leaders may in fact have seen each other—not only as threats and potential enemies—but also as possible allies whose cooperation in the form of an alliance could enhance security without the necessity of increasing arms expenditures. To be sure, they might have reasoned that an alliance would imply the reduction of national autonomy in various policy areas (Altfeld, 1984); they most certainly would have recognized that the commitment of their potential allies might be more than a little uncertain. Nonetheless, as a number of analysts of the balance of power have argued, alliances might have offered the leaders of the major European powers during the 1870–1914 era the opportunity to enhance their security in a way that was both rapid and which avoided the necessity of costly new budget allocations. To the extent that unallied majors remained available and they were willing to ally, a given nation could substitute—or at least complement—an increase in its own weapons and troops by moving to form an alliance.[9]

Finally, we should say that we are attracted to the pre-1914 European context precisely because substitution seems likely to have occurred in that setting. If the current understanding of most observers of the period is accurate, it seems clear that the decision makers in the six major European powers apparently did perceive that they had national security problems. To varying degrees and at differing points in time, moreover, those leaders attempted to manage those difficulties by increasing arms levels and altering their alliance commitments.

The importance of this should be clearly understood. To the extent that substitution cannot be found even where it seems that we should be most likely to find it, we might begin to question our ability to probe or understand the effect. We might continue to argue that trade-offs between arms and alliances occur as the literature suggests, but we might also begin to infer that the nature of the relationship between those two options is more subtle—and more elusive—than the existing arguments would lead one to expect. If leaders can substitute one foreign policy means for another but evidence of the relationship between arms and alliances is difficult to find even in the context of pre-1914 Europe, to put the point differently, it may be necessary to rethink the current conceptions of the extent of such trade-offs and the conditions under which they occur.

There is little in the existing literature, and certainly nothing in the Most and Starr argument as it has been developed to date, for example, which suggests that all nations substitute across the same alternatives to the same degree; there is nothing that suggests that given nations substitute identically through time. Thus, for example, one might expect that one or another of the six European states could have used the alliance option, while others did not. Similarly, it is possible that a given state allied at one time, but eschewed that alternative when it became involved in subsequent security crises. The implication of such possibilities, of course is that a consideration of *whether or not* substitution occurred may also entail the development of an understanding of *how* different decision makers in different states choose from among different options at different points in time. We may not see it unless we know fairly clearly just exactly what we are looking for.

The Data

The data used in this analysis are drawn from several sources. First, the list of states which were major powers throughout the 1870–1914 period was taken from Small and Singer (1982, Table 2.1). While it would have been preferable in our view to employ data which directly reflected the size and state of mobilization of each nation's military—for example, numbers of troops or ships, their state of readiness, their deployment, and so on—it was decided to limit this exploratory analysis to a focus on military expenditure data. That spending information for the states in question was derived from the data set generated by Choucri and North (1975) in their study of the dynamics of conflict among the major powers between 1870 and 1914. For Russia, Germany, France and the United Kingdom, the yearly military expenditure data represent national currencies expressed in constant 1906 United States dollars. The data on Austria–Hungary are more problematic. As far as it is possible to acertain, given the explanation provided by Choucri and North, they represent Austria's military expenditures, standardized by the wholesale price index multiplied by $100/2.46.[10]

The alliance data, of course, are taken from the comprehensive list of international alliances between 1815 and 1965 compiled by Singer and Small (1966) and Small and Singer (1969). Codings were made to reflect alliance formations and dissolutions and also changes in the class— entente, neutrality or nonaggression, and defense—of an existing alliance.[11] Consistent with the argument in the foregoing section, only alliances involving at least two major powers were utilized. Thus, alliances between a major power and a minor power were not included in the data set. Again, the rationale for excluding such pacts is based upon the assumption that in the international system of this era, minor powers would have afforded major powers with very little in the way of security; consequently an alliance with a minor power would not, in all likelihood, have been seen by a major power as anything that it could substitute for military expenditures.

Finally, data on interstate conflicts which involved the major powers between 1870 and 1914 were coded from Siverson and Tennefoss (1982).[12]

A Brief Aside

Before turning to the empirical analyses, it may be useful to pause briefly in order to underscore just what we are—and are not—up to in this chapter. The first point to note is that this effort is indisputably a comparative study of nations' foreign policies. It focuses on defense expenditure decisions and alliance behaviors, phenomena which have, in the main, fallen primarily in the domain of international relations specialists rather than foreign policy scholars. The work takes as its base, however, an explicit foreign policy approach. While it deals with international relations phenomena, in other words, it departs from much of the current international relations literature by conceiving those phenomena in foreign policy terms.

We should note, however, that this effort also departs in several ways from much of the work in comparative foreign policy. While most empirical comparative foreign policy analyses have used events data drawn from the post-1945 era, for example, our own effort deals with an earlier, historically important, epoch which has been largely unexplored by comparative foreign policy scholars.

Second, much of the empirical work in comparative foreign policy which has been completed to date has been based on what are by now fairly well known events data sets. There was considerable justification for that practice. The carefully compiled collections seem, in effect, to have provided at least a rough operational definition of "foreign policy." For an emerging field that would not have gotten far without it, they provided a tangible dependent variable which could be measured, studied and ultimately explained. The collections reflected the broad range of behaviors which nations can exhibit.

While the existing events data collections have thus been critically important, however, it is our view that the absence of events data sets for selected eras or sets of nations need not totally forestall useful empirical research. It would be preferable in a more perfect world to have traditional events data collections, but our research environment is far from perfect. Progress may be made, we believe, by focusing on narrower and more limited ranges of behavior for which data are more readily available.

The final point to note is that, while we do deal with two types of events, we depart from much existing work by focusing our interest, less on those crude empirical events, *per se*, and more on the abstract and overarching concept which we theorize is reflected by the empirical behaviors. Put differently, much of the early work in the field was pitched at a relatively low level of abstraction; different types of behaviors were seen, quite simply, as different. In contrast, our own effort begins the other way around. In our argument, apparently diverse acts—that is, defense spending and alliance management—are conceived as fundamentally similar. To us, events are important insofar as they are indicators of explicit concepts. It is this move to embed empirical events in more overarching theoretical concepts which is the central thrust of the alternative trigger and foreign policy substitution argument.

With all of that in mind, therefore, let us proceed with the actual analyses.

The Analyses

Three distinct types of preliminary analyses have been completed to date. The first explores the relationship between arms and alliances by employing straightforward cross-tabulations. The second utilizes a series of equally simple regression techniques. Finally, a third approach examines states' behaviors—generalized security responses—after they became the targets of conflict initiations by other major powers. Each type of analysis will be discussed in turn.

Arms and Alliances: Cross-tabulation Results

Simple chi-squared tests were made initially to explore the relationship between defense spending and alliance formations. The analyses utilized a variety of operationalizations of defense spending: increases or decreases in the annual percent change; less than or greater than the median annual percent change; and, annual percent changes by quartiles. (Median and quartile values were calculated separately for each nation.) Alliance formations were lagged zero years (Table 8.1) and one year (Table 8.2).[13] Analyses were conducted on each nation separately and also on all six majors taken collectively.

One potentially important caveat should be noted immediately: even if the major European states utilized alliance behavior as one means for managing their security problems during the 1870–1914 period, alliance formations were an extremely rare event in comparison with increases in defense spending. Budget limitations permitting, states could increase military expenditures in each year, but they did not forge a new set of alliance ties with equal frequency. Most nations in most years did not form alliances.[14] As a result, there is relatively little variance in alliance formation, relative to that in the defense spending. When situations such as that develop, in turn, the sensitivity of standard statistical procedures begins to be eroded. Tests of the sort employed here typically fail to detect subtle statistical—but important substantive—differences.[15]

With that statistical aside in mind, the point to note is that, regardless of how defense spending is treated and regardless of whether or not alliance formations are lagged, the tests reveal little support across the six states for the arms/alliance relationship.[16] There is little that suggests that the six majors, either individually or collectively, substituted between defense spending and alliance formations. Except for Germany, each formed alliances both when it was and was not simultaneously increasing its own defense spending. Each entered into such bonds both when its expenditures were both above and below its median rate of annual change.

Only one somewhat interesting set of findings emerges: as an examination of the quartile analyses in Table 8.1 (zero lag) suggests, the six nations showed a modest tendency to refrain from forming alliances when their defense spending was rising sharply (i.e.,

143

Table 8.1   *Defense Spending and Alliances: Cross-Tabulations*

Alliances formed	*Defense spending at t : alliance formation at t* *Defense spending*					
	− % change		*+ % change*		*Chi sq.*	*df*
	0	*≥ 1*	*0*	*≥ 1*		
Overall	75	15	149	25	0.24	1
Germany	18	0	22	4	3.05	1
Italy	11	3	28	2	2.07	1
UK	12	2	26	4	0.01	1
France	13	3	25	3	0.56	1
Russia	13	3	20	8	0.52	1
Austria	8	4	28	4	2.55	1

Alliances formed	*Defense spending at t : alliance formation at t* *Percent change in defense spending*					
	≤ median		*> median*		*Chi sq.*	*df*
	0	*≥ 1*	*0*	*≥ 1*		
Overall	113	19	111	21	0.12	1
Germany	21	1	19	3	1.10	1
Italy	18	4	21	1	2.03	1
UK	19	3	19	3	0.00	1
France	18	4	20	2	0.77	1
Russia	19	3	14	8	3.03	1
Austria	18	4	18	4	0.00	1

Alliances formed	*Defense spending at t : alliance formation at t* *Percent change in defense spending, by quartiles*									
	Q1		*Q2*		*Q3*		*Q4*		*Chi sq.*	*df*
	0	*≥ 1*	*0*	*≥ 1*	*0*	*≥ 1*	*0*	*≥ 1*		
Overall	54	11	59	8	53	15	58	6	4.48	3
Germany	11	0	10	1	8	3	11	0	6.60	3
Italy	8	3	10	1	10	1	11	0	4.29	3
UK	9	2	10	1	9	2	10	1	0.77	3
France	8	2	10	2	11	0	9	2	2.37	3
Russia	10	1	9	2	6	6	8	2	5.89	3
Austria	8	3	10	1	9	3	9	1	2.05	3

Quartile 4). Neither Germany nor Italy, for example, formed any alliances at all in those years in which its annual change in defense spending was increasing sharply (Quartile 4). Of the 40 formations recorded during the 1870–1914 period, only 6 (15%) occurred when nations were simultaneously effecting major increases in their own

Table 8.2　*Defense Spending and Alliances: Lagged Cross-tabulations*

	Defense spending at t : alliance formation at t+1 Defense spending					
Alliances	− % change		+ % change			
formed	0	≥ 1	0	≥ 1	Chi sq.	df
Overall	76	14	148	26	0.02	1
Germany	16	2	24	2	0.15	1
Italy	13	1	26	4	0.36	1
UK	11	3	27	3	1.06	1
France	14	2	24	4	0.03	1
Russia	11	5	22	6	0.52	1
Austria	11	1	25	7	1.08	1

	Defense spending at t : alliance formation at t+1 Percent change in defense spending					
Alliances	≤ median		> median			
formed	0	≥ 1	0	≥ 1	Chi sq.	df
Overall	112	20	112	20	0.00	1
Germany	20	2	20	2	0.00	1
Italy	21	1	18	4	2.03	1
UK	19	3	19	3	0.00	1
France	18	4	20	2	0.77	1
Russia	16	6	17	5	0.12	1
Austria	18	4	18	4	0.00	1

	Defense spending at t : alliance formation at t+1 Percent change in defense spending, by quartiles									
	Q1		Q2		Q3		Q4			
Alliances formed	0	≥ 1	0	≥ 1	0	≥ 1	0	≥ 1	Chi sq.	df
Overall	54	11	58	9	58	10	54	10	0.33	3
Germany	10	1	10	1	11	0	9	2	2.20	3
Italy	10	1	11	0	9	2	9	2	2.48	3
UK	8	3	11	0	10	1	9	2	3.86	3
France	9	1	9	3	10	1	10	1	1.81	3
Russia	7	4	9	2	8	4	9	1	2.67	3
Austria	10	1	8	3	10	2	8	2	1.26	3

defense expenditures. Such a result makes intuitive sense. Nations which want to increase their defense capability and which are capable of doing so by simply budgeting sharp increases in their own defense spending may not need to substitute (or augment) their own efforts by moving to form alliances with other states.

One might expect that that logic could be extended to states which effect a large decrease in expenditures (i.e., those which fall in Quartile 1 in Table 8.1). Put simply, such states might be much more prone to offset spending limitations by forming alliances. The results, however, do not support that thesis; only 11 (27.5%) formations involved states which were budgeting first-quartile spending changes.

While that result is somewhat disappointing from the perspective of the arms/alliances hypothesis, it suggests several considerations which are potentially important for efforts to understand substitution processes. First, large decreases in defense spending are, in at least some circumstances, intentional.[17] The point is important because some cases may fall in Quartile 1 because leaders in those states are anxious to lower spending while other first-quartile spending changes are unintentional results of budget constraints or other similar limitations. Cases in which leaders want to enhance their defense capabilities but must instead effect Quartile 1 spending decreases would appear likely to be among those in which efforts to form compensating alliances might be most common.[18]

All states which fall in even this category, however, should not be expected to complete an alliance. Alliances, unlike increases in a state's own arms stocks, are by definition at least bilateral. Thus, even though a state in Quartile 1 may want to form alliances to offset a spending decrease, the potential allies may find the suitor unattractive, *precisely because* the state in question is unable to maintain its own defense. If that were the case, of course, Quartile 1 spending changes would once again *not* necessarily lead to alliance formations.[19]

Even if the Quartile 1 state is an attractive suitor, however, another problem could develop. The Quartile 1 suitor might not, if its leaders were calculating carefully, want to ally with another, equally pressed, Quartile 1 state. They might be likely to prefer instead to ally with a stronger state effecting a Quartile 2–4 spending change. If that were the case and the leaders of the would-be alliance creator were successful, for example, any dyadic alliance thus formed would involve a Quartile 1 state and a *non*-Quartile 1 state. If all efforts by Quartile 1 states to form alliances would not necessarily lead to actual formations, as was said above, then it also appears likely that Quartile 1 formations might be extensively offset by formations involving nations whose spending changes put them in the other quartiles.

Before one ascribes too much to these results, however, two additional points should be noted. First, there appears to have been no general pattern of arms/alliances trade-offs which held across all of the major powers. Second, and perhaps more important, whatever substitution effects appear in the zero-lag quartile analyses (Table 8.1), they disappear entirely in the lag-one quartile analyses (Table 8.2). Even if one wants to argue that there is at least some support for the argument that alliance formations at *t* affected spending at *t*, in other words, these preliminary tests yield no evidence at all that defense spending at *t* affected alliance formations at *t*+1.[20]

Regression Analyses: Alliance Formations as Interventions in Nations' Defense Budgeting Processes

An alternative approach for exploring the relationship between states' arms and alliances entails the application of a few simple regression procedures. Described briefly, the first step is to regress a state's spending, first on a naïve model which includes the year as the only predictor variable and then on a second model which includes the year and a dummy variable coded to reflect the formation of an alliance.[21]

The results shown in Table 8.3 illustrate the results obtained. The six equations revolve around a class 1 defense alliance which was formed between Germany and Austria in 1879 and which was subsequently joined by Italy in 1882. The findings for Germany are particularly interesting. In the first equation, the R^2 is fairly low and it is not possible to reject the hypothesis of positive first-order autocorrelation. Insertion of a dummy variable to reflect the formation of the pact with Austria in 1879, however, alters the situation in several important ways. First, the proportion of variance explained rises sharply. Second, it becomes possible to reject the hypothesis of positive first-order autocorrelation.[22] Third, all three terms in the second equation for Germany have highly significant *t*-values.

Unfortunately, less satisfactory results are obtained when efforts are made to understand the Austrian and Italian experiences with this alliance. It is possible to reject the hypothesis of positive first-order autocorrelation even in connection with the naïve, time-only model, for example, when it is estimated on the Austrian data. The *t*-values obtained for the intercept and year terms in the dummy variable equation in that case are also lower and less significant than in the initial naïve formulation; respecifying the model in order to make it sensitive to the alliance formation, in other words, does not really improve the situation. The results are equally problematic in the Italian case. In that instance, inclusion of a variable to tap the formation fails to reduce the initial autocorrelation problem.

Perhaps the most intriguing result to be noted in connection with these equations, however, is the sign of the dummy variable when it is inserted. In the case of Germany, it is negative; formation of the alliance shifted German defense spending downward in a manner consistent

Table 8.3   *Selected Regression Analyses*

Nation Period (n)	Dependent variable R^2 (Adj. R^2) Durbin-Watson d	Intercept coefficient Stand. dev. t-value Sig.	Year coefficient Stand. dev. t-value Sig.	Dummy coefficient Stand. dev. t-value Sig.
Germany 1876– 1887 (12)	Expenditures 50.2 (45.2) 0.88	−4882156 157.228 3.11 .01	2651.3 835.7 3.17 .01	– – –
Germany 1876– 1887 (12)	Expenditures 93.9 (92.5) 1.86	−11516446 1010777 11.39 .001	6188.5 538.4 11.50 .001	a −31614 3942 8.02 .001
Italy 1870– 1887 (18)	Expenditures 89.8 (89.2) 0.61	−4370081 371930 11.75 .001	2348.5 198.0 11.86 .001	– – –
Italy 1870– 1887 (18)	Expenditures 96.5 (96.0) 0.75	−2887969 358267 8.06 .001	1557.8 191.0 8.16 .001	b 11788 2212 5.13 .001
Austria 1870– 1887 (18)	Expenditures 76.2 (74.7) 1.66	−1566698 225110 6.96 .001	856.9 119.8 7.15 .001	– – –
Austria 1870– 1887 (18)	Expenditures 90.1 (88.8) 1.43	−397514 294317 1.35 .20	232.7 157.0 1.48 .20	c 7561 1639 4.61 .001

a The dummy variable in the German equation for 1876–1887 is coded to reflect a class 1 defense alliance which was formed with Austria in 1879. 0: 1872–1879; 1: 1880–1887.

b The dummy variable in the Italian equation for 1870–1887 is coded to reflect a class 1 defense alliance which was formed with Germany and Austria in 1882. 0: 1870–1882; 1: 1883–1887.

c The dummy variable in the Austria equation for 1870–1887 is coded to reflect a class 1 defense alliance which was formed with Germany in 1879. 0: 1870–1879; 1: 1880–1887.

with the substitution hypothesis. In the case of Italy and Austria, however, the opposite is found. The sign is positive. If the results are to be believed, formation of the pact did not relieve Italian and Austrian decision makers. While the alliance might have enabled decision makers in both states to forgo new allocations that they would have *otherwise* been forced to make, it did not allow them to reduce already-existing expenditure levels.

Procedures which parallel those presented here have been applied to all of the class 1 alliance formations involving two or more of the major European powers between 1870 and 1914. The results roughly parallel those already shown. In some cases attention to the formation of pacts seemed to enhance our ability to understand the trends; in other cases the pacts seemed irrelevant. More important, no clear substantive picture emerged. In some cases, the results were consistent with the substitution hypothesis; states did decrease spending in the wake of alliance formations. In other instances, however, such reductions did not develop; expenditures proceeded to rise to a higher level or climbed at a more rapid rate.

That said, however, the tentative nature of the results discussed in this section should be emphasized. The time periods utilized are extremely short because nations seldom allowed long intervals to elapse between the formation of one alliance and their entry into another. Some periods were also shortened because efforts were made to avoid the inclusion of nations' wartime or immediate postwar years when decision makers were making extraordinary increases or decreases in spending levels.[23] It should also be emphasized that the regression approach used here is sensitive to only slope and intercept changes. More subtle effects of alliances such as learning or decaying patterns might be detected if alternative techniques are utilized.

Even with those caveats in mind, however, the dominant pattern here should be underscored once again. Put simply, the results are at best ambiguous; while some evidence of arms/alliance substitutions can be found, it does not appear from these analyses that such trade-offs were general either across the states in question or even within given states through time.

Generalized 'Security' Responses

One final, highly exploratory, type of preliminary analysis should be mentioned. Put simply, the focus here is on states' responses to security threats.

If we presume that the fact that being a target of at least one Siverson and Tennefoss (1982) conflict may be taken provisionally as a "trigger" which would be likely to induce national security concerns, it is possible to examine the patterns in the targets' responses. (Although we use the term "response," readers should note that the initial analyses

149

deal with zero-lag relationships.) One possibility, of course, is the familiar tit-for-tat response: states which are targets of conflict become initiators. Somewhat surprisingly, however, that pattern did not develop at all in the analyses (see Table 8.4).[24] States might also respond to conflict by elevating military expenditures; alternatively, they might move to form alliances. As the results in Table 8.4 suggest, the evidence is consistent with the hypothesis that both of those options were occasionally utilized.

The point to note, however, is that the substitution argument suggests that states may respond to conflicts in *any* (or even all) of these

Table 8.4 *Generalized 'Security' Responses to Conflict*

Target of conflict at t^1: initiator of conflict at t

Initiator of conflict	Target of conflict				Chi sq.	df
	0 times		≥ 1 times			
	0	≥ 1	0	≥ 1		
Overall	229	18	17	0	1.33	1

Target of conflict at t: percent change in defense spending at t

Median defense spending	Target of conflict				Chi sq.	df
	0 times		≥ 1 times			
	≤	>	<	>		
Overall	124	123	8	9	0.06	1

Target of conflict at t: alliance formation at t

Alliances formed	Target of conflict				Chi sq.	df
	0 times		≥ 1 times			
	0	≥ 1	0	≥ 1		
Overall	209	38	15	2	0.16	1

Target of conflict at t: 'security behavior' at t^2

'Security behavior'	Target of conflict				Chi sq.	df
	0 times		≥ 1 times			
	None	Some	None	Some		
Overall	96	151	7	10	0.04	1

a Distinctions between the different levels of conflict—threat, unreciprocated military action and reciprocated military action—were not utilized in the analyses presented in this table.

b Codings of "none" or "some" on the "security behavior" variable were made in the following fashion. None, if: the percent change in defense spending was less than or equal to the median for the nation in question, zero alliances were formed, and zero conflicts were initiated. Some, if: the percent change in defense spending was greater than the median for the nation in question, at least one alliance was formed, and/or at least one conflict was initiated.

fashions. If one codes nations as exhibiting "some" security-related behavior when they initiate conflict, increase spending above the median, and/or form an alliance, somewhat better results are obtained. A focus on this sort of generalized response, in contrast with a concern for either the tit-for-tat pattern or any single type of behavior, does slightly better.

Once again, however, the improvement is less than one would expect under the substitution hypothesis.[25] If being the target of a conflict did indeed trigger national security concerns among the major European powers during the 1870–1914 period, the preliminary analysis in Table 8.4 does little to support the contention that the leaders of those nations responded in a variety of alternative ways.

Summary, Conclusions and Suggestions for Further Research

The analyses presented here fail to reveal consistent patterns of substitutions between arms and alliances. Null findings, particularly in the face of significant theoretical suggestions, are never very satisfactory. These are clearly no exception. Given the frequency with which observers of the balance of power suggest that a relationship exists between arms and alliances in at least some historical periods, our negative findings are likely to generate one or the other of two rather different reactions. The first might be that the case for substitution has been overdrawn in the existing literature; it does not take place at all, is not very widespread, or operates in ways which the existing arguments do not make clear. The second reaction might be that analysts are quite correct in their contention that arms and alliances are related, but we fail to detect the relationship as a result of deficiencies in the research design and/or data which are employed. Let us consider each of these points.

Given what we know about international relations in general and nations' foreign policies in particular, it seems only remotely possible that substitution does not take place. The literature is simply too filled with examples of its occurrence to believe that it is not present in some form or another. To believe that it does not take place, moreover, would be to assume implicitly that decision makers have no choices (and hence, are unable to substitute), have infinite resources (and hence, face no necessity to substitute), or they are simply not very imaginative (and hence, fail to see the opportunities to substitute). None of those possibilities seems plausible.

Given the relative absence of the patterns which we predicted, some would undoubtedly have us adopt what Bueno de Mesquita (1985b, p. 122) has recently called the "dogmatic falsificationist" conclusion that the single counterexample discovered here should lead to the abandonment of the argument (see also Popper, 1959). According to that view, the evidence conclusively demonstrates that substitution does not occur.

We quite clearly repair to a rather different position. We argue that it might be more reasonable to suppose that substitution occurs, but its extent has been overgeneralized by those who are devoted to either the balance of power or the idea of systemic determination of national behavior. If this view is correct, then the research design needs to be recast in ways which would permit a focus on the conditions under which substitution takes place. If it is unreasonable to expect that substitution effects hold every time a nation enters an alliance but it is nevertheless the case that such relationships do exist some of the time in some contexts, to put the point differently, then we need to understand exactly which circumstances will produce the dynamic in which an alliance will lead to a decrease in military spending, or slightly differently, under which circumstances a desire to reduce military spending will lead to a nation's entry into an alliance.

Turning to the issue of the research design, it is not difficult to find several ways in which our approaches appear in retrospect to be flawed. First, it may well be the case that there is not sufficient variation in the power of the states we have studied. All of them were major powers. Within a certain range, they were all relatively equal in their abilities to afford security to their friends and insecurity to their enemies. This situation stands in sharp contrast to the situation in alliances such as NATO where there is a marked disparity of power and a widely recognized tendency for the smaller members of the alliance to "free ride" on the resources of the larger or largest member of the alliance. Stated differently, the smaller members of NATO are alleged to substitute the alliance for some of their defense expenditures. However, when an alliance is formed of only a few nations of relatively equal power, it may be that there are severe limits to how much a nation may "free ride" or substitute without fear that its partner will retaliate by either reducing its own level of commitment or seeking another partner. If this is correct, then substitution among the major powers of the 1870–1914 era may have been exaggerated; we will need to look at relationships that are more unequal.

Another possibility is that substitution takes place in ways to which military budgets are not necessarily sensitive. Military budgets, like many components of a national budget, are not usually as flexible as the substitution argument suggests. If this is so, then it may be that even if substitutions occur, they may be so much around the margins of the budget that our research design will not be sensitive enough to pick them up.

Related to this is the possibility that substitution may take place in areas that are not related to the budget. For example, as a consequence of their 1904 alliance with Japan, the British were able to withdraw five battleships from the Far East, where their interests would be protected by the Japanese, and add them to the Channel Fleet. The First Lord of the Admiralty, Lord Tweedmouth, wrote at the time: "Japan is our ally and her Navy is an element in our strength on the seas for ten years to come" (Nish, 1966, p. 353). This withdrawal was made with a view to keeping the traditional British standard of naval strength in relationship to possible opponents. Nonetheless, there was no decrease in military expenditures. If such occurrences are fairly common and substitution effects thus fail to appear in states' budgets, then we may need to formulate a research design based on a large set of rigorously designed case studies in which each opportunity for choice is studied and the constraints on choices are clearly delineated.

Finally, we need to recognize that the research design used here is preliminary and, in fact, leaves out a number of variables which might reasonably be thought to have an impact on choices involving alliances or military expenditures. We have given, thus far, scant attention to the environment of the international system. For example, it might be helpful to measure the level of tension in the international system. Or, it might be appropriate to examine each nation's national budget or economic health. Nations running significant budget deficits might be much more willing to substitute an alliance for military expenditures than a nation whose budget is robust.

Two additional points might be briefly made. First, we remain convinced about the utility of focusing on new time frames, new types of data, and efforts to embed raw empirical events in more overarching concepts. And second, as much of the foregoing suggests, this discussion is only one small portion of an ongoing research program which attempts to combine sophisticated theorizing, extensive attention to epistemology, and empirical testing. If the overall results of the program are indicative, they suggest that progress requires attention to all three concerns.

Notes

The authors would like to thank Richard Rosecrance and Harvey Starr for their helpful comments on an earlier draft. The efforts of the editors and other contributors to this volume are also greatly appreciated. Siverson's research was supported by the Institute for Governmental Affairs, University of California, Davis.

1 In addition to the Hermann and Peacock chapter in this volume, see Kegley *et al.*, 1975; East, Salmore and Hermann, 1978; Kegley, 1980; and Rosati, 1985.

2 The cyclical nature of this tradition might be noted. As Jervis notes:

> it is not clear whether we can make progress toward a scientific understanding of international politics. Indeed, it is not clear, at least not to me, whether we can make much progress in our discussions of this subject. Interest in it seems to go in cycles. The subject occupied much of our journals—and our PhD examinations—at the end of the 1960s and, after a period in which we tired of examining our epistemological and methodological assumptions, seems to be receiving more attention again. Whether we will do better this time around remains to be seen.
>
> (1985, p. 145)

3 For useful assessments of cumulation in international relations in general see Phillips, 1974; Starr, 1974, 1978; the articles in Rosenau, 1976a; Bueno de Mesquita, 1980, 1985a, 1985b; Hopmann, Zinnes and Singer, 1981; Krasner, 1985; and Jervis, 1985. For the record, the reader should perhaps be aware that both of the present authors have endeavored to make their own contributions to the so-called "cumulation" literature. See Most and Starr, 1982, 1983, 1984, 1985; Sullivan and Siverson, 1981; and Siverson and Sullivan, 1983.

4 While our commission here is not to assess just how much progress has been made, it might at least be observed in passing that today's analysts have a better decriptive feel of the world and better data. They are also better positioned than their predecessors to identify the important "puzzles" on which they may focus the next wave of research. See Zinnes, 1980, for a discussion of the utility of knowing "something" when one begins to theorize. Her observations parallel those of Lave and March, 1975, in their description of the approach to model building; somewhat interestingly, they also fit nicely with Waltz's assertion that the explanatory process begins with—rather than ends with—a statistical correlation (1979, ch. 1).

5 As one of the present authors likes to tell his students, "Anyone can tell a complex story, adding in all manner of possible additional explanatory factors, arguments, and perspectives. The trick is to tell a simple—what we used to call 'parsimonious'—story that is worth telling." The goal, as Waltz (1979, p. 4) suggests, is to avoid useless details that we neither really want nor need.

6 While we are not formalists and make no pretense that we are, the groundwork to which we refer develops a logical proof to demonstrate the incompleteness and inconsistency of the two hypotheses which exist in the literature. The unified argument is, at one level, an attempt to eliminate the inconsistencies. In this way, we agree wholeheartedly with Bueno de Mesquita when he observes:

> internal, logical consistency is a fundamental requirement of all hypotheses. To the extent that logical consistency is accepted as an

154

elemental requirement of all research, *formal, explicit theorizing takes intel-lectual, if not temporal, precedence over empiricism.*

(1985a, p. 128)

It might be noted in passing that our initial model of decision making is largely cognitive. As such, it contrasts with the more "social process" formulation suggested by Anderson in Chapter 15.

7 The outlines of this demonstration can be found in Starr, 1978, and Most and Starr, 1982, 1983, 1984, 1985. We would be remiss, however, if we failed here to note that a similar logical demonstration of this point was made in the foreign policy literature by Harold and Margaret Sprout, 1957, 1965. More than the better-known work of Snyder, Bruck and Sapin, 1962a, the Sprouts showed not only why analysts might want to include decision makers in their analyses, but also why their inclusion was an absolute necessity for analysts interested in understanding foreign policy outputs (as opposed to outcomes). That point in place, the argument should not have continued to be waged over *whether or not* decision makers should be somehow embedded in our models. Rather, the issue should have become centered on *how* they should be included, what conception(s) of them are best, what sorts of complexity are needed, whether their inclusion would require such vast amounts of detailed information that comparative research would be impeded (Rosenau, 1967c) or analysts would be able to make progress by specifying simplified models of decision processes, and so on. The Sprouts' demonstration should have allowed us to move beyond the initial question, in other words.

8 Most and Starr describe two distinct variations of the alternative trigger problem. Only the one which is more straightforward and more easily managed will be discussed here.

9 Two additional points might be made. First, it might have occurred to leaders that they could enhance their security by moving to deny their major opponents an ally; they might therefore have formed an alliance for that reason and that reason alone. Second, it should be clear that alliance dissolution could have important security-enhancing effects for certain states insofar as rupture of a tie implies a reduction in the defense burdens of such states.

10 While it is not clear what this multiplier represents, it appears that it is an attempt to standardize to the 1906 United States dollar. Insofar as the initial analyses focus more on the behaviors of given nations through time—as opposed to comparisons across nations—the ambiguity on this point is not particularly critical. It is only important to know that each nation's military expenditure series is treated in a consistent way. In extending this research, however, the ability to aggregate data across nations will likely be important.

11 Unless specifically noted in the discussion below, however, alliances of all three classes were included in our initial analyses.

12 Codings were made to reflect which state acted as the initiator and which as the target; entries also were made to reflect the level of conflict—threat, unreciprocated military action, reciprocated military action—involved in each dispute. Unless specifically noted in the discussion below, however, neither type of distinction was utilized in the initial analyses.

13 All types of alliance formations were included in these analyses. Analyses were also completed on the relationships between alliance formations at *t*

and defense spending at $t+1$ and are available on request. Suffice it to say that those tests yielded results which were generally identical to those shown in the tables.

14 While the lack of variance in the data should be apparent in Tables 8.1 and 8.2, it may be most obvious in the context of Note 9 above.

15 See Most and Starr, 1985, for an explanation of this difficulty and suggestions about what procedures may be adopted when it arises.

16 The displays in Tables 8.1 and 8.2 are simply collapsed cross-tabulation tables. The tally for the overall tabulation of the relationship between defense spending at t and alliances formation at t, for example, would have appeared as in Table 8.5.

Table 8.5   *Relation of Defense Spending at t to Alliance Formation at t+1*

| | | Overall alliances formed at t | |
		0	≥ 1
Overall defense spending at t	– % Change	75	15
	+ % Change	149	25

Chi square = 0.24, df = 1

17 Some rather large decreases in spending developed in the data set being utilized here: for example, as states emerged from conflicts and moved to demobilize.

18 It follows from this that it may be useful to build data on states' budget deficits into our subsequent analyses.

19 One might expect, however, that Quartile 1 states would have had a disproportionate propensity to *attempt* alliance formations. Thus, one might like to complement the existing Singer and Small, 1966, and Small and Singer, 1969, data with reports on unsuccessful attempts to form alliances. (Alternative arguments in favor of the need for such data would parallel the reasoning developed in Most and Starr, 1982, 1983.) In addition, it would also be helpful if it were possible to discern which state(s) were most desirous of forming each alliance.

20 As Table 8.6 should make clear, there also appears to be no relationship between alliance formation at t and defense spending at $t+1$. Additional analyses are available on request.

21 For an explanation of dummy variable regression analyses, see for example Johnston, 1972. While the procedures employed here are sensitive only to intercept and slope changes, they appear sufficient for at least a first pass at our problem. Dummy variables were entered in both additive and multiplicative fashion. The latter terms which would have detected slope changes invariably failed to load.

22 The procedures here are consistent with Johnston's interpretation of autocorrelation as an indication of an incorrect specification of the form of a relationship, 1972, pp. 243–4. Presuming that an alliance formation altered

Table 8.6   *Relation of Alliance Formation at t Defense Spending at t+1*

Alliance formation at t: defense spending at t+1

	Alliances formed									
	0				≥ 1					
Defense spending Percent change by quartiles	Q1	Q2	Q3	Q4	Q1	Q2	Q3	Q4	Chi sq.	df
Overall	51	58	56	53	12	9	11	8	1.13	3
Germany	8	11	9	11	2	0	2	0	–	–
Italy	10	10	10	8	1	1	1	2	0.89	3
UK	8	10	9	10	3	1	1	1	2.19	3
France	8	10	9	10	2	2	2	0	2.16	3
Russia	8	7	10	7	2	4	2	3	1.44	3
Austria	9	10	9	7	2	1	3	2	1.06	3

the level of a nation's defense spending (intercept), its rate of increase (slope) or both, but a model fails to include a variable which taps the effect, nonrandomly distributed error terms will develop when the first or time-based equation is estimated. One procedure is to move beyond the naïve first model by specifying a second equation which includes a dummy coding for the alliance effect. Positive first-order autocorrelation problems should be reduced and the sampling variance of the estimates should be reduced.

23 The decision to base Germany in Table 8.3 on the 1876–87 period illustrates both difficulties. In 1870–1, Germany was involved in the Franco-Prussian war (Small and Singer, 1982; Interstate War #58). Following the cessation of hostilities, German defense spending fell sharply (1873–5), presumably as the Prussian authorities moved to demobilize. The end point for the period, 1887, was chosen because Germany augmented its class 1 alliance with Italy with a class 2 pact in that year and also moved to reaffirm previously existing class 2 bonds with Russia and Austria.

24 It is probable that this result is an artifact of the coding procedures utilized by Siverson and Tennefoss and also of the focus in Table 8.4 on zero-lag relationships.

25 Efforts to account for the disappointing results are currently in progress. At the moment, the following explanations are being considered: (1) conflict as it has been coded to date is not sufficient to induce insecurity; distinctions need to be made for each level of Siverson and Tennefoss event; (2) conflict may, as the alternative triggers argument suggests, be only one type of insecurity-inducing phenomenon; more progress might be made by expanding the trigger focus to include a wider range of potential trigger phenomena; (3) the zero lags currently employed here need to be replaced with $t+1$ lags (one problem, of course, is that different responses may have different sorts of lag patterns); (4) finally, it may be possible that the behaviors described in Table 8.4 fail to encompass the full range of options across which leaders substituted.

PART III

Foreign Policy as an Interactive Process

9

Dyadic Case Studies in the Comparative Study of Foreign Policy Behavior

NEIL R. RICHARDSON

James Rosenau's (1966) persuasive call for "pre-theory" in the study of foreign policy two decades ago was instrumental in the drive for disciplined scholarship in the field. Since then, so many scholars have adopted the "scientific consciousness" of systematic comparisons he advocated as to change the field's emphasis. The resulting transformation in foreign policy studies has been most salutary.

This impressive change of intellectual disposition has nevertheless been hampered by theoretical conceptions that have encouraged a useful but, ultimately, an insufficient research strategy. In this chapter, I will specifically take issue with the proclivity of this scholarship to assume that the state is a solitary (or monadic) actor, an assumption that has led to a widespread reliance on cross-national, correlational empirical research. I will develop a competing research strategy based on the following logic:

(1) The immediate cause of foreign policy behavior lies in the calculations of decision makers.
(2) Decision makers are goal-directed.
(3) At least some decision outcomes are different from the additive sums of the outputs of the pertinent state actors.
(4) Therefore, case studies of decision making are needed to probe the causes of foreign policy behavior.
(5) Furthermore, such decision-making case studies must investigate the interdependent decisions of (minimally) two state decision-making leaderships simultaneously.

I should acknowledge at the outset that statements (1) through (4) repeat positions taken by others. What I hope to show is that, by

161

combining the first four observations, statement (5) follows logically. Moreover, in the final pages, I will then proceed to suggest how such dyadic case studies can complement correlational empirical research in the search for a theory of foreign policy behavior.

Monadic Conceptions of Foreign Policy

Early studies adopting a scientific mode of foreign policy analysis commonly explored hypothesized relations between national attributes and foreign policy behavior (e.g., Choucri and North, 1969; Feierabend and Feierabend, 1969; Salmore and Hermann, 1969). McGowan and Shapiro's (1973) assessment of this stream of empirical work was that little progress toward understanding comparative foreign policy had been achieved. In retrospect, it is not surprising that such cross-national studies failed to find persuasive correlational patterns linking societies' holistic attributes—size, wealth and political accountability, for example—to their states' foreign policy behaviour.[1] For one thing, little attention was initially paid to the conversion processes by which national attributes are harnessed to foreign policy purposes. Instead, the state was at least implicitly assumed to be a unitary actor that would employ holistic attributes similarly regardless of state apparatus or foreign policy circumstances.

Now this flaw was hardly monopolized by those whose research is under consideration here. Adherents of political realism, long the dominant paradigm, were no less guilty of making the same assumption. Modern analysts have self-consciously unburdened themselves of most of realism's least attractive features—hazy theory, tautological concepts and uncertain rules of evidence. But they often retained the assumption of the state as a unitary actor.

The assumption of unitary decision making has long been challenged. The unitary actor is now called into question regularly. Allison's (1969) presentation of organizational processes and bureaucratic politics galvanized most subsequent treatments of foreign policy decision making, and several contributions to this volume (Chapters 13–16) explore alternatives to the unitary actor perspective.

Thus, more recently the unitary actor assumption has regularly been abandoned. But yet another unpersuasive assumption remains prevalent. This is the belief that the state is a solitary actor, that its foreign policy decisions are rendered in isolation from its environment. In broadest terms, this assumption asserts that a state's decisions are made independently of other actors. Crucial to the thesis of this chapter are two types of objections to the solitary actor assumption.

162

The first type rests on the belief that elites make foreign policy decisions only with specific targets and goals in mind.

In order to develop this thesis, we should first remember that decision makers are required to choose among alternatives. Moreover, the alternatives available to the officials of any specific state will depend upon that society's national attributes. Soviet decision makers, for example, prospectively include among their real alternatives conventional offensive or defensive warfare with any of several European neighbors in view of the USSR's force levels. The Swiss, on the other hand, have no realistic military capacity to initiate an expansionist, offensive war, although they demonstrably retain the option of defensive warfare. Thus, a theory of comparative foreign policy needs to incorporate military and other pertinent national attributes in an explanation of why nations act as they do toward one another; an accounting of holistic national attributes permits us to estimate the number and qualitative range of alternatives that a particular state's decision makers can realistically entertain.

With this in mind, however, we can appreciate that such an accounting can only provide a first approximation; much remains before we can hope to understand why one particular alternative is more likely to be selected than another. The national attribute basis of early empirical studies led some commentators to an objection that echoes this concern. The lament of East and Winters (1976) was that the solitary actor assumption denied the importance of the target as another ingredient in the state's decisional calculations. Their position was that, as an actor faces a foreign policy decision, its resultant behavior will ultimately be determined by not only the array of alternatives its national attributes permit, but also by choice making that accounts for characteristics of the target of its behavior.

A broader reflection on the matter was offered in Kegley and Skinner's (1976) discussion of alternative "case for analysis" conceptions. What I have to this point subdivided into the unitary and solitary actor assumptions is merged into their "monadic" case for analysis. They point out that a monadic perspective implies several assumptions. It inclines the investigator to put foreign policy making into a "black box," as indicated by allusion above to the compatibility between assumptions of unitary actor and solitary actor. Thus, decision making is unscrutinized, implying further that different states are alike in this regard, each with a unitary and identical process. The monadic view, they remind us, also assumes that any given state is "predisposed to act in some characteristic way, and that [the resultant] behavior pattern is regarded as invariant with respect to any foreign actor" (p. 308). This, as we have seen, is one of the ways in which the state is assumed

163

to be an isolate. It is insensitive to variations among "targets" of its external behavior; the state is indiscriminant with respect to prospective targets when choosing among behavioral alternatives.

Finally, they argue that the monadic perspective inclines researchers to assume that the nation is significantly influential over other members of the system and even over the system as a whole. They say that this is in keeping with the denial that a state's behavior is affected by the behavior of other states toward it. Whether one accepts their view on this point is much less important for present purposes than is the prospect that states may seek to influence one another by means of foreign policy behavior.[2] For, whether the actor or instead its target is the more influential, in either case there is implicit a companion assumption that the state's foreign policy is goal-directed; its behavior is meant to influence others in desired ways. Thus the issue of goals is also relevant to our initial objection to the widespread assumption of the state as a foreign policy isolate.

Raymond (in Chapter 6) makes a good case for accepting the assumption of goal-directedness, and his position on this is not dependent on the question of policy evaluation that is his ultimate purpose. He concedes that goals may be elusive, that decision makers may sometimes lose sight of them, that some goals may be particularistic rather than consensual, and that they may be shortsighted or imprudent. Nevertheless, behavior initiated in their pursuit is still purposeful.

Illustrating how the assumption of goals can be incorporated into an analytic scheme, Hudson, Hermann and Singer (1985) begin by defining a decision occasion. Such an occasion arises whenever policy makers perceive that they face a "problem." In turn, "[a] problem exists when the authorities of a government perceive a discrepancy between present (or anticipated) conditions and those that they would prefer" (p. 3). Their subsequent actions are intended to reduce or eliminate that discrepancy. In short, policy makers are assumed to be goal-directed in that they have preferences with respect to their conditions. Said differently, perceived external conditions contribute to goal-directed behavior. Leaders thus do not function in isolation. In what follows I will be accepting the assumption that foreign policy decision makers are goal-oriented.

Kegley and Skinner's (1976) incisive dissection of the monadic perspective leads directly to advocacy of possible dyadic conceptions. The argument will be considered next, and it will bring the discussion to the second general category of objection to the solitary actor assumption, namely, that decision makers are more interested in the consequences of their actions than in the actions themselves. But, in fairness, it should first be acknowledged that the problematic assumptions of the monadic conception were not altogether lost on other researchers. Indeed, even before such criticisms were crystallized in systematic overviews of the mid-1970s, at least a few scholars were adopting dyadic conceptions of foreign policy (e.g., Rosenau and Hoggard, 1974; Rummel, 1972). Nevertheless, the monadic perspective was predominant to that time, and it has by no means since relinquished its hold on a large share of comparative foreign policy analysts.

In sum, another way of characterizing much of the research to date is to say that it conceives of foreign policy behavior as an "output." That is, this work has placed too much emphasis on what states do and not enough emphasis on the "outcomes" or consequences of their acts. Dye's (1972, p. 292) homily is that "[w]e cannot be content with measuring how many times a bird flaps its wings, we must assess how far the bird has flown." Reasons for this misplaced emphasis on outputs stem from the adoption of the solitary actor assumption, often even to the exclusion of target specification or presumed purposefulness.

I will next argue that this foreign-policy-behavior-as-output view represents a weakness not entirely overcome by the adoption of target-specific and goal-directed assumptions about actors, useful as they are. Indeed, even the slowly increasing adoption of a dyadic conception of foreign policy behavior will be portrayed as has having major promise in only some of its possible configurations.

Dyadic Conceptions of Foreign Policy

In order to develop this assertion, let us return to the outlines of Kegley and Skinner's (1976) discussion. They advance two variants on the dyadic possibility, the "directed dyad" and the "summed dyad." These variants share three assumptions: (1) that an actor's behavior is target-specific, (2) that an actor's behavior is goal-directed, and therefore (3) that an actor's behavior is influenced by the (goal-directed) behavior of others.

With these assumptions in hand, the summed dyad treats the behavior of the two actors toward each other as a (summed) aggregate. Adopting the summed dyad suggests two restrictive assumptions, namely, (1) that one actor's behavior will elicit a response from the other, and (2) that the latter will respond in kind. Because these assumptions are dubious, Kegley and Skinner clearly prefer the directed dyad as the case for analysis. The directed dyad is defined by

165

unidirectional target specificity, A→B. They point to its harmony with "who-does-what-to-whom" questions, its correspondence to empirical demonstrations of dimensionality in foreign policy behavior, and its capacity to expand geometrically the number of cases available for analysis by comparison to a monadic conception.

Central to what follows, however, is Kegley and Skinner's final observation on the advantages of the directed dyad. They emphasize that this configuration is especially well suited to examining the *consequences* of foreign policy behavior. They observe that, by treating each of the two dyadic partners as an actor that initiates behavior toward the other, the analyst can explore "outcome" questions of symmetry and reciprocity that are concealed by the summed dyad (also see East, 1972). We might call such an overlay of two directed dyads a "mutually directed dyad," wherein A→B is juxtaposed with B→A.

Symmetry and reciprocity in mutually directed dyads are potentially useful foci (e.g., Richardson, Kegley and Agnew, 1981). But there are other outcomes of interest that are not conceptually the simple additive intersection of two countries' behaviors toward one another. One example of a nonadditive consequence is the phenomenon of war, as carefully articulated by Most and Starr (1983), and it illustrates one reason to amend Kegley and Skinner's presentation.

Most and Starr point out that systematic scholarship on the causes of war has usually searched for associations between various national attributes and the nation's war involvement. A principal purpose of their article is to pinpoint the logical error of this procedural strategy. War, they argue, is a phenomenon minimally requiring that two nations' policy makers both agree to fight each other. Failing that condition, the decision by one state to risk—or even initiate—warlike hostilities will not result in a war as generally defined. Instead, the target of the first state's behavior will acquiesce when faced with the threat of war, while the initiator will then not need to incur the costs of warmaking because it need not do so in order to achieve its goal with respect to the target. Thus, the phenomenon of war illustrates that a dyadic outcome may differ from the simple addition of the two parties' outputs.

Of course, Most and Starr's broader point is that war as a dependent variable cannot logically depend on the attributes and decisions of any one actor. Rather, war is a product of (at least) the joint occurrence of some attributes and decisions of both parties to the fighting. The joint occurrence of these attributes is necessary to war, and war is an outcome rather than simply the sum of two states' behavioral outputs.

Notice how this conception of war differs from the directed dyad. They share the idea that the first actor's behavior depends on some properties of the second party. What is different about war as an outcome is that it also depends on the second party's behavior toward the first (that is, as opposed to the second party's attributes alone). In this sense, the mutually directed dyad may interact to produce an outcome that is qualitatively different from the simple output of either one taken singly in its behavior directed toward the other.[3]

Because outcomes can be qualitatively different from the addition of mutually directed outputs, we face the prospect that policy makers in state A must directly contend with the calculations of their counterparts in state B. Schelling (1960, ch. 4) has referred to this complication as the process of "interdependent decisions," and herein lies a different way to object to the mere juxtaposition of directed dyads. Viewed as a result of interdependent decision making, foreign policy behavior is still the product of actor choices. However, each actor's thoughts on its own best choice of action depend on the action it expects the other actor to take, action that it knows will depend, in turn, on the other actor's expectations of the first actor's choice.

So it is that even the salutary growth in directional dyadic studies can overlook a potentially crucial question in our search for understandings of foreign policy. Insofar as such research adopts a unidirectional perspective, it cannot explore outcomes that are qualitatively different from additive outputs of actors. Moreover, this remains true of mutually directed dyadic studies if they are insensitive to interdependent decision-making processes.

Parenthetically, it may be worth noting that these considerations argue against using the terms "actor" and "target" altogether. As interdependent participants, they are in fact simultaneously both actors and targets. The policy makers in one state may view themselves as people in need of reaching a decision, but they will make that decision conscious of what the other party expects them to do and what it will therefore probably decide to do toward them as *its* target.

To summarize the discussion to this point, I have agreed with earlier assessments that urge the adoption of this directed-dyadic case for analysis in comparative foreign policy research. This posture is supported on several grounds, the most important of which is the assumption that decision makers are goal-directed, and that they are therefore more interested in outcomes than in outputs. In view of (1) the observation that outcomes are sometimes non-additively related to pertinent outputs, and (2) the prospect that leaders in different countries may be making interdependent decisions, I further conclude that the "mutually directed dyad" is an especially important case for analysis. In addition, there is implicit in much of the preceding discussion the idea that theories of foreign policy necessarily entail social, political

167

and psychological components internal to national societies and their decision-making routines.

It is important to bear in mind that the advocacy of case study design in the next section is driven by the theoretical and conceptual issues just reviewed. If we believed instead that nations' foreign policy choices and acts could be explained merely by understanding the ranges of their respective choices, if we could believe that their goals were invariant and quite clear, if we conceived of their actions as resulting in outputs to the exclusion of considered outcomes, and if we only believed that their decisional calculations were never interdependent, then we would not need to engage in intensive case studies in search of explanations for why certain individual actors took certain actions toward certain targets. It is in one sense unfortunate, then, that the combined observations of other scholars lead us to reject these beliefs. Such beliefs are, after all, very convenient theoretical departures for empirical research. As we confront the apparent need for a particular form of case study, we must complicate the empirical research agenda.

Case Study Design

I will propose here the utility of dyadic case study design. Later, I will suggest how case studies can complement correlational research. The case study proposal rests on the need to examine intensively aspects of foreign policy decision making, a task not easily achieved by designs using numerous empirical cases.[4]

Decision-making processes have quite commonly been subjected to case study research, of course. And, usually, they have been defended as serving what Eckstein (1975, pp. 104–108) labels a "heuristic" function in theory development. George (1979, pp. 51–52) synopsizes the heuristic potential of the case study as follows:

> [T]he case study is used as a means of stimulating the imagination in order to discern important *new* general problems, identify possible theoretical solutions, and formulate potentially generalizable relations that were not previously apparent . . . [T]he case study is regarded as an opportunity to learn more about the *complexity* of the problem studied, to develop further the existing explanatory framework, and to refine and elaborate the initially available theory employed.

This heuristic value of case studies is the most intuitively obvious research purpose to which the design may be put. Moreover, in practice, case study research by political scientists has usually been non-cumulative. Indeed, methodological treatments of case study design typically label it "pre-scientific" (e.g., Campbell and Stanley, 1963). However, both the practice and presumption are unfortunate because, in principle, case study design can fruitfully be employed in the scientific enterprise. What is necessary to *scientific* case study is an *a priori* "scientific consciousness." Rosenau (1971a, p. 31) defines this to mean "an automatic tendency to ask, 'Of what larger pattern is this behavior an instance?'" This of course entails moving away from a heuristic intention, treating the case as a datum from among a "larger pattern" of data. This tendency toward scientific consciousness is an admirable one, but it is not very specific. It leaves for the comparative foreign policy analyst the remaining need to ask, "What is it that I need to know about the case as a datum?" The broadest answer is, "I need to know how this case compares to the other pertinent cases."

I have already suggested a more specific answer to this question. The analyst must determine what effect was made upon one party's final choice by considerations of what the other party's decision makers were likely to do under the circumstances at hand. However, this undertaking need not lead back to a heuristic approach to the case under scrutiny. The apparent complexity of the case materials is now guided by theoretical expectations—formulated in advance— regarding the interdependence of decisional calculations by decision makers for each state. Thus, a particular piece of information from a case might indicate which of its alternative choices the other party believed would be selected, rather than simply discovering that such a question was entertained. Indeed, positing goals within the pre-existing theory would yield propositions about the respective actors' preferred outcomes. In turn, these propositions would point to alternatives that each party should prefer in order to elicit a choice by the other that would contribute to the joint outcome preferred by the first.

In the current application, the dyadic case can serve to understand the intervening, causal relationship between, say, holistic national attributes as independent variables and state behavior as output. As noted at the outset, the comparative study of foreign policy is marked by a great many statistically based generalizations associating national attributes with foreign policy behavior. "Statistical generalizations . . . say nothing about the actual inner or interpersonal transactions that bring them about" (Diesing, 1971, p. 287; see also Russett, 1970a, p. 428). The case study, by contrast, appears as a remedial design.

[In order] to assess whether a statistical correlation between independent variables and the dependent variable is of causal significance, the investigator subjects a single case in which that correlation appears to more intensive scrutiny . . . in order to establish whether there exists an *intervening process*, that is, a causal nexus, between the independent variable and the dependent variable. If a connection between the two variables can be established in this way, then it comprises relevant evidence of the causal importance of the independent variable—at least in that single case and, therefore, *possibly* in other cases in which the statistical correlation was established.

(George, 1979a, p. 46, italics in original)

As Raymond (in Chapter 6) develops an analytic scheme for policy evaluation, he confronts the identical concern. The evaluator wants to know why a certain treatment or circumstance was followed by a certain action. S/he must develop a theory that links treatment to output (or outcome). Then, a microscopic perspective must be adopted in order to examine for the presence of hypothesized "bridging variables" that represent the causal link internal to the unit of analysis. In the present context, this intervening causal bridge refers to decision-making processes. It is precisely these microscopic processes that the dyadic case study can ferret out.

As an example, we might consider relations between the United States and the Soviet Union. Correlational evidence aggregated by three-month intervals (Richardson, 1982, 1986) has shown that the Nixon–Kissinger strategy for achieving superpower détente had a marked impact on Soviet behavior for almost three years spanning 1972 through 1974. In this period, the USA offered unprecedented economic incentives to Moscow, in return for which it expected more conciliatory diplomatic behavior from the Kremlin. The evidence shows that the United States provided economic welfare benefits to the Soviets and in return received (1) increases in both verbal and non-verbal cooperative behavior and (2) major decreases in verbal and non-verbal conflictive behavior from Moscow.[5] After 1974, dyadic relations worsened once again.

This evidence follows the mutually directed dyadic conception, and the empirical pattern is clear.[6] The 1972–4 period marks the heights of both sustained US economic inducements and Soviet conciliatory behavior in the decades of the 1960s and 1970s, the period studied. What this correlational evidence cannot document is the tempting inference that the presumed independent variable, US economic rewards, caused the presumed dependent variable, diplomatic behavior, to change in the direction of greater Soviet conciliation.

It is widely understood that Kissinger predicated his linkage strategy for détente on precisely this causal relationship. As Raymond (in Chapter 6) indicates, Kissinger believed that the provision of economic incentives would trigger a causal process in Soviet policy-making circles that encouraged reciprocity in diplomatic form. A pertinent dyadic case study would seek to discover whether (1) Washington policy makers believed that economics and diplomacy were linked (they certainly appear to have believed this) and whether, in fact, (2) Soviet leaders accepted the terms of Kissinger's linkage between US economic provisions and Soviet diplomatic behavior because (a) they believed a more conciliatory posture was necessary in order to maintain access to US credit and the goods it would allow them to purchase, and (b) they believed the diplomatic "costs" for these economic benefits were preferable to the costs of forgoing the opportunity. Kissinger was counting on such a reckoning by his Soviet counterparts in order to succeed in linking economic and diplomatic relations.

On what basis, then, should one select a case for intensive examination? Standard writings on case study design often proffer two answers, namely, the "typical" and "deviant" cases. Furthermore, these two possibilities are discussed as companions to correlational research involving large numbers of cases.

Deviant cases can be selected on the basis of independent variables or on the basis of dependent variables (see George, 1979a, pp. 7–12). Thus, the case selected for close study may share with other cases the same foreign policy behavior while differing from the others with respect to values of the independent variables. On the other hand, the selected case may share with others the values of independent variables while deviating in presumed foreign policy consequence. In either instance, theoretical advance is gained by close examination of the intervening decision processes. Those processes may indicate that a wider range of values on independent variables can be converted into the same behavioral result than was anticipated by the theory. Alternatively, the investigator may learn that similar values on independent variables can be associated with deviant foreign policy behavior when decisional procedures are also unusual. Either way, theory is thereby enriched. In other words, and without elaborating all the possible permutations, close analysis of a deviant case can produce theory enlightened by revisions pertaining to independent variables, intervening decision processes, and/or the dependent variable. Statements of empirical domain within the theory can then be more correctly bounded (Russett, 1970a, p. 429).

Notice that the deviant-case strategy is inherently comparative. One must know the observed values of independent and dependent variables for a number of observations in order to identify a deviant case. Verba (1967, pp. 160–1) and Smelser (1973) make this point; as Smelser comments (p. 56):

> The investigator takes two "groups" that differ in outcome (dependent variable) and attempts to locate differences in conditions between them (independent variable) [or intervening variable]. In deviant case analysis, one "group" is comprised of the deviant case itself, and the other by the majority of cases expressing the general finding.

171

As noted earlier, case study in the analysis of foreign policy behavior allows for incorporation of empirically based process variables (and should proceed dyadically). Now it can also be seen that deviant case study permits refinement of theory by identifying more carefully its empirical domains, that is, expanding the theory's typological properties by specifying more completely the conditions of the independent and intervening variables under which particular outcomes will occur (see George, 1979a, pp. 58–9). Such "enrichment" of theory is not without cost, however, for it also entails complicating the theory by typological qualifications. Y is no longer simply a function of X; Y is now a function of X within only a certain range of Y, and/or only as Z (process) is engaged, or only within a certain range of Z, and so forth. Such typological complications are in opposition to the goal of theoretical parsimony, of course, and so a balance must be struck.

The "typical" case, on the other hand, does not promise the same theoretical payoff. Selected because its association of independent and dependent variables is typical of a class of cases, it is therefore among the subset of cases that are most likely to yield expected findings upon closer examination. It is a most highly likely candidate to display causal bridges on the microscopic variables related to decision-making processes.

Accordingly, the typical case study can yield but two possible results. First, it may persuasively disconfirm the hypothesized causal linkages between independent and dependent variables. In the Popperian tradition of falsificationism (Popper, 1959, chs 1, 4), this is a powerful discovery that would cast grave doubt on the causal theory.[7]

The second possibility is that the case study will support theoretical expectations as to cause. That said support comes from the typical case may seem to weaken its value greatly. But this complaint should weigh heavily only insofar as what is revealed is redundant of prior empirical knowledge. In view of the paucity of empirically framed dyadic case studies of comparative foreign policy, the criterion of typicality for case selection has considerable appeal.

We often operate in the absence of prior correlational studies that would permit designations of "deviant" and "typical" cases, however. Under these circumstances, we may instead infer types of cases on theoretical grounds, labeling them "least likely" and "most likely." Returning to the détente example may clarify this possibility.

From some theoretical perspectives, Kissinger's strategy for modifying Soviet behavior would appear to be a "least likely" candidate for successfully evoking the desired outcome. An interdependence theory, say, might stress the importance of symmetrical and extensive economic relations as conditions enhancing diplomatic cordiality.

Such a theory would clearly suggest that the linkage strategy of the early 1970s was built on "least likely" foundations of asymmetrical and very modest economic intercourse. Case study materials documenting that the proposed causal sequence actually occurred would cast doubt on the theory, perhaps encouraging its modification to account for unexpected values on the independent variables.

From a different theoretical perspective, this episode would qualify as a "most likely" case instead. For example, Kissinger's effort would be a very likely case for a bargaining theory wherein explicit communication and clarity of the terms of exchange are deemed crucial to a successful outcome. Case evidence that the proposed causal sequence occurred would provide unsurprising support for the theory.

In short, theoretical inferences from "deviant" and "least likely" case evidence are similar, as are inferences drawn from "typical" and "most likely" studies. The "deviant"—"typical" pairing differs from the "least likely"—"most likely" pairing in that the former rests on prior correlational empirical bases whereas the latter rests on theoretical expectations alone.

A Research Strategy

The emphasis I have placed on the theoretical utility of case study design should not be allowed to obscure the important roles fulfilled by cross-dyadic correlational research. Because the latter identify regularities in relationships between dependent variables and certain independent ones, correlational studies can serve to test hypotheses. In addition, I have meant to indicate their importance in identifying both typical and deviant members of samples or populations as candidates for dyadic case studies of foreign policy making. Third, they are equally valuable for retesting relations between independent and dependent variables when the initial theory has been reformulated in line with case study findings.[8] In sum, these prescriptions translate into several steps in an iterative research agenda.

A piece of Niccolo Machiavelli's advice to his prince can serve to illustrate a research sequence. Machiavelli counseled that, if there appeared signs of dissension or dissatisfaction among his subjects, the prince should identify a foreign enemy as a perceived threat and thereby congeal support once again for his leadership. This advice has been translated by social scientists into a foreign policy proposition: A government experiencing domestic turmoil will engage in foreign conflict (as a diversionary tactic). Although Machiavelli's concern was with domestic tranquility, the other prospective outcome was a more conflictual relationship with the foreign country chosen as the target of the diversion.

A first step in research would be to select a sample or population of mutually directed dyads as cases for statistical analysis. The proposition would lead us to expect that those dyads in which at least one country featured high levels of domestic conflict—a holistic national attribute—would tend to experience high levels of foreign conflict. Moreover, while the foreign conflict might more likely be initiated by dyad members suffering domestic turmoil, further expectations of affective reciprocity would allow for unidirectional dyadic conflict to evolve into reciprocal conflict for pairs of countries.

Of course, only some fraction of those dyads where domestic turmoil is present would be expected to show high foreign conflict behavior since the proposition does not predict that a troubled government will initiate foreign conflict toward all, or even toward many of its foreign policy partners.[9] Nevertheless, this first step provides a general sense of the frequency of the proposed domestic-foreign conflict link. More importantly, this statistical survey also identifies candidates for dyadic case study.

The second step might appropriately delve into a "typical" dyadic case as identified by high domestic conflict for one party and high foreign conflict between them. The guiding research question at this juncture concerns the "causal nexus" of decision makers' calculations. Did the elites in state A initiate conflict with state B in the belief that they could divert the attentions of discontented citizenry? Was foreign conflict also undertaken because state A's leaders doubted their capacity to repress domestic turmoil, an intervening variable suggested by prior statistical studies of monads (Hazelwood 1973; Kegley, Richardson and Richter 1978)? Did A's leaders anticipate that conflict towards B would elicit B's reciprocal conflict toward A? In turn, did B's decision makers understand A's motive as a domestic one? If so, were they inclined to "forgive" A its belligerence, at least for a time or to some degree?

These are the questions of immediate cause as defined by decisional calculations. The answer to them from intensive case study can then be used to reassess dyadic theory of foreign policy. If, for example, our hypothetical case study uncovered basically affirmative answers to the above questions, the proposition would be corroborated further. Under these circumstances, the researcher might provisionally revise the theoretical expectations by incorporating military preparedness more explicitly as an intervening concept.

Case study corroboration and modest theoretical alteration in hand, the fourth step should probably be to re-examine the proposition in a "deviant" dyad, perhaps now defined as a like dyad differing only in that state C's repressive capacity is manifestly very great. Did C's leaders consider domestic repression as an alternative to initiating foreign conflict. If not, then the intervening variable loses credence. If, on the other hand, repression had been considered and rejected, then the theoretical status of this factor would remain unresolved.

If the deviant dyad were defined instead as one in which domestic conflict was much less pronounced, either positive or negative results would yield useful information on the range of domestic conflict values over which the domestic-foreign conflict proposition applies. That is, the empirical domain of the relationship could more surely be bounded and, if narrowed, retested statistically for the smaller set of dyads still eligible. Here, deviant case results would provide expectations of a stronger domestic-foreign conflict correlation across the remaining pairs of states.

Next, consider the possibility that the typical case study—the second step—revealed negative answers that contradict the initial proposition. Did state A's leaders initiate foreign conflict for reasons other than diversion? Or, did B's leaders actually initiate the conflict, perhaps seeing in A's domestic turmoil a weakness they could exploit?

Contrary findings such as these, when taken from a typical case, would lead research on a very different tack. It would then seem most prudent to return to a correlational mode that incorporates alternative incentives that seemingly caused A or B to initiate foreign policy conflict. In other words, the theory would be changed in that the immediate causes, decision makers' calculations, would be revised.

In sum, this illustrative sequence identifies two obvious examples of how the case study mode, in concert with correlational evidence, can advance theoretical understanding in ways that correlational studies alone cannot. Case studies can document the presence of diversionary conflict toward a particular dyadic partner that would be so restrictively target-specific that its occurrence would fail to register in statistics. If, say, all 30 countries in a sample that were experiencing domestic conflict were initiators of diversionary foreign conflict behaviour, but each toward only one target, then those 30 corroborating cases would be lost amidst correlations across the 870—that is, $N(N-1)$—directed dyadic possibilities constituted of these 30 countries' mutual interactions alone, even though the proposition was correct in all 30 cases. Case study could give new life to a statistically moribund proposition.

A second example is seen in the instance where negative findings from a typical dyad might indicate that B initiated the conflict in view of A's domestic difficulties. This revelation could also go unnoticed in correlational research, especially as time intervals of data observations are

175

typically of fairly long duration. In this example, theory revision would be straightforward. Unlike statistical disconfirmation, negative case study discoveries can readily point to plausible rival propositions that guide further correlational and case study research.

To conclude, I am advocating an iterative research agenda that moves from one design type to another and includes both data-based correlation probes and intensive case studies as complementary activities in the search for an improved comparative theory of foreign policy. The most efficient sequence of designs clearly defies *a priori* specification; the sequence must depend upon what the researcher learns at each step. On the other hand, several conceptual considerations strongly indicate that both correlational and case study inquiries should adopt mutually directed dyads as the case for analysis if the enterprise of comparative foreign policy reseach is to move ahead more quickly.

Notes

I am indebted to Jack Levy for some preliminary thoughts and to the editors and other conference participants for their many valuable comments, but none of them is liable for anything written here.

1 Selection of size, wealth and political accountability variables can of course be traced to Rosenau's (1966) initial conception of pre-theory. Rosenau himself may have had these categories brought to mind by the "attribute space" dimensions distilled in Rummel's (e.g., 1972) massive factor analytic studies.
2 One could as easily come to the opposite conclusion on this point. Denying that others have influence over the first state is equally consistent with the assumption that the state's actions have *no* impact on others and, therefore, that the system is either static or that it changes for reasons independent of the foreign policy behavior of any states.
3 Most and Starr's (1983) analysis of war also illustrates that policy makers must be cognizant of outcomes, not merely of their own outputs. Again, we see the assumption of goal-directedness at work.
4 For present purposes, I will restrict the discussion to the single case study design. Multiple, "comparative" case study strategies are considered by Verba, 1967; Lijphart, 1971, 1975; and George, 1982.
5 Moreover, because "détente" connotes a change in officials' dispositions, a sustained détente between traditional antagonists implies more than the additive sum of their mutually directed interactions, including such additional consequences as increased domestic welfare if military expenditure burdens are lessened and greater security for yet other societies.
6 In Chapter 5 Dixon uses the US–Soviet dyad to illustrate a novel and intriguing alternative correlational technique with which to examine interaction sequences as departures from null expectations.
7 Cook and Campbell (1979, pp. 20–1) synopsize the antidotal "Quine-Duhem

thesis" to the effect that apparent empirical falsification is particularly susceptible to error. Thus, the point here should be taken with appropriate caution.

8 As Russett (1970a, p. 437) ably illustrates, statistical studies can help to determine that a cause is necessary after a case study has erroneously suggested that it is sufficient. But this opportunity arises when, as he suggests, one begins the research sequence with a heuristic case study. He ends by proposing a research agenda similar to that which follows.

9 This observation may help to account for the weakness of statistical relationships uncovered in most monadic studies of the domestic-foreign hypothesis (e.g., Rummel 1963, 1964; Tanter, 1966).

10

Structure and Action in Militarized Disputes

RUSSELL J. LENG

The structure of any international crisis is organic rather than artificial; it is the result of gradual growth; and however much one may seek to detach and mount the specimens for purposes of exposition, it must never be forgotten that at the time they were part of the thought, feeling, and action of sentient human beings, exposed to all the impulses and fallibility of human nature.

Harold Nicolson, *The Congress of Vienna*

Introduction

This research is an attempt to "detach and mount" international crises, to classify them as one would biological specimens. Such an undertaking assumes that the evolution of each crisis can be reconstructed and classified as a distinct behavioral type, represented by the actions of the participants, and linked to their perceptions of the structure of the dispute. As an example of applied comparative foreign policy research, this study illustrates some of the advantages and limitations of the macro quantitative research strategy it represents.

Three years ago Charles Gochman and the present author published a paper (Leng and Gochman, 1982) describing a typology of militarized disputes, or crises,[1] based on three behavioral dimensions: militarization, escalation and reciprocity. One purpose of this study is to revise and refine that typology. As such it is an extension of an effort in description, classification and comparison. But it is also one step in a larger cumulative research effort—the Behavioral Correlates of War project—to determine the most salient differences between those militarized disputes that end in war and those that do not.

178

The earlier Leng and Gochman (1982) study ranked the behavioral types according to their relative war-proneness. The pattern of dispute behavior described by each category was treated as a predictor of the relative likelihood of the dispute ending in war. This study begins one step earlier in the hypothetical causal chain to consider possible links between the structure of the dispute and the bargaining behavior of the participants. The approach is similar to that taken by Snyder and Diesing (1977) in their comprehensive qualitative study of interstate crises. Dispute behavior is viewed as determined to a large extent by the participants' perceptions of the dispute *structure*, that is, of their relative motivation and usable military capability.

In sum, the unit of analysis is the dispute dyad (see the Richardson chapter above); the dependent variable is the dispute type, which is based on the actions of the disputants over the course of the dispute; and the independent variable is the dispute structure, which is based on each disputant's perception of its motivation and usable capability relative to the other.

Although the study focuses on the dispute structure as the independent variable, the intent is not to deny the potential salience of predictors of behavior mentioned elsewhere in this volume, such as variations in the attributes of decision units (Chapter 16), in the decision-making process (Chapter 13), or role conceptions (Chapter 14). Rather, the approach is to investigate the research problem one link further along in the assumed causal chain that leads from the attributes of the disputants, and the situations with which they are confronted, to the link between the resulting perceptions of the dispute structure and dispute behavior.

The Original Study

The typology presented in the earlier Leng and Gochman (1982) study provides the departure point for this chapter, so I will begin by describing its principal characteristics. The three behavioral dimensions led to eight categories of disputes, with each category defined according to whether it scored above or below the mean (for a sample of thirty militarized disputes) on each of the three dimensions. The "Fight" category, for example, was characterized by scores above the mean on all three dimensions: highly militarized, escalating upward in conflictive actions, and with a high level of reciprocity in the exchange of conflictive acts. All but one of the seven cases falling into this category ended in war. At the other end of the scale, each of the four cases falling into the "Prudence" category, with its low scores on all three dimensions, was resolved short of war.

The thirty cases were randomly drawn from lists of militarized disputes occurring between 1816 and 1975. Events data tracing the behavior of the disputants in each case were generated from the accounts of journalists and historians, then coded according to the Behavioral Correlates of War typology designed by Leng and Singer (1977). The coded events served as the raw data for computing the measures of militarization, escalation and reciprocity. Militarization tapped the relative prominence of threats, demonstrations and uses of military force; escalation focused on increases in the number, magnitude and mix of conflictive versus cooperative acts over the course of the dispute; reciprocity measured the extent to which the disputants responded to each others' actions in kind and magnitude.[2]

We found that different behavioral patterns were associated with different propensities for disputes to evolve into wars, and that the ordering of these propensities closely corresponded to what we had hypothesized in ranking the dispute types according to their expected war proneness. There was, of course, some variance within the categories, as well as between them, and we explored the reasons for the within-category variance in a follow-up study using nonbehavioral variables (stakes and capabilities) as predictors (Gochman and Leng, 1983).

In the second study we dropped the militarization dimension because it was positively correlated ($r = 0.53$) with the degree of escalation.

Revisions and Refinements in the Typology

The revised typology contains two major substantive changes. (1) As in the study mentioned above, the militarization measure has been dropped, leaving two dimensions of interest: escalation and reciprocity. (2) The measurement of escalation has been changed to take account of differences in the mix of cooperative and conflictive actions of *each* of the parties. In the original typology (Leng and Gochman, 1982), the dispute remained the unit of analysis throughout, so that a single measurement was taken of the escalation of the dispute based on the aggregate actions of the two parties. The current study employs separate measures of the levels of conflictive/cooperative actions for parties on each side. Dividing levels of escalation in conflictive behavior for each of the parties into three classes (high, moderate and low) yields an exhaustive and mutually exclusive typology based on the six most useful types in the Leng and Gochman (1982) study. As a result of these changes, six of the eight ideal types appearing in the original Leng and Gochman (1982) typology are retained in the current version: Fight, Resistance, Standoff, Put-down, Dialogue, and Prudence.[3]

Dispute Behavior and Structure

Because the revised typology is based on separate measures of each disputant's actions, it is logically possible to link the behavior of each to its perception of the dispute structure. The best-known attempt to make such a connection through a comparative study is that of Snyder and Diesing (1977).

Snyder and Diesing (1977) view the *structure* of the dispute as a function of the relative (1) motivation or interests (strategic, reputational and intrinsic), and (2) usable military capabilities of the opposing sides. The intersection of the interests and usable capabilities of the two sides determines the overall structure of the dispute, which in turn determines their respective preference orderings regarding the dispute outcome: that is, a political victory, submission, compromise, or deadlock (war).[4] Each party's preference ordering—and its perception of the opponent's—is presumed by Snyder and Diesing to be the primary determinant of its behavior over the course of the dispute. Thus when one side views itself as having an advantage in the interests/capability balance, it is more likely to bargain in a more aggressive, coercive manner than a party that sees itself at a disadvantage. Of course, it is also possible for the perceptions of the interests/capability balance to be symmetrical, with each side having the same preference orderings. In these instances we would expect the pattern of dispute behavior to be roughly the same for the two parties.

Just as we would expect the proportions in the use of coercive behavior by the two sides to reflect the structural interests/capability balance, we would expect the *magnitude* of the use of coercive actions by each side to reflect the importance of the interests at stake. That is, we would assume that states will accept a higher risk of war when more vital interests are at stake. Policy makers may even decide to go to war when they perceive their state at a serious military disadvantage if the stakes are high enough.

Each of the six behavioral types can be linked logically to the dispute structure as perceived by the participants; then the hypothesized linkages can be tested against real-world cases.[5] Although a rigorous test of the hypothesized relationship is not attempted in this study, some promising associations with selected real-world cases are illustrated in the manner described in the next section.

Method

The taxonomic effort begins with the construction of models of the six ideal types which form the revised dispute typology. Following the description of the ideal types, a candidate case is chosen from those real-world cases in the original Leng and Gochman (1982) study that fell into that type. The candidate case is *not* selected randomly. Rather it is based on the scores it received on the three dimensions in the original study, and on the accounts of the interactions provided by diplomatic historians. Those which appear to conform most closely to the ideal type are chosen. By the same token, the candidate cases are also those where the structural properties of the disputes—the motivation/capability balance and the importance of the stakes—are relatively unambiguous.

For each of the cases selected, a smoothed plot of the patterns of actions by the participants (weighted according to the mix and magnitude of conflict and cooperation within one-week intervals) is compared to the ideal type to see if it is possible to obtain a real-world referent from the sample cases. The comparisons provide an initial test of the correspondence between the ideal behavioral types and presumably representative cases from the real world, and a visual comparison of the differences in patterns of conflict behavior across categories.

Finally, these observed patterns of behavior are compared to what one would expect to find given the structural characteristics of each dispute. At this stage of the research, the observed relationship between the dispute structure and the behavior of the participants in the selected real-world cases can be no more than suggestive; nevertheless, the findings offer an indication of the potential value of the approach to students of comparative foreign policy.

Revised Typology of Militarized Disputes

Figures 10.1–6 illustrate the expected behavior patterns for each of the parties in the six ideal types. These are followed by a brief description of each dispute type, and its presumed relationship to the dispute structure. A summary of the behavioral characteristics of the six ideal types appears in Table 10.1.

Fight

Behavior In the original study (Leng and Gochman, 1982, p. 675) we described a Fight as a dispute in which the "antagonists employ mutu-

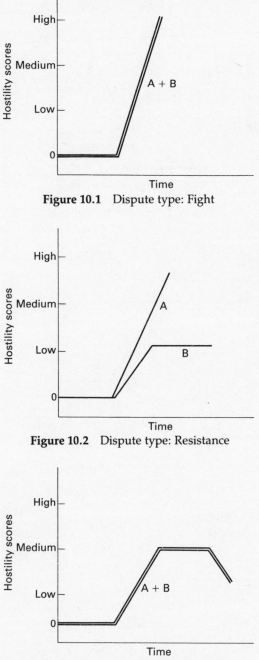

Figure 10.1 Dispute type: Fight

Figure 10.2 Dispute type: Resistance

Figure 10.3 Dispute type: Standoff

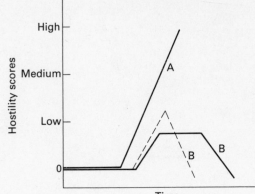

Figure 10.4 Dispute type: Put-down

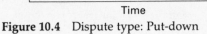

Figure 10.5 Dispute type: Dialogue

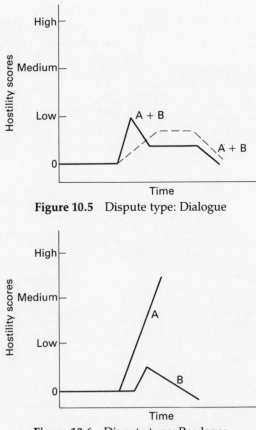

Figure 10.6 Dispute type: Prudence

ally coercive (bullying) influence strategies *or* one antagonist employs a bullying strategy while the adversary responds in a tit-for-tat manner." The level of conflict spirals upward to a very high level of conflictive behavior on both sides. There is an abrupt and continuing pattern of increasingly conflictive behavior for both sides, with a high degree of reciprocity in the mix and magnitude of conflictive and cooperative actions.

Structure   One would expect this interaction pattern to be associated with a structurally symmetrical dispute, where each party is highly motivated and each views its military capabilities as at least the equal of the other. Each is willing to assume a high risk of war to achieve victory.

Resistance

Behavior   One antagonist pursues a coercive strategy, while the other stands firm. One party's behavior is much like that seen in a Fight: an abrupt and continuing pattern of increasingly conflictive actions. Its adversary responds in kind, but at a more moderate rate of escalation. The level of reciprocity in the mix and magnitude of behavior is relatively low.

Structure   This dispute type should be structurally asymmetrical as well. Both parties are highly motivated, but one party has a significant edge in usable military capability.

Standoff

Behavior   The parties demonstrate their firmness through threats or military displays, but the pattern of escalation becomes asymptotic. Neither party is willing to retreat from its stand, yet neither is willing to increase the level of tension beyond a certain point. The dispute remains for some time near the peak level of hostility, then tapers off, moving slowly to a compromise, or ending in a stalemate. The behavior patterns are roughly the same for both parties: an abrupt upward movement in the magnitude of conflictive actions levels off as an asymptotic curve.

Structure   The dispute structure should be symmetrical. Each party is sufficiently motivated and confident of its capabilities to prefer war over surrender, but each is willing to accept a compromise to avoid a costly war.

Put-Down

Behavior In a Put-down one antagonist employs a coercive bargaining strategy with increasingly severe threats or displays of force; its adversary does not respond in kind, but yields after only a modest attempt to demonstrate resolve. Thus the observed patterns of action should be asymmetric. A's actions can be described as an abrupt or gradual pattern of increasingly conflictive actions; B may exhibit one or two short upward 'pulses' of more conflictive actions, but soon moves to a downward pattern of more accommodative actions.

Structure There is considerable asymmetry in the motivations or military capabilities—or both—of the two parties. One side submits after only a moderate demonstration of resolve in the face of a much more powerful and/or determined adversary.

Dialogue

Behavior The Dialogue has the greatest proportion of mutually accommodative behavior of any of the six types. Both sides pursue accommodative bargaining strategies either through conciliatory influence attempts by each, or by one party employing an appeasing strategy and the other succumbing to its appeal. The level of escalation is low, while the level of reciprocity is high.

Structure This should be a structurally symmetrical dispute. The most likely candidate would be a dispute where the stakes are not high enough for either party to accept a high risk of war, that is, where motivation is relatively low and usable military capabilities are evenly matched.

Prudence

Behavior Assertiveness by one party results in early submission by the other. Party A abruptly, or gradually, escalates the level of its conflictive actions; B does not reciprocate, but responds with abruptly or gradually more accommodative behavior. The level of reciprocity is quite low.

Structure One party enjoys a significant edge in usable military capabilities, and the level of motivation for the weaker party is low.

Table 10.1 *Dispute Types and Behavior Patterns*

Dispute type	Parties	Hostility level	Escalation pattern
Fight	A & B	High	Abrupt, continuing
Resistance	A	High	Abrupt or gradual, continuing
	B	High or moderate	Abrupt or gradual, levels off
Standoff	A & B	Moderate	Gradual, asymptotic
Put-down	A	High or moderate	Abrupt or gradual, continuing
	B	Low	Short upward pulse, or gradual and asymptotic
Dialogue	A & B	Low	Abrupt and quickly levels off, or gradual and asymptotic
Prudence	A	Moderate	Abrupt or gradual, continuing
	B	Low	Very little, if any

Hypothetical and Real-World Disputes

Having described the ideal types, the next step is to see whether they conform to disputes that might be observed in the real world. Six candidate cases have been chosen from the sample that was used in the original study. Each candidate had scores on the original three dimensions that placed it in the appropriate category in the 1982 (Leng and Gochman) study, and each has been described by observers or scholars as possessing behavioral and structural characteristics that are consistent with the types as they are described above. With these similarities already in hand, the question is whether the observed time series of conflictive and cooperative actions for each of the respective participants approximate the ideal types described in Figures 10.1–6.

As in the Leng and Gochman (1982, p. 674) study, individual actions by each party are assigned to a weighted category on a hostility-friendliness continuum developed by Rubin and Hill (1973) and modified to fit the Behavioral Correlates of War typology. These are then aggregated into weekly time intervals by summing the resulting scores, which range from +3 (most hostile) to −3 (most friendly).

To obtain a plot of behavioral patterns of escalation and de-escalation that may be easily compared to the simplified models in Figures 10.1–6, a compound resistant smoother[6] is employed to reduce the effects of outliers on the time series.

187

Fight: The Six-Day War, 1967

Narrative accounts of the dispute between Israel and Egypt that immediately preceded the Six-Day War of 1967 suggest that it would be an excellent candidate for the prototypical pattern of rapidly spiraling escalation associated with a Fight. The dispute yielded the highest combined escalation score for any of the thirty cases in the original study (Leng and Gochman, 1982, p. 676), and contemporary accounts (Yost, 1968; Lacqueur, 1969) described this as a dispute where escalating tensions and patterns of threat and counterthreat developed a momentum of their own.

Structurally it was a symmetrical dispute where the stakes were extremely high for both sides. The territory in question was of vital strategic importance for both sides, with the outcome of the dispute determining the future balance of power in the region. Both also saw a strong stand as critical to their reputation for resolve in future conflicts. Each assumed that it was at least the military equal of the other.

The smoothed time series for the weighted actions of each side appear in Figure 10.7.

There is virtually no interaction between the two parties prior to Egypt's decision to place its forces on a war footing and to move troops into Sinai on May 14. Those actions initiated the abrupt and continuing pattern of escalation in conflictive actions for both parties that is indica-

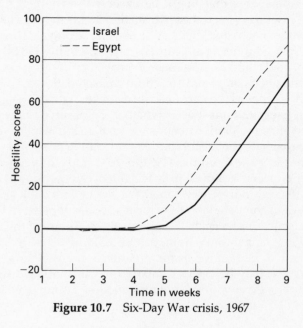

Figure 10.7   Six-Day War crisis, 1967

188

tive of a Fight. Israel's weekly scores lag behind those of Egypt in the magnitude of conflictive actions, indicating that Egypt is taking the lead in escalating the crisis. Otherwise the pattern is identical to that in Figure 10.1. There is a very high degree of reciprocity in the mix and magnitude of conflictive actions, $r = 0.75$.[7]

Resistance: The Italo-Ethiopian War, 1935

The interactions between the bullying Italians and the militarily weaker, but highly motivated, Ethiopians would appear to provide an excellent illustration of the asymmetric pattern of escalation expected of this type.

Structurally, the dispute is asymmetrical because of the decided Italian advantage in military capability. On the other hand, the Ethiopians correctly perceived that failure to resist would mean that Ethiopia would lose a significant portion of its territory, whereas Mussolini was in a position to compromise without serious diplomatic consequences. Thus, while Mussolini preferred war to compromise, the Ethiopians preferred war to submission.

The smoothed time series of weighted actions for the two parties are depicted in Figure 10.8.

The patterns of escalating conflict for the two sides are both less

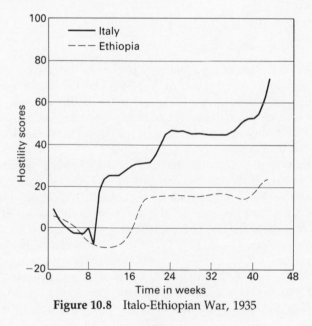

Figure 10.8 Italo-Ethiopian War, 1935

189

symmetrical and less consistent than in the case of the crisis preceding the Six-Day War. There is a lull after the clash at Wal Wal, during which the Ethiopians bring the matter to the consideration of the League of Nations. Then there is an abrupt shift upward as Italy begins troop movements at about the same time that Ethiopian actions are becoming more accommodative. A month passes before the Ethiopians respond in kind. This is followed by another lull in activity as Britain and France pursue peace initiatives. The conflict remains at the new level of hostility through the summer; until the mass mobilization of Italian forces in early September presages the outbreak of war.

Aside from a short downward pulse indicating Italian efforts to reassure the British and French at the beginning of the crisis, the curve of escalation in coercive actions for Italy is steeper and more consistently upward. The pattern is consistent with findings by Maoz (1983) in a wider study of crisis bargaining: The initiator (Italy) controls the evolution of the dispute. Ethiopia stands firm, but Italy retains the initiative and is always the first to raise the level of coercive actions.

With some modest variations, the behavior pattern in Figure 10.8 is quite similar to that depicted in Figure 10.2. The latter does not take into account the possibility of either lulls in activity or the efforts at accommodation by the weaker party. However, when the efforts at compromise fail, the weaker party attempts to match the preparations for war rather than submit—a pattern consistent with the structure of the dispute.

Standoff: The Berlin Wall Crisis, 1961

The Berlin Wall crisis of 1961 has been chosen as the best candidate for a model Standoff. George and Smoke (1974, pp. 134–6) have described the careful probing actions of the two sides in this dispute as "controlled pressure," an apt label for our verbal description of the abrupt, but controlled, asymptotic pattern of escalation associated with this type.

The behavior patterns depicted in Figure 10.9 are remarkably symmetrical. The conflict escalates abruptly in mid-August with the Soviet erection of the Wall but the peak level of conflictive action is less than half of that reached just prior to the outbreak of the Italian-Ethiopian War and one-third the level of magnitude reached in the crisis leading to the Six-Day War. The dispute then de-escalates at a fairly rapid rate, but it does not return to the pre-crisis level. The one exception is a flare-up at the end of the crisis—by the Soviets just prior to Khrushchev's decision to abandon the ultimatum[8] that signaled the start of the escalation of the dispute. Otherwise, the pattern mirrors that of the

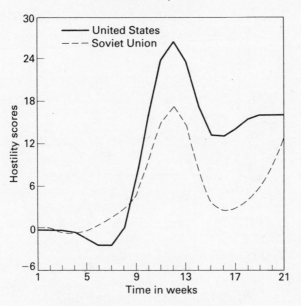

Figure 10.9 Berlin Wall Crisis, 1961

ideal type illustrated in Figure 10.3. The level of reciprocity is moderately high ($r = 0.49$ for first-order difference scores).

This is a structurally symmetrical dispute between evenly matched powers, with the USSR holding a slight local military advantage, and involves relatively high stakes for both sides. This dispute was included in the comparative qualitative study of Snyder and Diesing (1977), who described the structure as Prisoner's Dilemma for both sides, that is, each preferred a compromise over war, and war over submission—very much what one might expect in a Standoff as we have described it.

Put-Down: British-Russian Crisis, 1878

The British-Russian crisis that grew out of the Russo-Turkish War in the latter part of the nineteenth century represents a classic case of one great power "staring down" another through an impressive show of force. In this case it was the measured advance of a British naval squadron toward Constantinople. It has been chosen from among the four cases falling into the Put-down category in the earlier study for this reason, and because it represents the most purely dyadic of those four cases.

The patterns of weighted actions appearing in Figure 10.10 provide a

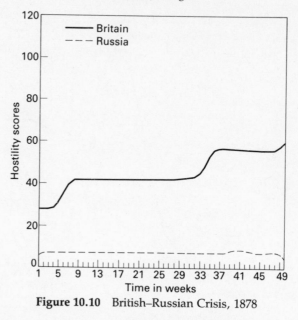

Figure 10.10 British–Russian Crisis, 1878

striking departure from the three previous disputes. Not only is the level of reciprocity low, but the Russians make only the most token response to the growing British threat until they quietly retreat at the end of the dispute. Britain, meanwhile, gradually ups the ante until the Russians yield to their demands. The markedly asymmetric pattern (r = 0.16) follows the broad curves depicted in Figure 10.4, but the British escalation is slow and deliberate, with two extended lulls interrupting the upward pattern. The Russian actions exhibit even less of an initial response in kind than the ideal model suggests, but this could be deceptive since the Russian behavior to which the British object is directed at a third party—Turkey.[9] Those actions do not appear in the dyadic representation of the dispute.

The lulls in the British actions, which reflect changes in the movements of the naval squadron, indicate a more calculated and cautious demonstration of force than the model suggests. This could be the result either of indecision on the part of the British government, or of an attempt to allow breathing periods for the Russians to seek a face-saving diplomatic retreat.[10] The low level of direct Russian response to the British actions is consistent with the purely defensive reactions of the militarily weaker party in a Put-down. It also indicates the limits of a purely dyadic representation of the dispute.

192

Dialogue: The First Moroccan Crisis, 1905–6

A dialogue, the mildest of the six militarized dispute types, is a symmetrical dispute with low levels of escalation for both sides. Of the cases falling into this category in the original study, the First Moroccan Crisis of 1905–6 yielded the lowest escalation score (22 with the mean for the sample being 49).

The dispute (see Figure 10.11) began with a German challenge to exclusive French influence in Morocco, when the Kaiser made a dramatic visit to Tangier at the end of March, 1905. The Kaiser's vague verbal warnings barely register on the smoothed plot. His demands for a European conference to settle the Moroccan question initially were rejected by the French, then accepted when France was assured of British backing. The conference at Algeciras in Spain began with a naval show of strength by the French and British, which appears as the upward pulse in conflictive action in early 1906. Once under way, it was clear that the Germans had been outmaneuvered. The conference ended in a diplomatic victory for the French, although Germany was allowed a face-saving "compromise."

Aside from the expected low level of conflictive activity for both sides, the most striking impression from the plot in Figure 10.11 is the predominantly accommodative pattern of behavior on the part of Germany. This indicates that the dispute was not as symmetrical as the

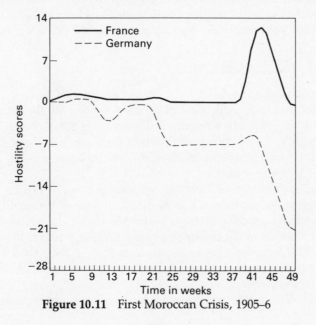

Figure 10.11 First Moroccan Crisis, 1905–6

ideal model for the Dialogue category would suggest. On the other hand, following the Kaiser's initial veiled threat, the only action that could qualify as militarily threatening is the French naval show of strength at the opening of the conference at Algeciras. The Germans are not coerced into accepting a face-saving compromise; they are diplomatically outmaneuvered by the French (and British). Thus, while the plot in Figure 10.11 is not as symmetrical as that in Figure 10.5, the overall pattern of very low escalation by both sides is consistent with the basic model. The question is whether the difference in the mix of cooperative and conflictive actions by the two sides is great enough to place the conflict on the borderline between a Dialogue and Prudence, the next category.

The dispute is structurally symmetric as far as the primary disputants are concerned; however, the diplomatic intervention of the British in support of the French swung the diplomatic balance at Algeciras toward the French position. Thus Snyder and Diesing (1977, pp. 118–19) classify the structure of the dispute as "Called Bluff": the French, with British support, prefer a compromise to war, but war to submission; the Germans prefer submission to war. The outcome, therefore, is a German submission to a face-saving compromise. That appears to be reflected in our purely dyadic plot of the dispute. Plots of the dispute with the French and British actions aggregated for one side and those of the Germans and Austrians on the other differ from Figure 10.11 only in the magnitude of the scores. Nevertheless, the introduction of the British into the dispute in its later stages also raises the question of whether the dispute belongs in the Prudence category.

Prudence: The Anschluss, 1938

The German-Austrian *Anschluss* crisis of 1938 typifies the case of a state prudently yielding, with little resistance, before an adversary with overwhelming military strength. Following von Schuschnigg's meeting with Hitler at Berchtesgaden, when the Austrian Chancellor was bullied into an agreement to bring Austrian Nazis into his cabinet, Austria's fate was sealed.

The smoothed plot of German-Austrian actions in Figure 10.12 is very close to the representation of the ideal type in Figure 10.6. Germany's actions describe a smooth upward curve of coercive actions. Hitler applied as much pressure as was necessary under the circumstances. The Austrian Chancellor protests at the outset, then attempts to offer a compromise, and, finally, submits to Germany's overwhelming military superiority.

The one element in the observed pattern that is not represented in

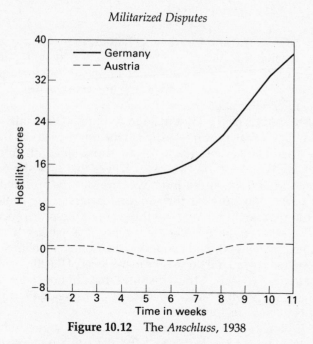

Figure 10.12 The *Anschluss*, 1938

Figure 10.6 involves the efforts by the less belligerent party, Austria, to encourage a compromise settlement through accommodative initiatives. This is an omission that was noted in the ideal model for Resistance, one of the two other asymmetric disputes.

The *Anschluss* is very asymmetric structurally as well. Germany not only has a tremendous military advantage; Austria also lacks the unity to establish any strong motivation to resist. A large portion of the Austrian nation welcomes the reunification of the German peoples.

Findings

Behavior Patterns   With the possible exception of the First Moroccan Crisis, the smoothed plots of the actions of the participants in the six real-world crises provide an excellent demonstration of the patterns exhibited in the abstract models.

The modest observed differences between the two, moreover, represent variations that are consistent with conceptual notions of the ideal types. In two (Italo-Ethiopian and British-Russian) of the three asymmetric disputes, there are extended "lulls," or static periods, in what is otherwise a consistent pattern of increasingly hostile moves by the stronger party. These are in no way inconsistent (the curve of escalation never moves downward) with the conceptual meaning of these

195

two types (Resistance and Put-down). Rather, they indicate breaks in the rising tension that allow time for deliberation by both parties. As such, they *could* provide "windows of opportunity" for diplomatic intervention to avoid a war. That was the intent in the British-Russian crisis; the Italian intentions were less salutary.

The ideal models also do not include accommodative initiatives by the weaker party that appear—as dips in the time series—in the asymmetric real-world disputes. These too are consistent with an intuitive notion of the types. In the two cases where this is observed (Italo-Ethiopian and *Anschluss*) the initiatives are not reciprocated by the stronger party. Nevertheless they suggest points in the evolution of the dispute that might tell us something about the preference orderings of the stronger party (whether or not it is willing to accept a compromise settlement), and about the likely outcome of the dispute. It is interesting to compare these dips in the level of hostility with those observed in the two symmetrical disputes that did not end in war (the Berlin Wall and the First Moroccan Crises). In those cases, dips in the level of hostility *are* reciprocated.

These findings are interesting in light of the suggested linkage between the observed patterns and the dispute structure. In those disputes where the stronger party preferred war over compromise (Italo-Ethiopian and *Anschluss*) the lulls are followed by an increase in coercive activity by the stronger party, and accommodative moves by the weaker party are not reciprocated. In the structurally symmetrical disputes that did not end in war (the Berlin Wall and the First Moroccan Crises), the accommodative moves *are* reciprocated.

The other variation observed in the real-world cases that does not appear in the ideal types is an upward or downward "tail" at the end of the crisis. These almost appear as flags indicating the outcome: both parties abruptly increase the level of hostility as war approaches in the Italo-Ethiopian dispute; one party's hostility scores go up and the other's drop signaling submission in the British-Russian crisis and the *Anschluss*; both drop prior to the compromise in the First Moroccan Crisis. The exception is the Berlin Wall Crisis where there is a brief rise in Soviet hostility prior to Khrushchev's withdrawal of his ultimatum. Whatever the specific reasons, the point of inflection of these changes suggest important turning points in the evolution of the disputes.

Structure and Behavior The observed patterns of behavior also are consistent with the structural characteristics of the disputes. The three disputes in which the military capabilities and motivations of the two sides are most evenly balanced (Six-Day War, the Berlin Wall, and the First Moroccan Crises) are also the disputes exhibiting the most symmetry in the observed patterns of behavior. The most dramatic escalation of conflictive behavior occurs in the two cases where the stakes are the highest—for both sides in the symmetrical Six-Day War crisis and for the weaker party in the asymmetrical Italo-Ethiopian War crisis. In the Berlin Wall and British-Russian crises, where important strategic issues are stake, but not survival itself, the pattern of escalation is more moderate. The disputes show the lowest patterns of escalation in the First Moroccan and *Anschluss* crises. The stakes were relatively low in the Moroccan crisis, and, if the long-term stakes were high in the case of the *Anschluss*, Austria was seriously divided over the issue.

Perhaps the most interesting aspect of the patterns of behavior depicted in Figures 10.6–12 is the relationship between the two parties in asymmetric disputes. The plots appearing in Figures 10.8, 10.10 and 10.12 all illustrate the extent to which the stronger party controls the escalation of the dispute. The Italian, British and German actions seem almost unrelated to those of the other party. They do not appear to be "reacting" to the responses of the other side, but to be following strategies of increasingly coercive actions until the other side submits to their demands. This underlines the importance that structural characteristics can exert on dispute behavior.

Conclusions

What has all this accomplished? First, as a representative categorization of the behavioral properties of militarized disputes, the current typology is a significant refinement of the original Leng and Gochman (1982) typology. It is more parsimonious; the measures of dispute behavior are more direct; differences in the behavior patterns for the two primary disputants are taken into account; and the behavior patterns exhibited in Figures 10.1–6 provide a visually suggestive means of comparing real-world cases with categories in the typology, as well as with each other.

Second, the validity of the ideal models presented in Figures 10.1–6 is supported by the correspondence between the models and the patterns of behavior observed in the six real-world cases. Moreover, as the departures from the basic pattern mentioned above suggest, the ideal models provide a useful benchmark to observe variations from the norm. Examining these variations should aid us in attempting to identify turning points in the evolution of disputes, or to discern significant behavioral differences between those disputes within particular categories that ended in war and those that did not.

A third finding was that the real-world cases demonstrated a high correspondence between the structural properties of the dispute and the expected observed patterns of behavior. This is not surprising, nor is the relationship between dispute escalation and the gravity of the issues at stake. The remarkable reciprocity shown in the plots of actions by the two parties in structurally symmetrical disputes is consistent with our findings in more comprehensive studies (Leng and Wheeler, 1979; Leng, 1984). The lack of reciprocity in structurally asymmetrical disputes is also consistent with our expectations regarding the structure of the dispute, as well as with findings by others (Maoz, 1983). This suggests that the decision makers' perceptions of the dispute structure act as important constraints on their behavior.

Future Research As suggestive as these findings may be, they represent only one step in an ongoing effort to discern the causes and consequences of the actions of states in militarized disputes.

The next steps will include a further refinement of the six basic dispute types, using a Box-Jenkins (1976) approach to modeling time series. Then the larger sample of real-world disputes from the Behavioral Correlates of War project will be classified according to their correspondence with particular types. With the dependent variable more precisely defined, the next step will be to develop operational measures of dispute structures to allow rigorous tests of the relationship between dispute structures and dispute behavior.

The final step will be to investigate the relationship between the attributes of the participants, broadly defined, and their perceptions of the structure of the dispute. This would entail moving one link back in the causal chain to consider the relative potency of the most promising idiosyncratic, role, governmental, societal and systemic variables on decision makers' perceptions of the dispute structure. A logical place to start would be with some of those mentioned in other chapters in this volume.

Notes

1 To insure clarity and to retain consistency with other Correlates of War studies, the term "militarized dispute" is used to describe conflicts in which an explicit threat of force is used by at least one of the two sides. For the full operational definition of a militarized dispute, see Leng and Gochman, 1983.
2 For a full discussion of sources and operational measures, see Leng and Gochman, 1982, pp. 674–5; Leng and Gochman, 1983, p. 101.
3 The two categories that have been dropped (Debate and Tirade) required an

unlikely mix of low militarization and high escalation; consequently they yielded only one borderline case from the sample of thirty (Leng and Gochman, 1982, pp. 677, 682).

4 Snyder and Diesing (1977, ch. 2) use game-theoretical terminology to describe the dispute structures. In a dispute described as Prisoner's Dilemma, for example, each player prefers victory over compromise, compromise over war, and war over submission; whereas in a Chicken game the ordering is victory first, compromise second, *submission* third, and war fourth. In Bully it is victory first, *war* second, compromise third, and submission fourth. And for Big Bully, it is *war* first, victory second, compromise third, and submission fourth. The dispute structure may be symmetric, say with both parties playing Prisoner's Dilemma, or asymmetric, with one party playing Prisoner's Dilemma and the other party playing Chicken in what Snyder and Diesing (1977) named "Called Bluff."

5 A preliminary test (Leng and Walker, 1982), which was limited to cases employed by Snyder and Diesing (1977), compared the behavior patterns predicted by Snyder and Diesing (1977) with those obtained in an overlapping sample of cases from the Behavioral Correlates of War project, with mixed results.

6 The formula is *4253H, Twice*. This combination starts by taking a running median over a span of 4 observations, re-centers each data point with a running median of the 2 middle-sized values, re-smooths using spans of 5 and 3, and ends with a combination of running weighted averages (H). Once the outliers have been smoothed by the process, the data are "re-roughed" to regain patterns in outliers lost to smoothing. For an easily accessible explanation of the process, see Velleman and Hoaglin, 1981, pp. 159–84. A more rigorous statistical examination appears in Velleman, 1980, pp. 609–15.

7 The reciprocity scores which are taken from Leng and Gochman, 1982, pp. 676–7, have been differenced once to remove serial correlations.

8 On June 4, Khrushchev reissued his 1958 threat to sign a separate peace treaty with East Germany and thereby end allied occupation rights in Berlin if the Western powers began negotiations to reach a permanent settlement. The deadline was now set for December 31, 1961.

9 The British concern is with the Russian advance toward Constantinople as the war intensified. These Russian moves do not appear as actions directed against the British, although it is British strategic interests in the area that prompt the show of force.

10 In this respect, the British strategy is not unlike that which they used during the crisis preceding the Falklands War a little over a century later.

PART IV

Cognitive Processes
in Foreign Policy Decisions

11

Opening the 'Black Box': Cognitive Processing and Optimal Choice in Foreign Policy Decision Making

CHARLES A. POWELL, JAMES W. DYSON
and HELEN E. PURKITT

Three main themes are developed in this chapter. First, the effort to develop a comparative theory of foreign policy at the micro level has been slowed by a lack of systematic research on how decision makers achieve an understanding of a problem, make choices, and justify those decisions to relevant client groups. Without such research, significant progress toward a general theory of foreign policy decision making is unlikely. More needs to be known about how individual decision makers use cognitions (i.e., behave mentally) to process information. Comparative foreign policy knows more about situational, organizational and systemic factors having the potential to influence decision output than about how policy makers gain problem understanding and select problem responses in specific decision-making situations.

Our second theme is that the time is now ripe for a renewal of research interest in the study of foreign policy decision making at the micro level. Although there has long been a recognition of the centrality of decision making to an understanding of foreign policy making, at least since the appearance of Snyder's (1954) decision-making framework, a research effort at the micro level is now more likely to produce useful results.

Optimism about the potential payoffs from future research on foreign policy decision making is tied to the remarkable convergence in research results that show patterned regularities in the ways people process information in making "intuitive" decisions. Research on human information processing in experimental cognitive and social psychology indicates that cognitive limitations and "cognitive conceit"

203

(i.e., an unwarranted faith in the adequacy of intuition in decision making) impose severe constraints on the individual's ability to formulate adequate, effective and "rational" solutions to complex problems. These insights about problem-solving behavior suggest some basic questions about the role of cognition, information processing, and the use of intuitively derived heuristics as fundamental constraints influencing the formulation of foreign policy, especially in cross-level and cross-national comparisons. The idea or image of the foreign policy decision maker as a limited information processor may serve a useful heuristic function in a variety of existing theoretical frameworks and methodologies currently used in the study of foreign policy decision making.

Thirdly, recent developments in game-theoretic techniques for modeling complex situations in a clear and easily communicated manner may provide an effective means for studying the actual behavior of decision makers under varying conditions of situational complexity. As Hudson, Hermann and Singer (1985) show, situational characteristics play an important role in foreign policy behavior. In addition, the internal structure and dynamics of the decision unit directly affect the final foreign policy outcome of the unit and also modulate the influence of external situational factors. For example, in the case of a decision unit characterized by multiple autonomous groups, there may be an internal "game" in which the outcome can be a conflictual deadlock or a more cooperative negotiated or bargained outcome depending on the "zero-sum" or "non-zero-sum" nature of the relationship among the groups (Hermann, Hermann and Hagan, Chapter 16). The structure and the stability of interactive situations affect both decision making at the micro level and foreign policy outputs at the aggregate level. At the micro level, game theory may be able to provide an apparatus for studying problem-solving heuristics employed by individual and group decision makers and the linkage between decisional processes and the foreign policy outputs of nation-states and other key aggregate actors in the international system. It may also provide a useful normative model of decisions under different conditions of situational complexity. That would help us to learn what information is selected and ignored by decision makers and how the selected information relates to their preferences.

Most research in comparative foreign policy has relied on some sort of input-output system model of the entire foreign policy process. The conversion process between inputs and outputs has been black-boxed or analyzed using "as if" logic based on the assumptions of one of the two dominant paradigms of political decision making (maximizing rational actor or satisficing/incrementalism). Our intent is to suggest a new logic for a rededicated research effort on foreign policy decision making.

Foreign Policy Decision Making
as a Micro Process

Research on comparative foreign policy behavior over the past several decades has been conducted predominantly at the aggregate level, focusing on nation-states and other important collectivities in the international system. Underlying much of this research is a macro-systemic model that conceptualizes the entire foreign policy process in terms of inputs and outputs. In this model, foreign policy decision making is usually viewed as a central aspect of the conversion process by which inputs are translated into the official foreign policy behaviors of nation-states. The use of this general systemic model has been useful for developing a general theoretical framework or factor theory of the major determinants of the foreign policy outputs at the aggregate level (McGowan and Shapiro, 1973). This general systemic model has also been helpful at the micro level in identifying potentially important aggregate and situational factors that may operate as determinants or constraints on the actual decisions undertaken by individual and small groups of foreign policy decision makers (Holsti, 1983, pp. 331–55).

The main limitation of this general model for enhancing our understanding of foreign policy decision making is that the foreign policy decision-making process is usually "black-boxed." Ironically, comparative foreign policy was part of a behavioral revolution in social science that asserted that only people, not nation-states, make foreign policy. Moreover, the central role played by individual decision makers in formulating foreign policy was clearly emphasized in the influential general decision-making framework developed by Snyder (1954), the most important early effort to study foreign policy decision making at the micro level. Concern for the need to open up the black box of decision making is also expressed in other chapters (13–16) of this volume. There is general agreement with Kegley's assessment (Chapter 13) of the current state of micro-analytical studies in comparative foreign policy that decision-making processes are ignored or discarded.[1]

Nevertheless, there has been some progress at the micro level among researchers who have incorporated insights from cognitive and social psychology into their research. For example, following the lead of Boulding (1971) and Jervis (1968, 1976), much of the literature in comparative foreign policy and international relations generally now routinely uses such "meta" concepts as decision-maker "perception" and "image" to describe the cognitive process of individual decision makers. Cognitive processes are widely viewed as an integral aspect of the decision-making process, and much of the past behavioral research at the micro level of foreign policy decision making has used a modified version of the psychological stimulus-response model. A variety of variables have been postulated as linking inputs with decision outputs: individual personality characteristics, roles, belief systems, situational factors, and a host of aggregate group and organizational factors that are viewed as important constraints to effective or rational decision making. (For further discussion of this research, see DeRivera, 1968; George, 1980; Hermann, 1980; Steiner, 1983; Sylvan and Chan, 1984; Hudson, Hermann and Singer, 1985; and the Kegley and Anderson chapters in this volume.)

Although a modified stimulus-response model has been used at the micro-analytic level to research the impact of such diverse factors as the attributes of specific personalities and situational factors, much of the research done in the past has focused on some aspect of cognition as a central feature of the mediating process between decision inputs and outputs. There has been some cumulative progress in understanding cognition even though researchers have used such diverse concepts as an individual's "belief system" (Abelson and Carrol, 1965; Chan, 1979), "operational code" (George, 1969) or "cognitive map" (Axelrod, 1976).

Past research on cognition shares a number of common working assumptions. First, there is general agreement that an individual's prior beliefs and expectations play a key role in structuring perceptions during all stages of the foreign policy decision-making process from the initial definition of the situation (Snyder, 1954) through problem understanding, analysis, evaluation of alternatives, and choice (Jervis, 1976, George, 1980). Secondly, selected aspects of cognition, such as prior beliefs, are generally viewed as playing a central role by serving as relatively stable filters (Boulding, 1959, 1971), or as stable sets of parameters affecting cognitions at all stages of decision making (George, 1969, 1979b). Thirdly, cognitions generally, and prior beliefs specifically, are often viewed as only one of several types of variables that influence foreign policy decision making.

This consensus on the role of cognition at a general level is not, however, matched by agreement on specifics. In fact, there is little agreement among researchers about the relative importance of cognitions for understanding specific foreign policy decisions or the official foreign policy acts of nation-states. This lack of agreement stems in part from a recognition that a variety of bureaucratic, domestic and international factors, as well as interactions among key actors, may influence the decision making of foreign policy officials and thus confound the cognitive decision making/output relationship posited in the mediated stimulus-response model. Ole Holsti succinctly summarized the general concern about this issue when he noted:

> It is not very fruitful to assume direct linkages between belief and foreign policy action [and] it is important to recognize the distinction between decisions and foreign policy actions. The literature on bureaucratic politics has illustrated the many potential sources of slippage between executive decisions and the implementation of policy in the form of foreign policy actions.
>
> (Holsti, 1976a, pp. 34–5)

Holsti suggests that the cognitions of key foreign policy decision makers may be relevant when one or more of the following conditions exist: innovative decision-making situations; long-range policy-planning situations; decisions under highly complex, ambiguous or unanticipated circumstances; decisions under stress; and decisions made by individuals at the top of an organization's hierarchy (Holsti, 1976a, p. 30). Several recent foreign policy studies have focused on the convergence between the prior beliefs of key foreign policy decision makers and selective aspects of foreign policy behaviors (e.g., Walker, 1977). Other research has attempted to identify the situations (i.e., crises) or conditions when the cognitions of policy officials might be expected to be an important factor in a particular foreign policy decision or in determining the direction of a country's foreign policy (Hermann, 1972a). More specific consensus among foreign policy researchers using the belief system concept has been retarded by the diversity of theoretical perspectives and methodologies used to study cognitive determinants of foreign policy (Holsti, 1976a; Bennett, 1981).

However, as we discuss in more detail elsewhere (Purkitt and Dyson, 1985a, 1985b), there are patterns in the results of past research on the role of beliefs and foreign policy decision making that are important for future directions in research on cognition and the decision-making process. Some research on beliefs uses an overarching concept such as a decision maker's "operational code" (George, 1969, 1979b) or "cognitive map" (Axelrod, 1976) to describe the cognitive processes of foreign policy decision makers. While there has been some convergence between selected components of such overarching frameworks (i.e., the instrumental beliefs in the George operational code perspective) and general patterns of nation-state behaviors (Walker, 1981; Rosati, 1984), there is little evidence that these general theoretical concepts adequately summarize the actual cognitions used

207

by decision makers in specific situations. (See Bennett, 1981, for a similar criticism of the cognitive mapping approach.)

The problem with such static belief system concepts is that they do not really help us to understand the actual decision processes of decision makers in specific situations. We do not know, for instance, how beliefs combine with prior experiences or other aspects of a person's cognitions, (for example, "schema", Schank and Abelson, 1977; Axelrod, 1981). Nor do we know how beliefs, or even which specific beliefs, are used in specific decision situations. We do not understand how beliefs are combined with incoming information, or how the cognitions of individual decision makers interact in the context of small group discussions of specific issues and decision situations. It is difficult to see how future progress at the micro level can be made using these static stimulus-response models of decision making.

In contrast to this static approach, a number of researchers working in this area are increasingly utilizing concepts and recent insights from psychological research on information processing to develop a process model of foreign policy decision-making. A process model conceives of political choice as a cognitively driven exercise in problem solving, executed through the use of a heuristic. Graber (1982a, 1982b), for example, used knowledge of information-processing research to study the actual strategies people use in processing political information. Heuer (1980) cites attribution errors in explaining why the Soviets intervened in Afghanistan. Heradstveit (1979) uses "observer-participant", "subject-actor" discrepancies (ideas borrowed from attribution research but increasingly used within an information-processing framework in psychology) to explain the continued polarization of Israeli-Arab relations.

More generally, Janis and Mann (1977) drew attention to the role of stress as an interfering mechanism in choice situations. Similarly, Janis's (1972) widely influential work on "groupthink" focused on the cognitive impact of group dynamics in decision making. Janis and Mann (1977) also explored the filtration function of prior beliefs in policy making, the importance of which was stressed by George (1980). Dyson *et al.* (1974), Kirkpatrick *et al.* (1976), Sylvan and Thorson (1979), and Thorson and Sylvan (1982) also demonstrated that cognition is integral to political decision making. All this has led to further research that increasingly relies on such central concepts as cognitive schema (Bennett, 1981), mental heuristics (Thorson, 1984), and information processing (Dyson and Purkitt, 1983; Purkitt and Dyson, 1985a).

Despite this increasing enthusiasm for cognitive process models, systematic research is still needed on such key aspects of cognition and foreign policy decision making as the role of prior experiences and beliefs, the impact of incoming information, and the problem-solving and choice heuristics actually used by decision makers in specific situations to understand political problems and to exercise choice. Moreover, research capable of extending insights from information processing and cognitive research into the actual decision-making process is relatively rare. Information diffusion and integration of research programs between psychology and political science is minimal. Differences in research questions and emphases create a wide gap between the two disciplines. (See Dyson and Purkitt, 1986a, for a comprehensive review of psychological research on information processing; and Rosenau, 1984a, for a discussion of related issues of decision quality.)

On the other hand, current experimental research across a number of fields dealing with processing of information by intuitive decision makers indicates an important convergence around a few basic insights. Some of these insights offer the promise of providing the basic building blocks of a general theory of intuitive decision making (Simon, 1978, 1980). This line of research has important implications for the future directions of micro-level studies of political decision making in general and foreign policy making in particular. As argued in the next section, the quality of policy decisions depends on both the information utilized and the problem-solving skills employed.

Cognition, Information and Future Research on Foreign Policy Decision Making

Our approach to political decision making is based on experimental evidence from research on human information processing in cognitive and social psychology and the convergence of results when applied to decision-making approaches grounded in intuitive logics. The three main insights from these bodies of research are that (1) individuals are selective information processors, (2) they have limited cognitive capabilities, and (3) they often use some sort of heuristic or mental aid to handle decision problems. In general, these research activities indicate that humans cannot process large amounts of information systematically without experiencing information overload. To compensate for the limitations of short-term memory and information-processing capabilities, people use intuitive mental heuristics as a problem attack plan to assist them in achieving problem understanding and to make choices or decisions.

This apparently universal reliance on intuitive heuristics to solve all types of problems is one of the most fundamental insights emerging from this line of research. People devise mental plans to solve problems, whether the task is an arithmetic problem, a consumer product choice, a decision about a personal question such as marriage, or the selection of a political candidate. Wildavsky's (1964, pp. 11–18) description of the incremental chooser underlines one of the intuitive heuristics frequently relied on by political decision makers. An intuitively grounded heuristic used across a wide variety of questions relies on past problem-solving experiences, a vague sense of the knowns and unknowns of a problem (i.e., topic/issue/question), what sort of data, conditions and situations are relevant to the problem, and a subjective estimate of the consequences that follow from alternative courses of action. Intuitive problem-solving approaches, therefore, are fundamentally based on one's subjective sense of familiarity with similar problems and on a rather unwieldly problem attack plan that lacks testability as to its effectiveness. As a result, the effort to understand complex problems such as those facing political decision makers flounders on the moorings of an unwieldy problem attack plan. Perhaps this system is also beset by what the cyberneticists term "noise"—which includes seemingly relevant information that actually has very little bearing on the development of effective responses to a problem.[2]

Although intuitive problem solving typically involves the use of what seems to be a simple heuristic, uncertainty over the effectiveness of various alternatives and inchoate problem attack plans often leads decision makers to seek increasing amounts of ostensibly relevant information before exercising a choice. However, the second fundamental insight from this line of research recognizes that people cannot process large amounts of information systematically without the aid of some sort of formal heuristic (e.g., an algorithm). In fact, the research to date indicates that the main effect of increasing information under conditions of decisional uncertainty is to increase one's subjective confidence in the adequacy of intuitively derived solutions while failing to improve the quality of decision making. Thus, cognitive limitations in processing large amounts of information mean that increases in information are often accompanied by increases in subjective confidence without a concomitant increase in the quality of a decision or problem response (Miller, 1956; Hayes, 1981; Payne, 1975, 1980; Heuer, 1978; Phelps and Shanteau, 1978).

The third insight from this line of research—concerning the use of intuitive heuristics to understand and to solve complex problems—often leads to fundamental errors or biases in the processing of information. The evidence to date suggests that the overutilization of simple intuitive heuristics and the underutilization of formal logical or statistical rules causes errors and biases at each of the following decision making stages (Nisbett and Wilson, 1977; Nisbett and Ross, 1980; Pitz, 1980):

(1) describing and coding information during the initial stage of problem identification,
(2) explaining important causal dimensions and making intuitive predictions during the initial stage of problem identification,
(3) explaining important causal dimensions and making intuitive predictions during the problem-evaluation stage,
(4) choosing among alternatives during the decision stage,
(5) evaluating, learning, integrating, and adapting to feedback information on the efficacy, adequacy and accuracy of prior behaviors and actions.

Although there is some recognition of these insights in current research on political decision making (e.g., George, 1980), there have been few efforts to date to apply these social psychological perspectives to a political context. George's work has been instrumental in translating such insights into the foreign policy literature, but it remains the case that there is little effort to examine systematically the basis of specific heuristics and beliefs and the role played by incoming information in the actual decision making process. Instead, George uses such "meta" concepts as "national interests" to describe the problem-understanding process of decision makers. Essentially, this means that their intuitive sense of national interest, regardless of how misguided it is as a basis for an effective problem response, dominates their use of a problem attack plan as well as the information they use to develop and justify conclusions.

Little is yet known about the content of the specific mental heuristics used by political decision makers. It is now reasonably clear, however, that individuals using intuitive problem attack plans can only utilize information on a few dimensions of a problem in attempting to gain understanding and develop responses. Thus, gathering a lot of information on more than a few dimensions leads to information overload. The collected information is ignored unsystematically so that individuals believe they have thoroughly analyzed the problem. Their confidence that they have reached a feasible choice after painstaking inquiry may harden their commitment to the option selected.

The recognition that political decision makers only use a few dimensions may be useful for guiding future descriptive studies of various stages of foreign policy decision making. This can be seen the problem-solving heuristic used by top spokespersons of both the Carter and Reagan administrations in their public articulations of United States foreign policy toward Southern Africa. Purkitt and Dyson (1986) found that spokespersons for both administrations used a few dimensions to analyze the key actors and problems of the region, one being a heavy reliance on prior beliefs (such as causal attributions) to analyze ongoing problems in the region. Furthermore, there were important differences across the two administrations in terms of their treatment of incoming information. Whereas the Carter administration officials tended to incorporate more problem-specific information into their statements about ongoing regional conflicts, Reagan officials consistently used a few simple and familiar themes: the need to contain the Soviets and their alleged surrogates in the region; the need to promote proven friends; and the important role played by the private sector in promoting development. Moreover, the study found linkages between the unique themes stressed by spokespersons for both administrations and changes in American foreign policy behavior towards South Africa (Purkitt and Dyson, 1986).

This research suggests that an information-processing perspective may be a useful theoretical approach for both describing the actual cognitive processes employed by foreign policy decision makers and for identifying cross-level linkages, although further systematic research will be required before its ultimate potential can be assessed. There is a possibility that these information-processing elements could form the core of a general theory of problem solving across levels and decisional contexts. Cognitive limitations and cognitive conceit may be fundamental constraints on foreign policy decision makers across cultures. The cross-cultural hypothesis is that decision makers adopt simple problem-solving heuristics to understand and make decisions about politics whether the actual participants in decision making are students or experts, American presidents or Soviet general secretaries.

Although situational factors and organizational constraints are clearly important factors influencing the decision-making process, it would be useful to study the actual cognitive processes of political decision makers across a variety of contexts and organizations in order to assess the role in shaping individual heuristics of such factors as bureaucratic standard operating procedures. Factors that have already been researched extensively, such as personality, role, situation and organization, may also be important sources of the specific heuristics of political decision makers. The information-processing approach to the study of comparative foreign policy may complement such "meta" concepts as "image," "operational code" and "cognitive map," or it may be fruitful on its own. An information-processing/problem-solving perspective could directly study the generally accepted view that "crisis" decision making involves significantly different information processes than other types of political situations, because of such factors as high stress, short decision time, and perceptions of threat. Cognitive research suggests that people are simple information processors during both routine and crisis decision periods. Crisis may even lead to more efficient problem identification activity ("it focuses the mind wonderfully") and thereby delimits the problem. Alternatively, as Janis (1972) has pointed out in his "groupthink" scenario, such delimiting in social processes may lead to policy fiascos. The conflict among these otherwise plausible assertions highlights the need for more data on how intuitive decisions are actually made, in terms of both information processing and traditional "meta" concepts.

That people always rely on simplifying mental heuristics and frequently misuse statistical and formal principles of inference may also be a useful insight. Computer data bases will soon provide policy makers with more information in a more efficiently retrievable form than before. The intended purpose is to improve the quality of decision making (Rosenau, 1984a). However, if the amount of information is increased, it is important to provide policy makers with explicit decision aids. Increasing information without such aids, as was discussed earlier, leads to information overload and faulty processing routines. Before we can be confident that technical improvements in data retrieval and processing will assist decision makers to understand and perhaps even solve political problems, more needs to be learned about the cognitive capacities, heuristics and routines by which political decision makers presently arrive at problem responses and political choices.

Finally, we need to know much more about how macro systemic factors impact on the micro process of foreign policy decision making and about relevant linkages across levels of analysis. Much of the macro work to date in comparative foreign policy can be applied at the micro level if there is an improvement in our ability to study foreign policy decision makers. In that regard, it is sometimes argued that systematic micro research is virtually foreclosed by the lack of "access" to high-level decision makers. This implies that the process of decision making at the highest levels of the foreign policy process differs distinctively from the way political decisions are made in other contexts. The information-processing literature suggests the opposite— that people generally, regardless of organizational status, are inefficient information processors. This and related issues can be examined using a variety of research techniques such as content analysis (Purkitt and Dyson, 1986) and case studies (Purkitt, 1984). As we suggest below, however, the potential may be greatest with experimentation, particularly with the ability of contemporary game theory to model and analyze complex situations.

213

Charles A. Powell, James W. Dyson and *Helen E. Purkitt*
Optimizing Decisions:
Structure and Stability in Complex Conflicts

Analytically, one of the biggest losses involved with the death of *Homo economicus* (Simon, 1985) at the hands of a throng of behavioral anomalies is that we can no longer think in terms of its well-developed apparatus for rational decision making, especially its battery of applied mathematical techniques. Unfortunately, the putatively emergent *Homo psychologicus* has nothing even remotely comparable with which to replace that lost apparatus. One might well turn back to elegance and away from relevance, leaving analyzing the "march of folly" (Tuchman, 1984) to the historians and policy analysts. But just as the Dark Ages had their rays of technological hope, some interesting and promising analytical developments for a new rational apparatus and analytical linguistics may well be emerging. The cluster of intellectual enterprises covered by the terms "artificial intelligence" and "cognitive science" constitutes a source of great potential for the study of foreign policy decision making. Others (Rosenau, 1984a; Mefford, in Chapter 12) discuss this more broadly, but one specific enterprise in this cluster has particular relevance for research at the micro level. We concur with Mefford that two pre-existing lines of inquiry converged with the computer technological revolution to form what is labeled "artificial intelligence": the mathematical theory of games and the general systems approach. It is the contemporary evolution of game theory that could provide a rational apparatus in the psychologically relevant analysis of decision making.

Rapoport (1964, 1986) notes that the first significant contribution of "classical" game theory originated with von Neumann in the 1920s and achieved considerable "policy-relevant" vogue in the 1950s. It was a taxonomy of complexity in interactive situations ("games"). However, until the late 1960s it was difficult to apply this taxonomy much beyond extremely simplified conflict situations. Nonetheless, game-theoretic concepts made their way even into nonscientific discourse, particularly the terms "zero-sum" and "non-zero-sum." These terms technically distinguished between simpler situations in which the positive or negative payoffs for all players add to zero (or some other constant sum) and more complex situations where they do not, implying the possibility of outcomes of mutual gain or loss, and therefore of cooperation as well as conflict.

The non-zero-sum game of cooperation/conflict known as the Prisoner's Dilemma became, to use Axelrod's (1984) characterization, the *"E. coli"* of social science. This game attracted interest as a conceptual or simple experimental model of an archetypal political choice situation, particularly because of a paradox that, from a formal logical perspective, constituted a crippling anomaly. Applying the theory of strategic decision developed in zero-sum (pure conflict) game theory to Prisoner's Dilemma, and the related game of Chicken, produced unsatisfactory rational prescriptions of mutual loss in these non-zero-sum situations while cooperation would produce mutual gain. In effect, the games demonstrated a "breakdown of rationality" (Howard, 1971).

The reason was that the alternative strategies for each player were only thought of as available for a one-shot choice, to be selected once and for all, ignoring the opponent's reaction. Situations originally depicted analytically as game trees (the "extended form") were reduced to a rectangular matrix (the "normal form"). But choices in game trees are most often arranged in temporal sequence, in which a completely informed permanent commitment to a set of automatic sequential choices is obviously unrealistic. Originally thought to be an innocuous mathematical convenience, it was subsequently discovered to affect the strategic properties of the game. Going beyond two alternative choices also increased the size of the tree or matrix explosively, which tended to restrict game theory to two-player, two-choice situations. Despite the superficial popularity of some of its concepts, and its intrinsic mathematical and theoretical interest, "classical" game theory had little practical applicability in the empirical study of decision making (Aumann and Maschler, 1972; Harsanyi, 1968, 1977, pp. 6–7; Howard, 1971, 1975).

Despite this limited immediate relevance, and even allegations of misuse (Rapoport, 1964), the potential of game theory continued to stimulate scholary interest, eventually bearing fruit in the mid 1960s. Stimulated by Rapoport, Isard, and others, the key breakthrough was made by Howard (1971) and extended by him and his colleagues (Mitchell, 1979, 1985; Fraser and Hipel, 1984; Fraser, Benjamin and Powell, 1985, forthcoming; Benjamin and Powell, 1986) with other convergent work by Axelrod (1984) and Brams (1977) and his colleagues (Brams and Kilgour, 1985; Zagare, 1985). A new view emerged of strategy as "policy," perhaps to be selected initially, but permitting the players the opportunity of changing at a later time. This new view of strategy implied and necessitated a change in the way outcomes are viewed. The key consideration is no longer what is maximally rational for a player as in classical game theory. Instead, the focus of this new view of strategy is on the characteristics of outcomes with particular attention to the issue of what makes outcomes stable.[3] The analytical focus shifts from the unilateral pursuit of individual or group optima to a multilateral search for equilibria involving uncertainty reduction and conflict resolution (Radford, 1976).

215

Allied with this fundamental shift from a concern with rational choice to an emphasis on strategy and stability were three additional changes in the game-theoretical framework. First, the applied game theorists tried to cut real-world scenarios to fit the properties of a mathematically intriguing model, like the bed of Procrustes. Now the cognitive representation of a real-world situation is taken as a given. A game-theoretic model is developed which summarizes the salient characteristics of the situational assessment.

Second, in providing his strategic solution to Prisoner's Dilemma, Howard (1971) also suggested a more analytically convenient notation than the game tree or pay off matrix by which situations could be described. He suggested that concrete choice alternatives be represented by "yes-no" *options*, using a simple (1,0) notation to indicate whether the option was taken (1) or not (0). A particular set of "yes-no" choices (a set of 1s and 0s; for instance: 00110) define a player's *strategy*. Taking all players' particular strategies together defines a particular *outcome* of the situation, also represented as a set of 0s and 1s. (Two actors, one with a five-option strategy 00110, and the other with a three-option strategy 010, produce an outcome 00110010.) There is a consequent brevity of notation, since n options, across all players, imply 2^n outcomes. Our two players have 8 options between them, so 2^8 means that 00110010 is one of 256 logically possible outcomes. Some outcomes are probably substantively absurd and can be removed as player preferences across outcomes are estimated.[4]

The third development in contemporary game theory has been the improvement in analytical methods. Originally, there was only one procedure relating a game model to the stability of a real world outcome—the "Nash equilibrium" (Nash, 1951). A Nash equilibrium is any outcome at which each player can be said to maximize his payoff, under the assumption that his opponent's strategy is fixed. In Prisoner's Dilemma, when conceived as an interaction of choices in original game theory, only the outcome of mutual loss is a Nash equilibrium. Howard (1971) resolved this evident breakdown of rationality by modeling the Prisoner's Dilemma as a matrix of interacting strategies, where one can locate mutual gain outcomes of co-operation that are also Nash equilibria. Even if Howard's solution is not accepted—and it clearly assumes that decision makers are capable of the conditional thinking required by the concept of strategy: "if I do this, then another player does that, . . ."—it is still possible to define plausible stability properties sufficient to power the analytical procedure. At a formal level, Fraser and Kilgour (1985) have described the universe of 726 2×2 ordinal games and assessed each outcome of each game in terms of 14 different aspects of stability.

216

Options analysis seems to have the potential to improve intuitive problem solving and perhaps also choice. Decision aids can only improve the quality of decision making to the extent that they recognize the fundamental insights from information-processing research. Human decision makers are only able to process systematically a few dimensions as binary choices without experiencing information overload. In the context of foreign policy behavior, Anderson in Chapter 15 shows empirically that the "courses of action" that constitute the basis of choice in Snyder and Paige's (1958) maximizing definition of decision can be seen not as "incompatible alternative courses of action, but rather [as] a sequence of binary yes-no choices over a wide array of independent actions" (below, p. 290). A chosen strategy constitutes a "mix" of "yes-no" options which are not necessarily mutually exclusive. In this way, options analysis, which utilizes Howard's binary (1,0) notation, more accurately reflects the actual thought processes of decision makers in their intuitive problem understanding (Newell and Simon, 1972).

Redefining "course of action" as strategy rather than as option responds to the additional problem noted by Anderson in his empirical critique of the Snyder framework that decision maker goals do not seem all that concrete. In this sense, a strategy might even *imply* an option before it is concretely defined, such as in the 1962 Cuban Missile Crisis when President Kennedy evidently decided on a strategy involving "doing something" short of an immediate attack on Cuba even before the concrete option of the naval blockade was defined. Howard (1971) emphasized that all options are ranges of options and can be collapsed together or broken out separately as seems appropriate to the decision maker or analyst. Similarly, all players can be seen as coalitions of players (as internal games) and combined or separated depending on the definition of the situation.

Most analytical procedures are initially intimidating, and game theory has a mythically formidable reputation in social science. The contemporary reality is considerably more user-friendly, particularly given that an actual decision maker does not have to understand the underlying theory or even a great deal of the analytical procedure. Although use of the decision tree in "departure game" analysis (Brams and Wittman, 1981; Zagare, 1985) requires more of the user (but has certain advantages), the procedures derived from the Howard (1971) options analysis application require relatively little. Nonetheless, this latter approach to modeling and structuring an interactive conflict situation could constitute a significant cognitive aid, in at least three significant ways:

(1) Because the real world can be more complex than any model could ever fully represent, the modeling process always may involve simplification. Structuring a conflict situation could help a decision maker by forcing an identification of the pertinent aspects of the situation.

(2) If the decision maker is missing important information, the model's requirement of completeness would seem to force either the necessary situational assessment or the recognition that action must be taken without it. Decision makers are likely to know their own options, and usually their own preferences for outcomes, but seem less likely to consider either the options available to other players in the situation or other players' preferences. Options analysis may force the decision maker to take into account the point of view of the other players, which is crucial from the standpoint of achieving better outcomes and stabilizing them in strategic *interaction* and *bargaining*.

(3) Situations beyond the very simple and obvious are virtually impossible for any human being to think about in a comprehensive, simultaneous manner. Structuring a situation in this manner should permit a decision maker to be consistent and comprehensive, while still considering a situation in terms of processible chunks.

Although problem understanding is an interesting experimental research and normative policy focus in and of itself, the process of interactive choice in social systems is even more intriguing and compelling, especially in the policy context of international relations. Moreover, both contemporary game theory and comparative foreign policy research argue persuasively that problem understanding and systems structure and stability are inextricably related. If options analysis can be utilized successfully for problem understanding, it should be possible to exploit the power of its structural and stability capabilities for the study of interactive choice:

(1) In some models there may be literally hundreds of possible outcomes. It may be important to identify which of these have particular relevance as unstable or stable outcomes (equilibria) in order to reduce the model to a reasonable size.

(2) Although just developing a good model may give a decision maker sufficient understanding of a situation to enable a decision and its implementation, an explicit analysis should allow that decision maker's assessments to be credibly communicated to others.

(3) If the goal of the decision maker is to forecast the future state of

218

the situation, the stability or instability of an outcome implies important assumptions about how the modeled players are expected to behave.

In order for applied game-theoretic analysis to yield an understanding of strategic interrelationships from which behavior could be explained or predicted (and might be assisted), there must be an accurate model of how decision makers assess their situation. Options analysts have typically sought to obtain these definitions of the situation from the best available source, optimally from decision makers in a direct client-interactive mode.[5]

Whatever the behavioral source, options analysis can provide a useful experimental context within which to study actual cognitive processes. Data could be collected on the actual behavior of participants to explore such questions as how (if at all) availability of a formal analytical technique helps people to process more information, helps them reduce processing errors, and helps them to arrive at internally consistent solutions/outcomes. It would also be a useful procedure with which to study cognitive conceit. An analysis of options could be used to elicit subjective assessments as to how much (more or less) information was used, how "good" their problem understanding and solution was both before and after exposure to the technique. More objectively, this would permit experimental analysis of how decision makers use this sort of technique, and what effect it has on their intuitive methods of problem solving and choice, especially in a social context (Anderson, Chapter 15). It would be particularly intriguing to test the assertion that people can process more dimensions of a problem systematically if they have an explicit algorithm. This would open the possibility that cognitively appropriate techniques like options analysis might accomplish the goal envisioned by George (1972) in his "multiple advocacy" prescription.

Albert Einstein was not unique in observing that while natural science and technology have developed explosively in the twentieth century, human beings have remained essentially the same, producing a dangerously lethal combination of human limitations and technical capabilities. Opening the "black box" of cognitive processing is not only a clear necessity for the study of foreign policy decision making to move forward, but also for an improvement of the "human factors" side of the modern global equation. Despite some differences in approach and terminology between us and other micro-oriented contributors to the present volume, there is a convergence on these main points. Increased availability of heuristics permits sophisticated but practical descriptive analysis, and offers thereby a potential improvement in

219

decision quality crucially needed to cope with the problems of the global system. The potential of artificial intelligence techniques in general—and game theory in particular—for the comparative study of foreign policy appears considerable.

Notes

We wish to thank the organizers and participants at the original conference for their invitation to prepare this paper and for their comments. Special thanks to Roger Wedberg, and to Niall Fraser and Charles Benjamin for contributions to the section on metagames and bargaining. The support for this effort from our institutions, and for Dyson and Purkitt from the National Science Foundation, is gratefully acknowledged.

1 Why the original decision-making approach failed to stimulate subsequent work at the micro level is an interesting question, albeit beyond the scope of the present discussion. Those unfamiliar with this framework are encouraged to review the original framework (Snyder, Bruck and Sapin, 1954) and the one empirical case study based on it (Snyder and Paige, 1958). For a contemporary discussion of this approach, see Rosenau, 1967. Key elements of the original framework, such as the importance of understanding a decision maker's "definition of the situation" and the key role of information variables, are presently being explored by the authors. A comprehensive analysis of the decision-making framework and the paradigmatic reasons why there has been little progress toward opening up the black box to date can be found in Powell, Dyson and Purkitt, 1985.

2 See Kahneman Slovic and Tversky (1982) and Dyson and Purkitt (1986a) for experimental research concerning intuitive decision making for the study of political choice.

3 Outcomes are stable where players prefer to remain rather than moving the system elsewhere.

4 Constraints across options both *within* a single player's strategy set and *across* options in different players' sets will identify logically impossible strategies and outcomes which can be explicitly eliminated from the analysis.

5 The practical application of options analysis continues to be enhanced by improved techniques, such as those developed by Fraser and Hipel (1984) and Howard (1986), including, most recently, personal computer programs. The approach can accommodate misperception ("hypergames") and the real and analytic combination of players into "coalitions," often an essential aspect of stability analysis. All of these developments have resulted from the actual use of the technique in real world, scholarly, and teaching contexts. (For a more detailed discussion with figures and examples, see Fraser, Benjamin, and Powell, 1985; Benjamin and Powell, forthcoming.)

12

Analogical Reasoning and the Definition of the Situation: Back to Snyder for Concepts and Forward to Artificial Intelligence for Method

DWAIN MEFFORD

Comparative foreign policy (CFP) is undergoing a most remarkable change. The earlier preoccupation with observable attributes and behavior is giving way to a new-found interest in cognitive mechanisms. Goal structures are allowed, if not in name, then at least in the guise of preference orderings (Hermann and Peacock, Chapter 2) and an overall problem-solving approach has been adopted in part (Hermann and Hermann, 1984). Discarding the atomism and behavioralist insistence that concepts correspond in some immediate way to objects that can be counted, researchers in the field are now freely experimenting with increasingly complex notions of how perception and preference interact in real contexts to shape behavior. Evidence of this thrust is apparent in the new direction the CREON project is taking, in particular the efforts to revitalize the notion of the decision maker's "definition of the situation" (Hermann and Coate, 1982; Hudson, 1983; Hudson, Hermann and Singer, 1985). Other essentially cognitive notions are also the subject of conceptual development and empirical test. These include the rules and mechanisms that circumscribe and guide choice among courses of action (Kegley, Chapter 13; Kegley and Raymond, 1981).

The Return to Cognitive Structures

All of this indicates that a number of the prominent theorists in the field are returning to their intellectural roots. As Hermann and Peacock point out in Chapter 2, we are witnessing a return to that type of broad-based conceptual program Richard Snyder laid out thirty years ago (Snyder, Bruck and Sapin, 1954, 1962a; Snyder and Robinson, 1961).

The substantive study reported in this chapter fits squarely within Snyder's "State as Actor in a Situation" frame (1954, p. 35). In particular it belongs to the program of situational analysis that Snyder *et al.* (1954, p. 54) originally adopted from Lewin's field theory (Lewin, 1936, 1951). To use the terminology of one of Snyder's other inspirations, Alfred Schuetz (1951, 1953, 1973), we focus on how key actors manage to "construct realities," that is, to select out what is critical in a situation (including evidence of threat or opportunity) and to formulate appropriate courses of action. We argue that much of the cognitive work involved in interpreting situations essentially entails posing and reworking historical analogies. In short, real or hypothetical situations—in our case a crisis—is understood against the backdrop of selected past incidents. Options are identified and decisions structured largely through the posing and juxtaposing of analogies. It is our contention that analogical reasoning is not simply one of the many cognitive processes at work in the activity of defining a situation, it is in fact the most fundamental and pervasive. The case study presented cannot prove this, but it does provide evidence.

Vis-à-vis Snyder's notion of the "definition of a situation" and the broader decision-analytic approach as a whole, the process of reasoning by analogy probably exerts greatest impact in the initial steps of the overall process. It helps shape the decision maker's initial orientation and posture. It is here that candidate interpretations are first marshaled, later to be scrutinized and reworked or rejected. Evaluation and calculation come later. While well within Snyder's framework, in breaking out of the process of analogical reasoning we are not only adding detail, but also implicitly arguing that the decision-analytic process is a sequenced one, with some cognitive activities contributing to initial structures and others functioning to refine and qualify such structures once recognized. Though analogies may play their most subtle and significant role in the early steps of decision making, they are also important factors in the other steps of the overall decision process. Analogical reasoning is ubiquitous. It enters into each of the intersecting cognitive processes that Snyder *et al.* identify:

- [The actors'] discrimination and relating of objects, conditions and other actors—various things are perceived or expected in a relational context;
- The existence, establishment or definition of goals—various things are wanted from the situation;
- Attachment of significance to various courses of action suggested by the situation according to some criteria of estimation;

222

- Application of "standards of acceptability" which

    (1) narrow the range of perceptions;
    (2) narrow the range of objects wanted; and
    (3) narrow the number of alternatives.

                                        (Snyder *et al.*, 1954, p. 37)

While Snyder emphasizes the primary function of perception and reasoning as a determinant of policy, he does not attempt to put forward a detailed theory of the processes involved. To the extent that we go beyond Snyder, the extensions lie in the effort to model one of the core cognitive mechanisms. The ambiguous and incomplete information that a new situation typically presents is often pieced together and completed on the basis of parallels drawn to past incidents. The parallels, once recognized, guide the actor's expectations as to what may ensue from the present situation if the parallel holds. In this manner several of the functions Snyder catalogues are accomplished through the act of identifying and exploring historical analogies. The how and the what of this process are the principal focus of the work reported here. The process is reconstructed experimentally in a realistic context through a case study of the formulation of Soviet policy. The particular case traces the formulation and reformulation of options from the Soviet perspective in the spring and summer of 1968 in Czechoslovakia. The changing interpretation of the situation is a complex function of both the stream of events and the propensity of various factions within the Politburo to selectively access different historical cases in their effort to interpret and anticipate events. In brief, the substantive problem involves how individuals and groups draw upon historical analogies in the effort to disambiguate a fast-breaking crisis situation and formulate policy.

The Step from Complex Theory to Computer Program

Substance aside, one of the chief objectives of this chapter is to illustrate a logic of inquiry that involves formulating concepts in the medium of a computer program. When dealing with a process model composed of several "moving parts," in our case including changing perceptions, changing objectives and changing contents of memory, there are definite limits to what can be captured with paper and pencil. The limitations of diagrams and textual descriptions are even more inhibiting when the object of interest changes its structure through time. In the face of such complexity, it becomes not only convenient, but ultimately necessary to shift from boxes and arrows drawn on paper to a program running on a computer. For the purpose of developing concepts and theory, viewed abstractly, flow charts and

diagrams like those often used in the comparative foreign policy literature are functionally equivalent to computer programs. The choice of
media for developing and pursuing ideas is essentially a practical one.
It is our view that the step from a complex model of interconnected
components, like that Snyder works with, to a computer program is
natural and immediate. In fact, cognitive processes like those pictured
but not specified by Snyder are already pressing the upper bound of
what can be expressed meaningfully in the form of static drawings and
textual description. Criticisms of Snyder indicate that he pushes the
medium of pen and ink beyond what it can effectively bear. This is the
message Hoffmann seems to be conveying in his cutting remark about
theory degenerating into "Chinese Boxes" (1977, p. 53). In his effort to
render multiple interdependence, Snyder transgresses the limits of
human attention and patience; at least this seems to be the case for
Hoffmann (1959), who is at a loss to visualize the process Snyder has in
mind. Rather than a multi-leveled interacting system, Hoffmann sees
only "boxes within boxes" that ultimately "have taken on a morose,
pointless life of their own, like the fascinating bones scattered on the
shores painted by Chirico" (1959, pp. 364, 370). The lesson in this is
that once the theorist abandons the realm of simple structure and
enters the world Weaver (1947) has called "organized complexity," the
traditional ways of developing and presenting concepts are likely to
fail. CFP, with its renewed interest in cognitive processes, has crossed
this conceptual frontier. If it is to develop further as a field its practitioners must either resort to poetic images or take seriously the notion
that computer programs can embody concepts and theories.

Stripped of journalistic hype, artificial intelligence (AI) proves to be
an expanding universe of serious applied and theoretical research.
Most definitions of the scope of the field are less than informative
because they generally assume a prior definition of what constitutes
"intelligence" (e.g., Barr and Feigenbaum, 1981, p. 3; Rich, 1983, p. 1;
Winston, 1984, p. 1). The variety of substantive, theoretical and formal
subfields within AI can best be inventoried by scanning the proceedings of the biennial International Joint Conference on Artifical Intelligence. The major areas of concentration include: natural language processing, problem solving, vision, learning and robotics. Each of these
subdivides into a myriad of special issues. (For a synoptic sense of
the universe of problems currently pursued in AI see Waltz's, 1985,
recent effort to erect a classification scheme.) Though politics does not
figure within this large universe, the cognitive themes that are central
to CFP, including human problem solving, planning and learning,
reside at the very core of AI. With the possible exception of Carbonell's
work (1979a, 1979b) and the earlier research of Abelson (1973, 1975;

224

Schank and Abelson, 1977), the AI systems that exist or have been proposed have little to do with substantive political questions. A handful of political scientists are now showing interest in the potential of AI concepts and methods, but these efforts are very preliminary and curiously diverse in focus.[1]

Given the considerable overlap in subject matter, it is ironic that the research communities associated with AI and foreign policy analysis are essentially unknown to each other. They use largely different technical and conceptual languages, they belong to different professional organizations and they publish in different journals. More than this, by virtue of training they subscribe to different notions of what constitutes excellence in research. Even when forced to work side by side, for example, in government-sponsored projects on strategic planning, political scientists and the AI engineers seem scarcely aware that they share a fundamental agenda. It may well be the case that the two fields were in closer intellectual proximity thirty years ago, before AI had a name and before CFP existed as a speciality. The fact that Simon's work figures prominently both in Snyder's thinking and in early and current AI is evidence of the overlap in ideas and problems. CFP's re-examination of Snyder may portend a return to those master themes that link AI and the comparative study of foreign policy. CFP stands to gain both an influx of concepts and a logic of inquiry appropriate to the development of sophisticated theory. One of the payoffs of returning to the decision-analytic framework as developed by Snyder is that it may serve as a conceptual bridge into the sizeable literature on problem solving that AI has generated.

Analogical Reasoning and the Structure of Decisions

In foreign policy, as in everyday life, analogies are used to understand the present in terms of the past. The practice is ubiquitous and serves the purpose of reducing a new and possibly threatening situation to a variation of something familiar. For better or worse, what is known or believed is often transferred wholesale to new contexts. While the parallels drawn might be apt in some cases in some respects, the overall resemblance may well be superficial, with differences and discrepancies overwhelming similarities. As a consequence, analogies are simultaneously powerful mechanisms for orienting policy and grave sources of misperception and error. Much of the research on human judgment stresses the detrimental character of drawing explicit or implicit analogies (Tversky and Kahneman, 1971, 1973, 1979; Kahneman and Tversky, 1972, 1973; Einhorn and Hogarth, 1978). But, recent work by a number of psychologists interested in problem solving and processes of attribution emphasize the more positive aspect by which analogies provide an initial structure for the situation or problem (Simon and Kotovksy, 1963; Simon, 1977; Jones et al., 1971; Mischel, 1973; Sternberg, 1977). Without this, reasoning cannot proceed. Some linguists and theorists concerned with the formal and computer replication of human reason and the use of natural language take a more radical position. Not only is the use of analogies seen as a recurrent strategy for guiding inference, but analogies are recognized as among the most powerful mechanisms devised by the human mind for coping with complex and ambiguous information (Ortony, 1979; Rumelhart and Ortony, 1977; Lakoff and Johnson, 1980; Lehnert and Ringle, 1982).

In the study of political decisions, in particular in the effort to reconstruct judgments that have precipitated military action, historians and political scientists have documented the costs of the uncritical use of analogies (Jervis, 1968, 1970, 1976; May, 1973) These treatments are generally anecdotal in nature. The historical record, in particular the memoirs material, is searched for instances in which policy is determined by the likeness a decision maker sees between one case and another. A classic example is Truman's initial reaction to the aggression by North Korea: he claims to have seen immediate and profound parallels between the challenge posed by the communists in Northeast Asia in 1950 and the German reoccupation of the Rhineland in the 1930s (Truman, 1956, Vol. II, p. 333; May, 1973; Paterson, Clifford and Hagan, 1983, pp. 472 ff.). Some of the most insightful accounts of the inner workings of policy making and problem solving characteristic of administrations or key individuals have focused upon the repertory of historical examples that are repeatedly invoked (Gardner, 1970; McLellan, 1976).

Whereas the psychological and historical literature provides a surfeit of examples of individuals using analogies to choose among options and solve problems, efforts in these fields to provide a systematic conception of how the process operates remain rudimentary. The work with human problem solving in cognitive science and artificial intelligence recognizes the importance of analogy and metaphor but, to date, has produced little general theory that is immediately relevant to political analysis.[2] It suffices to report that while the work with concept attainment is suggestive, formal work in this area has been confined to specialized data structures and their manipulation (Evans, 1968; Winston, 1970, 1978, 1979, 1981; Kling, 1971; Hayes-Roth, 1973; Hayes-Roth and McDermott, 1977, 1978; VanLehn and Brown, 1978; Mitchell, 1978; McDermott, 1979; Dieterich and Michalski, 1981;

Michalski, Carbonell and Mitchell, 1983). The work with extracting rules from examples and inducing correspondences between problems (Simon and Lea, 1974; Waterman and Hayes-Roth, 1978; Anzai and Simon, 1979; Quinlan, 1979; Newell and Rosenbloom, 1981; Carbonell, 1981, 1982, 1983) is intriguing but ultimately sheds little light on the type of judgment and reasoning at work in drawing political-historical analogies.

For reasons presented at length elsewhere (Mefford, 1982a), the various treatments of analogical reasoning as it pertains to algebraic word problems, the understanding of metaphor, and other research areas within cognitive science and artificial intelligence are ultimately inadequate. Such analogical reasoning, though suggestive, fails both conceptually and computationally as an approach to the question of analogies as they function within political settings. Of the approaches available we will argue that the work on sequence comparison within the broad field of pattern recognition is the most promising. Historical cases, viewed as sequences of events, can be compared and aligned in a natural way using procedures developed in this field.

Comparing Processes versus Comparing Attributes and Events

Extending and Generalizing "Structured, Focused, Comparison"

In an important article on the utility of case studies as building blocks for theory, George (1979a) attempts to merge the skills of the historian and the political scientist. He calls for an analytic strategy that is a cross between the broad, but shallow, statistical study of events and the detailed, but confined, recounting of single cases. His objective is to create a "differentiated" theory of foreign policy behavior that is relia-ble, that is, informed by a significant number of instances, and at the same time sophisticated and "focused" in terms of the questions it asks. It might seem that in wanting the best of what the political scientist and historian have to offer, he is proposing to square the circle. But his strategy is based on the sound proposition that systematic comparison is dependent upon the deliberate manner in which each case is described using a common set of categories, and not upon the number of cases (Russett, 1970a; Lijphart, 1971, 1975; Campbell, 1975, 1978; Eckstein, 1975; Verba, 1967). In short, the number of cases can be small and highly selected, yet still constitute an adequate base for extracting propositions regarding the correlation of factors and the manner and degree to which selected factors cause or condition others.

This chapter presents a technique for implementing the type of data

227

analysis that George envisions. It also goes beyond George's program by fashioning a research question that radically shifts the focus of comparison. In addition to events and the attributes of actors, we add the actor's cognitive processes including how the actor compares events and attributes. This involves a "doubling up" of the phenomena under investigation. Where the issue of comparison is generally approached as a question of method, as in George's discussion, we consider it as part of the object of research itself. The actor's cognitive process of searching for patterns among cases is an essential part of the decision-making process to be described and explained. Stepping from comparative case analysis to the study of how cases are compared by decision makers effectively transforms a question of method into a question of substance. How this is to be realized and what it represents as a bridge from conventional data analysis to cognitive modeling is the subject of this chapter. Here at the outset a diagram (Figure 12.1) may help make the general point regarding how the type of research George represents fits within the more inclusive research problem we have in mind.

Conceptualizing the Process of Analogical Reasoning

We have argued to this point that the field of comparative foreign policy is engaged in expanding its object of inquiry to embrace the cognitive processes by which actors interpret situations. To accomplish this requires a conception of the processes at work. Since this interpretive act often involves the drawing of historical analogies, the construction of historical analogies by political actors in real contexts should be examined. In drawing an analogy one case is used to inform the interpretation of another on the basis of parallels and discrepancies. Historical analogies are so ubiquitous in political debate that they often go unnoticed.

For example, in the case of Czechoslovakia in 1968, *Pravda* and *Izvestia* articles of July and early August were laced with explicit and coded references to the Polish and Hungarian precedents. Personal accounts by participants or witnesses to the internal debates within the Czech and Soviet parties and government bodies were also filled with examples in which historical parallels are drawn. A pair of analogies that recur in Czech and Soviet deliberations, as well as in subsequent commentary and analysis, involve matching the situation in Czechoslovakia as of mid-August 1968 to that of Hungary and Poland in October 1956. Although the decision problem was an extremely com-

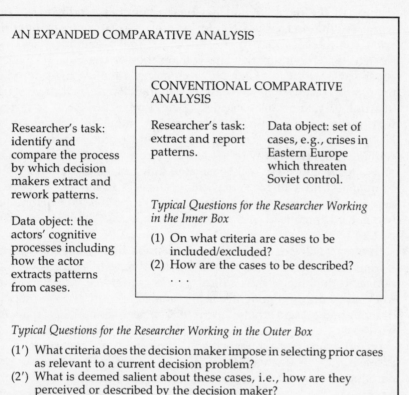

Figure 12.1   From comparative case analysis to the study of how cases are compared and used by decision makers

plex one for the Soviet leadership, analysis indicates that the decision to use military force in Czechoslovakia largely hinged on Soviet, Polish and East German leaders' judgments as to whether that country was another Poland or another Hungary (Robinson, 1968; Schmidt-Hauer and Muller, 1968; Ermath, 1969; Tigrid, 1969; Windsor and Roberts, 1969; Pelikan, 1976; Mlynar, 1978; Valenta, 1979; Tatu, 1981).

Other precedents are mentioned, including that of the ejection of Tito's Yugoslavia from the Cominform in 1948 and the Soviet use of troops to re-establish order following the Berlin uprising in 1953, but the studied opinion gravitates to the crises in Poland and Hungary in October and November 1956. There is abundant evidence for this reading in the memoirs and personal accounts by individuals who witnessed the internal debates. An example is a diary entry made by an arms control specialist of the Soviet Central Committee, Mikhail Voslensky, who summarized his conversation on the situation in Czechoslovakia with V. V. Zagladin, Ponomarev's deputy. In response to the report Voslensky made on his return from Prague in the first week of April, Zagladin capsulated the Soviet problem in terms of factors that distinguished the Czechoslovakian situation from that of Hungary. To him the parallels with Poland were overriding. "It is certainly possible that with some turn of events anti-socialist forces may appear, but these will be isolated individuals, and are not to be compared with Hungary. Regarding Dubcek, it should be remembered that there were panicky voices in 1956 and 1957 when Gomulka was named party head, and yet nothing happened"[3] (Voslensky, 1978, p. 126).

In short, analogies recur repeatedly in published media, transcripts, communiqués, and, if we believe first-hand reports, in the conversations and thinking of the political figures closest to crucial decisions. They also figure prominently in the analyst's effort after the fact to describe and explain what transpired. The parallels and discrepancies between cases are seized upon to explain the twists and turns of events. The analogy or juxtaposition is not simply a turn of phrase, but is integral to the analysis. Analogies are not only used to focus the description of events, but serve as a basis for exploring what might have been the case had certain factors or accidents not intruded. Valenta's (1979) post mortem on Dubcek's strategic errors is an example. By contrasting Dubcek to Tito, and to a lesser extent to Gomulka, Valenta concludes that Dubcek failed to learn the cardinal lesson of effective resistance to Soviet military intervention: a small state must maintain the credible possibility that force will be resisted by force. (At an early point in the course of events Dubcek denied himself this option by offering up General Prchlik in the effort to placate Warsaw Pact criticism.) Analogies are used by the decision makers and by the analysts attempting to understand the decision makers' reading of their situation and options. More than this, analogies are not simply rhetorical devices, but play a commanding role in shaping decisions by imposing certain options while masking others (Jervis, 1968, 1976; May, 1973).

From Coding Scheme to Language of Description

Before a correspondence between a pair of cases or situations can be recognized, the two must be described or perceived in common terms. This requirement, which of course holds for all systematic analysis as George (1979a) and others make abundantly clear, raises a number of preliminary issues regarding the language of description to be employed.

As demonstrated in George's (1979a, pp. 54–9) outline of the steps involved in conducting systematic comparison, the choice of cases and the selection of variables follow immediately from the substantive questions that motivate the research. The cases selected must be described in such a manner that generalizations can be drawn that satisfy the purpose of the study. For this reason it is instructive to work backwards from what the investigation seeks to find or demonstrate, to the question of how the data should be selected and arranged. Practical matters of convenience and availability intrude, but ultimately the research question is master. In the present case the underlying question involves the use of past histories to inform decisions in new, but similar, situations. The end product is a set of contingency plans or possible futures that emanate from a given situation. The situation that initially defines and motivates the decision problem is itself a sequence of events.

For example, the situation that confronted the Soviet leadership as of the second week of August 1968 was the product of the events that had transpired from the spring of that year up to that point in time. With the current situation as a given, the object of the analysis is to generate a set of strategies or courses of action that issue from that situation. In structuring the decision problem, each of these strategies is to be evaluated in terms of the costs and risks entailed with the result that options are criticized and ranked as they might be analyzed in a planning document or briefing book. In effect, the purpose is to replicate the way in which the decision problem takes on structure and definition, that is, the way in which options are created and deemed realistic and worth entertaining. It is the working hypothesis of this chapter that this process is to a significant extent driven by the explicit or intuitive matching of features of the current situation against those of other situations real or imagined. The dynamism and complexity of this process is best captured in the form of a programable procedure. When applied to a situation and equipped with a memory containing some set of case histories, the program pieces together strategies, each of which is qualified on the basis of what the histories have shown to be the result of pursuing similar strategies in similar contexts.

Using the history of Soviet responses to crises in its East European bloc as a laboratory, the purpose of the program is to re-create strategies that the Soviet leadership may have entertained at particular points in time. Of special interest are those turning points at which the Soviet Union weighed the prospect of outright military intervention. In approaching this problem the program exploits the role of historical analogies as they are used in identifying and choosing among hypothetical courses of action. Sequences of events representing past cases are fed into memory. The program matches the current situation, for example, the events of July and August 1968, against these histories. Once precedents have been found, they are assembled into a composite graph representing courses of action leading from the present into possible futures. These paths are then inspected for costs and risks, and an analysis is printed out which contains recommendations as to how the Soviet Union should proceed and why.

A Language of Events for the Soviet Case

Before it is possible to compare histories and construct contingency plans, the histories must be described in some uniform way. Much of the systematic comparative work on crisis behavior encodes cases as lists of values on variables without regard for an ordering across the variables; the information intrinsic to the temporal ordering of events is disregarded. There are numerous examples of this approach (George and Smoke, 1974; Blechman and Kaplan, 1978; Kaplan *et al.*, 1981). Some work exploits the information inherent in the temporal ordering of the events (or phases, or stages) that make up the crisis (Barringer, 1972; Bloomfield and Liess, 1969; Farris *et al.*, 1980). The present study follows the second practice, treating historical cases as sequences of situations or events chained together by, at a minimum, an ordering in time. Whereas it seems highly artificial to suppress the varieties of causal and intentional relations that transform mere chronology into interpreted history, for the present purpose it suffices to recognize only the relation of temporal succession. The data are thereby restricted to the merest skeleton of a chronicle. In the range of historical accounts, the data structure assumed in this study most closely resembles those simple chronicle-like entries compiled in such yearbooks as *Keesing's Contemporary Archives*. In short, in our usage a historical case is a sequence of events or actions ordered in time.

As a matter of convenience, and to facilitate manipulations involved in extracting patterns and constructing strategies, the events are recorded using a standardized set of phrases. These, in turn, are affixed with simple labels to speed the process of matching and to better reveal patterns and regularities.[4] This process of encoding can be illustrated using a fragment of the Czechoslovakian case. First, a raw précis is needed. Starting the case history with Novotny's appeal to Brezhnev, an abbreviated account of the course of events is extracted from case analyses (Robinson, 1968; Ermath, 1969; Windsor and Roberts, 1969; Remington, 1969, 1971; Tigrid, 1971; Pelikan, 1971, 1976; Golan, 1973; Simes, 1975; Skilling, 1976; Mlynar, 1978; Valenta, 1979; Tatu, 1981). In the effort to standardize and encode the case of the Soviet involvement in Czechoslovakia, the account is partitioned into paragraphs or propositions, each expressing an action from a predefined list. These propositions are then rewritten in a stylized form for the convenience of translating into an internal representation to be used by a computer program. Without loss of information, these propositions are further encoded by assigning unique symbols to each.[5] A segment of the narrative précis serves to illustrate how a case can be partitioned into events and rewritten as a sequence of stylized propositions to which labels have been assigned. The segment records the events between December 1967 and the end of March 1968. The encoded event follows the corresponding sentence in the narrative account.

December 1967:   The Stalinist head of the Czechoslovak Communist Party, Antonin Novotny, calls on Brezhnev to support him against the challenge to his leadership posed by the reform-minded opposition within the party; Brezhnev travels to Prague but adopts a "hands off" policy.

K42 [NATIONAL CP/GOVERNMENT ACTION :INVOLVING THE S.U. :APPEALS :FOR SUPPORT AGAINST CHALLENGE WITHIN THE PARTY]

D22 [CPSU/SOVIET ACTION :BETWEEN S.U. AND BLOC MEMBER(S) CONCILIATORY :NEGOTIATIONS WITH NATIONAL CP LEADER(S) POLITBURO :LEADING TO CHANGE IN NATIONAL CP LEADERSHIP :SOVIETS ACQUIESCE TO THE RISE OF A NEW LEADER]

January 1968: Novotny replaced as First Secretary by the head of the party in Slovakia, Alexander Dubcek.

L46 [NATIONAL CP/GOVERNMENT ACTION :LIBERALIZING SHIFT OR INITIATIVE :INVOLVING THE BALANCE BETWEEN FACTIONS :INDIVIDUAL LEADER DEMOTED OR EXPELLED]

Ultimately, there are two purposes in devising a coding scheme of this type: one concerns the fullness of the description it permits, and the other involves the effectiveness with which the descriptions can be searched for patterns and parallels. By generalizing the conventional notion of a coding scheme (Leng and Singer, 1970; Kegley, 1973; Hermann *et al.*, 1973) to the related but more encompassing concept of a formal language, both objectives can be met. The primitives of the language, its basic vocabulary, and the organization of the language reflect the purpose of the investigation, that in the present case is focused on Soviet strategic planning as it applies to Eastern Europe.[6]

The language devised must be capable of adequately expressing those factors that are likely to affect Soviet calculations. More than this, the language must be designed in such a way that the process of drawing analogies can be replicated, along with the subsequent activity of piecing together options and contingency plans informed by such analogies.

The lexicon used by the system reported in this chapter consists of an inventory of predicates that, taken together, make up a rudimentary language for describing political events of concern to the Soviet Union in Eastern Europe.[7] This language can be easily expanded to embrace a wider domain of events. Moreover, because the procedures for searching the case histories are independent of the way in which the cases are encoded, the language of description can be altered as desired. The lexicon assumed in this paper, although limited and inelegant, serves the present purpose. The bulk of the terms denote political actions exerted by one regime or political faction against another. These actions are sorted into four groupings by agent; for example, the Soviet Union, East European communist parties, and so on. A substantial fragment of the lexicon is displayed in Figure 12.2.

Once encoded on the basis of this lexicon, a case is expressed compactly as a sequence of symbols. With the case histories in this form it is possible to proceed to the issues of search, comparison and manipulation intrinsic to the creation of historical analogies.

Matching, Splicing and Rewriting Histories

The procedure described enables the researcher to represent cases as sequences of discrete symbols. At this point the problem of capturing the type of comparison and inference involved in the use of historical analogies becomes formally identical to a type of problem that is of central concern to a number of fields. Though there are important variations, the general task involves finding that subset from a sequence that best matches a given sequential pattern (Sellers, 1974a, 1974b, 1979, 1980; Hall and Dowling, 1980; Goldberg, 1982; Erickson and Sellers, 1983). In our working example, Czechoslovakia 1968, the sequential pattern to be matched is the encoded set of events preceding the Politburo decision of August 17, 1968. This sequence is to be compared against seven historical cases that, like the situation, have been rendered as sequences of symbols in accordance with the coding instrument described in the previous section. The cases include:

Czechoslovakia 1948 (culminating in the bloodless coup of February 25, 1948, in which the Communist Party takes over control from Benes's coalition government)

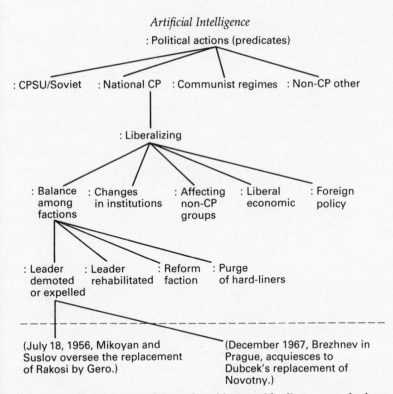

Artificial Intelligence
: Political actions (predicates)

: CPSU/Soviet : National CP : Communist regimes : Non-CP other

: Liberalizing

: Balance   : Changes   : Affecting   : Liberal   : Foreign
among   in institutions   non-CP   economic   policy
factions   groups

: Leader   : Leader   : Reform   : Purge
demoted   rehabilitated   faction   of hard-liners
or expelled

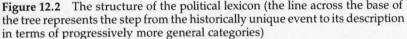

(July 18, 1956, Mikoyan and   (December 1967, Brezhnev in
Suslov oversee the replacement   Prague, acquiesces to
of Rakosi by Gero.)   Dubcek's replacement of
                                      Novotny.)

Figure 12.2 The structure of the political lexicon (the line across the base of the tree represents the step from the historically unique event to its description in terms of progressively more general categories)

Yugoslavia 1948 (the tension in Soviet-Yugoslav relations resulting in the expulsion of Tito's Yugoslavia from Cominform)

East Germany 1953 (triggered by the Berlin uprising in June 1953)

Poland 1956 (the Natolin faction surrenders power to Gomulka and Marshal Rokossovsky is recalled to the Soviet Union)

Hungary 1956 (Nagy's reform movement erupts into anti-Soviet rebellion)

Albania 1960 (a function of the Sino-Soviet rift and Soviet rapprochement with Yugoslavia)

Romania 1964–8 (over questions of Romanian sovereignty in matters of Council on Mutual Economic Assistance policy and the stationing of Warsaw Treaty Organization forces on Romanian territory)

Measures of Discrepancy and Deformation

Although the essential task is conceptually straightforward, sequence comparison in rich domains encounters a number of complications. These stem from the problem of evaluating partial matches, when the notion of resemblance is ill-defined. Much of the current work in this area derives from a strategy developed in the theory of error-correcting codes and parsers (Levenshtein, 1965a, 1965b; Ulam, 1972; Fu, 1982, pp. 246–75).[8] Levenshtein defines a general measure of difference between two sequences in terms of the number of insertions, deletions and substitutions required to transform the one into the other. Each of these operations is assigned a cost function; the "distance" between two sequences is set equal to the minimum cost set of transformations required to convert the one into the other. (If the weights are properly chosen such that the conditions of positive definiteness, symmetry and the triangle inequality hold, then the measure so defined becomes a true metric.)

The essential idea of Levenshtein's procedure can be conveyed using a parlor game where the object is to change one word into another by successively altering letters. In his example, Kruskal (1983) converts "WATER" into "WINE," whereas Schreider (1975) uses the Russian terms for "BLACK" and "WHITE." An illustration is useful because it conveys not only the basis for indexing the similarity of two sequences, but introduces a notation that has several uses. Following Kruskal (1983), a succession of letter-by-letter changes (that happen to be minimal) can be displayed using the following "listing":

WATER
  Substitute I for A
WITER
  Substitute N for T
WINER
  Delete R
WINE

Two, more compact, notations are those of a "trace", for example:

WATER
| |
| |
WINE

and an "alignment", for example:

[WATER]

[WINE–]

Each representation has its uses. The listing, while more cumbersome, is sometimes of theoretical interest because, as in computer science and microbiology, it can be construed as recording a sequence of physical processes and their intermediate products. In short it can be conceived as a process model where the individual transformations correspond to physical or computational transformations that exist within a substantive domain. Though they fail to express this aspect, the trace and alignment are convenient structures for reporting the matches found by some procedure.

The more compact notational forms of the trace and alignment can serve to describe the procedure used to render comparative process at work in the construction of historical analogies. In fashioning its recommendation for Soviet policy in the Czechoslovakian crisis in the summer of 1968, the system finds partial matches between the situation it is given and sequences of events within the East German, Polish, Romanian and Hungarian cases. The closeness of the resemblance varies, however; the events in Hungary following October 24, 1956 most closely approximate the Czech case. The match found between the Czechoslovakian case prior to invasion and the Hungarian case can be conveniently expressed as an alignment in which the symbols in the respective sequences represent actions and events as encoded by the lexicon discussed in the previous section:

Hungary (Oct. 29–Nov. 2, 1956) [D M F P F C]

Czech.   (Aug. 4–Aug. 14, 1968) [D' – F' – – C']

With the costs associated with insertions, deletions and substitutions each set to 1, the system determines that the best match aligns the events on the eve of the invasion of Czechoslovakia with events just prior to the Soviet invasion of Hungary, with the publication of the "New Chart" [D] in the Hungarian case identified with the Bratislava Declaration [D'], with the Soviet decision to cancel the evacuation of troops [F] from Hungary on October 30, 1956 matched with the announcement of troop maneuvers [F'] on the Czech frontier on August 11, 1968, and, finally, with the warnings in *Pravda* [C], November 2, 1956 aligned with the shrill warnings in *Literaturaya Gazata* [C'] on August 14, 1968.

It should be noted that, within the architecture of the coding instrument, the symbols that make up the sequences do not denote individual types of events, but categories of types of events. They are in a sense "middle-level". As noted in the section on the language of description, it is organized in this fashion to sustain richly differentiated description, in George's (1979a) sense of the term, while at the same time supporting the matching and reasoning procedures described in this and the next sections.

The alignment reveals several of the complications that typically arise in this type of matching problem. One involves the difference in the number of symbols in the two sequences. With historical data, like with data encountered in a number of domains, it would be highly restrictive to permit only correspondences between sequences of exactly the same length. In working with political histories it is likely

237

that one account may be richer in detail than another and yet the two may be deemed to be structurally quite similar. The problem is to construct a matching procedure that is insensitive to minor differences in the detail of the reportage. In the continuous case this issue is called "time warping" and arises in many areas of research, particularly that of speech recognition. The technical problem of constructing the best alignment(s) given an initial sequential pattern and a set of sequences to be inspected is solved using a dynamic programing strategy (Sellers, 1974a, 1974b; Wagner and Fischer, 1974; Erickson and Sellers, 1983). This work is motivated by the problem typical of the comparison of RNA, DNA and protein sequences in microbiology (Smith and Waterman, 1980, 1981; Friedland and Kedes, 1985).

At the formal level, given an encoding like that described earlier, the problem of comparing political case histories replicates the essential features of some of the most recent work in mathematical microbiology. The basic data structure in both domains is that of a sequence. The one is ordered in space, that is, from first to last or left to right, corresponding to the physical object suitably stretched and oriented. The other is ordered in time. The number of articulated elements or events that comprise a typical sequence are of similar magnitude. In the study of proteins and nucleotides the vocabulary consists of either four or twenty terms; there are roughly thirty distinct terms in the political lexicon we employ in the case study. The length of the typical sequence in the work in molecular biology ranges from less than one hundred molecules to thousands in the case of RNA, and to millions in the case of DNA. A typical political history may include one hundred or more events or actions. In short, at an abstract level, the isomorphism between the essential features of the two research problems suggests that the formalism and procedures that have proven effective in the one may hold out promise for the other. We believe this to be likely.

The programed procedure initially used to search the case descriptions for matching subsequences of events is based on work with error-correcting parsers (Aho and Peterson, 1972; Aho, Hirschberg and Ullman, 1974; Aho, Hopcroft and Ullman, 1974; Tanaka and Kasai, 1976; Tanaka and Fu, 1978; Fu, 1982). The formally less involved and computationally cheaper procedure that the system presently uses is based on algorithms and theorems developed by Wagner and Fischer (1974) and by Sellers (1974a, 1974b).[9] Our problem differs from that confronting the mathematical microbiologist in that we are interested not only in identifying and comparing patterns, but in using them to fashion strategies. This adds an additional step to the analysis, as becomes apparent in the case study of Soviet policy in Eastern Europe.

Analogies in Action: Constructing Contingency Plans

Rethinking Soviet Strategy on the Eve of the Invasion

On occasion a computer program solves a problem with an elegance and novelty that surprises the programmer. An example is the solution devised by the program reported in this chapter to the strategic problem the Soviet leadership faced on the eve of the military intervention in Czechoslovakia. Effectively freezing the stream of events that preceded the Politburo session of August 17, 1968—the date on which the fated decision to invade was reached—the system is set to the task of reconstructing the strategies that Brezhnev, Shelest, Suslov and other key Soviet officials may have individually or collectively raised and dismissed on that date. After identifying several feasible actions and dismissing them on grounds of cost or risk, the program fixed upon a strategy of steadily incrementing the Warsaw Pact troop level of the forces then engaged in "staff maneuvers" on Czechoslovak territory. The recommendation is that this force be increased until it equaled the number of armored divisions that had been assembled on Hungarian territory in the first week of November in 1956. While this preferred strategy is historically wrong, since the Soviets in fact chose to invade in dramatic fashion with a force twice that used in Hungary twelve years before, the system's solution to the strategic problem seems superior to the actual Soviet decision for a number of reasons. It is equally ruthless, yet more subtle, not incurring many of the costs and risks incumbent in a massive military action. The program in effect rediscovers Tatu's criticism of the Soviet Politburo's suboptimal decision. Rather than applying force in the dramatic and politically costly form of an outright invasion "one can argue that a steady reinforcement of [the contingent introduced at the end of May] similar to what took place in Hungary on October 30 to November 1, 1956, might have been another course of action. The maneuvers could have evolved into a creeping invasion of the country with the same outcome as the August intervention but with less dramatic overtones" (1981, p. 224).

Constructing analogies is only a preliminary part of the overall activity of creating and evaluating possible courses of action. Although analogies act to focus the imagination, their relation to the actual process of decision is unclear. Although on occasion they may exert such control on imagination and debate that they effectively exclude all other possibilities and, thereby, dictate policy by default, in the normal case the analyst or policy maker entertains several analogies that vie for consideration. This exercise of the imagination is clearly at work in preparing what is considered to be relevant to the decision problem. It

239

defines the landscape or world of possibilities, which, subsequently, may be examined in an articulated way.

As Steinbruner (1974) and others have argued, this preliminary structuring of the imagination or effort to manage the "structural" uncertainty of the decision problem is woefully under-studied and yet is of intrinsically equal or greater importance when compared to subsequent steps in the decision activity involving the application of optimal or satisficing decision rules. Possibly the neglect occurs because the process goes largely unnoticed by the decision makers themselves. The initial way in which a problem is conceived and explored is often relegated to the realm of intuition and *Fingerspitzengefuhl*. It is our contention that the activity of evoking analogies is central to the way in which a strategic problem takes on definition.

To this point we have concentrated on the procedure by which the historical record or memory might be searched in the effort to extract analogies. The question now arises as to how these historical parallels, each loaded with different semantic content and judged to be of varying relevance as indexed by the metric imposed, are utilized in the process of defining and judging options. In short, the theoretical problem becomes one of integrating the analogies identified into the more articulate and self-aware process in which considerations and arguments are explicity raised in the effort to construct and choose among strategies. In our working example, Zagladin's reasoning, cited earlier, illustrates this activity. He explicitly imposes a pair of analogies, the Hungarian and Polish precedents, juxtaposing the Czechoslovakian situation against the factors and risks identified with the two prior experiences (Voslensky, 1978).

Because both the situation and the case histories can be presented in a natural way as sequences of events and actions, if the connections among individual events are construed as simple asymmetric relations, a multitude of cases can be represented simultaneously as a directed graph. This involves no more than aggregating the sequences already extracted from the histories deemed relevant to the situation in question. Using arbitrary numbers to designate types of events (1, 2, 3, . . . etc.), if the analogies returned by the procedure described in the previous section were to be written out, they might yield a configuration like that in Figure 12.3, where each sequence of numbered nodes represents a fragment of a case history identified as analogical to the situation. The sequences are in effect assembled in computer memory as a composite graph (Ore, 1962).

If we assume a composite graph of this form, constructed on the basis of fragments of the past (and possibly other scenarios supplied by ideology or professional training), then the decision problem amounts

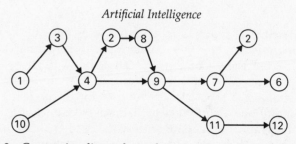

Figure 12.3   Composite directed graph aggregating event sequences from case histories

to exploring and evaluating the sometimes overlapping and cross-cutting event sequences that are expressed in the graph. This throws light on how analogies, though rooted in unique events, can stimulate the creation of strategies that, although they resemble the precedent, are nevertheless distinctive. In effect they are informed by the analogy, but represent an inventive variation that takes into consideration other analogies and factors particular to the situation at hand. The resulting scenario or contingency plan is, thus, an amalgram. The strategy reported at the outset of this chapter is an example. Although based on five historical cases, it is not a slavish copy of any one. In short, the analogies serve to define the problem space; they only indirectly determine the set of strategies that emerge from the exploration and inspection of this space of possibilities.

In terms of the work in artificial intelligence and cognitive simulation, the approach departs from the conception of problem solving inherent in the work with "weak" methods like that of means-ends analysis identified with Newell and Simon and their students. Whereas the work on problem solving is reviewed elsewhere as it may apply to the study of foreign policy (Mefford, 1982a, 1982b), it suffices here to contrast the more general approach to that used by the system reported in this chapter.

In solving a problem a program searches a "problem space" seeking a sequence of actions (or a least costly sequence of actions) that leads from a state described in terms of a set of initial conditions to a state that is defined as within the solution or goal set (Newell and Simon, 1972; Sacerdoti, 1977). The problem space consists of all permitted combinations of the actions available to the program and, in general, is of such size that it cannot be exhaustively inspected. Hence the need for heuristic strategies for paring down the search space. In a certain sense the use of historical analogies to structure a decision problem can be construed as the imposition of heuristics. The better interpretation, however, is to view the pattern-matching procedures in the current system as a method for constructing a highly constrained problem space. In this fashion the computational task of searching for viable

241

political strategies is kept within bounds. Going beyond the technical issue, the manner in which this problem space is constructed is significant as a partial theory of the problem-solving processes actually engaged in by decision makers and analysts. There is, therefore, a computational and a theoretical payoff. As in the modeling of weak methods, a solution is defined as a path, that is, sequence of actions, that traverses the graph. In keeping with worst-case analysis, a strategic solution to the problem posed by a situation is defined in essentially negative terms. It must traverse the graph without entering into a prohibited event (or into the *k*-diameter neighborhood of a prohibited event). In the present example two events are considered prohibited due to their negative impact on Soviet interests: a national communist party's decision to share power, that is, to default on its role as the leading political force; and the outbreak of a bloody, anti-Soviet rebellion. In the search for a viable strategy, if the system encounters either of these event types, it discards its current plan and backs up a safe distance from the disturbing event. In addition, it reports out the failed strategy, providing the likelihood or possibility of encountering such an eventuality as grounds for dismissing the strategy under consideration. In terms of these costly events the system is risk-averse: if at all possible it searches for a course of action that safely avoids such outcomes.

The analysis produced by the system takes the form of an initial description of what it identifies as the commanding parallels between the crisis situation and the best analogy it can draw from the historical cases. In this description, particularly adverse events are flagged as presenting dangers to be avoided. Dismissing courses of action that lead ineluctably to such negative outcomes, the system attempts to piece together a path or contingency plan that leads from the description of the current situation to a terminal point. In the Czechoslovakian example, the strategy devised approximates that which Tatu (1981) has called "creeping invasion." It is modeled after the Hungarian precedent, but contains a unique twist not present in the case histories. It is both historically informed and innovative like the best foreign policy problem solving it is intended to explain.

Evaluating this system's performance raises several questions pertaining not only to its accuracy and reliability, but to its rightful use. It is one thing to replicate Soviet behavior, but quite another to make improvements upon it. While the political and ethical questions entailed in the design of machines that plot strategies are of serious concern, they are not broached in this chapter. Our purpose here has been to explain how the system works and, more importantly, spell out how it captures several large issues regarding theory building and data analysis that arise in the study of foreign policy.

Notes

On the theme of scenarios and analogies, I have benefited from lengthy discussions with Alex Hybel and Ward Edwards. Alexander George and Hayward Alker gave me written comments on the sections of comparative method and logic of inquiry in general. My special thanks goes to Charles F. Hermann for his editorial efforts: with his help the chapter is now half its original length. The programming reported was supported by a grant from the University of Southern California Faculty Research and Innovation Fund. That support is gratefully acknowledged.

1 These efforts range from semantic models (Bennett, 1984, 1985; David Sylvan, 1984) to data analysis (Schrodt, 1984, 1985) and policy studies (Donald Sylvan, 1985a, 1985c). Efforts include the simulation of political argument (Majeski, 1984; Mefford, 1985). The earliest work by a political scientist is Alker's studies of "precedent logics" (Alker and Christensen, 1972; Bennett and Alker, 1977; Alker, Bennett and Mefford, 1980). The volume edited by Sylvan and Chan (1984) also contains efforts by these and other political scientists, including Thorson and Tanaka, as does the volume edited by Cimbala (1986). The most ambitious effort to date is probably the natural-language-based system designed by Duffy and Mallory (1984), which is intended to serve as a medium in which political reasoning can be modeled.
2 For a review of this literature with special attention to subfields within machine learning, including learning by example and the induction of classifications, see Mefford (1982a).
3 "Freilich koennen bei einem Umschwung auch antisozialistische Kraefte auftauchen, aber das sind Einzelpersonen, mit Ungarn ist das nicht zu vergleichen. Im Zusammenhang mit der Ernennung von Gomulka . . . gab es 1956/57 auch panische Stimmungen, und es ist doch nichts passiert." Michalik Voslenski, "Das wird nur den Amerikanern helfen," Tagebuch-Notizen des sowjetischen Funktionars Michael Woslenski ueber die Hintergrunde der Prag-Invasion, ["That Will only Help the Americans". The Diary of the Soviet Functionary, Michael Voslenski, regarding the Background of the Prague Invasion.] *Der Spiegel* 32. Jahrgang (August 21, 1978): 126–129, p. 126.
4 For proposals on how to represent the internal structure of events, see Mefford (1982b).
5 The program reported in this paper uses a subset of the 255 distinct bit strings used to encode the ASCII character set, but this choice is arbitrary, dictated solely by the desire to efficiently compare and manipulate the cases once encoded.
6 We resist the notion that some set of semantic primitives is canonical in an absolute sense. On this issue, see Mefford (1982b).
7 Those actions indicative of the Soviet Union or its leadership are grouped under one heading, as are those actions initiated by individual Eastern European communist parties and those involving the collective participation of several communist regimes operating formally or informally under the guise of the Warsaw Treaty Organization (WTO) or the Council for Mutual Economic Assistance (CMEA). A final group involves actors within socialist societies which are neither affiliated with the Communist Party nor identified with other states. Examples include unions, spontaneous mob

violence, public pressure, and the like. Several difficult-to-categorize actions are also included in this set, for example, economic crisis. The division into these four groupings is a matter of convenience and does not signify a serious nomenclature. We have experimented with more differentiated lexicons patterned after case grammars (Fillmore, 1968; Winograd, 1972, 1983), but a relatively simple inventory of political actions suffices as a base for the present study of analogical reasoning and planning (Charniak and Wilks, 1976; Mefford, 1982b). The lexicon is available from the author, Department of Political Science, Ohio State University, Columbia, Ohio 43210.

8 This issue and others intrinsic to sequence-based pattern recognition are discussed at length in a paper in which the algorithm and LISP code are presented (Mefford, 1983). It suffices here to provide the motivation for the algorithm.

9 For a full account plus a listing of the code, see Mefford (1983).

PART V

The Collective Process of Foreign Policy Decision Making

13

Decision Regimes and the Comparative Study of Foreign Policy

CHARLES W. KEGLEY, JR.

Introduction: The Incarceration of Theories of Foreign Policy

In what new directions might research in the comparative study of foreign policy most productively move? What paths, if pursued, are likely to provide more valid generalizable findings and more potent predictors of the external behavior of states than those emerging from prevailing research strategies and conventional conceptualizations?

This paper heuristically and didactically advances one among many potential responses to these questions. Before proceeding with this proposal, some characterization of the primary obstacles to be overcome must be identified.

Two propensities in comparative research practice may have contributed especially to the loss of momentum which our research movement is presently experiencing (see Ashley, 1976; Faurby, 1976b; Harf, Moon and Thompson, 1976; Kegley, 1980). Our genre of research has become imprisoned, in the first instance, by its overwhelming reliance on a particular kind of data, events and national attribute data (for example, see Kegley *et al.*, 1975). In the second instance, its progress has been blocked by the lack of systematic attention to the foreign policy-making process: to the decisions and the policy makers who make them. Many in the field have proceeded as if those individuals who make foreign policies—their characteristics, as well as the procedures they follow in the formulation and implementation of foreign policies—do not count.

These symbiotically related proclivities have locked our investigations of foreign policy into a mode of inquiry that has allowed for only

247

incremental discovery. On the basis of the findings that available data bases disclose, we have been asked to believe that foreign policy behaviors are influenced almost exclusively by the internal characteristics of nations or the attributes of those nations' external environments. This narrow supporting logic has required us to think in terms of bivariate relationships and causal linkages between policy inputs and outputs. The foreign policy-making process—occurring in what Easton (1953, 1965) termed the "black box," which converts policy inputs to policy outputs—has been discounted. The policy-making process *has* been like a black box to many of us since we see what comes out but not much of what happens inside. We have often dealt with these secretive features and functions by ignoring them or failing to incorporate them into our models, forgetting that the absence of evidence is not evidence of absence. Surely studies conducted within the confines of this research perspective fail to tap much of the variance in the real world of foreign policy making and enable only a limited range of phenomena to be adequately explained.

Thus, our habits of inquiry have imprisoned us. We have repeated our inquiries so often to ourselves—using the same framework to analyze the same kinds of limited data—that we have come to believe them and even to mistake them for reality. Our findings are to some degree artifacts of the methods and data that generated them. Even where these findings have converged, their ability to account for and predict foreign policy outcomes has not been very impressive and their validity has remained contingent upon the intellectual orientation that produced them. The tale our findings tell and the image of foreign policy they convey fail to approximate the real world of foreign policy determination. Have our models imposed a shape on events that is merely a figment of our imagination or, more accurately, a product of our methodological routines?

Liberating Theories of Foreign Policy: Decision Regimes

One avenue of escape is to follow the suggestion of Marcel Proust, who observed that "The life of nations merely repeats, on a larger scale, the lives of their component cells; and he who is incapable of understanding the mystery, the reactions, the laws that determine the movements of the individual, can never hope to say anything worth listening to about the struggles of nations."

Policy makers' behaviors and cognitions may be assumed to be the factors that directly determine foreign policy behavior—not the internal and external conditions operative at the point of decision. National and international circumstances do not make decisions and forge foreign policy; decision makers alone do this. How decision makers perceive the positive and negative incentives of foreign policy options determines the ultimate course of action. In theorizing about the sources of foreign policy behavior, we should begin with individuals, because only persons think, prefer and act. We can agree categorically with the view that "all factors that influence what foreign policy organizations actually do must somehow be filtered or translated into the psychological environment through . . . the attitudinal prisms of decision makers" (Hermann and Hermann, 1984, p. 2).

The suggestion that we watch and listen to individuals is hardly original. Our field has been aware of this need for decades.[1] This prescription evokes a sense of *déjà vu*, in that it returns us to the phenomenologically oriented and idiographically rich approaches recommended three decades ago (recall Snyder, Bruck and Sapin, 1954, and Snyder and Robinson, 1961). Yet, it does point to a direction which can restore some balance in how we seek to explain foreign policy behavior—providing the problems (see McClosky, 1956, and Rosenau, 1967c) associated with the application of those earlier, non-parsimonious and nonoperational decision-making frameworks emphasizing individuals and their perceptions can be overcome. In asking us to take into account human actions, it demands that we escape the deterministic logic that has attempted to explain national behavior abroad by reference exclusively to the political, social and economic forces that influence decisions, but not by reference to the decision makers who, in the last analysis, do the deciding. Only by incorporating decision-making-level phenomena can domestic and international factors be causally linked to foreign policy behavior. What is needed to include human beings and their decisions and motives in accounts of foreign policy is an integrating concept which can combine the multiple sources of influence operating on foreign policy from different levels. The field has suffered from the absence of such a construct.

Circumstantial experience invites the approach that is recommended in this chapter as a response to the problem identified. In interviews with twenty-six heads of state, foreign ministers or ambassadors visiting the University of South Carolina between 1982 and 1984, this author was struck with the uniformity with which these policy makers described how their decision behaviors were shaped. Although these descriptions differed in important ways, these policy makers all noted that for many policy issues with which they dealt decision making was *governed by rules*. Even though their positions allowed them a wide range of discretion (what we are accustomed to calling "decision latitude"), with respect to some policy questions these policy makers perceived incentives to make decisions in conformity with salient prescriptions. Because making important decisions was so difficult, policy makers acknowledged the need to reduce the task by placing it within a set of rules. In disclosing their reliance on decision rules (whether tacit or explicit), these policy makers seemed to agree with the observation that "it is so hard to make important decisions that we have a great urge to reduce them to rules" (Hacking, 1984, p. 17).

To the extent that this tendency is an empirical regularity, it provides a clue as to how we might proceed. Presumably, if we can identify the decision rules that are topically operative for different central policy makers, might we better predict and explain the kind of foreign policy likely to emanate from the countries these leaders represent? Let us pursue that possibility by explicating the assumptions surrounding the orienting-concept that it introduced here, which is termed a "decision regime."

Unlike the common use of the term *regime* to refer to the central political leadership of a national government (as is used by Hagan in Chapter 17), students of transnational relations recently have broadened the definition of "regimes." So-called "regime analysis" has generated a burgeoning literature (exemplary are Ruggie, 1972; Haas, 1975, 1980; Keohane and Nye, 1977; Young, 1980; Dolman, 1981; Coate, 1982; Krasner, 1982a; Puchala and Hopkins, 1983; Keohane, 1984). As a concept, *international regimes* have been usefully applied to analyze the collection of rules, norms and decision-making procedures that members of the international political system are sometimes observed to support in order to regularize behavior and to cooperatively resolve issues that surface on their common agendas. Although many definitions of such regimes can be found, most converge on the notion of a regime as an institutionalized system of cooperation between or among interacting parties, usually with respect to a given issue or issue-area. As defined by Krasner (1982a, p. 2), international regimes are composed of principles, norms, rules and procedures: "Principles are beliefs of fact, causation, and rectitude. Norms are standards of behavior defined in terms of rights and obligations. Rules are specific prescriptions or proscriptions for actions. Decision-making procedures are prevailing practices for making and implementing collective choice."

At the international level, regimes are generally believed to come into being in response to perceived problems, to develop among parties that share a common problem, and to be created from the mutual interests of these parties to cooperate in order to find solutions to the shared problem. Grounded in self-interests, the rules of international regimes take on quasi-legal authority, but usually in the absence of machinery to enforce compliance with those agreed-upon norms for behavior. International regime analysis assumes that, once formed, such international regimes constrain the behavior of members agreeing to adhere to them.

According to this analytical innovation, sovereign states are perceived to be the critical members of international regimes. Young (1980), in fact, argues that "the members of international regimes are always sovereign states," but quickly adds that "the parties carrying out the actions governed by international regimes are often private entities." In this sense, nonstate actors are often included in discussion of international regimes as key participants in those sectors of contemporary transnational relations where collaboration for concerted action based on shared purposes is emergent.

Might the comparative study of foreign policy profit by transferring the regime concept to the level of foreign policy making? Could it be employed to analyze the norms that may structure the making of decisions among participants in the foreign policy-making process of states? To this author's knowledge, up to this time the concept of an international regime has not been directly applied to the level of foreign policy making within nation-states. The application appears potentially appropriate, however.

Part of what makes this transfer inviting is the possibility that the formation of a regime is probable in *any* situation where there is a need for rules and procedures to regulate collective problem solving. Presumably, this recommendation would assert, the concept of a regime can in principle set the "rules of the game" among actors in *any* environment or in any group, providing such groups do indeed make decisions in compliance with rules, even when such norms are neither written nor legally binding. "People," it has been said (Harris, 1979, p. 275), "have a rule for everything they do." Collectivities, like individuals, almost invariably establish rules and procedures in order to plan, coordinate and reach decisions for at least some issues. (For instance, can any marriage survive without the creation of rules and procedures to manage decisions regarding some kinds of problems?) Decision regimes may be ubiquitous: "For every political system, be it the United States, New York City, or the American Political Science Association, there is a corresponding regime . . . Statesmen nearly always perceive themselves as constrained by principles, norms, and rules that prescribe and proscribe varieties of behavior" (Puchala and Hopkins, 1983, pp. 62, 86).

Can we not assume that those who make the foreign policies of

251

states, similarly to unitary state and nonstate transnational actors, confront some issues that promote the establishment of rules, norms and procedures for the formulation of their nation's foreign policy toward them? Do they not also often face problems from abroad that require cooperation among participants for solution and that make the achievement of consensus a precondition for success? Is there not in this environment also a great need for regularity, for order, for predictability? Are not such environments conducive to the formulation of decision rules, even where conflicts, bargaining and infighting over the values directing policy are endemic? Could it be that here—like within the competitive self-help international system—actors' self-interests are ultimately served by their ability to arrive at agreement about the decision rules which should define the boundaries of permissible action? If so, the resultant regime within such policy-making systems—when emergent—should be no less potent in constraining the behaviors of participants than are the kind of international regimes that have emerged in the Hobbesian, anarchical international system.

In fact, decision-making systems within states could prove to be even *more* conducive to the formation of regimes than is the system of relations between states. The formation of shared preferences and respected rules—whether formal or informal, written or unwritten, explicit or implicit, specific or general—for the making of foreign policy decisions is especially likely, given the overwhelming need for them. It is difficult to imagine the foreign policy-making process unfolding in the absence of decision rules and norms to make that task manageable. Let us elaborate.

Why Decision Regimes Tend to Form

A cluster of premises about the nature of the process of foreign policy decision making as it unfolds in national capitals encourages consideration of the proposition that decision regimes tend to materialize to shape foreign policy making. Those assumptions posit that foreign policy making routinely:

- evolves from the cumulative impact of a large number of decisions built up over time; foreign policy—rarely the product of a single isolated decision—has an accretional character and defers to principles of action that have been legitimized by many previous decisions and their outcomes: choices create precedents.
- is created by the articulation and aggregation of interests, but once created, past policies in turn generate institutions and interests that sustain them: the result is that the range of policy choice considered legitimate is thereafter reduced.

- is the product of a social process (see Anderson in Chapter 15) taking place in a group context that exerts pressure for the attainment of consensus on rules and for obedience to norms within its culture.
- demands organization, which in turn requires the formation of standard operating procedures, the identification of goals, and specification of sanctioned practices for realizing them.
- occurs in a relatively stable institutional setting that requires the clarification of value criteria and the offering of some rationale for them.
- requires planning, which is intellectually and politically impossible in the absence of some ground rules.
- defers to decision rules to simplify the task of choice, thus enabling policy makers to cope with the problems of insufficient information or information overload, ambiguity, problem recognition, insufficient time for the making of decisions, and the like.
- requires collaboration, which fosters the formation of agreement on rules and encourages the observance of those rules (because their violation would challenge that collaboration and generate costly conflict).
- is animated by the instilled need to establish policy continuity and predictability, thereby constraining the number of alternative paths that might be considered or followed under various contingencies.

As a caricature of the process of policy making, these assumptions, to a degree, may exaggerate the degree to which commonalities in the process of foreign policy decision making are extant. They depict a Weberian 'ideal type', describing a level of coordination, control and order that is always sought in administrative settings but rarely achieved.

Moreover, these assumptions implicitly challenge the "rational" choice model of decision making in foreign affairs. The "task environment" (Dill, 1958) for foreign policy makers is not conducive to pure rationality (see Rowe, 1974); it encourages decision making by deference to rules rather than by a cost-benefit analysis of the relative merits of all possible options. Rationality is described as "bounded" because the need to take shortcuts in calculating decision costs encourages the acceptance of satisfactory rather than maximal options. Thus, the assumption is made that policy makers often select less-than-optimal foreign policy options in conformity with the entrenched customs and practices of a consensually grounded decision regime, in part because that behavior avoids stimulating domestic political opposition or adverse redistributive costs (Lamborn, 1985, p. 41). Deference to sanctioned rules for choice thus serve policy makers' interests, even though rationality is compromised. And yet, the routinization of choice and standardization of practice does not preclude the capacity of policy makers to establish rationally new rules or to reorder preference structures; thus a decision regime is not necessarily incompatible with a rational model's assumptions.

253

In addition, to claim that decision making is often governed by rules is not to say that rulers do not rule. To possess a code of behavior is not to eliminate the possibility that the code can be violated or compromised, or that participants in the policy-making process will so value consensus that they will not take parochial positions. Such a claim would be a gross simplification. Still, people with power often *do* act on principle and do resist the temptation to make decisions arbitrarily. They are rewarded for such conduct politically. Policy makers succeed in rising to positions of power, in part, by their ability to represent themselves as leaders who understand the rules and customs supported broadly by their society. Their ability to build winning coalitions for their policy preferences depends on their ability to know the rules and utilize that knowledge to their competitive advantage. Accordingly, decision makers are inclined to study and to respect established practices and to allow their behavior to be circumscribed by voluntary deference to them because their personal interests are served by such submission. Thus, it is important to acknowledge that policy-making organizations are arenas for conflict, but the propensity with which coalitions within them form to resolve conflicts and arrive at rules for the setting of policy priorities is remarkable.[2] Bargaining does occur in policy making, but this can contribute to the formation of consensus as well as its erosion.

Definitional Clarifications and Measurement Implications: Decision Regimes and the Study of Foreign Policy

As conceptualized here, decision regimes, like operational codes, are composed of cognitive beliefs emerging from a relentlessly political process. Two major types of decision regimes may be identified, although, as shall be seen, they tend to be connected causally. Decision regimes may emerge when there is leadership consensus regarding the substance of policy as well as the process by which it is made. The former are termed *substantive* decision regimes, the latter *procedural* decision regimes. Substantive decision regimes are predicated on a negotiated view of global reality and a nation's place in it; through it the ambiguities of a complex international environment are interpreted and the range of a state's foreign policy response to the challenges perceived are framed. By operating as an expression of the broad aims of a society in its relations with actors beyond its borders, substantive decision regimes contribute to the definition of a nation's foreign policy goals. They arise from the need for any society to come

254

to terms with its core values and to arrive at some modicum level of agreement if it is to deal adaptively with the threats to survival and sovereignty confronting it from abroad. Often, but not always, the processes through which decisions are reached which may culminate in a substantive decision regime are themselves governed by the decision rules of a procedural regime.

Although these conceptions of regimes may open up some promising research possibilities if transferred from the study of relations *between* states to the study of decision processes *within* states, it would be a serious mistake to inadvertently transfer the deficiencies of international regime analysis and permit them to afflict the comparative study of foreign policy as well. Those deficiencies are multiple (see Strange, 1982). Conspicuous among them and most pertinent for our purposes has been the tendency for international regime analysis to employ elastic definitions of the concept and to implicitly assume that nearly all global issues addressed through collaborative endeavors are governed by shared principles within a regime. Clearly, regimes are not universal and do not automatically arise whenever international cooperation surfaces to concertedly confront a common problem. Some issues do not benefit from the formation of international regimes (Rothstein, 1984), and where shared purposes and practices are exhibited there also may not be emergent a regime to manage the collective aims that are perceived.

Similarly, it would be a mistake to assume that the need for consensus and rules for foreign policy making necessarily assures that agreement about beliefs surrounding a state's position on a foreign policy issue will materialize. The formation of decision regimes in foreign policy may *not* be assumed to be ubiquitous. To avoid falling into that trap, a nonelastic definition of a decision regime needs to be provided, one which allows for those dimensions of foreign policy behavior that are products of a consensually based set of decision rules to be differentiated from those which are not. To tighten the definition of the concept, two questions must be addressed: "Of what are decision regimes an instance?" and "How can we recognize when a state is acting in conformity with one, as opposed to when it is not?"

Regime Indicators

First, how can we operationally define a foreign policy decision regime so as to delineate what it is meant to include and exclude? At its root, by a substantive decision regime we mean nothing more or less than a set of consensually based rules for action which limit a state's range of permissible options in its conduct abroad. Such a regime refers to those important sets of issues on which policy makers hold in common values or rules that legitimate principles for the making of foreign policy decisions. They exist when policy makers' images of the external environment are so convergent that a set of established prescriptions and ground rules may be said to govern decision making regarding policy planning and policy implementation with respect to a given feature of that environment.

Notice that this definition does not make a substantive decision regime synonymous with foreign policy writ large. It confines its meaning to that *subset* of issues on which central policy makers hold highly shared and strongly felt convictions about the norms that should shape the position of their state toward them. Incentives for and the achievement of shared beliefs are not expected to arise for all issues which populate a state's foreign policy agenda. Indeed, the level of shared belief required to enable a decision regime to materialize is so high that for most states the formation of a decision regime may be expected to be a relatively rare occurrence. Nonetheless, when convictions about decision rules and procedures with respect to an issue do crystallize and stabilize, then (and only then) a coherent regime for the pursuit of shared purposes can be identified. In those exceptional cases we may have a powerful predictor, for knowledge of these shared beliefs will enable us to forecast with some measure of confidence that state's likely posture toward any policy choice confronting it on that issue. Rules and procedures shape behaviors, shared preferences lead to stable practices, and prescriptions exert force (Kratochwil, 1984).

It follows that before one can hope to analyze why states sometimes follow decision regimes, or what the consequences will be for foreign policy outcomes when different regimes exist, it is necessary to break the complex web of rules within a decision regime into its component parts. This partitioning cannot be accomplished without prior empirical analysis, because the subset of issues around which policy makers' images converge in a given issue area cannot be identified *a priori*.

To clarify the potential range of possibilities, let us for the moment assume that a state's foreign policy decisional pattern may conform to several models. At one extreme, consensus about policy priorities may be so fragile and/or unstable that a state may not be said to have developed norms for the management of the various foreign policy choices facing it; no decision regime of rules for hierarchically arranging goals around a monolithic preference ordering may be operative. At the other end of this hypothetical continuum, a state's ruling elite may so share preference hierarchies about national goals and strategies that a homogeneous set of decision rules may be said to have taken root with respect to that state's foreign policy; objectives to which policy makers are strongly committed that can be easily discerned by any observer are present. In such a case a substantive decision regime of underlying principles of, and priorities for, action is operative and is amenable to categorization. Finally, intermediate between these extremes may exist the most frequently emergent type of foreign policy decision regime: states that embrace multiple objectives, many of which are incompatible and none of which so overrides the others that any single set gains dominance. Under this situation of value variation, policy makers' beliefs will be insufficiently homogeneous and stable to enable a scale of priorities and rules to be identified. Nonetheless, this situation does not preclude the possibility that consensus about norms may emerge with respect to particular policy sectors or selected issues. Comparative analysis may show that policy sectors do vary, and that for some no regime has materialized whereas for others a distinct set of beliefs and rules governs decision making with respect to them.

This crude typology of possibilities underscores the view that decision regimes may or may not materialize to govern a state's decisional procedures, and that when they do principles for action may be operative and vary across issue-areas. It is, then, the burden of the investigator to ascertain the scope of a decision regime's applicability when it arises. At issue in determining the domain of a decision regime is not the isolation of the areas in which bargaining occurs—for bargaining may be assumed to occur with respect to every issue on a state's foreign policy agenda. Rather, what requires isolation are the issues and policy areas *where the bargains are made*. When struggles are resolved and consensus among a state's leadership about the norms that should govern the formation of policy is achieved, then the existence of a decision regime in that specified area may be discerned. In general, it may be hypothesized that the more intense the level of debate about the principles advocated to shape a policy sector, and the greater the number of actors and channels of access available for the exercise of influence over the direction of policy within it, the less likely will be the prospects for a decision regime to form, although these same factors may increase the intensity of the policy maker's desires to establish a regime particularly if the issue is recurrent.

When they do emerge, decision regimes in foreign policy making may be assumed to be arrived at and continually modified through a gradual accommodation of divergent opinions and to be under constant pressure to adapt themselves to evolving new circumstances. Decision regimes will often vary in their scope, type, degree of generality, specificity and their tolerance for rule violation. Like personal motivations and preferences generally, the rules of a regime may evolve and undergo modification without requiring the conclusion that noncompliance assures the termination of a rule.

To argue that decision regimes tend to form is not to contend that the rules of a regime, once formed, are not open to political challenge or do not coexist alongside alternative formulations. This may be assumed to be an ever-present (if sometimes latent) condition for even the most entrenched set of shared norms. The capacity for some dissent from a prevailing regime is always endemic. But in those exceptional circumstances where substantial consensus develops around the position a state should take on a foreign policy issue, a decision regime will arise and its perpetuation becomes a possibility.

Regime Identification

Our second question concerns how the existence of a decision regime can be identified. What are the criteria by which we can determine if a state is acting in adherence to a decision regime?

In general, the nature of a nation's substantive decision regimes will be captured by the distributionary pattern of its overall diplomatic activity. When the positions taken on global issues by the state and the postures that state assumes abroad toward global issues are governed by repetition and regularity, a decision regime may be said to have formed. These states' foreign policy profiles will exhibit durability and continuity over time, indicating that they operate from a consistent set of shared beliefs and a characteristic pattern of policy choice. Established norms *of* diplomatic practice suggest the existence of instilled norms *for* diplomatic practice. Conversely, it is where such persistence in foreign policy conduct is absent—where states display marked variation and discontinuity in their pattern of external behavior—that the absence of a decision regime regarding the substance of policy will be indicated.

To identify the content of a substantive decision regime and to evaluate the degree of variability in it over time requires attention to observed behaviors, both words and deeds. It may be assumed that where a vocabulary becomes widely used, a norm is operative that makes that language repetitive; where a practice becomes frequent, a norm is extant that renders it customary. Repeated behaviors tend to become obligatory.

But the problem of how to employ previous patterns of diplomatic activity as a source of evidence for the existence of a state's substantive decision regime is troublesome. The relationship of a decision regime to overt state practice may be likened to the relationship at the systemic level between international law and interstate custom. Like inter-

258

national law (see Onuf, 1982), decision regimes emerge from the precedents of state practice as a function of time, the volume of a type of
behavior, and the consistency of its repetition. Generally, it may be
assumed that the longer a practice is exhibited, the more frequently a
type of action is initiated, and the less the incidence of actions that depart
from the customary practice, the greater is the evidence that a particular
decision rule of a regime is in force. Furthermore, an inverse relationship may be assumed to exist between the duration and volume of
behavior for a given norm to become a decision rule: the more frequent
the behavior, the less the amount of time that must pass for the rule to
become entrenched. Likewise, the more consistent the practice, the less
the volume over time is required for it to be accepted as a norm for
behavior in a state's decision regime. And, of course, the more vocal
policy makers are in articulating that a practice is a custom to which their
state feels itself morally bound, then the duration, frequency and
consistency assumes proportionately less importance in contributing to
the definition of the core beliefs and values within a state's decision
regime.

These dynamic interacting dimensions of foreign policy behaviors
should be considered in any effort to uncover the characteristics of a
state's substantive decision regime and to identify the rules that embody
it (although how the dimensions should be weighed is difficult to
determine in the abstract). Because the principles of decision regimes
are a component of policy makers' perceptions and motivations, we are
dealing with an elusive phenomenon. Identifying the rules that inhere
in a state's foreign policy *goals* and estimating its leaders' *commitment* to
them pose special problems (see Brady, 1982, for a discussion of the
former, and Callahan, 1982, for approaches regarding the latter).

An inductive approach is required to draw valid inferences about the
existence and attributes of different types of decision regimes. Although
substantive decision regimes have no single compelling empirical
referent, they nonetheless may be measured by reference to a series of
indicators. In addition to the general pattern of its diplomatic behavior,
the content and degree of a nation's substantive foreign policy decision
regime is revealed by: (1) the elite articulations and policy declarations of
its leaders; (2) the doctrine it announces (for example, the Monroe,
Truman, Eisenhower, Nixon, Carter and Reagan doctrines, each of
which expressed the intent and limit of American diplomatic practice at
the time it was enunciated); (3) the treaties and formal agreements
to which it commits itself and binds its subsequent behaviors; (4) its
pattern of voting on resolutions in multilateral organizations such as
the General Assembly of the United Nations; (5) the distribution of its
budgetary allocations for competing instruments in the conduct of its

foreign policy; (6) the ongoing negotiations followed by the mass media which contributes to the setting of national agendas and delineates the key issues for debate; and (7) the formation of political coalitions among like-minded individuals to lobby for either a departure from or the preservation of a prevailing program of action.

Similarly, *procedural* decision regimes are amenable to observation and measurement, even if investigation in this category requires us to probe phenomena occurring largely behind closed doors. To identify the procedural rules of decision regimes, we will be dependent upon the detailed knowledge best derived by specialists through case studies (see Anderson, 1985). Their nature can be probed by looking for information in a variety of places and with a diverse set of methodological approaches. Perhaps most promising for this purpose is the emerging ethnographic approach—a form of naturalistic-qualitative method guided by anthropological theory whose roots stem from the phenomenological philosophical orientation (see Dorr-Bremme, 1985). In this regard, content analyses of memoirs and public statements of officials, methods for the "decomposition of historical narratives" (Burnstein and Berbaum, 1983), analysis of records of past voting on decision options, procedures for studying "cultures [and subcultures] at a distance" (Mead and Metraux, 1953), the use of Delphi techniques for estimating decisional procedures with expert-generated data, and elite and specialized interviewing are available. All of these approaches invite the use of primary sources, field methods, historical reconstruction, and comparative evaluation of multiple case studies. Particularly useful for cross-national studies are the emergent methodologies associated with "meta-analysis" (see Glass, 1978; Glass, McGaw and Smith, 1981; Hunter, Schmidt and Jackson, 1982; Light and Pillemer, 1984). For those less concerned with the problem of empirically tracing the existence of previous procedural decision regimes than they are with theoretically examining the dynamics of regime formation and decay (how rules develop and erode in different circumstances), simulation and gaming suggest themselves. For purposes of data-generation in the study of decision regimes, the possibilities opened by "the microelectronic revolution" (see Rosenau, 1984a) may be of potential use as well, as may applications of the "lag sequential" analysis of foreign policy that Dixon recommends in Chapter 5 of this volume.

The availability of a variety of fungible observational and measurement procedures would appear to make the operationalization of the decision regimes concept possible. At the very least, the study of decision regimes can be empirical; the existence of multiple indicators should further the comparative study of decision regimes and not doom the concept to operate without real-world referents.

An Agenda for Research

If the proposition is plausible that the game of foreign policy making tends to be played according to identifiable rules, some serious work awaits those analysts persuaded and willing to pursue the possibilities for research that the decision regime concept opens. One perspective on the research program that potentially can be pursued may be outlined as follows.

First, pilot studies are needed to estimate the extent to which, and the conditions under which, policy making is actually governed by shared decision norms or rules (a decision regime) in various foreign policy settings. The empirical existence, operation and impact of such regimes needs to be demonstrated through comparative case studies to produce evidence that decision regimes do, indeed, tend to materialize to regulate many components of foreign policy making. The potential promise of the concept's utility needs to be demonstrated. This task may be interpreted as a response to Lowi's (1972) challenge to classify policy issues according to the level of conflict they are likely to generate and policy-making structures according to the capacity for conflict resolution that they can mobilize. Should case studies reveal the operation of a culture supporting a decision regime for the making of foreign policy in several national settings, then more rigorous theory building can commence, encouraged by knowledge that we are dealing with a nonartifactual phenomenon that may be widespread.

Second, the problem of empirically identifying and categorizing the content of exhibited regimes—the rules and procedures outlining the behaviors permitted and prohibited in each national setting—will then have to be confronted (see Ranney, 1968, for a discussion of policy content). That task would require research to determine if a nation approaches the broad spectrum of its external concerns in a uniform set of decision rules, with a comprehensive regime that coherently shapes its general posture and energizes its policy product. Or, alternatively, do different decision regimes govern policy making for different purposes of its policy, with characteristics described as a "garbage can" decisional mix (Cohen, March and Olsen, 1972)? If the latter is the case, then a more restrictive concept of a regime will have to be constructed, which separates the body of decision rules made for the specific purposes of one aspect of foreign policy (such as defense), from the body of rules emergent in other substantive components of foreign policy (such as trade, immigration or foreign assistance). The content of a state's decision regime may also prove to be spatially specific, with different rules operative for its relations with different geographic regions of the globe or with particular international actors. And it also may be temporally specific, with its rules disrupted from time to time by new stimuli and choice opportunities. In addition, case studies will be needed to differentiate and estimate hierarchies among principles, the likelihood for each principle's enforcement, and the *extent* of a state's commitment to its various rules. These bear upon the potential for change of decision regimes, inasmuch as the important decisions policy makers make are concurrently choices of the kind of regime to which they subscribe. Thus, it is necessary to "contextualize" the domain of application for the rules of a state's decision regime. The information extracted from "focused comparisons" (see George, 1979a) of different cases would enable various modes of decision regimes to be detected and some general models of rule and procedure change and continuity to be constructed. Consideration could be given to the dynamics of rule subscription, acquisition, abandonment, redistribution, rescaling, redeployment, restandardization and retargeting (see Rescher, 1969). In this way some general propositions about the circumstances in which regimes are sustained and those in which regimes undergo modification can be extracted.

Third, exploratory case studies should also distinguish the *substantive* rules of a decision regime (those accepted as inexorable givens for the state's conduct involving the core values to which policy makers are deeply committed) from its instrumental or *procedural* rules (those defining not what to decide, but how to decide and who will do so). The latter can be expected to influence the former because rules for making decisions often shape the kinds of policy decisions that are reached. By extension, this distinction calls for the careful differentiation of the set of rules that comprise a state's formulation of its grand strategy from the set of rules governing the organization of rites, rituals and rules for participation in and control over the process of foreign policy determination. Foreign policy making entails choices about goals as well as procedures, and comparative case studies can reveal if different sets of rules define the regime which governs both types of decision. Both types of decisional behaviors will have to be inspected to determine if either substantive or procedural decision regimes have formed, and, if so, what their characteristics and interrelationships are.

Finally, similarities and differences of identified decision regimes of states will need to be systematically compared in order to ascertain if a general typology of the decision regimes of nations can be empirically constructed, so that substantive and procedural decision regimes can be classified according to type. Classification is a prerequisite for and a task preliminary to comparison for the construction of nomethetic knowledge (see McGowan, 1975). This general taxonomy of decision regime types could be developed if national preference orderings are sufficiently uniform to delineate universal theoretical concepts of decision regimes and to classify, based on invariances and differences, their major types. Such a typology could then be employed in comparative studies of the determinants and consequences of foreign policy behavior. Like the classification of nations' foreign policies (see Hermann, 1972b, and Baldwin, 1984) and of national role conceptions (see Holsti, 1970, and Walker's discussion in Chapter 14), so, too, the classification of types of decision regimes would allow these types to be used for subsequent theory building in much the same way the former have been used.

Potential Applications of the Construct

In contemplating the sequence of tasks outlined in this proposed research agenda, it is doubtful whether exploratory case studies will provide the evidence to suggest that decision regimes can be serviced to perform as a true umbrella concept (that is, as a composite construct that can account for, or predict, a large proportion of the variance in cross-national patterns in foreign policy behavior). But when conditions hold that allow for decision regimes to form, we may have before us a potentially powerful new variable that can give our field the leverage to explore heretofore unexamined questions or to account for phenomena which until now have defied adequate explanation. In particular cases, it may allow us to uncover the sources of some aspects of a state's foreign policy behavior that until now have resisted adequate treatment.

Consider three illustrative types of uses for the construct. First, decision regimes can be used to perform as *independent* variables. When they form, they can be employed as causal variables to explain facets of foreign policy behavior of states subscribing to them, under the adages that decision rules will determine policy outcomes and that decision characteristics can predict policy attributes. That which is to be explained, foreign policy behavior (Hermann, 1978b), may be accounted for by the attributes of decision regimes. Moreover, the consequences for states subscribing to the principles of various foreign policy decision regimes can be subjected to the kinds of evaluation research that Raymond recommends in Chapter 6.

Secondly, decision regimes can be treated as *dependent* variables. The dynamics of rule formation, maintenance and revision can be explored in efforts to model the factors that influence these regime dynamics. For example, the concepts suggested by Hermann, Hermann and

Hagan in Chapter 16 can be employed to analyze whether different types of "decision units" tend to generate a decision regime, and, if so, what the characteristics and consequences are for each type.

And thirdly, the typification of substantive foreign policy decision regimes and the procedural ones for states can facilitate analysis of the nexus between the two (the symbiotic relationship that conjoins them within Easton's (1953; 1965) "black box"). The causal linkage between policy-making procedures and policy outcomes can be explored in a manner and from a perspective that up to this time has not been possible within the confines of our present stock of concepts. Because procedural rules are made within the framework of a substantive decision regime, the consequences of procedural decision norms for change in substantive regimes can be traced over time, and the causal connection can be modeled. Thus the troublesome questions raised by the fact that "outcomes are not a direct consequence of process" (March and Olsen, 1976) can be addressed, and perhaps the rudiments of an acceptable model of the relationship between policy-making process and policy outcome can be developed. In this way the domestic sources of foreign policy can be approached from a fresh perspective, one that includes motives and values in the analysis and thereby reduces our field's emphasis on domestic constraints (rather than addressing the goals and strategies of governments and leaving us with the puzzling question of how a government would behave if it did not face those constraints).

The potential capacity of decision regimes to operate as a parsimonious explanatory and predictive construct that can subsume a large set of more amorphous and less composite concepts, and to serve as a common denominator encompassing a wider set of explanatory factors underlying the external behaviors of states, can be estimated by considering the range of linkages that are opened to investigation. The range of relationships amenable to examination with the regime concept may be grasped by inspection of Figure 13.1.

This figure places the "source" of foreign policy action in the norms adhered to by central decision makers, whose perceptions and assumptions about the appropriate and inappropriate will determine the probable external orientation of a state toward a set of discrete policy issues. The rules governing procedures for making decisions will shape this substantive decision regime, and these, in turn, will be given shape by the impact of perceived aspects of domestic and international reality. So, too, will the characteristics of a substantive decision regime be influenced substantially by perceptions of the internal and external circumstances prevailing at the point of decision. Needless to say, numerous feedback loops among these levels may be

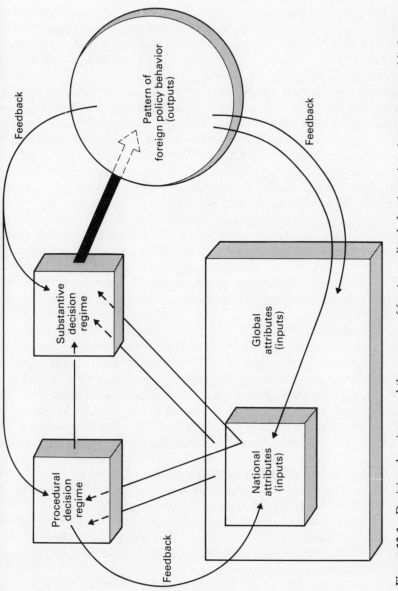

Figure 13.1 Decisional regimes and the sources of foreign policy behavior: picturing some causal linkages

envisioned, with a secondary series of connections emerging with time lags between rules within regimes and subsets of national and international attributes.

For instance, the pressure exerted by domestic interest groups to shape specific rules, substantive and procedural, would require examination. No country's foreign policy program is based on absolute consensus, because all policy-making groups consist of a collection of ambitious people, many competing with each other, some with their head of state, and all representing diverse economic, class and political interests. Therefore, no substantive decision regime will be the product of a unified, disinterested decision-making body, and decision regimes will always be the subject of controversy and be amenable to modification through political bargaining.

Similarly, changes in systemic circumstances, such as the level of international trade and debt, can be expected to provoke changes for every state's substantive foreign policy decision regime and in its norms and processes for making decisions. The limits to these kinds of potential relationships are confined only by the analyst's imagination, although some relationships will warrant more attention than will others. Readers are invited to join in the generation of propositions linking various components of this very preliminary model for comparatively studying the determinants and consequences of foreign policy behavior.

The potential theoretical payoff that might materialize from the departure in prevailing investigative practice through attention to decision regimes may be estimated from inspection of recent studies which fall somewhat loosely into the research program that has been outlined here (in that each of these studies has used decision norms to advantage). For instance, the rudiments of this mode of inquiry provided by Nitze (1980), Jönsson (1982b) and Kennan (1983) in analyzing the substantive program of the Soviet Union's foreign policy, or by Roeder (1984) to examine statistically the Soviet Union's procedural decision-making processes as a determinant of changes in the Soviet Union's foreign policy "syndrome," are suggestive of the kind of power that attention to decisional norms can yield.

George's (1985) analysis of the norms that have been embraced by the United States and the Soviet Union to govern their global rivalry illustrates the power that knowledge of substantive rules can provide to explain interactive patterns between competing states.[3] So, too, are analyses which indicate the outlines of foreign policy decision regimes with respect to particular issue areas (see Fraser, 1986, for an application of the concept to the study of intervention). Many Third World countries' strategies toward the agenda of the New International

Economic Order (NIEO) have been accounted for by reference to the decision rules those states have been observed to embrace (see Murphy, 1984, and Rothstein, 1984). Similarly, Western collaboration on East-West trade negotiations recently has been interpreted by reference to a consistent "decision mode" (Crawford and Lenway, 1985). So, too, have patterns in the causes of war been explicated by reference to procedural regimes (see Levy, 1986).

The possibilities of application abound, only depending on how far the analyst is willing to carry the need to specify the context of national decision regimes across time, issues and circumstance. As has been noted, comparative case studies are needed in order to refine the concept and to determine if it can indeed contribute to the explanatory power of theories and models of foreign policy behavior. But what on the surface renders the proposal inviting is the possibility that the norms of a foreign policy decision regime, when operative, may subsume a large number of interacting explanatory variables under a compound construct. This construct incorporates many factors that heretofore have been treated independently or, like motives and intentions, have been left untreated. If and when research can isolate decision regimes, and can ascertain their existence and the nature of their operation, then it might be possible to account for exhibited foreign policy behaviors that have resisted explanation with our field's present repertoire of concepts. For when decision regimes form and stabilize, we are very unlikely to witness departures in behavior from the boundaries they posit. For example, Brecher (1975) has shown that the emergence of a set of widely and intensely held beliefs about Israel's foreign policy made only a narrow range of foreign policy outcomes possible. To the extent that such confining "decision regimes" can be discovered for other states, we may be able to obtain unprecedented predictive leverage of foreign policy outputs by reference to them. That possibility certainly warrants experimentation to determine if the concept of a decision regime can open windows to foreign policy phenomena whose sources have yet to receive adequate illumination.

Instead of preparing the way for the emergence of still another framework that will confine and imprison theorizing in new, albeit different, ways, it is hoped that this recommendation and invitation will open the way for more productive theorizing. The prescription advanced must for the moment remain speculative. If it provokes more thought and manages to have identified some suggestive lines of inquiry, this essay will have served its primary purpose.

Charles W. Kegley, Jr.

Notes

Earlier versions of this paper were presented at the Annual Meeting of the American Political Science Association, September 1, 1984 (Washington, DC) and at the Faculty Colloquium of the Institute of International Studies, University of South Carolina, April 15, 1985. The present version of this greatly abridged paper has benefitted from the comments and assistance of Linda P. Brady, William A. Clark, Cheryl A. Fischer, Joe D. Hagan, Margaret G. Hermann, Charles F. Hermann, Donald B. Hottel, Jr., Donald J. Puchala, Lucia Wren Rawls, Jerel Rosati, James N. Rosenau, Joseph Sausnock, Peter Schraeder and Gregory A. Raymond. Their contributions are greatly appreciated. None of these bear any responsibility for the deficiencies of the reasoning presented.

1 For example, a decade ago Wittkopf (1976) recommended punching some pin-holes that would allow some light into the "black box" and would thereby restore the policy maker and the processes which govern his or her behavior back into the conceptual equation. The field has benefited immeasurably from the advice of those who have reminded us of our errors (see Simon, 1957; Singer, 1965; DeRivera, 1968; Bloomfield, 1974; Isaak, 1974; Hermann, 1980) and from those who have provided clues as to how this recommendation could be followed (see George, 1969, 1980; Hermann, 1976, 1978, 1980; Holsti, 1976b; Jervis, 1976; Kinder and Weiss, 1978; Falkowski, 1979; Janis, 1982; Steiner, 1983; Walker, 1983a; Chan and Sylvan, 1984; and Anderson, 1985). By and large the fact remains: the process in which those officials responsible for the making of foreign policy engage in reaching decisions has remained outside our models. When they have been treated (for example, Allison, 1971), these models have rarely described processes as they unfold in most foreign policy-making settings, and empirically these models can be shown to be bound by place for their validity (Brady and Kegley, 1977).

2 Another way of saying this is to note that groups, like individuals, energetically strive for rules to order beliefs, maintain cognitive consistency and fulfill expectations (see Janis, 1982, and Anderson, Chapter 15). Even though members of policy-making bodies are notorious for maintaining divergent perspectives, and such organizations are rarely monolithic, nonetheless these entities exert pressure for consensus even in the absence of their ability to attain unanimity. To get along, participants must go along. As they enter into decision-making roles, they are further imbued by an inherited culture, and as they become inured to it, they tend subconsciously to take its norms for granted and allow it to structure their activity. Collective actions ultimately result from individual preferences (Coleman, 1966), as the need for rules and consensus leads to the aggregation of individual preferences into a coherent policy product. Macro behaviors thus result from micro motives (see Schelling, 1978).

3 Also instructive in this context is the possibility that an informal decision regime for the negotiation of Soviet-American agreements on arms control exists, and that the rules of this regime [(1) "negotiate only from a position of strength;" (2) "do not negotiate away any achieved advantage;" (3) "negotiate for a reduction of the adversary's strategic advantage"] help explain why efforts to reduce armaments levels routinely have resulted in failure.

14

Role Theory and the Origins of Foreign Policy

STEPHEN G. WALKER

One of the enduring puzzles confronting the cross-national study of foreign policy is the relationship between environmental and dispositional explanations of foreign policy. As Sprout and Sprout (1956, 1965) posed it, the issue is how the "operational milieu" and the "psychological milieu" affect foreign policy. Their thesis is that the attitudes and decisions comprising a state's foreign policy are affected by environmental factors to the extent that the state's foreign policy makers perceive them and take them into account as they formulate policy. Within the context of this "larger" puzzle, there are two "smaller" puzzles. The first one is: how and when do domestic and international environmental characteristics, respectively, affect foreign policy? The second one is: how and when do two types of psychological characteristics, idiosyncratic and role, affect foreign policy? Implied by these questions is the premise that there is likely to be a state of tension between the members of each pair. By extension we may allow for the possibility of tensions across the pairs as well.

Different analysts have handled these questions in a variety of ways (e.g., Rosati, 1985; Kegley, in Chapter 13). One strategy is to introduce a set of auxiliary conditions which specify the circumstances under which one or the other type of factors is more influential. An early ambitious attempt at a solution by this strategy (Rosenau, 1966) suggested that the relative potency of these factors depends upon the foreign policy issue, plus the size, level of economic development, and the political organization of the country. A second strategy is to resolve the puzzle by excluding or confounding some factors and focusing upon the remainder. The initial efforts of Rummel (1972), Vincent *et al*. (1973) and Galtung (1964) to apply field theory and relative status theory are examples of this approach. Domestic environmental factors in the form of national attributes are used as indicators of psychological dispositions to direct conflictual or cooperative foreign policy behavior either toward particular target countries or into the general international environment. The International environmental characteristics are either excluded or confounded with domestic characteristics by introducing the relational property "distance" into the analysis. The distinction between role and idiosyncratic factors is never made, although the concepts of "field" and "status" imply psychological assumptions and processes as they are applied to the analysis of foreign policy.

I propose to explore solutions to these puzzles by means of a third strategy: the application of role and exchange theory which together incorporate environmental and dispositional explanations. The concepts of role expectations and role conceptions from role theory distinguish between role and idiosyncratic dispositions, respectively, whereas propositions from exchange theory specify the primacy of domestic and international sources of foreign policy under different conditions. The definition of role concepts and the statement of exchange propositions have been developed and elaborated elsewhere (Walker, 1979, 1981, 1983b). I will emphasize here their application to a series of studies by other scholars with a focus upon role analysis and the study of foreign policy (Holsti, 1970; Wish, 1980; M. Hermann, 1987a, 1987b; Singer and Hudson, 1987; C. Hermann, 1987).

The work of these authors represents stages in the evolving application of role analysis to the understanding of foreign policy. The first stage involves exploration, in which scholars have adopted an inductive, descriptive approach to the identification of national role conceptions and their behavioral correlates within a framework inspired by the development of role theory in social psychology. In the second stage, simplification of the role location process occurs as part of a strategy to map the sources of role conceptions and the impact of different situations upon role enactment. The third stage is characterized by efforts to develop a synthesis of the simple models generated during the second stage and by attempts as well to relate this complex model to a general theory of politics.

Exploration

Some years ago Holsti (1970) identified a set of national role conceptions in a content analysis of speeches by the leaders of seventy-one states between 1965 and 1967. Holsti (1970, pp. 245–6) defined a national role conception as including "the policymakers' own definitions of the general kinds of decisions, commitments, rules, and actions suitable to their state, and of the functions, if any, their state should perform on a continuing basis in the international system or in subordinate regional systems." His content analysis identified seventeen types of national role conceptions, which are listed here in Table 14.1. Holsti compares these to the roles that he uncovered from a review of the previous international politics literature and concludes that there is some overlap but also significant differences as well:

> Balances of power or balancing roles are not an important part of the vocabulary of contemporary international politics . . . The national roles of *regional or subsystem leader* and *regional collaborator* are seldom mentioned in descriptions or models of past or contemporary international systems . . . Other national role conceptions such as *liberator-supporter, anti-imperialist agent, defender of the faith, developer, bridge, example* and *internal development* are not discussed in the literature, but they appear prominently in the foreign policy statements of contemporary political leaders . . . The number [of identifiable national role conceptions] is almost double that derived from past and contemporary treatises on international politics. (Holsti, 1970, pp. 272–3, italics in original).

Holsti's (1970, pp. 247–56) inductive strategy for the identification of role conceptions differs from the efforts in the previous literature, which deduced roles from the implications of classical balance of power theory and its derivatives. Here we confront an apparent gap between idiosyncratically based or domestically based national role conceptions and the role expectations consistent with a balance of power system. Holsti (1970, p. 273) attributes this incongruity to the tendency of previous international politics theorists to focus upon the activities of the major powers and neglect regional systems outside Western Europe where cooperative ventures are quite important (1970, p. 273). The implication of this analysis is that balance of power theory is inadequate in scope and needs to be revised or replaced with a theory that will subsume the variety of foreign policy phenomena uncovered by his use of role as a concept to study foreign policy.

Wish has advocated a social-psychological approach to provide such a theoretical context:

> If the international system is perceived as a social structure, each nation would occupy many social positions or national roles in relationship to other nations. National role conceptions are defined as foreign policy makers' perceptions of their nations' positions in the international system.
>
> (Wish, 1980, p. 533)

Wish argues that the role conceptions of national leaders should be analyzed and classified according to three properties which social psychologists find important in understanding role-based behavior in interpersonal situations. These variables are status, motivational ori-

271

Table 14.1   National role conceptions and balance of power role conceptions

Balance of power role conceptions	National role conceptions																	
	Other	Bastion of the revolution/liberator	Regional leader	Regional protector	Active independent	Liberator/supporter	Anti-imperialist agent	Defender of the faith	Mediator/integrator	Regional collaborator	Developer	Bridge	Faithful ally	Independent	Example	Internal development	Isolate	Protectee
Revolutionary imperialist		X																
Bloc leader			X															
Balancer	X*																	
Bloc member ally													X					
Mediator									X									
Nonaligned														X				
Buffer																		
Isolate																	X	
Protectee																		X

X indicates overlapping definitions for a pair of role conceptions.
* Holsti (1970, p. 271) reports that "balancer" was a role conception appearing only for one nation and, therefore, not frequently enough to be included in his taxonomy of national role conceptions

entation and the substantive content of the role conception. In making this argument, Wish equates national role conceptions with the role conceptions of the nations' leaders; she also does not distinguish between the role conceptions of these leaders and either the role itself as a component of a social system or the role expectations held by other members of the international system regarding the occupant of the role.

With these steps Wish closes the gap between inductively defined role conceptions and the enactment of roles in the international system. She postulates that in order to understand foreign policy behavior, one should look for linkages between the status, the motivational orientation and the content of national role conceptions, and the following aspects of foreign policy behavior: international participation, independence of action and resource commitment. Wish does a content analysis of the role conceptions in the rhetoric of the leaders from seventeen nations between 1959 and 1968 and links them with measures of participation, independent action and resource commitment for these nations from the CREON data set. No hypotheses guide the selection of these aspects of foreign policy behavior nor are the expected relationships specified in advance of the test, a bivariate correlational analysis of the behavior and role conception variables.

Wish judges some of the results of this analysis as intuitively plausible, for example, the direct correlation between high status and high participation. Other results were judged counterintuitive, for example, the absence of a strong direct correlation between status and resource commitment (Wish, 1980, pp. 544–5). In the absence of a theory to guide the analysis, the findings are inconclusive. Forty Pearsonian rs are reported—nineteen significant at $p \leq 0.05$ level and eighteen which account for at least 10 per cent of the variance. However, without a "strong" theory to indicate whether one should expect only these relationships to be significant, the theoretical value of these findings is difficult to assess.

A "strong" role theory would answer four questions. What is a "role"? How do roles come into existence? Under what conditions are different roles enacted and, at least by implication, other roles not enacted? Why are these conditions the relevant ones? These questions do not exhaust those which a strong theory would answer, but they are the ones most directly relevant to the comparative study of foreign policy. Their answers should provide what Waltz (1979, pp. 8–10) maintains is legitimate to expect from a theory:

> A theory is a picture, mentally formed, of a bounded realm or domain of activity . . . A theory indicates that some factors are more important than others and specifies relations among them . . . A theory is *not* (italics added) the occurrences seen and the associations recorded, but is instead the expla-

273

nation of them . . . Theories are combinations of descriptive and theoretical statements. The theoretical statements are non-factual elements of a theory.

If "strong" theories are indeed combinations of descriptive and theoretical statements, then we may classify the exploratory efforts of Holsti and Wish as examples of relatively "weak" theory. These early inductive studies of national role conceptions and foreign policy behavior provide some answers to the first question expected from a "strong" role theory, that is, what is a "role"? A "role" in their research is the interface of a role conception and the behaviors associated with its enactment. Holsti (1970) and Wish (1980) report "occurrences seen" and "associations recorded," in Waltz's words, between role conceptions and role behaviors, but they do not offer clear explanations of them. They do not offer satisfactory answers to the other three questions expected from a "strong" role theory: how do roles come into existence, under what conditions are different roles enacted, and why are these conditions the relevant ones? Holsti is essentially content to reject balance of power theory as the traditional source of theoretical statements to explain role-based descriptions of foreign policy, while Wish does not make explicit the social-psychological theoretical context which influenced her descriptions of foreign policy roles.

Answers to these latter questions begin to tap what Waltz calls the "non-factual" elements of a theory, which are invented by the intellectual processes of speculation and the exercise of the imagination (Waltz, 1979, pp. 5–7). The theorist exercises these intellectual processes to "find the central tendency among a confusion of tendencies, to single out the propelling principle even though other principles operate, to seek the essential factors where innumerable factors are present . . . Both induction and deduction are indispensable in the construction of a theory, but using them in combination gives rise to a theory only if a creative idea emerges." (Waltz, 1979, pp. 10–11).

Recent efforts by research associates of the CREON project at the Ohio State University have yielded three such creative ideas (see Hudson, Hermann and Singer, 1985; Hermann and Peacock, Chapter 2 above). Each of these ideas provides different answers to the questions regarding the sources and the conditions associated with the definition and enactment of roles. Collectively, these ideas address what role theorists call the process of "role location," the matching of role with situation. In the social psychology literature this process is a function of the interaction between prescriptions previously communicated from the environment and the perceptions, values and attitudes of the individual occupying a position in a social structure (Sarbin and Allen, 1968, pp. 489–90). This conceptualization of the role

274

location process is consistent with the three ideas emerging from the CREON project, although the relative weight assigned to situational and individual sources varies across them.

The simplest formulation of the role location process is to assign an almost exclusive weight to one of these sources. This approach is the one pursued by the associates of the CREON project in the early phases of their investigations. Either the situational or the individual source becomes their theoretical focus which, incidentally, they recognize is a simplification of the complex process that they seek to model. However, this move is consistent with Waltz's contention that theorizing inevitably involves simplification. Leaving some things aside in order to concentrate on others and then viewing them as though in the meantime other things remain equal are two strategies of simplification that facilitate the emergence of theory (Waltz, 1979, p. 10).

Simplification

The work by Margaret Hermann (e.g. 1987a, 1987b) emphasizes the impact of individual perceptions, values and attitudes upon the determination of foreign policy orientations. The individual's needs for power and affiliation, belief in the ability to control events, degree of nationalism, willingness to trust others, and conceptual complexity are hypothesized as determinants of orientations toward the conduct of foreign policy. Depending upon the mix of high and low values along these dimensions of the individual's dispositions, s/he may exhibit an expansionist, active independent, influential, mediator/integrator, opportunist or developmental orientation toward foreign policy. M. Hermann (1987b) acknowledges that many of the ideas for these orientations came particularly from the literature dealing with national role conceptions. Indeed, a review of Hermann's description for these orientations shows at least some correspondence between them and the following role conceptions identified by Holsti: expansionist and bastion of revolution-liberator; active independent; influential and regional leader; mediator-integrator; opportunist and independent; developmental and developer.

If individuals with these orientations occupy leadership positions in countries with political systems characterized by personal rule, then the role conceptions become likely to influence domestic and foreign policy behavior (M. Hermann, 1987a). In this model of the role location process, therefore, an individual's role conception defines the country's foreign policy role, and this conception is influenced heavily by a mix of perceptions, values and attitudes rather than prescriptions previously communicated from the environment. However, the distinction between individual and environmental sources is not so simply drawn as this model would imply. In an analysis of twelve leaders of African governments characterized by personal rule, the role conceptions of these individuals changed as the issues facing each of them varied (M. Hermann, 1984). This volatile pattern is also consistent with an interpretation of the role location process as dominated significantly by situational influences.

The work by Singer and Hudson (1987) represents an attempt by other CREON associates to reverse the emphasis from role conceptions to situationally defined roles. They argue that:

> [T]here are really two levels of national roles. The first represents the broader ideological and instrumental beliefs of a national regime and corresponds to Holsti's framework as well as the concept of "regime orientation" developed in Hagan, Hermann, and Hermann (1982). The second identifies situationally defined roles that shift as the situation does. *The outcomes of the actor's role playing in these situations can be seen as shaping the broader roles* (italics added).

Their conceptualization of the role location process postulates that role conceptions are shaped by the experiences associated with situationally defined roles, a thesis that is refined in other CREON papers (e.g., C. Hermann, 1987).

Again, this premise simplifies the process being modeled: however, the theoretical justification is in the creative idea that flows from this simplification. In this case, it takes the form of a typology of situations defined according to four roles: actor, source, subject and facilitator/ aggravator. Singer and Hudson (1987) hypothesize that a nation's foreign policy behavior is a function of its occupation of one or more of these roles, plus the record of friendship and hostility between the country and the occupants of other roles (prior affect), the degree to which the country requires their support to realize basic values (salience), and the country's capabilities relative to them.

The situations in this typology are defined as problems in which one of the following sets of values becomes "problematical" either for the country under analysis or for others that seek its assistance: security/ physical safety, economic wealth, respect/status, well-being/welfare, and enlightenment. Value deprivation, in other words, creates one of the following situations: a *confrontation* situation between the country (X) under analysis and one or more others; an *intervention* situation in which X must decide whether to choose sides in a confrontation between others: an *assistance* situation in which X either seeks aid or provides aid in a cooperative relationship with others: a *collaboration* situation in which X cooperates in a mutual assistance relationship with others (Singer and Hudson, 1987).

With their definitions of role, situation, prior affect, salience and relative capabilities, the authors construct an "external predisposition model," so-called ". . . because it addresses the question: how does the immediate nature of the problem and the resulting configuration of roles establish a general predisposition for a regime to act in a given way?" They relate these situational attributes to four aspects of foreign policy behavior: its target, its affect, its commitment and its instruments of implementation (Singer and Hudson, 1987). They report good success in predicting the target and instrument of implementation, fair results in predicting affect, and poor performance in predicting the level of commitment in an analysis of 622 cases of behavior by the Ivory Coast, Guinea, Ghana, Kenya, Uganda and Zambia in situations between 1959 and 1968 (Singer and Hudson, 1987).

Their ability to predict all four aspects of behavior per case is, therefore, rather low (8 per cent of the cases), but they are able to make correct predictions for three of the four behavior attributes in 33.2 per cent of the cases. This success rate exceeds substantially the random probability of 5.6 per cent for getting three out of four correct. They evaluate these results as promising "since the model only examines external variables" (Singer and Hudson, 1987). The obvious next stage is to synthesize the models which have emphasized dispositional and situational variables, respectively, a task which one of the other members of the CREON project has already begun.

Synthesis

In an exploratory analysis of the roles of the United States and the Soviet Union in the Horn of Africa, Charles Hermann (1987) begins a synthesis of the two uses of "role". One "employs role as a basic element in establishing the relationship of other international entities to the acting government in dealing with transitory situations . . . [In the other] national role is used as part of a larger conceptual structure to establish the shared preferences of policy makers for foreign policy" (C. Hermann, 1987). The latter construct is called "regime orientation" and "can be defined as the shared political system belief of authoritative decision makers about their country's relationship to its external environment and the roles of government appropriate for pursuing the belief" (C. Hermann, 1987). In this conceptualization there is a distinction between "situational roles" and "decision-making roles." One is the country's role defined by the type of situation: confrontation, intervention, assistance, collaboration. The other is the decision-making group's shared expectations about the foreign policy behavior that their government will adopt in the situation based upon their shared beliefs.

The distinction between "decision-making roles" and "situational roles" is a crucial one. The former provide the basis for an answer to the question of how role conceptions come into existence, while the latter account for the selection of one role rather than another for enactment. The immediate sources of role conceptions are the shared beliefs of a country's authoritative decision makers. These beliefs and role conceptions may vary across nations, but they are often either shared or have analogs in more than one country. These role conceptions constitute the repertoire of roles that a set of decision makers can bring to bear upon a particular situation.

The definition of the situation as a confrontation, intervention, assistance or collaboration type occurs according to the logic of Singer and Hudson's "external predisposition model." As particular countries are assigned the situational roles of actor, source, subject and facilitator/aggravator, however, this process also activates shared beliefs about these countries along with the role conceptions associated with each belief. At this point, the role location process expands beyond the assignment of situational roles to identify the appropriate role conception and the foreign policy behavior that the country should follow in order to enact this role conception. In order to model this process, C. Hermann (1987) articulates decision rules for establishing the priority of alternative political beliefs for a given situation, the priority of alternative role conceptions associated with the appropriate political belief, and the foreign policy behavior associated with each role conception.

For example, if one of the shared political beliefs of US decision makers is "oppose traditional enemy," and: (1) the traditional enemy is the occupant of the source or the subject role in a collaborative situation; (2) it is the only entity in that role; (3) the basic value of the problem is not economic; (4) then the traditional enemy belief prevails. Associated with this belief are the following role conceptions: combatant, conciliationist, defender of the faith, opponent and policeman. In a collaborative situation, however, only one of these is appropriate, namely, the conciliationist role conception. Here we have an illustration of the interaction between the definition of the situation and the identity of the occupants for the roles that define the situation. Together they pose the question: how should the country act toward a traditional enemy in a collaborative situation?

The conciliationist role conception answers this question because its definition contains the expectation that "the government, while doing everything necessary to protect the security, welfare, and international interests of the country against the enemy, also will pursue opportunities to resolve or limit the disagreements with it" (C. Hermann, 1987). It assumes that the conflict with the traditional enemy is not zero-sum. Consequently, in collaboration or assistance situations, where the enemy is the source or the subject of the problem, the following foreign policy behavior is appropriate: the recipient of the behavior will be the enemy, and the behavior will involve diplomatic instruments applied with neutral affect and low or nonexistent commitment (C. Hermann, 1987).

For other combinations of core beliefs and situations, additional information may be required in the use of decision rules, including the salience of the occupants in situational roles and their capabilities relative to the country under analysis (C. Hermann, 1987). No systematic test of this complex model of the role location process is reported, but its applicability to several illustrations drawn from Soviet–American actions in Africa is demonstrated.

Conclusion

In this review of the evolving application of role analysis to the study of foreign policy, we have observed three stages: exploration, simplification and synthesis. Holsti (1970) and Wish (1980) explored the initial problems of definition and description associated with answering the question: what is a foreign policy role? M. Hermann (1987a, 1987b) and Singer and Hudson (1987) pursued strategies of simplification which yielded preliminary answers to the questions of how roles come into existence and under what conditions they are enacted. C. Hermann (1987) has begun the task of synthesizing these preliminary answers into a complex model of role location.

As the evolution of role theory has passed through these stages, therefore, it has assumed some of the characteristic elements of a strong theory. It has also begun to offer solutions to the puzzling relationship between environmental and dispositional explanations of foreign policy. The synthesis offered by C. Hermann (1987) addresses directly the issue of how the psychological and operational milieus, respectively, affect foreign policy behavior. The origins of foreign policy are in the interaction between the shared core beliefs of a country's authoritative decision makers and the external situation that they find problematical. This interaction evokes a definition of the situation and a national role conception that shape the enactment of behavior with a hypothetical level of affect, commitment and type of instrumentality toward a specific recipient.

While these efforts have provided answers to most of the questions associated with a strong role theory of foreign policy, there is one which still needs to be addressed and explicated. It is the "why" question. The foregoing analyses have focussed upon "what" a role is, "how" roles come into existence and "when" they are enacted. However, there is no clear answer as to *why* roles come into existence and are enacted. These analyses have produced statements of highly probable relationships without an explicit rationale for their occurrence. In other words, these efforts have produced hypothetical, lawlike statements without identifying the concepts and assumptions which explain them (Waltz, 1979, pp. 5–7). Instead, the decision rules that link the dispositional and situational components of the role location process are formed with the *ad hoc* introduction of concepts such as problem, prior affect, salience and relative capabilities. We are not told *why* these are important; however, it is my contention that they can and should be justified in order to be able to characterize the CREON model of role location as a strong theory.

In order to accomplish this task, I would suggest that it is desirable to integrate this model within the broader theoretical context provided by exchange theory. The seeds of integration are already contained in the point of departure for the CREON "external predisposition model" of situational roles. Both C. Hermann (1987) and Singer and Hudson (1987) assume that foreign policy behavior occurs only in response to a "problem" perceived by the nation's decision makers. A problem, in turn, is "any perceived discrepancy between present or anticipated states of affairs and what is envisioned as desirable" (Singer and Hudson, 1987). A discrepancy may involve the present or anticipated deprivation of one of the following sets of values: security/physical safety, economic wealth, respect/status, wellbeing/welfare, and enlightenment (Singer and Hudson, 1987; C. Hermann, 1987).

Elsewhere (Walker, 1983b; 1987) I have argued that a theory of foreign policy should be a variant of a general theory of politics, in which politics is assumed to be the process of authoritatively allocating values for a society (Easton, 1953). Derived from this assumption are four subprocesses: the *exchange process* in which values are allocated among the participants in the political process: the *role location* process in which a shared set of authoritative expectations is established and maintained among the participants in the exchange process; the *conflict process* in which enmity among these participants may occur when either existing terms of allocation are disrupted or else terms fail to be established when the participants first encounter one another; the *institution-building process* in which the terms of allocation and their accompanying shared expectations persist long enough to be formalized as organizations (Walker, 1983b, 1987).

From this perspective, the CREON model's components are elements of the role location process in this general theory of politics. The introduction of prior affect, salience, and relative capabilities into the CREON model as aids in formulating decision rules for the role location process are no longer *ad hoc* when viewed within the broader context provided by this theory, which offers answers to the question of why they are important and relevant determinants in the role location process. "Prior affect" and "relative capabilities" are important concepts in the conflict process, which is modeled by coalition theory and classical balance of power theory (Riker, 1962; Waltz, 1979). The concepts of "salience" and "problem" are at the heart of the exchange process because the CREON model defines them, respectively, as "the degree to which one country requires the support of another to realize basic values" and "value deprivation."

The selective introduction of these concepts into the CREON model's decision logic permits *ad hoc* variations in the role location process across confrontation, intervention, assistance and collaboration situations. The underlying theoretical rationale for these variations can be captured by relating the situations to one of the four processes associated with a general theory of politics. For example, the CREON confrontation situation has decision rules which introduce prior relative capabilities as one relevant condition in selecting a role for enactment (Singer and Hudson, 1987). Because a confrontation situation is defined as one in which a country either deprives another or is itself deprived by another, it is also by definition a situation in which the conflict process occurs. Consequently, the relative capabilities component of the balance of power model becomes relevant.

In addition to addressing the "why" question, the subsumption of the CREON role theory under a general theory of politics allows it to be reformulated more parsimoniously in some respects. This feature is desirable, because the number of national role conceptions is particularly unwieldly both in the CREON model and in Holsti's exploratory study upon which CREON builds. By realizing that the role location process is normally imbedded in either the exchange process or the conflict process, it is possible to subsume the role conceptions in the CREON model under one of the types of basic roles that define each of these processes. It is the perspective provided by the following theory of foreign policy as a variant of a general theory of politics that permits such a realization.

The central proposition in this theory of foreign policy is that a state's foreign policy is an instrument for the pursuit or maintenance of domestic political goals. It can be inferred either as a corollary of Waltz's theory of international politics or as a corollary of a theory of domestic politics (Walker, 1983b, 1987). From this proposition other postulates follow:

(1) States with the most pressing domestic problems of value allocation take the initiative in establishing exchange relations with other states.
(2) The targets of these initiatives can either respond with aid or refuse the request.
(3) If the response is positive, it is contingent upon the fulfillment of conditions that will benefit the domestic situation of the respondent.
(4) If the response is negative, the initiator can either ask some other state or press the request.
(5) If the latter option is selected, a conflict becomes more probable.
(6) In order to pursue or maintain domestic policy goals a state may also act to establish, maintain, or disrupt a shared set of expectations or the allocation of values among other states (Walker, 1983b, 1987).

According to the logic of these propositions, the role location process becomes imbedded in either an exchange process or a conflict process as one state takes the initiative and one or more others respond. Across these two processes five basic types of roles can be identified: consumer, producer, belligerent, facilitator and provocateur. The first two roles are associated with the exchange process, the third one with the conflict process, and the last two may be associated with either the exchange process or the conflict process. If we juxtapose these basic roles with the role conceptions identified for the types of situations in the CREON model, we get the pattern shown in Table 14.2.

The content of the role conceptions tends to vary, but they are all instances of decisions to occupy one of the roles in either the exchange process or the conflict process. They are subsumed in Table 14.2 under one of the four basic role types according to their assigned situations in the CREON model and the definitions of the basic roles elaborated in Walker (1983b, 1987). The latter are as follows:

(1) *Consumer*: describes a policy to establish or maintain assistance from another state.
(2) *Producer*: describes a policy which supplies assistance to another state.
(3) *Belligerent*: describes a policy either to resist requests for assistance or to press demands for assistance in spite of resistance.
(4) *Facilitator*: describes a policy that attempts to establish or maintain exchanges or shared expectations among other states.
(5) *Provocateur*: describes a policy that attempts to disrupt already existing exchanges or shared expectations among other states.

If the CREON role conception is assigned to a collaboration or assistance situation, then it is subsumed under either the consumer or the producer role in the exchange process. If the CREON role conception is associated with a confrontation situation, then it is subsumed under the belligerent role in the conflict process. If the CREON role con-

282

Table 14.2 *CREON role conceptions and the basic roles in an exchange theory of foreign policy*

| | | BASIC ROLES | | |
Consumer	Producer	Belligerent	Facilitator	Provocateur
Conciliationist (CO/AN)	Conciliationist (CO/AR)	Combatant (CF)	Combatant (I)	Defender of the faith (I)
Defender of the faith (CO)	Defender of the faith (AR)	Defender of the faith (CF)	Godfather/protector (I)	Opponent (I)
Donor (CO)	Donor (AR)	Opponent (CF)	Liberator (I)	
Godfather/protector (CO)	Godfather/protector (AR)		Mediator (I)	
Recruiter/promoter (CO)	Liberator (AR)		Policeman (I)	
	Policeman (AR)			
	Recruiter/promoter (AR)			

CO = *Collaboration* situation in which each assists the other regarding the same value
AN = *Assistance needed* situation in which one state requests assistance regarding a value
AR = *Assistance resource* situation in which one state provides assistance in response to another state's request regarding a value
CF = *Confrontation* situation in which one state attempts either to deprive another state of a value or else attempts to resist such deprivation
I = *Intervention* situation in which one state decides to choose sides in a confrontation between others

Sources: Walker, 1987; C. Hermann, 1987

ception is assigned to an intervention situation, then either the facilitator or provocateur role is the appropriate type of basic role.

There are other national role conceptions identified in the CREON project's analysis of American and Soviet shared political beliefs; however, they have not yet been fully defined or reported as associated with one of the four types of situations in the CREON model (C. Hermann, 1987, appendix 4). For the ones for which we do have this information, however, their placement under the basic roles does not appear to do violence to their original meanings. This judgment reinforces the contention that the CREON model's theory of role location is compatible with an exchange theory of politics and the theory of foreign policy derived from it and summarized above.

Overall, the application of role theory to the study of foreign policy has generated the combination of descriptive and theoretical statements that Waltz (1979, pp. 8–10) has argued are legitimate to expect from a strong theory. Much empirical work remains to be done in order to test the explanation that role theory offers for the origins of foreign policy, but it is a promising new direction in the comparative study of this puzzling topic.

15

What Do Decision Makers Do When They Make a Foreign Policy Decision? The Implications for the Comparative Study of Foreign Policy

PAUL A. ANDERSON

The variety of approaches to the study of the foreign policy behavior of governments is enormous. Instead of adding another potential solution to the list, this paper makes a modest proposal, asserts a strong claim, and presents some empirical results. The modest proposal is that at least a few individuals should focus on developing theories which describe the process of policy making in foreign affairs. The strong claim is that any theory of foreign policy inconsistent with those theories of the decision-making process is inadequate. The empirical results suggest that we have misrepresented what it is decision makers do when they make foreign policy decisions.

Although the argument represents a return to the roots of the study of foreign policy (the decision-making framework of Snyder, Bruck and Sapin, 1962a), unlike that earlier effort there is no suggestion here that decision making is the cornerstone for understanding everything of interest. Decision making is not being proposed as an alternative to "large-n" cross-national studies or to efforts which focus on the external environment of governments. Nor is this an argument that theories in comparative foreign policy must be reducible to theories of the foreign policy decision-making process. The fundamental argument is that adequate theories at one level cannot be inconsistent with what we know about the next lowest level. In other words, theories in comparative foreign policy behavior are not neutral with respect to theories of the process which generates that behavior.

For example, while neither Kegley's concept of decision regimes in foreign policy in Chapter 13 nor Rosenau's (1970) concept of national political adaptation is itself a theory of the decision-making process, both assume the underlying process is strongly goal-directed. If it were to turn out that the best theories of the underlying process were inconsistent with that proposition, then both theories would stand in need of modification.

There has been a long tradition in the comparative study of foreign policy going back to Rosenau (1966) and Wilkenfeld (1968) that governments are not identical. This tradition is well represented in this volume by the contributions of Hagan (Chapter 17), Hermann, Hermann and Hagan (Chapter 16) and Walker (Chapter 14). The evidence from studies of US foreign policy (Johnson, 1974; Kohl, 1975; George, 1980) suggests that foreign policy is generated by a variety of processes. There is no reason to suppose the USA is alone in this respect. Moreover, growing argument and evidence (Sylvan, 1985b; Hermann, Hermann and Hagan in Chapter 16) point to the conclusion that different processes make a difference. Thus, one way in which an improved understanding of the underlying process can make a difference in the large-scale theories of foreign policy behavior is in identifying the implications of the different decision-making processes of governments.

Whatever the differences in the processes that generate foreign policy behavior, they all reflect the limited information-processing capacity of individuals (Simon, 1979). The overwhelming cognitive demands of decision making guarantee that individuals must adopt strategies that fall short of the optimal, comprehensive ideal. Most of the time the simplifying strategies will produce acceptable outcomes. But sometimes, when the strategy is inappropriate for the task environment (Simon, 1981; Anderson, 1983b), the simplified decision strategy will make itself known in the form of biases, mistakes and errors. It is then that the shortcuts and simplifications reflected in the process are critical in understanding why particular decisions deviate from the norm. Both Kegley (Chapter 13) and Raymond (Chapter 6), for example, reject the general claim that foreign policy action is but the resultant of a set of small, uncoordinated decisions, without any sense of direction. And, they are on solid ground in rejecting it as a *general* description. But, it is equally clear that sometimes (and for generally understandable reasons) goals are left purposely vague and non-operational with the underlying conflict only partly resolved (Cyert and March, 1963). Under circumstances where goal conflict is hidden rather than resolved, it will be critical to understand process in order to understand why governments are acting as they are.

Thus, the call for attention to the underlying process that generates foreign policy behavior is a call for some foundation building that will make a difference in the large-scale theories of the foreign policy behavior of governments to which the field aspires. One of the fundamental issues that needs to be addressed is what it is that decision makers do when they make a foreign policy decision.

Introduction

Representations of Decision Making

Between the time of the discovery of Soviet missiles in Cuba and the imposition of a naval blockade of Cuba by the United States there were two significant delays in the US decision-making process. The first delay occurred when President Kennedy decided not to react immediately, but to plan the US reponse in secret (Abel, 1966; Allison, 1971). The second delay occurred on the third day of the crisis when the President decided to let the Executive Committee of the National Security Council (ExCom) continue to debate the issue even though a straw vote had shown a two-thirds majority in favor of a blockade (Allison, 1971; Detzer, 1979). Why did the President delay? The evidence suggests he could have acted earlier. The first delay did not occur because the President was at a loss as to what could be done. He is reported to have remarked to Adlai Stevenson, US Ambassador to the United Nations, "We'll have to do something quickly. I suppose the alternatives are to go in by air and wipe them out, or to take other steps to render the weapons inoperable" (Abel, 1966, p. 36). Thus he could have chosen an air strike on the first day. And why the second delay? The evidence suggests that the delay was not for the President's benefit; he had decided on a blockade (Sorensen, 1965; Allison, 1971). By the time the choice finally was made it was anticlimatic: Allison (1971, p. 208) described the meeting at which the official decision was made as a "Greek drama" where players maneuvered toward the predetermined outcome.

Are the delays inexplicable? Certainly not. But there are two different explanations for the delays and the difference between them points to an important bias in the way we represent foreign policy decision making. The most obvious explanation for the two delays is a cognitive explanation: Kennedy wanted to be sure that his choice would be the best available course of action, that a wide variety of goals and objectives had been considered, that the full range of alternatives had been examined, and that the consequences of following each

287

possible course of action had been carefully considered. Only with full and complete knowledge of goals, alternatives and consequences would he be in a position to choose the best course of action in light of US goals and objectives. To have chosen immediately would have been to choose in the face of profound ignorance and uncertainty. The second delay was Kennedy's attempt to make sure the apparent consensus behind a blockade was well founded; he had, after all, experience with a consensus of experts in the Bay of Pigs debacle.

A second explanation for the two delays is based upon the view that decisions are a product of a social process. From this perspective the delays were not really delays at all, but reflections of an incomplete and unfinished social process. The concept of a well-founded decision is widespread in the culture of bureaucracy, and among the attributes of well-founded and appropriate choice are consensus, coalition building and reasoned reflection. For President Kennedy to have reacted immediately upon receiving news of the missiles in Cuba would have violated shared interpretations of proper and appropriate decision-making behavior. From this view, the second delay was not for Kennedy's sake, not to reassure him that the blockade was the best course of action, but for the sake of the losers, the air-strike advocates. The additional time gave them a final opportunity to present their case. They could not later claim their views had been ignored, for they had been given every opportunity to justify their preferred course of action. The fact the final choice resembled a staged drama only reinforces the social character of the process. Everyone knew what the outcome would be; it was done as a symbolic end to the social process of decision making.

The justification for examining decision making from a social perspective is simple: some, but not all, political phenomena are cognitive phenomena. Those political phenomena that are largely cognitive, for example, an individual in a voting booth deciding which candidate to vote for, deserve a cognitive analysis: what cognitive representations do individuals use to store information about political objects, how do they allocate their attention, what mechanisms do they use to interpret new information, how do they store and retrieve political knowledge, in what ways are their information-processing strategies prone to error and bias? But not all political phenomena are purely cognitive, and one pre-eminently noncognitive political phenomenon is governmental action where political institutions stand between individual cognition and foreign policy outputs.[1]

While the view that governmental decision making is as much a product of a social process as it is an individual-level cognitive process has a long history—Snyder, Bruck and Sapin (1962a), Lindblom (1965),

Robinson and Majak (1967) and Allison (1971) all recognized the importance of social processes in shaping governmental action—most current research on foreign policy decision making adopts a strongly cognitive perspective as reflected in the works of Jervis (1976), Holsti (1976a), George (1980) and Larson (1985). Although there are a variety of reasons for the emphasis on individual cognition, including the fact that cognitive psychology is a high-growth area with recent substantial theoretical progress and growing influences in social psychology,[2] an important reason for the relative lack of emphasis on decision making as a social process is that we lack appropriate data on the social process of decision making. The data that we do have on foreign policy decision making is almost entirely based upon interviews, participant memoirs and second-hand journalistic accounts. While these data sources are not without their problems, in the hands of careful re-searchers they provide some basis for making tentative conclusions about the beliefs and attitudes of the participants. Even though we might be willing to take a decision maker's recollections as evidence for what he thought and believed, it requires a far greater leap of faith to take his recollections of the process (of which he is but a single biased observer) as good data.

The situation, however, is changing. Newly available (and still slowly emerging) empirical data on the decision-making process is of a far higher quality than that which was available in the past. The process of declassification is making more and more primary source information available on postwar US decisions in presidential libraries and archives. For example, we no longer need to rely upon Sorensen (1965), Schlesinger (1965) or Abel (1966) for information about how the USA made decisions during the Cuban missile crisis. Instead, we can read the verbatim transcripts of the meetings of the ExCom and read the memos and reports used by the decision makers.

High-quality archival data stands to rejuvenate the study of foreign policy decision as both a cognitive and a social process. We are in a position to reconstruct the flow of information upon which decisions are based, to read the transcripts of meetings at which decisions are made, and to quote directly the words of decision makers from private diaries and memos. The implications of these data are particularly striking for attempts to study decision making as a social process. Detailed case studies are no longer the only method available for studying the process of decision making. It is within our ability to draw a random sample of postwar face-to-face decision-making meetings in the United States executive branch, and to study in detail the processes of choice in a variety of settings. While the new data and more general methods will not automatically make the classic case studies of Snyder and Paige (1958), Paige (1968), Allison (1971) and Janis (1982) obsolete, the detailed case study will be supplemented by more general characterizations of the process of decision making in foreign policy based upon higher-quality data.

The potential for major revision of our basic understanding of the decision-making process is foreshadowed by the empirical results presented below that suggest that we have been mistaken on some of the fundamental aspects of decision making in foreign affairs. Consider, for example, Snyder's (1958, p. 19) (admittedly tentative) definition of decision making:

> Decision-making results in the selection from a socially defined, limited number of problematical, alternative projects (i.e., courses of action) of one project to bring about the particular state of affairs envisaged by the decision-makers.

While we all might quibble with bits and pieces of the definition, on the whole it seems quite reasonable. However, the empirical results presented below suggest the definition is inadequate in at least three important respects:

(1) Decision makers consider a surprisingly large number of alternatives. The average number of unique alternatives presented in 13 high-level decision-making sessions was 15.2.
(2) Very few of the alternatives were actually mutually inconsistent. Of the average 15.2 alternatives per meeting, only 2.4 (or 15.7%) were inconsistent. Thus decision making does not involve choices between incompatible alternative courses of action, but rather a sequence of binary yes-no choices over a wide array of independent actions.
(3) Statements of goals tend to produce and be produced by statements of alternatives. Thus, the temporal relationship between statements of goals and alternatives suggests that the particular state of affairs envisaged by the decision makers is not all that concrete. It appears that decision making involves the discovery of goals as much as it involves using decisions to achieve particular outcomes.

What is striking is that the second of these inconsistencies, the fact that mutually incompatible alternative courses of action are not a universal feature in foreign policy decision making, was a characteristic of the Korean decision analyzed by Snyder and Paige (1958). As Powell, Dyson and Purkitt suggest in Chapter 11, the first real test of the decision-making approach contained a clear falsification of one of its key assumptions. While Snyder and Paige do not ignore the fact that competing alternative courses of action were absent, that striking finding lay dormant because of the problems inherent in making general inferences from a single observation. It is only with the availability of comparable data from other decisions that the single isolated finding of the Korean decision takes on a new significance.

These three inconsistencies between our ordinary understanding of what the task of decision making involves and the evidence from actual decision making suggest that the basic representations we have been using to understand governmental action are not particularly appropriate. Thus, the need arises to reopen the question of what exactly decision makers do when they make a decision.

Empirical Research and the Social Process of Decision Making

If a social-process view of decision making is to result in an improved theory of foreign policy decision making that can support theories of the foreign policy behavior of governments, then it is critical that high-quality empirical data be brought to bear. Good theories are unlikely without high-quality data, and all too frequently anecdotes and rhetoric are substituted for data and careful analysis. Until relatively recently high-quality high-density records (e.g., verbatim transcripts) of decision making in foreign policy have been relatively hard to come by. While the situation is far from ideal, particularly for other countries, a great amount of information on the US foreign policy process has become available through the National Archives and the various presidential libraries. Memos, cables and working papers fill seemingly endless rows of shelves in the archives waiting for analytically minded social scientists to exploit them. Figuring out how all that information could be used to build and test theories is a real challenge. To make progress in developing general theories of the foreign policy process a way must be found to go beyond the standard narrative case study: we have to use the archival information to do more than tell a good story.

As a step in the direction of bringing more powerful methods to bear for using the available archival data, and to provide a descriptive picture of the behavior of real decision makers making real decisions, this author performed a content analysis of the transcripts of thirteen high-level crisis decision-making meetings. They included two meetings involving Truman and his advisers immediately after the invasion of South Korea by the North (Jessup, 1976a, b), three meetings immediately after the Chinese intervention in Korea (Jessup, 1976c,d,e), four meetings involving Eisenhower and his advisers in which they decided on the US response to the eventual collapse of the French at Dien Bien Phu (Gleason, 1982a,b,c,d), and four sessions of the ExCom during the Cuban missile crisis (Smith, 1962a,b,c,d).

The documents are memoranda for the record prepared by White House and State Department staff members. The style of the documents, which is consistent across all the meetings, is that of a third-party transcript. While they are not verbatim accounts of the meetings, they are detailed, chronological records of the statements of the decision makers. The following quotation from the first meeting on the Korean crisis provides a sense of the quality of the data:

> The President called on the Secretary of State to open the discussion.
>
> Mr. Acheson summarized the various problems which he thought the President should consider. The first point was the question of authorizing General MacArthur to supply Korea with arms and other equipment over and above the supplies of ammunition presently authorized under the MDAP program. He recommended that this be done. He suggested that our air cover should be used to aid in the evacuation of the women and children from Seoul and that our air force should be authorized to knock out northern Korean tanks or air force interfering with the evacuation. He then mentioned the resolution adopted by the [UN] Security Council and suggested that consideration should be given to what further assistance we might render to Korea in pursuance of his or a supplementary Security Council resolution. He next suggested that the President should order the Seventh Fleet to proceed to Formosa and prevent an attack on Formosa from the mainland. At the same time operations from Formosa against the mainland should be prevented. He said that he did not recommend that General MacArthur should go to Formosa until further steps had been decided upon. He said that the United States should not tie up with the Generalissimo. He thought that the future status of Formosa might be determined by the UN.
>
> The President interposed "or by the Japanese Peace Treaty".
>
> Mr. Acheson finally suggested that our aid to Indochina should be stepped up.
>
> General Bradley said that we must draw the line somewhere.
>
> The President stated he agreed on that.

Although these records are not as good as actual verbatim transcripts, they are as close to verbatim transcripts as we ever will have for many decisions.[3]

At the time these records were written, they were highly classified. The accounts of the Korean and Dien Bien Phu decisions have been completely declassified. The accounts of the ExCom meetings still contain some classified material, which has been deleted from the copies of the records open for research through a process called "sanitizing." The deleted portions of the documents generally pertain directly to intelligence sources and methods and do not represent more than 10 per cent of the material available.

Table 15.1   *Categories for Coding Decision-Making Sessions*

Task description	A description of a task facing the decision makers: For example, "A decision must be made by 2:00 AM this morning if we want to stop the ship outside Cuban territorial waters."
Task goal	A goal which refers to a task facing the decision makers: "He added that if there was any prospect of success in following a political track, we would have to keep heavy pressure on the Russians."
Outcome goal	A goal which refers to an external state of affairs: "Both General Taylor and Secretary Dillon pointed out that we could not permit Soviet technicians to go through the quarantine even though technicians are not on the embargo list."
Alternative	An explicit course of action which is capable of being performed "Secretary McNamara recommended that the East German ship not be stopped because it might be necessary for us to shoot at it or to ram it."
Description, own	A description of behavior by the decision unit: "The destroyer *Pierce* is following the ship which is still outside the barrier."
Description, other	A description of the behavior of an external actor: "The Attorney General said that fifteen ships have turned back, which is an impressive action taken by the Russians."
Prediction	A statement of possible future action by an external actor: "We could expect a veto from the Russians in the Security Council."
Consequence, own	A description of the consequences of an action by the decision unit: "Director McCone agreed that such action would be effective because it would greatly reduce imports into Cuba and also take away from the Cubans their outgoing cargoes."
Consequence, other	A description of the consequences of an action by an external actor: "He said the Soviet weapons in Cuba were pointed at our heart and put us under great handicap in continuing to carry out our commitments to the free world."
Decision	An authoritative decision: "The President again said we should let the East German passenger ship go through."
Interpretation, own	An interpretation of the reasons for an action by the decision makers: "The purpose of these talks is to arrive at a solution of the crisis or, if no solution is possible, to provide a basis for later action, having been unable to negotiate a settlement."
Interpretation, other	An interpretation of the reasons for an action by an external actor: "He said he believed the Soviets had turned their ships around because they did not want us to see what was on them."

Each sentence in the original document was categorized, using a computer-assisted content analysis procedure, into one of the twelve decision-relevant categories displayed in Table 15.1. A fuller description of the coding method can be found in Anderson (1983a). The counts and relative frequency of each statement type for each meeting are presented in Table 15.2.

The Structure of Alternatives

Immediately striking in Table 15.2 is the high number of alternatives. Alternatives accounted for 14.1 per cent of the statements with an average of 21.1 alternatives per meeting. Even after eliminating statements which repeat alternatives, the numbers remain high (as is shown in Table 15.3), with an average of 15.2 alternatives per meeting. Given the limits on the ability of individuals to process information, it is somewhat surprising that the decision makers could consider an average of 15.2 alternatives per meeting. If the basic model that decision makers choose alternatives by examining their consequences for achieving their goals is anywhere near correct, that means the decision makers confronted decision trees with 15 major branches. If the uncertain consequences of each alternative are included the decision tree would be of immense proportions. And, if decision makers can cope with gargantuan decision trees, then bounded rationality cannot be right.

A closer examination of the structure of alternatives reveals that it is

Table 15.2 *Mean Frequencies and Percentages of Interactions in Foreign Policy Decision-Making Groups*

	Korea		Vietnam		ExCom		Total	
	mean	%	mean	%	mean	%	mean	%
Task Description	22.6	14.1	28.3	14.5	10.3	11.2	20.5	13.7
Task Goal	24.4	15.2	18.3	9.4	10.0	10.9	18.1	12.1
Outcome Goal	4.8	3.0	9.8	5.0	3.0	3.3	5.8	3.9
Alternative	29.2	18.2	11.8	6.0	20.3	22.1	21.1	14.1
Description, Own	10.8	6.7	12.3	6.3	5.8	6.3	9.7	6.5
Description, Other	8.2	5.1	45.5	23.4	5.5	6.0	18.8	12.6
Prediction	14.6	9.1	26.3	13.5	5.8	6.3	15.5	10.3
Consequence, Own	9.6	6.0	7.5	3.9	5.8	6.3	7.8	5.2
Consequence, Other	1.0	0.6	6.0	3.1	1.0	1.1	2.5	1.7
Decision	4.6	2.9	5.8	3.0	6.5	7.1	5.5	3.7
Interpretation, Own	1.0	0.6	1.5	0.8	2.0	2.2	1.5	1.0
Interpretation, Other	1.2	0.7	1.8	0.9	2.0	2.2	1.6	1.1
Unclassified	28.2	17.6	20.3	10.4	14.0	15.3	21.4	14.3
n	801		779		367		1947	

What Do Decision Makers Do?

Table 15.3   Frequencies and Percentages of Alternatives

Group	Unique alternatives	Incompatible alternatives	Percentage of incompatible alternatives
Korea1	14	2	14.3
Korea2	23	3	13.0
Korea3	18	1	5.6
Korea4	17	1	5.9
Korea5	31	6	19.4
Korea mean	20.6	2.6	12.6
Vietnam1	11	5	45.5
Vietnam2	5	0	0.0
Vietnam3	6	0	0.0
Vietnam4	8	3	37.5
Vietnam mean	7.5	2.0	26.7
Excom5	13	0	0.0
Excom6	17	6	35.3
Excom7	18	1	5.6
Excom8	16	3	18.8
Excom mean	16.0	2.5	15.6
Grand mean	15.2	2.4	15.7

Key:
Korea1 – Blair House meeting, June 25, 1950
Korea2 – Blair House meeting, June 26, 1950
Korea3 – NSC meeting, November 28, 1950
Korea4 – Pentagon meeting, December 1, 1950
Korea5 – Pentagon meeting, December 3, 1950

Vietnam1 – 192nd meeting of the NSC, April 6, 1954
Vietnam2 – 194th meeting of the NSC, April 29, 1954
Vietnam3 – 195th meeting of the NSC, May 6, 1954
Vietnam4 – 196th meeting of the NSC, May 8, 1954

Excom5 – NSC ExCom meeting #5, October 25, 1962
Excom6 – NSC ExCom meeting #6, October 26, 1962
Excom7 – NSC ExCom meeting #7, October 27, 1962
Excom8 – NSC ExCom meeting #8, October 27, 1962

the standard decision-tree representation of choice which is inadequate, not bounded rationality. Although decision makers considered an average of 15.2 alternatives per meeting, only 15.7 per cent of the alternatives, or 2.4 alternatives per meeting, were incompatible. The vast majority of the alternatives were not mutually inconsistent, but represented independent courses of action. Thus the decision problem confronting the participants was not one of selecting the best from an array of 15 incompatible alternatives, but was instead a problem of choosing some subset of the 15 alternatives.

295

Although choosing a subset from a group of 15 alternatives is far simpler than performing a comparative evaluation of 15 alternatives, it is still no easy task. There are, after all, 32,767 unique subsets of 15 alternatives. The evidence suggests that decision makers do not consider each subset, but instead sequentially consider each alternative as it is introduced and make a relatively quick, yes-no decision whether to pursue that particular course of action.

A closer examination of the structure of incompatible alternatives reveals further interesting patterns. Incompatible alternatives almost always emerge in reaction to a previous suggestion. Participants rarely say "We could do X or else we could do Y." Instead, one participant says "We could do X," and then another individual says either "No, we shouldn't" or "No, we shouldn't do X, we should do Y." Thus, incompatible alternatives are produced through the interaction of decision makers. What is striking about the structure of incompatible alternatives is that the majority are simple objections to pursuing a course of action and not full-fledged alternative courses of action. Of the 31 inconsistent alternatives identified in the 13 meetings, 54.8 per cent were simple objections to a proposed course of action, that is, "We should not do X," 32.3 per cent represented positive suggestions, that is, "We should do Y rather than X," and 12.9 per cent identified mutually exclusive courses of action "We could do X or we could do Y."

The structure of the alternatives facing the decision makers was not so much a branching decision tree as a binary maze. The decision makers did not first explore the maze and then sit down to plan a path through it, but instead, they crept along through the maze making a series of independent judgments as to whether to go straight or take a left. Moreover, it appears that they do not find very many "Y" intersections that call for a comparative decision. Instead the maze appears to be a collection of long corridors with a series of paths branching to the side.

The Structure of Decisions

A second striking aspect of the data is the relatively low frequency of decisions, given the high number of alternatives. While there were an average of 21.1 alternatives per meeting, each meeting averaged 5.5 decisions. When repetitions of decision are deleted (as shown in Table 15.4), the average drops to 4.5 decisions per meeting. Using this accounting, only 29.4 per cent of the alternatives result in decisions.

However, that figure is somewhat misleading. There is nothing in the structure of decision-making meetings that requires that an alternative be described before a decision can be made. Even though each

Table 15.4   Frequencies and Percentages of Alternatives and Decisions

Group	Unique decisions	Decisions preceded by alternatives	Unique alternatives	Percentage of decisions preceded by alternatives
Korea1	12	5	14	35.7
Korea2	6	6	23	26.1
Korea3	1	1	18	5.6
Korea4	0	0	17	0.0
Korea5	0	0	31	0.0
Korea mean	3.8	2.4	20.6	11.7
Vietnam1	5	1	11	9.1
Vietnam2	1	1	5	20.0
Vietnam3	3	1	6	16.7
Vietnam4	11	8	8	100.0
Vietnam mean	5.0	2.8	7.5	36.7
Excom5	2	2	13	15.4
Excom6	6	4	17	23.5
Excom7	3	3	18	16.7
Excom8	8	6	16	37.5
Excom mean	4.8	3.8	16.0	23.4
Grand mean	4.5	2.9	15.2	19.3

Key: See Table 15.3.

meeting averaged 4.5 decisions (see Table 15.4), only 2.9 of those decisions were preceded by explicit statements of alternatives.[4] Using the actual number of decisions preceded by an alternative as a basis, only 19.3 per cent of the alternatives actually result in formal presidential decisions.

The high number of alternatives, the low number of incompatible alternatives, and the low frequency of decision, taken together suggest that what happens at these meetings is that a large number of alternatives are proposed and then simply ignored. They die for what amounts to the lack of a seconding motion (i.e., further consideration).

The Structure of Goals

A third striking number in Table 15.2 is what seems to be a low frequency of statements describing outcome goals (descriptions of desirable external states of affairs). There were on average 5.8 statements of outcome goals or 3.9 per cent of the statements in the

297

meetings. In comparison, there were considerably more statements that described goals specific to tasks facing the decision makers: an average of 18.1 per meeting, or 12.1 per cent of the total. In the context of the relatively low frequency of decisions and the low incidence of inconsistent alternatives, the relative emphasis on tasks facing the decision makers as opposed to outcomes in the external environment is not that surprising. The decision process does not appear to be particularly oriented toward long-term outcomes; far more attention is paid to the issue of what to do next.

This is not to say that goals are irrelevant to the decision-making process. Each of the decision meetings was held for a clear purpose; these were not routine discussions held according to a fixed schedule. For each meeting there was a problem to be confronted that served as a global goal or stimulus that was clear to all participants. But the shared concerns were not sufficient to uniquely determine action (if the consensus were that strong, there would have been little decision-making justification for the meetings). What is critical in understanding the decisions reached were the goals which were discovered in the course of the discussions (Anderson, 1983b).

The close relationship between goals and alternatives can be seen by examining the frequency with which goal statements occur in the context of other goal statements or alternatives. Averaged across all the meetings, 39.9 per cent of the goals were preceded by a statement of a goal or of an alternative, and 51.8 per cent of the goal statements were followed by an alternative or another goal statement. The breakdowns across the three decision settings are displayed in Table 15.5. Thus, goals tend to produce and be produced by goals and alternatives.

Bureaucratic Expertise and Participation

A final general characteristic of the decision-making meetings is the role of expertise in structuring the interactions of the participants. Expertise has been recognized as an important influence on decision

Table 15.5 *Sequential Patterns of Goals and Alternatives*

	Alternatives or goals followed by goals	Goals followed by alternatives or goals
Korea	44.5%	58.1%
Vietnam	29.8	37.1
ExCom	60.4	81.3
Total	39.9	51.8

making in the literature on both organizational theory and bureaucratic politics. Dearborn and Simon (1958) found that organizational participants tend to frame problems in terms of the specialization and expertise of their subdivision in the organization. March and Simon (1958) make a general argument about the importance of specialization and division of labor in fostering a tendency of organizational participants to focus upon the goals of their subunit rather than the goals of the organization as a whole. In addition to increasing identification with subunit goals, the bureaucratic politics literature (Allison, 1971) has noted the degree to which bureaucratic expertise can be a source of power and influence in the bureaucratic bargaining game.

In order to assess the influence of expertise on the interaction in the decision-making meetings, all of the statements of alternatives, and consequences or predictions were examined and the expertise of the speaker was compared with the content of the statement. If the person's expertise was in the military (including civilians in the Defense Department) and the alternative involved a military action, the alternative was coded as being within the person's domain. If on the other hand a person with military expertise proposed an alternative having to do with a purely diplomatic action, which would be implemented by the Department of State, then the alternative was coded as being outside the person's domain. The President was treated in a special category because there is nothing which is outside of his proper domain.

Table 15.6 contains the results of the supplementary coding. The results show the importance of bureaucratic expertise in that 59.5 per cent of the alternatives and 71.9 per cent of the consequences or predictions were consistent with the speaker's domain. If presidential statements are removed, then 56.2 per cent of the alternatives and 68.4 per cent of the consequences and predictions were consistent with the speaker's domain.

Variations across Meetings

The counts and frequencies show a considerable variation across the thirteen meetings as well as across the three decision settings. While the results suggest some intriguing differences in decision style, it is important to keep in mind that the results are based upon an extraordinarily small sample and the differences must not be over-interpreted: four meetings each from the missile crisis and the Dien Bien Phu crisis and five meetings from the Korean crisis (two meetings immediately after the initiation of the conflict and three meetings some months later after the intervention of the Chinese).

The most striking differences in Table 15.2 are between the Dien Bien

Table 15.6 *Bureaucratic Expertise and Statements in Decision-Making Groups*

Group	Alternatives					Consequences and Predictions				
	Presidential	Within domain	Outside domain	Percentage outside domain	Percentage presidential	Presidential	Within domain	Outside domain	Percentage outside domain	Percentage Presidential
Korea1	2	15	5	22.7	9.1	0	6	1	14.3	0.0
Korea2	3	16	18	48.6	8.1	1	8	0	0.0	11.1
Korea3	0	10	8	44.4	0.0	2	16	5	21.7	8.7
Korea4	0	15	6	28.6	0.0	0	14	5	26.3	0.0
Korea5	0	26	22	45.8	0.0	0	49	19	27.9	0.0
Korea mean	1.0	16.4	11.8	40.4	3.4	0.6	18.6	6.0	24.4	2.4
Vietnam1	2	8	9	47.4	10.5	9	35	12	21.4	16.1
Vietnam2	1	6	4	36.4	9.1	11	25	33	47.8	15.9
Vietnam3	1	2	4	57.1	14.3	2	14	3	15.8	10.5
Vietnam4	0	6	4	40.0	0.0	3	7	5	33.3	20.0
Vietnam mean	1.0	5.5	5.3	44.7	8.5	6.3	20.3	13.3	39.6	15.7
Excom5	0	12	8	40.0	0.0	0	18	1	5.3	0.0
Excom6	4	6	9	47.4	21.1	3	7	4	28.6	21.4
Excom7	5	9	8	36.4	22.7	3	2	3	37.5	37.5
Excom8	5	10	5	25.0	25.0	3	2	3	37.5	37.5
Excom mean	3.5	9.3	7.5	37.0	17.3	2.3	7.3	2.8	22.4	18.4
Grand mean	1.8	10.8	8.5	40.1	8.4	2.8	15.6	7.2	28.1	11.1

Key: see Table 15.3.

Phu decisions and the Korean and Cuban decisions. The Dien Bien Phu decisions were characterized by far fewer statements of alternatives and far more statements devoted to descriptions of other actors, predictions, and consequences of the actions of other actors: only 6 per cent of the statements in the Dien Bien Phu decisions referred to alternatives as compared to 18.2 per cent for the Korean decisions and 22.1 per cent for the Cuban ExCom decisions; 23.4 per cent of the statements in the Dien Bien Phu decisions were descriptions of the behavior of other actors as compared to 5.1 per cent for Korea and 6.0 per cent for the ExCom; 13.5 per cent of the statements involved predictions compared to 9.1 per cent for Korea and 6.3 per cent for the ExCom; and 3.1 per cent of the statements in the Dien Bien Phu decisions described the consequences of the actions of other actors as compared to 0.6 per cent for the Korean decisions and 1.1 per cent for the meetings of the ExCom.

Even though there were far fewer alternatives in the meetings relating to the Dien Bien Phu crisis, there was far more conflict as measured by the frequency of incompatible alternatives. During the Dien Bien Phu meetings, 26.7 per cent of the alternatives were incompatible with other alternatives as compared to 15.6 per cent for the missile crisis meetings and 12.6 per cent for the Korean meetings. A closer examination of the basis for these averages shows a striking pattern. For two of the Dien Bien Phu meetings no incompatible alternatives were proposed, while in the other two meetings the rate of incompatible alternatives was 45.5 and 30.0 per cent. The missile crisis decisions also show this variation, with the proportion of incompatible alternatives ranging from 0 to 35.3 per cent. Thus the conflict in the meetings varied considerably.

The meetings prompted by the imminent collapse of the French at Dien Bien Phu showed a tendency to devote more time to describing the external environment (descriptions of the actions of other actors, descriptions of the consequences of the actions of other actors, and predictions) than did the decisions surrounding the Korean crisis or the Cuban missile crisis. This is not particularly surprising given the nature of the decision problem facing the US government. In the Korean and Cuban situations, whether the US government should take any action was not a serious issue; in both cases, the USA was going to act.[5] The issue for the United States in the Dien Bien Phu crisis was very different. The French clearly had an important stake in the issue and would have to be treated as a partner in any American action. Thus much of the discussion during the Dien Bien Phu meetings was focused on the actions of the French government and its call for help. In the missile crisis, the participation of other actors was minimal (the only coordination issues that arose had to do with the Jupiter missiles in Turkey). In the Korean crisis, South Korea was in no position to defend itself. Thus it is not surprising to find the meetings pertaining to the collapse of the French forces at Dien Bien Phu involved far more external references than in the Korean and Cuban missile crises. In the later crisis the primary issue was to determine what American actions were appropriate, not whether any US action was appropriate.

The gross differences between the Dien Bien Phu meetings and the Korean and Cuban crisis meetings reinforces a critical issue which has long been recognized in studies of individual problem solving and decision making (Newell and Simon, 1972): behavior is sensitive to the task environment. The relationship between task environments and decision making suggests that if we are to understand the foreign policy decision-making process, it will be necessary to identify how differences in the task environment influence the process of foreign policy decision making.

One approach to distinguishing differences in the process of decision making is to classify meetings according to the relative frequency of different types of interactions. The twelve categories were recoded according to whether they involved goal statements (task goals and outcome goals), decision-relevant statements (task descriptions, alternatives and decisions), or external references (descriptions of behavior, predictions, consequences and interpretations). The results of the frequency of each type of interaction for each meeting are shown in Table 15.7. If a group devoted equal amounts of attention to goals, decisions and external references, then each category would account for one-third of the statements. The extent to which the pattern deviates from equal shares for each category is an indication of the relative orientation of the meeting. The first pass at a classification of meetings was to use 33 per cent as a cutoff criterion. If a category accounted for more than 33 per cent of the statements, then the category applied to a meeting. If the category accounted for less than 33 per cent of the statements, then the meeting did not reflect the category. This procedure results in six possible meeting types representing all possible subsets from the three-element set, only three of which are represented in the thirteen meetings in the data set.

Using this procedure, the seventh and eighth meetings of the Cuban ExCom and the first two meetings immediately after the outbreak of the Korean conflict fall into the decision category. The fifth and sixth meetings of the ExCom, the three meetings after the Chinese intervention in Korea, and the last meeting of the Eisenhower National Security Council before the fall of Dien Bien Phu fall into the decision-external

Table 15.7   *Classification of Types of Decision-Making Groups*

Group	Goal references	Decision references	External references	Type
Korea1	24.1%	55.4%	20.5%	decision
Korea2	16.3	58.2	25.5	decision
Korea3	29.4	33.1	37.5	decision-external
Korea4	18.7	46.2	35.2	decision-external
Korea5	21.0	36.5	42.5	decision-external
Vietnam1	18.4	32.1	49.5	external
Vietnam2	11.9	17.7	70.4	external
Vietnam3	16.7	19.6	63.7	external
Vietnam4	19.6	45.7	34.8	decision-external
Excom5	16.7	36.5	46.9	decision-external
Excom6	20.8	42.9	36.4	decision-external
Excom7	16.7	51.4	31.9	decision
Excom8	12.1	65.2	22.7	decision

Key: see Table 15.3.

category, and the first three meetings on the Dien Bien Phu crisis fall into the external oriented category.

While there are clear problems with this classification procedure, the groupings do have a certain face validity. The early meetings on the Korean crisis were clearly involved with determining the initial US response and naturally belong in the decision-making category. The meetings after the Chinese intervention fall into the decision-external category and reflect the twin problems faced by the United States of assessing the meaning of the Chinese intervention and determining the appopriate US response. The fifth and sixth meetings of the Cuban ExCom, which fall into the decision-external category, were primarily concerned with enforcing the blockade and maintaining the pressure on the Soviet Union. The seventh and eight meetings of the ExCom occurred after the conciliatory "Friday Night Letter" from Khrushchev (the public hard-line Soviet offer to trade missiles in Cuba for missiles in Turkey was received during the seventh meeting) and the attention of the ExCom focused most directly on decision-making tasks. The first three meetings on the Dien Bien Phu crisis fall into the external category and reflect the preoccupation of the decision makers with the deteriorating situation in Vietnam and the French request for aid. The fourth meeting falls into the decision-external category and reflects the pressures on the US government to take some action both in response to the situation in Vietnam and the Geneva negotiations.

Implications and Derivations

While it is clear that the whole of the foreign policy process is not captured in the records of group discussions, the records provide some of the best high-density observations of what decision makers do when they make a foreign policy decision. An earlier analysis (Anderson, 1983a), using only the records of the Cuban ExCom, suggested the following description of the decision-making process:

(1) A problem is defined and a global goal is identified, which produces a rough description of an acceptable resolution to the problem.
(2) A course of action is proposed. The alternative will be accompanied by an argument describing the positive outcomes associated with undertaking the action.
(3) The proposed course of action will produce one of three responses:
    (a) If there is general agreement on the desirability of following the course of action, it will be ratified.
    (b) If there is no support and no formal opposition, the alternative will die for what amounts to the lack of a second.
    (c) The third and most interesting case is when there is an objection to the alternative. Objections are framed in terms of the negative or undesirable consequences of the alternative, and the effect is to propose constraints, beyond the global goal, that further define an acceptable resolution of the problem.
(4) If there is disagreement over the newly introduced constraint, a secondary discussion on the merits of the new goal may ensue. Only if there is an imperative to act will a competing course of action be proposed.
(5) In the absence of an imperative to act, the original alternative is generally discarded and a different independent course of action is proposed.

(Anderson, 1983a, p. 217)

The analysis of the thirteen meetings suggest a few additions to this basic description:

Step 1:   While the initial problem focuses the attention of the various parts of the government on the issue, each subcomponent interprets the problem in light of its particular subgoals. Each part of the organization looks for actions within its repertoire which might be appropriate under the circumstances. The representatives of the organizational subunits attend the meeting to get authorization to implement their proposed courses of action, and to keep informed about the actions of other parts of the government.

Step 2:   Once at the decision-making meeting, the representatives of the institutions of the government ask permission to implement their proposed courses of action.

Step 3:   The President has the task of keeping collective action coherent and enforcing a common set of goals, while the representatives of other subunits have the task of ensuring that other subunits do not act in ways which make achieving their subgoals more difficult. Thus the meetings provide a mechanism for achieving a degree of coordination and control without overwhelming the cognitive capacity of the participants.

This description of the process of decision making must only be considered partially correct. More research is required before we will be in a position to state with some confidence what it is decision makers do when they make a foreign policy decision. The imperative is clear: more data. A central difficulty in interpreting the results of the content analyses is the complete lack of any base rate information. Is 15.2 unique alternatives per meeting anywhere near typical? Do all meetings have an average of 2.4 incompatible alternatives? Without more data on more meetings there is no way to tell whether we are trying to explain the outliers or the main effect. The first meeting on Dien Bien Phu that was content-analyzed was the 192nd meeting of the National Security Council, so there is no lack of available information on the process buried in the archives.

More data is not the only imperative. We also must be more systematic in the data we examine. There is an unfortunate tendency (which also shows up in this paper) to focus attention on the "interesting" cases: the Korean decisions, Dien Bien Phu, the Cuban missile crisis. While there are sound reasons for focusing upon critical events where war and peace are at stake, there are equally compelling reasons to focus on the mundane, routine and mediocre decisions. If we are interested in understanding the effects of crisis on decision making, we cannot understand them unless we understand how crisis decision making differs from noncrisis decision making. If we are interested in why decision processes go wrong and produce fiascos like the Bay of Pigs, we cannot understand the failures unless we understand how the failures differ from successes or from mediocre, run-of-the-mill decisions. In the final analysis, this is just a sampling problem and the solution is to draw a systematic sample of the meetings in the archives.

The third imperative is to develop new research techniques for exploiting the vast amount of material in the archives. Not all of the foreign policy process occurs in formal meetings where careful notes are kept. Most of what is in the archives represents the waste products of the process: old drafts of position papers, cables giving instructions to diplomats, reports from the field, and interorganizational memos and notes. We have no well-developed research technology for dealing with this mass of paper. Because these waste products represent the best information we have on the making of foreign policy decisions, it is imperative that we develop techniques that will allow this information to be exploited in systematic ways.

Paul A. Anderson
Conclusions and Implications for the Future

The three directions for the future seem clear. The first imperative is to expand the data base to include other governments and other decision settings. While detailed information about decision making in other governments is not as readily available as is information about US decision making, the work of Axelrod (1977), Levi and Tetlock (1980) and Steiner and Dorff (1980) demonstrate that high-quality, high-density observations are available for non-US cases. The second imperative is to determine how decision-making processes influence foreign policy behavior. Although the task is not a simple one, the work of Hermann, Hermann and Hagan (in Chapter 16) and Sylvan (1985b) represents impressive beginnings. The third imperative is to determine the conditions under which different decision-making processes are used. Ideally, we would have at our disposal a set of measurement tools that would allow the particular decision-making process in use to be identified without requiring detailed case studies of each decision. Knowing the range of decision-making processes, what difference those different processes make for external foreign policy behavior, and which process is at work in particular decision settings, will allow the full power of our knowledge about how decision makers make decisions to shape and inform theories of the foreign policy behavior of governments.

Although the description of the decision-making process that emerges from this research is not wildly inconsistent with the prevailing image of the process, it does differ from the prevailing image in a number of respects: decision makers consider far more alternatives than a conventional interpretation of bounded rational decision-making processes would suggest, the great majority of the alternatives are not mutually incompatible, and most alternatives do not result in decisions. These differences, however tentative and subject to revision, do have some implications for developing theories of the foreign policy behavior of governments.

First, understanding the structure of the mechanism that generates foreign policy behavior can aid in the construction of theories in the area of comparative foreign policy without requiring a reduction of comparative foreign policy to foreign policy decision making. Any theory of the comparative foreign policy of governments makes some implicit claims about the process of policy making in foreign affairs. While any particular theory will be consistent with a broad range of underlying processes, there will be some processes that are inconsistent with the higher-level theory. When a higher-level theory is inconsistent with the best available theory of the decision-making process, then the higher-level theory suffers because of it.

The description of the foreign policy process that emerges from the research reported here is one in which the foreign policy behavior of a government is the product of a set of binary choices over an array of noncompeting courses of action implemented by a collection of loosely coupled governmental subunits. On this description, foreign policy behavior is not a planned undertaking designed to achieve a set of clear objectives, nor is it the product of a process that weighs the desirability of a set of competing courses of action. Even in crisis situations it is the product of a set of loosely coordinated, nearly autonomous actions of governmental subunits. Thus theories that presume foreign policy behavior to be coherent and planned are problematic.

A second implication for comparative foreign policy that follows from this research is the possibility that an understanding of the underlying process will provide the basis for theories of biases and errors in the foreign policy behavior of governments. Research on the limited cognitive capacity of individuals has provided behavioral decision theory with a modest ability to predict the likely biases and errors in choice behavior (Nisbett and Ross, 1980; Kahneman, Slovic and Tversky, 1982). Although individuals have a limited ability to process information, they are not stupid; in simple situations their behavior is largely indistinguishable from that which would be produced by a mechanism with unlimited cognitive capacity. But sometimes, when the complexities of the task overwhelm our limited capacity to process information, something of the underlying process shows through in the form of biases, mistakes and errors. If we could develop an understanding of the policy process that was as rich as the understanding cognitive psychologists are developing of individual decision making, then we may be in a position to illuminate some of the mistakes and biases in foreign policy.

But before any of these implications for theories of the comparative foreign policy behavior of governments can come to pass, we need to improve our understanding of the underlying process, and the way to that understanding is in theories based upon high-density observations of real decision makers making real decisions. Anything less seems somehow second-rate.

Notes

I would like to thank Robert Coulam, Margaret Hermann, Timothy McKeon and Harvey Starr for their comments on some of the ideas presented here.

1 Robert Jervis is among the best-known scholars who view foreign policy from a cognitive perspective. His comments (Jervis, 1986, pp. 324–25) on the

utility of cognitive understandings of political behavior echo the present argument:

> My own work yields ambivalent results. On the one hand, a great many incidents in diplomatic history seem best explained by the dynamics of social cognition, but, on the other hand, a close examination of some particular cases shows that the impact of cognitive factors is minor compared to the brute force of obvious political imperatives and the workings of informal organizational norms and incentives.

2 Powell, Dyson and Purkitt provide a useful summary in Chapter 11 of the recent advances in our understanding of individual cognition.

3 Although tape recordings were made of the meetings of the ExCom, at the time the information was collected from the Kennedy Library they had not been declassified.

4 Three factors account for the "missing" alternatives: some of the decisions are unilateral presidential decisions directing that certain actions be taken, some of the decisions may have been discussed outside the formal meeting with the decision being announced by the President in the course of the meeting, and finally, because the accounts of the meetings are not verbatim transcripts, the statements of the "missing" alternatives may not have made it into the record. Discovering the true cause for the missing options will require an investigation that goes beyond the formal record of the meetings.

5 It should be kept in mind that the meetings on the Cuban missile crisis that were content-analyzed occurred in the later stages of the crisis. At the time the data were collected from the Kennedy Library, all the earlier records were classified and not open to research. In time a more complete picture of the missile crisis will emerge.

16

How Decision Units
Shape Foreign Policy Behavior

MARGARET G. HERMANN, CHARLES F. HERMANN
and JOE D. HAGAN

Who makes foreign policy decisions? What is the effect of the decision unit on the resulting foreign policy? An examination of how governments and ruling parties around the world make foreign policy decisions suggests that authority is exercised by an extensive array of different entities. Among the decision units are prime ministers, presidents, politburos, juntas, cabinets, interagency groups, coalitions and parliaments. Moreover, within any one government the pertinent decision units often change with time and issue. When cross-national comparisons of governmental decision-making bodies are contemplated as in the comparative study of foreign policy, the number of possible kinds of decision units becomes formidable.

The thesis of this essay is that there is a way of classifying decision units that can enhance our ability to account for governments' behavior in the foreign policy arena. Although we recognize that numerous domestic and international factors can and do influence foreign policy behavior, these influences must be channeled through the political apparatus of a government which identifies, decides and implements foreign policy. Within that apparatus is a set of authorities with the ability to commit the resources of the society and, with respect to a particular problem, with the authority to make a decision that cannot be readily reversed. We call this set of authorities the "ultimate decision unit," even though in reality the unit may consist of multiple separate bodies rather than a single entity. It is our contention that the structure and dynamics of such an ultimate decision unit help shape the substance of foreign policy behavior.

Participants experienced in the foreign policy-making process as well as those involved in decision making in large, complex organizations often remind us of the elusive nature of decision. They point out that in contrast to many theories of decision the actual process of choice may not be a clear, clean occurrence. Instead it may be a gradual, incremental process that transpires over an extended period without anyone being able to say that "X" made the decision on a given date. They note that those who gather and analyze the information supplied to policy makers shape and narrow subsequent options by determining what is passed along and how it is interpreted. Moreover, the implementors of someone else's decision may totally modify the original intent.

It takes nothing away from these important caveats about decision making, however, to observe that in the life of every organization actual points of decision do occur, although not always in a fashion visible to all who have participated in the process. Certainly key decisions and those who make them are constrained by available inputs and the subsequent implementation may lead to distortion, but nonetheless choice points do occur with some regularity. Despite the need to recognize that decisions do not always get executed as intended, knowledge of how decisions are made remains a powerful source of insight into what complex entities, such as governments, do.

These same participants in the policy-making process also feel uncomfortable with the requirement of decision theories that all decisions result from a similar process. In the reality of governmental foreign policy making—as in any entity dealing with numerous different kinds of issues of considerable complexity—we know that a singular approach to all problems is extremely improbable. A contingency approach to decision making is needed that indicates under what conditions decision units will follow one process and under what other conditions alternative specifiable processes probably will be operative. This essay advances such a contingency approach, proposing how different kinds of decision units lead to varying types of decision-making processes.

In differentiating decision units, we build upon the growing research about foreign policy making that focuses on competing bureaucratic organizations, on small groups and on powerful individuals. Many analysts have employed notions from bureaucratic politics to explain foreign policy (e.g., Neustadt, 1970; Allison, 1971; Destler, 1972; Halperin and Kanter, 1973; Halperin, 1974; Steinbruner, 1974; Allison and Szanton, 1976; Brady, 1976). Interest has also focused on the role that small groups (e.g., Janis, 1972; C. Hermann, 1978a; Tetlock, 1979; George, 1980; Semmel, 1982; Anderson, Chapter 15) and single individuals (e.g., Holsti, 1976a; Walker, 1977; Etheredge, 1978; M. Hermann, 1978, 1980; Stuart and Starr, 1981-2; Jonsson, 1982a;

Rosati, 1985) play in shaping foreign policy. Most of the work to date, however, has tended to consider each configuration—competing agencies, small groups or individuals—in isolation without asking when this unit rather than another comes into play and with what consequences for foreign policy behavior.

In this essay we will show that all three types of decision units are relevant to a cross-national study of foreign policy. We also will articulate how each kind of unit can affect a government's foreign policy behavior. The following are the conceptual underpinnings of the arguments in this essay.

Definition   At the apex of foreign policy decision making in all governments or ruling parties is a group of actors—the ultimate decision unit—who, if they agree, have both the ability to commit the resources of the government in foreign affairs and the power or authority to prevent other entities within the government from overtly reversing their position. The unit having these two characteristics obviously varies with the nature of the problem. For issues of vital importance to a country, the highest political authorities will be part of this ultimate decision unit. With more routine problems, the ultimate decision unit may actually be at a much lower level. For technical issues in some governments, the ultimate decision unit will vary depending on the type of problem the government is facing (military, economic, scientific, and so on). In governments where policy normally involves multiple bureaucratic organizations, the problem may be passed among many different units—within one agency, across agencies, or between interagency groups. The basic point, however, remains that eventually for most foreign policy problems, some person or persons finally authorizes a decision and they constitute for that issue the ultimate decision unit.

Classification   A comprehensive set of ultimate decision units can be developed such that one type is applicable in any given foreign policy case. If we postulate that it is always possible in principle to define the set of actors that comprise the ultimate decision unit with regard to a foreign policy issue, then the task becomes one of describing the relationship among the actors in that set. We believe that the research literature, previously noted, has isolated the major alternative types of ultimate decision units. They are:

(1) Predominant leader—a single individual has the power to make the choice and to stifle opposition.
(2) Single group—a set of interacting individuals, all of whom are

311

members of a single body, have the ability to select a course of action and obtain compliance.

(3) Multiple autonomous groups—the important actors are members of different groups or coalitions, no one of which by itself has the ability to decide and force compliance on the others; moreover, no overarching body exists in which all the necessary parties are members.

In cases of foreign policy decision making, the actors who can make authoritative decisions for the government should correspond to one of these three configurations. In some countries, the same ultimate decision unit may prevail in nearly all foreign policy matters; in other countries the unit may change depending on the issue under consideration or the point in time in the evolution of the regime.

Conceptualizing Control Variables   Each kind of ultimate decision unit exists in one of several states or conditions that determines not only the unit's direct impact on the final policy outcome but also the extent to which factors outside the decision unit must be considered in understanding what will happen in the foreign policy-making process. For each type of ultimate decision unit there is a key piece of information that enables the analyst to know when to focus only on the decision unit itself to determine the nature of the foreign policy decision and when there is a need to look outside the unit for the factors that will influence the decision. We call these "key control variables" because the status of these variables determines how other elements enter into the decision calculus for that unit. The key control variables for each of the three types of decision units have two conditions as shown in Table 16.1.

Table 16.1   *Key Control Variables*

Unit	*Control variable*	*Alternative conditions*
Predominant leader	Contextual sensitivity	(A) Insensitive
		(B) Sensitive
Single group	Concurrence	(A) Agreement
		(B) Disagreement
Multiple autonomous groups	Relationship among groups	(A) Zero-sum
		(B) Non-zero-sum

The conditions for each control variable that are labeled "A" in the table are the conditions in which the primary source of explanation for foreign policy resides in the decision unit itself—the internal dynamics of the unit shape the decision. By contrast the conditions of the control

312

variables that are designated "B" create circumstances in which the unit is penetrable, that is, it is far more susceptible to outside sources of influence in determining its decision. Thus, we can identify self-contained or externally penetrable conditions for each of the three kinds of ultimate decision units depending on the state of the key control variables. As we shall see, these alternative conditions lead to different decision-making processes in affecting foreign policy. But before going further in elaborating the theoretical implications of the key control variables, a description of the three types of decision units and the key control variables will prove helpful.

Three Types of Ultimate Decision Units

Predominant Leader

When the ultimate decision unit is a predominant leader, a single individual has the power to make the choice for the government. After such a leader's preferences are known, those with differing points of view stop public expression of their own alternative proposals out of respect for the leader or fear of political reprisals. Even if others are allowed to continue discussing alternatives, their points of view are no longer relevant to the political outcome. The predominant-leader decision unit is illustrated by a statement attributed to Abraham Lincoln in a cabinet meeting: "Gentlemen, the vote is 11 to 1 and the 1 has it." Only Lincoln's vote mattered; in this case he was the predominant leader.

In this type of decision unit, the critical set of variables for explaining the decision becomes the personal characteristics of the predominant leader. The leader's personal characteristics shape his initial inclinations and determine whether and how the leader will regard advice from others, react to information from the external environment, and assess the political risks associated with various actions (M. Hermann, 1978, 1984). Of particular importance in trying to explain a predominant leader's reaction to a foreign policy problem is knowledge about the leader's orientation to foreign affairs. By orientation to foreign affairs is meant the leader's views about how governments should act in the foreign policy arena. An orientation defines the leader's view of his own nation's and other nations' positions and roles in the world, and it presupposes a specific political style in dealing with foreign policy problems (George, 1979b; M. Hermann, 1980; Walker, 1983a; Rosati, 1985). Orientations also indicate how sensitive the leader will be to advice and information from the environment when making a foreign policy decision.

313

If a leader's orientation indicates that he has a well-defined view of the world and uses his view as a lens through which to select and interpret incoming information, the leader is likely to be looking for cues that confirm his beliefs when making foreign policy decisions. As a result, he will be relatively insensitive to discrepant advice and data. Stoessinger (1979) has called such leaders "crusaders." In effect, the leader selectively uses incoming information to support his predispositions. Such leaders tend to choose advisers who define problems as they do and are generally enthusiastic about the leader's ideas. Libya's Qaddafi and Cuba's Castro are examples of predominant leaders whose orientations appear to predispose them to be relatively insensitive to the variety of information in their external environments. By knowing the foreign affairs orientations of these two leaders, we have clues about what their governments will do in their foreign policy activities—for example, whom they are likely to confront, what problems they are likely to attend to, how much of their resources they are likely to commit to dealing with a problem or an opportunity. In short, we only have to know what the leader is like to be able to explain his government's foreign policy behavior.

If, however, the leader's orientation leads him to be sensitive to others' opinions and incoming information, we will need to know something about the environment in which the predominant leader is operating to say what the government is likely to do. Because such leaders are more "pragmatic," our analysis must take into account the context in which the leader finds himself. The sensitive leader will want to ascertain where others stand with regard to the problem and to consider how other governments are likely to act before making a decision. China's Zhou En-lai and Zambia's Kaunda are examples of this type of leader. Knowing the orientations of leaders like these two will provide us with clues about what part of the environment will be most influential on the leader, but we must still learn about that part of the environment to understand what the leader will do.

In sum, when the ultimate decision unit is a predominant leader, the key question we must ask in ascertaining how important the leader's personality will be in determining his government's foreign policy behavior is whether or not the leader's orientation to foreign affairs leads him to be relatively sensitive or insensitive to information from the political environment. If the leader is relatively insensitive, knowledge about the leader's personality will provide us with cues about what his government's foreign policy behavior is likely to be. If the leader is more sensitive, we will have to find out information about other aspects of the political system in order to suggest what the government will do in response to a foreign policy problem—personality data will not be enough.[1]

314

Single Group

When no one individual alone has the ability to routinely determine the position of the government on a class of foreign policy issues—or if such an individual declines to exercise authority—then an alternative ultimate decision unit must operate. The single group represents one option. A single group acts as the decision unit if all the individuals necessary for allocation decisions participate in the group and the group makes decisions through an interactive process among its members.

Single-group decision units are frequent in contemporary governments. The Politburo of the Communist Party in the Soviet Union, the Standing Committee of the Communist Party in China, the National Security Council in the United States, the cabinet or subcabinet groups in various parliamentary governments illustrate single-group decision units. To be the ultimate decision unit a single group does not have to be legally or formally established as an authoritative agent. Instead it must have, in practice, the *de facto* ability to commit or withhold resources without another unit engaging in the reversal of its decision at will. Moreover, it is not necessary for all group members to concur on every decision of the unit nor to have equal weight in the formation of group decisions. However, if some formal members of the group are never essential to establishing a group decision, then it would be more accurate to recognize the existence of a subgroup that excludes such persons.

When the ultimate decision unit for a particular foreign policy problem is a single group, the analyst must determine if the group can achieve a prompt consensus about the disposition of the problem under consideration (Janis, 1972; C. Hermann, 1978a, 1979; George, 1980). If substantial agreement is achieved quickly among the members (that is, typically in the course of one meeting), factors outside the group that can affect the decision are limited. With prompt consensus members of the group do not look elsewhere for either recommendations or support for their positions. As a result, elements outside the group remain excluded from the process. The members reinforce each others' predispositions and feel secure in their collective decision. Should disagreement persist, however, other aspects of the political system outside the group can become influential. Members of the group become attuned to outside political pressures as they seek supporting information for their positions, reinterpretation of the problem, or ways to resolve the conflict.

We hypothesize that prompt consensus is more likely if the group has certain structure and process characteristics (C. Hermann, 1979).

315

Consensus is more likely if the information the group receives is from a common source, is shared among group members, and is similarly interpreted by members. Consensus is also more likely if the group is small, if members have their primary loyalty to the group, and if power is unequally distributed among group members (that is, there is a strong, but not predominant, leader).

In sum, the key to understanding the foreign policy behavior that will be advocated when a single group is the ultimate decision unit is information on the promptness with which the group can achieve consensus. When consensus occurs quickly, we need to learn about the group's internal dynamics in order to say how the group is likely to deal with the foreign policy problem. If, on the other hand, group members have difficulty reaching consensus, we need to ascertain what other aspects of the political system are likely to be drawn into the consensus-building process or are likely to try to affect that process in order to determine what will happen in foreign policy making.

Multiple Autonomous Groups

It should be evident that another major alternative exists when the ultimate authority in foreign policy making is neither a single individual nor a single group. In this case we have multiple—two or more—separate groups, none of which can commit the resources of the regime without the support of all or some of the others. To be one of the groups in the set classified as the ultimate decision unit, a group must be capable of giving or withholding support that when combined with the support (or lack thereof) from other groups is sufficient to determine whether regime resources will be allocated. One group can block another group's initiatives by: (1) using a formal, sometimes constitutionally defined, veto power; (2) threatening to terminate the ruling coalition by withdrawing from it or overthrowing it with force; or (3) withholding part of the resources necessary for action or the approval needed for their use. For a set of multiple autonomous groups to be the ultimate decision unit, the decision cannot involve any superior group or individual that can independently resolve differences existing among the groups or that can reverse any decision the groups reach collectively. Representatives of the multiple autonomous groups can meet, so long as any decision the delegates reach must be approved by each constituent party.

The classic example of a decision unit composed of multiple autonomous groups is the coalition government in a parliamentary system (e.g., those in Fourth Republic France, in Italy during the past two decades, and in Israel under the Labour-Likud coalition). In these governments, cabinets are composed of members from several parties, none of which has a majority of seats in the parliament. The members of the coalition depend on each other to retain control of the government. This situation gives each party the ability to block policies of the others with the threat of bringing down the government by withdrawing from the coalition.

Ultimate decision units composed of multiple autonomous groups are not limited to parliamentary regimes. In presidential democracies, even with their independent executive, decision making can involve multiple autonomous groups on those issues where the president must receive the approval of the legislature. Multiple autonomous groups as ultimate decision units can also exist in authoritarian regimes. Following Perlmutter (1981), we note that authoritarian regimes typically consist of three types of structures—the state or governmental apparatus; the single, official party; and a variety of "parallel" or "auxiliary" structures which support the regime (e.g., militant gangs, the secret police and the military). Generally, a stable authoritarian regime like that in the Soviet Union is characterized by the dominance of one structure—a cohesive, strong single party. During certain periods, however, relations among these structures, or groups, can become unstable with none of the competing groups having dominance—particularly if there are no accepted rules or procedures for allocating or transferring political power. The government takes on the form of an unstable coalition. Such unstable coalitions are commonplace among current Third World regimes, many of which are internally fragmented and continuously threatened by military intervention.

Clearly for a foreign policy behavior to occur when multiple autonomous groups form the ultimate decision unit, an agreement must be forged among the set of groups involved. And often multiple autonomous groups are unable to reach agreement on any substantively meaningful course of action; they deadlock. Deadlocks result because by definition no group has the capacity to act alone on behalf of the regime. One or more groups are always in a position to block the initiatives of the others. Groups may take action on their own (typically in the form of verbal pronouncements), but no coordinated regime foreign policy activity is possible and meaningful actions and commitments are usually postponed.

We do not mean to indicate, however, that deadlock is automatic. The relationship among the multiple autonomous groups determines when deadlock will or will not occur. Groups that have an underlying acceptance of the right of the other groups to exist in the power structure or some formal or informal "rules of the game" for reaching agreement have a better chance of reaching accord than those that deny each other's legitimacy and seek every opportunity to keep the others from participating politically. In cases where the groups have granted each other political legitimacy, there is an incentive to interact with one another to resolve the problem. Such groups, in effect, have a non-zero-sum relationship. For those groups with formal or informal rules of the game, the invocation of the rules provides further reason for the groups to cooperate. The groups whom the rules will not favor in a given instance have added incentive to bargain with the others.

The alternative values of the key control variable when multiple autonomous groups are the ultimate decision unit are revealed by the question: Is the political relationship among the multiple autonomous groups zero-sum or non-zero-sum with respect to recognizing the legitimacy of each group to seek and share power? When the multiple autonomous groups have a zero-sum relationship, they try to destroy each other and see each group benefiting at the other's expense. Usually such groups can do nothing or almost nothing in the foreign policy arena. They tend to engage in verbal behavior that in no way commits the regime to a particular solution of the basic problem or they maintain the status quo. Deadlock is avoided only when an external source with the power to intervene does so and forces agreement on the groups. When multiple autonomous groups, however, have a non-zero-sum relationship, there is a basis for agreement. In order to ascertain the nature of the agreement and their foreign policy behavior, we have to examine the bargaining process among the groups and the nature of any formal or informal rules of the game governing such a process.

Effects of Decision Units on Foreign Policy Behavior

To be useful our classification of decision units and associated control variables must lead to insights about foreign policy behavior. In the discussion to follow we will use the distinction noted earlier between self-contained and externally penetrable units to forge some hypotheses about how decision units shape foreign policy behavior. Because it is easier to indicate what each type of decision unit will decide with regard to a foreign policy problem when the influences of other parts of the political process are muted—the linkages between the ultimate decision unit and foreign policy behavior are simpler and more straightforward—we will begin our discussion of how the units shape foreign policy behavior by examining the conditions where the ultimate decision units are self-contained. In other words, we will examine first the units that involve a predominant leader who is relatively insensitive, a single group that can reach prompt consensus, and multiple autonomous groups that have a zero-sum relationship. We will use illustrative case studies to demonstrate the effects that each of these decision units can have on foreign policy behavior.[2]

Effects of Self-Contained Decision Units

Insensitive Predominant Leader Suppose a government has a predominant leader whose orientation to foreign affairs suggests little sensitivity to incoming information from the environment. The leader has strongly held beliefs about the world by which he interprets political events. Such a leader selectively perceives and retains information about any new problem so that it substantiates previously held opinions and beliefs. Incompatible information or analysis from advisers is ignored or reinterpreted. In this case foreign policy actions are shaped by the leader's view of the world which, in turn, is influenced by the leader's more basic personal characteristics. An example of this type of leader is Romulo Betancourt, President of Venezuela from 1959 to 1964 (M. Hermann, 1984).[3]

Betancourt perceived the world divided into "us" and "them"—the democratic governments in the Americas formed the "us" and the dictatorships the "them." He (1968, p. 252) believed that "only governments born of legitimate elections, respectful of the rights of man and guaranteeing public liberties could form part of the regional community. That against dictatorial governments which do not conform to those norms there be established not only the collective sanction of non-recognition but also that of isolation in the economic field." Betancourt's philosophy became known throughout Latin America as the Betancourt Doctrine. To Betancourt, actions in the international arena took on a black/white character—with us or against us.

And Betancourt's personal beliefs became a primary determinant of Venezuelan foreign policy during the early 1960s. Betancourt was interested in seeing other Latin American countries adopt democratic procedures and became quite confrontational when democratically elected leaders in the Western Hemisphere were overthrown by coups. He broke relations with the following countries during his tenure as a result of his position: Argentina, the Dominican Republic, El Salvador and Peru. Cuba with its seemingly left-leaning and well-entrenched dictatorship became a pre-eminent problem for Betancourt during the last part of his tenure in office. In particular, Betancourt perceived that Castro was exporting revolution to Venezuela through

319

alleged aid to communist guerrillas. Drawing on his orientation, not only did Betancourt break diplomatic relations with Cuba but he urged countries in the Organization of American States (OAS) to withdraw their embassies from Cuba and to institute an economic boycott against it. In addition, the Betancourt regime exercised leadership in the 1962 Punta del Este Conference of the OAS where Cuba was excluded from membership (Thomas and Thomas, 1963; Betancourt, 1968). Betancourt broke off relations with Cuba even though there was opposition within his party to the move (Alexander, 1982, p. 442).

In effect, when an insensitive predominant leader like Betancourt is the ultimate decision unit, we can learn about the nature of the government's foreign policy behavior by examining the leader's personal characteristics and orientation to foreign affairs. The leader's view of the world will shape the government's foreign policy activity.

Single Group with Prompt Consensus   We suggested earlier some factors that we hypothesize promote prompt consensus when the ultimate decision unit is a single group—a common source of information, small size, members with their primary loyalty to the group, and unequally distributed power among group members (C. Hermann, 1978a, 1979). When factors such as these contribute to rapid consensus within a group, what kind of foreign policy might we expect to come from the interaction among the members of the group?

Exactly such a quick consensus occurred in the Israeli cabinet in December 1969 in response to a problem created for it by the United States (Brecher, 1975). The United States and the Soviet Union had been conferring on the accelerating war of attrition in the Middle East that followed the 1967 war. On October 28, 1969, the United States proposed a plan for a Middle East political settlement to the Soviet leadership which US Secretary of State William Rogers formally disclosed in an address in New York on December 9. When the report of Rogers' speech reached Jerusalem, an emergency session of the Israeli cabinet was convened. The cabinet, which represented virtually the entire political spectrum in Israel, quickly rebuffed Secretary Rogers' proposal. When the United States persisted by presenting an elaboration of the plan at the United Nations Four Power Talks on December 18, the Israeli government recalled its ambassador from the United States. On December 22, the cabinet met and made its position clear in a blunt statement: "The Cabinet rejects these American proposals, in that they prejudice the chances of establishing peace" (Brecher, 1975, p. 485). The Israeli cabinet as the ultimate decision unit reached agreement at its first meeting on the matter and did not hesitate to express its position in a most assertive way when the United States seemed slow to get the message.

When a group readily achieves consensus, as the Israeli cabinet did in this case, the deliberations leading to consensus reinforce the prior inclinations of members of the group. When members find their own interpretations and recommendations shared by others, it tends to confirm their conclusions. Members become more sure of themselves and the course of action or inaction they advocate. As discussion continues, participants express less qualification and more unequivocal declaration in support of the recommended means of treating the issue. The group deliberations make the results more certain—and possibly more extreme—than the members would have advocated individually before the group meeting. The theoretical underpinnings for such group dynamics is found in a broad range of research (e.g., George, 1972; Janis, 1972; Lamm and Myers, 1978; Semmel, 1982).

To declare that a decision will be more certain does not indicate the direction or content of the decision. A single group in consensus can be certain about the absolute necessity of doing nothing whatsoever about the issue they face. Conversely, they can be certain about the need for action and extreme in their choice of actions. Knowledge of individual members' preferences provides clues as to the probable content of the decision. Where such information on members of the group is not available, the direction of the group consensus can be estimated from other data on the group. For example, if the issue deals with a matter about which there is a shared set of beliefs among members of the group, then this regime orientation will dictate the direction in which the group dynamics will amplify the predisposition for decision (C. Hermann, 1983b; Walker and Simon, 1983). Thus, if the problem concerns a traditional adversary and there is a shared belief among members of the group that it is the enemy, action is likely to be assertive and negative in tone. If the problem involves an entity upon whom members of the group perceive their government is economically dependent, the action will probably be highly cautious and positive in tone. Such a widely shared set of political beliefs about the approach for dealing with the Arabs (or, perhaps more accurately, about unacceptable approaches) among members of the Israeli cabinet facilitated their quick rejection of the 1969 American peace proposal. The American proposal conflicted with the minimal terms for peace over which there was little dispute.[4]

If no prior shared beliefs provide the basis for decision, then the group may key on the orientation of a strong leader in the group. We have excluded by definition the existence of a predominant leader, but that does not mean there cannot be a person in the group with more power and influence than the others. When a prompt consensus occurs in a single-group ultimate decision unit with such a strong individual among its members, that person's preferences will likely be shared by the group and affect the foreign policy behavior.

In summary, with knowledge that members of a single group as the ultimate decision unit reached a quick consensus, we can say that the consensus will amplify the initial inclinations of the members and that we will get a more certain and probably more extreme response than if the decision were made by one member alone. Moreover, we can suggest what the nature of the decision is likely to be, based on members' general preferences regarding the problem at hand, by determining if members of the group have a shared set of beliefs that are triggered by the problem the group is facing, or by seeking information on the orientations of any strong leaders in the group.

Multiple Autonomous Groups with Zero-Sum Relationship Deadlock is the frequent result of decision making when multiple autonomous groups with a zero-sum relationship form the ultimate decision unit. Without some recognition of the other groups' rights to exist and participate in decision making, multiple autonomous groups are generally unable to reach agreement on any substantively meaningful course of action. Since by definition no group has the capacity to act alone on behalf of the regime, one or more of the groups are always able to block the initiatives of the others. Decisions tend to be postponed, and groups can, at most, engage in varying degrees of verbal behavior together or on their own.

A dramatic instance of an ultimate decision unit composed of multiple autonomous groups with a zero-sum relationship occurred in Iran during the "hostage crisis" with the United States. Recall that on November 4, 1979, militant Islamic students seized the American embassy in Teheran and took about sixty Americans captive. They threatened to try the Americans on espionage charges if the United States did not return the deposed Shah and his wealth. When the Carter Administration refused to comply, the crisis persisted, ending fourteen months later with the release of the hostages.[5] For our purposes here, the striking feature about the hostage crisis is the Iranian government's inability to act. It failed to gain the early release of the captives, to bargain for an acceptable response from the United States, or to place the hostages on trial. At times at least some groups in power favored each of these options and yet they were impotent to realize them.

The immobility of the Iranian government was in large part the result of the multiple autonomous groups that were engaged in making decisions and their reluctance to acknowledge each other's authority. Although at first glance Ayatollah Khomeini might appear a single predominant leader, closer examination suggests that his involvement (and even influence) in the crisis was limited. For the first year of the crisis, political authority within the Iranian regime was ambiguously defined and spread across different institutions. No one group could carry out its professed desires. Among the groups involved in decision making in addition to Khomeini were the relatively "moderate" members in the Prime Minister's office and the Foreign Ministry (e.g., Bazargan, Bani Sadr, Ghotbzadeh, Yazdi), the "radical" clergy led by Ayatollah Behesti, and the student militants. For much of the crisis these groups found themselves unable to arrive at a significant agreement over the fate of the American hostages.

When there are no institutionalized procedures or "rules of the game" governing how political authority is allocated and how policy differences are resolved among multiple autonomous groups, there is little incentive for agreement. Likelihood of deadlock is acute if there are real and unbridgeable differences on substantive policy matters among the groups or if the groups are in direct competition for control of the regime. Under these circumstances the wider membership of each political group retains careful oversight over its representatives in any intergroup discussions, instructing them on how to respond to important issues. Leaders that appear to be compromising face the difficult (and, perhaps, even politically suicidal) task of getting the approval of the wider membership of their groups. Leaders and members of the various groups, therefore, find it easier to discredit their opponents' initiatives than to try to work with the other groups to reach a decision.

All these effects were evident in the Iranians' inability to take effective action to resolve the hostage crisis. During the first six months moderates within the leadership took at least six major initiatives to break the impasse with the United States. In each case the initiatives were blocked by radical opposition in the Revolutionary Council, the intransigence of the student militants, and the subsequent withdrawal of Khomeini's earlier approval (or tolerance) of the initiative. Finally in March 1980, Khomeini ended further initiatives by postponing the entire issue until a parliament was elected and could decide what to do. The organization of the parliament was itself a drawn-out process, as once again the multiple autonomous groups vied for control. The hostages' release only came about after the radical clergy had consolidated their authority with the removal of the moderates.

Multiple autonomous groups in deadlock are not stagnant actors. Even the foreign policy behavior of certain deadlocked groups can be strikingly active as each group tries to assert its power and influence. The conflict among the groups can become quite public, including the

323

use of verbal foreign policy pronouncements by each of the groups in the ultimate decision unit. The behavior of the Iranian government in the hostage crisis fits this pattern. Foreign policy issues were central to the struggle for control of the new regime. The political infighting led to a continuous flow of bellicose rhetoric toward the United States— despite the basic reality that the Iranian leadership remained deadlocked and could do little to resolve the crisis.

Only three conditions seem likely to enable multiple autonomous groups with a zero-sum relationship to escape deadlock. If all the groups share beliefs or orientations about foreign policy issues (e.g., about what needs to be done to assure the country's immediate survival) and the situation invokes this shared belief, there is a basis for agreement among the groups. If any of the groups have exclusive or primary access to a coercive means of violence (e.g., the military, armed citizens, terrorists, an alliance with an outside country), the threatened use of such a weapon can induce concessions needed for agreement. A group or individual unaligned with any of the multiple autonomous groups forming the decision unit may also possess a means of coercive violence and respond to the deadlock by assuming control of the government and changing the nature of the ultimate decision unit. The military coup often plays this role in Third World countries.

In summary, when multiple autonomous groups form the ultimate decision unit, deadlock is the most likely outcome if the groups do not accept the rights of the others to share power or participate in decision making—that is, if the groups have a zero-sum relationship. Almost nothing beyond rhetoric will happen in response to the foreign policy problem. By almost nothing we mean largely caretaking operations that a head of state, foreign minister or senior civil servant may feel qualified to undertake to continue agreements previously established if these precedents are not challenged. Such actions might include continuation of the status quo, appeals for more time, requests to others to handle the problem temporarily, and very broad and vague policy declarations (or extreme threats as in the Iranian situation) that in no way resolve the issues in conflict. Any foreign policy behavior that does occur will involve minimal commitment of the government's resources.

Effects of Externally Penetrable Decision Units

In the previous section we suggested how the three types of ultimate decision units shape foreign policy behavior when each is configured in such a way as to preclude the influence of external factors outside the decision unit itself. Now let us briefly explore the effects each type of ultimate decision unit has on foreign policy behavior when its configuration permits more influence from other aspects of the political system. In other words, what happens in the foreign policy arena when the ultimate decision unit is a predominant leader who is sensitive to the immediate political environment, a single group whose members disagree, or multiple autonomous groups who have a non-zero-sum relationship? In each of these cases the analyst will need to invoke explanations that involve the context in which the decision unit is operating in order to account adequately for foreign policy. Again we will use illustrative case studies to indicate the effects that each of the externally penetrable decision units can have on foreign policy behavior.

Sensitive Predominant Leader   When faced with a foreign policy problem, the sensitive predominant leader looks to the situation to provide clues on what is happening and what needs to be done to deal with the problem. Such a leader monitors the environment to see what groups may perceive themselves affected by the problem and the nature of their reactions. The sensitive predominant leader seeks a consensus in dealing with the foreign policy problem that has a broad base of support. In effect, he protects his position by being constantly aware of the shifting opinions and coalitions among those he is leading within his regime, in the society at large, and (when necessary) in foreign constituencies as well. The positions of these various relevant constituents, their interpretation of the problem, and areas of disagreement among them have important implications for the foreign policy behavior the leader will advocate.

We assume that those sources of conflicting interpretations about the problem closest to the sensitive predominant leader will have the greatest impact on what he does. That is, the sensitive predominant leader will attend first to disagreement within his advisory group and those in a position to challenge his authority before paying attention to opposition in the government outside his advisory group or in the society at large. Opposition in the regime outside the advisory group or in the society at large will have more of an effect on a sensitive predominant leader's behavior the stronger and more generalized it is.

Leaders have a repertoire of possible ways of coping with opposition, including ignoring it, suppressing it, diverting attention from it, highlighting differences between their position and that of the opposition, compromising with it, and coopting the position of the opposition. Ignoring the opposition usually results in the opposition having little effect on foreign policy behavior; suppression diverts resources away from the foreign policy arena during the time it takes to restrain the opposition and, thus, is likely to reduce foreign policy activity; diverting attention from the opposition often involves the use of foreign policy activity as the leaders try to find an external scapegoat on which to focus public attention; both compromise and cooptation suggest that the opposition's position on the foreign policy issue becomes part of the leader's solution to the problem. We hypothesize that sensitive predominant leaders will adjust their strategy for dealing with opposition to the nature of that opposition. Such leaders are more likely to use suppression against challenges to their authority, particularly when the challenges occur within their advisory group and have some chance for success; to try scapegoating tactics if the opposition resides in the society outside the government but has little representation inside the government; and to seek a compromise if the disagreement focuses on a specific foreign policy issue and is lodged within the advisory group or government. Figure 16.1 displays in broad brush strokes the sequence of considerations that we propose comes into play when a predominant leader is responsive to the immediate political environment.[6]

President Kenneth Kaunda's management of Zambian responses to Rhodesia's Unilateral Declaration of Independence (UDI) provides us with an example of how opposition and ways of dealing with opposition can affect the foreign policy making of a sensitive predominant leader. Elsewhere we have established that Kaunda is a sensitive predominant leader (M. Hermann, 1984). Kaunda and his advisers on the Foreign Affairs Committee of the Cabinet shared three beliefs regarding Zambian foreign policy during the initial stages of the Rhodesian UDI crisis: humanism, nonalignment and pan-Africanism (Mtshali, 1973; Hatch, 1976; Anglin and Shaw, 1979). In working toward the goals embedded in these beliefs after UDI, they walked a tightrope trying to decrease Zambia's dependence on Rhodesia and South Africa by turning toward its East African neighbors while not incurring extreme economic costs to the country. This balance proved difficult to achieve given Zambia's landlocked position, its dependence before UDI on rail shipping through Rhodesia to the coast, and its large trade with South Africa. It was made even more difficult by Kaunda and his advisers' outspoken support for the liberation struggles in Southern Africa. How to manage the balance after UDI became a recurring source of division.

In such instances Kaunda was quick to listen to his advisers' concerns and to try to reach some consensus among those whose support he considered critical to implementing the decision. One particular problem that caused dissension concerned which of the two Rhode-

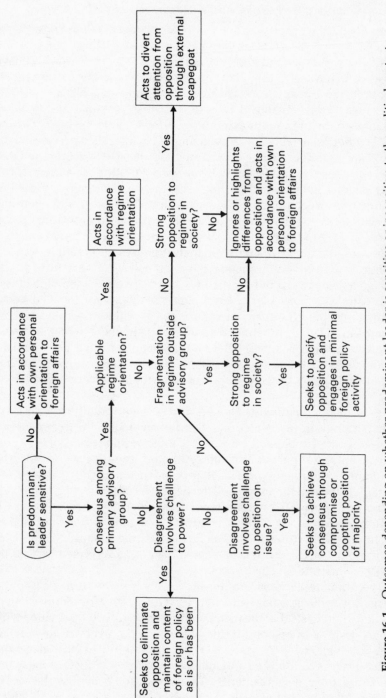

Figure 16.1 Outcomes depending on whether predominant leader is sensitive or insensitive to the political context

sian liberation groups Zambia should support. After "months of agonizing appraisal," Kaunda and his advisers chose Nkomo and ZAPU over Sithole and ZANU. Anglin and Shaw (1979, p. 247) have observed, however, that Kaunda worked ceaselessly to seek unity between these two Rhodesian liberation groups, ZANU and ZAPU, "because ZANU managed to establish close personal and political relations with an influential minority in the Cabinet."

The Rhodesian crisis also served Kaunda as a scapegoat for overcoming domestic opposition within Zambia. Mtshali (1973) has argued that Kaunda used the Rhodesian UDI as a way of uniting the various tribes and regions with their differing beliefs and customs into a nation. Kaunda, in effect, built a consensus within Zambian society around a foreign policy by diverting attention from strong domestic opposition in the society to the need to deal with a threatening external enemy.

In sum, the sensitive predominant leader uses information from the political environment to shape the foreign policy behavior he urges on the government. To determine how a sensitive predominant leader will react to a particular foreign policy problem, we need to know something about the current relations he has with those individuals or groups in the government and society who are likely to have a vested interest in what is done. The strategies the sensitive predominant leader uses in building a consensus among these individuals and groups will affect the foreign policy behavior he will advocate.

Single Group in Continuing Disagreement When the ultimate decision unit is a single group whose members are divided on the treatment of a foreign policy problem, the means of conflict resolution become important in interpreting the outcome. Although these processes may be contained within the group itself, group division greatly increases the potential effect of forces outside the decision unit. Bureaucratic politics offers one approach for characterizing the interplay of these forces. In effect, the forces are various political organizations seeking to build coalitions with sufficient power to resolve the dispute. The Soviet invasion of Czechoslovakia in August 1968—as interpreted by Valenta (1979)—illustrates such a process.

The ultimate decision unit in the Soviet Union with respect to the crisis in Czechoslovakia was the Politburo of the Communist Party. Evidence suggests that the membership of this group was divided with regard to how to respond to the liberalization movement in Czechoslovakia (Valenta, 1979, pp. 20–1). In June and July of 1968 the Soviet Politburo was deadlocked and members were searching for a means of resolving their disagreements. Thus, on July 29 almost the entire Soviet Politburo traveled to the Czech town of Cierna to negotiate some type of accommodation with their Czech counterparts. Forty-eight hours after the meetings concluded, both sides reconvened with representatives from Bulgaria, East Germany, Hungary and Poland to ratify the bilateral compromise they had concluded and to issue the Bratislava communiqué. A diplomatic solution had been reached. The Czechs pledged—among other things—their commitment to the Warsaw Treaty Organization and to the foreign policy leadership of the Soviet Union. A strong case can be made that nothing happened in Czechoslovakia in the weeks following this agreement of which the Soviets were not aware on August 3 in Bratislava. In fact, very little happened objectively outside the Soviet Union concerning Czecho-slovakia in the 17 days between the Bratislava agreement and the invasion on the night of August 20–21, 1968. Yet the Soviet leadership appears to have changed its collective judgment and reached a very different decision about how to handle the crisis. Why?

When a single group is severely divided over how to deal with a foreign policy problem, there is an opening for forces elsewhere in the political system to attempt to persuade members of the group to move in their direction. Such is particularly the case when the time for decision is long enough that these other parties can make their positions known. Members of the group become more susceptible to outside influences as they seek support for their ideas or some way to resolve the disagreement. The question becomes whether politically effective groups or individuals in the society or elsewhere in the government strongly advocate a common position or whether such groups and individuals are themselves divided on what should be done. If the political forces outside the single group for and against the various positions are roughly balanced, their attempts to influence group members may very well cancel each other out. Each faction in the decision unit will have its positions reinforced by these outside groups and individuals. No realignment will occur within the group. Such appears to have been the case for the Soviet Politburo in the Czech situation prior to the negotiations in Cierna and Bratislava. The groups outside the Politburo favoring and opposing intervention were roughly balanced (Valenta, 1979).

Under such circumstances, the presence of a strong leader or an influential subgroup within the decision unit may offer one means of resolving the conflict. A strong leader or subgroup has an incentive to do something if they have a definite preference with regard to the foreign policy problem under discussion. The strong leader or subgroup can mix persuasion, log-rolling, compromise and coercion to work toward agreement. If, however, forces outside the single group that is in disagreement over what to do are roughly balanced and there is no strong leader or influential subgroup (or as in the case of the Soviet Politburo in the Czech situation, the strong leader refuses to make a choice), minimal action or compromise seem likely. Any foreign policy activity will probably be diplomatic in nature and involve little commitment as well as neutral affect. If any action occurs, it will keep options open and be reversible. The negotiations at the end of July and the beginning of August at Cierna and Bratislava respectively would seem consonant with this characterization.

Valenta (1979) argues that the very act of a negotiated settlement galvanized those political influentials in the Soviet Union and Eastern Europe who opposed such an outcome. In the 17 days after the Bratislava declaration, a critical change took place in the strength of the domestic political groups and individuals favoring intervention. After Bratislava, the opponents of the diplomatic course of action had a concrete example of the kind of agreement they feared and as a result they were better able to dramatize their fears more effectively to others. According to Valenta (1979, ch. 4), their appeal had an effect on (1) bureaucrats responsible for ideological affairs in the Soviet Union, (2) members of the Ukrainian Party bureaucracy who feared the spread of Czech reforms into their republic, (3) sections of the KGB who saw a decrease in their ability to conduct intelligence operations in Eastern Europe, and (4) some segments of the Soviet armed forces who anticipated a change in their ability to maintain an effective presence in Eastern Europe. The increased strength of these proponents of intervention forced a realignment in the Politburo. "The advocates of military intervention in Moscow won the debate only during the last round of their offensive, which began around August 10. From this date until August 17 the pressure of the interventionist elements grew so strong that some of the wavering decision makers shifted to the side of the interventionists" (Valenta, 1979, p. 145). What had been a balanced opposition outside the decision unit became unbalanced with more individuals and groups favoring one option over the other. And the Politburo members seized on the swell of consensus outside the decision unit adopting the position of the strongest block—intervention.

Although Soviet Union decision making during the 1968 Czechoslovakian crisis is but a single example, we believe that the interplay of forces it suggests is part of the more general pattern shown in Figure 16.2. As the figure suggests, when a single group with the ultimate authority to make a decision is divided, three things can happen. A strong leader in the group, a subgroup, or some other elements within the group may devise a means to overcome the deadlock. Alternatively, political forces outside the group may pressure a preferred solution—provided these outside influences generally coalesce

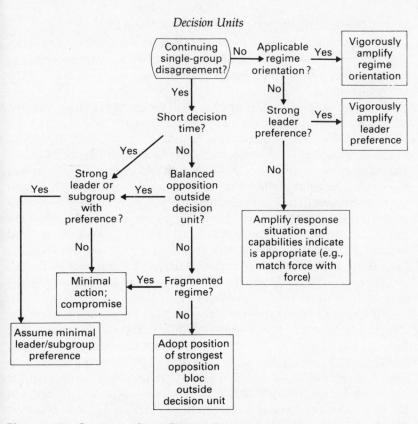

Decision Units

Figure 16.2 Outcomes depending on disagreement or consensus in a single group with authority to make decisions

around a preferred option. If neither of these developments transpires, no foreign policy action is likely to occur; or if the problem is too important to ignore, then minimal diplomatic action that involves limited commitments and is reversible can be expected.

Multiple Autonomous Groups with Non-Zero-Sum Relationship When multiple autonomous groups forming the ultimate decision unit have a non-zero-sum relationship, the groups recognize each other's legitimacy and are willing to interact with each other and to engage in bargaining. Such groups are generally able to reach some agreement with regard to a foreign policy problem because they have developed some formal or informal "rules of the game" that structure the interaction among the groups. In effect, their acceptance of each other's legitimate right to participate in decision making prods the groups to work out a process that facilitates policy making. To illustrate a

331

situation in which multiple autonomous groups with a non-zero-sum relationship formed the ultimate decision unit, we will examine the struggle within the United States government over ratification of the 1963 Nuclear Test Ban Treaty.

The treaty banned the testing of nuclear weapons in outer space, the oceans and the atmosphere and was initialed on July 23, 1963, by officials of the United States, the United Kingdom and the Soviet Union. For the United States, formal acceptance of the treaty awaited a second hurdle—ratification by a two-thirds majority vote of the Senate. It is because of the "checks and balances" nature of the American Constitution that US decision making on this issue takes the form of multiple autonomous groups, involving the Senate and the President along with his advisers and the national security bureaucracies. And across time a set of rules of the game has developed between the President and Senate with respect to treaty ratification with both sides accepting the legitimacy of the other to exercise bounded authority over such matters.

In the case of the Test Ban Treaty the rules are summed up in the adage that "the President proposes and Congress disposes." The American Constitution, in effect, stipulates rules for resolving disagreements between the executive and legislative branches with regard to ratification of treaties that can be construed as favoring the legislative branch because only one-third plus one of the members of the US Senate are needed to block a treaty drafted by the executive. When, in a given situation, the rules appear to favor one group over the others, there is incentive for the other groups to try to bargain with the favored group to achieve some of their ends before the rules are set in motion and the favored group's position is adopted. Generally at issue is whether the less favored groups can offer some concessions or a trade-off to save some of their position.

Lepper (1971) notes that although the Kennedy Administration was jubilant about completing the negotiations with the Soviets on the Test Ban Treaty, they perceived that the general climate of opinion in the Senate opposed any treaty with the Soviet Union. Certain key senators on the important military and foreign affairs committees that were having hearings on the treaty (e.g., Jackson, Stennis and Russell) declared their hostility to the treaty openly. Realizing he had an uphill battle, Kennedy mobilized those in the executive branch who favored the treaty to campaign for it. "The Administration witnesses for the Congressional hearings were carefully selected and scheduled for their appearances before the committees" (Lepper, 1971, p. 84). But Kennedy's most important action involved the assurances he offered to the Senate when the treaty appeared to be getting bogged down in one particularly hostile committee. He stated publicly that a number of safeguards would be taken to ensure that the United States was not disadvantaged by the treaty. These safeguards included promises that underground testing would be vigorously carried out, that the United States would actively watch for and strongly protest any Soviet violations of the treaty, and that the government would maintain a strong weapons research program. Lepper (1971) observes that these assurances helped convince undecided senators. Moreover, these assurances made the treaty more palatable to skeptical senators. And when the Senate vote was finally taken, it was 80 for ratification and 19 opposed. A mutually acceptable position had been reached among a working coalition on both sides. Kennedy traded the assurances for the treaty.

The Test Ban Treaty ratification illustrates some basic features of the multiple-autonomous-groups mode of decision making under non-zero-sum conditions. Bargaining and negotiation among the parties become important tools for resolving differences among the groups. Compromise between the preferred positions of the various parties is likely to be evident in the foreign policy outcome. Which parties can be expected to offer concessions more readily and more extensively depends upon who appears to be favored by the rules of the game as applied in the immediate situation. If the rules of the game are clear but the favored party seems uncertain, then bargaining among the parties still can be expected although the concessions may be more evenly matched. Where adequate rules do not yet exist, or are in the process of being institutionalized, multiple autonomous groups with a non-zero-sum relationship will have more trouble reaching agreement. Although the incentive to bargain will be present, the process may take longer, is more susceptible to outside manipulation, and still has some chance of deadlock. Figure 16.3 suggests what some of these possible outside forces are and their effect on foreign policy as well as summarizes our discussion of multiple autonomous groups with a non-zero-sum relationship.

Conclusions

In this essay we have argued that at the apex of foreign policy making in all governments or ruling parties there are a group of actors with the ability to commit the resources of the government and with the power to prevent other entities within the government from reversing their position—the ultimate decision unit. Although this decision unit may change with the nature of the foreign policy problem and across time,

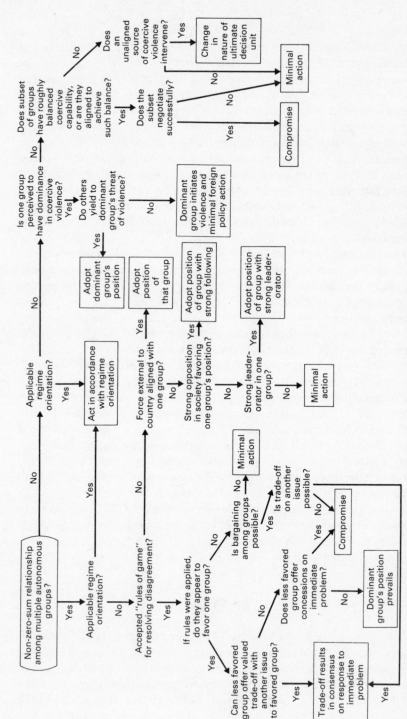

Figure 16.3 Outcomes depending on whether relationship among multiple autonomous groups is zero-sum or non-zero-sum

how it is structured will shape what a government does in the foreign policy arena. Our proposal is that the decision process in each type of decision unit channels and molds the impact of the wider domestic and international environment on foreign policy behavior. In other words, the ultimate decision unit serves either to "amplify" or "dampen" a government's initial predisposition to act on a foreign policy problem. In effect, the government's definition of internal and external pressures may predispose it to act in a particular manner, but the precise character of its actions will be modified by properties of the ultimate decision unit.

We have postulated that there are three types of ultimate decision units—predominant leader, single group and multiple autonomous groups. Each of these types of ultimate decision units exists in one of several states or conditions that help to determine whether the decision unit directly affects foreign policy making or whether factors outside the decision unit must be taken into consideration in understanding the decision-making process. By ascertaining which of the three types of decision units is the ultimate decision unit for a particular foreign policy problem and its state or condition, we have shown how an analyst can narrow the range of variables that need to be considered in explaining the nature of the resulting foreign policy behavior.

The framework we have outlined in this essay provides some basis for making cross-national comparisons among governmental decision-making bodies. It contains concepts that can be applied to a variety of different types of political systems. And it enables us to put into perspective the extensive array of different entities within a government that can make foreign policy. Furthermore, the framework gives us a means for comparing and contrasting different types of decision units. In effect, it makes the decision unit a more accessible unit of analysis for the student of comparative foreign policy.

Notes

Earlier versions of this chapter were presented at the International Studies Association meeting in Cincinnati, March 24–27, 1982, and at the International Society of Political Psychology meeting in Mannheim, West Germany, June 24–27 1981. Work on the chapter was supported by the Mershon Center of Ohio State University. The authors would like to thank Lloyd Etheredge, Richard Herrmann, Terrence Hoppmann, Steve Ropp and Dina Zinnes, as well as members of their research group (Aaron Adler, Valerie Hudson, Greg Peacock and Eric Singer) for their helpful comments on previous drafts of the chapter.

1 To make our presentation less complicated we have been discussing here

leaders who are either sensitive or insensitive. In actuality, there is probably a continuum of sensitivity with leaders differing in their degree of openness to information from the environment. Sensitivity also may not be a general phenomenon but change with issues or by level of interest or expertise in the area of the foreign policy problem. We will use the term "relatively" sensitive or insensitive to indicate that we realize sensitivity has some subtle nuances we are not confronting directly in what is described in this chapter.

2 In another place (M. Hermann and C. Hermann, 1982), we have described a way of determining which of the three types of decision units is the ultimate decision unit for a particular regime in a given situation. Through the use of a decision tree, we can ascertain for a particular foreign policy problem and regime whether the ultimate decision unit is likely to be a predominant leader, single group or multiple autonomous groups.

3 In this case illustration, as in the others presented in this chapter, we have depended on specific sources for interpretation of the events that took place. We are not experts on the various cases and are, therefore, not able to evaluate the analyses. We, however, have found these particular descriptions of the cases useful in our own thinking about decision units and as examples of the conceptual material.

4 In June 1970, the United States government made a new proposal to the Israelis that fulfilled the peace conditions of some of the members of the cabinet but not those of other members and, therefore, did not enable an appeal to a regime orientation nor such a prompt consensus.

5 Useful treatments of the Iranian political scene, the events surrounding the hostage crisis, the Iranian decision making during the crisis include Rouleau, 1980; Keddie, 1981; Kifner, 1981; Smith, 1981; Stempel, 1981; and Sick, 1985. For more limited coverage, see Rubin, 1980; and Ledeen and Lewis, 1981.

6 In this figure as well as in the two other figures presented in this essay, a "yes" answer to the first question leads into the series of questions that determines foreign policy behavior for the externally penetrable decision unit while a "no" answer leads into the questions appropriate to determining foreign policy behavior for the self-contained decision units.

PART VI

Domestic Influences on Foreign Policy

17

Regimes, Political Oppositions, and the Comparative Analysis of Foreign Policy

JOE D. HAGAN

Although it is often assumed that "politics stops at the water's edge," domestic politics and foreign policy are typically closely interwoven. For Americans, this has become particularly apparent over the past decade. Constrained by the breakup of the Cold War consensus and the reassertion of congressional powers, presidents have found it increasingly difficult to cope with the ambiguities and interdependencies of the international system in the 1980s. Nor are these pressures unique to the pluralist American political system. Few governments, democratic or authoritarian, appear to be immune from domestic political constraints. Many are weakened by internal divisions and/or lack of support from the wider polity. Domestic politics further complicates foreign policy making, leaving these governments even less capable of coping with an already complex array of foreign policy problems.

This chapter is concerned with the status of political explanations in the field of comparative foreign policy. It begins with a brief summary and critique of existing comparative foreign policy research on political influences, noting that most empirical studies have addressed mainly the role of accountability, often using it as a surrogate measure of domestic constraints. It seeks to develop more precise indicators of domestic political constraints, ones based on actual, existing political oppositions that can potentially occur in any type of political system. Conceptualizations of two kinds of regime-level opposition are offered—regime fragmentation and vulnerability. A brief empirical analysis is presented, one identifying and classifying regimes and another examining their correlations with several dimensions of foreign policy behavior. This analysis serves two purposes. First, it illustrates how one can effectively collect cross-national data on political oppositions through a focus on a nation's central political leadership, or "regime".[1] Second, the findings from this analysis point to the complexity of the linkage between internal politics and foreign policy and, as such, suggest several specific directions for future research on domestic political influences and foreign policy.

Comparative Research on Domestic Politics and Foreign Policy: A Critique

Comparative research into political influences and foreign policy is not new. Each of the major comparative foreign policy frameworks gives a central role to political influences. Rosenau (1966) posits that a political variable—accountability—is one of the three most important foreign policy influences and, as such, determines the relative "potency" of other sources of foreign policy. More recent efforts have sought to conceptualize a wider array of political phenomena. Salmore and Salmore (1978), in their development of the CREON (Comparative Research on the Events of Nations) project's "regimes perspective," identify three groups of regime "constraints:" the ability of the regime to extract resources from society, political constraints, and the leadership's disposition to use resources. Wilkenfeld et al. (1980), in the political component of their IBA (Interstate Behavior Analyses) model, posit another set of influences: "formal institutional factors" such as bureaucracies and legislatures, "linkage mechanisms" concerning the effects of wider polity such as public opinion, and "political system aggregate descriptor variables" referring to the over-all features of the political system such as shared elite traits. Clearly, there is a consensus that political variables constitute an important, although complex, cluster of influences on foreign policy. Still, even with these innovative conceptual efforts, "large gaps appear in the existing literature on foreign policy and political phenomena" (Wilkenfeld et al., 1980, p. 53).

The gap is most apparent in the empirical literature, where most of the political concepts proposed in the above frameworks have remained undeveloped. Much of the current empirical knowledge about political influences on foreign policy centers around a single variable—accountability and, in particular, the distinction between open and closed (or democratic and authoritarian) regimes (see Salmore and Hermann, 1969; Salmore and Salmore, 1970; Moore, 1974a, 1974b; East and Hermann, 1974; Russett and Monsen, 1975; Butler and Taylor, 1975). In these studies the foreign policies of open regimes are assumed to be constrained by domestic political influences, whereas closed ones are not.

The primacy given to accountability reflects a conventional wisdom that political conditions in open and closed systems are fundamentally different. Open polities are assumed to have much opposition, because they have, according to one widely cited scheme (Farrell, 1966, p. 168), "competitive, regular electoral contests, legalized two- or multi-party organizations aimed at offering alternative governmental leadership, a high degree of toleration for autonomous groups in politics, and an acceptance of constitutional restraints on governmental power." Closed systems, in contrast, are pictured as being largely immune from domestic constraints. Comparativists have drawn upon Friedrich and Brzezinski's (1956) "totalitarian model" and have assumed the following conditions are characteristic of closed political systems: "an official ideology, a single mass party, a system of terroristic policy control, near complete party control of all means of effective mass communication, and central control of the entire economy." Few political constraints are likely to occur under these conditions; opposition outside of the regime cannot exist and power remains highly concentrated in the hands of the seemingly monolithic party leadership. Compared to leaders in closed political systems, those in open ones are thought to be subject to far greater constraints because, first, only they confront "significant" oppositions (autonomous interest groups and competing parties) and, second, only they have constitutional procedures guaranteeing the expression of domestic dissent.

The premise of this paper is that accountability is a simplistic conceptualization (and measure) of domestic constraints and, in particular, political oppositions. A reading of the "areas studies" literature on the politics of foreign policy in a variety of non-American settings suggests there are at least two problems with the use of accountability as a surrogate measure of political oppositions.[2] First, such a measure assumes that oppositions are equally pervasive in all democratic systems. This is a dubious assumption because opposition levels vary significantly across different democratic polities. Regimes such as those of Britain's Thatcher and West Germany's Kohl are fairly cohesive and retain stable parliamentary majorities, whereas Israel's Labour-Likud coalition and Italy's Socialist-led five-party coalition are internally fragmented with tenuous parliamentary majorities. Even within a single nation there can be dramatic changes in domestic oppositions. Compare, for instance, the cohesiveness and stability of French governments between the Fourth and Fifth Republics, or similarly the growth of opposition in the United States since the Vietnam

341

War and Watergate. The basic point is simple—significant variances in domestic oppositions occur both within and across democratic polities.[3]

The weakness of accountability becomes even more apparent if we recognize a second limitation in its use as a measure of domestic constraints—it assumes that "significant" oppositions cannot occur in closed political systems. This, too, is a tenuous assertion. Recent research on foreign policy making in the Soviet Union, China, and several other authoritarian states disputes the notion that leaders in closed regimes operate free of political constraints.[4] This literature consistently points to the occurrence of significant oppositions in closed regimes, not in the form of competing interest groups or political parties but rather as political divisions within the regime. These divisions are due, in part, to the diffusion of political power across institutional and bureaucratic groups in larger, established authoritarian systems such as that of the Soviet Union. Equally important, however, is that many authoritarian regimes are ruled by collective leaderships in which the leader must share power with other politically powerful individuals. Indeed, Valenta (1979, p. 27) asserts, the seemingly dominant Soviet leader is, at most, a first among equals and "compared with such chief executives in Western political systems as the American president, the Soviet secretary general probably has somewhat limited decision making power and enjoys fewer prerogatives."

Political conflict within the regimes of authoritarian political systems can be rather intense and foreign policy decision making highly political. Two factors contribute to this. First, there are often different policy positions within a leadership, reflective of competing belief systems and institutional interests. Ideology provides few concrete solutions on specific problems, and as another Soviet specialist notes, there can be "a predisposition to make different assessments of the 'correlation of forces' in world politics" (Dallin, 1969, p. 46). Second, political debates are intensified by the competition for power and position within leadership circles, especially during periods of succession crises. As one China observer notes about that country's factionalized leadership, "at a critical point in any policy debate between leaders at the pinnacle of power, differences over issues become so intense that it is not the policy itself which is paramount, but rather the authority, power, and influence of the leader advocating policy" (Brown, 1976, p. 10). In such an environment foreign policy making can become highly politicized, giving us reason to suspect that leaders in closed regimes often face the kinds of political pressures which constrain their democratic counterparts.[4]

Summarizing then, the argument thus far is that accountability is an inadequate concept for assessing cross-national differences in political constraints emanating from domestic oppositions. Although it might tell us much about the wider context in which political actors operate (it will be used in this manner in the empirical analyses later in the chapter), knowledge of accountability *by itself* tells us little about the more basic question of whether or not opposition actually exists. Indeed, accountability can mislead us into assuming erroneously that opposition exists in regimes where it actually does not (in stable, cohesive democratic regimes) and ignoring it where it actually does exist (in fragmented or unstable authoritarian regimes). Thus, we should change our basic assumption about political conditions in open and closed regimes. It should be assumed that oppositions can potentially occur in any type of regime and influence its foreign policy—regardless of the regime's accountability or other aspects of its formal structural arrangements. The implication of this is that we should attempt to conceptualize and measure actual, existing political phenomena, such as divisions within regimes and actors and pressures in the wider political environment.

Conceptualizing Political Oppositions for Comparative Analysis: Regime Fragmentation and Vulnerability

Political opposition is a complex phenomenon, a reality that accounts for the difficulty of developing broad, cross-national measures. As the IBA and CREON frameworks have made clear, there is a wide variety of political actors that seemingly affect foreign policy. At least four basic sets of actors come to mind: (1) divisions within the leadership stemming from personality, factional and bureaucratic differences; (2) legislative actors and other nonexecutive actors sharing power with the executive; (3) politically active segments of the society in the form of bureaucratic and interest group actors; and(4) the less structured activity of the mass public in the form of public opinion and sometimes widespread civil unrest. Rigorously observing all of these actors is quite difficult. This task is compounded by phenomena such as bureaucratic politics, interest group influence, and public opinion which fluctuate across specific issues and different situations. Such variation greatly hinders the development of broad, aggregate measures of oppositions and their activities, and it is not surprising that there has been a dearth of successful measurement efforts.

343

By way of illustrating how measures of actual, existing political oppositions can be developed for comparative analysis, we present two measures of regime level oppositions, ones within or closely proximate to the central political leadership. Although fragmentation and vulnerability clearly are not comprehensive measures of domestic opposition, they are especially important because they capture oppositions most proximate to a nation's top political authorities. As such, these variables are most likely to constrain foreign policy makers because they (1) strike directly at the ability of authorities to reach a consensus among themselves and (2) bring in to play most directly the question of these leaders' continued control of the regime. Knowledge of a regime's internal strength can also tell us something about the leadership's ability to resist the pressures of actors outside of the regime, such as interest groups and public opinion.

Regime Fragmentation

This concept concerns the degree to which a government's central political leadership is fragmented by persisting, internal political divisions in the form of competing personalities, institutions/bureaucracies, factions, or competing parties or other such political groups. (Alternatively, regime fragmentation can be thought of as a measure of the single leader's ability to dominate his or her immediate political environment.) Political divisions within a regime are important because they frequently give rise to debates over foreign policy issues in the actual decision-making process. Given that power to allocate the nation's resources lies in the authoritative positions constituting the regime, deep leadership cleavages can prevent foreign policy makers from committing their nation's resources to a particular course of action. Even if not all members of a regime's coalition actually participate in the making of policies, decision makers must still be concerned that their decisions do not alienate crucial members of the ruling coalition.

It is, of course, quite difficult to observe the generally hidden political processes internal to a government, particularly when one is collecting data across a wide array of national political systems. However, a crude—but workable—strategy can be used for extensive cross-national data collection. Regimes can be classified in terms of observable political divisions occurring within three basic political arenas: the cabinet, the legislature and the leader's own political party. At least five basic levels of political fragmentation are identifiable in a way that captures the broad mix of cabinet, legislative and party oppositions to the leader. Ranging from very cohesive regimes to highly fragmented ones, the five types of regimes are:

(1) *Regimes dominated by a single, individual leader.* Little power within the regime exists independently of the leader, who can remove any other individuals from office if he so wishes. The leader dominates his own party/group, and bureaucracies and institutions have little autonomy. Examples include the Soviet Union under Stalin, Spain under Franco, and Third World regimes such as Touré's Guinea, Castro's Cuba and Libya's Qaddafi.

(2) *Regimes dominated by a single, cohesive party/group in which there exist established, autonomous bureaucracies and institutions.* Although ruled by a single, politically cohesive group, a leader in this type of regime does not have complete dominance over other party, cabinet or legislative actors. These other leadership roles are institutionalized and have some influence on policy making. Examples include relatively cohesive regimes in advanced industrial states (e.g., the Soviet Union under Brezhnev and Britain under Thatcher) and some Third World regimes where there is some pluralism (e.g., Kenya and Zambia).

(3) *Regimes dominated by a single party/group that is itself internally divided by established political factions.* These factions are organized for competition for the party leadership, and often they might also differ on substantive policy matters. Examples of such regimes include the Liberal Democratic Party in Japan, the Christian Democratic Party in Italy, and the Chinese Communist Party in the 1960s prior to the Cultural Revolution.

(4) *Regimes in which the ruling party/group shares power with one or more minor parties/groups.* Here there is a sharing of authority with one or more minor, or junior, members, usually because of the dominant party's inability to obtain an absolute majority of legislative seats. Examples include the current West German coalition between the Christian Democrats and the Free Democrats, as well as the present American situation in which the presidency is held by the Republicans and the Congress is partially controlled by the Democrats.

(5) *Regimes in which there is no clear dominant party or group—there exists a coalition of autonomous political groups.* Policy making is fragmented with the absence of any one group able to assert leadership and direction within the regime. Any group within the regime can block policy initiatives by threatening to dismantle the regime by withdrawing from the coalition. Examples include the cabinets of Fourth Republic France, Israel's current Labour-Likud coalition, and West Germany's "Grand Coalition" of the late 1960s. Also included are unstable authoritarian regimes such as Indonesia under Sukarno, China during the Cultural Revolution, and Iran during Khomeini's first two years in power.

These groups of regimes are the basis of the five-point regime fragmentation/cohesion scale to be used later in this paper. Along this scale it is assumed that the intensity of political constraints varies significantly, becoming progressively more pronounced as one moves from more cohesive regimes (ones dominated by a single leader or group) to more fragmented (ones internally divided by factions or competing political groups). The assumption is that political constraints become more severe as we move from institutional to factional and party/group divisions because factional and party/group divisions are indicative of (1) greater substantive policy splits and/or (2) more intense competition for political power.

Regime Vulnerability

Whereas regime fragmentation taps political constraints resulting from divisions within the leadership, regime vulnerability focuses broadly on the strength of the regime as it relates mainly to the wider political environment. In essence, it asks what is the likelihood that the current leadership will be removed from political office. Clearly, leaders seek to stay in office, and it is reasonable to expect that they will conduct foreign policy in a way that will be consistent with their retaining political power. If a leadership does face significant challenges to its position, it will likely avoid actions that could provoke controversies that, in turn, might help opposing political parties or other groups (e.g., the military) to force its removal from office.

As with the fragmentation concept, it is difficult to observe precisely the political strength of regimes in a way appropriate for comparative analysis. As Americans are well aware, the political situation of any administration can literally vary month by month in public opinion polls. Thus, for the purpose of developing broad, cross-nationally useful measures, it is necessary to once again adopt a less than perfect, but realistic, strategy. Namely, we focus on the question of whether the current regime—and ones before it—have been able to stay in office for extended periods of time. This kind of strategy has gained credibility in the literature on democratic stability, where the frequency of cabinet changes has been treated as a general indicator of domestic political pressures, or at least, a measure of executive strength *vis-à-vis* the legislature (see Hurwitz, 1971; Lijphart, 1984). However, we must expand the focus from just parliamentary cabinets to other types of political systems and consider changes in powerful political roles lodged in the party or legislature, and not just the executive. Still, the logic behind "cabinet" durability is applicable to other political systems—namely, that the persistent control of a regime by a single group or leader over an extended period of time is a good indicator of its ability to resist domestic oppositions.

The most basic means for measuring regime vulnerability is in terms of the frequency of changes in the top leadership over a particular period of time (or, alternatively, the present regime's time in office as well as the average tenure of preceding regimes). In addition, as the above literature on democratic stability points out, it is necessary to look more closely at the types of regime changes that have occurred. Often a regime change simply involves the replacement of an individual leader, with the same political group or coalition remaining in power. Other regime changes are far more dramatic and reflect a more intense competition for political dominance, ones involving the coming to power of an entirely new political group or party. The means by which a regime comes to power (as well as the kinds of changes that have preceded it) is broadly indicative of the intensity of political challenges it can expect during its tenure of power.

There are at least five basic (and really observable) types of regime changes. The most dramatic of these occurs when an entire ruling group is overthrown through illegal, sometimes violent, means. The mildest involves only the change in one of the top non-head-of-state officials in the government in a way that does not alter the regime's basic political make-up. Ranging from the mildest to the most severe, these types of regime changes are:

(1) *Regime changes limited to the removal or resignation of a top political leader, but one who is not the effective head of state.* One example is a president's removal of an institutionally subordinate premier, as in the case of de Gaulle's removal of Premiers Debré and Pompidou. In communist systems changes in a premier or president (both of whom are subordinate to the party secretary) fall into this category, if they do not reflect broader changes in the interfactional balances.

(2) *Regime changes involving a change in the effective head of state, but no change in the basic political make-up of the ruling group.* Examples are changes in Japanese prime ministers, all of whom have been heads of the Liberal Democratic Party, and in Indian prime ministers during the 1960s, all of whom were leaders of the then relatively cohesive Congress Party.

(3) *Regime changes due to adjustments in the mix of groups/factions that constitute the ruling coalition, but that do not alter the essential political make-up of the regime.* These are signified by the continuation in office of the dominant ruling party or faction or, if no such group exists, a similar mix of coalition members. Examples are the rotation of cabinet positions in the multi-party coalitions of Italy,

347

Lebanon, and Fourth Republic France; the resignation of a minor, or junior coalition member, a role often played by West Germany's Free Democratic Party; or a change in the interfactional balance of a fragmented, authoritarian regime, as occurred with Khrushchev's consolidation of power over the factionalized Soviet Politburo of the mid-1950s.

(4) *Regime changes involving the replacement of one political group (or set of groups) by another, occurring through routinized, constitutionally sanctioned procedures.* The typical case is an election resulting in the removal from office of one party by another—for example, the 1977 defeat of the Indian Congress Party by the Janata Party and the 1985 Israeli election replacing the Likud government with a Labour-Likud coalition.

(5) *Regime changes in which an entire ruling group is forced from office by another group through illegal or irregular means.* Examples include any *coup d'état* (e.g., the Ghanaian military's overthrow of Nkrumah in 1966 and the numerous government changes in Bolivia) or any other irregular means such as those surrounding the removal of the Shah of Iran and the coming to power of Khomeini.

The frequency and type of regime changes in a political system are the basis for measuring regime vulnerability. *Our assertion is that a regime will be highly constrained if it exists in a political system that has recently experienced (1) frequent regime changes with regimes retaining power for relatively short periods of time, and (2) dramatic changes involving the rotation of different political groups in power and/or challenges involving illegal political means.* As discussed below, the political vulnerability of a regime can be measured in terms of how it came to power along with the pattern of regime changes in, for example, the decade prior to its coming to power. In the analyses below, it is hypothesized that high levels of vulnerability will place considerable constraints on a regime's foreign policy behavior.

Linking Domestic Politics to Foreign Policy: Political Constraints

Pronounced political divisions within a regime and the occurrence of strong political pressures threatening to remove the regime from power are likely to have a broad impact on foreign policy. The dynamics of these effects center around political constraints (i.e., prohibitions on certain foreign policy options), because they are likely to upset the domestic political balance or because the leadership simply does not have the complete political authority necessary for the implementation of such actions.

Political constraints on a regime's conduct of foreign policy represent a blend of two decision-making dynamics: controversy avoidance and consensus building. At one level, the leadership is hindered from taking actions that it expects to be controversial. Politically "risky" actions can provoke public debate over the leadership's policies and ability to lead the country. Foreign policy controversies can be particularly costly if they alienate important political support groups, and in the case of a very weak regime, such pressures can pose a threat to its very survival by upsetting tenuous interfactional/interparty balances and weakening slim legislative majorities. To the degree a regime is capable of pursuing a policy, it will carefully attempt to build a consensus among those political actors upon which it depends for the implementation of policy and/or its own continuation in office. This decision-making dynamic is largely one of resolving differences among relevant actors through an often drawn-out process of "accommodation, involving negotiation, persuasion, and a variety of related techniques" designed to arrange maximum compromises among political adversaries (Hilsman, 1959, pp. 366–7).

The logic of political constraints suggests that the foreign policies of politically fragmented and vulnerable regimes will be distinctive with respect to ambiguity, commitment, and style of diplomacy. Ambiguity refers to the manner in which a regime communicates its policy positions and intentions, with ambiguous behavior taking the form of either vague or contradictory statements about policy positions or intentions. Fragmented and vulnerable regimes are likely to engage in highly ambiguous behavior. In part this results from their need to avoid specific statements that could provoke public criticism on specific points of policy as well as future direction of government policies. Fragmented regimes are also likely to engage in highly contradictory and inconsistent verbal behavior, because of the tendency of different groups within a regime to make pronouncements (often politically motivated) on their own that reflect their own particular policy position.

The foreign policies of politically constrained regimes are also likely to be marked by an inability to make substantively meaningful commitments, at least in the sense of using material resources or even publicly threatening or promising such action. Political constraints restrict the leader's ability to commit the nation's resources—or even express intentions to do so—because the diversion of resources to an international venture could prove to be controversial and materially costly. Also, leaders of fragmented regimes are sometimes unable to act because the commitment of actual resources often requires the formal approval of opposing groups within the regime.

349

The final element of foreign policy influenced by domestic politics is what might be referred to as a regime's "style of diplomacy" which encompasses such behaviors as independence, conflict and intensity in a nation's foreign policy. Fragmented and vulnerable regimes are likely to engage in passive or quiet behaviors, that is, diplomacy marked by few initiatives, low intensity and occasional hostility. In part, this passivity stems from the "watering down" process inherent in bargaining and compromise when a consensus is developed. Perhaps more importantly though, quiet diplomacy stems from the imperative that highly constrained governments must avoid controversies that could disrupt tenuous public support and interfactional/intergroup balances.

Measuring Regime Characteristics and Testing Some Basic Hypotheses

In this section we present an illustrative, cross-national examination of the association between political constraints and foreign policy behavior. The purpose of this exercise is to demonstrate procedures for identifying actual regimes and classifying them by levels of fragmentation and vulnerability. The sample of regimes used here is for the 38 nations in the CREON data set (the foreign policy data set used in the analyses below) for the 9-year period 1959–67. In addition, we examine the broad association between these patterns of oppositions and several dimensions of foreign policy behavior. This enables us to test basic hypotheses and present certain findings about the cross-national linkage between domestic politics and foreign policy. The findings, in turn, point to specific directions for future comparative foreign policy research on political influences.

Identifying Political Regimes

In the empirical analyses, we want to be able to compare the foreign policy behavior of regimes classified in terms of fragmentation and vulnerability. Thus, the "regime", as opposed to the "nation-state", must serve as the unit of analysis for this research. Even though it is used in most cross-national research, the nation-state is not an appropriate unit of analysis for research on regimes and oppositions. The attributes of nations are not subject to changes except over very extended periods of time. It is too gross a unit of measurement for the kinds of comparisons we will be making, because within any nation there can be, over time, major changes in the level of domestic opposition and other political conditions.

The use of the regime as a unit of analysis in comparative research does, however, present some difficulties: namely, what exactly constitutes a "regime change?" In other words, what types of events would we want to treat as indicators of the termination of one regime and the beginning of another? The most basic procedure for delineating regimes is to focus simply on the head-of-state position, with a regime change occurring in the event of a change in the individual occupant of this position. This criterion is relatively easy to employ, and it results in the identification of regimes that have a degree of "face validity," as it deals with the coming and going of more or less well-known political leaders. More importantly, this criterion can be used because changes in the head of state often correspond to changes in the level of regime fragmentation and vulnerability.

The "head-of-state criterion," however, is not sufficiently precise for measuring oppositions. Used by itself, it can blur major changes in oppositions that might occur during the tenure of a particular head of state. Accordingly, a supplementary rule for identifying regimes is needed. For the purposes of this research, the best strategy is to focus directly on the occurrence of significant changes in the level of regime fragmentation and vulnerability. Where there is a change in the level of fragmentation or vulnerability (with the exception of changes in non-head-of-state officials), that event will be considered to mark the termination of one regime and the beginning of another. Specific political events that signify the beginning of a new regime are: (1) a gain or loss of a majority of legislative seats by the ruling party, (2) the rise or demise of competing factions within the leader's party, and (3) the formation or dismantling of a coalition government involving a redistribution of cabinet seats among major coalition members under the same leader. These criteria, along with the main criterion of a change in head of state, constitute the indicators by which regimes are identified.

The regimes identified for the 38 nations in the CREON sample for the 9-year period, 1959–67, are listed in Table 17.1. Included under each country is the name of the regime's leader, serving as the label of the regime. (In the case where a leader is the head of more than one regime a number follows the name of the regime—for example, for the two de Gaulle regimes we have "de Gaulle-1" and "de Gaulle-2.") Adjacent to the label of the regime are the dates during which the regime was in power. For the 9-year period under consideration, ninety-two regimes were identified for the 38 nations in our sample. For all but ten of the nations, there was more than one regime. Four countries had five or more different regimes. In most cases, regime changes were marked with the coming to power of a new head of state, although in nine cases the regime change was ascertained solely on the

Table 17.1 *Regimes in the CREON Sample of Nations, for the Years,
1959–1967.*

Belgium
Eyskens (pre-1959 to April 1961)
Lefevre (April 1961 to July 1965)
*Harmel (July 1965 to March 1966)
Boeynants (March 1966 to
post-1967)

Canada
Diefenbaker-1 (pre-1959 to June
1962)
Diefenbaker-2 (June 1962 to April
1963)
Pearson (April 1963 to post-1967)

Chile
Alessandri (pre-1959 to Nov. 1964)
Frei (Nov. 1964 to post-1967)

China, People's Republic of
*Mao Zedong (pre-1959 to April
1959)
Lui Shaoqi and Mao Zedong
(April 1959 to July 1966)
Collective leadership (August 1966
to post-1967)

Costa Rica
Echandi (pre-1959 to May 1962)
Orlich (May 1962 to May 1966)
Trejos (May 1966 to post-1967)

Cuba
*Castro-1 (Jan. 1959 to May 1959)
Castro-2 (June 1959 to post-1967)

Czechoslovakia
Novotny-1 (pre-1959 to Sept. 1963)
Novotny-2 (Sept. 1963 to Jan.
1967)
Novotny-3 (Jan. 1967 to post-1967)

Egypt
Nasser (pre-1959 to post-1967)

France
de Gaulle-1 (pre-1959 to Nov.
1962)
de Gaulle-2 (Nov. 1962 to
post-1967)

Federal Republic of Germany
Adenauer-1 (pre-1959 to Sept.
1961)
Adenauer-2 (Sept. 1961 to Oct.
1963)
Erhard (Oct. 1963 to Oct. 1966)
*Interregnum (Oct. 1966 to Dec.
1966)
Kiesinger (Dec. 1966 to post-1967)

German Democratic Republic
Ulbricht (pre-1959 to post-1967)

Ghana
Nkrumah (pre-1959 to Feb. 1966)
Ankrah (Feb. 1966 to post-1959)

Guinea
Touré (pre-1959 to post-1967)

Iceland
Jonasson (pre-1959 to Nov. 1959)
Thors (Nov. 1959 to Aug. 1965)
Benediktsson (Aug. 1965 to
post-1967)

India
Nehru-1 (pre-1959 to Aug. 1963)
*Nehru-2 (Aug. 1963 to June 1964)
Shastri (June 1964 to March 1966)
Gandhi (March 1966 to post-1967)

Israel
Ben-Gurion (pre-1959 to June
1963)
Eshkol (June 1963 to post-1967)

Italy
*Fanfani-1 (pre-1959 to Feb. 1959)
Segni (Feb. 1959 to March 1960)
Tambroni (April 1960 to July 1960)
Fanfani-2 (July 1960 to June 1963)
Leoni (June 1963 to Dec. 1963)
Moro (Dec. 1963 to post-1967)

Ivory Coast
Houphouet-Boigny (pre-1959 to
post-1967)

Japan
Kishi (pre-1959 to July 1960)
Ikeda (July 1960 to Nov. 1964)
Sato (Dec. 1964 to post-1967)

Kenya
  Kenyatta-1 (Dec. 1963 to April
    1966)
  Kenyatta-2 (April 1966 to
    post-1967)

Lebanon
  Karami-1 (pre-1959 to May 1960)
  al-Da'uq (May 1960 to Aug. 1960)
  Salaam (Aug. 1960 to Oct. 1961)
  Karami-2 (Nov. 1961 to Feb. 1964)
  Queini (Feb. 1964 to July 1965)
  *Karami-3 (July 1965 to April 1966)
  Yaffi (April 1966 to Dec. 1966)
  Karami-4 (Dec. 1966 to post-1967)

Mexico
  Lopez-Mateos (pre-1959 to Dec.
    1964)
  Diaz-Ordaz (Dec. 1964 to
    post-1967)

New Zealand
  Nash (pre-1959 to Dec. 1960)
  Holyoake (Dec. 1960 to post-1967)

Norway
  Gerhardsen-1 (pre-1959 to Aug.
    1963)
  *Lyng (Aug. 1963 to Sept. 1963)
  Gerhardsen-2 (Sept. 1963 to Nov.
    1965)
  Borten (Nov. 1965 to post-1967)

Poland
  Gomulka (pre-1959 to post-1967)

Philippines
  Garcia (pre-1959 to Dec. 1961)
  Macapagal-1 (Dec. 1961 to Nov.
    1963)
  Macapagal-2 (Dec. 1963 to Nov.
    1965)
  Marcos (Dec. 1965 to post-1967)

Spain
  Franco (pre-1959 to post-1967)

Switzerland
  Collective leadership (pre-1959 to
    post-1967)

Thailand
  Thanarat (pre-1959 to Dec. 1963)
  Kittikachorn (Dec. 1963 to
    post-1967)

Tunisia
  Bourguiba (pre-1959 to post-1967)

Turkey
  Menderes (pre-1959 to May 1960)
  Gursel (May 1960 to Nov. 1961)
  Inonu (Nov. 1961 to Feb. 1965)
  Urguplu (Feb. 1965 to Oct. 1965)
  Demirel (Oct. 1965 to post-1967)

Uganda
  Obote-1 (Sept. 1962 to Feb. 1966)
  Obote-2 (Feb. 1966 to post-1967)

USSR
  Khrushchev (pre-1959 to Oct. 1964)
  Brezhnev (Oct. 1964 to post-1967)

United States
  Eisenhower (pre-1959 to Jan. 1961)
  Kennedy (Jan. 1961 to Nov. 1963)
  Johnson-1 (Nov. 1963 to June
    1966)
  Johnson-2 (June 1966 to post-1967)

Uruguay
  *Fisher (pre-1959 to Feb. 1959)
  Etchegoyen (March 1959 to Feb.
    1963)
  Crespo (March 1963 to Feb. 1965)
  Beltran (March 1965 to Feb. 1967)
  Gestido (March 1967 to post-1967)

Venezuela
  *Larrazabal (pre-1959 to Feb. 1959)
  Betancourt (Feb. 1959 to March
    1964)
  Leoni (March 1964 to post-1967)

Yugoslavia
  Tito (pre-1959 to post 1967)

Zambia
  Kaunda (Oct. 1964 to post-1967)

---

* Asterisks indicates that the dates of the regime's tenure in office did not include any
of the months covered in the CREON events data set.

basis of nonleadership political changes. All but two democratic polities (Zambia and Switzerland) had multiple regimes, while about half (seven) of the fifteen continuously nondemocratic polities had more than one regime.

Classifying Regimes by Political Oppositions

Having identified regimes, the next step is to categorize each of them by levels of fragmentation and vulnerability. Information on political conditions for each regime was drawn from several types of sources. News chronologies (e.g., *Keesing's Contemporary Archives, Facts on File* and the *New York Times Index*) were used to identify members of ruling coalitions as well as changes in regimes. Certain volumes on political parties (e.g., Janda, 1980; McDonald, 1971) provided additional details on the precise distribution of seats in multi-party cabinets and legislatures. In the case of regimes with single ruling parties, it was usually necessary to consult detailed case studies of these governments to discern the existence of a dominant leader or permanent factions. Here again, case study research proves essential to capturing the complexities of domestic phenomena cross-nationally.[5]

Turning first to fragmentation, regimes were assigned scores along the five-point fragmentation scale, ranging from highly cohesive regimes at the low end of the scale to highly fragmented regimes at the high end. A series of questions was asked in the process of classifying each regime. The most basic question was whether there was a single party or group in control. In the case of single-party/single-group regimes, it was asked if a single leader dominated the cabinet, ruling party and legislature to the degree that he or she could remove any other leader from power. If that was the case then the regime was assigned a value of 1. Where there was no dominant leader, it was then ascertained if formal factions existed. Nonfactionalized regimes were assigned a value of 2; if factions were identified the regime received a ranking of 3. In the case of those regimes ruled by multiple parties/ groups, it was necessary to determine the extent of power sharing among the coalition members. Regimes with a single, dominant party that shared power with one or more junior members were assigned a score of 4. The final group of regimes included those with multi-party coalitions with no single dominant party or group. Those regimes were ranked as being the most highly fragmented and were assigned a value of 5. The distribution of the 92 regimes in our sample across the five-point regime fragmentation scale is presented in Table 17.2.

The regime vulnerability measure has two components. The first component is simply the length of time that regime was in power,

Table 17.2 Distribution of Regimes across Five Levels of Regime Fragmentation

I — Highly cohesive regimes — Regimes dominated by a single individual leader	II — Regimes constrained by established and autonomous actors and institutions	III — Regimes controlled by a single group which is internally fragmented (factionalized)	IV — Regimes in which the ruling party shares power with minority party(s)	V — Highly fragmented regimes — Regimes in which there is no clear single dominant party
CUB/Castro-2	USA/Kennedy	USA/Johnson-2	USA/Eisenhower	FRG/Kiesinger
MEX/Lopez-Mateos	USA/Johnson-1	URU-Etchegoyen	CAN/Diefenbaker-2	NOR/Borten
MEX/Diaz-Ordaz	CAN/Diefenbaker-1	URU/Gestido	CAN/Pearson	ICE/Jonasson
SPN/Franco	COS/Orlich	CZE/Novotny-3	COS/Echandi	TUR/Inonu
GDR/Ulbricht	FRN/de Gaulle-2	GHA/Ankrah	COS/Trejos	TUR/Urguplu
CZE/Novotny-1	FRG/Adenauer-1	KEN/Kenyatta-1	VEN/Betancourt	LEB/Karami-1
YUG/Tito	POL/Gomulka	ISR/Eshkol	VEN/Leoni	LEB/al-Da'uq
IVR/Houphouet-Boigny	CZE/Novotny-2	PRC/Lui and Mao	CHL/Alessandri	LEB/Salaam
GUI/Touré	USR/Khrushchev	IND/Shastri	CHL/Frei	LEB/Karami-2
GHA/Nkrumah	USR/Brezhnev	IND/Gandhi	URU/Crespo	LEB/Queini
TUN/Bourguiba	NOR/Gerhardsen-1	JAP/Kishi	URU/Beltran	LEB/Yaffi
TUR/Gursel	UGA/Obote-2	JAP/Ikeda	BEL/Eyskens	LEB/Karami-4
EGY/Nasser	KEN/Kenyatta-2	JAP/Sato	BEL/Lefevre	SWI/Collective
(n=13)	ZAM/Kaunda	(n=13)	BEL/Boeynants	PRC/Collective
	TUR/Menderes		FRN/de Gaulle-1	(n=14)
	TUR/Demirel		FRG/Adenauer-2	
	ISR/Ben-Gurion		FRG/Erhard	
	IND/Nehru-1		ITA/Segni	
	THI/Thanarat		ITA/Tambroni	
	THI/Kittikachorn		ITA/Fanfani-2	
	PHI/Garcia		ITA/Leoni	
	PHI/Macapagal-2		ITA/Moro	
	NZE/Nash		NOR/Gerhardsen-2	
	NZE/Holyoake		ICE/Thors	
	(n=24)		ICE/Benediktsson	
			UGA/Obote-1	
			PHI/Macapagal-1	
			PHI/Marcos	
			(n=28)	

including any years before and/or after the 9-year period under consideration in this chapter. The second component of the vulnerability measure is based on the fivefold classification of regime changes listed earlier in the chapter. Specifically, a regime's score on this aspect of vulnerability is based on examination of the manner in which that regime came to power and a consideration of the number and types of regime changes that occurred during the 10 years prior to its coming to power. Each of these regime changes was assigned a weighted score according to the following scheme: a regime change occurring as the result of illegal or irregular procedures was assigned a value of 5, a change involving a legal transfer of power from one party/group to another was assigned a value of 4, a change in only the power distribution among coalition members received a value of 3, a change in simply the top leader was given a value of 2, and a change in other, lesser leaders—that is, relatively minor adjustments—in the coalition was assigned a value of 1. These scores were then summed to give the regime an overall score on this component of vulnerability.

The scores for these two vulnerability components were then combined in a manner that resulted in an ordinal vulnerability scale with values ranging from 1 to 5—one comparable to the five-point fragmentation scale. Specifically, the scores for each of the two vulnerability components were collapsed into five-point scales.[6] These scores were then summed and finally divided by 2. The result is a nine-point vulnerability scale. Low scores on this scale indicate regimes that are highly durable with extended tenures in office and having been preceded by few dramatic regime changes. The distribution of regimes in our sample across this regime vulnerability scale is presented in Table 17.3.[7]

The collapsing of the vulnerability measure allows for the creation of a third opposition measure—a composite fragmentation/vulnerability variable. This combined measure is computed simply by adding the values of each regime for the five-point fragmentation scale and the nine-point vulnerability scale.

A Test of Hypotheses and Some Suggestive Findings

In this section we report on some basic findings about the effects of fragmentation and vulnerability on three dimensions of foreign policy behavior. These dimensions of foreign policy behavior are taken from the CREON data set and are specificity, commitment and independence of action. They are, respectively, indicators of the three elements of foreign policy behavior discussed above—ambiguity, commitment and diplomatic style. Measures of foreign policy behavior have been

Table 17.3   *Distribution of Regimes across Levels of Vulnerability*

Highly vulnerable regimes	5.0 = ITA/Segni; ITA/Tambroni; BEL/Boeynants; LEB/Karami-1; LEB/al-Da'uq; LEB/Salaam; LEB/Queini; LEB/Karami-3; LEB/Yaffi; LEB/Karami-4
	4.5 = BEL/Eyskens; FRN/de Gaulle-1; ITA/Fanfani-2; TUR/Urguplu; LEB/Karami-2
	4.0 = VEN/Betancourt; URU/Gestido; FRG/Erhard; FRG/Kiesinger; ITA/Moro; ICE/Jonasson; UGA/Obote-2; TUR/Demirel; PHI/Macapagal-1
	3.5 = USA/Johnson-2; CAN/Diefenbaker-2; VEN/Leoni; URU/Etchegoyen; URU/Crespo; URU/Beltran; BEL/Lefevre; FRN/de Gaulle-2; CZE/Novotny-3; NOR/Gerhardsen-2; TUR/Gursel; TUR/Inonu; ISR/Eshkol; JAP/Kishi; IND/Shastri; PRC/Collective; NZE/Nash
	3.0 = USA/Kennedy; USA/Johnson-1; CAN/Pearson; CUB/Castro; COS/Echandi; COS/Orlich; COS/Trejos; FRG/Adenauer-2; USR/Khrushchev; NOR/Borten; ICE/Thors; EGY/Nasser; ISR/Ben-Gurion; JAP/Ikeda; THI/Thanarat; THI/Kittikachorn; PHI/Macapagal-2; PHI/Marcos
	2.5 = CHL/Alessandri; CHL/Frei; SWI/Collective; CZE/Novotny-2; ICE/Benediktsson; GHA/Ankrah; UGA/Obote-1; KEN/Kenyatta-1; JAP/Sato; PHI/Garcia; NZE/Holyoake
	2.0 = CAN/Diefenbaker-1; FRG/Adenauer-1; CZE/Novotny-1; NOR/Gerhardsen-1; TUR/Menderes; IND/Gandhi
	1.5 = USA/Eisenhower; MEX/Lopez-Mateos; MEX/Diaz-Ordaz; GDR/Ulbricht; POL/Gomulka; USR/Brezhnev; GHA/Nkrumah; KEN/Kenyatta-2; ZAM/Kaunda; PRC/Lui and Mao
Highly durable regimes	1.0 = SPN/Franco; YUG/Tito; GUI/Touré; IVR/Houphouet-Boigny; TUN/Bourguiba; IND/Nehru

aggregated for the 92 regimes in our sample, and our focus will be on correlations between regime attributes and their mean scores for each foreign policy behavior.

Also examined are the mediating effects of political accountability, which concerns whether the regime's political system is democratic or authoritarian (i.e., an open or closed polity). Although earlier we criticized the preoccupation with accountability in empirical comparative foreign policy studies, we did not suggest that it is not an important concept, useful in combination with others. We argue that it mediates the impact of oppositions on foreign policy behavior. We hypothesize that the effects of fragmentation and vulnerability will be greater in democratic polities, where the open political process and the wider array of political actors force leaders to be especially attentive to domestic oppositions.

Our first foreign policy dimension, specificity, concerns the degree to which a government communicates information about its actual or potential use of resources in a foreign policy action. As such, it is one indicator of ambiguity in foreign policy behavior. The CREON specificity measure, as developed by Swanson (1982, p. 225), is based on a five-point scale ranging from *high* specificity to *low* specificity: (1) the actual use of resources, which is maximum specificity; (2) specificity in time or conditions for the use of resources; (3) specificity of the kinds of resources to be used; (4) specificity of the problem, issue, or topic; and (5) the absence of any relevant information. We hypothesize that regime fragmentation and vulnerability are positively correlated with this specificity measure.

The correlations for mean specificity and the fragmentation, vulnerability and composite measures are reported in the first column of Table 17.4. (The second and third columns are for subsamples of open and closed regimes.) The coefficients for the overall sample of regimes indicate a moderate association between specificity and each of the three regime measures. These correlations are also in the hypothesized positive direction, indicating that higher levels of fragmentation and vulnerability are associated with increased foreign policy ambiguity. However, the findings reported in the other two columns of Table 17.4 indicate that the link between regimes and specificity holds mainly for democratic regimes. Statistically significant associations occur only for the sample of open regimes, suggesting that leaders in closed regimes are less pressured to alter their policy pronouncements given, perhaps, the absence of high-pressured media and legislative criticism.[8]

As developed by Callahan (1982), "commitment" concerns the degree to which a government's current actions limit its future options through the allocation of resources or the generation of expectations in

Table 17.4 *Correlations between Regimes' Attributes and Specificity*

	Entire sample (n=92)	Open regimes (n=67)	Closed regimes (n=25)
Regime fragmentation	0.28*	0.28*	0.01
Regime vulnerability	0.34*	0.31*	0.25
Composite measure	0.33*	0.33*	0.14

* Pearson's correlation coefficient is significant at the $p=0.05$ level

others. The CREON commitment measure is based on an eleven-point scale, with its highest points being actions that involve the transfer of resources, are specific in intent or purpose, are without conditions, and are not easily reversed. The correlations between the three regime measures and the commitment variable are reported in Table 17.5. These coefficients are for the relationship between the opposition measures and mean commitment scores.

The findings for the regime characteristics and commitment are largely unexpected and difficult to interpret, at least according to the logic of political constraints. The correlations for the vulnerability measure and the composite measure are statistically significant for the full sample of regimes. However, these correlations are positive, suggesting that politically constrained regimes in our sample display relatively high levels of commitment in terms of the eleven-point CREON scale. This clearly disputes our view that political constraints on regimes would preclude major commitments (particularly ones involving resources) on the part of fragmented and vulnerable regimes. Also perplexing is the fact that if we control for accountability, the relationship becomes weaker and is no longer statistically significant. Clearly, the findings for commitment are puzzling and require further analysis.

The CREON *independence of action* measure concerns the 'degree of autonomy a government tries to maintain in its foreign policy actions' (M. Hermann, 1982, p. 254). Independence of action (IOA) has two elements: an "initiative-reactive" dimension and a "unilateral-multilateral" dimension. Each dimension is indicative of the degree of passivity in foreign policy and, as such, is one measure of a nation's "style of diplomacy." The results of the analysis of regime characteristics and independence of action are reported in Table 17.6. Note that two coefficients are reported in each cell of the table. These are for the separate measures of IOA's two dimensions: mean self-initiated behavior (or percentage of the regime's behavior that was self-initiated) and mean unilateral behaviors (or percentage of the regime's behaviors

Table 17.5 *Correlations between Regimes' Attributes and Commitment*

	Entire sample (n=92)	Open regimes (n=67)	Closed regimes (n=25)
Regime fragmentation	0.16	0.05	−0.15
Regime vulnerability	0.23*	0.14	0.09
Composite measure	0.21*	0.11	−0.10

* Pearson's correlation coefficient is significant at the $p=0.05$ level

that were unilateral). If the logic of political constraints is accurate, we should find negative correlations between the regime measures and these two IOA measures.

Examination of the first column of coefficients in Table 17.6 points to an absence of an overall relationship between regime traits and the two IOA dimensions, with the exception of weak correlations in the case of regime vulnerability. However, if we control for the effects of accountability, the tie between regimes and IOA becomes clearer. As with specificity, the effects of vulnerability are limited to open regimes. More intriguing, though, is that the correlations of the fragmentation and composite regime measures to IOA are in opposite directions for the two types of polities. For open systems, there are, as expected, negative correlations between the opposition measures and initiative and unilateralism in foreign policy. However, in the case of closed regimes the reverse is true. Here there are sizeable positive correlations between oppositions (particularly fragmentation) and both dimensions of independence of action. Contrary to our hypotheses, politically pressured regimes in closed polities appear prone to engage in a highly assertive style of diplomacy marked by much self-initiated and unilateral behavior.

Table 17.6   *Correlations between Regimes' Attributes and Two Dimensions of Independence of Action—Initiative and Unilateralism*

	Entire sample (n=92)	Open regimes (n=67)	Closed regimes (n=25)
Regime fragmentation	−0.12/−0.05	−0.24*/−0.11	0.31*/0.47*
Regime vulnerability	−0.18*/−0.18*	−0.23*/−0.23*	0.13/0.18
Composite measure	−0.16/−0.12	−0.26*/−0.19	0.35*/0.42*

The first coefficient in each cell is for percent self-initiated behaviors and the second is for percent unilateral behavior
* Pearson's correlation coefficient is significant at the $p=0.05$ level

Conclusions and some New Directions for Comparative Research on Political Oppositions and Foreign Policy

This chapter has offered a reassessment of comparative foreign policy research on domestic political influences. The premise of this effort has been that empirical research in this area has been overly simplistic, mainly because it has focused on political structure and assumed that political constraints occur mainly in some types of political systems and not others. We have pointed out that oppositions can exist (or not exist) in any type of political system. We have offered two conceptualizations of existing political oppositions. These are regime fragmentation and vulnerability, both of which center on political constraints most immediate to a nation's central political leadership, and in a way that captures oppositions in both democratic and nondemocratic systems.

Included in this chapter is a brief, illustrative analysis of the effects of fragmentation and vulnerability on several basic dimensions of foreign policy behavior—specificity, commitment and independence of action. The purpose of this analysis is to demonstrate a viable strategy for collecting opposition data for cross-national studies. The foreign policy behaviors of 92 regimes for 38 nations were analyzed. The results are suggestive. Although the findings for commitment are puzzling (and even indicate that constrained regimes engage in higher levels of commitment), the results indicate that fragmentation and vulnerability are significantly associated with specificity and independence of action in meaningful ways. Across the entire sample of 92 regimes, fragmented regimes and politically vulnerable ones displayed the expected tendency towards diminished specificity, although these effects held mainly for democratic polities. The findings for independence of action were more complex but quite interesting. The impact of oppositions on IOA became evident mainly when we controlled for accountability. IOA was affected by a regime's opposition in the case of both open and close polities, *but* the direction of the relationships differed for the two subsamples of regimes. For open regimes, fragmentation and vulnerability were, as hypothesized, associated with low levels of initiative and unilateralism in foreign policy. In contrast, these regime traits (primarily fragmentation) were associated with greater independence of action in the case of closed regimes. These findings, as well as those for specificity, suggest that accountability plays an important mediating role as suggested by Rosenau (1966), although these effects extend not only to "potency" but also to the direction of a source variable's influence on foreign policy behavior.

Clearly these findings are preliminary, but they do provide some basis for pointing out specific directions for future comparative foreign policy research on domestic politics and foreign policy. The first area for future inquiry is in the continued conceptualization of political oppositions, in particular measures of powerful societal (or corporatist) interests, party system traits and mass political unrest. It is possible that

361

fragmentation and vulnerability will prove to be valuable devices for linking these other kinds of oppositions to foreign policy because they can tell us something about the degree to which a regime will be able to resist pressures from outside the regime. Attention also should be given to the refinement of opposition measures—especially regime fragmentation—in a way that would encompass substantive policy positions of competing political groups. The measures used in this chapter assume that leaders from different factions and parties do, in fact, have fundamental differences over policy matters. The constraining implications of fragmentation would seem to be greatly intensified in those cases where there was no consensus on basic foreign policy problems and strategies, as is quite evident if we look at the rise of congressional constraints on American presidents with the demise of the cold war consensus in the period following the Vietnam War. A more powerful measure of domestic constraints would incorporate substantive policy differences in the manner so effectively done by Holsti and Rosenau (1984) in their recent study of American foreign policy elites.

The second area of needed inquiry concerns the dependent variable, foreign policy behavior. Clearly, additional consideration needs to be given to the link between political constraints and foreign policy commitments in order to dissect the puzzling results presented in this paper. Other, more complex "second-order" measures also deserve attention. For example, fragmentation and vulnerability are likely to be associated with adaptability and consistency in foreign policy across time. Similarly, the regime traits presented in this chapter could prove useful in explaining the linkage between regime change and the kinds of basic shifts in foreign policies alluded to by Moon (1985a) and Rosati (1985). There is strong reason to expect that only the more dramatic regime changes discussed above (for example, those involving the replacement of one political group by another) would account for foreign policy changes, whereas milder changes (those where the same party retains power but with a new leader) would indicate relatively little change in foreign policy. Attention should also be given to what might be called "regime orientation," that is the shared foreign policy perceptions and interests of the leadership. Presumably, if we are to assess fully the impact of political constraints, we must know something about the initial preferences of the regime leadership. The effects of fragmentation and vulnerability could then be assessed by examining the degree to which leaders were able to diverge from their original preferences. The foreign policy effects of leaders' preferences suggested by Kegley's "decision regimes" (Chapter 13), Papadakis and Starr's 'opportunity and willingness' (Chapter 20), or Walker's "role" preferences (Chapter 14), are likely to be mediated by regime constraints.

A third task for further research is the continued development of explanations of "how" oppositions influence foreign policy. It is important that the field moves beyond explanations which assert that politically constrained regimes simply have less of everything—less independence, less commitment, and so on. This chapter's comparison of open and closed systems shows that the same types of oppositions can give rise to opposite kinds of behavior in different settings. These results indicate that leaders of closed polities are likely to respond with more assertive foreign policies, at least in the form of greater independence. Such a finding should not come as a complete surprise. Cases such as China during the Cultural Revolution and Iran during the "hostage crisis" show that sometimes highly fragmented and unstable governments engage in dramatically active foreign policies for domestic political purposes. Future studies must recognize the task of accounting for both the amplifying and diminishing effects on foreign policy of domestic oppositions. The theoretical question is not simply "if" oppositions affect foreign policy; it also concerns "how" they influence those external behaviors.

A fourth task for comparative foreign policy research is that of integrating political explanations with those from other theoretical perspectives in the field. Not only would multivariate explanations place the "potency" of political effects in proper perspective, they could also provide the key to accounting for "how" oppositions are linked to foreign policy. Along with political accountability (and other aspects of political structure such as institutionalization of the regime), other nonregime attributes would seem very important. For example, one important mediating influence is leader personality as developed by M. Hermann (see Hagan and Hermann, 1984). The presence of an experienced and active leader is likely to mitigate against political constraints. Leaders with different personalities are likely to respond to domestic oppositions in contrasting ways with varying effects on foreign policy behaviors. A leader with an aggressive, confrontational political style is likely to ignore domestic oppositions or even assertively use foreign policy as a means of mobilizing domestic support for the regime. Other leaders with a more compromising, pragmatic orientation to politics are likely to be quite sensitive to political constraints and thus respond with more restrained foreign policy actions. In sum, the introduction of multivariate schemes, along with further work on political concepts and how they are linked with foreign policy behaviors, could prove to be useful paths to understanding the apparently complex linkage between domestic politics and foreign policy, particularly as we move towards the more elaborate, situationally based and decision-making-oriented models of foreign policy behavior suggested by Hermann, Hermann and Hagan (Chapter 16), and Powell, Dyson and Purkitt (Chapter 11).

Notes

An early version of this chapter was presented at the Southern Political Science Association meeting, Atlanta, November 1983. The author is very grateful to those individuals who have commented on previous drafts, including Maurice East, Albert Eldridge, Kenyon Griffin, Charles Hermann, Margaret Hermann, Charles Kegley, Maria Papadakis, Donald Puchala, Steve Ropp, Jerel Rosati and James Rosenau. A special debt of gratitude is owed to Barbara Salmore who introduced the author to the concept of regime in foreign policy and who, along with Stephen Salmore, generously provided him with an earlier and perhaps now unrecognizable data set on regimes. The author alone remains responsible for any deficiencies in this research.

1 This definition of regime simply refers to the nation's central political leadership and is drawn from Salmore and Salmore (1978). It is more general than the one presented by Kegley (Chapter 13), whose concept of "decision regime" is concerned with certain of the leadership's substantive and procedural norms. My use of the term draws upon its conventional usage in comparative politics, whereas Kegley's reflects its development in the international relations literature.

2 This author strongly agrees with Anderson's (1985) arguments about the importance of case studies to comparative foreign policy research. A number of detailed, theoretically informed case studies of non-American foreign policy decision making—especially Weinstein, 1976; Destler, Fukui and Sato, 1979; and Valenta, 1979—have been essential to developing this paper's arguments about the linkage between politics and foreign policy. These studies are analyzed in detail in Hagan (1985).

3 Valuable analyses of policy making in democratic settings, other than the United States, include Andrews, 1963; Waltz, 1967; Neustadt, 1970 and Vannicelli 1974. The literature on Japanese foreign policy is remarkably rich, and useful surveys of that country's foreign policy making are Hellman, 1969, ch. 1; Destler *et al.*, 1976; Ori, 1976 and Hosoya, 1976. This literature is reviewed in Hagan (1980).

4 General statements of the applicability of political conceptions of the foreign policy-making process in the Soviet Union can be found in Dallin, 1981; Schwartz, 1975; Spielman, 1978; and Valenta and Potter, 1984. The literature on domestic political influences in other closed regimes is rather scattered, with the exception of Chinese foreign policy making where there is a rich body of material on the influence of Communist Party factional politics. See, for example, Gottlieb, 1977; Terrill, 1978; and Sutter, 1978. This literature is also reviewed in Hagan (1980).

5 The data on the identification of regimes and their classification by fragmentation and vulnerability were collected by the author according to rules developed by him. This data collection effort, however, was facilitated by related efforts on the part of his colleagues on the CREON project—

specifically earlier regime data collection efforts by Barbara Salmore and Stephen Salmore and the 1977 CREON Summer Seminar. These efforts provided clues in researching the situations of specific regimes. My identification of regimes and their classification are in many cases different from these other efforts, reflecting differences in measurement schemes, coding rules, and primary source materials.

6 Regime values for vulnerability's *first* component were collapsed in the following way. Regimes lasting more than 12 years were given a value of 1, those lasting between 6 and 12 years received a score of 2, those lasting 4–6 years were given a value of 3, those lasting 2–3 years received a score of 4, and finally those that survived less than 2 years were given a score of 5. Regime scores for the *second* component of the vulnerability measure were collapsed in the following manner. Regimes with scores in the range 0–4 were assigned a final value of 1, those with scores in the range 5–8 were given a value of 2, those with scores between 9 and 12 were assigned a value of 3, those with scores between 13 and 20 received a value of 4, and those remaining highly vulnerable regimes with scores ranging from 21 to 59 received a value of 5.

7 The author recognizes problems underlying the additive combining of ordinal scales. However, at this stage of research this would seem valid because of the face validity of the resulting combined measures and, more importantly, because there is little in the comparative politics literature to suggest an alternative weighting scheme. However, one task for future research is the development of empirically more sophisticated schemes for combining measures of different types of oppositions.

8 In this analysis of regimes *in closed polities,* as well as the subsequent ones, the data on fragmentation is changed, slightly. Namely, the fragmentation value for the third Chinese regime—"PRC/Collective"—is changed from 5 to 3. This prevents distorted correlations for the closed subsample of regimes, resulting from the "outlier effects" of this unusually fragmented closed regime. This regime is the only closed regime ruled by multiple groups and having a fragmentation value greater than 3.

18

Foreign Policy, Learning and War

JOHN A. VASQUEZ

The Neglect of Foreign Policy
in the Study of War

Although various aspects of the causes of war have been studied by those taking a scientific approach to international relations, the domestic prerequisites for war have received little attention. This is true not only for those, such as Bueno de Mesquita (1981), who boldly argue that all decision makers can be treated as the same rational calculators regardless of the domestic political context, but also for those who treat domestic factors primarily in structural terms (Choucri and North, 1975). With the exception of some of the excellent work on perception and war (Holsti, North and Brody, 1968; Jervis, 1976), little consideration is given to foreign policy questions, especially how leaders try to mobilize a society for the decision to go to war and more importantly how the domestic political environment encourages or restrains a government from making a foreign policy that is apt to lead to war. It is as if the decision to go to war were not a foreign policy problem at all, and that the factors that affect foreign policy behavior and decision making, including the previous foreign policy, have no impact on the outbreak of war. Indeed, the widespread notice, if not acclaim, for Bueno de Mesquita (1981), who black-boxes the domestic political environment, demonstrates the meager impact the comparative study of foreign policy has had on our colleagues. All we have learned about foreign policy since the publication of Snyder, Bruck and Sapin (1954) seems of little use to them.

In this chapter I hope to begin to rectify this situation by showing the importance of domestic politics in making decisions about war and the role foreign policy plays in the outbreak of war. In this first section I will briefly discuss the limitations of attempting to black-box the domestic political environment. Next, I will try to identify the kinds of foreign policy practices that foster the outbreak of war. In the third section, I will focus on how societies learn to use the institution of war and create foreign policies to deal with it. Of particular importance is the balance between hard-liners and accommodationists both in terms of what lessons are learned and the kinds of policies that are adopted. In the last section I will present some theoretical hunches about the conditions under which hard-liners or accommodationists are likely to dominate a state's political environment and its leadership, and the factors that change the balance between hard-liners and accommodationists.

The most recent attempt to black-box the domestic environment is that of Bueno de Mesquita (1981). His effort illustrates both the merits and limits of treating decision makers as rational utility maximizers. The explanation he offers is, as he makes clear, confined to an analysis of the necessary conditions for the outbreak of war and not the sufficient conditions. Thus, while he can account empirically for a number of cases of war by demonstrating that the initiator (because of greater capability as weighted by several factors) had a utility for the war, he does not attempt to explain why in the many cases where a deductive utility for war could be found, war was not initiated. Clearly, other factors than just the ability to win a war play a role, and I want to suggest that at least some of those factors lie in the domestic political context in which leaders must operate.

War cannot be initiated, as Bueno de Mesquita would have us believe just by a simple decision of the leader. The public must be mobilized not only to accept the decision, but to fight and sacrifice enthusiastically in order to give the state the highest chances of success. For this reason, even if the decision maker wants to go to war, he (or she) may not initiate it because of domestic constraints. This was certainly the case with Franklin Delano Roosevelt prior to the attack on Pearl Harbor, and it was also the case with Bethmann-Hollweg, who in 1914 wanted the war to come in a way that would make it clear to the Social Democrats that Germany was not at fault. An analysis of domestic politics is important, however, not just for understanding how leaders may feel constrained or may manipulate the public, but for apprehending how aspects of the entire society come to the decision to go to war. In this sense, the decision to go to war is rarely made by a single leader as if he (or she) alone had this thought and informed the country of it. Instead, what happens is that a growing number of people begin to feel that war may be necessary and this shift in attitude convinces the leadership that certain actions can be taken. These actions, in turn, produce consequences which in turn convince more people and groups that war is justified. All this is missed by black-boxing the domestic environment.

But Bueno de Mesquita and others would argue that we can live without this detail, even without knowing the actual decision rules leaders take, if we have a deductive set of rules with which the actions of leaders are consonant and which therefore accurately predict their behavior (Singer, 1984, p. 20). Has Bueno de Mesquita been able to predict, as he wants, who will be the initiator and victor in a war? He has in many cases, but not in all. And the ones in which he has not turn out to be very interesting and very important. The critical ones are the two world wars, both of which he treats as dyadic cases in which he accurately predicts that the stronger Austria–Hungary will initiate war against Serbia and the stronger Germany will initiate war against Poland, but he fails to predict the outcome.[1] He omits from his data analysis the Japanese attack on the United States and the equally flawed decision of Hitler to invade the USSR, although he states that his theory explains the Japanese decision (Bueno de Mesquita, 1981, pp. 85–6). In all of these cases the initiator lost the war, a set of serious deviations from his theory that need to be explained.[2] If we add to this the fact that the theory incorrectly predicts the outcome of the Vietnam War and the data analysis omits the American and Chinese interventions in the Korean War, we begin to wonder whether the theory can only explain the easy cases. More critically, can we accept a theory that provides us with no aid in avoiding the great mistakes (and miscalculations) of our recent past?

This is not to say that this approach should be abandoned or that Bueno de Mesquita has not made an important and in many ways a brilliant contribution to the literature. It is to say that the claims for the theory must be qualified and the domain of its applicability found. One begins with cost-benefit analysis, to see how much that explains. Then one looks at the deviations. In the end probably more will be learned by explaining deviations from rational behavior than by expected-utility theory itself (Rapoport and Chammah, 1965, p. 11). I want to argue that Bueno de Mesquita's analysis only applies to certain kinds of wars—primarily wars between unequals, which I call wars of oppor-tunity (see Vasquez, 1986a). It is less applicable to wars between equals, which I call wars of rivalry, particularly when these are complex wars involving more than two parties.

If we assume that there are different types of war, then the foreign policy processes that precede them are probably also different. Like-wise, the relevant domestic factors for these different wars will also be different. One can mentally compare factors and interactions associated with imperial wars as opposed to general great-power wars like the

Second World War to see how this might be the case. In this analysis, I will confine myself to explaining the role foreign policy and domestic political factors play in the wars Bueno de Mesquita has most difficulty in black-boxing—the wars between equals, the wars of rivalry.

The specification of the relationship between foreign policy and the outbreak of war is an important task for those of us in comparative foreign policy because it provides an opportunity to build a bridge between our subfield and quantitative studies of war, particularly since the Correlates of War project is now making critical research decisions about how to treat domestic politics and foreign policy (see Singer, 1982). In this situation, it is important not only that the case against black-boxing the domestic politics environment or treating political leaders as rational utility maximizers be made, but that an alternative conceptual 'model' be put forth.

Foreign Policies that Lead to War

Singer is interested in explaining the foreign and national security policies that lead to war. Unfortunately, there has been little research on what kinds of foreign policy or what characteristics of foreign policy behavior are most apt to lead to war. The early studies on foreign policy behavior that examined national attributes, although successful in finding an association between size and participation and in making some inroads in analyzing cooperation-conflict (see Rosenau and Hoggard, 1974), were unable to find any correlation for the use of military force (East and Hermann, 1974). Singer (1981, p. 11) is probably correct in assuming that national attributes are unrelated to war. What is more likely is that certain kinds of foreign policies, when viewed in a dyadic context, do encourage war. The problem here is that only recently have we devoted any attention to conceptualizing and classifying policies as opposed to discrete characteristics of behavior (see Vasquez, 1986b).

The easiest way to begin is to try to identify a set of practices that seem to be related to the use of force and the outbreak of war. Elsewhere I have argued (Vasquez, 1983, pp. 215ff.) that power politics behavior is a series of steps to war and not to peace. Power politics or *realpolitik* behavior may be defined as actions based on an image of the world as insecure and anarchic (the security dilemma) which leads to distrust, struggles for power, interest taking precedence over norms and rules, the use of Machiavellian strategems, the presence of coercion, attempts to balance power, reliance on self-help, and the use of force and war as the *ultima ratio* (Vasquez, 1983, p. 216). Power politics behavior can be distinguished from power politics theory or realism,

369

which is an abstract body of generalizations and prescriptions derived from and intended to shape practices in the world (see Ashley, 1981, pp. 211, 215 for a similar distinction).[3] Leng (1983, 1986) has provided evidence that one aspect of power politics behavior, *realpolitik* bargaining—which he defines as "strategies that demonstrate power and a willingness to use it" (Leng 1983, p. 381)—does tend to lead to war. He finds that states that pursue *realpolitik* bargaining practices with equals end up going to war rather than nonviolently resolving serious disputes.

If we piece together some of the other findings and theoretical suggestions made within the Correlates of War project, we get the following picture of the kind of foreign policy that leads to war among equals. As a situation develops that might portend the use of force, leaders and various policy influencers become concerned primarily with security goals and/or using military force to gain stakes which they have been unable to attain up to this point.[4] In order to test their rival (Rummel, 1979b) and demonstrate resolve (Maoz, 1983), leaders rely on threats and coercive tactics, which involve them in crises (or serious disputes). Leaders respond to a crisis and to security issues that are perceived as posing a long-term threat by attempting to increase their military power through alliances and/or a military build-up (Singer, 1983; Choucri and North, 1975). In a tense environment, military build-ups lead to arms races, and alliance-making may result in a polarization (of blocs), both of which increase insecurity. In serious disputes between equals, actors employ *realpolitik* tactics (Leng, 1983). Eventually a dispute arises that escalates to war. Disputes or crises are most apt to escalate if there is an ongoing arms race (Wallace, 1979, 1982) and if: (1) they are triggered by physical threats to vital issues (Gochman and Leng, 1983; James and Wilkenfeld, 1984), (2) they are the second or third crisis with the same rival (with *realpolitik* tactics becoming more coercive and hostile in each succeeding crisis) (Leng, 1983),[5] and (3) a hostile interaction spiral emerges during the crisis (Holsti, North and Brody, 1968).

Each of these actions must be viewed as foreign policy decisions that are interrelated and cumulative. They are not statistically independent, but reflect a process of increasing hostility between rivals and a mobilization of domestic resources and public attitudes in preparation for war. The taking of one step does not require the taking of the next, but each step that is taken makes it more difficult to turn back and reverse the process. On this basis, we might hypothesize that not all foreign policies are equally likely to lead to war, but that power politics practices are in the long run highly associated with the outbreak of war.

The reason these power politics practices (from alliances to military build-ups) are not independent is that they have global consequences that lead the rival to take actions that are even more threatening. This in turn produces domestic reactions in the first country that stiffen its determination not to give in. When policy actions fail to produce the desired outcomes, more costly and riskier policies are tried. In addition to this underlying logic, there is an intellectual coherence that binds the actions together. Leaders do not take actions through trial and error, but have learned from their own experience and the storehouse of traditional 'wisdom' what to do in certain situations. The pre-eminent intellectual tradition that has guided leaders in their relations with equals (at least in the West for the last two centuries) has been power politics theory, or its twentieth-century variant—realism. Given this coherence in action and the presence of a rationale, it makes sense to identify power politics as *one kind* of foreign policy (see Vasquez, 1986b), since it brings together a set of related practices that define goals and means within a single tradition. In this sense, foreign policy is formulated by decision makers drawing upon a catalog of *realpolitik* practices and its traditions to deal with current situations. In the process they reinforce, adapt, build upon and change those practices and traditions, and thereby draw upon lessons of the past and create new lessons for the future.

My contention is that realism is a set of prescriptions that leaders imperfectly follow and that usually lead to an intensification of hostility and not to peace.[6] The importance of power politics is not that it provides an accurate explanation (which it does not), but that it is a form of behavior that must itself be explained (see Vasquez, 1983, pp. 215 ff.). If we conceptualize power politics as one image leaders can have of the world and as a set of practices that constitute one kind of foreign policy, then we can develop a more complete explanation of the steps to war by discovering what external and domestic factors give rise to leaders who will adopt this foreign policy. One way of approaching this question is to examine how leaders and their societies learn to go to war.

Learning to Fight

About forty-five years ago, Margaret Mead (1940) argued that war is a cultural invention that is learned. Taking this perspective, one of the things we want to know is how societies learn to fight. What is it in a people's experience that makes them accept war as an institution and adopt ideologies, like power politics, that provide a rationalization for and legitimation of the use of force?

371

The most notable proponents of power politics—Thucydides, Machiavelli, Prussian *realpolitik* theorists, and Hans Morgenthau—all lived during periods of major warfare and a breakdown of their regional or global order. They were seared by those experiences and derived from them the fundamental lessons that became the hallmark of a power politics image of the world. Their worlds were *realpolitik* worlds and the lessons they derived from their experiences captured a historical reality, but not all history, not all worlds.

Other worlds have existed. The *Pax Romana* provided stability and order unknown in the fifth century BC of Thucydides. Italy after unification was not Machiavellian Italy. The world of the Concert of Europe was not the world of Adolf Hitler. Long-distance global trade in the nineteenth century lacked the peril of trade with the Orient in the days of Marco Polo. What is significantly different about these other worlds is that they have ways of making authoritative allocations without going to war. In addition, the issues they resolve are issues that the loser can afford to lose. In the long run the loser expects to derive benefits from the stability of the system and future victories that will outweigh any current loss. Not only do *realpolitik* worlds lack nonviolent allocative mechanisms, but they raise life and death issues, which make it difficult for actors to live with each other. Clearly the practices of foreign policy in *realpolitik* worlds are going to be different, as will be the frequency of war.

If this analysis is correct, then not all periods should experience the same amount of war. The empirical evidence supports this expectation. Not all historical periods (see Levy, 1983; Wallensteen, 1984) and not all actors (or dyads) experience the same amount of war (see Bremer, 1980; Small and Singer, 1982, ch. 10). This suggests that war is not as culturally acceptable in some times and places as in others. In fact, not only does the frequency of war differ, but the goals of war, the rules of its conduct, perhaps even the reasons justifying war vary from time to time.

All this underlines the fact that war is part of a political culture and that the practices derived from the lessons of war are meant to cope with and survive war, not avoid it. In that sense, it is not surprising that a power politics image of the world and a foreign policy based on it will lead actors to take steps that will bring them progressively closer to the brink of war. The culture of war, like the culture of vendetta and dueling, is a trap. Once in the culture one must adopt the image and practices of the culture in order to survive, but to do that one must fight. Realism may provide clues to the dynamics of processes that lead to war, but it will provide little aid into understanding how such worlds of war originate or can be superseded.

In general we can conclude that people have learned to fight by fighting. From major wars they have developed a set of lessons that recommend certain practices for dealing with war-threatening situations. In the West much of this folklore is embodied in power politics "theory." Upon critical reflection, it appears that these practices, rather than averting war, bring the parties closer to it. The reason for this is that, among equals, the practices of power politics are answered in kind: threats producing counterthreats, alliances producing counter-alliances, military build-ups leading to arms races, defeat of moderate strategies in one crisis leading to escalation in the subsequent crisis. A learning model is probably the best way to account for how one action (or step toward war) leads to the next. It seems leaders learn, in Singer's (1984, p. 6) words, "to behave in certain ways under these conditions, and those certain ways lead to escalation of these disputes, culminating in war." The point here is that the ways leaders behave is a function of learning to employ certain *realpolitik* practices in certain situations.

Domestic Prerequisites of War

What kinds of leaders and domestic political contexts are necessary for power politics to be implemented as the state's official foreign policy? In order to answer this question we need some classification system for differentiating leaders, elites and policy influencers according to whether they will be apt to adopt *realpolitik* practices. Historians have often recognized this need and indicate that among European monarchies the court was frequently divided over whether a policy of war or peace should be pursued. Typically these factions are referred to as the war party and peace party (see Braudel, 1966, p. 940). This nomenclature appears tautological for our purposes in that it does not precisely identify the characteristics of each faction that lead them to advocate their respective policies. The work of Frederick Hoffmann (1970) provides some insight on this question. In an analysis of legislative arms debates, he finds that conservative and radical arguments are always presented and seem unaffected by external factors. This leads him to conclude that a person's security views are not derived from "objective" factors, but are a function of individual beliefs and predispositions. Hoffmann's analysis suggests that *realpolitik* practices may in part be advocated because of personal predispositions, but his labels of conservative and radical seem much too broad, especially to describe arguments over military expenditures.

More precise and clearly focusing on personal predispositions is the hard-line/soft-line distinction (see Snyder and Diesing, 1977, pp. 297–310). It is much clearer that hard-liners as opposed to soft-liners are prone to adopting *realpolitik* practices, whereas either conservatives or radicals can be hard-liners. However, both the terms hard-liner and soft-liner can be regarded as somewhat pejorative from at least some point of view. An alternative would be to use the more neutral "hawk-dove" distinction but this is too time-bound to the Vietnam debate for an analysis meant to explain nineteenth- and twentieth-century wars. The term soft-liner can be replaced by "accommodationist," following the lead of Wittkopf and Maggiotto (1983) who compare hard-liners and accommodationists within the public and the elite. This seems appropriate, since no one ever says they are advocating a "soft line," but policy influencers often express the need to take a "harder line." In addition, the term hard-liner, although pejorative, seems less pejorative than other terms such as militarist, the latter being widely used in the period following the First World War. Finally, the hard-liner/accommodationist distinction is compatible with Singer's (1982, p. 43) proposal to delineate the conditions that generate "hawkish and doveish moves."

If in fact hard-liners and accommodationists are rivals who will continually debate with one another because of personal predispositions, it will always be difficult to avoid negative connotations from arising since each faction will always impugn the motives and policies of the other. The responsibility of the analyst is to define recognizable labels in a manner that is fairly neutral and precise enough so that one faction can be empirically distinguished from the other. For the purpose of this analysis, an accommodationist can be defined as an individual who has a personal predisposition that finds the use of force, especially war, repugnant, and advocates a foreign policy that will avoid war through compromise, negotiation, and the creation of rules and norms for nonviolent conflict resolution. Conversely, a hard-liner can be defined as an individual who has a personal predisposition to adopt a foreign policy that is adamant in not compromising its goals and who believes in the efficacy and legitimacy of threats and force. Although hard-liners have a general predisposition to *realpolitik* practices, the two positions are not identical. Realism is a detailed intellectual position that is more subtle and sophisticated than the general stance connoted by the term *hard-line*. This means that hard-liners will tend to emphasize the coercive aspects of power politics and neglect advice on prudence (see Leng, 1983) and messianism. This suggests, of course, that there can be both hard-line (i.e., militant) idealists and accommodative realists. In any case, what is of interest here is that a distinction can be made in the foreign policy elite and the public between accommodationists (and all other non-hard-liners) on the one hand, and hard-liners, on the other.[7]

It is likely that once hard-liners are in power, or are highly influential in the domestic environment, *realpolitik* practices will be implemented. So to uncover the domestic political (as opposed to structural) roots of war we must explain the rise of hard-liners. It can be assumed that there are always hard-liners and accommodationists within a population and what Mannheim (1952, pp. 304–7, 315–18) calls the "spirit of the times" will determine which will prevail. It is this nebulous spirit of the times that must be more precisely analyzed if we are to discover under what domestic and global conditions hard-liners are likely to be influential within the elite and in the public. It is not inconceivable that these conditions are so powerful that hard-liners will push accommodationists out of the body politic. We will begin by looking at an initial domestic political context and then see how that is changed by external factors.

To determine whether a domestic political context is initially more favorable to the influence of hard-liners or accommodationists all one has to do is to look at the "lessons of the past" that prevail in the political culture. This is not a difficult task since these lessons are reflected in the popular media and the publications of the intelligentsia. The crucial question is: Where do these lessons come from? It seems that in all societies these lessons are derived from the most traumatic experiences that the society as a whole goes through. For most, this is the last major war. Subsequent events, particularly more limited wars, will affect those lessons, but for the generation that lived through the traumatic experience only another major war will lead to an opportunity for rethinking the lessons. Using a general learning model (Vasquez, 1976) one can assume that these lessons will be passed on to the next generation through socialization and will be accepted, although with less emotional attachment.

Lessons of history (May, 1973; Jervis, 1976, ch. 6) seem to be debated just before, during, and/or just after a major war, and then once again as a new war looms. Whether hard-liners or accommodationists are favored in the postwar environment depends on whether hard-line policies are judged to have succeeded or failed during the last war. The key variables in making this assessment are whether the war was won or lost and whether the effort was regarded as being worth the costs in terms of what was gained. This produces four possible outcomes, as illustrated in Figure 18.1.

The more determinative variable is costs, with casualties being the major factor (Mueller, 1971). Extreme hard-liners will always see the war as worth the costs, in part because of their attitude toward force

Figure 18.1   Prevalence of hard-liners/accommodationists in
the domestic political environment

and in part because they attach a higher value to what is at stake in a war. Extreme accommodationists will always find the costs too high because they generally regard war as a repugnant if not immoral practice that produces few benefits. Which position will prevail will be determined by how most people between these two extremes adduce the costs. Wars that are adduced as *not* having been worth the costs lead to a postwar domestic political context in which accommodationists tend to prevail. Conversely, wars that are adduced to have been worth the costs lead to a domestic political context in which hard-liners prevail.

The second variable, victory or defeat, determines the stability of the domestic political context and the extent to which the derived lessons are susceptible to internal debate and external influence. A victory that is seen as not worth the costs and a defeat in a war that is seen as worth the effort are highly volatile domestic situations filled with cognitive dissonance. Such situations tend to divide the population more than the cognitively consistent situations and lead to recriminating questions, such as why was an unnecessary war fought, why was an important war lost. The First World War produced such a situation, with each of the major victors feeling the victory was not worth the costs (so that their interwar leaderships and domestic political environments were dominated by accommodationists), and with Germany having important segments of its society feeling that the war was worth the costs, and had been lost because of a stab in the back.

Of course the outcomes and assessments of some wars are clearer than others, so that each variable is treated as a continuum with a

376

stalemate demarked at the origin of the y-axis. The less drastic the victory or defeat, the less stable the subsequent domestic political context. In this sense, it is interesting to compare the Second with the First World War, and Figure 18.1 portrays the postwar domestic environment of the winners and losers. The second war was not only a more drastic defeat for Germany, but a clearer victory for the allies. In Germany, as well as Japan, the hard-liners were purged by the victors so that there was no one left to make the case that the war was worth the costs, although the tremendous costs would have made it difficult for the hard-liners to regain power after the disgrace of such a defeat. In the allies, accommodationists were soundly defeated because they and their policies were seen as bringing about the war in the first place, which hard-liners (probably incorrectly) believed could have been avoided by a hard-line policy. Such a situation is less likely to lead to a repeat of war between the same two parties than the situation produced after the First World War.[8]

Figure 18.1 provides a framework for determining and predicting the initial domestic political context prior to the rise of a new critical issue and external threat. It is hypothesized that after an appropriate time lag,[9] the domestic political context will be determined by whether the war was won or lost and whether it was adduced as worth the costs. The analysis assumes that a kind of law of political inertia will operate, allowing hard-line or accommodationist tendencies to prevail and be played out in a state's foreign policy until disturbed by some external factor or by a non-foreign-policy domestic issue.[10] For accommodationists, *ceteris paribus*, the rise of an external threat and involvement in crisis tend to lead to a rethinking of previous lessons and an increase in the influence of hard-liners among the elite, the public at large, and the opposition. Conversely, for hard-liners, defeat in a crisis leads to a more coercive strategy in the next crisis (see Leng, 1986) so that only a terrible defeat in a war leads to a rethinking of a hard-line position, *ceteris paribus*.

Having outlined the general tendencies of the domestic political context, I will now delineate the factors that will encourage the adoption of power politics. All other factors being equal, hard-liners will prefer *realpolitik* practices over all other options, but will adopt the least costly first. Once *realpolitik* practices are adopted by one side it is difficult for the target not to eventually respond in kind. This is because, if the target is accommodative, that will only encourage the initiator to repeat its previously successful strategy. If the strategy is repeated, then the accommodationists in the target will lose influence to the hard-liners. Conversely, if the *realpolitik* practices are resisted, this leads to an escalation in means (see Vasquez and Mansbach, 1984,

377

pp. 428–9). The introduction of power politics, then, drives out accommodative influences and leaders on both sides and increases the influence and power of hard-liners in each rival. This is reinforced by the tendency of both sides to introduce more symbolic and transcendent stakes.[11]

A domestic context dominated by hard-liners will constantly push the leadership to take actions that are riskier and more hard-line than they would normally take. In order to keep domestic support, leaders try to placate hard-liners, but in the absence of success this is difficult since policy influencers always tend to advocate riskier policies than leaders adopt. If a crisis drags on or there is a series of crises, the leadership will try to get out of a situation that portends to drain domestic support by adopting any policy or strategy that may result in victory, despite the risks.[12] Likewise, the leadership will be less likely to oppose the bold action that holds out the promise of victory for fear of loss of support. These domestic factors reinforce the tendency produced by crisis interactions to escalate moves that fail either within a crisis or from one crisis to the next. If leaders resist these domestic pressures and do not produce a success, then they are apt to be replaced by hard-liners.[13]

Similar factors are at work at the bureaucratic level. Each bureaucracy as well as each bureaucratic decision maker wants to avoid failure. In a crisis or war, the military will push for the use of the greatest firepower because they regard this as the most likely to produce victory (and therefore for them the least risky). They are aided by hard-liners in the public and legislature (or party) who demand all possible means be used. In addition, in the military and the foreign policy-making establishment some individuals see the crisis (or war) as an opportunity for rapid career advancement if they can develop a successful solution to the foreign policy (or military) problem. These individuals, who are probably risk-acceptant, advocate the bold action. Thus, the prevalence of hard-liners in the domestic political environment not only increases the probability that the leadership will be hard-line, but sets up partisan and bureaucratic incentives for taking harder and riskier policies.

The probability that an actor will employ any *realpolitik* practices in order to gain stakes must be discounted by whether a global institutional context exists with effective procedures for resolving issues, especially security issues (see Lee, Kegley and Raymond, 1985). Since states, including those led by hard-liners, will always adopt the strategy that seems to be the most effective, but least costly, they will use the non-violent "rules of the game" first. But if the system is too rigged and the issues too fundamental, then they will resort to the various unilateral means within the power politics arsenal (see Mansbach and Vasquez, 1981, pp. 310–13).

This suggests that all other factors being equal, hard-liners have a more difficult time than accommodationists in getting policies accepted because the rules of the game are usually followed first, and force is both costly and risky. Accommodationists maintain their influence by using both these factors to their advantage. When accommodationists prevail after a war their main concern is to establish a postwar order that will prevent the use of force and war. This can lead to an attempt to create a new global order, including a system of rules and norms that preserves it but allows for the settlement of disputes (as at Versailles and the Congress of Vienna); or to an attempt to prevent national participation in another war (as in the Neutrality Acts and constitutional provisions in the Federal Republic of Germany and in Japan after the Second World War). In either case, accommodationists establish a set of rules (or laws) that correct the errors (or conditions) that led to the previous war. Just as the military prepares to fight the previous war, accommodationists try to prevent the last war. The Neutrality Acts provide an excellent illustration of this. Correctly assessing that the United States became involved in the First World War because of its insistence on trading with belligerents, the acts prohibited actions on the part of the USA which accommodationists felt led to the previous war. In the Vietnam War, accommodationists passed the War Powers Act not only to prevent the President from unilaterally involving the country in a war, but also to prevent the nation from gradually becoming involved in a war without an explicit decision by Congress.

The rules accommodationists establish, whether at the global or domestic level, have the effect of preserving their influence and reducing that of hard-liners. Domestically their rules are obstacles to implementing previous practices or positions that led to war, and these usually include either explicitly or indirectly a variety of hard-line options. At the global level, the new norms and rules have a legitimacy that requires that they must be first tried before any unilateral (and hence hard-line) action can be initiated.[14] This means that accommodative actions will always be taken first, and hard-liners will not be in a position to influence policy unless those actions fail. Learning theory suggests that failure must be persistent before there is a drastic change in policy, since the initial response to failure is incremental change (see Vasquez, 1976).

Accommodationists also establish their prevalence more directly by creating a dominance over the intellectual and popular opinion about the lessons to be derived from the previous war. Often finding hard-liners responsible for the war, they take direct measures against the potential allies of hard-liners. This usually involves a drastic reduction in the military and a disparagement of its values. Similar sentiments are directed toward defense industries who are regarded as war profiteers and may as in the First World War be regarded as one of the causes of war. The end of the war and these sentiments lead to a reduction in the size and influence of the two natural institutional bases of hard-line support—the military and defense industries.[15] In addition, these reductions in capability make it more difficult to take hard-line actions.

The prevalence of accommodationists is also aided by the fact that the use of force and war is an almost irreversible act and hence requires a high degree of commitment and certainty to overcome the natural inertia and conservativeness of collectivities (see Singer, 1984, pp. 23–4), a conservativeness that has been immeasurably increased by the negative lessons associated with the last war. This effect will be particularly powerful within the bureaucracy, who take their cue from the accommodationist leadership that hard-line advocacy will not advance one's career. Even within the military, there will be an unwillingness to become involved in any action unless it is clear that there will be a rapid and clear victory that will lead to a rehabilitation of the military's lost reputation in the previous war. The unwillingness of the foreign policy bureaucracy and the military to advocate risky hard-lines will be reinforced by popular sentiment which, under accommodationist sway, will be seen as difficult to mobilize for war, thereby making hard-line actions more costly and uncertain.

These internal actions are not without external effects. A state with a reduced military, low military expenditures, and a public that is difficult to mobilize is not very threatening. The willingness of the leadership to take accommodative actions also makes war less likely. More important, however, is that if the decision to go to war involves a series of steps, the prevalence of accommodationists delays the onset of war by their reluctance to take steps that lead to war and increase the influence of hard-liners in the opposing side. Such steps include an unwillingness to compromise, the use of coercion and force, the making of alliances and the decision to build up the military. Of course, if the opponent takes advantage of the accommodationists to push too far, then support for accommodationist policies declines and the sentiment for a change in policy rises. Accommodationists have a difficult time in maintaining influence in the face of coercion and hostility. The human tendency to strike back in the face of persistent hostility overwhelms accommodationists' ability to control the situation and plays into the hands of hard-liners.

Conclusion

The above analysis is meant to demonstrate that opening up the black box can provide a more complete and accurate account of the outbreak of wars of rivalry by identifying the kind of foreign policy that leads to war and the domestic political context that encourages the adoption of that foreign policy. The driving out of accommodationist influences in the domestic environment of both rivals is an important step toward war and a domestic prerequisite for public mobilization. The introduction of each new realist practice—alliance formation, trickery, military build-up, crisis diplomacy and arms races—has domestic consequences in the other side that increase the influence and support of hard-liners and the support of more escalatory actions. Simultaneously, these practices lead to an increase in hostility between rivals, greater insecurity and the propensity to overreact (Holsti, North, Brady, 1968). The outbreak of war between equals must be seen in this light. It is a process that produces a situation that each side has learned can only be handled by going to war (Mead, 1940).

This act is rare within the global system, because even hard-liners will only adopt it after the more available, less costly means have failed, and only after they have learned that the *realpolitik* practices short of war fail to bring about their goals. But if rivals are to avoid war altogether, their leaders must learn that power politics is part of the culture of war and will tend to bring them closer to war than to peace. If peace is to be maintained among equals, especially in the nuclear age, then new institutions for resolving issues must be invented and new ways of contending for stakes must be learned.

Notes

An earlier version of this chapter was presented to the World Congress of the International Political Science Association, July 17, 1985, Paris, France. Support for this work has been provided by a Fulbright research grant, a Rutgers competitive fellowship, and the Rutgers University Research Council. My thanks to each of these sponsoring groups for their support and to Marie Henehan, J. David Singer, Peter Wallensteen, and the editors of this volume for valuable suggestions. The sole responsibility for the chapter is mine alone, however.

1 To treat these wars in this manner does not tell us very much. In particular to use only dyads for the two world wars (even though the possibility of intervention is measured) produces an expected-utility score that is too high, in that it makes the initiation of the war appear as a much more rational and calculating decision than it was. My argument is that the 'calculations' in complex wars involving more than two parties are so

381

difficult for leaders to make that explanations other than expected-utility must be introduced to account for their behavior. Bueno de Mesquita, 1981, pp. 158–9, does recognize that in certain circumstances (e.g., when nonaligned states) utility calculations may become so difficult that leaders are either behaving less like utility maximizers or are more prone to miscalculate. For his justification of the way he treats the two world wars, see pp. 99–100.

2 These cases pose a problem for Bueno de Mesquita because if he succeeds in predicting the initiation, as he does in the way he treats the two world wars, then he fails in predicting the outcome. There are times when his theory would not predict that the initiator would win, but he does not tell us if the two world wars fall into this category (p. 153). For his discussion of the Second World War see pp. 173–6.

3 The critical distinction is between theory and practice and not among power politics, *realpolitik* or realist, all of which tend to refer to the same phenomenon. In this analysis, I try to reserve the term "realism" for an intellectual body of thought, whereas "power politics" and "*realpolitik*" (which I use synonymously) can refer to a body of practices or theory, depending on the context.

4 The point that needs to be emphasized is that power politics behavior only occurs in certain contexts, namely, those involving security issues of the highest salience. Further, not all international politics or even most of international politics is devoted to these issues, as realists contend. Hence, it is incorrect to assume that security is the only or main goal of decision makers in any given historical period or interstate relationship (see Vasquez, 1983, pp. 216–17). Indirect support for this assumption is provided by Gochman and Leng (1983) who find that the initial use of threats leads to an escalation in hostile bargaining techniques only when "vital" issues (political independence and control of domestic and contiguous territory) are at stake and not when other issues are under contention. This suggests that *realpolitik* practices are likely to be employed only in response to certain threats and are not used to deal with just any political situation, an important qualification that is overlooked by the notion that "all politics is a struggle for power" (Morgenthau, 1960, p. 27).

5 For evidence that often more than one confrontation occurs before war breaks out, see Wallensteen, 1981.

6 This is even true when short-term serious disputes lead to a victory. The resentment produced by Prussian victory in the Franco-Prussian war, by French victory in the two Morocco crises, and by Austro-Hungarian victory in the 1908 Bosnia and Herzegovina crisis were critical in producing the hostility vented in 1914.

7 I include this parenthetical remark to indicate that the main opponents of hard-liners may not be accommodationists, but isolationists. Since in this analysis I am primarily interested in the rise of hard-liners, I have not sought to construct a complete typology. See Wittkopf and Maggiotto, 1983, for such an effort; it includes hard-liners as one type among four. In addition to isolationists and accommodationists, they identify internationalists. In normal times this is a clearly identifiable opinion group, but as war approaches I believe internationalists become increasingly difficult to differentiate from hard-liners the way I define them and describe their behavior in this chapter. The primary example that supports my point is Franklin D. Roosevelt.

8 Although the main purpose of Figure 18.1 is to analyze domestic political factors and the adoption of foreign policy practices, it also provides a framework for examining the effects of the postwar domestic environment on the stability of the peace and the likelihood of war recurring. In this sense, the least stable peace would be a postwar situation in which hard-liners prevailed in both rivals, or a situation that subsequently changed to that. Next, would be one in which hard-liners prevailed in the losers and accommodationists in the winners, followed by the situation in which hard-liners prevailed in the winners and accommodationists in the losers. Finally, the most stable peace would be one in which accommodationists prevailed in both. Such a framework may help elucidate how successful universalistic policies and regimes (see Doran, 1971; Wallensteen, 1984) are in preserving a postwar peace and order. Although a detailed case study would need to be conducted to see whether a war produced a particular combination of postwar environments, the Six-Day War, the First World War, the Second World War and the Congress of Vienna seem to be examples of each of the four types listed above.

9 This analysis assumes that there may be a time lag before the predicted group prevails, but that by the time a new issue and threat arises (around fifteen years after the war) the domestic context should be clear. Thus after 1918, Lloyd George and the French took a hard line, while the Germans were accommodative during the Weimar Republic. This was to change in each side, thereby sustaining the description given in Figure 18.1. In the United States the change in sentiment was heralded by the defeat of the Versailles Treaty and Wilson's League of Nations, but even more significant were the Neutrality Acts of 1935-9.

10 While the domestic political environment will favor either a hard-line or an accommodationist tendency, the leadership of a state may not hold the prevalent position if it was brought to power on a non-foreign policy issue. Such a leadership, however, will still be constrained by the domestic context.

11 Hard-liners also gain in influence because their predictions that the other side poses a threat seem to be confirmed by the actions the other side takes. The success of these predictions, however, rests *in part* on a self-fulfilling prophecy.

12 These same factors play a role in the escalation of techniques during a war, and appear to apply to both open and closed polities.

13 The classic example is Churchill replacing Chamberlain, but such actions are not confined to democracies. Bethmann-Hollweg was driven from office in the midst of the First World War, in part, for opposing unrestricted submarine warfare, a policy which hard-liners knew would risk American intervention, but which they thought would bring victory before American participation could make a difference (Fischer, 1967, pp. 288–93).

14 Kegley and Raymond, 1982, and Lee, Kegley and Raymond, 1985, provide some evidence to support the notion that the discussion of norms and rules as legitimate restraints is associated with a reduction in the escalation of disputes to war.

15 These reductions, however, may not be to the prewar levels (see Russett, 1970b).

19

Cultural Influences on Foreign Policy

MARTIN W. SAMPSON III

In *Comparing Public Policy* Douglas Ashford (1978, p. 82) comments that "there is probably more similarity across policies for one country in how policies are formed and implemented than there is for the same policy across several countries". The growing interest in decision making may result in some attention to the accuracy and implications of this surprising comment, for the decision-making topic has recently become more prominent in numerous contexts. Command and control have become a significant issue in the nuclear deterrence literature; the notion of a monolithic state seems less satisfactory than it once did in the political economy literature; interest in policies and decision making have supplanted the fixation on behavior in the comparative foreign policy field; and in ways unimagined thirty years ago the business administration field has become concerned with questions of how foreign businesses operate and what US businesses can absorb from those practices. Among these trends the latter is interesting in that it directly confronts the question of whether cultural differences temper decision-making processes in various national settings. Such an inquiry is not yet evident in the comparative foreign policy literature, and there has been little effort to understand how much is indeed foreign about foreign policy decision-making practices in various countries and whether comparative studies can demonstrate that such differences matter.

This chapter considers the importance of culture as an influence on foreign policy decision making. There are two general rationales for this study. One is the possibility that cultural differences have an important impact on organizational behavior and thus are an element of national foreign policy decision-making processes. The second rationale for this inquiry is that cultural differences are observable in a variety of settings, such as businesses, educational institutions, voluntary organizations, and the like. As a phenomenon that stretches across a wide variety of functional settings, cultural factors should be relatively easy to study and analyze, thus providing a set of ideas for thinking about the less accessible realm of foreign policy decision making within a particular nation.

For relatively homogeneous nations national culture is a more meaningful term than it is for nations with numerous ethnic groups. For that reason, the cases selected for this preliminary study are France and Japan, which are also roughly comparable as noncommunist, industrial, and parliamentary democracies. The first section of the chapter discusses basic aspects of the approach developed in the subsequent discussion. The second section focuses on certain cultural features of individuals in each of the two nations and then discusses the effects of these features on organizations. In the third section these effects are compared with the generalizations in the existing literature on the foreign policy decision-making process in each of these nations to ascertain whether there seems to be a general congruence between the processes of other organizations and the processes found within the foreign policy decision-making arena. The concluding section considers the implications of the study.

Introduction

LeVine (1973, p. 104) defines culture as an organized collection of rules focusing on the ways in which members of a population should communicate, think, and interact with one another and their environments. Nadler, Nadler and Broome (1985, p. 89) describe culture as a "system of socially created and learned standards for perceiving and acting shared by members of an identity group." Barnlund and Araki (1985, p. 25) say "in a sense the rules that govern human interaction within a community are the culture. Intangible and vague as they may seem, they make a meaningful existence possible for the members of any human community." Hofstede (1980, p. 43) refers to culture as "collective mental programming of a group of people in an environment." He also states (1980, p. 13) that "societies, organizations, and groups have ways of conserving and passing on mental programs from generation to generation with an obstinacy which many people tend to underestimate."

As used in the present study, this set of norms, standards, rules or collective mental programing refers to a national culture that has certain properties. First, these socially created and learned factors exist

385

across a variety of institutions within a single nation-state; one may detect them in many different functional settings—families, associations, businesses and governmental organizations—and one may also detect them over a large range of time periods. Second, these factors are not rigidly binding upon all people of that society at all times. Cultural norms are typical and are common within the population, but they are not deterministic in the sense of being equally binding upon all relevant people at all times. One expects them in a probabilistic fashion; certain tendencies are more likely in one culture than in another. Third, the norms and practices are familiar to people of that particular culture. Those people routinely encounter and deal with, respond to, and act upon these particular norms, whether their own behaviors are accurately described by the norms or not. Fourth, as sets of rules these aspects of culture can be appropriately regarded as incentives which have the effect of organizing the structuring behavior.

Process, Not Content

In asking how national cultural variables affect foreign policy decision making it is important to distinguish the present study from a different tradition in the study of foreign policy and international relations. This earlier tradition finds direct links between individuals' characteristics in a national population and the content, not the process, of that nation's foreign policy. Its concern is with the details of the policy choice, not with how the choice was made.

Akira Iriye's analysis illustrates this approach. In his view

> it becomes obvious that the question of the relationship between domestic culture and external affairs has been at the core of historical debate on the foreign policies of Nazi Germany, Stalinist Russia, Wilsonian America, and many other societies. The debate between A. J. P. Taylor and his critics has centered around the degree to which Nazi culture can be said to have preconditioned Hitler's foreign policy, and the debate between the exponents of what Daniel Yergin has called the "Riga Axioms" and the "Yalta Axioms" has involved differences of opinion regarding the cultural foundations of Soviet foreign policy.

(Iriye, 1979, p. 116)

Iriye (1979, p. 129) links the "isolationist and exceptionalist impulse" in US foreign policy to the importance in American culture of "private initiatives, where power was equated with commercial and economic development." Iriye (1979, p. 125) also quotes writers in the United States during the Second World War who found explanations for the bombing of Pearl Harbor in " 'ingrown cultural, non-material tendencies . . . [that are] a tremendous danger inherent in the traditional

Japanese frame of mind'." The gist is that characteristics of individuals in certain cultures explain the prominence of certain values in the content of foreign policies.

The present study lacks confidence in such direct jumps from individuals to policy content. Its concern is the rather different matter of whether cultures affect the decision-making process in certain identifiable and analytically useful ways. The underlying proposition here is in some ways akin to the conclusions of Child and Kieser (1979, p. 267) whose article on German and British workers observes that "there can be no question that, contrary to the view implied in some recent writings, a sociologically valid theory of organizations must take cultural settings into account." Thus this discussion is concerned with policy content only insofar as it is a reflection of the policy process.

Processes, Not Structures

A study of decision making and culture could focus on either decision-making structures or decision-making processes (or both). Work such as Steiner's compendium on foreign ministries of the world (1982) demonstrate that there are potentially interesting differences of structure between various foreign ministries. Aiken and Bacharach (1979, p. 216) review recent research on the impact of culture on the internal functioning of organizations (not foreign policy organizations). They juxtapose studies that "generally conclude that there was little evidence for any cultural impact on the behavior of organizations" with other studies that emphasize "how the social and cultural context affects the behavior of organizational members" (1979, p. 216). Their judgment is that studies that found little or no relationship between culture and organizations tended to focus on structure, while the studies that did find strong relationships between culture and organizations focused instead upon process aspects of those organizations. (In Aiken and Bacharach's terms structure includes size, differentiation and specialization, while process includes influence and decision making.) Aiken and Bacharach conclude that "it is probably the failure to draw this distinction between structure and process which has contributed to the difference in findings . . . as well as the relative neglect of the wider culture context in which organizations function." Consistent with Aiken and Bacharach's interpretation of a relevant but non-foreign-policy literature, this discussion emphasizes organizational processes rather than organizational structures and leaves that topic for future exploration.

This study looks for some kind of bridge between ways in which individuals of a particular culture operate, the consequent characteristic aspects of the organizations within that culture, and the implications of those characteristics for the outputs of those organizations. In other words there are three underlying questions here. Is national culture an important—but not exclusively important—source of variance among decision-making structures of various countries? If that premise is correct then can information that can be learned about decision making in easily studied organizations and settings within a nation help us understand decision making in the less accessible setting of a ministry of foreign affairs? Are there logical relationships between those aspects of the decision process and policy outputs?

Culture and Organization

Japan

An essay by Japanese psychiatrist L. Takeo Doi (1976, p. 89) argues that *amae* pervades and actually makes the Japanese patterns of communication. Doi observes that there is a rich Japanese vocabulary surrounding this concept, which is the idea of depending and also presuming upon another person's love. The emphasis given to unanimous agreement or consensus in Japanese culture is in a sense "a token that the mutuality of all members has been preserved." Doi goes on to observe that the "well known Japanese fondness for hesitation or ambiguity of expression can also be explained along the same line. Japanese hesitate . . . when they fear that what they have in mind might be disagreeable to others."

Empathy and communication are important for the maintenance of group identities, and Barnlund (1975) offers some useful observations about Japanese culture in regard to communication. What Americans disclose about themselves in average, routine discussions exceeds what the Japanese disclose about themselves in intimate discussions. Japanese culture favors evasion or silence rather than frank, open conflict, and Japanese people prefer formal, regulated encounters rather than informal contacts. Cushman and King (1985, p. 127) state that empathy is also a significant device for conflict avoidance in Japan, and that communications "take place in *kuuki*, a term that refers to human atmosphere or the similar vibrations that create a feeling of commonality or that all are moving in a common direction."

Cathcart and Cathcart focus on the family and refer to *keifu*, bond, and *on*, indebtedness. *Keifu* is important because of the permanence of the family as an institution, which is not necessarily limited to biological kinship. Indebtedness or dependency "in Japan is considered a natural and desirable trait capable of producing warm human relationships" and is something that is not to be escaped. *On*, the Cathcarts note,

388

Should be viewed as part of a group structure and not as a relationship between two persons only. Everyone in a group is at the same time an *on*-receiver and an *on*-giver . . . [*On*] is based upon the natural dependency inherent in human relationships rather than upon inherent individual qualities or attributes that enable some human beings to assume superior positions to others.

(Cathcart and Cathcart, 1976, pp. 61–2)

Another theme the Cathcart study emphasizes is *oyabun-kobun*. A superior person empathizes and appreciates the role of the inferior; the inferior receives support from the superior whom he or she serves and in return gives loyalty to the superior. This "makes for a unique structure in Japanese groups . . . not found in American groups, where relationships are dependent on changing role functions and where the ideal group is one in which every person is considered equal to every other one" (1976, p. 62).

Across these studies of Japanese culture are certain themes that pertain to communication patterns, authority relationships, and/or conflict resolution. There is commitment to avoidance of open, harsh conflict, a commitment that coincides with other factors, such as recognition of dependence upon people as a normal, positive circumstance. There seems to be no jarring transition from discussion of Japanese culture in general to discussion of how Japanese groups function, for the culture is heavily oriented toward groups. Indeed, it has been observed that Japan may have only one basic kind of group, namely the family, and that other groups in Japanese society, including the nation, are fundamentally a replication of that institution.

That certain things follow for Japanese business organizations is logical but also empirically clear from studies of business organizations in Japan. Kume (1985, p. 235) presents a list of cultural factors in the USA and Japan that are reflected in business organizations. Kume describes the Japanese practice for reaching decisions as consensual, reflecting cultural factors such as "acceptance of a given option, conformity, tentativeness." The locus of decision making is the group, with leaders facilitating shared responsibility; the attendant cultural factors are collectivism, interdependence and group orientation. Kume describes the criteria of decision making as "intuition, group harmony," reflecting cultural factors of "holistic, spiritual consistency."

Illustrative of management techniques that are congruent with Japanese social norms is *ringesi* or the practice of circulating documents among relevant people within an organization, eliciting ideas from each person prior to the finalization of the document. Tsuji (1968, p. 457) describes this as "literally a system of reverential inquiry about a superior's intentions . . . although seldom defined, it is a . . . word to refer to a system whereby administrative plans and decisions are made through the circulation of a document called ringisho." He goes on to note that this process, beginning with a document originally drafted by a low-level official, then discussed "by the officials of all relevant bureaus and divisions," and finally approved by the top person who typically approves it "without change or modification because of this long process of prior scrutiny" is "a fundamental characteristic of Japanese administrative behavior, organization, and management" (1968, p. 458).

The *nemawashi* mechanism is discussed in numerous studies of Japanese organizations, including Ting-Toomey (1985), Cushman and King (1985) and Kume (1985). This is a cultural process in which extensive consultation occurs among people and problems are resolved "gradually and subtly, and the final solution has the widespread support from all parties concerned" (Ting-Toomey, 1985, p. 74). The term literally refers to the process of trimming roots as a tree is transplanted so that in time the main root of the tree can flourish. "Through *nemawashi* or personal interaction, one seeks to improve the empathy and cooperation necessary to attain group harmony" (Cushman and King, 1985, p. 127).

Thus in Japanese organizations efforts are made to avoid circumstances that produce clear-cut winners and losers within the organization or that force consensus to coincide with approval. Japanese organizations have a predictable deference to seniority, a practice of people attaching themselves to mentors, and patterns of employees devoting careers to one organization. This is a system that is typically dominated by the upper level, but that domination exists in a style that does not maximize speed or minimize dispersal of information. The inclusion of a wide array of people implies a relatively cumbersome process that Americans would regard as too time-consuming and Japanese would regard as insulation against the apparent carelessness of rapid, high-handed decisions by Americans (Barnlund, 1975). The dispersion of information within such a system also suggests that consideration of options and consideration of details that pertain to a general, unanimously accepted course of action will be more informed and careful than would otherwise be the case. Within such systems jarring inconsistencies are unlikely between what Westerners would describe as decision and implementation stages of policy processes. What Stewart (1985, pp. 193–6) calls "radical empiricism" may also follow; in his view Japanese businesses rank very high in uncertainty avoidance, carefully considering details and then preferring to adopt a course of action and stay with it rather than completely rethink a basic approach. In sum, one would expect that such a setting would produce a stream of decisions that as a whole reflect less conceptual flexibility, less inconsistency, and more attention to implications of choices than would be true of organizations found in some other cultural settings.

France

Crozier (1964, p. 227) states that "French successes have always been most conspicuous at the two ends of the scale—individual explorations in science and adventures where man is complete master of his own endeavor; and large scale routine operations where a bureaucratic system of organization that protects the individual completely from human interference is more efficient than more flexible competitive systems." The individual-as-master extreme would seem very different from what one would expect of Japanese culture, and a preliminary examination of literature on French cultural values produces a quite different impression from the literature on Japan. Major themes include a markedly different capacity to form and belong to groups and very different mechanisms for avoiding conflict.

Crozier's study of France offers extensive information about French culture. Clark notes from that work five enduring cultural traits:

(1) France is essentially a congery of households containing the major unit of all social strategies—the family. This has a strong hold over its members and possesses a negative attitude to the collective action of outsiders.

(2) The individual becomes isolated and consequently avoids having face-to-face relationships and finds difficulty in co-operating. The individual depends for protection on the impersonal rules which free him or her from interference by superordinates.

(3) Authority is highly centralized and yet its operation is constrained by extensive impersonal rules. This means that the leadership styles associated with the American executive do not have the same esteem because superordinates are most often involved in semi-judicial activities arbitrating between contending groups.

(4) The formal aspects always dominate the informal so that spontaneous social structures are always precarious. The informal associations are more often negative than constructive.

(5) France is typified by isolated strata which constrain the individual. Within any strata there are strong norms of equality and liberty, but the strata compete with one another to achieve greater privileges.

(Clark, 1979, p. 275)

A quick, superficial comparison of this list with what has been said about Japan would note sharp differences between the two cultures in regard to items (2) and (3). Item (1) which emphasizes the importance of the family also seems more a contrast than a similarity, for the family unit seems to generalize less well to other contexts in French than in

391

Japanese culture. Item (5) may also be very different. The egalitarian theme in French culture is very strong, yet Crozier labels it a jealous egalitarianism which becomes an important protection against external authority as well as a barrier to individual leadership.

Crozier argues that there is a dearth of informal groups in French society, whether one looks at the interactions of small children or at adult citizens confronted with a common problem. Drawing upon research by Wylie, Bernot, de Tocqueville, Goblot and Pitts, Crozier (1964, p. 219) agrees with Pitts that informal groups generally exist as "negative, unstable, and never expressed openly," something that has long been characteristic of France, and has contributed to a pattern in which leadership across different groups emerges in the culture only at the last possible moment.

An apparently different theme is the argument that philosophical diversity is acceptable in ways that behavioral diversity is not. Thus there is potential for conflict over forms and designs that does not exist as clearly for questions involving detail, substance and interaction modes. This point reflects Schonfeld's (1976, p. 63) observations about education in France: "within the authority-laden mode, there is a very high level of attempted and effective control over what to do, how to do it, and how to behave in class, but a very low level of idea control." He pushes this idea further with is comments about an instructor who disliked the system: "since he did not normatively approve of this system, he behaved as people who have dual guides to action behave under routine conditions—i.e., they strongly condemn a system in which they participate while adhering to that system's rules, even though, in fact, they are not forced to do so" (1976, p. 86). Nor in Schonfeld's (1976, p. 64) view is this normative tension atypical:

> The French secondary school students tend to have a dualistic normative structure. This permits those who desire serious modifications in the nature of the unit to remain behaviorally within the bounds of the actual system without suffering from cognitive strain . . . Such dual guides to action seem to have a particular value in a regimented social unit, the function of which is highly valued and in which the subordinates have developed a strong critical spirit.

When, then, does such a situation become untenable? His view is that the line is crossed "when the unit and/or its superordinates are perceived as not functioning effectively to achieve the goal sought through membership in the organization" (1976, p. 180).

Conflict in French culture is avoided in part through reliance upon formal structures and forms, which set ground rules that reduce the potential for open conflict. Conflict is acceptable in formal settings established to deal with conflict but the expression of conflict is much less acceptable in informal settings. Another mechanism for conflict reduction is apathy, which enables a person to avoid both conflict and dependency relationships. Another is the tendency of people to remain aloof, at least aloof in contrast to what Americans would expect from one another.

From these general observations certain implications might follow for French organizations. One, certainly, is a lack of underpinnings for consensual organization in the Japanese sense of that idea. Antipathy to informal organizations, the value of analytic diversity, difficulties of developing and accepting task-based leadership, and concern for remaining within established, general, formal guidelines are a combination that would seem to thwart both trust among people and extensive, creative and task-oriented communication within the groups. It should be expected that such organizations would be relatively weak in their capacity to disperse information widely, to absorb extensive amounts of information at the upper levels, or to implement a significant portion of the decisions that are taken. With upper-level people whose selection and advancement is heavily related to criteria external to the organization, there is relatively little scope for spectacular advancement based upon merit. By the same token one might anticipate that the incentives for people at the top to use or creatively seek more information from people lower down are muted. One would expect substantial resentment and complaint on the part of lower-level people but very little expression of that between levels, so that this tension would rarely become a force for positive change. The outputs of such an organization would presumably not be well tailored to the task of implementation. The preference for the general, overarching and abstract focus instead of attention to detail hardly leaves the implementation people high and dry; after all, they, too, can abide by the philosophic principles. The lack of incentives for focusing on detail, however, may mean that the philosophic tenets are ill-suited to the issue that has just been decided.

Granick (1979, pp. 88–9) notes in a typology of organizations that in France ascriptive criteria are very important in deciding who is to be hired for various positions. Moreover, the extent to which the "promotion of managers relies heavily on individual characteristics established prior to the beginning of the [person's] career" is especially pronounced in France (1979, pp. 88, 91). On this dimension he ranks France ahead of the United States and seven countries of Eastern and Western Europe examined in his study. It may be that this factor is akin to Maurice's report (1979, p. 52) that the authority and the technical hierarchies overlap much less in French than in German firms. According to Granick's typology France also ranks high in income differentials between manual workers and managers (as does the USA), and France ranks relatively low on the dimension that "a successful managerial career tyically includes holding responsible posts in three or more different job functions." Finally, France ranks low with respect to rapid turnover of managerial posts. The upshot, then, is a very formal, stratified, ascriptive and rigid setting for organizations.

Foreign Policy Decision Processes and Outputs

It seems evident that decision processes typically work in distinctive ways in France and in Japan for reasons of culture (as well as other factors that are beyond the scope of the present paper). The next step is to ascertain whether there is evidence of these kinds of features in the foreign policy decision making of France and Japan. That topic is a prelude to the subsequent consideration of how these kinds of factors affect foreign policy outputs.

Japan

Holland (1984) contrasts the US Department of State with the Japanese Ministry of Foreign Affairs. Primarily concerned with the structures, personnel practices and resources available to each of the two organizations, he pays less attention to the dynamics of decision making. And yet in his study are numerous indications of the kinds of organizational characteristics that were noted in the previous discussion of Japan. The importance of seniority, hierarchy, membership in a particular class of trainees, harmony, elitism and conformity are mentioned. So too is the notion that overly ambitious foreign service officer trainees do not fit in if their ambition is self-focused; instead, the proper expression of ambition is to work hard and to ensure that the entire training class succeeds and distinguishes itself as an outstanding group.

Holland states that there are substantial tensions between people who successfully moved through training programs into career positions and, on the other hand, noncareer foreign service officers. The noncareer people are likely to advance less rapidly than career people. A kind of second-class citizens in the Japanese foreign ministry, typically the noncareer people are specialists. Efforts to encourage career people to develop specialties have met extensive opposition (Holland, 1984, pp. 153–4); that role is thus relegated to people who have less stature and will not be competitors for the career people. Holland also notes that there tends to be extensive opposition to the inclusion of people from other ministries. (Thus a practice that is

394

commonplace in the United States is a challenge to the group identity of Japanese foreign service people.) The theme of loyalty to the group, then, has implications for behavior toward both insiders and outsiders.

One of the few other studies of foreign policy decision making in Japan is Fukui (1977), whose discussion of the decision-making process points at various aspects that would result in a relatively slow decision-making process. He characterizes decision as evolving, not made, and refers to the foreign ministry as subsystem-dominated. He notes a tendency to focus on one issue at a time. If that issue is routine and noncontroversial, then the process is akin to the *ringesi* process mentioned above. If the issue is more political and less routine, then the involvement of interest groups, members of the Diet, cabinet members and the like, may result in a process that seems quite unlike the *ringesi's* high degree of structure and excludes lower-ranking officials in the foreign ministry. Even so, however, a division head with jurisdiction over such an issue is rarely bypassed in the course of what appears to be a largely informal process.

Fukui observes that the number of people who work on an issue inside the foreign ministry seems to vary inversely with the number of outside officials and politicians who are concerned about the issue. This may mean that Japanese culture complicates the task of running an efficient foreign policy. On the other hand, implementation probably proceeds more smoothly in this setting than in many others. The effort devoted to consultation and development of a policy greatly facilitates the implementation of that policy, reducing the potential for slippage, disruption and policy subversion as the policy is carried out.

Both Holland and Fukui refer to staff shortages and a Japanese foreign service that is overworked, Holland providing data to compare Japan with other major nations in this regard. In Fukui's view the resource shortages are a major explanation of a tendency to deal with one issue at a time. Many cultural factors would, however, seem to exacerbate these problems, such as exclusion of noncareer people and the time devoted to decision making.

Fukui comments that the Treaties Bureau is in many respects the most powerful organization within the foreign ministry and that it "exerts a substantial unifying influence, no doubt contributing to the 'legalistic' mentality so often attributed to the ministry and its officials." This characteristic is in part reflective of the constraints imposed on Japanese foreign policy in the aftermath of the Second World War. At the same time it may also be the case that the leverage of this part of the foreign ministry is reflective of certain other factors. Given the bias against nongeneralist, noncareer people, it may follow that the Treaties Bureau encounters fewer opponents and obstacles than it would in a milieu in which inputs from accepted, respected specialists were expected and used. In a sense, then, there is a culturally related explanation of why few other bases of expertise can be advanced as alternative ways of organizing and unifying the Japanese foreign ministry.

These paragraphs have discussed culturally related features of the Japanese foreign ministry. The discussion is cursory, handicapped in part by the dearth of studies of routine decision making in Japan. Even so, it does provide some glimpses of a process that seems in many respects congruent with what one would observe in other organizations in Japan. Whether these factors have an impact on the outputs of Japanese foreign policy is a subsequent question.

Destler *et al.* (1976) suggest an affirmative answer to that question, as do some brief case studies by Watanabe (1978) and Holland (1984). According to Destler *et al.* (1976, p. 107):

> The line between what is political and what is cultural is not easy to draw. But certain characteristics of Japanese and American policy behavior appear to be based on deep-rooted cultural values and patterns of interpersonal relationships; thus they are not adequately explained by the structure of the two political systems.

The authors suggest that Japanese diplomats seem much more comfortable adapting themselves to what other people have proposed, ascertaining what the other side will yield or not yield on, then formulating a proposal of their own—even if the discussions were requested by Japan in the first place. Similarly, Prime Minister Sato made specific proposals on the Okinawa question only after several years of talks (Destler *et al.*, 1976, p. 108). The point may in part pertain to a concern about gathering all relevant details prior to committing Japan to a particular course of action. Holland describes negotiations for a consular convention in the 1960s as lasting two years and involving extensive clarification of detail. Put differently, these examples illustrate—but do not demonstrate—a characteristic that typifies Japanese foreign policy, namely a tendency to retrospectively develop a logic that ties earlier choices together.

These authors also detect an expectation that the stronger party will adapt itself to the weaker party, acknowledging the need of the other and making concessions specifically because it is the stronger of the two groups. Another factor is the importance of ambience among negotiators; if there is appropriate rapport, then trust rather than the details of specific agreements become the major element in the negotiation. Both points are evident in the textile negotiations of the early 1970s according to Destler *et al* (1976).

These authors also see Japanese policy as prone to a kind of immobility, transitory perhaps, but also predictable, while internal processes slowly work themselves out. Leaders among a Japanese policy group do not press each other inappropriately hard for solutions or decisions; thus discord within the Japanese government will typically not be resolved by a leader taking a firm, controversial stand that others are forced to accept. Holland describes negotiations about the visit of a US submarine to Japan in the 1960s, a process that lasted 21 months. The Japanese negotiators kept returning with questions

> that obviously had their genesis in earlier discussions between the ministry and the Science and Technology Agency, the Fishermen's Association, or the Defense Agency, or had resulted from queries from the Liberal Democratic Party or opposition parties.
>
> (1984, p. 129)

Holland (1984, p. 133) also describes a dispute in the 1980s between the Foreign Ministry and the Defense Agency over whether the Soviet Union is a major threat to Japan or not. The Foreign Ministry argued that the USSR is not a serious threat because it does not have a hostile intent, while the Defense Ministry argued that the threat exists because the USSR has weapons. The result was the production of a "Potential Threat Doctrine."

The tenor of Watanabe's (1978, pp. 81–3) discussion of currency revaluation issues in the early 1970s is similar. In two episodes Japan suffered because no decision could be reached to counter the prevailing policy of never closing currency markets. In 1972 the market finally was closed when another serious threat to the yen seemed imminent. These last cases illustrate another point: once a course of action is chosen the tendency is to persevere with that course of action, modifying it as necessary rather than making sharp, unexpected changes in the policy formed. Such changes are probably difficult to mesh with the highly consensual kind of system, which encourages expression of ideas but extensive acceptance by younger officials of the choices made by senior people and is also characterized by the ascription of second-class status to people who are specialists. In this regard Holland notes that an outcome of the nearly two years of negotiations about the consular treaty was that Japan then used the resulting document as the basis for negotiations with other countries on the same topic.

Each of these cases suggests a careful, lengthy process. None of the cases is characterized by flamboyant use of abstract principles or rapid, decisive intervention by top-level people or a closely held coordination process. The cases seem to reflect Fukui's idea that the cultural norms on consultation and development of consensus reinforce the involvement of domestic political forces in Japanese foreign policy.

397

France

Even fewer studies exist on French foreign policy decision making than on Japanese foreign policy decision making. The literature on the content, strategy or constraints operative on French foreign policy typically ignores details of a policy process. A few years ago William Wallace (1980, p. 289) noted that no full-scale study of the Quai d'Orsay, the French foreign ministry, has been done since 1961. Nor do there seem to be many case studies of episodes or issues in French foreign policy that shed much light on the process. For example, the French case (Farrands, 1985) in a recent volume devoted to the general topic of foreign policy implementation looks at external factors that complicated the implementation of French security policy in regard to Africa, not internal factors. A comparison of French organizations in general with French foreign policy decision making in particular can therefore draw upon only a modest number of studies of the foreign policy process.

In an earlier study Wallace (1978, p. 43) observed that among Bonn, London and Paris are "marked differences between . . . structure, status, and ethos which help to account for divergences in the management of foreign policy between the three governments." One of those differences is that in France the legislature plays a modest role in foreign policy matters; reportedly there is typically one plenary session a year that deals with foreign policy, and the foreign affairs committee has little information or clout. Officials of the Quai d'Orsay are thus far less preoccupied with parliamentary business than their opposite numbers in Bonn or London. A related point is emphasized in Smouts's (1977, p. 38) discussion of French foreign policy formulation and public opinion:

> In a general way, in France the feeling that politics is a dubious and rather obscure activity is accompanied, paradoxically enough, by a certain respect for the majesty of power. It is therefore easy to concede that "the high-ups" should keep certain pieces of information to themselves . . . Such an attitude means that restrictions on information arising from the specific exigencies of foreign policy are readily understood, the need for discretion is recognized, and public opinion is relatively unexacting.

Smouts goes on to observe that "in France the obvious imperatives of foreign policy are augmented by a cult of security extending throughout the entire administration and developed to the highest degree for questions affecting foreign relations."

In a fashion that is symmetric with the great-man interpretations of the foreign policy content of the de Gaulle era, studies of the French foreign policy decision-making process report that presidents under the Fifth Republic have been able to dominate the foreign policy arena and have chosen to do so. Kaminsky (1975, p. 55) comments that de Gaulle and Pompidou both preferred to personally make decisions and implement them rather than attempt to satisfy the diverse views of a council of ministers, a foreign affairs bureaucracy, or even an informal group of advisors. "De Gaulle, he notes, often made sudden, unilateral decisions." Wallace (1978, p. 43) offers a slightly different interpretation, namely that de Gaulle placed control of the direction of foreign policy in the Elysée, his own office, but felt that management of foreign policy belonged at the Quai d'Orsay. In a different study Wallace (1980, p. 277) states that the "Quai d'Orsay, in de Gaulle's presidency, had . . . an assured bureaucratic role in the preparation of dossiers for submission to the Elysee and the execution of Presidential decisions, even if its political role had been reduced from that which it played under the Fourth Republic."

These studies have very general references to bureaucratic resistance; issues in which the Elysée decision-making machinery fails to coordinate policy because it is either unaware of what is happening or insufficiently staffed to act; and issues in which the policy apparatus is stunned by a presidential decision. Two points might follow at this juncture. First, in Wallace's (1980, p. 278) view the overall structure is efficient because of effective presidential leverage on the lower levels:

> This structure, with its intense personalization of policy making and centralization of authority, allows for great flexibility in the management of selected issues for rapid initiatives taken with the President's authority and under his personal control. It is less a matter of bypassing the bureaucracy, as Presidents are forced to do in Washington when they are determined on initiatives, than of overriding a bureaucracy which accepts the ultimate authority of the Elyseé.

One can here suspect that there is a congruence between the apparent resilience of the structure to this kind of leadership and some aspects of French culture regarding philosophic ideas, doing things properly, and avoidance of conflict.

A major reform of the Quai d'Orsay occurred during the Giscard years. This reform resulted in increased numbers of personnel and in a reorganization to replace certain functional divisions with geographic divisions. It would be most interesting to know what explains the pattern of post-de Gaulle presidents bypassing the Quai d'Orsay, who initiated the reform, and what kinds of expectations surrounded the reform effort. Hypothetically the reform might be the outgrowth of extensive discussions between top-level and lower-level people, but a comparison of Japanese and French cultural influences on organizations does not exactly point toward France as the country where that kind of reform would occur. Two other possibilities are more likely: the reform may have been mandated from the top or it may have resulted from a major crisis lower down that produced some reform initiatives from the Quai d'Orsay itself.

These comments about the process can be juxtaposed with what one might expect to find based upon the earlier discussion of French culture and French organizations. From the organization literature one might expect a very centralized process. One would anticipate that top-level people would rely to only a limited extent on the lower levels, giving them fewer incentives to be pragmatic or constructively aware of contradictory details than is the case in Japan. The importance of criteria external to the job setting for establishing the prestige of a person would produce influential people at the upper level whose clout is based neither upon longevity nor upon expertise. This situation is the opposite of that found in Japan, where there are very strong norms against outsiders who have not come through the ranks or are not career people. The implication for France is a lesser quality of information and knowledge that can be brought to bear upon a particular issue and less capacity of the apparatus to gather information. Another implication might be significant frustration at lower levels stemming from violations of the general structure or from nearly automatic deference to the President. Another characteristic, summarized by Stewart's (1985, p. 187) references to the importance of logical considerations, principles and concepts in devising strategy, is a process that devotes attention to abstract formulations that are guidelines rather than precise answers for specific circumstances. Clearly the consideration of information available about French foreign policy decision making provides less than is needed to cogently substantiate these ideas, yet there does seem to be a congruence between foreign policy decision making and other kinds of French organizations.

What should be expected about the output of the French foreign policy process if those expectations are extrapolations from the studies of French organizations? Stewart refers to an emphasis on logic, concepts and theories, and also to leadership as a function of role. Those points imply a propensity for an abstract foreign policy. Abrupt changes in content of such formulations are also to be expected when the top person changes an opinion. Certainly there might be a pattern of choices that require no implementation (e.g., declarations) and, alternatively, other choices that lack workable, tractable guidelines. Farrands (1985, p. 76), for example, refers to Giscard d'Estaing's early policy toward Africa as

> conducted in the light of events elsewhere. It had three faces: liberalism, economic self-interest, and strategic insecurity. Each of these was a

"rational" response, given France's history and perceived situation, but these did not add up to an implementable policy programme even where the separate elements could be pursued.

(Judging from the consideration of French culture and organizations one would expect that the lower levels would complain about this kind of problem but not in ways that would challenge the authority of the upper-level people, improve subsequent policy, or force any drastic reform of the foreign policy process.)

These kinds of factors are apparent in a comparison of US and French policies that Hoffmann (1967, p. 66) made during the Vietnam War. In his view American policy tends to be very pragmatic, less concerned about the long run, and at least partially rooted in intra- and interagency bargaining. The qualities of French policy are very different. A long-range vision is manifest, there is a remarkable capacity for short-run flexibility, and there may be numerous short-run conflicts in what is done. That assessment is an apt generalization about French policy many years later. The grand-theme idea appears in general assessments of French foreign policy (e.g., Hanreider and Auton, 1980; Macridis, 1985) and is most eloquently stated by Chirac (1978). It is also evident in more specific studies. For example, de La Serre and Defarges (1983, p. 62) note that the Quai d'Orsay welcomed the establishment of the European Political Cooperation (EPC) as a means of increasing its participation in European politics but that things did not work out that way, since the EPC has subsequently been used as a presidential platform "for affirming principles . . . while reserving for France the possibility of independent policy making" (1983, p. 66). In that context they identify examples of France staking out its own, independent positions, such as Mitterrand's (1983, p. 68) renunciation of the 1980 Venice Declaration and Mitterrand's policy toward El Salvador.

One can assume that a continuity between earlier eras and the Mitterrand era is a foreign policy apparatus whose lower and middle levels are rarely asked for advice and continually expected to cope with abstract, forthrightly logical policy ideas from on high that pose implementation problems. But there are no studies that substantiate or undermine that assumption. Clearly some continuities exist between the Mitterrand foreign policy and that of his predecessors, including the extensive use of personal diplomacy and the appearance of a President dominating the foreign policy process. Whether the content of Mitterrand's policy is vintage Gaullist (Hoffmann, 1984–5) or is a sharp change in the direction of "realism" (DePorte, 1984), aspects of Mitterrand's policy seem very reminiscent of Hoffmann's 1967 observations about the nature of French foreign policy. DePorte argues that less attention is now devoted to the proclamation of grand themes, but there continues to be a short-run compartmentalization of the policy, such that there is a clear logic within each category and yet extensive short-run clash between categories. Examples include France's strong support for US deployment of missiles in Europe coupled with an opposite stance toward US foreign economic policy, or a variety of rationales for seeking constructive relationships with certain countries, which, in the aggregate, have had French diplomats pursuing Algeria, Libya, Israel, the PLO, Egypt and Iraq almost simultaneously.

France, of course, is not the only nation whose foreign policy has tensions of these kinds. In the United States one would likely ascribe them to bureaucratic politics and the impact of domestic pressure groups working through the Congress. The Japanese environment has those factors, too, and yet its process reduces the potential for contradictions within the foreign policy. The French environment lacks these factors, but some aspect of the well-insulated French process seems conducive to persisting tensions of these kinds. Much more work is needed to ascertain how and to what extent cultural variables play a role in this apparently durable theme of French foreign policy.

Conclusions and Observations

If it were possible to unplug the cultural factor from Japanese foreign policy decision making, do the same for France, and then put those plugs back in the wrong places, would there be significant changes in the foreign policy output of each nation? Have we obtained some understanding of whether such an operation would have any impact at all?

As indicated by the title, the first task of the paper has been to demonstrate that there are significant differences between decision-making activities in France and Japan and that those differences are reflections of cultural distinctiveness. The second task has been to look for congruence between organizations in general within each nation and foreign policy decision-making processes in particular. The effort has yielded a glimpse of such a relationship. Various Japanese cultural attributes that pertain to group harmony seem to resonate in descriptions of Japanese organizations in general and in descriptions of the Japanese foreign ministry in particular. Various points about French cultural norms and organizations, including those pertaining to the mode of separation between upper and lower levels, do not seem contradictory with what is available on French foreign policy decision-making processes. It is easy to read too much into those processes, more than can be substantiated by the information gathered for this discussion. The comparisons between Japan and France are asymmetrical in this regard. Japan may be slightly easier to fathom because of the apparent consistency of cultural norms based on family structures, the many studies that exist on Japanese culture and business practices, and the trail left by an inherently slow-moving process involving many people. Circumstances such as those of France in which the top person gets rapid and extensive support from lower levels on almost all decisions present a tight, less easily fathomed system. The implication, then, of the previous section is that there may be some intriguing congruence between national culture, consequent widespread organizational processes, and foreign policy decision making.

The third task has been to find relationships between culturally rooted features of the foreign policy decision apparatus and foreign policy outputs. For the Japanese example there seems to be a degree of fit. With so little information on French foreign policy decision making an assessment is difficult; the relationships suggested in the present chapter are illustrative but correspond to what is suspected to be true of the French foreign policy process.

It should be noted that the study at this stage does not demonstrate that such relationships characterize a significant portion of either Japan's or France's foreign policy output. Nor does this discussion take the subsequent step of demonstrating that output characteristics of French foreign policy or Japanese foreign policy do not also appear in culturally different nations. Nor has this discussion confronted plausible rival hypotheses, such as assertions that the nature of the political system is more important than culture, that there is more variance between national cultures than within them (in other words, how valid are the studies of businesses and organizations in national settings), or that the impact of functional subcultures of foreign ministries or leadership staffs overwhelms the effects of national cultures. These tasks may benefit from a variety of kinds of information on foreign policies, including events data, and much remains to be done. As a preliminary look, however, the chapter has found some interesting illustrations of relationships between the respective organizational cultures and the foreign policy outputs of Japan and France. In more systematic studies this dimension may explain some of the variance in foreign policy decision making by nation-states; how much of the variance it explains cannot be determined on the basis of this discussion.

Put differently, the study suggests that reversing the culture plugs would make sharp differences in the foreign policy processes and outputs of these two nations. It is difficult for foreign policy scholars, who confront a chronic problem of a very small n, to think about such an operation because the number of foreign policy cases is limited and much is hidden. Scholars interested in cultural differences among more numerous and open kinds of groups such as educational organizations or businesses might more readily imagine the effects of such a change. If, as this discussion has suggested, it is reasonable to draw upon that kind of material for clues about differences between foreign policy decision-making processes of specific states, then at least better questions can be asked about that which is hidden.

If the overlooked variable of culture is an important aspect of foreign policy decision making and outputs, then it may be possible to do more with this approach than simply ask better questions. The approach is tangential to some ideas presented elsewhere in this volume. Kegley's concept of a decision-making regime (Chapter 13) would from the perspective of this study refer to something that is at least partially grounded in a cultural context that also influences decision making in businesses, voluntary organizations, local government, and the like. (How much of such a regime would be cultural and how much would be the result of cohort groups, policy inertia, political structures and other factors, is the research question noted above.) The Hermann, Hermann and Hagan discussion (Chapter 16) of decision units and foreign policy behaviors presents logical relationships between foreign policy processes, issues, and resulting behaviors of states. The relationship of that study to this discussion is intriguing. Logical possibilities such as "predominant decision maker" and "single-group decision maker" appear to be less than pure chance occurrences in Japan and France; instead, in cultures such as that of France the predominant decision maker will be the prevalent mode, while in some other cultures such as that of Japan a variant of the single group will be more prevalent and also possibly more viable politically and administratively. This discussion thus may elucidate where one encounters certain forms of decision making, and, similarly, where leader sensitivity and "concurrence" are likely to exist at high levels. By the same token, the Hermann, Hermann and Hagan study (Chapter 16) contributes extensively to understanding what the logic and results might be of certain kinds of norms and patterns that are conveyed by national cultures.

Notes

An earlier version of this chapter was presented at the Annual Meeting of the American Political Science Association, New Orleans, September 1985. This research was supported by an Undergraduate Research Opportunities Program (UROP) grant at the University of Minnesota. I wish to thank John Turner for helpful comments and Nancy Hynes for research assistance. The chapter is the responsibility of the author.

PART VII

International Influences on Foreign Policy

20

Opportunity, Willingness, and Small States: The Relationship Between Environment and Foreign Policy

MARIA PAPADAKIS and
HARVEY STARR

After a fierce burst of research activity during the late 1960s and early 1970s, the comparative study of foreign policy as a *field* of study currently suffers from a certain lack of theoretical and methodological unity. Although Rosenau (1975) optimistically concluded that comparative foreign policy had arrived as a field of academic inquiry, the state of affairs within this field is not particularly satisfying.[1] Ashley grimly concludes that "the comparative foreign policy area is (at least if taken as a whole) an example of a static or degenerating research nucleus," and Moon asserts that "comparative foreign policy research has long been marked by the absence of any organizing macro-theory, and . . . there is no sense of a cumulative enterprise centered around a coherent and widely shared set of assumptions" (Ashley, 1976, p. 155; Moon, Chapter 3).

Assuming that Rosenau was correct and comparative foreign policy *is* a field of study, the stagnation of the research nucleus is perplexing. The volume of ongoing research in international conflict, foreign economic policies, decision-making processes, peace research, and a myriad of other topics which include studying foreign policy from a comparative perspective would seem to indicate that the comparative study of foreign policy is a dynamic and vital field of inquiry (see Hermann and Peacock, Chapter 2, for another overview of the field; also Starr, 1985).

However, these studies do not relate to and build upon each other in a way necessary for theory building. The clue to this puzzle is one which was mentioned earlier—that there is no truly common theoretical and methodological framework within which all of these comparative studies operate. The one major exception may be those studies manipulating events data, but as will be argued below, events data analysis represents only one of several useful comparative methods, and it cannot provide all of the analysis necessary for generating and testing theories.

It is the major contention of this chapter that the comparative study of foreign policy is frustrated by three interrelated weaknesses. First, there has been an insufficient conceptualization of the state, foreign policy, and the foreign policy *process*, which leads to the general problem of dependent variable identification in many studies. Second, and as a consequence of the first weakness, the phenomena under study have not been rendered as comparable as they need to be for a systematic application of scientific inquiry. Finally, and as a consequence of the first two problems, multiple, rigorous comparative methods have been slow to develop (again, with the possible exception of events data analysis).

This chapter proposes to develop and apply a model based on the concepts of environment, opportunity and willingness, in order to help resolve the problems noted above. The model is both theoretic and pre-theoretic because it acts simply as an organizational device which structures and orders variables affecting foreign policy, and says nothing about the actual foreign policy "output"; (e.g., see the similar discussion in Starr, 1978). Yet it is also theoretical in that it makes assumptions and generates theories about foreign policy and the foreign policy process. In this way, the environmental model may serve as an analytical tool and not just as an organizational device.

To illustrate how the environmental model works in terms of structuring and ordering variables, generating theories about foreign policy, and availing itself of comparative methods, it will be applied to the foreign policy of small states. The use of small states as the "test" of the model is appropriate for two major reasons. First, size is one variable which is consistently significant in distinguishing differences in foreign policy behavior (e.g., Sawyer, *et al.* 1967; Rummel, 1969; Salmore and Hermann, 1970; Weede, 1970; East, 1973; Jensen, 1981). Second, accounting for all possible nation-state environments, small states would possess the most constrained opportunity sets; therefore, it may be possible to control the factors affecting foreign policy more easily.

410

The Comparative Study of Foreign Policy

Although we now tend to associate the comparative study of foreign policy with a particular stage of the study of foreign policy, specifically cross-national descriptive studies, this need not be the best we can do in advancing our understanding and theorizing about the foreign policy of nation-states. Before assessing the problems within the comparative study of foreign policy to date, there needs to be some appreciation of the implications of "comparative foreign policy" for scholarly endeavor. First and foremost, the ultimate goal of comparative foreign policy should be to elucidate the concept "foreign policy" and to generate theory about foreign policy phenomena. The "comparative" aspect of this interpretation should be understood from a methodological perspective: comparison is the primary method for analyzing foreign policy, and the results of this methodological comparison may be either "substantive" or "theoretical."

As such, however, comparative foreign policy requires that the phenomena under study be sufficiently conceptualized and operationalized as to lend themselves to comparative analysis. Or, to paraphrase Rosenau (1966, p. 40), the "raw materials need to be rendered comparative and ready for theorizing." In this sense, comparative foreign policy is more than simply applying the scientific method to foreign policy, as implied by McGowan (1975). Rather, comparative foreign policy requires a "conceptual paradigm" of foreign policy itself before the comparative method should ever be applied. Comparative foreign policy as a field of inquiry thus has a dual purpose in the study of international politics: to conceptualize and theorize about "foreign policy," and, as a result of this first purpose, to develop rigorous comparative methods which will contribute to our understanding of foreign policy phenomena.

In order to accomplish these goals, it is important that the comparative study of foreign policy be generous enough to accommodate several "scientific" comparative methods: i.e., events data analysis, case studies, quantitative analysis and variations upon these methods. What distinguishes the scientific method from "nonscientific" analysis are the procedures—conceptualization of a problem, operationalization and measurement, and hypothesis testing. There is nothing in these procedures which requires one form of method (i.e., quantitative analysis) or precludes another (i.e., case studies). As Russett notes (1974), quantitative research methods and traditional case analyses are *both* necessary and methodologically complementary approaches.[2] The discussion/understanding of comparative foreign policy presented is neither new nor unique. Rosenau (1966, 1975), McGowan (1975),

411

Hermann and East (1978) and Kegley (1980) all address these points in some fashion. What then has rendered comparative foreign policy a "static and degenerating research nucleus?" Ashley (1976, p. 155) has noted that "this group has never exhibited any uniform, sustained selective cumulation." Yet cumulation is a clearly necessary process in theory building. Its absence in comparative foreign policy may be a manifestation of deeper problems within the field.[3]

Zinnes (1976b, p. 162) has distinguished between "additive" and "integrative" cumulation. Additive cumulation occurs when a study adds to and builds upon the existing literature through such activities as citing previous research, using previously collected data, re-analyzing extant data, and incorporating new variables into the analysis. With integrative cumulation, a new study goes beyond earlier analyses by "[tying] together and *explain[ing] a set* of research findings" (italics in original). While each form of cumulation has its role in the development of the discipline, it is integrative cumulation which most clearly indicates the maturation of a science, and it is the scarcity of integrative cumulation that has concerned international relations scholars.

Many factors may contribute to the lack of integrative cumulation, but the present discussion makes some attempt to resolve one in particular: the inability for theory building to take place.[4] As Hopmann, Zinnes and Singer (1981, p. 4) state, "for cumulation to proceed . . . there must be consensus within the field about the nature of the puzzle under investigation and researchers must be willing to relate their own work to a larger body of knowledge." Yet, as noted earlier, there has been a lack of consensus within the comparative foreign policy field about the nature of the puzzle (foreign policy); as a consequence, the problem of missing dependent variables arises.

In other words, competing conceptualizations of "foreign policy" and limited conceptualizations of the foreign policy process have created problems with comparing studies as well as with operationally defining what is to be explained—the dependent variable, foreign policy. In this situation it is difficult to cumulate because (1) the dependent variable is either inadequately conceptualized and operationalized, or (2) studies are only minimally comparable because the dependent variables are different. As Rosenau would say, the raw materials have not been rendered sufficiently comparable. There also seems to be a related lack of willingness (or ability) on the part of scholars to relate their own work to a larger body of knowledge. One of the present authors has elsewhere (Most and Starr, 1984, p. 404) *demonstrated* that a major impediment to cumulation is "the general failure to conceptualize questions and indicators broadly enough to capture the relationships and processes that scholars are actually interested in studying."[5]

412

Reflecting this failure to conceptualize more broadly, comparative foreign policy according to Moon (Chapter 3) has been characterized by the absence of macro-theory and a coherent, widely shared set of assumptions. This lack of a unifying theoretical framework stems in large part from the various scholarly perceptions of foreign policy: while foreign policy may be minimally understood as purposeful state action with respect to its external (as opposed to domestic) environment, beyond this minimum our understandings of foreign policy begin to diverge. In addition, in the absence of a model which structures and orders independent variables *and* theorizes about foreign policy phenomena, our attempts to evaluate competing conceptualizations and to relate studies and theories to one another are hampered (see, for example, Chapters 2, 3 and 15).

With regard to competing conceptualizations of foreign policy, it appears that there are essentially three predominant understandings of the phenomena: (1) foreign policy as output (e.g., the actual decision, the substantive content of foreign policy), (2) foreign policy as process (e.g., the processes of making and implementing foreign policy), and (3) foreign policy as behavior (e.g., the implementation of output, a tangible act). These distinctions follow from Robinson and Majak's (1967) decomposition of the total decision-making process into "output", "outcome" and "effect," in which outputs are intermediate products *within* the decision unit and lead to later outcomes which are "imposed upon the environment external to the decision unit" (Robinson and Majak, 1967, p. 185). The actual consequences of implementation are then seen as effects.

In essence, each of these understandings of foreign policy is correct—the task is to develop a theoretical framework which can incorporate all three concepts (yet can look at them separately as needed) and which will encourage use of comparative methods. It is on this count that comparative foreign policy as a field has been amiss. There has been little theoretical effort to integrate these perceptions into a dynamic model of foreign policy as output, process and behavior. Although Rosenau's pre-theories, attribute theory, and events data analysis have been successful in identifying foreign policy outputs and structuring key independent variables, the overall dynamic understanding of foreign policy is missing. Any thorough or general theory of foreign policy must incorporate these three perceptions, and the pursuit of foreign policy analyses without the broader theoretical framework has contributed to the seeming lack of direction and progress in the comparative approach to foreign policy. The environmental model developed below hopes to provide an overall structure and theory for a dynamic understanding of foreign policy as output, process and behavior, and to provide more focused direction in the comparative study of foreign policy.

The Environmental Model

The use of an environmental approach to the study of foreign policy is not new. The Sprouts (1957), Snyder, Bruck and Sapin (1962b), and Brecher *et al.* (1969) have been the most prominent scholars who employ environmental analysis—the central thesis is that environmental factors influence foreign policy by being perceived and reacted to by foreign policy decision makers. Understood in this manner, the environmental perspective is very much a decision-making approach to the study of foreign policy (a perspective that is developed and stressed in Chapters 13, 15 and 16).

Other scholars have also, to a lesser extent, applied an environmental framework in their analyses of foreign policy and comparative foreign policy. Rosenau's (1966) pre-theory represents an attempt to structure the environment into groups of variables of increasing comprehensiveness (i.e., individual, governmental, societal, systemic). This, and forms of attribute theory (e.g., East, 1978b), represent an attempt to identify key environmental factors/variables which provide a "capacity to act" on the part of a nation-state. In addition, in a series of discussions, Most and Starr (1982, 1983, 1984) advance the environmental approach by developing the *logic* of the interaction between the environment and decision makers. By looking at the logical connections between the opportunity for interaction provided by the environment, the willingness of decision makers to pursue certain policies (and choice of foreign policy tools), the substitutability of those policy tools, and the interdependent nature of foreign policy "effects," the basis for an environmental model was constructed.

Although the theories of attribute theorists (the Sprouts, Snyder, Brecher and Rosenau—including the latter's conceptualization of "adaptation" as developed, for example, in Rosenau, 1981) have done much to elucidate the importance of "environment" and to identify key variables, there is still a lack of clarity with respect to the specific linkages between environment and foreign policy. Thus, the environmental model presented here proposes to (1) provide a theoretical framework for analyzing foreign policy, (2) act as a pre-theoretic structuring and ordering device for analyzing "foreign policy" as output, process and behavior, and (3) provide for a more rigorous comparative method by allowing for a more systematic and explicit conceptualization of foreign policy as a dependent variable.

414

The model which will be developed emerges from a synthesis of previous "environmental" approaches to international relations. The Sprouts' (1957) concept of "milieu," Singer's (1969) "levels of analysis," Rosenau's (1966) "pre-theories," and Starr's (1978) "opportunity and willingness" serve to form a cohesive analytic framework, and in all four concepts the phenomena of international relations take place in a particular environmental context. The concept of environment, or "milieu," includes all phenomena to which the environed unit's activities may be related, including the psychological or perceptual environment. In this environmental model, foreign policy derives from a state's capacity to act and its willingness to avail itself of particular opportunities. However, a state's capacity to act is not derived simply from its material resources, but rather by its relationship with all aspects of its environment, both tangible and relational.

To understand the nature of foreign policy and the foreign policy behavior of states, it is therefore necessary to understand the relationship between the state and its environment, for the milieu establishes the range of possibilities for action. The Sprouts provide three particularly useful concepts for studying the relationship between the entity and its environment—environmental possibilism, environmental probabilism and cognitive behaviorism.

With environmental possibilism, the environment is conceived as a "sort of matrix which limits the operational results of whatever is attempted"; thus, the environment may be seen as providing the parameters, or constraints, on the range of action available to the entity. In a more positive sense and as Starr would say, the environment provides the state with a set of *opportunities* for action.[6] Environmental probabilism is based on the assumption that given a set of opportunities, or a particular environmental matrix, certain behaviors are probable because of patterns of predictability in human—and consequently nation-state—behavior. Critical to this "environmentalism" is the notion of cognitive behaviorism: an entity relates to its environment as that environment is perceived.

Starr's concepts of opportunity and willingness are relevant to and refine the Sprouts ecological approach. For Starr and the Sprouts, the environment constrains and provides opportunities to international actors (environmental possibilism/opportunities), but actions are ultimately predicated upon how an actor perceives its environment (cognitive behaviorism/willingness). However, "willingness" (which deals with psychological goals and motivations) is not directly employed by the Sprouts and is more useful than simply subsuming the psychological milieu into the environment. This position highlights the important mediating role that the foreign policy

415

decision-making process plays between the set of foreign policy environments and the set of outputs, outcomes and effects.[7]

Singer's "levels of analysis" and Rosenau's "pre-theory" (which is meant to apply specifically to foreign policy) add texture to the more abstract concepts of milieu and environment. Individual, role, governmental, societal and systemic variables comprise unique environmental levels, each more comprehensive than the previous level.[8] What Singer and Rosenau are essentially conceptualizing is the broader environment of the Sprouts broken down into smaller units, for example, to levels or sub-environments. This renders the milieu more manageable from a theoretical and empirical standpoint, since it allows us to "operationalize" the environment into distinct levels and variables as well as to theorize about the effects of different levels of the environment on foreign policy. Rosenau and Singer provide the means for us to take the ecological perspective one step further by specifically delineating the hierarchical relationship between layers of the environment. The task for Rosenau and Singer, as opposed to the Sprouts and Starr, is to identify specific levels of the environment and to consider how to treat variables characteristic of these levels in relation to one another.

Thus, we have an environmental framework for analyzing the foreign policy of states. The state is an entity in an environment, and the environment may be divided into different levels with different sets of variables characterizing each level.[9] The environment defines the context within which a state may act, but how the state *actually acts* or deals with its environment depends upon a number of factors: the sets of opportunities that the characteristics of the sub-environments "objectively" provide the state, how the state perceives its environment, its willingness to take a particular course of action, and so on. In addition, states may overcome initial environmental constraints by exploiting other opportunities within their environment, especially technological changes that may expand the "menu for choice." Nevertheless, while there are a variety of foreign policy tools that may be substituted for one another to create "foreign policy" opportunities, characteristics of "larger" environments (e.g., systemic polarity) establish constraints on the range of possible behaviors that can and do, indeed, occur (see Most and Starr, 1985). We can safely argue that while the characteristics of the environment may provide an unlimited number of possible combinations of opportunities, in all probability there will be consistent patterns of behavior because of the logic of environmental probabilism and because some variables of the environment will be consistently more important than others.

Figure 20.1 is a schematic representation of the environmental

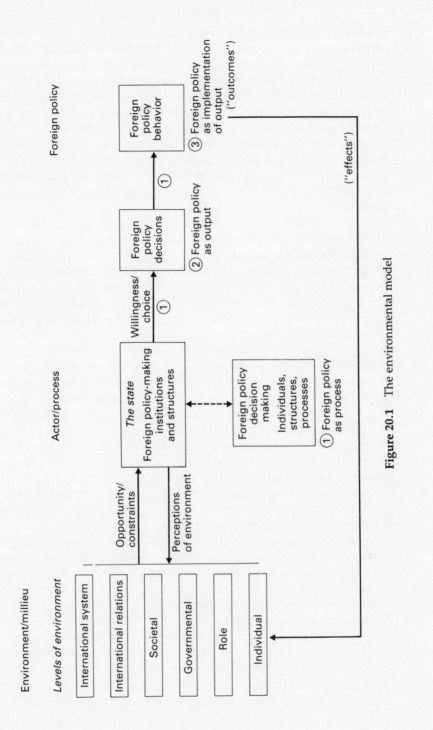

Figure 20.1 The environmental model

model, and illustrates more clearly the dynamic relationship between its components. It is important to note that in this model foreign policy may be perceived as process, output and behavior, with the relationship between the environment and foreign policy being mediated to a great extent through the decision-making process (see below). In terms of Figure 20.1, we can see that events data analysis and attribute-oriented analyses have (at least in the past) attempted to directly correlate variables/attributes in the environment (i.e., size, wealth, level of development, military strength) with foreign policy as output and as behavior by *assuming* that these environmental characteristics affect decision making in a systematic, and therefore controllable, manner.

With attribute theory and events data analysis, it is possible to skip the foreign policy decision-making process by postulating the relationship between environmental factors and decision choices. In this way, the relationship between the environment and decision making is assumed, and the relationship between environmental factors (the independent variables) and foreign policy (the dependent variable) as output or behavior may then be tested. Interestingly, any lack of statistical association between environmental factors and foreign policy as output or behavior should not imply that there is no relationship between these variables; rather, it should be presumed that the impact of attributes on the decision-making process is not as systematic *nor as direct* as it was supposed.[10] Given the need for decision makers to perceive their environments, and the variety of factors that comprise any decision-making calculus, there is no reason to expect that the same environmental factors have equal significance for all states, or that foreign policy decisions must be based upon a material capacity to act (as is assumed by attribute theory).

The environmental model reflects and tolerates a number of disparities between nation-states and their environments and imparts a new focus on the decision-making aspect of foreign policy. Nation-states have substantial differences in their environments in terms of material resources, relations with other states, positions in various international hierarchies, and domestic conditions; because of these differences it is not reasonable to assume that all states pursue the same foreign policy goals or have the same interests. Consequently, the environment may affect states in different ways, even though they may possess similar environmental factors. What is important is the overall environmental *matrix*, and not the collection of factors themselves. Constraints implied by one set of factors can be overcome by the opportunities provided by another; for example, a resource-poor nation may benefit economically by a fortuitous geostrategic position,

418

by a particularly industrious labor force, by diplomatically skilled leadership, and so on. This is not to assert that because each nation possesses a different environmental matrix that no theories, generalizations or patterns of foreign policy may be detected; the principle of environmental probabilism maintains that some characteristics of the environment will be consistently more important than others and therefore predictability can be achieved.

We can see that the environment both creates and constrains opportunities for nation-state activity—states are restricted by the real possibilities of the "objective" environment (e.g., a state without a nuclear weapon cannot use it), but the existence of other environmental conditions creates new capabilities for action. Willingness, which is based on cognitive behaviorism and environmental probabilism, equates with the process of choice taking, and decision makers, either consciously or unconsciously, *perceive* and are *shaped by* the environment. Their perception of the environment, available choices, opportunities and existing constraints determines the range of possible foreign policy action. But, the environment also indirectly shapes the decision-making process in an idiosyncratic fashion by influencing individual personalities and cognitive processes, group decision-making behavior (i.e., "groupthink") and role perceptions. In this way the environment's influence on foreign policy making has a dual nature: it provides opportunities and constraints for actual choices and establishes the human dynamics of the decision-making (willingness) process itself.

From this discussion we can see that there is no deterministic relationship between the environment, the foreign policy process, and the outcome of that process. Opportunity and willingness operate as mediating variables between the environment and foreign policy, and the task is to relate specific environmental characteristics to specific opportunities, to identify particular opportunities with particular kinds of willingness, and to specify how often and under what conditions these relationships will occur. While environmental factors in this model are independent variables, opportunity and willingness may be dependent (*vis-à-vis* the environment) or independent (*vis-à-vis* the foreign policy process) variables. We need to begin structuring and ordering environmental factors in a way that we can operationalize them into "opportunity" and "willingness" variables. At this point it should then be possible to identify the major influences on the foreign policy process, delineate and test the impact of various combinations of opportunity and willingness variables, and determine which combinations make certain decisions and behaviors more or less likely.

Maria Papadakis and Harvey Starr
Environment, Small States and Foreign Policy[11]

In the study of international relations, a nation's resources are frequently assumed to define its capacity for action, and power is often assumed to be exercised for its own sake. As a consequence, our scholarly endeavors have tended to reflect an acceptance that some states matter more than others, that large states matter more than small states because their size provides them with more resources and more power. Handel (1981, p. 3) admits that "the study of the weak states [in comparison to great powers] has been sorely neglected," and Amstrup (1976, p. 128) complains that although more research effort has now been directed toward small states, "the confusion seems greater today than, say, ten years ago."

Yet in spite of the seeming confusion over the comparative lack of attention given to small states, quantitative studies indicate that there *is* something about small states which distinguishes them from larger states. In a review of the literature of comparative foreign policy behavior, Sullivan (1976, p. 135) concludes that "economic development and size appear to be the strongest influences across more types of foreign policy," and Jensen (1981, pp. 222–4) notes that smaller powers are more likely than large powers to abstain from conflict, vote less often in the UN, favor multilateral organizations over bilateral, and confine themselves to diplomatic instruments of foreign policy.

However, analyzing small states and their foreign policy requires more than an application of traditional power assumptions about the behavior and goals of states. Rather, the whole range of assumptions about size, power and behavior must be called into question. Traditional theories about the relationship between size, power and behavior lack the ability to explain three conditions: (1) that power can emerge from factors other than material resources and that "nonpower" activity is possible, (2) that the size of states makes a qualitative difference in the nature of states beyond raw power capabilities, and (3) that power and influence can be exercised "selectively" and at less than system level. To phrase this another way, the environment of small states provides them with a different set of opportunities and constraints than larger states; consequently, we should not expect, as traditional power theory does, that small states desire the same goals, have the same interests, utilize fewer of the same resources, execute their foreign policies at the same levels as large powers, or in any way operate as "mini" versions of larger states.

A discussion of power is not completely irrelevant to the comparative study of foreign policy, since it is not unusual to find the view that the foreign policy of states is merely a formalized process of exercising

420

power and influence in international relations. In addition, as with attribute theory, the foreign policy of a state is thought to be associated with its resource base; that is, its foreign policy is based upon its material capacity to act. There is thus a frequently implied association between power and foreign policy.

The utility of the concept of power and its relationship to foreign policy depends upon how it is conceptualized. Traditional power theory asserts that states are motivated by power maximization, and this power maximizing behavior is the result of systemic anarchy in which states employ a strategy of self-help to gain security. The use of force is the *modus operandi* of power, and the more material resources a nation has, the greater its ability to exercise power. Yet in the post-1945 system, the predominance of security considerations on the foreign policy agenda and the utility of force as an instrument of policy are questionable. As Keohane and Nye (1977) stress, the growth of complex interdependence has structurally induced constraints on the range of choice of nation-states. The lack of fungibility of military power, in addition to the presence of multiple global common goods, has dictated changes in the priorities nation-states establish as well as their means of influencing world politics. What has happened, in a process of slow change, is that a wide variety of "issues" and their accompanying regimes are dominating the international arena, rather than the traditional military and security concerns.

In addition, power as the motivating force behind behavior seems to be missing from cooperative international behavior, in which states actually seem to abrogate their power. If events data are to be trusted, cooperative interaction constitutes the majority of international interaction. Specific and "extreme" forms of cooperation, such as economic and political integration, and the creation of Deutschian "security communities," especially among the OECD states (see Russett and Starr, 1985, ch. 15), are even more anomalous. Although such collective security arrangements may be partially explained by power theory, they still violate the self-help assumptions intrinsic to power theory.

Traditional power theory also has a difficult time accounting for the impact of interdependence, issue regimes and transnational relations on international politics, especially in the sense of modifying our conceptions of the sources of power and influence (see also Hart, 1976). Keohane and Nye's conception of power as originating from asymmetric interdependent relationships is a major conceptual change from the realist notion of power as attributes and military might. Importantly, through this conceptualization of power we obtain a new perspective of power as emanating from *relationships* between states instead of a *comparison* of their relatively fixed resources. With respect to issue regimes and global collective goods—monetary and trade regimes, oceans, pollution, food, population—the nature of the problems themselves and the anarchy of the international system imply that only the cooperative and voluntary agreements are useful.

The power of small states under these circumstances is not based on resources, but what Rothstein (1977, p. 25) calls "disruptive potential." As he notes, for traditionally powerless states:

> The underdeveloped countries may not have the power to achieve many of their external goals, but in a number of important cases they may have the power of preventing any other group of states from achieving theirs . . . where only cooperative and voluntary agreements are useful . . . the underdeveloped countries may have a strong veto or delaying power.

The character of the contemporary international system seems to be one in which the concepts of "influence" and "interdependence" are appropriate alternatives to the concepts of "power" and "sovereignty." The development of theories about interdependence, regimes, transnationalism, and so on, has simultaneously refined and expanded our understanding of international politics. In addition, as we shift our level of analysis and get into alternative explanations for the foreign policy outputs of states such as role, societal, governmental and decision-making factors, it is not so clear that power has anything to do in the calculus of decisions at the subnational level. It seems necessary then to re-evaluate the traditional assumptions about the relationships between size, power and behavior.

Size, Power, and Foreign Policy

Since the extant small-state literature tends to analyze small states in the context of traditional power theory, small states become, by definition, *weak states*. Although there is, quite literally, no duplication of definition from one work to another, a certain conceptual consistency does exist in these definitions. Because of their limited material resources, small states are defined as having virtually little or no power, as being "system takers," and as always being on the policy "defensive." Naturally then, small states can exercise influence only when they are able to exploit competing great-power interests, and in this context their foreign policies should reflect great-power manipulation.

In addition, small states are presumed to be overwhelmingly preoccupied with maintaining their territorial security, so much so that most of the small-state literature addresses this question exclusively, for example, Fox (1959), Rothstein (1968), Vital (1967), Sveics (1970), Mathisen (1971), De Raeymaeker *et al.* (1974), Menderhausen (1980), Pearson

(1981). The logical conclusion that many scholars draw is, as stated above, that small states can exercise influence only when they are able to exploit competing great-power interests. Implicit in much of this literature is the perception that small states are merely diminutive versions of the great powers with the same interests and goals, only with fewer resources for achieving the desired ends.

However, as Rothstein (1968, pp. 2–3) argues,

> If small powers were nothing more than less powerful great powers, there [is] surely little point in attempting to study them as a distinct kind of unit. The contemporary status and influence of small powers apparently signifies a major revolution in their role in world politics. At the very least, contemporary developments indicate the necessity of analyzing small powers on the basis of something other than traditional power factors.

Because small states tend to rank so low on the traditional power hierarchy, they were understood to have no ability to exercise power because they had no ability to coerce other states. But as Rothstein points out, small powers have been successful in influencing world politics in spite of their seeming lack of power, so the question becomes, then, what is an appropriate analytical alternative to traditional power theory for understanding the position, influence and foreign policies of small states in the international system?

What is required is a model which will take into account the distinct environments of small states, the changing nature of the international system (i.e., a more cooperative, issue-oriented system which condemns the use of military force except in self-defense), and the perception of the international system by foreign policy decision makers. Keohane (1969), in an earlier challenge to size based on physical resources, stressed the perception of "systemic role" by the leaders of states as a major approach to the goals and needs of states (see also Walker, Chapter 14). In addition, an analytic scheme is required to structure and order our present understanding of small states and to pull together this disparate body of literature. The environmental model presented in the previous section seems appropriate, and small states will be analyzed with this model in terms of their environment, opportunity *and* willingness, and their foreign policy.

The Environment of Small States

Although the environmental matrices of small states may vary widely, all small states have in common minimal populations, resources and geographic area. Indeed, most small states are characterized by a limited pool of human and material resources which may be brought to bear for the benefit of the state and its citizens. For the most part, small states fall into two broad categories, that of the older European small states and that of the newer developing small states of Afro-Asia. These two categories of states differ from one another in major ways, especially with regard to their levels of economic development, concern with security issues, historical association with one another, degree of political stability, cultural homogeneity, age of independence and their perception of their role in the international system. These major differences between small states prevent them from being lumped together as one type of international entity; consequently, their various environments provide them with distinct types of opportunities and foreign policy stimuli. How then may we understand the opportunities and willingness of small states in terms of their range of foreign policy choices and their ability to exercise influence in the international system? First and foremost, size reduces the resources which can be brought to bear on the formulation and execution of foreign policy, and there is a general, limited capacity for influence and interaction with other states. Indeed, De Raeymaeker *et al.* (1974, p. 18) goes so far as to state "small states lack the capacity to act offensively and to exert a decisive influence on other nations." However, to pursue this line of argument is to fallaciously equate capacity for action with the capacity to coerce. Rothstein (1968, p. 25) is more optimistic, and although he recognizes that "few small powers enjoy the luxury of possessing enough strength to handle all problems on their political horizons, they may be able to confront and survive the most serious problems, provided they perceive them correctly." What, then, are the specific constraints facing small states, and what counter-opportunities may they have for influencing international politics?

Small states are generally limited in personnel, both in number and in skill, and financial/wealth constraints provide for only a small-scale foreign policy apparatus. Consequently, small states will have difficulty in obtaining and interpreting information from the external environment, causing them to be "slow to perceive various opportunities and constraints" (Reid, 1974, p. 46). These bureaucratic and personnel factors limit the ability of small states to have a high degree of international interaction with a large number of states, causing most small states to have a low level of international involvement. In addition, a small domestic economy, a small military and limited wealth imply that small states do not normally have a wide range of tools with which to implement their foreign policies.

The instruments of foreign policy are few, and Barston (1973, p. 19) maintains that "small states, having less margin for error than the more powerful states, must carefully manage their external relations in order to minimize risks and reduce the impact of policy failures." Finally, the small domestic economies of these states cause them to have a high degree of dependence on foreign trade, but with low levels of economic diversification and concentrated export markets. This condition leaves small states vulnerable to fluctuations in the world economy and open to domination by their trading partners.

The general "opportunity" picture for small states is thus quite grim. Small geographic size makes these states vulnerable to invasion and conventional military attack, leaving small states with—perhaps—a permanent environment of insecurity. The small state tends to be dependent on its external environment for political and economic support, and the bureaucracy and machinery for conducting foreign policy tend to be small and weak in terms of efficiency, research capacity and timely policy responses. Small states cannot afford many embassies, causing information about international affairs to be limited and controlled by external sources. As a result, the decision calculus involved in willingness will be incomplete and/or distorted. Perceptions may be incorrect or states may be slow to detect opportunities or problems in formulating policy choices. It is here that we see the importance of studies contrasting the conditions under which cognitive/idiosyncratic factors come to the fore as opposed to role/ governmental factors (e.g., see Holsti, 1976b).

In light of these constraints, it seems almost impossible that small states should be able to exert influence on other states and maintain independent foreign policies. When scholars have considered just this issue, they have almost always done so in terms of the small state as David facing the large state as Goliath. That is, small states are assumed to have, almost exclusively, reactive foreign policies—they rarely take the foreign policy initiative—and they are invariably reacting to pressure from a much larger power. The ability of a small state to exercise influence is thus usually understood as its ability to resist the demands of a larger state.

What do small states have going for them that allow them such resistance? From a systemic perspective small states have the ability to appeal to world opinion, and in the contemporary international system there are substantial constraints on the larger powers themselves, for example, norms against the use of force, imperialism and interventionism. Small states can also focus attention on specific local issues, and mobilize the resources and will to back policy, as opposed to global powers whose attention and resources are spread thin. Indeed, Mack (1975) makes such an argument for explaining small-power victory over locally intervening great powers. What is required is simply not fighting the enemy on its own terms and not losing the conflict (but not necessarily winning the conflict either).

Small states can exert influence and leverage on a larger state by appealing to mutual interest. The power of persuasion may be substantial if a small state can convince a larger power that a particular action is also in the interest of the bigger state. This may especially be the case if the small state has something to offer the larger state—such as a strategic location, a valuable commodity or a prestigious political association. In this sense, strength on the part of the small state emanates more from its relationship with the other state than by any raw measure of power.

Moving to the governmental level of analysis, small size may be an asset. As Rapoport *et al.* (1971, p. 148) notes, "smallness can facilitate administrative coordination and integration and promote the responsiveness of public servants." The military and economic constraints of size may thus become a diplomatic strength. By developing and encouraging a small but efficient bureaucracy, a small state may *concentrate* its diplomatic efforts on key international "pressure points" and be all the more successful for its trouble. If one is a small state, this is in fact a rational policy response—instead of overextending valuable resources at a number of missions around the globe, concentrating the staff and their energies in the capitals of the most consequence can be more productive. A reputation of diplomatic effectiveness can be a valuable bargaining strength, and selective placement of embassies and personnel may help overcome the information and communications constraints of size.

There are additional societal factors which may overcome primary size constraints and provide opportunities for the small state. Andrew (1970) notes that internal political stability may provide confidence and flexibility in policy making (see also Hagan, Chapter 17), and domestic intellectual and cultural resources may contribute to a prestigious international reputation. Also, domestic economic constraints may be overcome by location, market access and historical ties.

There are thus many opportunities for a small state to circumvent the limitations of size to exert influence on other states in the international system. Jensen (1981, pp. 228–9) succinctly explains how the will of a small state may prevail: (1) the small state is able to concentrate its energies on a single issue while a larger state must deal with many foreign policy issues concurrently, (2) the small state may be willing to take greater risks and to pursue its goals indefatigably since it has less to lose than a great power—the small state has nowhere to go but up, (3) the small power may prevail because of its greater tolerance for sacrifices in a conflict situation, as was the case with North Vietnam, (4) the small state may benefit from a centralized and concentrated decision-making structure when confronting a more pluralistic, fragmented structure, (5) the small state may possess a desired "resource," be it a valued commodity or strategic location, and (6) the small state may threaten to align with the other side if satisfaction is not obtained.

However, the "willingness" of small states to undertake such efforts is not clear. Although willingness depends primarily on the willingness of foreign policy leadership to avail itself of particular foreign policy options and alternatives, some scholars who address this question with regard to small states assert that these states are generally "unwilling." For example, De Raeymaeker *et al.* (1974, p. 18) argue that "small states lack the political will to act offensively and to exert a decisive influence on other nations . . . [they] will usually hold to the status quo." Barston (1973, p. 19) adds that "the cost of viability [for the small state] is often political quiescence and compromise." This, however, depends considerably on the idiosyncratic characteristics of individual leaders, especially their tolerance of risk and uncertainty (due to poorer information-processing capabilities). Such willingness also depends on the systemic role that leaders see their states following in world politics.

The Foreign Policy of Small States

Given the preceding discussion of a small state's environment and the opportunities and constraints which are presented by such an environment, it is possible to construct some understanding about the foreign policies of small states—an understanding about foreign policy as decision making, output and behavior.

With respect to foreign policy decision making in small states, and following Rosenau's pre-theory, we perceive this process as one in which individuals rather than groups dominate, and in which the individual decision-making style is personalized and perhaps authoritarian (see also Hermann, Hermann and Hagan, Chapter 16). The process tends to be one which is in reaction to external events and behaviors, rather than an "offensive" policy-making process. A limited human and material resource base requires that the decision-making structure be limited in size and scope, with the result that decision-making personnel operate with information that is controlled by outside sources and with information that can often be untimely or incomplete. The consequence is that small states may not be able to perceive their environment correctly, or may not be able to respond immediately to a foreign policy problem or opportunity. However, small size may benefit the decision-making process: administration may be more centralized and more efficient, and time and resources may be concentrated on the most important issues.

The actual output/substance of small-state foreign policies is not entirely clear. Many authors (e.g., Andrew, 1970; Barston, 1973; De Raeymaeker *et al.* 1974; Rothstein, 1977) argue that the foreign policies of small states are preoccupied with protecting their territorial integrity and independence, and that the major substantive thrust is on sovereignty, equality and justice. Because small states lack the traditional instruments of power and influence, they emphasize their sovereign equality with the larger powers as their main justification for being "heard" in the international arena. As Andrew (1970, p. 32) puts it, small states have an "exaggerated reliance on demands for formal recognition of status." However, East (1975) finds that a substantial proportion of small-state foreign policies are concerned with economic issues. The foreign policy outputs of small states is clearly one area which requires more investigation, since most of the arguments presented here are theories not substantiated with empirical evidence.

A fairly standard picture of the foreign policy behavior of small states emerges from the current literature. East (1975) summarizes the orientation of this literature with regard to the foreign policy behavior of small states and finds that a particular "model" of behavior emerges. East's points are presented below with some elaboration. Small states are expected to demonstrate the following kinds of foreign policy behavior (East, 1975, p. 160):

(1) "low levels of overall participation in world affairs"—because small states have limited human and material resources with which to conduct their foreign affairs, they will have fewer opportunities to interact with other states. This is substantiated by empirical evidence (Salmore and Hermann, 1970; East, 1975).
(2) "high levels of activity in intergovernmental organizations"—because small states have limited diplomatic resources they will use them in the most cost-efficient manner by preferring multilateral ties to extensive bilateral associations. See, for example, Reid (1974), Plischke (1977), Karns and Mingst (Chapter 22).
(3) "high levels of support for international legal norms"—since the present norm of sovereign equality is to the benefit of small states, they will be highly supportive of a system which grants them the same recognition as larger states. J. Rapoport *et al.* (1971) notes that small-state survival depends upon respect for international law and the practice of international cooperation.
(4) "avoidance of the use of force as a technique of statecraft"—because small states do not have the capacity to maintain a large military, they will not attempt to use force in their international relations since there is a high chance of military defeat.

428

(5) "avoidance of behavior which tends to alienate the more powerful states in the system"—small states are dependent upon and threatened by the larger powers; consequently, they would not wish to challenge them. See, for example, Vital (1967, p. 12).

(6) "a narrow functional and geographic range of concern in foreign policy activities"—since the small-state capacity for international interaction is limited, it is most likely that their interaction will be regionally located, and that small states will concentrate their resources on the few major substantive issues which involve them.

We thus have a general theme of the small state as an inactive (but reactive) submissive state in international affairs. Small states do not challenge the status quo—are in fact supportive of it—and try to cultivate the goodwill of the larger powers. Small states are dependent upon international law and normative principles for this status, and naturally they attempt to encourage other states to abide by the same principles. Because of its environment and the constraints which are placed upon the small state, the logical, expected foreign policy behavior may be summarized as "low-key." Small states carefully manage their foreign policies to avoid risky behavior, they are careful not to aggravate other states, and they are generally unwilling to either exert influence on other states or to disrupt the balance of the international system. This model of small-state behavior is consistent with a view of the world which sees material power as the major instrument of foreign policy and which sees a world in which large states are the major actors in a never-ending quest to increase their spheres of influence. In this kind of world, the rational small-state response is to be cooperative, to interact only with those states with which it must come in contact, and to avoid conflict with larger powers. This is the model of small-state behavior when the international system is dominated by security concerns and when the small state has no coercive ability.

How does this model stand up to empirical tests? East (1975) finds that small states do tend to be less active in international politics and they do tend to engage in multilateral diplomatic activity. *However*, small states engage in much higher levels of nonverbal conflict behavior than do the larger states, and their foreign policies are specific and avoid ambiguity. In addition, East discovers that small-state foreign policies reflect a high level of involvement by the economic bureaucracies. Bailey (1966, p. 241) also reports that the developing small states in the UN tend to demonstrate flagrant disregard for the institution's rules of procedure and organization. What thus is tentatively suggested is a picture of small states that have so much at stake, and that have a foreign policy process which has such a limited ability to gather information and initiate policy responses that they must engage in high risk, active and conflictual behavior.

Conclusions

The preceding discussion of the foreign policy environment of small states and the general model of foreign policy decision making, substance and behavior which is traditionally asserted illustrate how the environmental model may be used to generate theories about foreign policy. However, what the preceding discussion and East's (1975) findings also illustrate is that our traditional assumptions about the relationships between size, power and expected foreign policy behavior *may not be appropriate* for analyses of small states. The opportunities for small states to exercise influence in world affairs appear to be different than those for larger powers, and tend to rely on the characteristics of the relationship between the small state and other states, rather than on the possession of any objective measures of power. The distinctive nature of the small state's foreign policy environment, especially with regard to the structural limitations on the foreign policy process, indicates that, as East found, the small state is much more willing to engage in high-risk, hostile behavior than would be theoretically supposed.

Although some aspects of the traditional theories are still appropriate (for example, very few small states could actually resist a major great-power aggression), it does not seem that the major assumptions about small states are valid in the contemporary international system. Small states do not seem to be overwhelmingly preoccupied with security concerns (economic issues appear to be more significant problems), and they do not necessarily have to be the submissive, legalistic states which they are thought to be. With so much emphasis on survival/security, scholars have overlooked the possibility that if the security of a state is not challenged, or if it is simply impossible to maintain, then theories generated on the basis of the security dilemma and self-help will not be useful for explaining or predicting behavior. When finally put to the empirical test, as by East (1975), it appears that there might be flaws in this logic.

What seem to be missing from these traditional theories are understandings of the motivation/willingness of small states—why are small states so active and aggressive when their environments would, at least superficially, indicate that they be otherwise? The contributions of several authors to this volume suggest several clues. The high activity levels and aggression of small states may reflect leader personality traits (e.g., Hermann, Hermann and Hagan, Chapter 16), intense political pressures in a fragmented or highly vulnerable regime (e.g., Hagan, Chapter 17), or the absence of a decision regime clearly defining the nation's foreign policy needs and procedures for making policies (e.g., Kegley, Chapter 13).[12] What is required is that, through environmental linkages, we repostulate the relationship between size and foreign policy, and submit these new theories, as well as the old, to further investigation.

While we have not provided solutions for all the problems in the study of foreign policy delineated in the first part of this chapter, we have tried to show that using an environmental model can cover the full range of the foreign policy process and can be used to provide a more holistic approach to the study of small states. The question of the nature of power and some basic assumptions concerning the foreign policy of small states were presented as a way to show how an environmental model can help to identify such assumptions and guide analyses. Although no dramatic new statements concerning small states have been presented, we have indicated how an environmental model can be used in the comparative study of foreign policy, reorienting our perspective on power and the performance of small states, and how the model can begin integrating previously noncumulative small-state theories. Certainly it enhances our ability to fit new studies into our understanding of small states.

Notes

1 Rosenau (1975, p. 35) states, "Kuhn's formulation of a normal science allows for a field to be said to emerge when the degree of methodological and philosophical consensus among researchers is such that their contributions are merely elaborations and refinements of each other's work."

2 Case studies can add refinements and further insights to quantitative studies, stimulate hypothesis development, sensitize researchers to particular issues and situations, accommodate multiple actors in the foreign policy process, and test inferences resulting from quantitative analysis. They cannot tell us anything about the likely frequency of events, or about the general conditions out of which particular events may come because of the level of analysis at which case studies are undertaken. Thus, quantitative analysis and case studies are interdependent methods, both necessary for advancing knowledge and theory building (see Starr, 1974, for further elaboration).

3 Students of foreign policy and international relations have been particularly fascinated with cumulation and its place in the development of the discipline (see especially Starr, 1974; Rosenau, 1976a, pt 2; Zinnes, 1980; Hopmann, Zinnes and Singer, 1981; Russett, 1983; and Most and Starr,

1984). Hopmann, Zinnes and Singer (181, p. 4), for instance, explain that the process of cumulation requires that "scholars, who seek to solve the same puzzles, build on their colleagues' findings" and that "it is necessary for scholars to relate their work explicitly to the large theoretical structure of which it is a part."

4 Another major factor contributing to the lack of integrative cumulation is an *insufficient incentive* to cumulate. The nature of political science/ international studies as a discipline tends not to reward the replication of research which is required by the cumulation and theory-building process. Additionally, once a scholar finds a research "niche" (theoretical and/or methodological), his or her cumulative endeavors tend to be narrow in scope (see also Starr, 1984, p. 8).

5 The argument was developed to show that a focus on middle-range and narrower hypotheses needed to be *re*-placed within the context of grand theory. By returning to *what* it is we are interested in, *and why*, we are forced to address the conceptualization of foreign policy and the foreign policy process.

6 Several chapters in this volume discuss specific aspects of the environment, such as Moon and economic structures, Karns and Mingst in regard to international organizations, or Hagan and domestic political conditions. Others, such as Walker's, provide a broader view of the environment.

7 Bueno de Mesquita has characterized the combination of willingness with the substitutability of different foreign policy tools (and goals) as a micro-level process subject to expected utility analysis and other rational choice models.

8 Rashid (1985) has discussed the question of whether foreign policy should be studied *across* all levels of analysis, or whether we should "seek the *linkages* between phenomena across each level" conceiving such linkages as "shared boundary points in two adjacent sets." In this sense, Rashid asks whether we should be talking of "levels" of analysis or "layers" of analysis.

9 Various decision units (see Chapter 16) may be conceived of as "entities" within larger governmental, societal or systemic environments (see also Starr, 1978).

10 This sort of indirect relationship was one conclusion of Starr's (1984) study of Kissinger's perceptions of the USSR and China, and the relationship between belief system/perception and foreign policy behavior/ implementation.

11 This section represents the preliminary results of a major research project of one of the authors. As such, it evaluates only the current international relations literature which *specifically* addresses the policy, status and concerns of "small states" as a group. The authors recognize that there is a recent body of literature on *individual* small states, especially Third World nations. These case studies are especially rich and insightful; however, to incorporate them into this chapter would far exceed the space available and they generally do not tend to direct themselves explicitly to "small-state" theory.

12 The authors would like to thank Joe Hagan for his suggestions on these points.

21

Soviet Behavior, Presidential Popularity, and the Penetration of Open Political Systems: A Diachronic Analysis

EUGENE R. WITTKOPF and
MARK J. DEHAVEN

Mikhail Gorbachev's offer in April 1985 to place a six-month moratorium on intermediate-range missile deployments in Europe was the latest in a series of public relations attempts by the highest echelons of Soviet leadership to affect negotiations regarding the European theater nuclear balance in a manner consistent with Soviet preferences. In March 1982 Leonid Brezhnev announced "a moratorium on the deployment of medium-range nuclear arrangements" in European Soviet Russia and "an end to the construction of launching positions" for such missiles. In December 1982 his successor, Yuri Andropov, announced a willingness "to agree that the Soviet Union should retain in Europe only as many missiles as are kept there by Britain and France" (cited in Sigal, 1984, pp. 107–8). In each of these instances the Western European countries scheduled to receive Pershing II and cruise missile deployments as part of the NATO force modernization program agreed upon in 1979 were the presumed targets of the Soviet diplomatic initiatives, whose apparent purpose was to drive a wedge between Washington and its European allies.

If correct, these observations suggest that Soviet leaders have sought to influence the contours of the arms control process in the Western alliance in a manner not unlike domestic political actors. Minimally, the Soviets appear to have sought to affect the "climate of opinion" in the Atlantic alliance, and they seem able to do so because of the susceptibility of open societies to penetration by extra-territorial actors.

How do external political stimuli interact with those generated at home to produce the political climate within which policy makers must formulate their foreign policy choices? This is a central but illusive and unresolved question in the comparative study of foreign policy (see also Hermann and Hermann, 1984). In this chapter we explore an approach toward solving this intriguing theoretical puzzle that builds bridges between domestic and foreign policy analysts and analyses. Its theoretical focus is the linkage between the purposeful behavior of extra-national actors and the policy-making environment of open political systems. Its empirical focus is the impact of Soviet foreign policy behavior (as measured by events data) on the policy-making environment of the United States (as measured by popular approval of incumbent presidents), which is hypothesized to be penetrable by foreign powers. We examine this hypothesis by comparing across the eight presidents who have occupied the White House since the Second World War.

The analysis is self-consciously longitudinal, multicausal and multilevel in its approach. Where we perhaps differ from the paradigmatic thrust of comparative foreign policy research is in our treatment of open political systems as permeable by extra-national forces and in our concern for the impact of foreign policy on domestic politics, rather than vice versa. Indeed, our theoretical thrust in the first instance is not Soviet foreign policy behavior but rather the way domestic and foreign policy stimuli interact to produce a climate of opinion within open political systems with which policy makers must cope if they are to succeed politically. In this sense the Soviet inputs are as much exemplary as are the domestic American responses to them. Ultimately, of course, if would be desirable to explore empirically the linkages between the climate of opinion in open societies, which external variables are hypothesized to affect, and the subsequent behavior of foreign policy makers as they seek to cope with external situations,[1] thus completing the loop between the external setting, the internal setting, decision makers, and state action about which Snyder, Bruck and Sapin (1962a) theorized two decades ago.

In a sense, ours is an effort to understand politics and foreign policy in an environment conceptualized by James Rosenau (1984c, p. 257) in his revisitation of his well-known pre-theories as "cascading interdependence," one characterized as "patterned chaos" in which "the advent of complex interdependence has expanded the boundaries within which systemic-subsystemic tensions unfold." In such an environment, Rosenau argues, new channels of influence allow for the

434

emergence of new global structures. We seek to explore empirical data that may bear on these structures and processes, thus charting new directions in the search for answers to the enduring question of how foreign and domestic policy environments interact with one another to stimulate foreign policy outcomes.

Open Political Systems: Penetrated or Permeable?

Penetration is a central concept in dependency theory that helps explain the structural position of Third World states in the international division of labor and the role they occupy in the world capitalist system. The concept describes processes whereby "nonmembers of a national society participate directly and authoritatively, through actions taken jointly with the society's members, in either the allocation of its values or the mobilization of support on behalf of its goals" (Rosenau, 1966, p. 65, italics removed; see also Rosenau, 1969b). It thus seems ill-suited to an understanding of the interface between foreign and domestic political forces among the open political systems of the Western industralized world. These societies generally possess the capabilities at home and abroad to thwart the most obvious and pernicious manifestations of external influences that Third World nations experience.

The post-industrial societies of the Western world are penetrable nonetheless. Interdependence, which implies the inability of nations to shield themselves from the effects of decisions made abroad over which they have no direct control, is the condition; it is often carried out through the mechanism of international regimes (see Keohane and Nye, 1977; Krasner, 1982b; and Keohane, 1984).[2] Rosenau argued specifically that "penetration" implied more than "interdependence." "Penetration" was to incorporate the participation of extra-national actors in the authoritative allocation of values domestically.[3] "Interdependence" was conceptualized as involving something less. But because the sensitivity and vulnerability of post-industrial societies to extra-national forces is so obvious today (the example of Japanese automotive exports to the United States comes readily to mind, but there are numerous others, ranging from shoes to steel), the distinction Rosenau drew nearly two decades ago no longer seems useful empirically. Perhaps we should conceptualize open political systems as *permeable* by *intrusive*[4] forces which, if successful in their efforts or effects, would transform open political systems into *penetrated* ones.

This is not meant to suggest that in the specific case examined here the United States is permeable by Soviet intrusive behavior in the same way that it has become sensitive and vulnerable to, say, Japan. Indeed, interdependence and the associated political economy research focus are peculiarly relevant to First World polities. Although the nuclear threat has clearly tied each superpower's security to the behavior of the other, the two remain essentially delinked insofar as the socioeconomic and welfare issues normally associated with political economy questions are concerned. Nevertheless, because open political systems are less able than others to cut themselves off from external influences, the potential exists for domestic groups to respond differently to external stimuli which may lead them to adopt and promote divergent policy prescriptions. The potential is greatest in an environment characterized by the absence of a foreign policy consensus. Such has been the case in the United States during the post-Vietnam decade where, within the mass public as well as elite circles, competing visions of the appropriate role of the United States in world affairs have persisted (Wittkopf and Maggiotto, 1983; Holsti and Rosenau, 1984; Wittkopf, 1984, 1985). Divergent views of the Soviet and communist threats and competing prescriptions for dealing with them are at the heart of the alternative world views.

Both theory and evidence suggest that world views are not easily changed, but the Soviet Union, like other external stimuli, has the capacity to subtly affect the orientation of domestic actors to the outside world by what it says and does or doesn't do. Presidents must under such circumstances cater to quite different groups with often quite different priorities if they are to gain support for their policies and programs; they can ignore those subscribing to different viewpoints only by risking great political peril (Kegley and Wittkopf, 1982–3). This is no less true of those who may be motivated by less tangible concerns than it is of those motivated by immediate self-interest, as we can assume to be the case with those touched by the welfare issues growing out of complex interdependence. The persistent debate in Washington about an appropriate American foreign policy toward Central America is illustrative (see also Cohen, 1983).

The Soviet Union as a Domestic Political Actor

Soviet leaders doubtless actively sought to affect the climate of opinion regarding the Euromissiles, and hence government decisions, in Western Europe in recent years. Whether their initiatives had the intended effect on the domestic political context in Western Europe is problematic, since attitudes toward the Euromissiles were intimately linked to concern about nuclear weapons and, perhaps more importantly, to the broader concern widely shared among key political

436

groups in Europe about dependence on American security guarantees.[5] As one observer concluded:

Some see opponents of nuclear deployments as victims of manipulation by a propaganda campaign from the East, but while evidence of such a campaign is incontrovertible, evidence of its success is not. Antinuclear sentiment is by no means confined to the left in Europe; it extends across the political spectrum to embrace Christian Democrats, Liberals and center party members, and Social Democrats, all of whom are historically unreceptive if not downright hostile to Communist appeals. Indeed, it is a sign of their self-confidence that some leaders in these parties have opposed the missile deployments in spite of the Soviet campaign. Moreover, Soviet propaganda has proved notably uninspiring among the one group from which it might have expected to command allegiance, Italy's Communist party.

(Sigal, 1984, p. 64)

What this does not disprove, of course, is that Soviet initiatives may have augmented antinuclear attitudes and sensitivities to dependence on America's security umbrella—which illustrates the reasoning underlying our theoretical and empirical research thrusts. But it is a task complicated by the fact that the Soviet Union is widely acknowledged to be involved in numerous endeavors designed to enhance its overseas influence, activities often viewed in value-laden terms as evidence of an expansionist power bent on conquest of the West. As the foreword to a recent Arms Control and Disarmament Agency report put it, "some of the major themes and tactics in the current Soviet propaganda campaign are far from new . . . Today, as in . . . previous propaganda efforts, the Soviets basically seek to mislead public opinion in the Western democracies" (US Arms Control and Disarmament Agency, 1983).

The Soviet Union is widely acknowledged to engage in "active measures," which refer to "a broad range of deceptive techniques—such as use of front groups, media manipulation, disinformation, forgeries, and agents of influence—to promote Soviet foreign policy goals and to undercut the position of Soviet opponents" (Soviet Active Measures, 1983, p. 1; see also Shultz and Godson, 1984). These efforts are intentionally deceptive and are usually "based on some unlawful act or . . . a misrepresentation of a lawful act or true situation" (Martin, 1982, p. 58).

The State Department has from time to time published reports on Soviet active measures. Their thrust is clear: beware, the Soviets are unscrupulous; they willingly and knowingly lie and cheat to attain their goals. Although the impact of active measures is admittedly difficult to assess, they have, in the words of former Under Secretary of State Lawrence Eagleburger, "a corrosive effect on open political

437

systems" (cited in Soviet Active Measures, 1983, p. 8). Diligent counter-intelligence efforts are therefore required to parry these often clandestine activities, and citizens in the "free world" must be educated about the deceptive practices to which they may be exposed.

While some Soviet practices are clandestine, others are not. "Public diplomacy" is practiced by both superpowers, and the periodic if infrequent interviews or other appearances of Soviet officials in the Western print and electronic media as well as in less visible (but perhaps more influential) forums suggest Soviet sensitivity to the politics of policy making in Western democracies.

Viewed as a whole, the record suggests that Soviet behaviors.differ in their intrinsic importance and in the importance policy makers ascribe to them. Furthermore, information about some of them are simply unavailable and thus impossible to treat analytically. As a first approximation toward analyzing the domestic impact of Soviet behavior, events data nonetheless commend themselves. Clearly events data do not capture all that would be desirable; clandestine acts, deliberate disinformation ventures, and other behaviors which may be shrouded in secrecy or produce unintended consequences may fail to be captured. At the same time, because events data are drawn from publicly available sources, they measure precisely the kinds of acts that are most likely to affect the climate of opinion in open political systems. Analytically, then, our task is to construct a model which enables us to consider simultaneously the effects of Soviet foreign policy acts and domestic political factors in shaping the climate of opinion within which foreign policy makers must act.

Modeling Presidential Popularity

A focus on presidential popularity allows us to build on a body of empirical inquiry that seeks to understand the confluence of internal and external stimuli on the domestic context within which foreign (and domestic) policy choices are formulated. The state of the economy, dramatic external events, war and domestic satisfaction with presidential performance have been shown to be systematically related to popular approval of presidents' performance (Mueller, 1970, 1973; Kernell, 1978; Hibbs, 1982b; Chappell and Keech, 1985; Ostrom and Simon, 1985).[6] Fluctuations in presidential popularity in turn have been shown to be related to congressional support of presidents' domestic and foreign policies (Edwards, 1981) and to the outcome of congressional and presidential elections (Kernell, 1977; Abramowitz, 1985).[7]

Our model of presidential popularity builds on the pioneering work of John E. Mueller. Like other critics of Mueller's early work, we found it necessary to pursue different measurement strategies and examine alternative functional forms to explain the relationship between the independent and dependent variables. But our principal interest is not in refining Mueller's model(s) but in exploring the effects of adding one additional factor to his conceptualization: the purposeful behavior of an external actor on the domestic politics of the target state. COPDAB (Conflict and Peace Data Bank) data from 1949 through 1978 and WEIS (World Event/Interaction Survey) data from 1979 through 1983 were used to assess the impact of external behaviors on presidential popularity from Truman to Reagan.[8]

Our dependent variable is the proportion of respondents registering approval of presidential performance in response to the periodic Gallup poll question, "Do you approve or disapprove of the way [the incumbent] is handling his job as president?"[9] To meet the assumption of equal time intervals on which our analytic technique rests, the data were gathered on a monthly basis using the last poll taken in a month. When no poll was taken during a month the data were estimated by taking an average of the nearest preceding and succeeding months. For those presidents for whom poll data were not available during the month of their initial inauguration, we used the first available poll. Our data set thus consists of 420 monthly observations, of which 55 (13%) were estimated.

Initially we sought to replicate Mueller's model of presidential popularity from Truman to Johnson by applying the same measurements to the Nixon to Carter years. The model performed poorly. Watergate and the Iranian hostage crisis seemed to distinguish the 1970s from previous decades, Vietnam notwithstanding. Mueller's model posited a linear decline in presidential popularity conceptualized as "coalition of minorities" effects (measured simply as time in office). Watergate and Iran were associated with much steeper declines; for both Nixon and Carter a quadratic term was necessary to fit the empirical data. Thus in both cases Stimson's (1976) cyclical model proved more applicable than Mueller's linear model. The serial correlation evident in Mueller's model and the way "time" was used as a surrogate for other variables also proved troublesome.

Together, these factors led us to seek an alternative model that would enable us to control confidently for domestic and dramatic external events so that we could focus on the behavior of external actors as domestic political actors. As a first approximation, we found Kernell's (1978) model and measurement strategies compelling.

Following Kernell, we first sought to describe presidential popularity as a function of the state of the economy and short-term surges due to dramatic international events and the "honeymoon" or "halo" effect which boosts a president's popularity early in his term. The state of the economy was measured using (1) a six-month moving average of the percentage unemployed and (2) a six-month moving average of the percentage change in the consumer price index. We expected both variables to affect presidents' popularity adversely. However, the collinearity between them led to inconsistent and unstable parameter estimates. We therefore turned to a single "misery index," which has been shown to discriminate nicely among voters' assessments of governmental performance cross-nationally (Lipset, 1982) and to account significantly for variations in public assessments of presidential performance in the United States (Ostrom and Simon, 1985). The index is simply the sum of monthly inflation and unemployment rates.[10]

The dramatic international events or "rally points" for the years 1949 through 1980 are identified by Brody (1984, p. 43). They parallel Mueller (1970) in that each directly involves the United States and is "specific, dramatic and sharply focused." For President Reagan we added the release of the American diplomatic hostages by Iran in 1981 and the invasion of Grenada in 1983. Following Kernell, we scored the events according to the assumption "that rally events have a decreasing impact on popularity over a five-month period only. After that period their effect is assumed to be nil and the rally variable is scored zero" (Kernell, 1978, p. 513). Also following Kernell, we treat each president's "honeymoon" separately from the international events (Mueller had lumped the two together), scoring the beginning of each term as 6 and then decreasing the value over a six-month period to 0.

The remaining variables in our basic model measure the "shocks" shown in previous analyses to be related to declines in presidential popularity, namely, the effects of the Korean and Vietnam wars on Truman's and Johnson's popularity and Watergate on Nixon's. (No attempt is made to model the effects of war on Eisenhower's and Nixon's popularity.) Following Mueller (1973), the impact of war is measured by the base-10 logarithm of the cumulative number of American casualties.[11] We begin cumulating Korean War casualties in July 1950. We assume the Vietnam War begins in August 1964, when the Gulf of Tonkin Resolution is adopted, and begin cumulating casualties at that time. Following Chappell and Keech (1985), we measure Watergate with a dummy variable, scoring it 1 beginning with the "Saturday night massacre" in the fall of 1973 and continuing through Nixon's resignation the following August, and 0 otherwise.

We assume with Kernell (1978) that "the president's current popularity reflects the level of approval during the preceding month. This proposition suggests that the president's popularity will respond sluggishly to environmental forces. During the brief intervals between observations, many citizens will maintain their assessment of the president's performance regardless of intervening events" (p. 515). In econometrics such dynamic processes are described as conforming to a "partial adjustment" model.[12] We use maximum likelihood (nonlinear least squares) methods to estimate its parameters. The model itself, in which lagged values of the endogenous variable are used as predictors, is an extension of the instrumental variable approach used by Kernell. It differs from Kernell's in that it does not depend on finding an instrument that is correlated with the dependent variable at t-1 but uncorrelated with the disturbance term. The structural equation for our model is:

$$Y_t = \alpha_0 + \alpha_1 X_t + \ldots + \beta Y_{t-1} + u_t$$

where

$$u_t = \varrho\, u_{t-1} + \varepsilon_t$$

For purposes of estimating the parameters of the model, the structural equation can be rewritten as follows:

$$Y_t = \alpha_0(1-\varrho)+\alpha_1(X_t-\varrho X_{t-1}) + \ldots + Y_{t-1}(\beta+\varrho)-\beta\varrho Y_{t-2} + \varepsilon_t$$

where ϱ is the correlation of the error terms at t and $t-1$.

The results of our analyses designed to model the confluence of domestic and external stimuli on presidential popularity are displayed in Table 21.1.[13] Clearly the explanatory power of the model is considerable, with the model as a whole accounting for substantial proportions of the variability in all presidents' popularity. Generally speaking, the conceptual appropriateness of the partial adjustment model is reinforced empirically. The coefficient reported under the column heading "Beta" indicates that for half of the presidents prior developments have a long-run effect on their popularity. For Kennedy and Ford these effects are positive. For Eisenhower and Nixon they are negative. There is an analog here with Mueller's "coalition of minorities" variable, which suggests that presidents' popularity will decay over time as their decisions (or nondecisions) alienate progressively larger numbers of groups and citizens. The positive signs for Kennedy and Ford, on the other hand, indicate that, other things being equal, their popularity increased over time. Contrariwise, the remaining variables, while correctly signed in most instances, are generally not significant statistically. The substantive inference is that Americans are indeed prone to change their evaluations of presidential performance only slowly in response to changing circumstances. Only in the case of the one

441

Table 21.1 A Dynamic Model of Presidential Popularity from Truman to Reagan

President	Rally	Misery index	Early term	War casualties	Watergate	Beta	Rho	Intercept	R²	N (months)
Truman	0.54 (2.87)	0.05 (0.07)	-0.17 (1.74)	0.84 (0.82)	—	0.11 (0.16)	0.92*	20.96	0.96	48
Eisenhower	0.32 (0.32)	-0.01 (0.12)	0.67 (1.71)	—	—	-0.31* (0.11)	0.91*	85.32	0.68	96
Kennedy	0.90* (0.33)	-0.10 (0.33)	0.48 (0.39)	—	—	0.80* (0.11)	-0.08	12.98	0.78	35
Johnson	0.41 (0.25)	-0.26 (0.17)	-0.29 (1.42)	-3.21 (3.34)	—	-0.23 (0.14)	0.95*	68.20	0.95	61
Nixon	0.75* (0.30)	-0.04 (0.10)	1.09 (1.21)	—	-5.21 (3.73)	-0.09 (0.04)	1.00**	-0.86	0.92	67
Ford	0.71 (0.54)	-0.68 (0.45)	0.48 (1.02)	—	—	0.72* (0.23)	-0.14	21.44	0.56	29
Carter	1.26* (0.43)	0.41 (0.27)	-3.87 (3.50)	—	—	0.10 (0.15)	0.89*	24.68	0.85	48
Reagan	0.84 (0.70)	-0.17 (0.17)	-3.44 (2.74)	—	—	0.11 (0.20)	0.91*	42.29	0.82	36

Cell entries are regression coefficients followed by their standard errors
* Statistically significant at $p \leqslant 0.05$
** Significantly different than 0.0 at $p \leqslant 0.05$ but not significantly different than 1.0. With rho set to zero, this is a first differences model

explicitly foreign policy variable, the "rally round the flag" measure, and only for Kennedy, Nixon and Carter, does it appear that the American public responds quickly (and positively, as theory predicts) to current developments.[14]

The Influence of Soviet Foreign Policy Behavior on Presidential Popularity: A First Approximation

What happens to our ability to explain presidential popularity when we add to the model the intentional acts directed by the Soviet Union toward the United States? Our expectation is that an increase in Soviet acts targeted at the United States will increase presidents' popularity. Although the thrust of the argument above suggests that Soviet leaders may believe they can affect the climate of opinion in open societies negatively as well as positively, we think this is unlikely at least insofar as the popularity of incumbent presidents is concerned. Previous research on the impact of external events on presidential popularity demonstrates that the American people are able to discriminate between foreign policy successes and failures, and that they do not uniformly follow the dictum "my country [or president], right or wrong" (Lee, 1977; Brody, 1984). The balance of evidence nonetheless points in that direction; dangerous developments abroad lead to a closing of the ranks around the president, who also benefits from efforts to attain peace. The implication from the point of view of Soviet behavior is that efforts to realize "détente" (i.e., increases in co-operative acts) will redound to a president's benefit, just as efforts to stoke the fires of "cold war" (i.e., increases in conflictual acts) will promote greater presidential popularity at home.[15] (The further implication is that the only way Soviet policy makers may be able to affect presidential popularity negatively is through a do-nothing strategy, which may deny a president the short-term boosts in popularity he would otherwise receive.)

To test our expectations, we first added to our model of presidential popularity the monthly frequency of Soviet conflictual and cooperative acts. The results were disappointing. The coefficients for the events variables were uniformly small, none was significant statistically, and the predictive power of the equations compared to that shown in Table 21.1 remained virtually unchanged. Accordingly, we examined several alternative specifications of the events variables. One measured the *cumulative* number of Soviet conflictual and cooperative events during each president's term in office. The assumption here is that 'history' may have an impact on public perceptions of Soviet-American rela-

443

tions, with the cumulative effects of "détente" and "cold war" redounding to a president's benefit. The results of these analyses are shown in Table 21.2.

The results suggest that a "history" of antagonistic Soviet behavior may have impacted meaningfully on the popularity of some presidents (Truman, Eisenhower, Johnson and Ford), suggesting that short-term deviations from established patterns may affect public perceptions of presidential performance. We must be cautious in making this inference, however, since our "history" variable may be picking up a temporal trend which matches a similar trend in the presidential popularity data. Furthermore, the direction of the relationship between Soviet behavior and presidential popularity is not what we anticipated. Only for Ford does conflictual Soviet behavior contribute positively to presidential approval. For others, successive increments in the direction of "cold war" contribute to declining presidential support, quite the opposite of what nationalistic "rally round the flag" sentiments would predict. Short-run changes in the cumulative record of Soviet cooperative behavior, on the other hand, have no significant impact on presidential popularity.[16]

Assuming our empirical results are not simply statistical artifacts, we can only speculate on the reasons for the differences in them for Ford, on the one hand, and Truman, Eisenhower and Johnson, on the other. For Ford they are perhaps located in growing elite dissatisfaction with the policy of détente Ford inherited from Nixon, which may have led the American public to rally behind their president as the long slide from détente gained momentum.[17] For the other presidents they may be located in the greater salience accorded foreign policy in American domestic politics in the 1950s and 1960s compared to the 1970s.[18] Ostrom and Simon (1985), for example, ascribe the relative stability of Eisenhower's and Kennedy's popularity to external factors, noting among other things that the event behaviors directed by their administrations toward the Soviet Union were primarily conflictual in nature. They conclude that "the Eisenhower and Kennedy popularity levels are a result of a relatively efficacious public primarily concerned with foreign policy issues, presidential behavior that reinforced these priorities, and the frequent occurrence of approval-enhancing events" (p. 352). In such an environment fear of war, reinforced by incremental contributions to a cumulative record of Soviet hostility toward the United States, might well be expected to erode a president's popularity.

We probed the comparative difference between the historical periods in postwar American foreign policy known as Cold War and Détente by repeating the analyses in Table 21.2 after rearranging our

Table 21.2 A Dynamic Model of Presidential Popularity from Truman to Reagan Incorporating the Cumulative Record of Soviet Foreign Policy Behavior Directed Toward the United States

President	Soviet conflict acts	Soviet cooperative acts	Rally	Misery index	Early term	War casualties	Watergate	Beta	Rho	Intercept	R²	N (months)
Truman	-0.20* (0.10)	0.48 (0.31)	0.24 (0.28)	0.05 (0.07)	-0.22 (1.68)	1.11 (0.80)	—	0.17 (0.17)	0.89*	32.24	0.96	48
Eisenhower	-0.18* (0.09)	0.20 (0.12)	0.29 (0.33)	-0.07 (0.13)	0.78 (1.81)	—	—	-0.28* (0.12)	0.81*	87.82	0.69	96
Kennedy	-0.00 (0.10)	-0.02 (0.17)	0.72 (0.46)	-0.17 (0.37)	0.07 (0.80)	—	—	0.71* (0.20)	-0.04	22.05	0.78	35
Johnson	-0.19* (0.08)	0.29 (0.19)	0.47 (0.24)	-0.26 (0.19)	0.50 (0.68)	-3.39* (1.38)	—	-0.02 (0.20)	0.55*	77.36	0.96	61
Nixon	-0.09 (0.16)	-0.09 (0.10)	0.80* (0.30)	-0.07 (0.11)	0.87 (1.72)	—	-6.04 (3.89)	-0.22 (0.13)	0.88*	84.92	0.93	67
Ford	0.38* (0.15)	-0.10 (0.13)	1.79* (0.60)	-0.09 (0.45)	4.03 (2.11)	—	—	0.12 (0.37)	-0.17	31.14	0.71	29
Carter	0.08 (0.08)	-0.28 (0.14)	1.15* (0.47)	0.33 (0.30)	0.90 (1.94)	—	—	0.23 (0.29)	0.60*	42.65	0.87	48
Reagan	0.04 (0.07)	-0.09 (0.17)	0.76 (0.74)	-0.03 (0.16)	0.53 (0.90)	—	—	0.83* (0.11)	-0.03	7.50	0.85	36

Cell entries are regression coefficients followed by their standard errors
* Statistically significant at p≤0.05

data into four clusters: (1) the Eisenhower and Kennedy years (the two nonwar presidencies in the pre-détente period); (2) the Truman, Eisenhower, Kennedy and Johnson years (the four pre-détente presidencies), (3) the Nixon and Ford years; and (4) the Nixon, Ford and Carter (through November 1979) years.[19] The results tended to confirm the patterns suggested in Table 21.2. During the Cold War the cumulative record of Soviet conflict behavior impacts presidents' popularity adversely at a statistically significant level ($p \leq 0.05$). During the era of Détente, defined narrowly as the Nixon and Ford years, it makes a positive contribution ($p=0.07$). When Carter is included, the variable becomes negative (and not significant statistically). Cooperative Soviet behavior, on the other hand, is related to presidential popularity negatively during the Détente period and positively during the Cold War era. In two of the four time periods (the Cold War years broadly defined and the Détente period narrowly defined) the variable is statistically significant (at $p \leq 0.05$).

The Influence of Soviet Foreign Policy Behavior on Presidential Popularity: A Second Approximation

The confrontation of theory and data often requires that one, the other, or both be revised. Because we believe our theoretical arguments are sound but have little empirical evidence that clearly confirms them, our first itch is to question our data, and perhaps our methods. Thus we wonder whether the appropriate measure of Soviet behavior is the frequency of Soviet conflictual and cooperative acts, whether measured monthly or cumulatively. It may be useful in some research environments to assume that one events datum is equivalent to another; in ours, because we are seeking to measure the effects of external behaviors on a domestic political environment, that assumption may be questionable. A clearly threatening event that increases the possibility of superpower war, for example, is likely to be perceived as more salient domestically than, say, a diplomatic protest. Some weighting scheme that accords relatively more importance to some behaviors than others may thus be preferable.

Fortunately, the COPDAB data set contains a series of weights which purport to differentiate empirically the relative importance of different event categories. We examined these weighted frequencies to determine if events with different relative importance produce different empirical consequences on the domestic environment within which presidential choices must be made. The answer is a qualified but essentially negative one. Using the monthly frequency of weighted cooperative and conflictual events as the predictors, the only significant coefficient was for Kennedy on the conflict variable. When we shifted to the "history" model and used the cumulative record of Soviet behaviors as predictors, the conflict variable for Truman, Johnson and Ford was significant, but with the sign for Ford positive and for the other two presidents negative. Again, then, we are left with the ambiguity of whether our negative conclusions about the impact of Soviet foreign policy behavior on the American domestic political environment are a product of theoretical or empirical shortcomings.

The second revision that flows naturally from our confrontation of theory and evidence concerns not the independent variables (i.e., the events data) but the dependent variable. It is well established that the American public responds differently to foreign stimuli, with some being relatively more "attentive" to the external environment than others, who may also hold different foreign policy attitudes than the bulk of the mass public. To the extent that attentives hold foreign policy attitudes more akin to those of elites or policy influentials, policy makers may also be more responsive to the opinions of the attentives than to others.[20]

Available data permit only a suggestive probe of this line of reasoning. Some of the Gallup data beginning with President Johnson can be matched with respondents' educational background. Assuming that education correlates with attentiveness, we would expect those with college educations to be more responsive to foreign initiatives than high school graduates, who in turn would be more responsive than those with only a grade school education.

Table 21.3 reports the analysis of presidential popularity from Johnson to Reagan by education group. (Because the available data appear at intervals too infrequent to permit replication of our earlier time-series methods, the results cannot be compared directly to those reported previously.) Once again the model accounts for a substantial proportion of the variation in presidential popularity, which is true for all educational groups, but the association between particular variables and presidential popularity is often incorrect, which is likewise true across the educational categories. Furthermore, it remains clear that overt Soviet behavior is only tangentially related to variations in presidential popularity, and that education, our surrogate for attentiveness, discriminates poorly among Americans' responses to presidential performance. This unexpected finding holds not only for the Soviet behavior variables (including the weighted events data, for which the analyses are not shown) but for the others as well. Indeed, perhaps the most striking finding in Table 21.3 is how little variability there is among the educational groups.

Table 21.3 A Model of Presidential Popularity from Johnson to Reagan Incorporating Soviet Foreign Policy Behavior Directed Toward the United States, by Educational Groups

President	Attained education	Soviet conflict acts	Soviet cooperative acts	Rally	Misery index	Early term	War casualties	Watergate	Intercept	R^2	N (of polls)
Johnson	College	-0.18 (0.24)	0.33 (0.57)	0.72 (0.54)	0.40 (0.55)	-3.22* (1.51)	-17.10* (1.90)	—	107.81	0.81	35
	High School	-0.09 (0.20)	0.05 (0.48)	0.33 (0.45)	0.19 (0.46)	-3.03* (1.27)	-17.20* (1.60)	—	113.41	0.87	35
	Grade School	-0.02 (0.24)	0.04 (0.56)	1.02 (0.53)	-0.26 (0.54)	-3.04* (1.49)	-14.84* (1.86)	—	106.21	0.78	35
Nixon	College	-0.30 (0.50)	-0.63 (0.40)	0.22 (0.75)	-0.89* (0.38)	1.58* (0.73)		-24.58* (3.93)	70.68	0.76	42
	High School	-0.06 (0.46)	-0.38 (0.37)	1.29 (0.69)	-0.56 (0.34)	1.46* (0.67)		-24.39* (3.61)	60.65	0.76	42
	Grade School	-0.06 (0.49)	-0.40 (0.39)	1.60* (0.73)	-0.41 (0.36)	1.83* (0.71)		-19.50* (3.81)	53.16	0.68	42
Ford	College	-0.35 (1.09)	-2.17 (0.98)	2.61 (1.31)	0.01 (1.32)	3.45 (1.97)			53.74	0.55	15
	High School	-0.09 (1.04)	-1.34 (0.93)	0.49 (1.24)	0.52 (1.25)	2.91 (1.86)			38.21	0.45	15
	Grade School	-0.23 (0.94)	-1.77 (0.84)	1.75 (1.13)	-0.48 (1.13)	4.72* (1.69)			44.54	0.62	15
Carter	College	2.16 (1.93)	-0.93 (1.20)	4.30 (3.45)	-2.09 (1.80)	6.76 (4.27)			61.91	0.56	12
	High School	1.40 (1.53)	-0.94 (0.95)	3.52 (2.73)	-1.63 (1.43)	7.01 (3.39)			60.46	0.63	12
	Grade School	2.97* (1.00)	-0.90 (0.62)	3.75 (1.78)	-2.92* (0.93)	3.04 (2.20)			74.87	0.80	12
Reagan	College	-0.18 (0.39)	-0.05 (0.69)	-18.61* (7.64)	0.52 (0.71)	15.94* (6.48)			49.08	0.60	16
	High School	0.13 (0.36)	-0.65 (0.66)	-18.33* (7.24)	0.10 (0.67)	17.19* (6.13)			44.85	0.69	16
	Grade School	-0.15 (0.49)	-0.16 (0.88)	-14.30 (9.71)	0.97 (0.90)	11.32 (8.23)			23.27	0.45	16

Cell entries are regression coefficients followed by their standard errors

* Statistically significant at $p < 0.05$

New Directions, Old Questions

If the bad news is that our explanatory models fail to match our expectations, the good news may be that the Soviet Union is unable to play an effective domestic political role and to affect the climate of opinion in the United States in a manner conducive to Soviet interests. That conclusion depends on a number of critical assumptions, of course. It assumes that events data capture the Soviet behaviors that are most likely to affect politics in open societies, for example. And it assumes that mass publics are both sensitive and responsive to external stimuli. Perhaps neither assumption is warranted. We may have asked more of events data than they can bear (McClelland, 1983), and mass publics are notorious for their lack of sustained interest and involvement in foreign policy issues.[21] It may be unreasonable to expect that they will give attention to the daily flow of foreign affairs captured in events data. Episodic and dramatic events, those captured in the rally-round-the-flag variable, are perhaps the only ones that can be expected to engage the attention of most people most of the time.

We are struck nevertheless by how extensive a role "word politics" seems to play in the interactions of the superpowers, and by how much those games seem designed to shape domestic decision-making environments (see, e.g., Talbott, 1979, 1984). If we are to understand how open political systems are penetrated by extra-territorial actors in issue-areas other than those normally embraced in political economy perspectives, perhaps what is required is a shift in both data and analytical focus toward what Kegley in Chapter 13 calls "decision regimes." Implicit in this view is a research agenda that focuses on individual policy makers and policy-making groups and on how they balance the competing demands of foreign and domestic politics. Case studies (of the sort suggested in Chapter 15 by Anderson) and memoir histories may prove more useful instruments to probe the balance than the kinds of data and analytical tools that have been used by comparativists in the wake of Rosenau's path-breaking pre-theoretical arguments.

However, before we abandon the ideas explored here as a way of examining how open political systems are permeated by intrusive forces, our diachronic comparative analysis should be extended cross-nationally. There is a substantial body of literature comparable to that on American presidential popularity for other open political systems. Comparative research on France (Lewis-Beck, 1980, 1984; Hibbs and Vasilatos, 1981; and Lafay, 1984), West Germany (Frey and Schneider, 1980; and Kirchgässner, 1985), and the United Kingdom (Hibbs, 1982a) supports the proposition that among Western democracies generally macroeconomic conditions have a significant impact on citizens' perceptions of their political leaders. When combined with idiosyncratic political variables and occasional rally points, the empirical evidence suggests that Western leaders can increase their popularity by appealing to improvements in the quality of life or high symbolic politics (Paldam, 1981; Ostrom and Simon, 1985). The principal remaining controversy concerns the appropriate measurement strategies and methodological applications (Norpoth and Yantek, 1983). The opportunity to draw this research into the comparative foreign policy domain and to learn if other open political systems are more permeable by extra-national forces than the American system presents an exciting and challenging research agenda. In the process we may find a key to unlocking the riddle about how domestic and foreign policy stimuli interact in an environment characterized as "cascading interdependence."

Notes

The research reported in this paper was supported by the National Science Foundation under grant SES-8311478. Thanks are due to Neil R. Richardson for providing the 1948–78 Soviet dyadic events data analyzed in the paper, William J. Dixon and other participants in the Conference on New Directions in the Comparative Study of Foreign Policy for their helpful comments on an earlier version, and John S. Shinkwiler for giving his time and expertise so generously.

1 See Ostrom and Job (1982) for an interesting probe of the linkage between presidential popularity and American intervention abroad.
2 The successful operation of the postwar international economic system in enhancing the free flow of capital goods and technology has been a major contributing factor to the growth of economic and political interdependence. The rise of neoprotectionist sentiments among key domestic actors throughout the Western world, in part a response to the very success in creating an open political economy, underscores the fact that interdependence is a force for nationalism as well as internationalism. See Holsti (1984) for an elaboration of this idea, with specific reference to the interesting case of Canadian-American interactions.
3 As Rosenau reasoned, penetrated systems exist when nonmembers participate "directly in a society's politics; . . . there must be intensive face-to-face interaction between members and nonmembers of a society. Values cannot be authoritatively allocated, or goal-attaining activities authoritatively mobilized, from afar" (Rosenau, 1966, pp. 68, 69).
4 Cantori and Spiegel (1970) use the concept of an *intrusive system*, defined as *"the politically significant participation of external powers in the international relations of the subordinate system"* (p. 25), in their comparative approach to the international politics of regions. Subversion and propaganda are among the methods of participation they cite.

The permeability of states, following Herz (1957), traditionally has referred to the threat of states' territoriality posed by modern weapons. States remain "conditionally viable" (Boulding, 1962), but the very destructive capacity of today's weapons has reduced the utility of force as an instrument of influence and enhanced the relative utility of other means, thus subjecting states to a broader array of intrusive forces.

5 Rosenau (1984) uses the idea of *role scenarios* or *action scripts* in an effort to infuse the role variable in his pre-theories with a dynamic quality. He argues that the response of the Western peace movements to the deployment of the Euromissiles provides "a good, current example of how the action scripts of publics can become inextricably linked into cascading processes . . . Both the ordinary citizen and the movements' leaders had to make choices among scripts in which their actions might differentially affect the coherence of their organizations, the effectiveness of their governments, the stability of NATO, the negotiating postures of the Soviets, the orientations of the Reagan Administration, and the prospects for cooling down or heating up the arms race" (p. 273).

6 There are a number of works on presidential popularity in addition to those cited here, including, for example, MacKuen (1983), and Norpoth and Yantek (1983), who provide research results germane to our analyses. A comparable body of literature exists for other Western nations, where particular attention has focused on the *responsibility hypothesis*, which states that voters hold governments accountable for the performance of the economy. Paldam (1981) surveys much of this literature, to which we will refer in our conclusion. Mueller's special contribution to this literature appears to be in his effort to bring explicitly political variables into the analyses.

7 More broadly, Richard Neustadt (1980) has argued that presidential prestige is an important source of presidential power generally. How prestige translates into power remains uncertain, however, just as the causal link between public opinion and foreign policy remains elusive.

8 The 1979–83 WEIS data were compiled and made available by Dr. Frederick A. Rothe. COPDAB data are available for 1948, but we chose to begin our analysis with 1949 since there were few polls on Truman's popularity taken in 1948.

9 Data were drawn from *The Gallup Opinion Index* (1980) and *The Gallup Report* (1984).

10 Monthly inflation rates were calculated from the changes in the consumer price index (for wage earners and clerical workers) reported in US Department of Commerce (1976, 1983) and *Survey of Current Business* (1984).

11 Casualties are the total number of hostile deaths, defined as the sum of those killed in action and those who died of wounds, died while missing, and died while captured. The data were provided by the US National Archives.

12 Durbin-Watson statistics range from 0.37 to 0.96 for each of the eight presidents under consideration, indicating the presence of positive autocorrelation. We tested the lag structure and found evidence that it conforms to a first-order autoregressive process. Although it is possible to transform the data to remove the serial correlation, the partial adjustment model is preferable conceptually for the reasons outlined by Kernell.

13 To preserve the sample size(s), the observations that would have been lost

by lagging the exogenous variables are estimated by using the next available data point.

14 There is considerable variation in the misery index, which, if smoothed, might change our estimates of the parameters and our corresponding interpretation of the partial adjustment model.

15 Although we believe these theoretical arguments are sound, the weak empirical confirmation of them led us to consider alternative specifications of the Soviet behavior variables, as noted below. One expressed Soviet conflict behavior as a proportion of the total number of Soviet events (conflict plus cooperation) directed toward the United States. The results generally paralleled those based on the disaggregated conflict and cooperation categories in that the coefficients were small for all of the presidents and statistically significant for none.

16 Paralleling the normalized conflict index discussed in Note 19, we constructed a similar index using the cumulative conflict and cooperation scores. The coefficient for the variable was significant for two presidents, Eisenhower and Ford, but with different signs. Eisenhower's popularity decreased as the cumulative balance of Soviet behavior moved toward conflict, while Ford's increased.

17 The sign on the Soviet conflict variable for Carter suggests that the same processes may have been at work during his administration, even though the coefficient is not significant statistically. The positive correlation is consistent with the argument that during the latter part of Carter's term the American people exorcised the ghost of Vietnam and adopted a more assertive and nationalistic posture toward external challenges generally, and alleged Soviet expansionism in particular (see Yankelovich and Kaagan, 1981a), which may have redounded to Carter's benefit.

Although we must be cautious in ascribing too much importance to the following, the absence of significance for Carter may be due to our measurement strategies, specifically the switch from COPDAB to WEIS data beginning in 1979. Available evidence (Howell, 1983; Vincent, 1983) suggests that the two data sets do not overlap completely. We sought to determine the import of using different data sets in our analyses by comparing the first two years of Carter's administration with the last two, but the results were inconclusive. The small number of cases and the obvious fact that the early term variable did not apply to the 1979–80 period were principal confounding factors.

18 Among some four dozen polls taken between 1949 and 1972, foreign or security policy issues received top billing two-thirds of the time when Americans were asked to name the nation's most important problem. In contrast, economic concerns were named most important from 1973 to 1978. Not until 1980, following the Iranian seizure of American diplomats and the Soviet invasion of Afghanistan, did a foreign policy issue once more top the list ("Opinion Roundup," 1980, p. 21).

19 Determining the appropriate categories for aggregation is difficult. The issue is relevant to our overall comparative strategy. We chose to analyze presidential popularity and report our results by president, since previous research generally shows that the functional form of the relationship between the independent and dependent variables varies from one president to the next. This implies that idiosyncratic factors are also at work, and that any aggregation across presidents should incorporate them. The usual

approach is to include dummy variables for each administration, which affect the 'starting values' for each president's popularity.

The foregoing problems are compounded when we talk about 'cold war' and "détente" as distinct historical periods. Kegley and Wittkopf (1982), for example, provide empirical and interpretive evidence to suggest that the détente phase of Soviet-American relations lasted from 1969 through 1978, but they acknowledge that the long slide from détente may have begun as early as 1974, when the Jackson-Vanik amendment to the 1974 US Trade Act effectively denied the Soviet Union most-favored-trade treatment. Other empirical inquiries (Dixon, 1983; Andriole, 1984) reinforce these alternatives but by no means provide conclusive cut-points.

20 See Maggiotto and Wittkopf (1981) and Wittkopf (1984) for examinations of the foreign policy attitudes of attentives, and Wittkopf and Maggiotto (1983) and Wittkopf (1985) for comparisons of the foreign policy attitudes of attentives and elites.

21 However, mass publics do have opinions about foreign affairs, and there is evidence that they are able to maintain coherent and consistent world views (Maggiotto and Wittkopf, 1981; Wittkopf and Maggiotto, 1983; Wittkopf, 1984, 1985).

22

International Organizations and Foreign Policy: Influence and Instrumentality

MARGARET P. KARNS and KAREN A. MINGST

States find themselves enmeshed in increasingly complex networks of organizations, both formal and informal, as a consequence of the tightening of their economic and security interdependencies. The majority of these organizations are limited in membership to small groups of states with common interests in enhancing predictability in their interactions, information sharing and problem solving, but with differing specific interests. Even for the major powers, "neither toughness nor unilateralism alone can deal effectively with complex problems that require international cooperation," as the Reagan Administration has discovered (Keohane and Nye, 1985, p. 149). Yet the utility and impact of multilateralism have frequently been misconstrued. A more realistic, yet expanded view of the dimensions of international cooperation requires a reassessment of the relationship between national policy making and international organizations and regimes.

We hypothesize that all states are influenced, though to varying degrees and in varying ways, by their participation in intergovernmental organizations (IGOs) with consequences for both the substance and processes of domestic and foreign policy. Secondly, we hypothesize that with the tightening of the networks of interdependencies, the impact of IGOs on all states will grow. Evidence of the former abounds in the increasing number of problems transcending national borders, for example, pollution; in the growth in volume and speed of international financial transactions which make regulation by one government alone difficult if not impossible; in the proliferation of nuclear and other sophisticated weapons that raise the risks to all nations of future conflicts; in the movement of ideas and information across national borders, for example, by satellite communication, in ways that make every polity more penetrable and thus compel joint action to regulate; and in the ability to tap previously inaccessible areas, for example, outer space, the seabed, and polar caps, whose colonization is precluded by changed international norms and which therefore invite joint exploration and exploitation. It is in this context that we suggest the need for more attention to the ways in which IGOs, as links between the international and domestic arenas, influence the foreign policies and policy processes of states.

Traditionally, scholars have treated the domestic and international influences on foreign policy as separate sets of variables. Whereas research has been conducted on the ways in which IGOs have been used as instruments of foreign policy by states, little attention has been paid to the influences of IGO participation on national policy and policy making. As Haas (1969, p. 272) suggests, it is "dangerous" to overlook this two-way flow of influence. This chapter is based on the hypothesis that the existence and outputs of IGOs do make a difference in the behavior of states, but that the impact varies along a series of different dimensions. In other words, some organizations linked to some issue-areas have more impact than others; certain states are more susceptible or receptive to IGO influences than others. We lay out these dimensions of variability and suggest, on the basis of our own and others' extant research, the nature and extent of impact. We argue that the efforts of governments to utilize international organizations as instruments of statecraft require adaptations in policy and/or policy-making processes and that the uses which states make of different IGOs as instruments affect their receptivity to IGO influences, generating unique patterns of interpenetration between the international system and the policies and policy processes of states.

It is necessary, however, to cumulate a considerable body of case study material and/or other data before the underlying hypotheses on the increasing influence of IGOs can be fully addressed. Therefore, while we start from a presumption of finding substantial impact, albeit variable, a counter-hypothesis would be that the nature of international politics and the primacy of domestic political constraints minimize the influence of IGOs on foreign policy.[1]

A review of previous efforts to conceptualize the role of IGOs as a source of policy informs the subsequent discussion. Since Rosenau (1966) outlined his pre-theory differentiating among the five source variables of foreign policy, comparative foreign policy scholars have devoted considerable attention to operationalizing these variables and testing their relative potency (among others, Powell *et al.*, 1974; Rosenau and Hoggard, 1974). Four of the variables (individual, role, governmental and societal), however, represent internal sources of a nation's foreign policy. As McGowan and Kegley (1983a, p. 7) lament,

> Surveys of the comparative foreign policy literature . . . clearly demonstrate that a great deal of attention has been devoted to the internal/societal nexus but that little progress has been made in thinking about, much less resear- ching, the external/systemic influences affecting foreign policy.

For East (1985) this means that international factors have actually been unnecessarily relegated to a lower status.

Harf *et al.* (1974, p. 236) noted that the systemic variable was nothing more than a "residual category for any potential influence not within the borders of a nation." They proposed differentiating between systemic variables (system-wide characteristics) and external variables ("exogenous attributes of individual nations irrespective of other units in the international arena") (p. 246). However, this distinction was largely ignored by fellow researchers. CREON participants have focused on the international situation (Brady, 1978) or external pre- disposition (Hudson, Hermann and Singer, 1985). Papadakis and Starr (Chapter 20), following in the tradition of Sprout and Sprout (1957), suggest utilizing an umbrella concept, the international environment.

Similarly, Gourevitch (1978) and Kahler (1984) argue that contempo- rary theory has surrounded societies with a "theoretical insulation from intrusions of the external" (Kahler, 1984, p. 17). Kahler asserts that success of penetration by external actors is determined by access and by skill in constructing domestic political alliances (p. 278). Gourevitch (1978, p. 882) posits, "International systems, too, become causes instead of consequences." Both suggest that greater attention be given to how international factors affect the domestic determinants of foreign policy.

Increased interest in international political economy has led to efforts to link political/economic systemic characteristics to types of foreign policy behavior. Operating from a liberal framework, Keohane and Nye (1977) suggest that the international system can best be characterized as one of complex interdependence. They and East (1981) trace the impact of interdependence on foreign policy and policy making. In the radical tradition, the contributions in McGowan and Kegley (1983a) seek to explain long-term trends in foreign policy beha- vior based on a state's position in the world economic system of capitalism.

It is apparent that dissatisfaction with the systemic concept and inadequate distinction among environment, system and external factors continue. Yet in none of this exploration of systemic/external sources have IGOs been considered except for the efforts of East (1978a) and McCormick (1980). East posits that systemic characteristics may include such variables as total number of IGOs, the amount of overlapping membership, and allocation patterns of IGOs, each measuring the degree of organization in the system. In an empirical study utilizing CREON events data, McCormick finds that levels of cooperation among nations can better be explained by IGO characteristics than by national attributes. Within the international organization literature, only Matecki (1957) and Meltzer (1976) have attempted previously to explore IGO impact on national policies in specific cases, although others have argued the desirability of doing so (Riggs, 1967; Kay, 1969).

IGOs are an integral part of a system characterized by complex interdependence. The latter, we argue, best describes the character of the contemporary international system and has consequences for foreign policy and policy making. IGOs provide the formal institutional components of "international regimes" by which states seek to provide order and reduce uncertainty. As Krasner (1982a, p. 186) suggests, international regimes include the collection of principles, norms and decision-making procedures that members utilize to regularize behavior and to resolve issues cooperatively. They may play a key role in affecting the incentives and costs, in creating the opportunities for and constraints on state cooperation.

Nonetheless, regimes as a concept have not been rigorously operationalized. Whether we know a regime when we see it is unclear (Strange, 1982). However, it is the IGOs that are the institutional components of many regimes and to which governments belong, around whose work portions of national bureaucracies are often themselves organized and driven, and whose budgets require governmental decisions on appropriations. Institutions, agendas, decisions on votes, occasions for speeches and for conferring with others all create opportunities for decision making within member states and for initiatives toward cooperation without. As components of regimes, as forums for the interactions of member states, and as international actors in their own right then, IGOs can be treated as variables within a complex interdependence system that impinges on national governments. They provide opportunities for national decision making at the same time that they add to the constraints under which states must operate.

The development of IGOs has led to the emergence of networks of transgovernmental and transnational relations, particularly involving governmental and IGO officials in the more developed pluralistic

457

states and international economic IGOs, and creating a high degree of interpenetration. The possibilities of such linkages and interpenetration were anticipated by Rosenau (1969a). Further work by Keohane and Nye (1974) and others focused on transnational and transgovernmental networks, but few analysts have systematically explored them and their impact on national policies and policy making. Yet, because of these complex patterns of linkage and interpenetration between IGOs and states—or more specifically, linkages to agencies within governments and groups within domestic societies—the influences of IGOs on foreign policy and policy making cannot be treated solely as "external" sources of foreign policy.

IGOs and Foreign Policy: The Dimensions of Variance

The patterns of influence between IGOs and foreign policy depend on seven sets of variables: the national attributes of a state; the nature of the domestic political system; the characteristics of particular IGOs; the perceived utility of an IGO as instrument for national policy implementation; the substantive differences among issue-areas; the diplomatic skills, personality and persuasiveness of individuals who serve as national representatives to IGOs, members of IGO secretariats, and as national decision makers; and the positions within IGO or national decision-making structures of such individuals.

In constructing hypotheses of the variations in IGO impact on states, we shall concentrate first on linking IGOs in general with the national attributes of different states and their domestic political systems. Then, we shall treat IGOs as variables and explore how the characteristics of particular organizations affect the ways and the degree to which member states find specific organizations useful tools of their foreign policies.

States are frequently differentiated by national attributes and by their roles in the international system. While the importance of the variable of state size is open to challenge, considerable work exists characterizing the behavior of small, middle-sized and large states. Hence, we have chosen to utilize these categories. In so doing, we follow the contention of Papadakis and Starr in Chapter 20 who reject past tendencies to characterize small states as "mini" versions of larger states with fewer resources for pursuing the same ends. While noting the substantial differences between older European small states and newer developing states in Afro-Asia, they describe how limited human and material resources contribute to a "highly individualistic, 'issue-oriented' style of foreign policy making" in small states generally.

With respect to middle-sized powers, Holbraad (1984, p. 76) suggests that they "do not constitute a class to nearly the same extent as the great powers do . . . the division between them and those below in the international hierarchy is far less marked than the distinction between the great powers and themselves . . . their shared interests are not so substantial and lasting as those of the great powers." Holbraad distinguishes the middle powers, then, in terms of "the strength they possess and the power they command" (p. 76) within the different geographical regions of the world.

Using this classification, there are only two large or great powers, the United States and the Soviet Union, with a third, China, being on the dividing line between large and middle powers.

In addition to the dimension of state size, level of development is an important national attribute. Various measures have been proposed for distinguishing developed from developing states. Coupling per capita GNP and the Physical Quality of Life Index (PQLI)[2] (with the relevant breakpoints being $3500 in per capita GNP and a PQLI of ±90) supplements the income measure with indicators of the level of progress in meeting basic human needs. Katzenstein (1978) has further singled out unique features of the foreign economic policies of the six advanced industrial states—those states within the OECD with the largest economies (the United States, the United Kingdom, West Germany, Italy, France and Japan) and characterized the behavior patterns of the small European corporatist states (Katzenstein, 1985). The latter are distinguished primarily by the extent of domestic political consensus on how to deal with the external environment and by less competitive bureaucratic politics.

National polities are also frequently characterized as open or closed, in reference to the extent of influence of internal groups on political processes. Krasner (1978) makes a related distinction between strong and weak states based on the degree of permeability by pressure groups.

States also vary by their relation to the international system, the nature and degree of their interdependence (that is, mutual dependence) with others, dependency, degree of penetration by external actors, sensitivity or vulnerability (Caporaso, 1978, pp. 13–43). The latter distinction—sensitivity or vulnerability—is particularly useful in identifying degrees of adaptability by states to costly changes precipitated by other actors' actions (Keohane and Nye, 1977, pp. 12–19), for the more vulnerable a state is, the more adaptive it must be.

Considerable attention has been paid recently to the position and behavior of a dominant or hegemonic state in the international system. Such a state had been widely postulated as playing a key role in the establishment of international regimes, particularly in international economic relations (Kindleberger, 1974; Krasner, 1976; Avery and Rapkin, 1982). The effects of a decline of hegemony on the underlying patterns of cooperation and conflict, however, do not necessarily conform to the theories of hegemonic stability insofar as the patterns of cooperation persist even in the face of the presumed decline of hegemonic power (Keohane, 1984).

We shall utilize the above distinctions of size, level of development, nature of the political system, and relation to/position in the international system in developing our hypotheses regarding the variable impact of IGOs on foreign policy and policy processes.

In analyzing the impact of IGOs, we consider their agenda-setting role, formal outputs such as norm-setting resolutions, rules and supervisory decisions, as well as the adaptations in patterns of policy implementation that may be required to facilitate participation on the one hand and optimum use of the IGO as an instrument of policy on the other. We are also concerned with the consequences of the informal interactions which IGOs facilitate, and the avenues through which IGO influences may be channeled: representatives and delegates, IGO secretariat officials, transgovernmental networks and coalitions.

IGOs as Influencers of National Policy and Policy-Making Processes: Impacts on Different Types of States

The fact that IGOs are an integral part of the network of international relations and that most states participate in multiple organizations not only enlarges the possibilities for national policy, but adds to the constraints under which states operate. The existence of these international institutions and the requirements of participation, we hypothesize, necessarily exert an impact of variable magnitude on the foreign policy behavior and decision-making processes of member governments. It is the variations in and significance of IGO impacts that principally concern us.

IGO Agenda-Setting/Decision-Forcing Impact

The most pervasive way that IGOs have a direct influence on national policies is through the establishment of international and hence of national agendas. Member governments must develop some type of response to IGO agenda items, even if an issue is one in which the state has no particular interest, or would prefer to avoid public discussion.

The hundreds of meetings, conferences, and regular and special sessions of IGOs which take place each year all create agendas for some portion of national bureaucracies. The number of times that this forces or stimulates a re-evaluation of policy itself appears to be limited; in some cases, governments are pressed to form responses on issues in which they have little interest, thus promoting the pretense of policy. On the other hand, governments are sometimes forced to mobilize resources to study issues not previously on their national agendas. For example, many environmental questions received attention for the first time as a result of the 1972 Stockholm Environment Conference, while an OECD decision to study positive adjustment policies in 1979 prompted member governments to gather information and think about these topics in ways which few, including the United States, had done before.

Large states are more apt than others to be affected by the agenda-setting/decision-forcing role of IGOs. In general, small states, because of limited manpower and monetary resources, cannot deal with all issues in depth, and must specialize (East, 1973, p. 559). With more resources to draw upon, middle powers, in general, can be more responsive to IGO agendas than small states, but less so than large states. The advanced industrial states regardless of size have a greater capacity to react to IGO initiatives and agendas. In contrast, less developed states, with their limited capacity to act and even to adapt to IGO participation through budgetary and bureaucratic expansion, will frequently do little more than follow the lead of the larger less developed states in the Group of 77. The extent of a state's response, however, will also depend on the salience of an issue to its national interest and the principal decision makers' perceptions of their ability to influence international actions. For example, the Scandinavian states were immediately galvanized by the Law of the Sea negotiations that were vital to their interests, while the equally small European land-locked states displayed considerably less interest in the issue.

Historically, dominant or hegemonic states have been able to a substantial degree to shape IGO agendas to suit their interests. The United States played a key role in the formation of the postwar economic institutions, regarding these institutions as important instruments for structuring an international order favorable to American interests. But while a hegemonic state is more apt to set IGO agendas than other states, and hence, be less subject to the agenda-setting/decision-forcing impact of IGOs, the case of the United States illustrates how readily even the hegemon can find itself as 'agenda-taker' (Pastor, 1984), once its ability to command a majority, especially in universal, one-state, one-vote IGOs diminishes.

461

Margaret P. Karns and *Karen A. Mingst*
The Impact of IGO Norm Setting

Norm setting is an important activity of many IGOs, although international law scholars debate whether IGO resolutions endorsing certain norms do, in fact, achieve this purpose. Nevertheless, norm-setting resolutions can determine the parameters of specific issues in ways that either present opportunities for governments to act or limit their freedom to respond. In general, those countries most supportive of and responsive to norm-setting resolutions, regardless of their content, are the middle powers. As Holbraad (1984, p. 209) suggests,

> Being weaker and more exposed than great powers, they are less able to override the law in their dealings with other states and more dependent on a system of rules and conventions protective of the sovereign rights of states. Being richer and less dependent on others than most small states, they have more to lose from a state of international lawlessness and perhaps also more to gain from a degree of international organization.

Hence, middle powers are more apt to initiate norm-setting resolutions and to circumscribe their actions in compliance with IGO-set norms to preserve a modicum of international order. Their responses, however, depend on the characteristics of the international system. In a unipolar international system, middle powers will tend to accommodate the dominant power and follow its lead concerning the content of norm-setting resolutions, whereas in a bipolar system, which course middle powers pursue may depend on geographic position and the relationship with the protagonists (Holbraad, 1984, pp. 114, 119–20). Or, middle powers may utilize norm-setting resolutions for bridge building, giving them greater responsibility than they might otherwise be expected to have. So middle powers are apt to be affected not so much by the content of the resolution, as by the function that norm-setting resolutions have in preserving their position in the international system.

In contrast, the hegemonic state and small states are both, for different reasons, less affected by norm-setting resolutions. Small states will be most responsive to norm-setting resolutions when they are produced by a coalition of small states (Katzenstein, 1985, pp. 46–7), witness UN General Assembly Resolution 2749 proclaiming the seas and seabed the "common heritage of mankind," which was initiated by Malta. In such cases, the norms will likely lessen the freedom of action of major powers *vis-à-vis* that issue-area and correspondingly enhance the potential influence of small weak states. A hegomonic state will tend to establish norms consonant with its interests, and, thus, not be required to adapt its behavior significantly. Small states, even when they play a key role in setting norms as above, face few constraints given the limited scope of their foreign policies.

The Impact of IGO Rule-Creating and Supervisory Decisions

A limited number of IGOs have the capacity to enact rules and interpret their application through dispute-settlement and supervisory processes. Rule-creating and supervisory decisions such as flow from the
General Agreement on Tariffs and Trade (GATT) or the International
Atomic Energy Agency (IAEA) directly affect national laws and regulations in their respective issue-areas. To fulfill their legal obligations to
these organizations, states have to incorporate IGO rules through
legislation or regulatory pronouncements. However, their motivations
for doing so will vary. Some states do so out of a sense of obligation;
others do so with more concern for reputation and the value of encouraging predictable cooperative behavior on the part of other states
through reciprocity. In still other cases, particularly that of a dominant
state, IGO rules will frequently coincide with existing national rules
(Henkin, 1979; Keohane, 1984). None of the above indicate that state
size has an effect on patterns of compliance and noncompliance with
IGO rules. The nature of the domestic political system and degree of
development appear to be the key variables.

Closed states and states not highly penetrated by external actors can
more effectively implement IGO rule-creating and supervisory decisions because of the relatively limited overt fragmentation within their
systems. In contrast, open political systems, particularly those with
federal and/or pluralist systems, are apt to encounter constitutional
impediments and/or cross-pressures from groups within the society to
adopting IGO decisions. Such groups may be especially sensitive or
vulnerable in opposing or supporting the actions of specific IGOs. The
openness of the system provides opportunities to influence both legislative and implementation processes giving legal effect to rule-creating
or supervisory decisions. Hence, domestic political factors will assume
substantial importance in shaping foreign policy decisions relating to
IGO-generated rule-creating and supervisory decisions. An exception
to this general point may well be the small, developed, European
corporatist states, who, having forged a high degree of national consensus about external conditions, may be in a better position to implement IGO decisions with less domestic bargaining and compromise
than larger states (Katzenstein, 1985).

Developed states are more likely to implement rule-creating and
supervisory decisions than developing states for several reasons. They
are more likely to have the specialized administrative apparatus capable of implementing such decisions, where developing states with

scarce manpower and resources often do not. Given the nature of rules generated by IGOs such as GATT, IMF (International Monetary Fund), WHO (World Health Organization), IMCO (Intergovernmental Maritime Consultative Organization) and IAEA, the adjustments required in the domestic policies of developed states, however, are likely to be less extensive than in developing states. Furthermore, Less Developed Countries (LDCs) are less likely to be parties to rule-creating IGOs that impact on foreign policy such as GATT and IMCO, and more likely to be subject to the stringent conditions imposed by the IMF which have not infrequently engendered violent domestic reactions to the changes imposed (Honeywell, 1983; Payer, 1974). Nonetheless, developed states also have more tools available to them to thwart or circumvent rule-creating measures when they so choose.

IGO-Influenced Adaptations in Foreign Policy Processes and Implementation

The influence of IGOs on methods of policy implementation and justification is less pervasive than agenda setting and of less direct impact than IGO legislative and regulatory changes. Nonetheless, such adaptations are a recurrent phenomenon. Inasmuch as IGOs are instruments or tools of national policy, the use of such tools often requires adaptation by the user.

At a minimum, member states must adapt their decision-making and implementation processes to accommodate IGO participation. Representational structures must be established and budgetary resources appropriated (Sundelius, 1983). The impact of such added bureaucratic structures and associated fiscal commitments depends on the relative influence of such units in the government and the importance attached to the IGO and the issues with which it deals. The potential for impact is significant. Where states are sufficiently developed and wealthy to have some bureaucratic and fiscal flexibility, the approach adopted by an IGO to dealing with an issue deemed important by a member government may influence the decision process or regime (Kegley, Chapter 13) for national policy making, that is, "who gets the action." Similarly, the existence of several IGOs in an issue-area, for example, trade, may lead to the emergence of multiple groups within a national government dealing with different but overlapping aspects of the issue-area (Zimmerman, 1973; Potter, 1980; Mansbach and Vasquez, 1981). The need for coordinating responses and representation may result in the creation of *ad hoc* coordinating groups.

At times, IGO decisions may be utilized by a group or individual in a domestic bureaucracy to enhance its position in seeking to implement or justify a policy change. Open pluralistic systems, especially those with highly developed bureaucracies, are most subject to such actions, sometimes involving a transgovernmental coalition. Such competitive bureaucratic politics are less likely to occur in the open systems of small corporatist states where bargaining is, by definition, more circumscribed and cooperation and compromise are highly valued (Katzenstein, 1985, p. 96). In such cases, as Kravik (1976, pp. 26–7, 156–8) suggests,

> Decisions are made with reference to some acceptable national standard . . . in such a way that the goals of voluntary associations are realized by accommodating private interests to an accepted and visible national interest . . . All participants (public and private) see themselves as responsible to both private and national constituencies. All participants in the system view themselves as sharers.

In general, the ability of national bureaucracies to adapt decision and implementation strategies to take advantage of IGOs as instruments of national policy will depend upon the receptivity of key decision makers to the requirements and opportunities of multilateral diplomacy, and their knowledge of and experience with IGO processes. This, in turn, may depend on whether the structures established by the government in managing its IGO participation can influence decision makers' knowledge and perception of IGOs. We shall delve further into the questions of receptivity and sensitivity after exploring the avenues of IGO influence on foreign policy.

Channels of IGO Influence

That IGOs serve as forums for the socialization and learning of representatives and delegates is well established (see, among others, Alger, 1963; Ernst, 1978; Peck, 1979; Riggs, 1981). Personal contacts and the necessity of operating in a "nonnational role" are particularly important in modifying a delegate's "affective map of the world," and increasing awareness of issues, the concerns of other nations, and the workings of IGOs (Alger, 1965). Delegate learning and socialization may lead to changes in behavior such as voting patterns, legislative or policy initiatives which in specific instances may alter national policy and behavior. Systematic studies linking attitude change and subsequent policy decisions are singularly lacking, however (for two exceptions see Karns, 1977, and Riggs, 1977). The potential importance of this channel will depend upon the present and subsequent status and influence of an individual, the salience of the specific issue(s) at stake and of the organization to national interests.

465

An unintended consequence of the growth and development of IGOs, but for many states, one of the most important consequences, is the emergence of networks of governmental and IGO officials (Keohane and Nye, 1974, p. 234). Empirical research on transgovernmental coalitions has been limited, however. Findings thus far suggest that members of such coalitions only partially determine the positions of their own bureaucracies and the policies pursued by their governments (Russell, 1973, p. 457); "participation by subunits of governments in transgovernmental networks and coalitions does not necessarily influence government policy decisions" (Crane, 1984, p. 401). It has been suggested that transgovernmental coalitions "are more likely to affect what governments decide to do than to impose restraints on what governments may do" (Keohane, 1982, p. 470). The formation and effectiveness of such coalitions depend on "the predisposition of heads of governments on the issues and their willingness to consult with other governments and accommodate themselves to their preferences" (Crane, 1984, p. 422). IGO secretariats are not regarded as critical either to coalition formation or to the deliberations of coalition members (Crane, 1984, p. 428).[3]

Transgovernmental coalitions have greater opportunity for affecting national policy in large, developed, and open pluralistic states, or in societies which are highly penetrated. In the former case, there are more points of access into the political process and less centralized state control. On the other hand, closed states, or small developing states fearing external penetration or conspiracy within, both sensitive and even vulnerable to manipulation from the outside, are less likely to be receptive to transgovernmental coalitions. Distrustful of such overtures, they also have less experience with operating in the bargaining environment. This stands in contrast to the expected behavior of small advanced industrialized societies which acknowledge external penetration, but seek domestic adjustments to compensate through consensual bargaining within tightly knit domestic political structures (Katzenstein, 1985).

Data on the interactions between secretariat and government officials is sparse, however, aside from isolated descriptions.[4] Explicit, direct efforts by secretariat officials to exert influence would violate the trust required for them to play mediating roles. If an executive head chooses an advocacy role, he may influence member state(s) by pressing for preferred proposals or creating a climate of favorable opinion. Raul Prebisch, the first Secretary-General of UNCTAD (United Nations Conference on Trade and Development), played such a role on the problem of trade preferences for developing countries. Amadou Mahtar M'Bow, the Director General of UNESCO, has clearly played a leading role in resisting pressure from the United States and other developed states to revise administrative procedures and management in that organization, while championing the proposals for a New World Information Order. In these cases, IGO officials used both the formal authority of office and personal suasion to influence changes in national policies (Cox, 1969; Keohane and Nye, 1974; Finkelstein, 1984).

The linkages between international and domestic nongovernmental groups, the media, and public opinion offer other channels for inputs from IGOs to foreign policy. Though the literature on these domestic sources of foreign policy is rather extensive, relatively little attention has been paid to the ways in which the activities of and participation in IGOs affect such domestic factors.

In examining the ways in which IGOs are hypothesized to influence national policies and policy making, we do not presume that IGOs are "superior" to states, although it is, in fact, possible for states to relinquish authority in certain areas as functionalism has always presumed. IGOs are not "elements of a new international order 'beyond the nation-state,' " (Keohane, 1984, p. 63), but elements of such an order of, by and for nation-states. They change "the context within which states make decisions based on self-interest," (p. 13) and contribute to a changed definition of state interests (p. 63). The key to IGO impact does not lie in the implementation and enforcement of rules, but in the opportunities that they offer for tapping additional sources of information, for the mutual adjustment of policies, and the negotiation of agreements which make other governments' policies more predictable.

We have delineated the variety of dimensions along which IGO participation may affect policy and policy-making in different types of member states. We direct our attention next to delineating the ways in which states use IGOs as instruments of statecraft and the characteristics of IGOs themselves. The character of particular IGOs and the issue-area(s) to which they are associated will affect both their use by member states and their variable impact upon those states.

IGOs as Variable Instruments and Influencers

Conceptually, then, IGOs are seen as integral parts of the contemporary system of complex interdependence. They can be a source of influence on foreign policy as shown above. However, they also differ from most other systemic variables in the extent of their interpenetration with their member states. They are both the creation of states and the tools of statecraft, available to states as part of their "menu of choices" (Russett and Starr, 1985).

IGOs offer opportunities for interest aggregation, collective influence and bargaining. Small states generally and developing states specifically are most apt to participate in such interest aggregation and to construct coalitions in IGO bodies to enhance their influence. Indeed, the formation of the Group of 77 by the developing states prompted changes in approach by the developed countries, including the use of the OECD as a vehicle for coordinating preparations for UNCTAD and the special UN sessions dealing with North-South issues. However, the developed countries have never succeeded to the extent of the developing (or the socialist) states in achieving a degree of cohesion over time and across issue-areas. Yet, over time, even the Group of 77 is likely to fragment as the newly industrializing countries (NICs) like the ASEAN states find their interests diverging. This has already begun to happen in GATT.

States frequently use IGOs as vehicles for securing collective legitimization of their own foreign policy actions and delegitimizing those of other states (Claude, 1967, ch. 4). Both major and middle powers, in particular, have sought IGO endorsement of their policies and responses to crisis, while new nations have viewed membership itself as a mark of legitimacy. Small states may seek such collective legitimization of specific actions as well, but their relative powerlessness to affect outcomes leaves them with little more than the moral high ground, witness Nicaragua's experience with the International Court of Justice after the US mining of its harbors. Yet, by mobilizing a progressively growing coalition in response to specific colonial problems over time, small states legitimized and sped the process of decolonization.

States may use IGOs both as vehicles for creating international public policy and for influencing other states' policies. In so doing, a variety of techniques may be employed, including agenda setting, coalition building, log-rolling, bilateral and multilateral discussion. By initiating policy proposals within IGOs, states set agendas for other member states who must decide how to respond. The role of dominant states in this respect is clear, especially in terms of establishing institutions within which specific policy initiatives may be developed. But IGOs open the possibility of initiation to all member states.

By providing a variety of different kinds of frameworks for multilateral cooperation in different issue areas, IGOs enhance the opportunities for different states to exercise influence within different issue-areas and organizations. Disaggregating power resources by issue and organization, or as Baldwin (1979) has suggested by the "policy-contingency framework" of each influence attempt, reduces the predictive power of structural realism by positing multiple hierarchies within the international system. Keohane (1983, p. 526) has suggested, however, that "modified structural models . . . may be valuable elements in a multilevel framework for understanding world politics."

The breadth of the agendas in UN bodies provide opportunities for linking issues, often in classic log-rolling fashion, hence permitting states to promote or safeguard specific foreign policy interests. Thus, in the Law of the Sea negotiations, landlocked states insisted on combining all other issues with the proposal for an international seabed authority in the disposition of whose revenues they had an interest. Other linkages have often provoked charges of politicization. Linked issues pose challenges to negotiators and decision makers alike. If the decisions involved are largely symbolic, then the outcome may simply be a bit of discomfort. When the decisions are as significant as those in the Law of the Sea Conference, however, the problem becomes more acute as security and economic interests are at stake.

Finally, IGOs may provide opportunities for bilateral and multilateral discussion. The annual UN General Assembly sessions are frequently cited as vehicles for the conduct of other business among representatives and ministers. This is an unintended consequence of the growth and development of IGOs, but for many states the opportunities so created are as important, if not more important, than the work of the IGO itself. In such a forum both individual and collective influence can be brought to bear on other member states' policies.

The general attitude of a government or administration toward multilateral diplomacy and toward specific IGOs has a major bearing on its receptivity and sensitivity to initiatives within or by those organizations and on its own efforts to use IGOs as instruments of policy. The task of interpreting and responding to the work of various IGOs falls to specific individuals and/or groups within member governments.

Little research exists, however, on what shapes the relative predisposition of governments and individuals toward multilateral collaboration. Some states clearly choose to resist collaboration and to minimize even the nominal intrusions of IGOs (as well as most external influences) while others follow adaptive strategies and responses maximizing the influences and even intrusions of IGOs.

Predisposition and receptivity to IGOs are not only a matter of general attitude toward external influence and multilateralism, but a function of the issue area and purposes of the IGO itself. Organizations vary in the functions they perform, in organizational structure and decision processes, and in scope of membership. Whether a state chooses to utilize a particular IGO as an instrument of its policy will depend on whether these characteristics are perceived to create a favorable forum in which to pursue national interests and objectives.

Different issue areas are apt to lead to different international arrangements (Lipson, 1984, p. 12). Although social welfare and human rights, security and economic issues constitute three broad categories of issues within IGOs, much more extensive categorizations are possible and, indeed, frequently necessary to capture the broad range of subject matter with which IGOs deal. The more salient the issue-area and multilateral cooperation to a member state, the more attention it will devote to ensuring that IGO structures favor its interests. When a member is basically disinclined to multilateralism, but feels it cannot afford not to participate, much of its effort will be devoted to limiting the role of the organization, as the Soviet Union has done on many occasions (Rubenstein and Ginsburgs, 1971).

Alternatively, states may seek out the most favorable forum, as small developing states have done in avoiding GATT and creating UNCTAD in order not to subject themselves to the rules of an open trading system that they regard as inimical to their interests.

IGOs also vary significantly by function, ranging from the ubiquitous information gathering, to norm setting, to the more authoritative functions of rule creating, supervising, or engaging in operational activities (Jacobson, 1984). Hence, a state's receptivity to a particular IGO will depend on its attitude toward multilateral (as opposed to bilateral or unilateral) performance of these various functions. Closed societies are more likely to thwart if not outright object to IGOs' information-gathering functions, while newly created states are more likely to object to IGOs performing the more decisive functions that impinge on fragile national sovereignty or state prerogatives.

Finally, organizations vary in their membership and structure. The less developed states prefer large, plenary bodies in which decision making is based on one-state, one-vote. Such forums provide maximum opportunities for coalition-building, linkage, and log-rolling. The developed states, particularly dominant ones, prefer those bodies in which their influence is greater by virtue of restricted membership and/or weighted voting, or to organizations with membership restricted to those directly involved with a particular issue. The latter facilitate bargaining on rules and procedures to extend cooperative pursuit of states' objectives. While the networks of such forums for developed states are more extensive in number and import, the basic principles behind the potential for greater cooperation among smaller numbers of states sharing common interests are well established.

Similarly, strength of IGO secretariats and executive heads varies widely among IGOs and over time. IGOs having strong secretariat leadership are apt not only to have more influence on national decision making, but more likely to be utilized by decision makers, whereas IGOs with weak secretariats, riddled by dissension on goals and administrative techniques, are less apt to be utilized, unless of course, a state or a group attempts to seize the organizational power vacuum and utilize the organization for its own purposes.

The examination of the variations among and between IGOs permits us to suggest for what purposes and under what conditions different types of states are more likely to utilize particular IGOs as instruments of their policy. Likewise, under conditions of complex interdependence, we hypothesize that IGOs influence policy and policy making in member states in varying ways and degrees as postulated above. As Riggs (1967, p. 106) has suggested, "the more useful it [an organization] becomes the greater the modification (in policy and behavior) may be."

The task of tracing influence flows, however, is one of the thorniest which political scientists face. What indicators can we devise for the responsiveness of national officials to multilateral institutions? How do we identify transgovernmental networks and coalitions? When do we know that states have accepted IGO rules and decisions? This is not the place for an extended treatment of these questions, but responsiveness of states to IGO norms and rules can be traced in the modifications of national behavior and references to IGOs in policy statements through content analysis, voting studies and systematic direct observation. Delegation sizes and voluntary contributions are indicators of the importance and utility states ascribe to IGOs as are changes in bureaucratic size and organization relevant to IGO participation. Similarly, the initiation of more (or fewer) agenda items is an indicator of state interest. Identification of transgovernmental networks and coalitions and their influence on policy will depend heavily on interview data with IGO and government officials and on transaction analysis. However, patterns of participation by national and IGO officials in multilateral meetings, not limited to formal IGO sessions where they can be traced in newspaper and documentary sources, will provide a rough outline. The acceptance of the rule-creating and supervisory decisions of an IGO will be evident in willingness of states to relinquish authority to the IGO. Cases of the latter are clearly limited, but not nonexistent, particularly in the European Community.

Conclusion

We have hypothesized that all states are influenced by their participation in IGOs and that as interdependence among states increases this

471

influence will grow. On the basis of extant work, we have also suggested a series of hypotheses on the dimensions of variance in the impact of IGOs. In summary, these assert that, among national characteristics, state size and level of development make a difference in the degree of responsiveness to IGO agenda setting, but that national interest is an important intervening variable. Size appears to make a difference in the responsiveness of IGO norms but not to rule creation and supervision. Implementation of the latter, however, is affected both by level of development and the nature of the political system, as is the likelihood that states will make adjustments in policy processes to facilitate IGO participation. Similarly, government officials from developed states with open political systems are more likely to participate in transgovernmental networks and coalitions and, hence, be subject to influences from IGO officials.

Size is also linked to the variations in the use states make of IGOs as instruments of statecraft for interest aggregation and legitimization. Level of development affects the former also and the type of IGO preferred as an instrument.

A hegemonic state which creates and uses IGOs to legitimate norms and policies will be minimally affected by IGO outputs until its dominance wanes as weaker states exploit the opportunities provided by some of the same IGOs (Krasner, 1981). Its attitude toward the utility of particular types of IGOs is likely then to undergo significant change.

For the task of addressing both our basic hypothesis that the existence and outputs of IGOs do make a difference in the behavior of states and the subsidiary hypotheses on the variable dimensions in IGO impact, a variety of methodologies will be useful, from case studies on the relations between states and IGOs, to content analysis of materials on national policies, to interviews, transaction analysis and direct observation. In concluding, however, we are led to suggest four substantive areas of future research for students of comparative foreign policy.

First, as we have hypothesized, different IGO characteristics are key variables affecting the predisposition of policy makers to multilateral diplomacy in general or to particular IGOs as tools of statecraft. This chapter only begins to uncover these variabilities. A more rigorous research cooperation with IGO scholars is required to link organizational characteristics to state behavior, thereby tapping work which has been done on IGO impact (see for example, Mingst and Schechter, 1985). Research is also needed on the sources and patterns of relative sensitivity and predisposition to multilateralism in general.

Second, we suggest the ways and degrees that IGOs are hypothesized to influence different types of states. While the classification of states is still at a rudimentary level, we have integrated the extant literature in

472

using national attributes and role in the international system. Are there characteristics other than these which are more central to explaining behavior as the political economists (e.g. Caporaso, 1985) argue with their attention to long-term structures? Do these classifications coalesce logically to form clusters of states with enough variability between clusters and enough within-cluster similarity to warrant cross-national comparisons?

Third, other IGO-related characteristics in the complex interdependence system merit further research, including the internationalization of domestic bureaucracies (Hopkins, 1976), transgovernmental coalitions and international regimes. Each of these characteristics and processes provides opportunities for and constraints on states, oft-times in much the same ways that IGOs do. Yet, heretofore, few have been systematically examined as sources of foreign policy.

Fourth, research needs to be continued on operationalizing the behavior component of foreign policy—a task central to CREON scholars at an earlier stage and urged by Baldwin (1984). In this chapter we have alluded to a variety of foreign policy behaviors associated with participation in IGOs—setting national agendas from IGOs or ignoring them, aligning or failing to align national policies to norm-setting resolutions, initiating (or not) national rules or directives in response to IGO-generated rule creation or supervisory decisions. However, these are all procedural dimensions of behavior. They tell us nothing about substance of behavior. Do IGOs influence states to be more aggressive or more amenable to peaceful settlement of disputes? More or less generous in providing economic assistance to the disadvantaged? More or less observant of human rights? More or less cooperative? These question beg systematic exploration.

Because of the proliferation of IGOs and their prominence as parts of the system of complex interdependence which characterizes contemporary international politics, we believe that students of foreign policy and policy making must take into account the ways in which IGOs impinge on different types of member states. Particular IGOs may or may not be significant. However, as integral components of the contemporary international system, as both influencers and instruments, IGOs have generated unique patterns of interpenetration between the domestic and systemic sources of foreign policy—patterns that have been inadequately explored to date.

Notes

The authors gratefully acknowledge the comments of Davis M. Bobrow, Harvey Starr, and the editors of this volume. This paper represents an offshoot of a

473

project dealing with IGOs as Instruments and Influencers of Policy, support for portions of which has come from the University of Dayton Research Council, the Roosevelt Center for American Policy Studies, the German Marshall Fund of the United States, and the University of Kentucky Research Foundation.

1 Kal J. Holsti, 1980, has also argued that states adopt strategies in the future to lessen their degree of integration and interdependence leading to fragmentation of the international system.
2 The Physical Quality of Life Index (PQLI) was developed by the Overseas Development Council. See Sewell *et al.*, 1983, for a discussion.
3 An important exception to this conclusion is contained in a case study of the role of IATA (International Air Transport Association) in mobilizing a coalition against the US effort to withdraw antitrust immunity for IATA's fare-setting framework (see Jonsson, 1984).
4 We shall address some of the methodological problems of gathering data on transnational coalitions and secretariat influence in the Conclusion.

References

Abel, Ellie (1966), *The Missile Crisis* (New York: Bantam).

Abelson, Robert P. (1973), "The structure of belief systems," in Roger C. Schank and Kenneth Mark Colby (eds), *Computer Models of Thought and Language* (San Francisco: W. H. Freeman), pp. 287–339.

Abelson, Robert P. (1975), "Concept for representing mundane reality in plans," in Daniel G. Bobrow and Allan Collins (eds), *Representation and Understanding. Studies in Cognitive Science* (New York: Academic Press), pp. 273–309.

Abelson, Robert P. (1981), "The psychological status of the script concept," *American Psychologist*, vol. 36, pp. 715–29.

Abelson, Robert P., and Carrol, J. D. (1965), "Computer simulations of individual belief systems," *American Behavioral Scientist*, vol. 8, pp. 24–30.

Abramowitz, Alan I. (1985), "Economic conditions, presidential popularity, and voting behavior in midterm congressional elections," *Journal of Politics*, vol. 47, pp. 31–43.

Adelman, I., and Morris, C. T. (1965), "A factor analysis of the interrelationship between social and political variables and per capita gross national product," *Quarterly Journal of Economics*, vol. 79, pp. 555–578.

Aho, Alfred V., Hirschberg, D. S., and Ullman, J. D. (1974), "Bounds on the complexity of the longest common subsequence problem," *Journal of the Association for Computing Machinery*, vol. 23, pp. 1–12.

Aho, Alfred V., Hopcroft, John E., and Ullman, J. D. (1974), *The Design and Analysis of Computer Algorithms* (Reading, Mass.: Addison-Wesley).

Aho, Alfred V. and Peterson, T. G., (1972), "A minimum distance error-correcting parser for context-free languages," *SIAM Journal on Computers* vol. 4, pp. 305–12.

Aiken, M., and Bacharach, S. (1979), "Culture and organizational structure and process: comparative study of local government administrative bureaucracies in Walloon and Flemish regions of Belgium," in C. J. Lammers and D. S. Hickson (eds), *Organizations Alike and Unalike* (London: Routledge and Kegan Paul), pp. 215–50.

Alexander, R. J. (1982), *Romulo Betancourt and the Transformation of Venezuela* (New Brunswick, NJ: Transaction Books).

Alger, Chadwick F. (1963), "United Nations participation as a learning experience," *Public Opinion Quarterly*, vol. 17, pp. 411–26.

Alger, Chadwick F. (1965), "Personal contact in intergovernmental organization," in H. C. Kelman (ed.), *International Behavior: A Social-Psychological Analysis* (New York: Holt, Rinehart and Winston), pp. 523–47.

Alker, Hayward R., Bennett, James, and Mefford, Dwain (1980), "Generalized precedent logics for resolving insecurity dilemmas," *International Interactions*, vol. 7, pp. 165–200.

Alker, Hayward R., Jr., and Christensen Cheryl (1972), "From causal modeling to artificial intelligence: the evolution of a UN peace-making simulation," in J. A. LaPonce and P. Smoker (eds), *Experimentation and Simulation in Political Science* (Toronto: University of Toronto Press), pp. 177–224.

Allan, Pierre (1983), *Crisis Bargaining and the Arms Race: A Theoretical Model* (Cambridge, Mass.: Ballinger).

Alliluyeva, Svetlana (1967), *Twenty Letters to a Friend* (New York: Harper and Row).

Allison, Graham T. (1969), "Conceptual models and the Cuban missile crisis," *American Political Science Review*, vol. 63, pp. 689–718.

Allison, Graham T. (1971), *Essence of Decision: Explaining the Cuban Missile Crisis* (Boston, Mass.: Little, Brown).

Allison, Graham T., and Szanton, P. (1976), *Remaking Foreign Policy: The Organizational Connection* (New York: Basic Books).

Allison, Paul D., and Liker, Jeffrey K. (1982), "Analyzing sequential categorical data on dyadic interaction," *Psychological Bulletin*, vol. 91, pp. 393–403.

Altfeld, Michael (1984), "The decision to ally: a theory and test," *Western Political Quarterly*, vol. 37, pp. 523–44.

Amstrup, Nils (1976), "The perennial problem of small states in international politics," *Cooperation and Conflict*, vol. 11, pp. 163–82.

Anderson, Charles W. (1979), "The place of principles in policy analysis," *American Political Science Review*, vol. 73, pp. 711–23.

Anderson, Irvine (1985), "In defense of case studies: an interdisciplinary analytical model for the study of foreign policy," paper presented at the Conference on New Directions in the Comparative Study of Foreign Policy, Columbus, Ohio.

Anderson, Paul A. (1983a), "Decision making by objection and the Cuban missile crisis," *Administrative Science Quarterly*, vol. 28, pp. 201–22.

Anderson, Paul A. (1983b), "Normal failures in the foreign policy advisory process," *World Affairs*, vol. 146, pp. 148–75.

Andrew, Arthur (1970), *Defense by Other Means: Diplomacy for the Underdog* (Toronto: Canadian Institute of International Affairs).

Andrews, W. (1963), *French Politics and Algeria: The Process of Policy Formation, 1954–1963* (New York: Appleton-Century-Crofts).

Andriole, Stephen J. (1984), "Detente: a quantitative analysis," *International Interactions*, vol. 11, pp. 381–95.

Anglin, D. G., and Shaw, T. M. (1979), *Zambia's Foreign Policy: Studies in Diplomacy and Dependence* (Boulder, Colo: Westview Press).

Anzai, Y., and Simon, Herbert A. (1979), "The theory of learning by doing," *Psychological Review*, vol. 36, pp. 124–40.

Aristotle (1963), "Ethics," in A. E. Wardman and J. L. Creed (trans.), *The Philosophy of Aristotle* (New York: Mentor).

Aron, Raymond (1966), *Peace and War* (New York: Praeger).

Ashford, D. (1978), "The structural analysis of policy or institutions really do matter," in D. Ashford (ed.), *Comparing Public Policies* (Beverly Hills, Calif.: Sage), pp. 81–98.

Ashley, Richard K. (1976), "Noticing pre-paradigmatic progress," in J. N. Rosenau (ed.), *In Search of Global Patterns* (New York: Free Press), pp. 150–7.

Ashley, Richard K. (1981), "Political realism and human interests," *International Studies Quarterly*, vol. 25, pp. 204–36.

Aumann, R. J. and Maschler, M. (1972), "Some thoughts on the Minimax Principle," *Management Science*, vol. 18, pp. 54–63.

References

Avery, William, and Rapkin, David P. (eds) (1982), *America in a Changing World Political Economy* (New York: Longman).
Axelrod, Robert (ed.) (1976), *Structure of Decision* (Princeton, NJ: Princeton University Press).
Axelrod, Robert (1977), "Argumentation in foreign policy settings: Britain in 1918, Munich in 1938, and Japan in 1970," *Journal of Conflict Resolution*, vol. 21, pp. 727–56.
Axelrod, Robert (1984), *The Evolution of Cooperation* (New York: Basic Books).
Azar, E. (1980), "The codebook of the conflict and peace data bank," mimeo.
Azar, Edward E., and Ben-Dak, Joseph D. (eds) (1975), *Theory and Practice of Events Research* (New York: Free Press).
Bailey, Sydney D. (1966), "UN voting: tyranny of the majority?", *The World Today*, vol. 22, pp. 234–41.
Bakeman, Roger (1978), "Untangling streams of behavior: sequential analysis of observational data," in G. P. Sackett (ed.), *Observing Behavior, Vol. II, Data Collection and Analysis Methods* (Baltimore, Md: University Park Press).
Bakeman, Roger (1983), "Computing lag sequential statistics: the ELAG program," *Behavioral Research Methods and Instrumentation*, vol. 15, pp. 530–5.
Bakeman, Roger, and Brown, Josephine E. (1977), "Behavioral dialogues: an approach to the assessment of mother-infant interaction," *Child Development*, vol. 48, pp. 195–203.
Baldwin, David A. (1979), "Power analysis and world politics: new trends vs. old tendencies," *World Politics*, vol. 31, pp. 161–94.
Baldwin, David A. (1984), "Statecraft and foreign policy analysis: whatever happened to outputs?", paper presented at the annual meeting of the American Political Science Association, Washington, DC.
Banks, A. S., and Gregg, P. M. (1963), "Grouping political systems: Q-Factor analysis of a cross-polity survey," *The American Behavioral Scientist*, vol. 9, pp. 3–5.
Barnlund, D. (1975), "Communication styles in two cultures: Japan and the US," in T. Williams (ed.), *Socialization and Communication in Primary Groups* (The Hague, Netherlands: Mouton), pp. 399–428.
Barnlund, D., and Araki, S. (1985), "International encounter: the management of compliments by Japanese and Americans," *Journal of Cross-Cultural Psychology*, vol. 16, pp. 9–26.
Barouch, Robert, McSweeney, A. J., and Soderstrom, E. J. (1978), "Randomized field experiments for program planning, development, and evaluation: an illustrative bibliography," *Evaluation Quarterly*, vol. 2, pp. 655–95.
Barr, Avron, and Feigenbaum, Edward A. (eds) (1981), *The Handbook of Artificial Intelligence*, Vol. I (Los Altos, Calif.: Kaufmann).
Barringer, Richard E. (1972), *War Patterns of Conflict*, (Cambridge, Mass.: MIT Press).
Barston, Ronald P. (ed.) (1973), *The Other Powers: Studies in the Foreign Policies of Small States* (London: Allen & Unwin).
Becker, David (1982), " 'Bonanza development' and the 'new bourgeoisie,' " *Comparative Political Studies*, vol. 15, pp. 243–88.
Benjamin, C. M., and Powell, C. A. (eds) (1986), "Modelling and experimentation in international relations," *Peace and Change*, Special Issue.
Bennett, James P. (1984), "No second thoughts about 'No First Use': How can the policy analyst undertake subjunctive reasoning in political argument?",

477

paper prepared for the annual meeting of the International Studies Association, Atlanta, Ga.

Bennett, James P. (1985), "Pre-theory for comparing national security policies," paper presented for the Conference on New Directions in the Comparative Study of Foreign Policy, Columbus, Ohio.

Bennett, James P., and Alker, Hayward R., Jr. (1977), "When national security policies breed collective insecurity: the War of the Pacific in a world politics simulation," in K. Fritsch Deutsch, H. Jaguaribe and A. Markovits (eds), *Problems of World Modelling* (Cambridge, Mass.: Ballinger), pp. 215–302.

Bennett, W. L. (1981), "Perception and cognition: an information processing framework for politics," in S. L. Long (ed.), *The Handbook of Political Behavior*, Vol. 1 (New York: Plenum), pp. 69–193.

Bernstein, Richard J. (1978), *The Restructuring of Social and Political Theory* (Philadelphia, Pa: University of Pennsylvania Press).

Best, Michael, and Connolly, William (1982), *The Politicized Economy*, 2nd edn (Lexington, Mass.: Heath).

Betancourt, R. (1968), *La Revolucion Democratica en Venezuela* (Caracas, Venezuela: Imprenta Nacional).

Bialer, Seweryn (ed.) (1981), *The Domestic Context of Soviet Foreign Policy* (Boulder, Colo: Westview Press).

Blake, David, and Walters, Robert (1983), *The Politics of Global Economic Relations*, 2nd edn (Englewood Cliffs, NJ: Prentice-Hall).

Blechman, Barry M., and Kaplan, Stephen S. (eds) (1978), *Force Without War: US Armed Forces as a Political Instrument* (Washington, DC: Brookings Institute).

Blondel, Jean (1969), *An Introduction to Comparative Government* (New York: Praeger).

Bloomfield, Lincoln P. (1974), *The Foreign Policy Process: Making Theory Relevant* (Beverly Hills, Calif.: Sage).

Bloomfield, Lincoln P., and Liess, Amelia C. (1969), *Controlling Small Wars: A Strategy for the 1970s* (New York: Knopf).

Bobrow, Davis B. (1968), "Liberation wars, national environments, and American decision-making," in T. Tsou (ed.), *China in Crisis*, Vol. 2 (Chicago: University of Chicago Press).

Bobrow, Davis B., Chan, Steve and Kringen, John A. (1979), *Understanding Foreign Policy Decisions* (New York: Free Press).

Boruch, Robert, McSweeney, A. J., and Soderstrom, E. J. (1978), "Randomized field experiments for program planning, development, and evaluation: an illustrative bibliography," *Evaluation Quarterly*, vol. 2, pp. 655–96.

Boulding, Kenneth E. (1959), "National images and international systems," *Journal of Conflict Resolution*, vol. 3, pp. 120–31.

Boulding, Kenneth E. (1962), *Conflict and Defense* (New York: Harper & Row).

Boulding, Kenneth E. (1971), "National images and international systems," in W. H. Hanreider (ed.), *Comparative Foreign Policy: Theoretical Essays* (New York: McKay), pp. 90–107.

Box, G. E., and Jenkins, G. M. (1976), *Time Series Analysis: Forecasting and Control* (San Francisco: Holden-Day).

Brady, Linda P. (1976), "Bureaucratic politics and situational constraints in foreign policy," *Sage International Yearbook of Foreign Policy Studies* (Beverly Hills, Calif.: Sage).

Brady, Linda P. (1978), "The situation and foreign policy," in M. A. East, S. A.

478

References

Salmore and C. F. Hermann (eds), *Why Nations Act* (Beverly Hills, Calif.: Sage), pp. 173–90.

Brady, Linda P. (1982), "Goal properties of foreign policy activities," in P. Callahan, L. P. Brady and M. G. Hermann (eds), *Describing Foreign Policy Behavior* (Beverly Hills, Calif.: Sage), pp. 137–52.

Brady, Linda P., and Kegley, Charles W., Jr (1977) "Bureaucratic determinants of foreign policy behavior: some empirical evidence," *International Interactions*, vol. 3, pp. 33–50.

Brams, S. J. (1977), "Deception in 2×2 games," *Journal of Peace Science*, vol. 2, pp. 171–203.

Brams, S. J., and Kilgour, M. (1985), "Optimal deterrence," paper delivered at the annual conference of the International Studies Association, Washington, DC.

Brams, S. J., and Wittman, D. (1981), "Nonmyopic equilibria in 2×2 games," *Conflict Management and Peace Science*, vol. 6, pp. 39–62.

Braudel, F. (1966), *The Mediterranean and the Mediterranean World in the Age of Phillip II*, Vol. II (New York: Harper & Row).

Brecher, Michael (1972), *The Foreign Policy System of Israel: Setting, Images, Process* (New Haven, Conn.: Yale University Press).

Brecher, Michael (1975), *Decisions in Israel's Foreign Policy* (New Haven, Conn.: Yale University Press).

Brecher, Michael, Steinberg, Blema, and Stein, Janice (1969), "A framework for research on foreign policy behavior," *Journal of Conflict Resolution*, vol. 13, pp. 75–101.

Bremer, S. (1980), "National capabilities and war proneness," in J. D. Singer (ed.), *The Correlates of War*, Vol. II (New York: Free Press), pp. 57–82.

Brody, Richard (1984), "International crises: a rallying point for the president?", *Public Opinion*, vol. 6, pp. 41–3, 60.

Brown, R. (1976), "Chinese politics and American policy: a new look at the triangle," *Foreign Policy*, vol. 23, pp. 3–23.

Browne, Malcolm W. (1985), "Hardest questions prove alluring," *New York Times*, April 23.

Budescu, David V. (1984), "Tests of lagged dominance in sequential dyadic interaction," *Psychological Bulletin*, vol. 96, pp. 402–14.

Bueno de Mesquita, B. (1980), "Theories of international conflict: an analysis and appraisal," in T. R. Gurr (ed.), *The Handbook of Political Conflict* (New York: Free Press), pp. 361–98.

Bueno de Mesquita, B. (1981), *The War Trap* (New Haven, Conn.: Yale University Press).

Bueno de Mesquita, B. (1985a), "Reply to Stephen Krasner and Robert Jervis," *International Studies Quarterly*, vol. 29, pp. 151–4.

Bueno de Mesquita, B. (1985b), "Toward a scientific understanding of international conflict: a personal view," *International Studies Quarterly*, vol. 29, pp. 121–36.

Burnstein, Eugene, and Berbaum, Michael L. (1983), "Stages in group decision making: the decomposition of historical narratives," *Political Psychology*, vol. 4, pp. 531–61.

Butler, F., and Taylor, S. (1975), "Towards an explanation of consistency and adaptability in foreign policy behavior: the role of political accountability," paper presented at the annual meeting of the Midwest Political Science Association, Chicago.

References

Callahan, Patrick (1982), "Commitment," in P. Callahan, L. Brady and M. Hermann (eds), *Describing Foreign Policy Behavior* (Beverly Hills, Calif.: Sage), pp. 177–206.

Callahan, Patrick, Brady, Linda, and Hermann, Margaret (eds) (1982), *Describing Foreign Policy Behavior* (Beverly Hills, Calif.: Sage).

Campbell, Donald T. (1975), "'Degrees of freedom' and the case study," *Comparative Political Studies*, vol. 8, pp. 178–93.

Campbell, Donald T. (1978), "Qualitative knowing in action research," in Michael Brenner, Peter Marsh and Marilyn Brenner (eds), *The Social Contexts of Method* (New York: St Martin's Press).

Campbell, Donald T., and Stanley, Julian C. (1963), *Experimental and Quasi-Experimental Designs for Research* (Chicago: Rand McNally).

Canada, Department of External Affairs (1970), *Foreign Policy for Canadians* (Ottawa, Canada: Queen's Printer).

Cantori, Louis J., and Spiegel, Steven L. (1970), *The International Politics of Regions: A Comparative Approach* (Englewood Cliffs, NJ: Prentice-Hall).

Caporaso, James A. (1978), "Dependence, dependency, and power in the global system: a structural and behavioral analysis," *International Organization*, vol. 32, pp. 13–34.

Caporaso, James A. (1982), "The state's role in Third World economic growth," *The Annals of the AAPSS*, vol. 459, pp. 103–11.

Caporaso, James A. (1985), Comments made at the Conference on New Directions in the Comparative Study of Foreign Policy, Columbus, Ohio.

Carbonell, Jaime G., Jr. (1979a), *The Counterplanning Process: A Model of Decision-Making in Adverse Situations* (Pittsburgh, Pa: Computer Science Department, Carnegie-Mellon University).

Carbonell, Jaime G., Jr. (1979b), "Subjective understanding: computer models of belief systems," doctoral dissertation, Yale University Research Report No. 150 (New Haven, Conn.: Department of Computer Science, Yale University).

Carbonell, Jaime G., Jr. (1981), "A computational model of analogical problem solving," in *Proceedings of the Seventh International Joint Conference on Artificial Intelligence*, pp. 147–52.

Carbonell, Jaime G., Jr. (1982), "Metaphor: an inescapable phenomenon in natural language comprehension," in W. Lehnert and M. Ringle (eds), *Knowledge Representation for Language Processing Systems* (Hillsdale, NJ: Lawrence Erlbaum), pp. 415–34.

Carbonell, Jaime G., Jr. (1983), "Learning by analogy: formulating and generalizing plans from past experience," in R. S. Michalski, J. G. Carbonell and T. M. Mitchell, *Machine Learning: An Artificial Intelligence Approach* (Palo Alto, Calif.: Tioga), pp. 137–61.

Cardoso, Fernando H. (1973), "Associated-dependent development: theoretical and practical implications," in A. Stepan (ed.), *Authoritarian Brazil: Origins, Policies, and Future* (New Haven, Conn.: Yale University Press), pp. 142–76.

Cardoso, Fernando H., and Faletto, Enzo (1979), *Dependency and Development in Latin America* (Berkeley, Calif.: University of California Press).

Cathcart, D., and Cathcart, R. (1976), "The Japanese social experience and concept of groups," in L. A. Smovar and R. E. Porter (eds), *Intercultural Communication* (Belmont, Calif.: Wadsworth), pp. 58–65.

Cervantes, Miguel de (1964), in W. Starkie (trans.), *Don Quixote of La Mancha* (New York: Signet).

Chan, Steve (1979), "Rationality, bureaucratic politics, and belief systems:

480

explaining the Chinese policy debate, 1964–1966," *Journal of Peace Research*, vol. 16, pp. 333–47.

Chan, Steve (1982), "Cores and peripheries: interaction patterns in Asia," *Comparative Political Studies*, vol. 15, pp. 314–40.

Chan, Steve, and Sylvan, Donald A. (1984), "Foreign policy decision making," in D. A. Sylvan and S. Chan (eds), *Describing Foreign Policy Behavior* (New York: Praeger).

Chappell, Henry W., Jr and Keech, William R. (1985), "A new view of political accountability for economic performance," *American Political Science Review*, vol. 79, pp. 10–27.

Charniak, Eugene, and Wilks, Yorick (1976), *Computational Semantics* (New York: North-Holland).

Chase-Dunn, Christopher (1978), "Core-periphery relations: the effects of core competition," in B. Kaplan (ed.), *Social Change in the Capitalist World-Economy* (Beverly Hills, Calif.: Sage), pp.159–76.

Chase-Dunn, Christopher (1981), "Interstate system and capitalist world economy: one logic or two?", *International Studies Quarterly*, vol. 25, p. 19–42.

Chilcote, Ronald, and Johnson, Dale (1983), *Theories of Development: Mode of Production or Dependency?* (Beverly Hills, Calif.: Sage).

Child, J., and Kieser, A. (1979), "Organization and managerial roles in British and West German companies," in C. Lammers and D. Hickson (eds), *Organizations Like and Unlike* (London: Routledge and Kegan Paul), pp. 251–71.

Chirac, J. (1978), "France: illusions, temptations, ambitions," *Foreign Affairs*, vol. 56, no. 3, pp. 489–99.

Choucri, Nazli, and North, Robert (1969), "The determinants of international violence," *Papers: Peace Society (International)*, vol. 12, pp. 33–63.

Choucri, Nazli, and North, Robert (1975), *Nations in Conflict: National Growth and International Violence* (San Francisco, W. H. Freeman).

Cimbala, Stephen J. (ed.) (1986), *Artificial Intelligence and National Security* (Lexington, Mass.: Lexington Books).

Clark, P. (1979), "Cultural context as a determinant of organizational rationality: a comparison of the tobacco industries in Britain and France," in C. J. Lammers and D. S. Hickson (eds), *Organizations Alike and Unalike* (London: Routledge and Kegan Paul), pp. 272–87.

Claude, Inis L., Jr (1967), *The Changing United Nations* (New York: Random House).

Coate, Roger A. (1982), *Global Issue Regimes* (New York: Praeger).

Cohen, Benjamin (1983), "An explosion in the kitchen?: economic relations with other advanced industrial states," in K. Oye, R. Lieber and D. Rothchild (eds), *Eagle Defiant: US Foreign Policy in the 1980s* (Boston, Mass.: Little, Brown), pp. 105–30.

Cohen, Bernard C. (1983), "The influence of special-interest groups and mass media on security policy in the United States," in C. W. Kegley, Jr and E. R. Wittkopf (eds), *Perspectives on American Foreign Policy* (New York: St Martin's Press), pp. 222–41.

Cohen, Michael D., March, James G., and Olsen, Johan P. (1972), "A garbage can model of organizational choice," *Administrative Science Quarterly*, vol. 17, pp. 1–25.

Cohen, Raymond (1981), *International Politics: The Rules of the Game* (New York: Longman).

References

Cohen, Stephen (1982), "Approaches to the international economic policy-making process," in W. Avery and D. Rapkin (eds), *America in a Changing World Political Economy* (New York: Longman), pp. 147–74.

Coleman, James (1966), "Individual interests and collective action," *Papers on Non-Market Decision-Making*, vol. 1, pp. 49–62.

Converse, Phillip, Miller, Warren, and Stokes, Donald (eds) (1969), *Elections and the Political Order* (New York: Wiley).

Conybeare, John (1983), "Tariff protection in developed and developing countries: a cross-sectional and longitudinal analysis," *International Organization*, vol. 37, pp. 441–67.

Cook, Thomas D., and Campbell, Donald T. (1979), *Quasi-Experimentation: Design and Analysis Issues for Field Settings* (Boston, Mass.: Houghton Mifflin).

Coplin, William D., Mills, Stephen L., and O'Leary, Michael K. (1973), "The PRINCE concepts and the study of foreign policy," in Patrick J. McGowan, Jr. (ed.), *Sage International Yearbook of Foreign Policy Studies*, Vol. 1 (Beverly Hills, Calif.: Sage), pp. 73–103.

Coplin, William D., and O'Leary, Michael K. (1972), *Everyman's PRINCE* (North Scituate, Mass.: Duxbury).

Cox, Robert W. (1969), "The executive head: an essay on leadership in international organization," *International Organization*, vol. 23, pp. 205–30.

Cox, Robert W., and Jacobson, Harold K. (eds) (1974), *Anatomy of Influence: Decision-Making in International Organizations* (New Haven, Conn.: Yale University Press).

Crabb, Cecil V., Jr (1972), *American Foreign Policy in the Nuclear Age* (New York: Harper & Row).

Crane, Barbara B. (1984), "Policy coordination by major Western powers in bargaining with the Third World: debt relief and the common fund," *International Organization*, vol. 38, pp. 399–428.

Crawford, Beverly, and Lenway, Stefanie (1985), "Decision modes and regime change: Western collaboration on East-West trade," *World Politics*, vol. 37, pp. 375–402.

Cronbach, Lee J., et al. (1980), *Toward Reform of Public Evaluation* (San Francisco: Jossey-Bass).

Crozier, M. (1964), *The Bureaucratic Phenomenon* (Chicago: University of Chicago Press).

Cupitt, Richard (1985), "Domestic determinants of import barrier dynamics," paper presented at the annual meeting of the International Studies Association, Washington, DC.

Cushman, D., and King, S. (1985), "National and organizational culture in conflict resolution," in W. Gudykunst, L. Stewert and S. Ting-Toomey (eds), *Communication, Culture, and Organizational Process* (Beverly Hills, Calif.: Sage), pp. 114–33.

Cyert, Richard, and March, James G. (1963), *A Behavioral Theory of the Firm* (Englewood Cliffs, NJ: Prentice-Hall).

Dallin, Alexander (1969), "Soviet foreign policy and domestic politics: a framework for analysis," in E. Hoffman and F. Fleron (eds), *The Conduct of Soviet Foreign Policy* (Chicago: Aldine-Atherton), pp. 36–49.

Dallin, Alexander (1981), "The domestic sources of Soviet foreign policy," in S. Bialer (ed.), *The Domestic Context of Soviet Foreign Policy* (Boulder, Colo: Westview Press), pp. 335–408.

482

References

Dallin, Alexander (1985), *Black Box: KAL 007 and the Superpowers* (Berkeley, Calif.: University of California Press).

Dearborn, DeWitt C., and Simon, Herbert A. (1958), "The identification of executives," *Sociometry*, vol. 21, pp. 140–4.

DeBastiani, Richard J. (1983), *Computers on the Battlefield: Can They Survive?* (Washington, DC: National Defense University).

de La Serre, F., and Defarges, P. (1983), "France: a penchant for leadership," in C. Hill (ed.), *National Foreign Policies and European Political Cooperation* (London: Allen & Unwin), pp. 56–70.

DePorte, A. (1984), "France's new realism," *Foreign Affairs*, vol. 63, pp. 144–165.

De Raeymaeker, Omer, *et al.* (1974), *Small Powers in Alignment* (Louvain, Belgium: Leuven University Press).

DeRivera, Joseph H. (1968), *The Psychological Dimensions of Foreign Policy* (Columbus, Ohio: Merrill).

Dessler, David, Krapela, Edward, and Doran, Charles (1983), "Political change and foreign economic policies," paper prepared for the annual meeting of the International Studies Association, Mexico City, Mexico.

Destler, I. M. (1972), *Presidents, Bureaucrats, and Foreign Policy* (Princeton, NJ: Princeton University Press).

Destler, I., Clapp, P., Sato, H., and Fukui, H. (1976), *Managing an Alliance: The Politics of US-Japanese Relations* (Washington, DC: Brookings Institute).

Destler, I., Fukui, H., and Sato, H. (1979), *The Textile Wrangle* (Ithaca, NY: Cornell University Press).

Detzer, David (1979), *The Brink: Cuban Missile Crisis, 1962* (New York: Crowell).

Deutsch, Karl W. (1966), *The Nerves of Government: Models of Political Communication and Control* (New York: Free Press).

Diamond, Stuart (1984), "Technology: advances stir global issues," *New York Times* May 24.

Diesing, Paul (1971), *Patterns of Discovery in the Social Sciences* (Chicago: Aldine Atherton).

Dietterich, T., and Michalski, R. (1981), "Inductive learning of structural descriptions," *Artificial Intelligence*, vol. 16, pp. 257–94.

Dill, William (1958), "Environment as an influence on managerial autonomy," *Administrative Science Quarterly*, vol. 2, pp. 409–43.

Dillon, William R., Madden, Thomas J., and Kumar, Ajith (1983), "Analyzing sequential categorical data on dyadic interaction: a latent structure approach," *Psychological Bulletin*, vol. 94, pp. 564–83.

Dixon, William J. (1983), "Measuring interstate affect," *American Journal of Political Science*, vol. 27, pp. 828–51.

Dixon, William J. (1985) "Action and reflection in US-Soviet relations: a discrete sequential analysis," paper presented at the annual meeting of the American Political Science Association, New Orleans, La.

Doi, L. (1976), "The Japanese patterns of communication and the concept of amae," in L. Samovar and R. Porter (eds), *Intercultural Communication* (Belmont, Calif.: Wadsworth), pp. 188–93.

Dolman, Anthony J. (1981), *Resources, Regimes, World Order* (New York: Pergamon).

Doran, C. (1971), *The Politics of Assimilation* (Baltimore, Md: Johns Hopkins University Press).

Dorr-Bremme, Donald W. (1985), "Ethnographic evaluation: a theory and

483

method," *Education Evaluation and Policy Analysis*, vol. 7, pp. 65–83.

Downs, Anthony (1967), *Inside Bureaucracy* (Boston, Mass.: Little Brown).

Duffy, Gavan (1984), "The tractability of macro applications of artificial intelligence: a reply to Rosenau," unpublished manuscript.

Duffy, Gavan, and Mallory, John (1984), "The social science workbench," unpublished paper, Cambridge, Mass.: MIT Press.

Duncan, George T., and Siverson, Randolph M. (1975), "Markov chain models for conflict analysis," *International Studies Quarterly*, vol. 19, pp. 344–74.

Dye, Thomas R. (1972), *Understanding Public Policy* (Englewood Cliffs, NJ: Prentice-Hall).

Dynes, Patrick S. (1983), *Program Evaluation: An Annotated Bibliography* (New York: Garland).

Dyson, Joseph, W., Godwin, H. B. and Hazlewood, L. (1974), "Group composition, leadership orientation and decisional outlaws," *Small Group Behavior*, vol. 7, pp. 114–28.

Dyson, J. W., and Purkitt, H. (1983), "An experimental study of cognitive processes and information in political problem-solving," grant proposal to the National Science Foundation, Florida State University and US Naval Academy (unpublished).

Dyson, J. W., and Purkitt, H. (1986a), "An experimental study of cognitive processes and information in political problem solving," final report to the National Science Foundation, Florida State University and US Naval Academy.

Dyson, J. W., and Purkitt, H. (1986b), "Review of experimental small group research," in S. Long (ed.), *Handbook of Political Behavior*.

East, Maurice A. (1972), "Stratification of world society and the international system," paper presented at the annual meeting of the International Studies Association (South), Atlanta, Ga.

East, Maurice A. (1973), "Size and foreign policy behavior: a test for two models," *World Politics*, vol. 25, pp. 556–76.

East, Maurice A. (1978a), "The international system perspective and foreign policy," in M. A. East, S. A. Salmore and C. F. Hermann (eds), *Why Nations Act* (Beverly Hills, Calif.: Sage), pp. 143–60.

East, Maurice A. (1978b), "National attributes and foreign policy," in M. A. East, S. A. Salmore and C. P. Hermann (eds), *Why Nations Act* (Beverly Hills, Calif.: Sage), pp. 123–42.

East, Maurice A. (1981), "The organizational impact of interdependence on foreign policy-making: the case of Norway," in C. W. Kegley, Jr. and P. McGowan (eds), *The Political Economy of Foreign Policy Behavior* (Beverly Hills, Calif.: Sage), pp. 137–62.

East, Maurice A. (1985), "Studying foreign ministries comparatively: an antidote for the malaise?", paper presented at the Conference on New Directions in the Comparative Study of Foreign Policy, Columbus, Ohio.

East, Maurice A., and Hermann, Charles F. (1974), "Do nation-types account for foreign policy behavior?", in J. N. Rosenau (ed.), *Comparing Foreign Policies: Theories, Findings, and Methods* (New York: Wiley), pp. 269–303.

East, Maurice A., Salmore, Steven, and Hermann, Charles F. (eds) (1978), *Why Nations Act: Theoretical Perspectives for Comparative Foreign Policy Studies* (Beverly Hills, Calif.: Sage).

East, Maurice, and Winters, Barbara Kay (1976), "Targeting behavior: a new direction," in J. N. Rosenau (ed.), *In Search of Global Patterns* (New York: Free Press), pp. 361–9.

Easton, David (1953), *The Political System: An Inquiry into the State of Political Science* (New York: Knopf).

Easton, David (1965), *A Framework for Political Analysis* (Englewood Cliffs, NJ: Prentice-Hall).

Eckstein, Harry (1975), "Case study and theory in political science," in Fred I. Greenstein and Nelson W. Polsby (eds), *Handbook of Political Science*, Vol. 7 (Reading, Mass.: Addison-Wesley), pp. 79–138.

Edwards, George C., III (1981), "Congressional responsiveness to public opinion: the case of presidential popularity," in N. R. Luttbeg (ed.), *Public Opinion and Public Policy* (Itasca, Ill.: Peacock), pp. 379–97.

Einhorn, H. J., and Hogarth, R. M. (1978), "Confidence in judgement: persistence of the illusion of validity," *Psychological Review*, vol. 85, pp. 395–416.

Erickson, Bruce W., and Sellers, Peter H. (1983), "Recognition of pattern in genetic sequences," in D. Sankoff and J. B. Kruskal (eds), *Time Warps, String Edits, and Macromolecules: The Theory and Practice of Sequence Comparison* (Reading, Mass.: Addison-Wesley), pp. 55–91.

Ermath, Fritz (1969), *Internationalism, Security, and Legitimacy: The Challenge to Soviet Interests in East Europe 1964–1968*, RM-5909-PR (Santa Monica, Calif.: RAND Corporation).

Ernst, Manfred (1978), "Attitudes of diplomats at the United Nations: the effects of organizational participation on the evaluation of the organization," *International Organization*, vol. 32, pp. 1037–44.

Etheredge, L. S. (1978), *A World of Men: The Private Sources of American Foreign Policy* (Cambridge, Mass.: MIT Press).

Etzioni, Amitai (1960), "Two approaches to organizational analysis: a critique and a suggestion," *Administrative Science Quarterly*, vol. 5, pp. 257–78.

Evans, Peter (1979), *Dependent Development: The Alliance of Multinational, State, and Local Capital in Brazil* (Princeton, NJ: Princeton University Press).

Evans, T. G. (1968), "A program for the solution of a class of geometric analogy intelligence test questions," in M. Minsky (ed.), *Semantic Information Processing* (Cambridge, Mass.: MIT Press), pp. 271–352.

Falkowski, Lawrence S. (ed.) (1979), *Psychological Models in International Politics* (Boulder, Colo: Westview Press).

Farrands, Christopher (1985), " 'Diamonds and impotence': the implementation of Giscard d'Estaing's African policies," in S. Smith and M. Clarke (eds), *Foreign Policy Implementation* (London: Allen & Unwin), pp. 72–94.

Farrell, R. Barry (1966), "Foreign policies of open and closed political systems," in R. B. Farrell (ed.), *Approaches to Comparative and International Politics* (Evanston, Ill.: Northwestern University Press), pp. 167–208.

Farris, Lee, Alker, Hayward R., Jr, Carley, Kathleen, and Sherman, Frank L. (1980), "Phase/actor disaggregated Butterworth-Scranto codebook," project working paper (Cambridge, Mass.: Center for International Studies, MIT).

Faurby, Ib (1976a), "The lack of cumulation in foreign policy studies: the case of Britain and the European Community," *European Journal of Political Research*, vol. 4, pp. 205–25.

Faurby, Ib (1976b), "Premises, promises, and problems of comparative foreign policy," *Cooperation and Conflict*, vol. 11, pp. 139–62.

Fay, Brian (1975), *Social Theory and Political Practice* (London: Allen & Unwin).

Feierabend, I. K., and Feierabend, R. L. (1966), "Aggressive behaviors within polities, 1948–62: a cross-national study," *Journal of Conflict Resolution*, vol. 10, pp. 249–71.

Feierabend, I. K., and Feierabend, R. L. (1969), "Level of development and international behavior," in R. Butwell (ed.), *Foreign Policy and the Developing Nation* (Lexington, Ky: University of Kentucky Press), pp. 135–88.

Fillmore, C. (1968), "The case for case," in E. Bach and R. T. Harms (eds), *Universals in Linguistic Theory* (New York: Rinehart & Winston), pp. 1–88.

Finkelstein, Lawrence S. (1984), "The political role of the Director General of UNESCO," paper presented at the annual meeting of the International Studies Association/West, Denver, Colo.

Finlay, David J., and Hovet, Thomas, Jr (1975), *7304: International Relations on the Planet Earth* (New York: Harper & Row).

Fischer, F. (1967), *Germany's Aims in the First World War* (New York: Norton).

Fox, Annette Baker (1959), *The Power of Small States* (Chicago; University of Chicago Press).

Frankel, Joseph (1979), *International Relations in a Changing World* (Oxford, England: Oxford University Press).

Fraser, Cleveland, R. (1986), "Decision regimes and intervention: inter-law as a mediating variable?" paper presented at the Annual Meeting of the International Studies Association (Anaheim: CA, March 25–29).

Fraser, N. M., Benjamin, C. M., and Powell, C. A. (1985), "Optimizing the decision process: structure and stability in complex conflict," *Proceedings, Society for General Systems Research*, pp. 1061–77.

Fraser, N. M., Benjamin, C. M., and Powell, C. A. (forthcoming), "New methods for applying game theory to international conflict," *International Studies Notes*.

Fraser, N. M., and Hipel, K. W. (1984), *Conflict Analysis: Models and Resolutions* (New York: North-Holland).

Fraser, N. M. and Kilgour, M. (1985) "Enumerating and evaluating the 726 non-strict ordinal 2×2 games," *Proceedings, Society for General Systems Research*, pp. 1086–94.

Freeman, Howard E. (1977), "The present status of evaluation research," in M. Guttentag and S. Saar (eds), *Evaluation Studies Review Annual*, Vol. 2 (Beverly Hills, Calif.: Sage), pp. 17–51.

Frey, Bruno (1978), *Modern Political Economy* (Oxford, England: Martin Robertson.)

Frey, Bruno, and Schneider, Friederich (1980), "Popularity functions: the case of the US and West Germany," in P. Whiteley (ed.), *Models of Political Economy* (Beverly Hills, Calif.: Sage), pp. 47–84.

Friedland, Peter, and Kedes, Laurence H. (1985), "Discovering the secrets of DNA," *Communications of the ACM*, vol. 28, pp. 1164–86.

Friedrich, C. and Brzezinski, Z. (1956), *Totalitarian Dictatorship and Autocracy* (New York: Praeger).

Friedrichs, Guenter, and Schaff, Adam (1983), *Micro-Electronics and Society: A Report to the Club of Rome* (New York: New American Library).

Fu, K. S. (1982), *Syntactic Pattern Recognition and Applications* (Englewood Cliffs, NJ: Prentice-Hall).

Fukui, H. (1977), "Policy making in the Japanese foreign ministry," in R. Scalapino (ed.), *Foreign Policy of Modern Japan* (Berkeley, Calif.: University of California Press), pp. 3–36.

The Gallup Opinion Index (1980), Report No. 182 (Princeton, NJ: The Gallup Poll).

References

The Gallup Report (1984), Report No. 231 (Princeton, NJ: The Gallup Poll).

Galtung, Johan (1964), "A structural theory of aggression," *Journal of Peace Research*, vol. 1, pp. 95–119.

Galtung, Johan (1971), "Structural theory of imperialism," *Journal of Peace Research*, vol. 8, pp. 81–117.

Gamson, W., and Modigliani, A. (1971), *Untangling the Cold War* (Boston, Mass.: Little, Brown).

Gardner, Lloyd (1970), *Architects of Illusion* (Chicago: Quadrangle).

General Accounting Office (1978), *Status and Issues: Federal Program Evaluation* (Washington, DC: US Government Printing Office).

George, Alexander L. (1969), "The operational code: a neglected approach to the study of political leaders and decision-making," *International Studies Quarterly*, vol. 13, pp. 190–222.

George, Alexander L. (1972), "The case for multiple advocacy in making foreign policy," *American Political Science Review*, vol. 66, pp. 751–85.

George, Alexander L. (1979a), "Case studies and theory development: the method of structured, focused comparison," in Paul Gordon Lauren (ed.), *Diplomacy: New Approaches in History, Theory, and Policy* (New York: Free Press), pp. 43–68.

George, Alexander L. (1979b), "The causal nexus between cognitive beliefs and decision-making behavior: the 'operational code' belief system," in L. S. Falkowski (ed.), *Psychological Models of International Politics* (Boulder, Colo: Westview Press), pp. 95–124.

George, Alexander L. (1980), *Presidential Decision Making in Foreign Policy: The Effective Use of Information and Advice* (Boulder, Colo: Westview Press).

George, Alexander L. (1982), "Case studies and theory development," paper presented at the Second Annual Symposium on Information Processing in Organizations, Pittsburgh, Pa.

George, Alexander L. (1983), "The Basic Principles Agreement of 1972: origins and expectations," in Alexander George (ed.), *Managing US-Soviet Rivalry* (Boulder, Colo: Westview Press), pp. 107–17.

George, Alexander L. (1985), "US-Soviet global rivalry: norms of competition," paper presented at the 13th International Political Science Association World Congress, Paris, France, July 10–15.

George, Alexander L., Hall, David K., and Simons, William E. (1971), *The Limits of Coercive Diplomacy: Laos, Cuba, Vietnam* (Boston, Mass.: Little, Brown).

George, Alexander L., and Smoke, R. (1974), *Deterrence in American Foreign Policy* (New York: Columbia University Press).

Gilpin, Robert (1975a), "Three models of the future," in C. F. Bergsten and L. R. Krause (eds), *World Politics and International Economics* (Washington, DC: Brookings Institute), pp. 37–60.

Gilpin, Robert (1975b), *US Power and the Multinational Corporation: The Political Economy of Foreign Direct Investment* (New York: Basic Books).

Gilpin, Robert (1979), "The computer in world affairs," in M. L. Dertouzos and J. Moses (eds), *The Computer Age: A Twenty-Year View* (Cambridge, Mass.: MIT Press), pp. 229–53.

Glass, Gene V. (1978) "Integrating findings: the meta-analysis of research," *Review of Research in Education*, vol. 5, pp. 351–79.

Glass, Gene V., McGaw, Barry and Smith, Mary Lee (1981), *Meta-Analysis in Social Research* (Beverly Hills, Calif.: Sage).

Gleason, S. Everett (1982a) "Memorandum of discussion at the 192nd meeting of the National Security Council, 6 April, 1954," *Foreign Relations of the United States, 1952–1954*, vol. 13, part 1, (Washington: Government Printing Office), pp. 1250–65.

Gleason, S. Everett (1982b) "Memorandum of discussion at the 194th meeting of the National Security Council, 29 April, 1954," *Foreign Relations of the United States, 1952–1954*, vol. 13, part 2, (Washington: Government Printing Office), pp. 1431–45.

Gleason, S. Everett (1982c) "Memorandum of discussion at the 194th meeting of the National Security Council, 6 May, 1954," *Foreign Relations of the United States, 1952–1954*, vol. 13, part 2, (Washington: Government Printing Office), pp. 1481–93.

Gleason, S. Everett (1982d) "Memorandum of discussion at the 194th meeting of the National Security Council, 8 May, 1954," *Foreign Relations of the United States, 1952–1954*, vol. 13, part 2, (Washington: Government Printing Office), pp. 1505–11.

Gobalet, J. G., and Diamond, L. J. (1979), "Effects of investment dependence on economic growth," *International Studies Quarterly*, vol. 23, pp. 412–22.

Gochman, C., and Leng, R. (1983), "Realpolitik and the road to war: an analysis of attributes and behavior," *International Studies Quarterly*, vol. 27, pp. 97–120.

Golan, Galia (1973), *Reform Rule in Czechoslovakia: The Dubcek Era, 1968–1969* (Cambridge, England: Cambridge University Press).

Gold, David, Lo, C., and Wright, Erik Olin (1975), "Recent developments in Marxist theories of the state," *Monthly Review*, vol. 27, nos 5/6, pp. 29–43, 36–51.

Goldberg, R. N. (1982), "Minimal string difference encoding," *Journal of Algorithms*, vol. 3, pp. 147–56.

Goodhart, C. A. E., and Bhansali, R. J. (1970), "Political economy," *Political Studies*, vol. 18, pp. 43–106.

Gottlieb, T. (1977), *Chinese Foreign Policy Factionalism after the Cultural Revolution*, R-1901-NA (Santa Monica, Calif.: RAND Corporation).

Gottman, John M., and Bakeman, Roger (1979), "The sequential analysis of observational data," in M. C. Lamb, S. J. Soumi and G. R. Stephenson (eds), *Social Interaction Analysis: Methodological Issues* (Madison, Wis.: University of Wisconsin Press), pp. 185–206.

Gottman, John M., and Notarius, Cliff (1978), "Sequential analysis of observational data using Markov chains," in T. R. Kratochwill (ed.), *Single Subject Research: Strategies for Evaluating Change* (New York: Academic Press), pp. 237–86.

Gourevitch, Peter (1978), "The second image reversed: the international sources of domestic politics," *International Organization*, vol. 32, pp. 881–912.

Graber, D. A. (1982a), "Have I heard this before and is it worth knowing? Variations in political information processing," paper presented at the annual meeting of the American Political Science Association, Denver, Colo.

Graber, D. A. (1982b), "Strategies for processing political information," paper presented at the annual meeting of the Midwest Political Science Association, Milwaukee, Wis.

Granick, D. (1979), "Managerial incentive systems and organizational theory," in C. Lammers and D. Hickson (eds), *Organizations Alike and Unalike* (London: Routledge and Kegan Paul), pp. 76–96.

References

Gross, Edward (1969), "The definition of organizational goals," *British Journal of Sociology*, vol. 20, pp. 282–93.

Gurr, Terry R., and Ruttenberg, C. (1971), "The conditions of civil violence: first tests of a causal model," in J. V. Gillespie and B. A. Nesvold (eds), *Macro-Quantitative Analysis* (Beverly Hills, Calif.: Sage), pp. 187–215.

Haas, Ernst B. (1969), *Tangle of Hopes: American Commitments and World Order* (Englewood Cliffs, NJ: Prentice-Hall).

Haas, Ernst B. (1975), "On systems and international regimes," *World Politics*, vol. 27, pp. 147–74.

Haas, Ernst B. (1980), "Why collaborate? Issue linkage and international regimes," *World Politics*, vol. 32, pp. 357–405.

Hacking, Ian (1984), "Winner takes less," *The New York Review of Books*, vol. 31, pp. 17–21.

Hagan, Joe (1980), "Regimes, oppositions and foreign policy: a cross-national analysis of the impact of domestic politics on foreign policy behavior," PhD dissertation, Lexington, Ky, University of Kentucky.

Hagan, Joe (1985), "Domestic political influences on foreign policy: revising and reviving themes for comparative analysis," paper presented at the annual meeting of the International Studies Association, Washington, DC.

Hagan, Joe, and Hermann, Margaret (1984), "Instability, leaders, and foreign policy: the influence of leader personality on the political use of foreign policy," paper presented at the annual meeting of the International Society of Political Psychology, Toronto, Canada.

Hagan, Joe, Hermann, Margaret, and Hermann, Charles (1982), "How decision units shape foreign policy behavior," paper presented at the annual meeting of the International Studies Association, Cincinnati, Ohio.

Hall, P. A. V., and Dowling, G. R. (1980), "Approximate string matching," *Association for Computing Machinery, Computing Surveys*, vol. 12, pp. 381–402.

Halperin, Morton H. (1974), *Bureaucratic Politics and Foreign Policy* (Washington, DC: Brookings Institute).

Halperin, Morton H., and Kanter, A. (1973), "The bureaucratic perspective: a preliminary framework," in M. H. Halperin and A. Kanter (eds), *Readings in American Foreign Policy* (Boston, Mass.: Little, Brown), pp. 1–42.

Handel, Michael (1981), *Weak States in the International System* (London: Cass).

Hanreider, W., and Auton, G. (1980), *The Foreign Policies of West Germany, France, and Britain* (Englewood Cliffs, NJ: Prentice Hall).

Harf, James E., Hoovler, David G., and James, Thomas E., Jr (1974), "Systemic and external attributes in foreign policy analysis," in J. N. Rosenau (ed.), *Comparing Foreign Policies: Theories, Findings, and Methods* (New York: Wiley), pp. 235–350.

Harf, James E., Moon, Bruce E., and Thompson, John E. (1976), "Laws, explanation, and the X-Y syndrome," in J. N. Rosenau (ed.), *In Search of Global Patterns* (New York: Free Press), pp. 271–81.

Harris, Marvin (1979), *Cultural Materialism* (New York: Random House).

Harsanyi, J. C. (1968), "Games with incomplete information played by 'Bayesian' players: Part II", *Management Science*, vol. 14, pp. 320–34.

Harsanyi, J. C. (1977), *Rational Behavior and Bargaining Equilibrium in Games and Social Situations* (New York: Cambridge University Press).

Hart, Jeffrey (1976), "Three approaches to the measurement of power in international relations," *International Organization*, vol. 30, pp. 289–305.

Hart, Jeffrey (1981), "Interpreting OECD policies toward the New International

References

Economic Order," in C. W. Kegley and P. McGowan (eds), *The Political Economy of Foreign Policy Behavior* (Beverly Hills, Calif.: Sage), pp. 215–31.

Hartmann, Frederick H. (1983), *The Relations of Nations*, 6th edn (New York: Macmillan).

Hatch, J. (1976), *Two African Statesmen* (Chicago: Henry Regnery).

Hauslohner, Peter (1981), "Prefects as senators: Soviet regional politicians look to foreign policy," *World Politics*, vol. 33, pp. 197–233.

Hayes, J. R. (1981), *The Complete Problem Solver* (Philadelphia, Pa: Franklin Institute Press).

Hayes-Roth, Frederick (1973), "A structural approach to pattern learning and the acquisition of classificatory power," in *Proceedings of the First International Joint Conference on Pattern Recognition, Washington, DC*, pp. 343–55.

Hayes-Roth, Frederick, and McDermott, John (1977), "Knowledge acquisition from structural descriptions," in *Proceedings of the Fifth International Joint Conference on Artificial Intelligence*, pp. 356–62.

Hayes-Roth, Frederick and McDermott, John (1978), "An interference matching technique for inducing abstractions," *Communcations of the ACM*, vol. 21, pp. 401–10.

Hazelwood, Leo A. (1973), "Externalizing systemic stress: international conflict as adaptive behavior," in Jonathan Wilkenfeld (ed.), *Conflict Behavior and Linkage Politics* (New York: McKay), pp. 148–90.

Helleiner, Gerald (1979), "Transnational enterprises and the new political economy of US trade policy," in J. Adams (ed.), *The Contemporary International Economy* (New York: St Martin's Press), pp. 97–110.

Hellman, D. (1969), *Japanese Domestic Politics and Foreign Policy: The Peace Agreement with the Soviet Union* (Berkeley, Calif.: University of California Press).

Henkin, Louis (1979), *How Nations Behave: Law and Foreign Policy*, 2nd edn (New York: Columbia University Press).

Heradstveit, D. (1979), *The Arab-Israeli Conflict: Psychological Obstacles to Peace* (Oslo: Universitetsforlaget).

Hermann, Charles F. (1972a), *International Crises: Insights From Behavioral Research* (New York: Free Press).

Hermann, Charles F. (1972b), "Policy classification: a key to the comparative study of foreign policy," in J. N. Rosenau, V. Davis and M. A. East (eds), *The Analysis of International Politics* (New York: Free Press), pp. 58–79.

Hermann, Charles F. (1978a), "Decision structure and process influences on foreign policy," in M. A. East, S. A. Salmore and C. F. Hermann (eds), *Why Nations Act* (Beverly Hills, Calif.: Sage), pp. 69–102.

Hermann, Charles F. (1978b), "Foreign policy behavior: that which is to be explained," in M. A. East, S. A. Salmore and C. F. Hermann (eds), *Why Nations Act* (Beverly Hills, Calif.: Sage), pp. 25–47.

Hermann, Charles F. (1979), "The effects of decision structures and processes on foreign policy behavior," paper presented at the annual meeting of the International Society of Political Psychology, Washington, DC.

Hermann, Charles F. (1983a), "Foreign policy," in Stuart S. Nagel (ed.), *Encyclopedia of Policy Studies* (New York: Dekker).

Hermann, Charles F. (1983b), "Super-power involvement with others: alternative role relationships," paper presented at the annual meeting of the American Political Science Association, Chicago, Ill.

Hermann, Charles F. (1987), "Super-power involvement in Africa: alternative role relationships," in Stephen Walker (ed.), *Role Theory and Foreign Policy Analysis* (Durham, NC: Duke University Press).

Hermann, Charles F., and Coate, Roger A. (1982), "Substantive problem areas," in P. Callahan, L. P. Brady and M. G. Hermann (eds), *Describing Foreign Policy Behavior* (Beverly Hills, Calif.: Sage), pp. 77–114.

Hermann, Charles F., and Dixon, William J. (1984), "The structure of foreign policy: from conceptualization to observation," paper presented at the annual meeting of the International Studies Association, Atlanta, Ga.

Hermann, Charles F., and East, Maurice A. (1978), Introduction, in M. A. East *et al.* (eds), *Why Nations Act* (Beverly Hills, Calif.: Sage), pp. 11–24.

Hermann, Charles F., East, Maurice A., Hermann, Margaret G., Salmore, Barbara G., and Salmore, Stephen A. (1973), *CREON: A Foreign Events Data Set* (Beverly Hills, Calif.: Sage Professional Paper Series 02–024; Vol. 2).

Hermann, Charles F., and Hermann, Margaret G. (1984), "Combining external and domestic factors in theories of foreign policy: the synthetic role of decisionmaking models," paper delivered at the annual meeting of the American Political Science Association, Washington, DC.

Hermann, Charles F., and Hermann, Margaret G. (1985), "The synthetic role of decisionmaking models in theories of foreign policy," in M. D. Ward (ed.), *Theories, Models, and Simulations in International Relations* (Boulder, Colo: Westview Press), pp. 223–48.

Hermann, Charles F., and Hudson, Valerie (1983), "A new round of foreign policy theory building: the CREON model," paper prepared for the annual meeting of the International Studies Association, Mexico City, Mexico.

Hermann, Margaret G. (1976), "When leader personality will affect foreign policy: some propositions," in J. N. Rosenau (ed.), *In Search of Global Patterns* (New York: Free Press), pp. 326–33.

Hermann, Margaret G. (1978), "The effects of personal characteristics of political leaders on foreign policy," in M. A. East, S. A. Salmore and C. F. Hermann (eds), *Why Nations Act* (Beverly Hills, Calif.: Sage), pp. 49–68.

Hermann, Margaret G. (1980), "Explaining foreign policy behavior using personal characteristics of political leaders," *International Studies Quarterly*, vol. 24, pp. 7–46.

Hermann, Margaret G. (1982), "Independence/interdependence of action," in P. Callahan *et al.* (eds), *Describing Foreign Policy Behavior* (Beverly Hills, Calif.: Sage), pp. 243–58.

Hermann, Margaret G. (1984), "Personality and foreign policy decision making: a study of 53 heads of government," in D. A. Sylvan and S. Chan (eds), *Foreign Policy Decision Making: Perception, Cognition, and Artificial Intelligence* (New York: Praeger), pp. 53–80.

Hermann, Margaret G. (1987a), "Assessing the foreign policy role orientations of Sub-Saharan African leaders," in S. Walker (ed.), *Role Theory and Foreign Policy Analysis* (Durham, NC: Duke University Press).

Hermann, Margaret G. (1987b), "Leaders' foreign policy role orientations and the quality of foreign policy decisions," in S. Walker (ed.), *Role Theory and Foreign Policy Analysis* (Durham, NC: Duke University Press).

Hermann, Margaret G., and Hermann, Charles F. (1982), "A look inside the 'black box:' building on a decade of research," in G. Hopple (ed.), *Biopolitics, Political Psychology, and International Politics* (New York: St Martin's Press), pp. 1–36.

Herrmann, Richard K. (1983), "Competing analyses of Soviet foreign policy: a

491

critical review," paper delivered at the 24th annual meeting of the International Studies Association, Mexico City.

Herring, Ronald (1980), "Structural determinants of development choices: Sri Lanka's struggle with dependency," paper prepared for the Postwar Economic Development of Sri Lanka Conference, University of Peradeniya, Sri Lanka.

Herz, John H. (1957), "Rise and demise of the territorial state," *World Politics*, vol. 9, pp. 473–93.

Heuer, R. J. (1978), "Do you think you need more information?" Unpublished mimeo.

Heuer, R. J. (1980), "Analyzing the Soviet invasion of Afghanistan: hypotheses from causal attribution theory," *Studies in Comparative Communism*, vol. 13, pp. 347–55.

Hibbs, Douglas A. (1982a), "On the demand for economic outcomes: macroeconomic performance and mass political support in the United States, Great Britain, and Germany," *Journal of Politics*, vol. 44, pp. 426–62.

Hibbs, Douglas A. (1982b), "The dynamics of political support for American presidents among occupational and partisan groups," *American Journal of Political Science*, vol. 26, pp. 312–32.

Hibbs, Douglas A., and Vasilatos, Nicholas (1981), "Economics and politics in France: economic performance and mass political support for Presidents Pompidou and Giscard d'Estaing," *European Journal of Political Research*, vol. 9, pp. 133–45.

Hicks, Alexander, Friedland, Roger and Johnson, Edwin (1978), "Class power and state policy: the case of the American states," *American Sociological Review*, vol. 43, pp. 302–15.

Hicks, Alexander, and Swank, Duane (1984), "On the political economy of welfare expansion: a comparative analysis of 18 advanced capitalist democracies, 1960–71," *Comparative Political Studies*, vol. 17, pp. 81–119.

Hilsman, Roger (1959), "The foreign policy consensus: an interim research report," *Journal of Conflict Resolution*, vol. 3, pp. 361–82.

Hirschmann, Albert (1945), *National Power and the Structure of Foreign Trade* (Berkeley, Calif.: University of California Press).

Hodnett, Grey (1981), "The pattern of leadership politics," in S. Bialer (ed.), *The Domestic Context of Soviet Foreign Policy* (Boulder, Colo: Westview Press), pp. 87–118.

Hoffmann, F. (1970), "Arms debates—a 'positional interpretation.' " *Journal of Peace Research*, vol. 7, pp. 219–28.

Hoffmann, Stanley H. (1959), "International relations: the long road to theory," *World Politics*, vol. 11, pp. 346–77.

Hoffmann, Stanley H. (1967), "Perceptions, reality and the Franco-American conflict," *Journal of International Affairs*, vol. 21, pp. 57–71.

Hoffmann, Stanley H. (1977), "An American social science: international relations," *Daedalus*, vol. 106, pp. 41–60.

Hoffmann, Stanley H. (1984), "Gaullism by any other name," *Foreign Policy*, vol. 57, pp. 38–57.

Hofstede, G. (1980), *Culture's Consequences* (Beverly Hills, Calif.: Sage).

Holbraad, Carsten (1984), *Middle Powers in International Politics* (New York: St Martin's Press).

Holland, H. (1984), *Managing Diplomacy* (Stanford, Calif.: Hoover Institution Press).

Hollander, Paul (1978), *Soviet and American Society: A Comparison* (Chicago: University of Chicago Press).

Holsti, Kalevi J. (1970), "National role conceptions in the study of foreign policy," *International Studies Quarterly*, vol. 14, p. 233–309.

Holsti, Kalevi J. (1977), *International Politics: A Framework for Analysis*, 3rd edn (Englewood Cliffs, NJ: Prentice-Hall).

Holsti, Kalevi J. (1980), "Change in the international system: interdependence, integration, and fragmentation," in O. R. Holsti, R. M. Siverson and A. L. George (eds), *Change in the International System* (Boulder, Colo: Westview Press), pp. 23–53.

Holsti, Kalevi J. (1983), *International Politics: A Framework for Analysis*, 4th edn (Englewood Cliffs, NJ: Prentice-Hall).

Holsti, Kalevi J. (1984), "Interdependence, integration, and fragmentation," in C. W. Kegley, Jr and E. R. Wittkopf (eds), *The Global Agenda: Issues and Perspectives* (New York: Random House), pp. 203–17.

Holsti, Ole R. (1976a), "Foreign policy formation viewed cognitively," in R. Axelrod (ed.), *Structure of Decision* (Princeton, NJ: Princeton University Press), pp. 18–54.

Holsti, Ole R. (1976b), "Foreign policy decision makers viewed psychologically: 'cognitive process' approaches," in J. N. Rosenau (ed.), *In Search of Global Patterns* (New York: Free Press), pp. 120–44.

Holsti, Ole R., Brody, R. and North, R., (1964), "Measuring affect and action in international reaction models," *Journal of Peace Research*, vols. 3–4, pp. 170–90.

Holsti, Ole R., North, R., and Brody, R. (1968), "Perception and action in the 1914 crisis," in J. D. Singer (ed.), *Quantitative International Politics* (New York: Free Press), pp. 123–58.

Holsti, Ole R., and Rosenau, James N. (1984), *American Leadership in World Affairs* (Boston, Mass.: Allen & Unwin).

Honeywell, Martin (ed.) (1983), *The Poverty Brokers: The IMF and Latin America* (London: Latin America Bureau).

Hoole, Francis W. (1977), "Evaluating the impacts of international organizations," *International Organization*, vol. 33, pp. 541–63.

Hopkins, Raymond F. (1976), "The international role of domestic bureaucracy," *International Organization*, vol. 30, pp. 405–32.

Hopmann, P. T., Zinnes, Dina, and Singer, J. David (eds) (1981), *Cumulation in International Relations Research* (Denver, Colo: Denver Monograph Series in World Affairs, University of Denver).

Hosoya, C. (1976), "Japan's decision making system as a determining factor in Japanese-United States relations," in M. Kaplan and K. Mushakoji (eds), *Japan, America, and the Future World Order* (New York: Free Press), pp. 117–24.

House, Ernest R. (1980), *Evaluating with Validity* (Beverly Hills, Calif.: Sage).

Howard, N. (1971), *Paradoxes of Rationality* (Cambridge, Mass.: MIT Press).

Howard, N. (1975), "Examples of a dynamic theory of games," *Papers of the Peace Science Society (International)*, vol. 24, pp. 1–27.

Howard, N. (1986), *CONAN: The Scientific Way of Gaining Co-operation and Avoiding Conflict* (Birmingham, England: Nigel Howard Systems).

Howell, Llewellyn E. (1983), "A comparative study of the WEIS and COPDAB data sets," *International Studies Quarterly*, vol. 27, pp. 149–59.

Hudson, Valerie M. (1983), "The external predisposition components of a

References

model of foreign policy behavior," unpublished doctoral dissertation, Columbus, Ohio, Ohio State University.

Hudson, Valerie, Hermann, Charles F. and Singer, Eric (1982), "Explaining the foreign policy behaviors of Ghana, Kenya, and Zambia: a test of the predictive power of the external predisposition component," paper prepared for the annual meetings of the International Studies Association, Cincinnati, Ohio.

Hudson, Valerie, Hermann, Charles F., and Singer, Eric (1985), "The situational imperative," paper presented at the Conference on New Directions in the Comparative Study of Foreign Policy, Columbus, Ohio.

Hunter, John E., Schmidt, Franck L., and Jackson, Gregg B. (1982), *Meta-Analysis: Cumulating Research Findings Across Studies* (Beverly Hills, Calif.: Sage).

Hurwitz, L. (1971), "An index of democratic political stability: a methodological note," *Comparative Political Studies*, vol. 3, pp. 41–68.

Hveem, Helge (1972), "Foreign policy as a function of international position," *Cooperation and Conflict*, vol. 7, pp. 65–86.

Hyde, Albert (1984), "A survey of the program evaluation and evaluation research literature in its formative stage," in G. R. Gilbert (ed.), *Making and Managing Policy* (New York: Dekker), pp. 219–37.

Iriye, A. (1979), "Culture and power: international relations as intercultural relations," *Diplomatic History*, vol. 3, pp. 115–28.

Isaak, Robert A. (1974), "The individual in international politics: solving the level-of-analysis problem," *Polity*, vol. 7, pp. 64–76.

Jacobson, Harold K. (1984), *Network of Interdependence: International Organizations and the Global Political System* (New York: Knopf).

James, P., and Wilkenfeld, J. (1984), "Structural factors and international crises behavior," *Conflict Management and Peace Science*, vol. 7, pp. 33–53.

James, Robert (1974), *Winston Churchill: His Complete Speeches* (London: Chelsea House).

Janda, K. (1980), *Political Parties: A Cross-National Survey* (New York: Free Press).

Janis, Irving L. (1972), *Victims of Groupthink* (Boston, Mass.: Houghton Mifflin).

Janis, Irving L. (1982), *Groupthink*. 2nd ed. (Boston, Mass.: Houghton Mifflin).

Janis, I. L., and Mann, L. (1977), *Decision-Making: A Psychological Analysis of Conflict, Choice and Commitment* (New York: Free Press).

Japan Economic Research Center (1983), *Japan's Economy in the World—1990* (Tokyo: JERC).

Jensen, Lloyd (1981), *Explaining Foreign Policy* (Englewood Cliffs, NJ: Prentice-Hall).

Jervis, Robert (1968), "Hypotheses on misperception," *World Politics*, vol. 20, pp. 454–79.

Jervis, Robert (1970), *The Logic of Images in International Relations* (Princeton, NJ: Princeton University Press).

Jervis, Robert (1976), *Perception and Misperception in International Politics* (Princeton, NJ: Princeton University Press).

Jervis, Robert (1978), "Cooperation under the security dilemma," *World Politics*, vol. 30, pp. 167–214.

Jervis, Robert (1985), "Pluralistic rigor: a comment on Bueno de Mesquita," *International Studies Quarterly*, vol. 29, pp. 145–9.

Jervis, Robert. (1986) "Cognition and political behavior," in R. R. Lau and D. O. Dears (eds), *Political Cognition* (Hillsdale, NJ: Erlbaum).

References

Jessup, Philip C. (1976a) "Memorandum of conversation, June 25, 1950," *Foreign Relations of the United States, 1950* (Washington: Government Printing Office), vol. 7, pp. 157–61.

Jessup, Philip C. (1976b) "Memorandum of conversation, June 26, 1950," *Foreign Relations of the United States, 1950* (Washington: Government Printing Office), vol. 7, pp. 179–83.

Jessup, Philip C. (1976c) "Memorandum of conversation, November 28, 1950," *Foreign Relations of the United States, 1950* (Washington: Government Printing Office), vol. 7, pp. 1242–9.

Jessup, Philip C. (1976d) "Memorandum of conversation, December 1, 1950," *Foreign Relations of the United States, 1950* (Washington: Government Printing Office), vol. 7, pp. 1276–83.

Jessup, Philip C. (1976e) "Memorandum of conversation, December 3, 1950," *Foreign Relations of the United States, 1950* (Washington: Government Printing Office), vol. 7, pp. 1323–34.

Jodice, David (1980), "Sources of change in Third World regimes for foreign direct investment, 1968–1976," *International Organization*, vol. 34, pp. 177–206.

Johnson, Richard T. (1974), *Managing the White House: An Intimate Study of the Presidency* (New York: Harper & Row).

Johnston, J. (1972), *Econometric Methods*, 2nd edn (New York: McGraw-Hill).

Jones, Edward E., Kanouse, David E., Kelley, Harold H., Nisbett, Richard E., Valins, Stuart, and Weiner, Bernard (1971), *Attribution: Perceiving the Causes of Behavior* (Morristown, NJ: General Learning Press).

Jönsson, Christer (ed.) (1982a) *Cognitive Dynamics and International Politics* (New York: St Martin's Press).

Jönsson, Christer (1982b), "The ideology of foreign policy," in C. W. Kegley, Jr and P. McGowan (eds), *Foreign Policy: USA/USSR* (Beverly Hills, Calif.: Sage), pp. 91–110.

Jönsson, Christer (1984), "Interorganization theory and international organizations: an analytical framework and a case study," paper presented at the annual meeting of the International Studies Association, Atlanta, Ga.

Kagan, Donald (1985), "The pseudo-science of peace," *The Public Interest*, vol. 7, pp. 43–61.

Kahler, Miles (1984), *Decolonization in Britain and France. The Domestic Consequences of International Relations* (Princeton, NJ: Princeton University Press).

Kahneman, Daniel, Slovic, Paul, and Tversky, Amos (eds) (1982), *Judgement Under Uncertainty: Heuristics and Biases* (Cambridge, England: Cambridge University Press).

Kahneman, Daniel, and Tversky, Adam (1972), "Subjective probability: a judgment of representativeness," *Cognitive Psychology*, vol. 3, pp. 430–54.

Kahneman, Daniel, and Tversky, Adam (1973), "On the psychology of prediction," *Psychological Review*, vol. 80, pp. 237–51.

Kaminsky, E. (1975), "The French chief executive and foreign policy," in P. McGowan (ed.), *Sage International Yearbook of Foreign Policy 3*, pp. 51–84.

Kaplan, Morton (1957), *System and Process in International Politics* (New York: Wiley).

Kaplan, Stephen S. (ed.) (1981), *Diplomacy of Power: Soviet Armed Forces as a Political Instrument* (Washington, DC: Brookings Institute).

Karns, David (1977), "The effects of interparliamentary meetings on the foreign policy attitudes of United States congressmen," *International Organization*, vol. 31, pp. 497–514.

Katzenstein, Peter (1978), *Between Power and Plenty: Foreign Economic Policies of Advanced Industrial States* (Madison, Wis.: University of Wisconsin Press).

Katzenstein, Peter (1985), *Small States in World Markets: Industrial Policy in Europe* (Ithaca, NY: Cornell University Press).

Kay, David A. (1969), *United States National Security Policy and International Organizations: The Changing Setting* (Cambridge, Mass.: MIT Press).

Kean, James, and McGowan, Patrick (1973), "National attributes and foreign policy participation: a path analysis," in P. McGowan (ed.), *Sage International Yearbook of Foreign Policy Studies, Vol. 1*, (Beverly Hills, Calif.: Sage), pp. 219–52.

Keddie, N. R. (1981), *Roots of Revolution* (New Haven, Conn.: Yale University Press).

Kegley, Charles W., Jr. (1973), "A general empirical typology of foreign policy behavior," Sage Professional Papers in International Studies 02-014 (Beverly Hills, Calif.: Sage).

Kegley, Charles W., Jr. (1976), "Selective attention: a general characteristic of the interactive behavior of nations," *International Interactions*, vol. 2, pp. 113–16.

Kegley, Charles W., Jr. (1980), "The comparative study of foreign policy: paradigm lost?", Institute of International Studies Essay Series, No. 10 (Columbia, SC: University of South Carolina).

Kegley, Charles, W. J. et al. (eds) (1975), *International Events and the Comparative Analysis of Foreign Policy* (Columbia, SC: University of South Carolina Press).

Kegley, Charles W., Jr., and McGowan, Pat, (eds) (1981), *The Political Economy of Foreign Policy Behavior* (Beverly Hills, Calif.: Sage).

Kegley, Charles W., Jr., and Raymond, Gregory A. (1981), "International legal norms and the preservation of peace, 1820–1964: some evidence and bivariate relationships," *International Interactions*, vol. 8, pp. 171–87.

Kegley, Charles W., Jr., and Raymond, Gregory A. (1982), "Alliance norms and war: a new piece in an old puzzle," *International Studies Quarterly*, vol. 26, pp. 572–95.

Kegley, Charles W., Jr., Richardson, Neil R., and Richter, Gunter (1978), "Conflict at home and abroad: an empirical extension," *Journal of Politics*, vol. 40, pp. 742–52.

Kegley, Charles W., Jr., and Skinner, Richard A. (1976), "The case-for-analysis problem," in J. N. Rosenau (ed.), *In Search of Global Patterns* (New York: Free Press), pp. 308–18.

Kegley, Charles W., Jr., and Wittkopf, Eugene R. (1982), *American Foreign Policy: Pattern and Process* (New York: St Martin's Press).

Kegley, Charles W., Jr., and Wittkopf, Eugene R. (1982-3), "Beyond consensus: the domestic context of American foreign policy," *International Journal*, vol. 38, pp. 77–106.

Kennan, George (1983), "Two views of the Soviet problem," in C. W. Kegley, Jr., and E. R. Wittkopf (eds), *Perspectives on American Foreign Policy* (New York: St. Martin's Press), pp. 40–6.

Keohane, Robert O. (1969), "Lilliputians' dilemmas: small states in international politics," *International Organization*, vol. 23, pp. 291–310.

Keohane, Robert O. (1979), "US foreign economic policy toward other advanced capitalist states: the struggle to make others adjust," in K. Oye, D.

Rothchild and R. Lieber (eds), *Eagle Entangled: US Foreign Policy in a Complex World* (New York: Longman), pp. 91–122.

Keohane, Robert O. (1982), "International agencies and the art of the possible: Case of the IEA," *Journal of Policy Analysis and Management*, vol. 1, pp. 469–81.

Keohane, Robert O. (1983), "Theory of world politics: structural realism and beyond," in A. W. Finifter (ed.), *Political Science: The State of the Discipline* (Washington, DC: American Political Science Association), pp. 503–40.

Keohane, Robert O. (1984), *After Hegemony* (Princeton, NJ: Princeton University Press).

Keohane, Robert O., and Nye, Joseph S. (1974), "Transgovernmental relations and international organizations," *World Politics*, vol. 27, pp. 39–62.

Keohane, Robert O., and Nye, Joseph S. (1977), *Power and Interdependence* (Boston, Mass.: Little, Brown).

Keohane, Robert O., and Nye, Joseph S. (1985), "Two cheers for multilateralism," *Foreign Policy*, vol. 60, pp. 148–67.

Kernell, Samuel (1977) "Presidential popularity and negative voting,' *American Political Science Review*, vol. 71, pp. 44–66.

Kernell, Samuel (1978), "Explaining presidential popularity," *American Political Science Review*, vol. 72, pp. 506–22.

Kifner, J. (1981), "How a sit-in turned into a siege," *New York Times Magazine*, May 17, p. 54–73.

Kinder, Donald R., and Weiss, Janet A. (1978), "In lieu of rationality: psychological perspectives on foreign policy decision making," *Journal of Conflict Resolution*, vol. 22, pp. 707–35.

Kindleberger, Charles P. (1974), *The World in Depression, 1929–39* (Berkeley, Calif.: University of California Press).

King, Alexander (1983), "Microelectronics and world interdependence," in G. Friedrichs and A. Schaff (eds), *Micro-Electronics and Society: A Report to the Club of Rome* (New York: New American Library), pp. 311–36.

Kirchgässner, Gebhard (1985), "Causality testing on the popularity function: an empirical investigation for the Federal Republic of Germany, 1971–1982, *Public Choice*, vol. 45, pp. 155–73.

Kirkpatrick, S. A., Davis, D. F., and Robertson, R. O. (1976), "The process of political decision-making in groups: search behavior and choice shifts," *American Behavioral Scientist*, vol. 20, pp. 33–64.

Kling, R. E. (1971), "A paradigm for reasoning by analogy," *Artificial Intelligence*, vol. 2, pp. 147–78.

Kobrin, Stephen (1980), "Foreign enterprise and forced divestment in the LDCs," *International Organization*, vol. 34, pp. 65–88.

Kochen, Manfred (1981), "Can the global system learn to control conflict?", in Richard L. Merritt and Bruce M. Russett (eds), *From National Development to Global Community: Essays in Honor of Karl W. Deutsch* (London: Allen & Unwin), pp. 379–403.

Kohl, Wilfrid L. (1975), "The Nixon-Kissinger foreign policy system in US-European relations: patterns of policy making," *World Politics*, vol. 28, pp. 1–43.

Koopmans, T. C., and Montias, J. M. (1971), "On the description and comparison of economic systems," in A. Eckstein (ed.), *Comparison of Economic Systems* (Berkeley, Calif.: University of California Press), pp. 27–78.

Korany, Bahgat (1983), "The take-off of Third World studies? The case for foreign policy," *World Politics*, vol. 35, no. 3, pp. 465–87.

Krasner, Stephen D. (1976), "State power and the structure of international trade," *World Politics*, vol. 28 (3), pp. 317–41.

Krasner, Stephen D. (1978), *Defending the National Interest: Raw Materials Investments and US Foreign Policy* (Princeton, NJ: Princeton University Press).

Krasner, Stephen D. (1981), "Transforming international regimes: what the Third World wants and why," *International Studies Quarterly*, vol. 25, pp. 119–48.

Krasner, Stephen D. (1982a), "Structural causes and regime consequences: regimes as intervening variables," in Stephen D. Krasner (ed.), *International Regimes* (Ithaca, NY: Cornell University Press), pp. 185–206.

Krasner Stephen D. (1982b), "Structural causes and regime consequences," *International Organization*, vol. 36, pp. 185–206.

Krasner, Stephen D. (1985), "Toward understanding in international relations," *International Studies Quarterly*, vol. 29, pp. 137–44.

Kratochwil, Friederich (1981) "Alternative criteria for evaluating foreign policy," *International Interactions*, vol. 8, pp. 105–22.

Kratochwil, Friederich (1984), "The force of prescriptions," *International Organization*, vol. 38, pp. 684–708.

Kravik, Robert (1976), *Interest Groups in Norwegian Politics* (Oslo: Universitetsforlaget).

Kruskal, Joseph B. (1983), "An overview of sequence comparison," in D. Sankoff and J. B. Kruskal (eds), *Time Warps, String Edits and Macromolecules: The Theory and Practice of Sequence Comparison* (Reading, Mass.: Addison-Wesley), pp. 1–44.

Kuhn, Thomas S. (1970), *The Structure of Scientific Revolution* (Chicago: University of Chicago Press).

Kume, T. (1985), "Managerial attitudes toward decision making," in W. Gudykunst, L. Stewart and S. Ting-Toomey (eds), *Communications, Culture and Organizational Process* (Beverly Hills, Calif.: Sage), pp. 231–51.

Lacqueur, W. (1969), *The Road to War* (London: Penguin).

Lafay, Jean Dominique (1984), "Political change and stability of the popularity function: the French general election of 1981," *Political Behavior*, vol. 6, pp. 333–52.

Lakatos, Imre (1970), "Falsification and the methodology of scientific research programmes," in Imre Lakatos and Alan Musgrave (eds), *Criticism and the Growth of Knowledge* (Cambridge, England: Cambridge University Press), pp. 91–196.

Lakoff, George, and Johnson, Mark (1980), *Metaphors We Live By* (Chicago: University of Chicago Press).

Lamborn, Alan C. (1985), "Risk and foreign policy choice," paper presented at the annual meeting of the International Studies Association, Washington, DC.

Larson, Deborah Welch (1985), *Origins of Containment: A Psychological Explanation* (Princeton, NJ: Princeton University Press).

Lave, Charles A., and March, James G. (1975), *An Introduction to Models in the Social Sciences* (New York: Harper & Row).

Ledeen, M., and Lewis, W. (1981), *Debacle: The American Failure in Iran* (New York: Knopf).

Lee, Jong R. (1977), "Rallying around the flag: foreign policy events and presidential popularity," *Presidential Studies Quarterly*, vol. 7, pp. 252–6.

Lee, K. C., Kegley, C. W., and Raymond, G. A. (1985), "Normative constraints on the use of force short of war: an empirical examination," paper presented at the World Congress of the International Political Science Association, Paris, France.

Lehnert, Wendy G., and Ringle, Martin H. (eds) (1982), *Strategies for Natural Language Processing* (Hillsdale, NJ: Erlbaum).

Lenat, Douglas, B., Borning, Alan, McDonald, David, Taylor, Craig, and Weyer, Stephen (1983), "Knosphere: building expert systems with encyclopedic knowledge," *Proceedings of the Eighth International Joint Conference on Artificial Intelligence*, vol. 1, pp. 167–9.

Leng, Russell J. (1983), "When will they ever learn?", *Journal of Conflict Resolution*, vol. 27, pp. 379–419.

Leng, Russell J. (1984), "Reagan and the Russians: crisis bargaining beliefs and the historical record," *American Political Science Review*, vol. 78, pp. 338–55.

Leng, Russell J. (1986), "Realism and crisis bargaining: a report on five empirical studies," in J. Vasquez (ed.), *Evaluating US Foreign Policy* (New York: Praeger), pp. 39–57.

Leng, Russell J., and Singer, J. D. (1970), *Toward a Multi-Theoretical Typology of International Behavior* (Ann Arbor, Mich.: University of Michigan, Mental Health Research Institute).

Leng, Russell J., and Singer, J. D. (1977), "Toward a multitheoretical typology of international behavior," in M. Bunge, J. Galtung and M. Malitza (eds), *Mathematical Approaches to International Politics* (Bucharest: Romanian Academy of Social and Political Science), pp. 71–93.

Leng, Russell J., and Wheeler, H. (1979), "Influence strategies, success and war," *Journal of Conflict Resolution*, vol. 23, pp. 655–84.

Leng, Russell J., and Walker, Stephen G. (1982) "Comparing two studies of crisis bargaining: confrontation coercion and reciprocity," *Journal of Conflict Resolution*, vol. 27, pp. 379–419.

Leng, Russell J., and Gochman, Charles S. (1982) "Dangerous disputes: a study of conflict behavior and war," *American Journal of Political Science*, vol. 26, pp. 664–87.

Lentner, Howard (1985), "The concept of the state in foreign policy analysis," paper presented at the Conference on New Directions in the Comparative Study of Foreign Policy, Columbus, Ohio.

Lepper, M. M. (1971), *Foreign Policy Formulation: A Case Study of the Nuclear Test Ban Treaty of 1963* (Columbus, Ohio: Merrill).

Lerche, Charles O., Jr, and Said, Abdul A. (1979), *Concepts of International Politics*, 3rd edn (Englewood Cliffs, NJ: Prentice Hall).

Levenshtein, V. I. (1965a), "Binary codes capable of correction deletions, insertion, and reversals," *Cybernetics and Control Theory*, vol. 10, no. 8, pp. 707–10, Russian original in *Doklady Akademii Nauk SSR 163*, vol. 163, no. 4, pp. 845–48.

Levenshtein, V. I. (1965b), "Binary codes capable of correcting spurious insertions and deletions of ones," *Problems of Information Transmission*, vol. 1, pp. 8–17, Russian original in *Problemy Peredachi Informatssi*, vol. 1, no. 1, pp. 12–25.

Levi, Ariel, and Tetlock, Phillip E. (1980), "A cognitive analysis of Japan's 1941 decision for war," *Journal of Conflict Resolution*, vol. 24, pp. 195–211.

LeVine, R. (1973), *Culture, Behavior, and Personality* (Chicago: Aldine Publishing Co.).

References

Levitan, Sar A., and Wurzburg, Gregory (1979), *Evaluating Federal Social Programs* (Kalamazoo, Mich.: W. E. Upjohn Institute).

Levy, Jack S. (1983), *War in the Modern Great Power System, 1495–1975* (Lexington, Ky: University Press of Kentucky).

Levy, Jack, S. (1986), "Organizational routines and the causes of war," paper presented at the annual meeting of the International Studies Association, (Calif. Anaheim).

Lewin, Kurt (1936), *Principles of Topological Psychology* (New York: McGraw-Hill).

Lewin, Kurt (1951), *Field Theory in Social Science* (New York: Harper).

Lewis-Beck, Michael S. (1980), "Economic conditions and executive popularity: the French experience," *American Journal of Political Science*, vol. 24, pp. 306–23.

Lewis-Beck, Michael S. (1984), "The economics of politics in comparative perspective: an introduction," *Political Behavior*, vol. 6, pp. 205–10.

Light, Richard J., and Pillemer, David B. (1984) *Summing Up: The Science of Reviewing Research* (Cambridge, Mass.: Harvard University Press).

Lijphart, Arend (1971), "Comparative politics and the comparative method," *American Political Science Review*, vol. 65, pp. 682–93.

Lijphart, Arend (1975), "The comparable-cases strategy in comparative research," *Comparative Political Studies*, vol. 8, pp. 158–77.

Lijphart, Arend (ed.) (1984), "New approaches to the study of cabinet coalitions," special issue of *Comparative Political Studies*, vol. 17, pp. 155–279.

Lin, S. A. Y. (1983), "Comparative economic development of Mainland China and the Republic of China," in T. B. Lee and K. Glaser (eds), *Taiwan and the Free World Security* (Taipei: Tamkang University), pp. 77–107.

Lindblom, Charles E. (1959), "The science of muddling through," *Public Administration Review*, vol. 29, pp. 79–88.

Lindblom, Charles E. (1965), *The Intelligence of Democracy* (New York: Free Press).

Lindblom, Charles E. (1977), *Politics and Markets: The World's Political-Economic Systems* (New York: Basic Books).

Lipset, Seymour Martin (1950), *Agrarian Socialism* (Berkeley, Calif.: University of California Press).

Lipset, Seymour Martin (1982), "No room for the ins: elections around the world," *Public Opinion*, vol. 5, pp. 41–6.

Lipson, Charles (1984), "International cooperation in economic and security affairs," *World Politics*, vol. 37, pp. 1–23.

Lowi, Theodore J. (1972) "Four systems of policy, politics, and choice," *Public Administration Review*, vol. 32 (July/August), pp. 298–310.

Mack, Andrew (1975), "Why big nations lose small wars: the politics of asymmetric conflict," *World Politics*, vol. 27, pp. 175–200.

MacKuen, Michael B. (1983), "Political drama, economic conditions, and the dynamics of presidential popularity," *American Journal of Political Science*, vol. 27, pp. 165–92.

Macridis, R. (1985) "French foreign policy: the quest for rank," in R. Macridis (ed.), *Foreign Policy in World Politics* (Englewood Cliffs, NJ: Prentice Hall), pp. 22–71.

Maggiotto, Michael A., and Wittkopf, Eugene R. (1981), "American public attitudes toward foreign policy," *International Studies Quarterly*, vol. 25, pp. 47–64.

Majeski, Stephen J. (1984), "Searching for generalizable decision rules: recommendations and forecasts in planning war involvement," paper prepared

500

References

for the annual meeting of the American Political Science Association, Washington, DC.

Mannheim, K. (1952), *The Problem of Generations. In his Essays on the Sociology of Knowledge* (London: Routledge and Kegan Paul).

Mansbach, Richard W., Ferguson, Yale H. and Lampert, Donald E. (1976), *The Web of World Politics* (Englewood Cliffs, NJ: Prentice-Hall).

Mansbach, Richard W., and Vasquez, J. A. (1981), *In Search of Theory: A New Paradigm for Global Politics* (New York: Columbia University Press).

Maoz, Zeev (1983), "Resolve, capability, and the outcomes of international disputes," *Journal of Conflict Resolution*, vol. 27, pp. 195–229.

March, James G., and Olsen, J. P. (1976), "Organizational choice under ambiguity," in James G. March and J. P. Olsen (eds), *Ambiguity and Choice in Organizations* (Bergen, Norway: Universitetsforlaget), pp. 10–23.

March, James G., and Simon, Herbert A. (1958), *Organizations* (New York: Wiley).

Martin, Andrew (1975), "Is democratic control of capitalist economies possible?", in L. Lindberg *et al.* (eds), *Stress and Contradiction in Modern Capitalism* (Lexington, Mass.: Lexington Books), pp. 13–56.

Martin, L. John (1982), "Disinformation: an instrumentality in the propaganda arsenal," *Political Communication and Persuasion*, vol. 12, pp. 47–64.

Matecki, B. E. (1957), *Establishment of the International Finance Corporation and United States Policy: A Case Study in International Organization* (Englewood Cliffs, NJ: Prentice Hall).

Mathisen, Trygve (1971), *The Functions of Small States in the Strategies of the Great Powers* (Oslo: Universitetsforlaget).

Maurice, M. (1979), "For a study of 'societal effect': universality and specificity in organizational research," in C. Lammers and D. Hickson (eds), *Organizations Alike and Unalike* (London: Routledge and Kegan Paul), pp. 42–60.

May, E. (1973), *Lessons of the Past: The Use and Misuse of Power in American Foreign Policy* (New York: Oxford University Press).

Mazmanian, Daniel, and Sabatier, Paul A (1983), *Implementation and Public Policy* (Glenview, Ill.: Scott, Foresman).

McClelland, Charles A. (1969), "International relations: wisdom or science?", in J. N. Rosenau (ed.), *International Politics and Foreign Policy: A Reader in Research and Theory*, rev. edn (New York: Free Press), pp. 3–5.

McClelland, Charles (1983), "Let the user beware," *International Studies Quarterly*, vol. 27, pp. 169–77.

McClelland, Charles A., and Hoggard, Gary D. (1969), "Conflict patterns in the interactions among nations," in James N. Rosenau (ed.), *International Politics and Foreign Policy* (New York: Free Press), pp. 711–24.

McClosky, Herbert (1956), "Concerning strategies for a science of international politics," *World Politics*, vol. 8, pp. 281–95.

McCormick, James M. (1980), "Intergovernmental organizations and co-operation among nations," *International Studies Quarterly*, vol. 24, pp. 75–98.

McDermott, J. (1979), "Learning to use analogies," *Proceedings of the Sixth International Joint Conference on Artificial Intelligence*, Vol. 1, pp. 568–76.

McDonald, R. (1971), *Party Systems and Elections in Latin America* (Chicago: Markham).

McGowan, Patrick (1974), "Problems in construction of positive foreign policy theory," in J. N. Rosenau (ed.), *Comparing Foreign Policies* (New York: Sage), pp. 25–44.

McGowan, Patrick (1975), "Meaningful comparisons in the study of foreign policy: a methodological discussion of objectives, techniques, and research designs," in C. W. Kegley, Jr., *et al.*, *International Events and the Comparative Analysis of Foreign Policy* (Columbia, SC: University of South Carolina Press), pp. 52–87.

McGowan, Patrick (1976), "The future of comparative studies: an evangelical plea," in J. N. Rosenau (ed.), *In Search of Global Patterns* (New York: Free Press), pp. 217–35.

McGowan, Patrick, and Kegley, Charles W., Jr. (1983a), *Foreign Policy and The Modern World System* (Beverly Hills, Calif.: Sage).

McGowan, Patrick, and Kegley, Charles W., Jr. (1983b), "Introduction: external influences on foreign policy behavior," in P. McGowan and C. W. Kegley, Jr. (eds), *Foreign Policy and the Modern World System* (Beverly Hills, Calif.: Sage), pp. 7–10.

McGowan, Patrick, and Shapiro, Howard B. (1973), *The Comparative Study of Foreign Policy: A Survey of Scientific Findings* (Beverly Hills, Calif.: Sage).

McGowan, Patrick, and Walker, Stephen (1981), "Radical and conventional models of US foreign economic policy making," *World Politics*, vol. 33, pp. 347–82.

McLellan, David S. (1976), *Dean Acheson: The State Department Years* (New York: Dodd, Mead).

Mead, Margaret (1940), "Warfare is only an invention—not a biological necessity," *Asia*, vol. 40, no. 8, pp. 402–5.

Mead, Margaret, and Metraux, Rhoda (eds) (1953), *The Study of Culture at a Distance* (Chicago: University of Chicago Press).

Mefford, Dwain (1982a), "Pattern matching and grammatical inference. Machine learning as the generalization of descriptive and exploratory data analysis," unpublished paper (Los Angeles, Calif.: University of Southern California).

Mefford, Dwain (1982b), "Case grammars and systematic case analysis," unpublished paper (Los Angeles, Calif.: University of Southern California).

Mefford, Dwain (1983), "Computational models of analogical reasoning using error-correcting parsers and a dynamic programming algorithm for sequence comparison," unpublished paper (Los Angeles, Calif.: University of Southern California).

Mefford, Dwain (1985), "Changes in foreign policy across time: the logical analysis of a succession of decision problems using logic programming," in Urs Luterbacher and Michael D. Ward (eds), *Dynamic Models of International Conflict* (Boulder, Colo: Lynne Rienner), pp. 401–23.

Meltzer, Ronald I. (1976), "The politics of policy reversal: the US response to granting trade preferences to developing countries and linkages between international organizations and national policy making," *International Organization*, vol. 30, pp. 649–68.

Mendershausen, Horst (1980), *Reflections on Territorial Defense* (Santa Monica, Calif.: RAND Corporation).

Merton, Robert K. (1957), *Social Theory and Social Structure* (Glencoe, Ill.: Free Press).

Meyer, John W., and Scott, W. Richard (1983), *Organizational Environments: Ritual and Rationality* (Beverly Hills, Calif.: Sage).

Michalski, Ryszard S., Carbonell, Jaime G., and Mitchell, Tom M. (1983), *Machine Learning: An Artificial Intelligence Approach* (Palo Alto, Calif.: Tioga).

Michels, Robert (1962), *Political Parties: A Sociological Study of the Oligarchical Tendencies of Modern Democracy*, originally published in 1915 (New York: Free Press).

Midlarsky, Manus (1974), "Power, uncertainty, and the onset of international violence," *Journal of Conflict Resolution*, vol. 18, pp. 395–431.

Miliband, Ralph (1969), *The State in Capitalist Society* (New York: Basic Books).

Millar, T. B. (1969), "On writing about foreign policy," in J. N. Rosenau (ed.), *International Politics and Foreign Policy*, 2nd edn (New York: Free Press), pp. 57–64.

Miller, G. A. (1956), "The magical number seven plus or minus two: some limits on our capacity for processing information," *Psychological Review*, vol. 63, pp. 81–97.

Miller, W. L., and Mackie, M. (1973), "The electoral cycle and the asymmetry of government and opposition popularity: an alternative model of the relationship between economic conditions and political popularity," *Political Studies*, vol. 21, pp. 263–79.

Mingst, Karen, and Schechter, Michael G. (1985), "Assessing intergovernmental organization impact: problems and prospects," *Review of International Studies*, vol. 11, pp. 199–206.

Mischel, Walter (1973), "Toward a cognitive social learning reconceptualization of personality," *Psychological Review*, vol. 80, pp. 252–83.

Mitchell, T. H. (1979), "Concession making as a determinant of vertical trade relationships," PhD dissertation (Toronto: York University).

Mitchell, T. H. (1985), "Systems planning as a bargaining process," *Proceedings, Society for General Systems Research*: pp. 1071–76.

Mitchell, T. M. (1978), "Version spaces: an approach to concept learning," PhD dissertation, Stanford University, Calif.

Mlynar, Zdenek (1978), *Nachfrost: Erfahrungen auf dem Weg vom realen zum menshlichen Sozialismus* (Cologne: Europaische Verlanganstalt).

Mohr, Lawrence B. (1973), "The concept of organizational goals," *American Political Science Review*, vol. 62, pp. 470–81.

Moon, Bruce (1982), "Exchange rate system, policy distortion, and the maintenance of trade dependence," *International Organization*, vol. 36, pp. 715–39.

Moon, Bruce (1983a), "The foreign policy of the dependent state," *International Studies Quarterly*, vol. 27, pp. 315–40.

Moon, Bruce (1983b), "The rise of interdependence and the fall of conceptual clarity," Northwestern University, mimeo.

Moon, Bruce (1985a), "Consensus or compliance? Foreign policy change and external dependence," *International Organization*, vol. 39, pp. 297–329.

Moon, Bruce (1985b), "World system effects on basic human needs," Northwestern University, mimeo.

Moon, Bruce, and Dixon, William (1985), 'Politics, the state, and basic human needs: a cross-national study," *American Journal of Political Science*, vol. 29, no. 4, pp. 661–94.

Moore, D. (1974a), "Governmental and societal influences on foreign policy in open and closed nations," in J. N. Rosenau (ed.), *Comparing Foreign Policies: Theories, Findings and Methods* (Beverly Hills, Calif.: Sage), pp. 171–99.

Moore, D. (1974b), "National attributes and nation typologies: a look at the Rosenau genotypes," in J. N. Rosenau (ed.), *Comparing Foreign Policies: Theories, Findings, and Methods* (Beverly Hills, Calif.: Sage).

Morgenthau, Hans J. (1960), *Politics Among Nations*, 3rd edn (New York: Knopf).

Morgenthau, Hans J. (1962), *The Impasse of American Foreign Policy* (Chicago: University of Chicago Press).

Most, Benjamin A., and Starr, Harvey (1982), "Case selection, conceptualization and basic logic in the study of war," *American Journal of Political Science*, vol. 26, pp. 834–56.

Most, Benjamin A., and Starr, Harvey (1983), Conceptualizing 'war': consequences for theory and research. *Journal of Conflict Resolution*, vol. 27: pp. 137–159.

Most, Benjamin A. and Starr, Harvey (1984) "International relations theory, foreign policy substitability, and 'nice' laws," *World Politics*, vol. 36, pp. 383–406.

Most, Benjamin A. and Starr, Harvey (1985), "Polarity, preponderance, and power parity in the generation of international conflict," paper presented at the annual meeting of the International Studies Association, Washington, DC.

Mosteller, Frederick, and Tukey, John W. (1977), *Data Analysis and Regression: A Second Course in Statistics* (Reading, Mass.: Addison-Wesley).

Mtshali, B. (1973), "Zambia's foreign policy: the dilemma of a new state," unpublished PhD dissertation, New York University.

Mueller, John E. (1970), "Presidential popularity from Truman to Johnson," *American Political Science Review*, vol. 64, pp. 18–34.

Mueller, John E. (1971), "Trends in popular support for the wars in Korea and Vietnam," *American Political Science Review*, vol. 65, pp. 358–75.

Mueller, John E. (1973), *War, Presidents and Public Opinion* (New York: Wiley).

Munton, Donald (1976), "Comparative foreign policy: fads, fantasies, orthodoxies, perversities," in J. N. Rosenau (ed.), *In Search of Global Patterns* (New York: Free Press), pp. 257–71.

Munton, Donald (ed.) (1978), *Measuring International Behavior: Public Sources, Events, and Validity* (Halifax, Canada: Centre for Foreign Policy Studies, Dalhousie University).

Murphy, Craig N. (1984), *The Emergence of the New International Economic Order Ideology* (Boulder, Colo: Westview Press).

Nadler, L., Nadler M., and Broome, B. (1985), "Culture and the management of conflict situations," in W. Gudykunst, L. Steward and S. Ting-Toomey (eds), *Communications, Culture and Organizational Process* (Beverly Hills, Calif.: Sage), pp. 87–113.

Nagel, Stuart S. (1982), *Public Policy: Goals, Means, and Methods* (New York: St Martin's Press).

Naisbett, John (1982), *Megatrends: Ten New Directions Transforming Our Lives* (New York: Warner).

Nash, J. F. (1951), "Non-cooperative games," *Annals of Mathematics*, vol. 54, pp. 286–95.

Neustadt, Richard E. (1970), *Alliance Politics* (New York: Columbia University Press).

Neustadt, Richard E. (1980), *Presidential Power* (New York: Wiley).

New York Times (1985) June 27, p. 1.

Newell, Allan, and Rosenbloom, P. (1981), "Mechanisms of skill acquisition and the law of practice," in J. R. Anderson (ed.), *Cognitive Skills and Their Acquisition* (Hillsdale, NJ: Erlbaum).

Newell, Allan and Simon, Herbert (1972), *Human Problem Solving* (Englewood Cliffs, NJ: Prentice-Hall).

Nicolson, Harold (1946), *The Congress of Vienna* (New York: Harcourt, Brace).

Nisbett, Richard E., and Ross, Lee (1980), *Human Inference: Strategies and Shortcomings in Social Judgement* (New York: Wiley).

Nisbett, R. E. and Wilson, P. P. (1977), "Telling more than we can know: verbal reports on mental processes," *Psychological Review*, vol. 84, pp. 231–59.

Nish, Ian H. (1966), *The Anglo-Japanese Alliance: The Diplomacy of Two Island Empires, 1894–1907* (London: Athlone).

Nitze, Paul H. (1980), "Strategy in the decade of the 1980s," *Foreign Affairs*, vol. 59, pp. 82–101.

Norpoth, Helmut, and Yantek, Thom (1983), "Macroeconomic conditions and fluctuations of presidential popularity: the question of lagged effects," *American Journal of Political Science*, vol. 27, pp. 785–807.

North, Robert C. (1969), "Research pluralism and the international elephant," in K. Knorr and J. N. Rosenau (eds), *Contending Approaches to International Politics* (Princeton, NJ: Princeton University Press), pp. 218–42.

Nye, Joseph S., Jr (1974), "UNCTAD: poor man's pressure group," in Robert W. Cox and Harold K. Jacobson (eds), *Anatomy of Influence: Decision-Making in International Organizations* (New Haven, Conn.: Yale University Press), pp. 334–70.

O'Connor, James (1973), *The Fiscal Crisis of the State* (New York: St Martin's Press).

Offe, Claus (1972), "Political authority and class structure—an analysis of late capitalist societies," *International Journal of Sociology*, vol. 2(1), pp. 73–108.

Offe, Claus (1975), "The theory of the capitalist state and the problem of policy formation," in Leon Lindberg *et al.* (eds), *Stress and Contradiction in Modern Capitalism* (Lexington, Mass.: Heath), pp. 125–144.

O'Leary, Michael (1976), "The role of issues," in J. N. Rosenau (ed.), *In Search of Global Patterns* (New York: Free Press), pp. 318–25.

O'Leary, Michael (1983), "Politics and policies as a component of international political economy: a cross-national statistical study," paper prepared for the annual meeting of the American Political Science Association, Chicago, Ill.

Olson, Mancur, Jr. (1963), "Rapid growth as a destabilizing force," *Journal of Economic History*, vol. 23, pp. 529–52.

Onuf, Nicholas G. (1982), "Global law-making and legal thought," in N. G. Onuf (ed.), *Law-Making in the Global Community* (Durham, NC: Carolina Academic Press), pp. 1–82.

"Opinion Roundup" (1980), *Public Opinion*, vol. 3, pp. 21–40.

Ore, Oystein (1962), *Theory of Graphs* (Providence, RI: American Mathematical Society).

Organski, A. F. K. (1958), *World Politics*, 2nd edn. (New York: Knopf).

Ori, K. (1976), "Political factors in postwar Japan's foreign policy decisions," in M. Kaplan and K. Mushakoji (eds), *Japan, America and the Future World Order* (New York: Free Press), pp. 145–74.

Ortony, Andrew (ed.) (1979), *Metaphor and Thought* (New York: Cambridge University Press).

References

Osgood, Robert E. (1953), *Ideals and Self-Interests in America's Foreign Relations* (Chicago: University of Chicago Press).

Ostrom, Charles W., Jr., and Job, Brian (1982), "The president and the political use of force," paper presented at the annual meeting of the American Political Science Association, Denver, Colo.

Ostrom Charles W., Jr., and Simon, Dennis M. (1985), "Promise and performance: a dynamic model of presidential performance," *American Political Science Review*, vol. 79, pp. 334–58.

Paige, Glenn D. (1968), *The Korean Decision* (New York: Free Press).

Paldam, Martin (1981), "A preliminary survey of the theories and findings on vote popularity functions," *European Journal of Political Research*, vol. 9, pp. 181–99.

Park, T. W., and Teng, C. C. (1983), "Between the North and the South: foreign policy of the newly industrializing countries," paper presented at the annual meeting of the International Studies Association, Mexico City, Mexico.

Parsons, Talcott (1956), "Suggestions for a sociological approach to the theory of organizations," *Administrative Science Quarterly*, vol. 1, pp. 64–7.

Pastor, Robert (1984), "The international debate on Puerto Rico: the costs of being an agenda-taker," *International Organization*, vol. 38, pp. 575–95.

Paterson, Thomas, G., Clifford, J. Garry, and Hagan, Kenneth J. (1983), *American Foreign Policy*, 2nd edn, vol. 1 (Lexington, Mass.: Heath).

Patton, Michael Quinn (1978), *Utilization-Focused Evaluation* (Beverly Hills, Calif.: Sage).

Payer, Cheryl (1974), *The Debt Trap: The International Monetary Fund and the Third World* (New York: Monthly Review).

Payne, J. W. (1975), "Relation of perceived risk to preferences among gambles," *Journal of Experimental Psychology: Human Perception and Performance*, vol. 21, pp. 286–94.

Payne, J. W. (1980), "Information processing theory: some concepts and methods applied to decision research," in T. S. Wallstens (ed.), *Cognitive Processes in Choice and Decision Behavior* (Hillsdale, NJ: Erlbaum), pp. 95–115.

Pearson, Frederic S. (1981), *The Weak State in International Crisis* (Washington, DC: University Press of America).

Pearson, Frederic S., and Rochester, J. Martin (1984), *International Relations: The Global Condition in the Late Twentieth Century* (Reading, Mass.: Addison-Wesley).

Peck, Richard (1979), "Socialization of permanent representatives in the United Nations: some evidence," *International Organization*, vol. 33, pp. 365–90.

Pelikan, Jiri (ed.) (1971), *The Secret Vysocany Congress: Proceedings and Documents of the Extraordinary Fourteenth Congress of the Communist Party of Czechoslovakia* (London: Allen Lane).

Pelikan, Jiri (1976), *Ein Fruhlung, der nie zu Ende geht: Erinnerungen eines Prager Kommunisten* (Frankfurt, Germany: Fischer).

Perlmutter, A. (1981), *Modern Authoritarianism: A Comparative Institutional Analysis* (New Haven, Conn.: Yale University Press).

Perrow, Charles (1961), "The analysis of goals in complex organizations," *American Sociological Review*, vol. 26, pp. 854–66.

Perrow, Charles (1970), *Organizational Analysis: A Sociological View* (Belmont, Calif.: Wadsworth).

References

Petras, James (1978), *Critical Perspectives on Imperialism and Social Class in the Third World* (New York: Monthly Review).

Phelps, R. H., and Shanteau, J. (1978), "Livestock judges: how much information can an expert use?", *Organizational Behavior and Human Performance*, vol. 21, pp. 209–19.

Phillips, Warren, (1974), "Where have all the theories gone?", *World Politics*, vol. 26, pp. 155–88.

Phillips, Warren (1978), "Prior behavior as an explanation of foreign policy," in M. A. East, S. A. Salmore and C. F. Hermann (eds), *Why Nations Act* (Beverly Hills, Calif.: Sage), pp. 161–72.

Pitz, G. F. (1980), "The very guides of life: the use of probabilistic information for making decisions," in T. S. Wallsten (ed.), *Cognitive Processes in Choice and Decision Behavior* (Hillsdale, NJ: Erlbaum), pp. 77–94.

Plischke, Elmer (1977), *Microstates in World Affairs* (Washington, DC: American Enterprise Institute).

Popper, Karl R. (1959), *The Logic of Scientific Discovery* (New York: Basic Books).

Popper, Karl R. (1963), *Conjectures and Refutations: The Growth of Scientific Knowledge* (New York: Harper Torchbooks).

Potter, William C. (1980), "Issue area and foreign policy analysis," *International Organization*, vol. 34, pp. 405–28.

Poulantzas, Nicos (1973), *Political Power and Social Classes* (London: New Left Books).

Powell, Charles, Andrus, David, Fowler, William A., and Knight, Kathleen (1974), "Determinants of foreign policy behavior: a causal modeling approach," in J. N. Rosenau (ed.), *Comparing Foreign Policies: Theories, Findings, and Methods* (New York: Wiley), pp. 151–70.

Powell, Charles A., Dyson, James W., and Purkitt, Helen E. (1985), "Foreign policy decision making: cognitive processing and optimal choice at the micro level," unpublished manuscript.

Price, James L. (1968), "The study of organizational effectiveness," *Sociological Quarterly*, vol. 13, pp. 3–15.

Puchala, Donald J. (1971), *International Politics Today* (New York: Dodd, Mead).

Puchala, Donald J., and Hopkins, Raymond F. (1983), "International regimes: lessons from inductive analysis," in S. D. Krasner (ed.), *International Regimes* (Ithaca, NY: Cornell University Press), pp. 61–91.

Purkitt, H. (1984), "A case study of the Angolan Civil War: an information processing perspective," unpublished paper prepared for the US Naval Academy.

Purkitt, H., and Dyson, J. W. (1985a), "Analyzing global systems: a problem solving perspective and some suggested applications," *Proceedings, Society for General Systems Research*, pp. 1077–85.

Purkitt, H., and Dyson, J. W. (1985b), "Understanding cognitive processes in foreign policy decision making: an information processing perspective," paper delivered at the annual conference of the International Studies Association, Washington, DC.

Purkitt, H., and Dyson, J. W. (1986), "The role of cognition in US foreign policy towards Southern Africa," *Political Psychology*.

Quinlan, J. R. (1979), "Discovering rules from large collections of examples: a case study," in Donald Michie (ed.), *Expert Systems in the Macro Electronic Age* (Edinburgh, Scotland: Edinburgh University Press).

Radford, K. J. (1976), "The treatment of complex decision, policy and planning problems," *INFOR*, vol. 14, pp. 86–94.

Rainey, Gene E. (1975), *Patterns of American Foreign Policy* (Boston, Mass.: Allyn & Bacon).

Ranney, Austin (1968), "The study of policy content: a framework for choice," in A. Ranney (ed.), *Political Science and Public Policy* (Chicago: Markham), pp. 3–22.

Rapkin, David (1983), "The inadequacy of a single logic: integrating political and material approaches to the world system," in W. Thompson (ed.), *Contending Approaches to World System Analysis* (Beverly Hills, Calif.: Sage), pp. 241–68.

Rapoport, A. (1960), *Fights, Games, and Debates* (Ann Arbor, Mich.: University of Michigan Press).

Rapoport, A. (1964), *Strategy and Conscience* (New York: Harper & Row).

Rapoport, A. (1986), "Problems and dilemmas of rationality and morality, particularly with respect to international conflict in a nuclear age," in C. M. Benjamin and C. A. Powell (eds), *Special Issue: Peace and Choice*.

Rapoport, A., and Chammah, A.J. (1965), *Prisoner's Dilemma* (Ann Arbor, Mich.: University of Michigan Press).

Rapoport, Jacques, *et al.* (1971), *Small States and Territories* (New York: Arno/ UNITAR).

Rashid, Taufiq (1985), Personal communication, Indiana University, Department of Political Science.

Reid, George L. (1974), *The Impact of Very Small Size on the International Behavior of Microstates* (Beverly Hills, Calif.: Sage).

Remington, Robin (ed.) (1969), *Winter in Prague: Documents on Czechoslovak Communism in Crisis* (Cambridge, Mass.: MIT Press).

Remington, Robin (1971), *The Warsaw Pact: Case Studies in Communist Conflict Resolution* (Cambridge, Mass.: MIT Press).

Rescher, Nicholas (1969), *Values and the Future* (New York: Free Press).

Reynolds, L. G. (1983), "The spread of economic growth to the Third World: 1859–1980," *Journal of Economic Literature*, vol. 21, pp. 941–80.

Reynolds, P. A. (1980), *An Introduction to International Relations*, 2nd edn. (London: Longman).

Rich, Elaine (1983), *Artificial Intelligence* (New York: McGraw-Hill).

Richardson, Lewis (1960), *Statistics of Deadly Quarrels* (Pittsburgh, Pa: Boxwood).

Richardson, Neil R. (1982), "Economic linkage as a detente strategy," paper presented at the annual meetings of the International Studies Association, Cincinnati, Ohio.

Richardson, Neil R. (1986), "Reagan's detente policy: economic linkage unchained," in John A. Vasquez (ed.), *Evaluating American Foreign Policy* (New York: Praeger), pp. 97–111.

Richardson, Neil, and Kegley, Charles, Jr. (1980), "Trade dependence and foreign policy compliance: a longitudinal analysis," *International Studies Quarterly*, vol. 24, pp. 191–222.

Richardson, Neil R., Kegley, Charles W., Jr. and Agnew, Ann C. (1981), "Symmetry and reciprocity in dyadic foreign policy behavior," *Social Science Quarterly*, vol. 62, pp. 128–38.

Riggs, Robert E. (1967), "The United Nations as an influence on United States policy," *International Studies Quarterly*, vol. 9, pp. 271–3.

Riggs, Robert E. (1977), "One small step for functionalism: UN participation and congressional attitude changes," *International Organization*, vol. 31, pp. 515–40.

Riggs, Robert E. (1980), "The FAO and the USDA," *Western Political Quarterly*, vol. 33, pp. 324–9.

Riggs, Robert E. (1981), "Civil servant attitudes toward the UN in Guatemala, Norway and the United States," *International Organization*, vol. 35, pp. 395–405.

Riker, William (1962), *The Theory of Political Coalitions* (New Haven, Conn.: Yale University Press).

Robinson, James A., and Majak, Roger (1967), "The theory of decision making," in J. C. Charlesworth (ed.), *Contemporary Political Analysis* (New York: Free Press), pp. 175–88.

Robinson, William F. (1968), "Czechoslovakia and its allies," *Studies in Comparative Communism*, vol. 1, pp. 141–70.

Roeder, Philip G. (1984), "Soviet policies and Kremlin politics," *International Studies Quarterly*, vol. 28, pp. 171–93.

Rosati, Jerel (1984), "The impact of beliefs on behavior: the foreign policy of the Carter Administration," in D. A. Sylvan and S. Chan (eds), *Foreign Policy Decision-Making* (New York: Praeger), pp. 158–91.

Rosati, Jerel (1985), "Continuity and change in American foreign policy: developing a theory of foreign policy," paper presented at the Conference on New Directions in the Comparative Study of Foreign Policy, Columbus, Ohio.

Rosecrance, Richard (1973), *International Relations: Peace or War?* (New York: McGraw-Hill).

Rosenau, James N. (1966), "Pre-theories and theories of foreign policy," in R. Barry Farrell (ed.) *Approaches to Comparative and International Politics* (Evanston, Ill.: Northwestern University Press), pp. 27–92.

Rosenau, James N. (1967a), *Domestic Sources of Foreign Policy* (New York: Free Press).

Rosenau, James N. (1967b), "Foreign policy as an issue area," in J. N. Rosenau (ed.), *Domestic Sources of Foreign Policy* (New York: Free Press), pp. 11–50.

Rosenau, James N. (1967c), "The premises and promises of decision-making analysis," in J. C. Charlesworth (ed.), *Contemporary Political Analysis* (New York: Free Press), pp. 189–211.

Rosenau, James N. (1968a), "Comparative foreign policy: fad, fantasy or field?", *International Studies Quarterly*, vol. 12, pp. 296–329.

Rosenau, James N. (1968b), "Moral fervor, systematic analysis, and scientific consciousness in foreign policy research," in Austin Ranney (ed.), *Political Science and Public Policy* (Chicago; Markham), pp. 197–236.

Rosenau, James N. (1969a), *Linkage Politics: Essays on the Convergence of National and International Systems* (New York: Free Press).

Rosenau, James N. (1969b) "Toward the study of national–international linkages," in James N. Rosenau (ed.), *Linkage Politics* (New York: Free Press), pp. 44–63.

Rosenau, James N. (1970), *The Adaptation of National Societies: A Theory of Political System Behavior and Transformation* (New York: McCaleb-Seiler).

Rosenau, James N. (1971), *The Scientific Study of Foreign Policy* (New York: Free Press).

Rosenau, James N. (1974), *Comparing Foreign Policies* (New York: Halsted).

Rosenau, James N. (1975), "Comparative foreign policy: one-time fad, realized fantasy, and normal field," in C. W. Kegley, Jr. *et al.* (eds), *International Events and the Comparative Analysis of Foreign Policy* (Columbia, SC: University of South Carolina Press), pp. 3–38.

Rosenau, James N. (1976a), *In Search of Global Patterns* (New York: Free Press).

Rosenau, James N. (1976b), "Restlessness, change, and foreign policy analysis," in J. N. Rosenau (ed.), *In Search of Global Patterns* (New York: Free Press), pp. 369–76.

Rosenau, James N. (1980), *The Scientific Study of Foreign Policy*, rev. edn. (New York: Nichols).

Rosenau, James N. (1981), *The Study of Political Adaptation* (New York: Nichols).

Rosenau, James N. (1982), "National and factional adaptation in Central America," in R. E. Feinberg (ed.), *Central America: International Dimensions of the Crisis* (New York: Holmes & Meier), pp. 239–69.

Rosenau, James N. (1983a), "The adaptation of small states," in B. A. Ince, A. T. Bryan, H. Addo and R. Ramsarian (eds), *Issues in Caribbean International Relations* (Lanham, Md: University Press of America), pp. 3–28.

Rosenau, James N. (1983b), "Breakpoints in history: nuclear weapons, oil embargos, and public skills as parametric shifts," Institute for Transnational Studies.

Rosenau, James N. (1984a), "The microelectronic revolution and the conduct of foreign policy," paper presented at the annual meeting of the American Political Science Association, Washington, DC.

Rosenau, James N. (1984b), "New natural resources as global issues," in C. W. Kegley and E. R. Wittkopf (eds), *The Global Agenda: Issues and Perspectives* (New York: Random House), pp. 390–7.

Rosenau, James N. (1984c), "A pre-theory revisited: world politics in an era of cascading interdependence," *International Studies Quarterly*, vol. 28, pp. 245–305.

Rosenau, James N. (1984d), "Role and role scenarios in foreign policy," paper presented at the annual meeting of the International Studies Association, Atlanta, Ga.

Rosenau, James N. (1985a), "Beyond imagery: the long-run adaptation of two Chinas," Institute for Transnational Studies.

Rosenau, James N. (1985b), "The state in an era of cascading politics, wavering concept, widening competence, withering colossus, or weathering change?", paper presented at the 13th World Congress of the International Political Science Association, Paris.

Rosenau, James N. (1985c), "Toward a single-country theory: the USSR as an adaptive system," paper presented at the Conference on Domestic Sources of Soviet Foreign and Defense Policies, University of California, Los Angeles, Calif.

Rosenau, James, Burgess, Philip M., and Hermann, Charles F. (1973), "The adaptation of foreign policy research: a case study of an anti-case study project," *International Studies Quarterly*, vol. 17, pp. 119–44.

Rosenau, James, and Hoggard, Gary (1974), "Foreign policy behavior in dyadic relationships: testing a pre-theoretical extension," in James N. Rosenau (ed.), *Comparing Foreign Policies* (Beverly Hills, Calif.: Sage), pp. 117–49.

Rossi, Peter H., and Freeman, Howard E. (1982), *Evaluation: A Systematic Approach* (Beverly Hills, Calif.: Sage).

Rothgeb, John (1985), "Trojan horse, scapegoat, or non-foreign entity: foreign policy and investment penetration in poor countries," paper presented at the annual meeting of the International Studies Association, Washington, DC.

Rothstein, Robert L. (1968), *Alliances and Small Powers* (New York: Columbia University Press).

Rothstein, Robert L. (1977), *The Weak in the World of the Strong* (New York: Columbia University Press).

Rothstein, Robert L. (1984), "Regime-creation by a coalition of the weak: lessons from the NIEO and the Integrated Program for Commodities," *International Studies Quarterly*, vol. 28, pp. 307–28.

Rouleau, E. (1980), "Khomeini's Iran," *Foreign Affairs*, vol. 59, pp. 1–20.

Rowe, Alan J. (1974), "The myth of the rational decision maker," *International Management*, vol. 29, pp. 38–40.

Rubenstein, Alvin Z., and Ginsburgs, George (eds) (1971), *Soviet and American Policies in the United Nations: A Twenty-Five Year Perspective* (New York: New York University Press).

Rubin, B. (1980), *Paved with Good Intentions* (New York: Oxford University Press).

Rubin, T., and Hill, G. (1973), *Experiments in the Scaling and Weighting of International Events Data* (Arlington, Va: Consolidated Analysis Center).

Ruggie, John (1972), "Collective goods and future international collaboration," *American Political Science Review*, vol. 66, pp. 874–93.

Rumelhart, David, and Ortony, Andrew (1977), "The representation of knowledge in memory," in Richard C. Anders *et al.* (eds), *Schooling and the Acquisition of Knowledge* (Hillsdale, NJ: Erlbaum).

Rummel, Rudolph J. (1963), "Dimensions of conflict behavior within and between nations," *Yearbook of the Society for General Systems*, vol. 8, pp. 1–50.

Rummel, Rudolph J. (1964), "Testing some possible predictors of conflict behavior within and between nations," *Peace Research Society Papers*, vol. 1, pp. 79–111.

Rummel, Rudolph J. (1968), "The relationship between national attributes and foreign conflict behavior," in J. D. Singer (ed.), *Quantitative International Politics: Insights and Evidence* (New York: Free Press), pp. 187–214.

Rummel, Rudolph J. (1969), "Indicators of cross-national and international patterns," *American Political Science Review*, vol. 63, pp. 127–47.

Rummel, Rudolph J. (1972), *The Dimensionality of Nations Project* (Beverly Hills, Calif.: Sage).

Rummel, Rudolph J. (1977), *Field Theory Evolving* (Beverly Hills, Calif.: Sage).

Rummel, Rudolph J. (1979a), *National Attributes and Behavior* (Beverly Hills, Calif.: Sage).

Rummel, Rudolph J. (1979b), *War, Power, Peace: Understanding Conflict and War, Vol. 4* (Beverly Hills, Calif.: Sage).

Russell, Robert W. (1973), "Transgovernmental interaction in the international monetary system, 1960–1972," *International Organization*, vol. 27, pp. 431–64.

Russett, Bruce M. (1967), *International Regions and the International System* (Chicago; Rand McNally).

Russett, Bruce M. (1968), "Components of an operational theory of alliance formation," *Journal of Conflict Resolution*, vol. 12, pp. 285–301.

Russett, Bruce M. (1970a), "International behavior research: case studies and cumulation," in Michael Haas and Henry S. Kariel (eds), *Approaches to the Study of Political Science* (Scranton, Pa: Chandler), pp. 425–43.

Russett, Bruce M. (1970b), *What Price Vigilance?* (New Haven, Conn.: Yale University Press).

Russett, Bruce M. (1974), "International behavior research: case studies and cumulations," in B. Russett (ed.), *Power and Community in World Politics* (San Francisco: W. H. Freeman), pp. 13–30.

Russett, Bruce M. (1978), "The marginal utility of income transfers to the Third World," *International Organization*, vol. 32, pp. 913–28.

Russett, Bruce M. (1983), "International interactions and processes: the internal vs. external debate revisited," in A. W. Finifter (ed.), *Political Science: The State of the Discipline* (Washington, DC: American Political Science Association), pp. 541–69.

Russett, Bruce M., and Monsen, R. Joseph (1975), "Bureaucracy and polyarchy as predictors of performance: a cross-national examination," *Comparative Political Studies*, vol. 8, pp. 5–31.

Russett, Bruce M. and Starr, Harvey (1985), *World Politics: The Menu For Choice*, 2nd edn. (New York: W. H. Freeman).

Rutman, Leonard (1980), *Planning Useful Evaluations* (Beverly Hills, Calif.: Sage).

Sacerdoti, Earl D. (1977), *A Structure for Plans and Behavior* (New York: Elsevier).

Sackett, Gene P. (1979), "The lag sequential analysis of contingency and cyclicity in behavioral interaction research," in J. D. Osofsky (ed.), *Handbook of Infant Development* (New York: Wiley), pp. 623–49.

Sackett, Gene P. (1980), "Lag sequential analysis as a data reduction technique in social interaction research," in D. B. Sawin, R. D. Hawkins, L. O. Walker and J. Hinson Penticuff (eds), *Exceptional Infant, Vol. 4, Psychosocial Risks in Infant Environment Transaction* (New York: Brunner, Mazel), pp. 300–40.

Sackett, Gene P., Holm, R., Crowley, C., and Henkins, A. (1979), "A FORTRAN program for lag sequential analysis of contingency and cyclicity in behavioral interaction data," *Behavior Research Methods and Instrumentation*, vol. 11, pp. 366–78.

Salmore, Stephen A., and Hermann, Charles F. (1969), "The effect of size, development, and accountability on foreign policy," *Peace Research Society Papers*, vol. 14, pp. 16–30.

Salmore, Stephen A., and Hermann, Charles F. (1970), "The effect of size, development and accountability on foreign policy," paper presented at the annual meeting of the American Political Science Association, Los Angeles, Calif.

Salmore, B. and Salmore, S. (1970), "Political accountability and foreign policy," paper presented at the annual meeting of the American Political Science Association, Los Angeles, Calif.

Salmore, B., and Salmore, S. (1978), "Political regimes and foreign policy," in M. East *et al.* (eds), *Why Nations Act: Theoretical Perspectives for Comparative Foreign Policy Studies* (Beverly Hills, Calif.: Sage), pp. 103–22.

Sarbin, Theodore, and Allen, Vernon (1968), "Role theory," in G. Lindzey and E. Aronson (eds), *The Handbook of Social Psychology*, vol. 1, 2nd edn. (Reading, Mass.: Addison-Wesley), pp. 488–567.

Sawyer, Jack, *et al.* (1967), "Dimensions of nations: size, wealth, and politics," *Journal of Sociology*, vol. 73, pp. 145–72.

Sayle, Murray (1985), "KA007: a conspiracy of circumstance," *New York Review of Books*, pp. 44–54.

Shanck, Roger. C., and Abelson, R. P. (1980), *Scripts, Plans, Goals and Understanding. An Inquiry into Human Knowledge Structures* (Hillsdale, NJ: Erlbaum).

Schelling, Thomas (1960), *The Strategy of Conflict* (Cambridge, Mass.: Harvard University Press).

Schelling, Thomas (1978), *Micromotives and Macrobehavior* (New York: Norton).

Schlesinger, Arthur M., Jr. (1965), *A Thousand Days: John F. Kennedy in the White House* (Boston, Mass.: Houghton Mifflin).

Schmidt-Hauer, Christian, and Muller, Adolf (1968), *Viva Dubcek: Reform und Okkupation in der CSSR* (Cologne, Germany: Kiepeneuer & Witsch).

Schonfeld, W. (1976), *Obedience and Revolt* (Beverly Hills, Calif.: Sage).

Schoultz, Lars (1981), *Human Rights and United States Policy Toward Latin America* (Princeton, NJ: Princeton University Press).

Schreider, Ju. A. (1975), *Equality, Resemblance, and Order*, trans. from the Russian by Marin Greenlinger, revised from the 1971 Russian edition (Moscow: Mir).

Schrodt, Philip A. (1984), "Artificial intelligence and international crisis: the application of pattern recognition to the analysis of event sequences," paper presented at the annual meeting of the American Political Science Association, Washington, DC.

Schrodt, Philip A. (1985), "Adaptive precedent-bases logic and rational choice: a comparison of two approaches to the modeling of international behavior," in Urs Luterbacher and Michael D. Ward (eds), *Dynamic Models of International Conflict* (Boulder, Colo: Lynne Rienner), pp. 373–400.

Schuetz, Alfred (1951), "Choosing among projects of action," *Philosophy and Phenomenological Research*, vol. 12, pp. 161–84.

Schuetz, Alfred (1953), "Common-sense and scientific interpretation of human action," *Philosophy and Phenomenological Research*, vol. 14, pp. 1–37.

Schuetz, Alfred (1973), "On multiple realities," in Maurice Natanson (ed.), *Alfred Schuetz, Collected Papers*, Vol. I, (The Hague: Martinus Nijhoff), pp. 207–59.

Schwartz, M. (1975), *The Foreign Policy of the USSR: Domestic Factors* (Encino, Calif.: Dickenson).

Scott, Richard W. (1977), "Effectiveness of organizational effectiveness studies," in P. S. Goodman and J. Pennings (eds), *New Perspectives in Organizational Effectiveness* (San Francisco: Jossey-Bass), pp. 63–95.

Scriven, Michael (1972), "Pros and cons about goal-free evaluation," *Evaluation Comment*, vol. 3, pp. 1–7.

Seabury, Paul (1963), *Power, Freedom, and Diplomacy* (New York: Random House).

Sellers, Peter H. (1974a), "An algorithm for the distance between two finite sequences," *Journal of Combinatorial Theory*, vol. A16, pp. 253–8.

Sellers, Peter H. (1974b), "On the theory and computation of evolutionary distances," *SIAM Journal of Applied Mathematics*, vol. 26, pp. 787–93.

Sellers, Peter H. (1979), "Pattern recognition in genetic sequences," *Proceedings of the National Academy of Sciences, USA*, vol. 76, pp. 3041.

Sellers, Peter H. (1980), "The theory and computation of evolutionary distances: pattern recognition," *Journal of Algorithms*, vol. 1, pp. 359–73.

Selznick, Philip (1949), *TVA and the Grass Roots* (Berkeley, Calif.: University of California Press).

Semmel, A. K. (1982), "Small group dynamics in foreign policymaking," in G.

Hopple (ed.), *Biopolitics, Political Psychology, and International Politics* (New York: St Martin's Press), pp. 94–113.

Sewell, John W., *et al.* (1983), *The US and World Development: Agenda 1983* (New York: Praeger).

Sharp, Mitchell (1972), "Canada-US relations: options for the future," *International Perspectives*, special issues, pp. 1–22.

Shevchenko, Arkady N. (1985), *Breaking with Moscow* (New York: Knopf).

Shultz, Richard H., and Godson, Roy (1984), *Dezinformatsia: Active Measures in Soviet Strategy* (Washington, DC: Pergamon).

Shurkin, Joel M. (1983), "Expert systems: the practical face of artificial intelligence," *Technological Review*, November/December, pp. 72–7.

Sick, G. (1985), *All Fall Down* (New York: Random House).

Sigal, Leon V. (1984), *Nuclear Forces in Europe* (Washington, DC: Brookings Institute).

Simes, Dimitri K. (1975), "The Soviet invasion of Czechoslovakia and the limits of Kremlinology," *Studies in Comparative Communism*, vol. 8, pp. 1, 2.

Simis, Konstantin (1985), "The Gorbachev generation," *Foreign Policy*, vol. 59, pp. 3–21.

Simon, Herbert A. (1957), *Models of Man* (New York: Wiley).

Simon, Herbert A. (1958), "The decision-making schema: a reply," *Public Administration Review*, vol. 18, pp. 60–3.

Simon, Herbert A. (1964), "On the concept of organizational goals," *Administrative Science Quarterly*, vol. 9, pp. 1–22.

Simon, Herbert A. (1977), "Artificial intelligence systems that understand," in *Proceedings, International Joint Conference on Artificial Intelligence*, pp. 1059–73.

Simon, Herbert A. (1978), "Information-processing theory of human problem solving," in W. K. Estes (ed.), *Handbook of Learning and Cognitive Processes*, vol. 5 (Hillsdale, NJ: Erlbaum), pp. 271–95.

Simon, Herbert A. (1979), *Models of Thought* (New Haven, Conn.: Yale University Press).

Simon, Herbert A. (1980), "Behavioral and social science," *Science*, vol. 209, pp. 72–8.

Simon, Herbert A. (1981), *The Sciences of the Artificial*, 2nd edn (Cambridge, Mass.: MIT).

Simon, Herbert A. (1985), "Human nature in politics: the dialogue of psychology with political science," *American Political Science Review*, vol. 79, pp. 293–304.

Simon, Herbert A., and Kotovsky, K. (1983), "Human acquisition of concepts for sequential patterns," *Psychological Review*, vol. 70, pp. 534–46.

Simon, Herbert A., and Lea, G. (1974), "Problem solving and rule induction: a unified view," in L. Gregg (ed.), *Knowledge and Cognition* (Hillsdale, NJ: Erlbaum).

Singer, Eric, and Hudson, Valerie (1987), "Role theory and African foreign policy," in S. Walker (ed.), *Role Theory and Foreign Policy Analysis* (Durham, NC: Duke University Press).

Singer, J. David (1965), *Human Behavior and International Politics* (Chicago: Rand-McNally).

Singer, J. David (1969), "The level-of-analysis problem in international relations," in J. N. Rosenau (ed.), *International Politics and Foreign Policy*, rev. edn (New York: Free Press), pp. 20–9.

References

Singer, J. David (1981), "Accounting for international war: the state of the discipline," *Journal of Peace Research*, vol. 18, pp. 1–18.

Singer, J. David (1982), "Confrontational behavior and escalation to war, 1816–1960: a research plan," *Journal of Peace Research*, vol. 19, pp. 37–48.

Singer, J. David (1983), "From war to war: the role of major power decline and response, 1816–1980: a research proposal," University of Michigan, mimeo.

Singer, J. David (1984), "Getting at decision rules in major power conflict," discussion paper presented at the ECPR workshops on decision making, Salzburg, Austria.

Singer, J. David, and Small, Melvin (1966), "Formal alliances, 1815–1939: a quantitative description," *Journal of Peace Research*, vol. 3, pp. 1–32.

Singer, J. David, and Small, Melvin (1968), "Alliance aggregation and the onset of war, 1815–1945," in J. D. Singer (ed.), *Quantitative International Politics: Insights and Evidence* (New York: Free Press), pp. 247–86.

Sivard, R. L. (1981) *World Military and Social Expenditures: 1981.* (Leesburg, Va: World Priorities).

Siverson, Randolph M., and Sullivan, Michael P. (1983), "The distribution of power and the onset of war," *Journal of Conflict Resolution*, vol. 27, pp. 473–94.

Siverson, Randolph, and Tennefoss, Michael R. (1982), "Interstate conflicts: 1815–1965," *International Interactions*, vol. 9, pp. 147–78.

Skilling, H. Gordon (1976), *Czecholovakia's Interrupted Revolution* (Princeton, NJ: Princeton University Press).

Sloan, Anne T. (1985), "Superpower interventionism: a model of US-Soviet intervention behavior," paper presented at the Conference on New Directions in the Comparative Study of Foreign Policy, Columbus, Ohio.

Small, Melvin, and Singer, J. David (1969), "Formal alliances, 1816–1965: an extension of the basic data," *Journal of Peace Research*, vol. 6, pp. 257–82.

Small, Melvin, and Singer, J. David (1976), "The war-proneness of democratic regimes, 1816–1965," *Jerusalem Journal of International Relations*, vol. 1, pp. 50–69.

Small, Melvin, and Singer, J. David (1982), *Resort to Arms* (Beverly Hills, Calif.: Sage).

Smelser, Neil J. (1973), "The methodology of comparative analysis," in Donald P. Warwick and Samuel Osherson (eds), *Comparative Research Methods* (Englewood Cliffs, NJ: Prentice-Hall), pp. 42–86.

Smith, Bromley (1962a), Summary Record of NSC Executive Committee Meeting #5, 25 October 1962: Executive Committee Meetings 1–5, 10/23/62 through 10/26/62 folder, National Security Files, papers of John F. Kennedy, John F. Kennedy Library.

Smith, Bromley (1962b), Summary Record of NSC Executive Committee Meeting #6, 26 October 1962: Executive Committee Meetings 6 through 10, 10/26/62 through 10/28/62 folder, National Security Files, papers of John F. Kennedy, John F. Kennedy Library.

Smith, Bromley (1962c), Summary Record of NSC Executive Committee Meeting #7, 27 October 1962: Executive Committee Meetings 6 through 10, 10/26/62 through 10/28/62 folder, National Security Files, papers of John F. Kennedy, John F. Kennedy Library.

Smith, Bromley (1962d), Summary Record of NSC Executive Committee Meeting #8, 27 October 1962: Executive Committee Meetings 6 through 10,

10/26/62 through 10/28/62 folder, National Security Files, papers of John F. Kennedy, John F. Kennedy Library.

Smith, Steve (1979), "Brother, can you paradigm? A reply to Professor Rosenau," *Millennium*, vol. 8, pp. 235–45.

Smith, Steve (1981), "Traditionalism, behaviouralism and change in foreign policy analysis," in B. Buzan and R. Jones (eds), *Change and the Study of International Relations* (London: Pinter), pp. 189–208.

Smith, Steve (1983), "Foreign policy analysis: British and American orientations and methodologies," *Political Studies*, vol. 31, pp. 556–65.

Smith, Steve (1985), "The hostage rescue mission," in Steve Smith and M. Clarke (eds), *Foreign Policy Implementation* (London: Allen & Unwin), pp. 11–32.

Smith, T. (1981), "Putting the hostages' lives first," *New York Times Magazine*, May 17, pp. 76–101.

Smith, T. F., and Waterman, M. S. (1980), "New stratigraphic correlation techniques," *Journal of Geology*, vol. 88, pp. 451–7.

Smith, T. F., and Waterman, M. S. (1981), "Identification of common molecular substances," *Journal of Molecular Biology*, vol. 147, pp. 195–7.

Smouts, M. (1977), "French foreign policy: the domestic debate," *International Affairs*, vol. 53, pp. 36–50.

Snyder, David, and Kick, Edward (1979), "Structural position in the world system and economic growth., 1955–1970: a multiple network analysis of transnational interactions," *American Journal of Sociology*, vol. 84, pp. 1096–1126.

Snyder, G., and Diesing, P. (1977), *Conflict Among Nations* (Princeton, NJ: Princeton University Press).

Snyder, Richard C. (1958), "A decision-making approach to the study of political phenomena," in R. M. Young (ed.), *Approaches to the Study of Politics* (Evanston, Ill.: Northwestern University Press), pp. 3–38.

Snyder, Richard C., Bruck, H. W., and Sapin, Burton (1954), "Decision-making as an approach to the study of international politics," Foreign Policy Analysis Project Series, No. 3, Princeton, NJ.

Snyder, Richard C., Bruck, H. W., and Sapin, Burton (1962a), *Foreign Policy Decision-Making: An Approach to the Study of International Politics* (New York: Free Press).

Snyder, Richard C., Bruck, H. W., and Sapin, Burton (1962b), "Decision making as an approach to the study of international politics," in Snyder, Bruck and Sapin (eds), *Foreign Policy Decision Making* (New York: Free Press).

Snyder, Richard C., and Paige, Glenn D. (1958), "The United States decision to resist aggression in Korea: the application of an analytic scheme," *Administrative Science Quarterly*, vol. 3, pp. 341–78.

Snyder, Richard C., and Robinson, James A. (1961), *National and International Decision-Making* (New York: Institute for International Order).

Sorensen, Theodore C. (1965), *Kennedy* (New York: Harper & Row).

Soviet Active Measures (1983), US Department of State, Bureau of Public Affairs, Special Report No. 110, September.

Spanier, John (1984), *Games Nations Play*, 5th edn. (New York: Holt, Rinehart & Winston).

Spielman, K. (1978), *Analyzing Soviet Strategic Arms Decisions* (Boulder, Colo: Westview Press).

References

Sprout, Harold, and Sprout, Margaret (1956), *Man-Milieu Relationship Hypotheses in the Context of International Politics* (Princeton, NJ: Princeton University Press).

Sprout, Harold, and Sprout, Margaret (1957), "Environmental factors in the study of international politics," *Journal of Conflict Resolution*, vol. 1, pp. 309–28.

Sprout, Harold, and Sprout, Margaret (1965), *Ecological Perspective on Human Affairs* (Princeton, NJ: Princeton University Press).

Sprout, Harold, and Sprout, Margaret (1971), *Toward a Politics of the Planet Earth* (New York: Van Nostrand).

Starr, Harvey (1974), "The quantitative international relations scholar as surfer: riding the 'fourth wave,' " *Journal of Conflict Resolution*, vol. 18, pp. 336–68.

Starr, Harvey (1978), " 'Opportunity' and 'willingness' as ordering concepts in the study of war," *International Interactions*, vol. 4, pp. 363–87.

Starr, Harvey (1984), *Henry Kissinger: Perceptions of International Politics* (Lexington, Ky: University Press of Kentucky).

Starr, Harvey (1985), "Rosenau, pre-theories and the evolution of the comparative study of foreign policy," Indiana University, Department of Political Science, mimeo.

Steers, Richard M. (1975), "Problems in the measurement of organizational effectiveness," *Administrative Science Quarterly*, vol. 20, pp. 548–58.

Steinbruner, J. D. (1974), *The Cybernetic Theory of Decision* (Princeton, NJ: Princeton University Press).

Steiner, Jurg, and Dorff, Robert H. (1980), *A Theory of Political Decision Modes: Intraparty Decision Making in Switzerland* (Chapel Hill, NC: University of North Carolina Press).

Steiner, Miriam (1983), "The search for order in a disorderly world: worldviews and prescriptive decision paradigms," *International Organization*, vol. 37, pp. 321–414.

Steiner, Z. (1982), *Times Survey of Foreign Ministries of the World* (Westport, Conn: Meckler).

Stempel, J. D. (1981), *Inside the Iranian Revolution* (Bloomington, Ind.: Indiana University Press).

Stephan, A. Stephen (1935), "Prospects and possibilities: the New Deal and the new social research," *Social Forces*, vol. 12, pp. 515–21.

Stephens, John (1979), *The Transition from Capitalism to Socialism* (London: Macmillan).

Sternberg, Robert J. (1977), *Intelligence, Information Processing and Analogical Reasoning: The Computational Analysis of Human Abilities* (Hillsdale, NJ: Erlbaum).

Stewart, E. (1985), "Cultures and decision making," in W. Gundykunst, L. Steward and S. Ting-Toomey (eds), *Communication, Culture and Organizational Process* (Beverly Hills, Calif.: Sage), pp. 117–209.

Stimson, James A. (1976), "Public support for American presidents: a cyclical model," *Public Opinion Quarterly*, vol. 40, pp. 1–21.

Stoessinger, John D. (1979), *Crusaders and Pragmatists: Movers of Modern American Foreign Policy* (New York: W. W. Norton).

Strange, Susan (1982), "Cave! Hic dragones: a critique of regime analysis," *International Organization*, vol. 36, pp. 479–96.

Stremlau, John J. (1982), "The foreign policies of developing countries in the

References

1980s," in J. J. Stremlau (ed.), *The Foreign Policy Priorities of Third World States* (Boulder, Colo: Westview Press), pp. 1–18.

Stremlau, John J. (1985), "Soviet foreign policy in an uncertain world," *Annals*, vol. 481, pp. 9–171.

Stuart, D., and Starr, H. (1981–2), "The 'inherent bad faith model' reconsidered: Dulles, Kennedy, and Kissinger," *Political Psychology*, vol. 3, pp. 1–33.

Sullivan, Michael P. (1976), *International Relations: Theories and Evidence* (Englewood Cliffs, NJ: Prentice-Hall).

Sullivan, Michael P., and Siverson, Randolph M. (1981), "Theories of war: problems and prospects," in P. T. Hopmann, D. A. Zinnes and J. D. Singer (eds), *Cumulation in International Relations* Research Monograph Series in World Affairs (Denver, Colo: Graduate School of International Relations, University of Denver), pp. 9–37.

Sundelius, Bengt (1983), "Interdependence, internationalization, and foreign policy decentralization," paper presented at the annual meeting of the American Political Science Association, Chicago.

Survey of Current Business (1984), vol. 64, p. 54.

Sutter, R. (1978), *Chinese Foreign Policy after the Cultural Revolution, 1966–1977* (Boulder, Colo: Westview Press).

Sveics, V. V. (1970), *Small Nation Survival: Political Defense in Unequal Conflicts* (New York: Jericho).

Swanson, D. (1982), "Specificity," in P. Callahan *et al.* (eds), *Describing Foreign Policy Behavior* (Beverly Hills: Sage), pp. 223–41.

Sylvan, David (1984), "Politicization dynamics," paper prepared for the Second World Peace Science Congress, Rotterdam, The Netherlands.

Sylvan, David, and Majeski, Stephen J. (1983), "A formalization of decision and measurement heuristics for war initiation: the 1961 Vietnam commitments," paper prepared for the annual meetings of the American Political Science Association, Chicago.

Sylvan, Donald A. (1985a), "A brief description of current research designed to construct a computational model of Japanese supply security decision making," paper prepared for the Merriam Seminar (Champaign, Ill.: University of Illinois).

Sylvan, Donald A. (1985b), "Output versus outcome: do US foreign policy organizational strategies make a difference?" paper presented at the annual meeting of the American Political Science Association, New Orleans, La.

Sylvan, Donald A., (1985c), *Understanding the Nature of Political Limits in the Global Energy Arena* (Columbus, Ohio: Ohio State University).

Sylvan, Donald A., and Chan, S. (eds) (1984), *Foreign Policy Decision Making* (New York: Praeger).

Sylvan, Donald A., and Thorson, S. J. (1979), "Measuring cognitive style at a distance," paper presented at the Joint National Meeting of the Operations Research Society of American and the Institute for Management Science, Milwaukee, Wis.

Talbott, Strobe (1970), *Khrushchev Remembers: With an Introduction, Commentary and Notes by Edward Crankshaw* (Boston, Mass.: Little, Brown).

Talbott, Strobe (1979), *Endgame: The Inside Story of SALT II* (New York: Harper & Row).

Talbott, Strobe (1984), *The Russians and Reagan* (New York: Vintage).

518

Tanaka, E., and Fu, K. S. (1978), "Error-correcting parsers for formal languages," *IEEE Trans. Comput.*, vol. C-27, pp. 605–16.

Tanaka, E., and Kasai, T. (1976), "Synchronization and substitution error-correcting codes for the Levenshtein metric," *IEEE Transactions on Information Theory*, vol. IT-22, no. 2, pp. 100–3.

Tanter, Raymond (1966), "Dimensions of conflict behavior within and between nations, 1958–60," *Journal of Conflict Resolution*, vol. 10, pp. 41–64.

Tatu, Michel (1969), *Power in the Kremlin: From Khrushchev to Kosygin*, trans. Helen Katel (New York: Viking).

Tatu, Michel, (1981), "Intervention in Eastern Europe," in Stephen S. Kaplan *et al. Diplomacy of Power: Soviet Armed Forces as a Political Instrument* (Washington, DC: Brookings Institution), pp. 205–64.

Terrill, R. (1978), *The Future of China after Mao* (New York: Delta).

Tetlock, P. E. (1979), "Identifying victims of groupthink from public statements of decision makers," *Journal of Personality and Social Psychology*, vol. 37, pp. 1314–24.

Thies, Wallace J. (1980), *When Governments Collide* (Berkeley, Calif.: University of California Press).

Thomas, A. V., and Thomas, A. J., Jr. (1963), *The Organization of American States* (Dallas, Tex.: Southern Methodist University Press).

Thompson, Kenneth W., and Macridis, Roy C. (1976), "The comparative study of foreign policy," in R. C. Macridis (ed.), *Foreign Policy in World Politics* (Englewood Cliffs, NJ: Prentice-Hall), pp. 1–31.

Thorson, S. J. and Sylvan, D. A. (1982), "Counterfactuals and the Cuban missile crisis," *International Studies Quarterly*, vol. 26, pp. 539–71.

Thorson, S. J. and Sylvan D. A. (1984), "Intentional inferencing in foreign policy: an AI approach," in D. A. Sylvan and S. Chan (eds), *Foreign Policy Decision Making* (New York: Praeger), pp. 280–309.

Tigrid, Pavel (1969), "Czechoslovakia: a post-mortem," *Survey*, no. 73, pp. 133–64.

Tigrid, Pavel (1971), *Why Dubcek Fell* (London: Macdonald).

Ting-Toomey, S. (1985), "Toward a theory of culture," in W. Gudykunst, L. Steward and S. Ting-Toomey (eds), *Communication, Culture and Organizational Process* (Beverly Hills, Calif.: Sage), pp. 71–86.

Todaro, Michael (1981), *Economic Development in the Third World*, 2nd edn. (New York: Longman).

Toffler, Alvin (1980), *The Third Wave* (New York: Bantam).

Tomlin, Brian (1985), "Measurement validation: lessons from the use and misuse of UN General Assembly roll-call votes," *International Organization*, vol. 39, pp. 189–206.

Truman, Harry S (1955–6), *Memoirs*, 2 vols (Garden City, NY: Doubleday).

Tsai, Wen-Hsiang, and Fu, King-Sun (1979), "Error-correcting isomorphisms of attributed relational graphs for pattern analysis," *IEEE Transactions on Systems, Man, and Cybernetics*, Vol. SMC-9, no. 12, pp. 757–68.

Tsuji, K. (1968), "Decision making in the Japanese government," in R. Ward (ed.), *Political Development in Modern Japan* (Princeton, NJ: Princeton University Press), pp. 457–75.

Tuchman, B. (1984), *The March of Folly: From Troy to Vietnam* (New York: Knopf).

Tukey, John W. (1962), "The future of data analysis," *Annals of Mathematical Statistics*, vol. 33, pp. 1–67.

References

Tukey, John W. (1977), *Exploratory Data Analysis* (Reading, Mass.: Addison-Wesley).

Tullis, F. LaMond (1985), "The Current View on Rural Development: Fad or Breakthrough in Latin America?" *International Political Economy Yearbook*, vol. 1 (Boulder, Colo: Westview Press).

Turner, Judith Axler (1985), "An enterprising 'scruffy' teaches computers to think . . . in English," *Chronicle of Higher Education*, April 17.

Tversky, Adam, and Kahneman, Daniel (1971), "Belief in the law of small numbers," *Psychological Bulletin*, vol. 76, pp. 105–10.

Tversky, Adam, and Kahneman, Daniel (1973), "Availability: a heuristic for judging frequency and probability," *Cognitive Psychology*, vol. 5, pp. 207–32.

Tversky, Adam, and Kahneman, Daniel (1979), "Judgement under uncertainty: heuristics and biases," *Science*, vol. 185, pp. 1124–31.

Ulam, S. M. (1972), "Some combinatorial problems studied experimentally on computing machines," in S. K. Zaremba (ed.), *Applications of Number Theory to Numerical Analysis* (New York: Academic Press), pp. 1–3.

US Arms Control and Disarmament Agency (1983), "Soviet propaganda campaign against NATO," (Washington, DC: ACDA).

US Arms Control and Disarmament Agency (1984), "World military expenditures and arms transfers, 1972–1982," (Washington, DC: US Government Printing Office).

US Department of Commerce (1976), "Business statistics 1975," (Washington, DC: US Government Printing Office).

US Department of Commerce (1983), "Business statistics 1982," (Washington, DC: US Government Printing Office).

Valenta, J. (1979), *Soviet Intervention in Czechoslovakia, 1968: Anatomy of a Decision* (Baltimore, Md: Johns Hopkins University Press).

Valenta, J., and Potter, W. (eds) (1984), *Soviet Decision Making for National Security* (London: Allen & Unwin).

VanLehn, K., and Brown, J. S. (1978), "Planning nets: a representation for formalizing analogies and semantic models of procedural skills," in R. E. Snow, P. A. Frerico and W. W. Montague (eds), *Aptitude Learning and Instruction: Cognitive Processes Analyses* (Hillsdale, NJ: Erlbaum), pp. 95–137.

Vannicelli, Primo (1974), "Italy, NATO, and the European Community: the interplay of foreign policy and domestic politics," (Cambridge, Mass.: Harvard Center for International Affairs).

Vasquez, John A. (1976), "A learning theory of the American anti-Vietnam War movement," *Journal of Peace Research*, vol. 13, pp. 299–314.

Vasquez, John A. (1983), *The Power of Power Politics: A Critique* (London: Pinter; New Brunswick, NJ: Rutgers University Press).

Vasquez, John A. (1986a), "Capability, types of war, peace," *Western Political Quarterly*, vol. 39, No. 2 (June), pp. 313–27.

Vasquez, John A. (1986b), *Explaining and Evaluating Foreign Policy: A New Agenda for Comparative Foreign Policy* (New York: Praeger).

Vasquez, John A., and Mansbach, R. W. (1984), "The role of issues in global co-operation and conflict," *British Journal of Political Science*, vol. 14, pp. 411–33.

Velleman, P. (1980), "Definition and comparison of robust nonlinear data smoothing algorithms," *Journal of the American Statistical Association*, vol. 75, pp. 609–15.

References

Velleman, P., and Hoaglin, D. (1981), *Applications, Basics, and Computing of Exploratory Data Analysis* (Boston, Mass.: Duxbury).

Verba, Sidney (1967), "Some dilemmas in comparative research," *World Politics*, vol. 20, pp. 111–27.

Vere, Steven A. (1978), "Inductive learning of relational productions," in D. A. Waterman and F. Hayes-Roth (eds), *Pattern-Directed Inference Systems* (New York: Academic Press), pp. 281–95.

Vincent, Jack E. (1971), "Predicting voting patterns in the General Assembly," *American Political Science Review*, vol. 65, pp. 471–98.

Vincent, Jack E. (1983), "WEIS vs. COPDAB: correspondence problems," *International Studies Quarterly*, vol. 27, pp. 161–8.

Vincent, Jack, Baker, Roger, Gagnon, Susan, Hamm, Keith, and Reilly, Scott (1973), "Empirical tests of attribute, social field, and status field theories on international relations data," *International Studies Quarterly*, vol. 17, pp. 375–404.

Vital, David (1967), *The Inequality of States* (Oxford, England: Clarendon Press).

Voslensky, Michail (1978), "Das wird nur den Amerikanern helfen: Tagebuch-Notizen des sowjetischen Funktionars Michael Woslenski ueber die Hintergrunde der Prag-Invasion," *Spiegel*, no. 34, pp. 126–9.

Wagner, R. A., and Fischer, M. J. (1974), "The string-to-string correction problem," *Journal of the Association for Computing Machinery*, vol. 21, pp. 168–73.

Walker, Stephen G. (1977), "The interface between beliefs and behaviors: Henry Kissinger's operational code and the Vietnam War," *Journal of Conflict Resolution*, vol. 21, pp. 129–68.

Walker, Stephen G. (1979), "National role conceptions and systemic outcomes," in L. Falkowski (ed.), *Psychological Models in International Politics* (Boulder Colo: Westview Press), pp. 125–68.

Walker, Stephen G. (1981), "The correspondence between foreign policy rhetoric and behavior: insights from role and exchange theory," *Behavioral Science*, vol. 26, pp. 272–80.

Walker, Stephen G. (1983a), "The motivational foundations of political belief systems: a re-analysis of the operational code construct," *International Studies Quarterly*, vol. 27, pp. 179–201.

Walker, Stephen G. (1983b), "The origins of foreign policy in a self help system: a postscript to Waltz's theory of international politics," paper presented at the annual meeting of the International Studies Association, Mexico City, Mexico.

Walker, Stephen G. (1987), "Role theory and the international system," in S. Walker (ed.), *Role Theory and Foreign Policy Analysis* (Durham, NC: University Press).

Walker, Stephen G., and Simon, S. (1983), "Role analysis and Asian security conceptions," paper presented at the annual meeting of the American Political Science Association, Chicago.

Wallace, Michael (1972), "Status, formal organization, and arms levels as factors leading to the onset of war, 1820–1964," in B. Russett (ed.), *Peace, War, and Numbers* (Beverly Hills, Calif.: Sage), pp. 49–70.

Wallace, Michael (1979), "Arms races and escalation: some new evidence," *Journal of Conflict Resolution*, vol. 23, pp. 3–16.

Wallace, Michael (1982), "Armaments and escalation: two competing hypotheses," *International Studies Quarterly*, vol. 26, pp. 37–51.

Wallace, W. (1978), "Old states and new circumstances: the international predicament of Britain, France, and Germany," in W. Wallace and W. Patterson (eds), *Foreign Policy Making in Western Europe* (New York: Praeger), pp. 31–55.

Wallace, W. (1980), "Independence and economic interests: the ambiguities of foreign policy," in P. Cerny and M. Schain (eds), *French Politics and Public Policy* (New York: St Martin's Press), pp. 267–90.

Wallensteen, Peter (1981), "Incompatibility, confrontation, and war: four models and three historical systems, 1816–1976," *Journal of Peace Research*, vol. 18, pp. 57–90.

Wallensteen, Peter (1983), "Economic sanctions: ten modern cases and three important lessons," in M. Nincic and P. Wallensteen (eds), *Dilemmas of Economic Coercion* (New York: Praeger), pp. 87–129.

Wallensteen, Peter (1984), "Universalism vs. particularism: on the limits of major power order," *Journal of Peace Research*, vol. 21, pp. 243–57.

Wallerstein, Immanuel (1974), *The Modern World-System I; Capitalist Agriculture and the Origins of the European World-Economy in the Sixteenth Century* (New York: Academic Press).

Wallerstein, Immanuel (1979), *The Capitalist World-Economy* (Cambridge, England: Cambridge University Press).

Wallerstein, Immanuel (1980), *The Modern World System II: Mercantilism and the Consolidation of the European World-Economy, 1600–1750* (New York: Academic Press).

Waltz, David L. (1985), "Scientific DataLink's artificial intelligence classification scheme," *The AI Magazine*, vol. 6, pp. 58–63.

Waltz, Kenneth (1967), *Foreign Policy and Democratic Politics: The American and British Experience* (Boston, Mass.: Little, Brown).

Waltz, Kenneth (1979), *Theory of International Politics* (Reading, Mass.: Addison-Wesley).

Wampold, Bruce E. (1984), "Tests of dominance in sequential categorical data," *Psychological Bulletin*, vol. 96, pp. 424–9.

Ward, Michael Don (1982), "Cooperation and conflict in foreign policy behavior," *International Studies Quarterly*, vol. 26, pp. 87–126.

Watanabe, A. (1978), "Foreign policy making Japanese style," *International Affairs*, vol. 54, pp. 75–88.

Waterman, Donald A. and Hayes-Roth, Frederick (1978), "Inductive learning of relational productions," in D. A. Waterman and F. Hayes-Roth (eds), *Pattern-Directed Inference Systems* (New York: Academic Press).

Weaver, James, and Jameson, Kenneth (1981). *Economic Development: Competing Paradigms* (Washington, DC: University Press of America).

Weaver, Warren (1947), "Science and complexity," in W. Weaver (ed.), *The Scientists Speak* (New York: Boni & Gaer), pp. 1–13.

Weber, Max (1947), *The Theory of Social and Economic Organization*, A. M. Henderson (ed.), T. Parsons (trans.) (New York: Oxford University Press).

Weede, Erich (1970), "Conflict behavior of nation states," *Journal of Peace Research*, vol. 7, pp. 229–35.

Weinstein, F. (1976), *Indonesian Foreign Policy and the Dilemma of Dependence: From Sukarno to Suharto* (Ithaca, NY: Cornell University Press).

Weiss, Carol (1972), *Evaluation Research: Methods of Assessing Program Effectiveness* (Englewood Cliffs, NJ: Prentice-Hall).

Wendzel, Robert L. (1981), *International Politics: Policymakers and Policymaking* (New York: Wiley).

References

Wholey, Joseph S., *et al.* (1971), *Federal Evaluation Policy* (Washington, DC: Urban Institute).

Wicker, Tom (1985), "A disintegrating story," *New York Times*, September 3, p. 29.

Wildavsky, Aron (1964), *The Politics of the Budgetary Process* (Boston, Mass.: Little, Brown).

Wildavsky, Aron (1979), *Speaking the Truth to Power* (Boston, Mass.: Little, Brown).

Wilkenfeld, Jonathan (1968), "Domestic and foreign conflict behavior of nations," *Journal of Peace Research*, vol. 1, pp. 56–9.

Wilkenfeld, Jonathan, Hopple, G., Rossa, P., and Andriole, S. (1980), *Foreign Policy Behavior: The Interstate Behavior Analysis Model* (Beverly Hills, Calif.: Sage).

Wilkenfeld, Jonathan, Lussier, Virginia Lee and Tahtinen, Dale (1972), "Conflict interactions in the Middle East, 1949–1967," *Journal of Conflict Resolution*, vol. 16, pp. 135–54.

Windsor, Philip, and Roberts, Adam (1969), *Czechoslovakia 1968: Reform and Resistance* (New York: Columbia University Press).

Winograd, Terry (1972), *Understanding Natural Language* (New York: Academic Press).

Winograd, Terry (1983), *Language as a Cognitive Process, Vol. I: Syntax* (Reading, Mass.: Addison-Wesley).

Winston, Patrick H. (1970), "Learning structural descriptions from examples," PhD dissertation, MIT, Cambridge, Mass.

Winston, Patrick H. (1978), "Learning by creating and justifying transfer frames," Artificial Intelligence Memo No. 520, Artificial Intelligence Laboratory (Cambridge, Mass.: MIT).

Winston, Patrick H. (1979), "Learning and reasoning by analogy," *Communications of the ACM*, vol. 23, pp. 689–703.

Winston, Patrick H. (1981), "Learning new principles from precedents and exercise," Artificial Intelligence Memo No. 632, Artificial Intelligence Laboratory (Cambridge, Mass.: MIT).

Winston, Patrick H. (1984), *Artificial Intelligence*, 2nd edn. (Reading, Mass.: Addison-Wesley).

Wish, Naomi (1980), "Foreign policy makers and their national role conceptions," *International Studies Quarterly*, vol. 24, pp. 532–54.

Wittkopf, Eugene R. (1976), "Politics and ecology, Easton and Rosenau: an alternative research priority," in J. N. Rosenau (ed.), *In Search of Global Patterns* (New York: Free Press), pp. 338–54.

Wittkopf, Eugene R. (1984), "Public attitudes toward American foreign policy in the post-Vietnam decade," paper presented at the annual convention of the International Studies Association, Atlanta, Ga.

Wittkopf, Eugene R. (1985), "Elites and masses: another look at attitudes toward America's world role," paper presented at the annual meeting of the American Political Science Association, New Orleans, La.

Wittkopf, Eugene R., and Maggiotto, Michael A. (1983), "Elites and masses: a comparative analysis of attitudes toward America's world role," *Journal of Politics*, vol. 45, pp. 303–34.

Wolfers, Arnold (1962), *Discord and Collaboration* (Baltimore, Md: Johns Hopkins University Press).

World Bank (1984), *World Development Report* (Washington, DC: World Bank).

Wright, Erik Olin (1978), *Class, Crisis, and the State* (London: New Left Books).

523

References

Yankelovich, Daniel, and Kaagan, Larry (1981a), "Assertive America," *Foreign Affairs*, vol. 59, pp. 606–713.

Yankelovich, Daniel, and Kaagan, Larry (1981b), *New Rules: Searching for Self-Fulfillment in a World Turned Upside Down* (New York: Random House).

Yeaton, William H., and Redner, Robin (1981), "Measuring strength and integrity of treatments: rationale, techniques, and examples," in Ross F. Conner (ed.), *Methodological Advances in Evaluation Research* (Beverly Hills, Calif.: Sage), pp. 61–76.

Yost, Charles (1968), "How it began," *Foreign Affairs*, vol. 46, pp. 304–20.

Yost, Charles (1972), *The Conduct and Misconduct of Foreign Affairs* (New York: Random House).

Young, Oran (1969), "Professor Russett: industrious tailor to a naked emperor," *World Politics*, vol. 21, pp. 486–511.

Young, Oran (1980), "International regimes: problems of concept formation," *World Politics*, vol. 32, pp. 331–56.

Yuchtman, Ephraim, and Seashore, Stanley E. (1967), "A system resource approach to organizational effectiveness," *American Sociological Review*, vol. 32, pp. 891–903.

Zagare, F. C. (1985), "The pathologies of unilateral deterrence," in U. Luterbacher and M. D. Ward (eds), *Dynamic Models of International Conflict* (Boulder, Colo: Lynne Rienner), pp. 56–75.

Zimmerman, William (1973), "Issue area and foreign policy process: a research note in search of a general theory," *American Political Science Review*, vol. 67, pp. 1204–12.

Zimmerman, William (1982), "What do scholars know about Soviet foreign policy?" *International Journal*, vol. 37, pp. 198–219.

Zimmerman, William, and Palmer, Glenn (1983), "Words and deeds in Soviet foreign policy: the case of Soviet military expenditures," *American Political Science Review*, vol. 77, pp. 358–67.

Zinnes, Dina A. (1976a), *Contemporary Research in International Relations: A Perspective and a Critical Appraisal* (New York: Free Press).

Zinnes, Dina A. (1976b), "The problem of cumulation," in J. N. Rosenau (ed.), *In Search of Global Patterns* (New York: Free Press), pp. 161–6.

Zinnes, Dina A. (1980), "Three puzzles in search of a researcher," *International Studies Quarterly*, vol. 24, pp. 315–42.

Zinnes, Dina A. (1983), "An event model of conflict interaction," in D. A. Zinnes (ed.), *Conflict Processes and the Breakdown of International Systems* (Denver, Colo: University of Denver), pp. 119–48.

Zinnes, Dina, North, Robert, and Koch, Howard (1961), "Capability, threat, and the outbreak of war," in J. N. Rosenau (ed.), *International Politics and Foreign Policy* (New York: Free Press), pp. 469–82.

About the Authors

PAUL. A. ANDERSON moved in 1986 to the faculty of Laurence University from that of the Carnegie-Mellon University. His research interests include organizational decision making with special emphasis on foreign policy decision making, and applications of artificial intelligence and computer simulation to the study of politics. He is currently completing work on an NSF-sponsored project to develop a bounded-rationality model of the outbreak of interstate war. He has published articles in *Behavioral Science*, the *American Journal of Political Science, Philosophy of the Social Sciences* and *Administrative Science Quarterly*.

DAVIS B. BOBROW is Professor of Government and Politics at the University of Maryland (College Park). He previously taught at the University of Minnesota, School of Advanced International Studies, and Princeton, and held senior staff positions in the Office of the Secretary of Defense and at the Oak Ridge National Laboratory. He has been a Visiting Professor in Japan and Israel. His publications include co-authorship of *Understanding Foreign Policy Decisions* and a series of articles with Robert Kudrle on various aspects of foreign economic policy.

STEVE CHAN is Professor of Political Science at the University of Colorado at Boulder. He was Fulbright Professor at Tamkang University in Taipei during 1984–5, and has also taught at the Texas A&M University, the University of Maryland and the Bowling Green State University (Bowling Green, Ohio). His publications include *International Relations in Perspective*, co-authorship of *Understanding Foreign Policy Decisions*, and co-editorship of *Foreign Policy Decision Making*.

MARK J. DEHAVEN is a graduate student in the Department of Political Science at the University of Florida.

WILLIAM J. DIXON is Assistant Professor of Political Science at Emory University (Atlanta, Georgia). His principle research interests are in the areas of international political economy and the dynamic modeling of foreign policy interaction. He has published in the *American Journal of Political Science, International Studies Quarterly* and *International Interactions*.

JAMES W. DYSON is Professor of Political Science at Florida State University. His research interests include political decision making, the role of mass media in politics, and the application of experimental methods to the study of politics.

JOE D. HAGAN is an Assistant Professor of Political Science at the University of Wyoming. He formerly taught at Goucher College, where he was a recipient of their award for "outstanding teaching in the social sciences." He is a managing editor of *International Studies Notes*. His current publications on domestic politics and foreign policy include articles in the *Journal of Asian and African Studies* and the *Social Science Journal*.

CHARLES F. HERMANN is Director of the Mershon Center at the Ohio State University, where he is also Mershon Professor in the Department of Political Science. He has served as Vice President of the International Studies Association, as a staff member of the National Security Council, and as a faculty member at Princeton University. His numerous publications include co-authorship of *Why Nations Act* and editorship of *International Crises: Insights from Behavioral Research*.

MARGARET G. HERMANN is a Research Scientist at the Mershon Center, Ohio State University. She has a PhD in psychology from Northwestern University (Evanston, Illinois) and was a National Institute of Mental Health Postdoctoral Fellow at the Educational Testing Service and Lecturer at Princeton University before moving to Ohio State. Her major research interests include political leadership, political personality, and the comparative study of foreign policy. She is the author or editor of a number of books, book chapters and journal articles, among which are *A Psychological Examination of Political Leaders*, *Describing Foreign Policy Behavior* and *Political Psychology: Contemporary Problems and Issues*. She has been Vice-President of the International Studies Association and of the International Society of Political Psychology as well as editor of *Political Psychology*.

MARGARET P. KARNS is Director of the Center for International Studies and Associate Professor of Political Science at the University of Dayton. She was a Fellow at the Roosevelt Center for American Policy Studies in Washington, DC in 1982–3. She is currently collaborating with Karen A. Mingst on a project on United States participation in international organizations and completing a monograph on the OECD under a grant from the German Marshall Fund of the United States. Her publications include editorship of *Persistent Patterns and Emergent Structures in a Waning Century*.

CHARLES W. KEGLEY, JR, is Director of the Byrnes International Center at the University of South Carolina, where he also is Pearce Professor of International Affairs in the Department of Government and International Studies. He serves as Associate Director of the International Studies Association and has held appointments on the faculties at Georgetown University (Washington, DC) and the University of Texas. His publications include co-authorship of *American Foreign Policy: Pattern and Process* and *World Politics: Trend and Transformation*, and co-editorship of *The Sage International Yearbook of Foreign Policy Studies*.

RUSSELL J. LENG is Professor of Political Science and Chair of the Division of Social Sciences at Middlebury College (Middlebury, Vermont). He also has held visiting appointments at American University and at the University of Michigan. His ongoing research on international crisis behavior has resulted in numerous articles in scholarly journals and anthologies. The most recent of these is "Reagan and the Russians: crisis bargaining beliefs and the historical record" in the *American Political Science Review*.

DWAIN MEFFORD is Assistant Professor of Political Science at the Ohio State University. His research into cognitive processes is sponsored by the National Science Foundation.

KAREN A. MINGST is Associate Professor of Political Science at the University of Kentucky and currently serving as Vice President of the International Studies Association-South. She has published work on international organizations and law, political economy, and Africa in *International Organization*, the *Journal of Common Market Studies, Review of International Studies, Journal of Peace Research, Africa Today*, and *East Europe Quarterly*, and is currently collaborating with Margaret P. Karns on a project on United States participation in international organizations. She has received financial support from the Carnegie Endowment, Ford Foundation and the Fulbright Program.

BRUCE E. MOON is Assistant Professor of Political Science at Northwestern University (Evanston, Illinois). He has taught previously at Duke University, Indiana University and the San Francisco State University. His research in international political economy and comparative foreign policy has been published in the *American Journal of Political Science, International Studies Quarterly, International Organization*, and in edited volumes. He is currently at work on a book on the political economy of basic human needs provision.

BENJAMIN A. MOST was an Associate Professor of Political Science at the University of Iowa. His publications include articles in the *American Journal of Political Science*, the *American Political Science Review, Comparative Political Studies, International Studies Quarterly, the Journal of Conflict Resolution* and *World Politics*.

MARIA PAPADAKIS is a PhD candidate in political science at Indiana University. She has taught international politics at the University of Kentucky and has served as an interim economic officer at the US Embassy in Harare, Zimbabwe. She is currently working as an international trade analyst for the US International Trade Commission in Washington, DC. Her analysis of the effects of ballistic missile defense on Soviet-American nuclear competition was recently published in *Third World Quarterly*.

GREG PEACOCK is a PhD candidate in Political Science from the Ohio State University. His dissertation work is an evaluation of the CREON research project as an example of work in comparative foreign policy studies. He has prior degrees in political science and international relations from Ohio State and Brigham Young University.

CHARLES A. POWELL is Associate Professor of International Relations at the University of Southern California. His research interests include contemporary game theory, bargaining, foreign policy analysis techniques, comparative foreign policy and experimental gaming simulation.

HELEN PURKITT is Associate Professor of Political Science at the United

States Naval Academy. Her research interests include comparative foreign policy, political decision making, the politics of South Africa and international terrorism.

GREGORY A. RAYMOND is Professor of Political Science at Boise State University (Idaho). His research on international norms has appeared in numerous journals and edited books. His most recent publications include authorship of *Conflict Resolution and the Structure of the State System*, co-authorship of *The Other Western Europe: A Comparative Analysis of the Smaller Democracies* and co-editorship of *Third World Policies of Industrialized Nations*.

NEIL R. RICHARDSON is Associate Professor of Political Science at the University of Wisconsin-Madison, where he also serves as Chair of the International Relations Program. He earlier held a faculty appointment at the University of Texas at Austin. His publications include *Foreign Policy and Economic Dependence*.

JAMES N. ROSENAU is the Director of the Institute for Transnational Studies at the University of Southern California as well as Professor of Political Science and International Relations. He is a past President of the International Studies Association and has also been a member of the faculties of Rutgers University (New Brunswick, New Jersey) and Ohio State University. He has published many books on the scientific study of foreign policy, global interdependence and political adaptation, including most recently co-authorship of *American Leadership in World Affairs* and co-editorship of *World Systems Structure: Continuity and Change*.

MARTIN W. SAMPSON III is an Associate Professor in the Political Science Department at the University of Minnesota. His publications include *International Policy Coordination*, an n-actor game theoretic study of OPEC and the East African Common Market, and "Rapid Deployment in Lieu of Energy Policy", a study of tensions in US policy toward the Persian/Arabian Gulf.

RANDOLPH M. SIVERSON is Professor of Political Science at the University of California, Davis where he is also Chair of the Department of Political Science. He is co-editor of *International Interactions*. His publications include articles in the *Journal of Conflict Resolution*, *International Studies Quarterly*, *American Journal of Political Science*, *American Political Science Review* and *World Politics*. He also co-edited *Change in the International System*.

HARVEY STARR is Professor and Chair of the Political Science Department at Indiana University. He has published widely on international conflict, alliance and foreign policy analysis, with current research focusing on the diffusion of war. His recent publications include *Henry Kissinger: Perceptions of International Politics* and co-authorship of *World Politics: The Menu for Choice* (2nd edn).

JOHN A. VASQUEZ is Associate Professor of Political Science at Rutgers University (New Brunswick, New Jersey) and is a specialist in international relations theory. His publications include *The Power of Power Politics: In Search of Theory*, and articles in *International Studies Quarterly*, *Journal of Politics*,

528

Journal of Peace Research, International Organization and *British Journal of Political Science,* among others. He is also editor of *Evaluating US Foreign Policy* and *Classics of International Relations.* He is currently working on a book on the steps to war.

STEPHEN G. WALKER is a Professor in the Department of Political Science at the Arizona State University. His publications have appeared in *World Politics, Journal of Politics, Journal of Conflict Resolution, International Studies Quarterly, Behavioral Science, Political Psychology, Journal of Peace Research, British Journal of Political Science* and the *British Journal of International Studies.* He is also the editor of *Role Theory and Foreign Policy Analysis.*

EUGENE R. WITTKOPF is Professor of Political Science at the University of Florida. He is a past President of the Florida Political Science Association and has been a Visiting Professor at the University of North Carolina at Chapel Hill. He is author and editor of several books in international politics and foreign policy, including *The Nuclear Reader: Strategy, Weapons, War.* His recent research on public opinion and foreign policy has been supported by grants from the National Science Foundation.

Index

Abel, E. 287, 289
Abelson, R. 206
Acheson, D. 292
accommodationists 376–81
accountability 341–3, 353–8, 438
action, measure of 359–60, 361
adaptability 71–2, 459
Adelman, R. L. 115
Adler, A. 335
agenda setting 460–1, 468, 469, 473
Aho, A. 238
Aiken, M. 387
Alger, C. 465
Alker, H. 232, 243
Allan, P. 80
Allen, V. 274
alliances 135, 138–40, 143–53
Alliluyeva, S. 56
Allison, G. 32, 34, 95, 268, 287, 289, 290, 299, 310
alternative triggers 88–9, 136–8, 142
Altfeld, M. 139
analogical reasoning 221–42
Anderson, C. 109, 217, 260, 286, 298, 304, 310
Anderson, I. 268, 364
Anderson, P. 9, 155, 268, 285–308
Andrews, W. 364
Andriole, S. 453
Andropov, Yuri 443
Anglin, D. 326, 328
Anzai, Y. 227
Aron, R. 102
artificial intelligence 214, 224–5, 227, 241–2
ASEAN 468
Ashford, D. 384
Ashley, R. 15, 370, 409, 412
autolag Z score profiles 92–4
Avery, W. 460
Axelrod, R. 206, 306
Azar, E. 26

Bacharach, S. 387
Bakeman, R. 81, 95
Baldwin, D. 263, 468, 473
Banks, A. S. 112

bargaining 125–8, 396
Barnlund, D. 385, 388, 390
Barr, A. 224
Barringer, M. 232
Becker, D. 36
Ben-Dak, J. 26
Benjamin, C. 215, 220
Bennett, J. 243
Berbaum, M. 260
Berlin crisis 190–1
Bernstein, R. 20
Best, M. 35
Betancourt, R. 319, 320
Bethmann-Hollweg 383
Bialer, S. 74
black box 248, 366, 367, 368–9, 381
Blake, D. 35
Bleckman, B. 232
Blondel, J. 45
Bloomfield, L. 232, 268
Bobrow, D. 8, 32, 111–57, 473
Boruch, R. 101
Boulding, K. 205, 206, 451
Box, G. 198
Brady, L. 103, 268, 310, 456
Brams, S. 215
Braudel, F. 373
Brecher, M. 17, 24, 25, 26, 27, 30, 31, 320, 414
Bremer, S. 372
Brezhnev, Leonid 62, 433
Brody, R. 17, 366, 381, 440
Broone, B. 385
Brown, R. 81, 342
Bruck, H. 22, 155, 220, 222, 249, 285, 288, 414, 434
Brzezinski, Z. 341
Bueno de Mesquita, B. 37, 154, 366, 367, 368, 369, 382, 432
Burgess, P. 14, 55
Burnstein, E. 260
Butler, F. 340

Callahan, P. 29, 358
Campbell, D. 169, 176
Cantori, L. 450
Caporaso, J. 36, 459, 473

Carbonell, J. 224, 227
Cardosa, F. 35, 50
Caribbean Basin Initiative 107
Carley, K. 232
Carrol, J. 206
Carter, Jimmy 452
case studies 171–2, 227, 231
Castro, F. 319
Cathcart, D. 388, 389
Cathcart, R. 388, 389
Chamberlain 383
Chan, S. 8, 11–57, 243, 268
change 2, 58, 70–1
Charniak, E. 244
Chase-Dunn, C. 35, 36
Chilcote, R. 35
Child, J. 387
China 342
Chirac, J. 401
Choucri, N. 32, 140, 366, 370
Christenson, C. 243
Churchill, W. 383
Cimbala, S. 243
Clapp, H. 396
Clark, W. 268
Claude, I. 468
Clifford, J. 226
closed systems 360, 463
Coate, R. 250
cognitive processes 206–9, 222–3, 228,
    230, 287–9, 376, 425
cognitive science 203–4, 209–11, 226,
    415
Cohen, Ben 35, 51
Coleman, J. 268
commitment, measure of 358–69, 361
communication networks 23, 78–9, 438
comparative foreign policy *see* foreign
    policy
Comparative Research on the Events of
    Nations (CREON) 28, 29, 32, 48, 50,
    132, 221, 273, 274, 275, 281–2, 340,
    343, 350, 356, 358, 359, 457, 473
computers 223–4
conflict processes 26, 280, 282
Congress of Vienna 379
Connolly, W. 35
Converse, P. 52
Conybeare, J. 41
Cook, T. 176
Coplin, W. 26, 27
Correlates of War (COW) project 198,
    369, 370
Coulman, R. 307
Cox, R. 467
Crabb, C. 102, 103
Crane, B. 466

Crawford, B. 267
crosslag Z score profiles 89–92
Crozier, M. 391
Cuba 287, 292, 301, 305, 319, 320
culture 384–6, 394–404; of war 372–81
Cupitt, R. 41
Cushman, D. 388, 390
cybernetic steering model 120
Cyert, R. 286
Czechoslovakia 228–30, 232–3, 237–9,
    242, 328–30

Dallin, A. 70, 73, 74, 342, 364
de Gaulle, Charles 351, 398, 399
De La Serra, F. 401
de Toqueville 392
Dearborn, D. 299
decision-making 22–3, 161–2, 296–7, 321,
    384, 402–4, 460–1; as subject of study
    203–5, 293–4; in France 398–402;
    in Japan 394–7; processes of 122,
    205–9, 286–307, 387–8, 418; units of
    309–35
decision regimes 133, 247–67, 404, 449
DeFarge, P. 401
DeHaven, M. 1, 433–53
dependency theory 435
DePorte, A. 401–2
DeRivera, J. 206, 268
Dessler, D. 41
d'Estaing, Giscard 400
Destler, I. 310, 364, 396
Detzer, D. 287
Deutsch, K. 17, 79
development theory 53–5
Diamond, L. 17
Diesing, P. 179, 199, 374
Dietterich, T. 226
Dill, W. 253
Dimensionality of Nations (DON)
    25–6
disputes 179, 181, 196, 197
Dixon, W. 8, 29, 37, 48, 77–95, 176, 450,
    453
Doi, L. T. 388
Dolman, A. 250
Doran, C. 383
Dorff, R. 306
Dorr-Breeme, D. 260
Downs, A. 110
Duffy, G. 243
Dulles, J. 114
Duncan, G. 83
Durbin-Watson 451
Dye, T. 165
Dynes, P. 109
Dyson, J. 9, 203–20, 290, 308, 364

East, M. 7, 28, 34, 40, 154, 340, 364, 410, 428, 429, 430, 456, 457, 460
Easton, D. 280
Eckstein, H. 55, 227
economic structures 3, 43–7, 214, 428
Edwards, W. 243
Einhorn, H. 225
Eisenhower, D. 104, 441, 444, 446, 452
El Salvador 319, 401
Eldridge, A. 364
environmental variables 24–5, 269, 270, 361, 414–19, 423, 430, 431, 434, 456
Erikson, B. 234
Ermath, F. 233
Ernst, M. 465
escalation 178, 179–81, 242–4
Etheredge, L. 310, 335
Etzioni, A. 109
Euromissiles 436–7
European Community 471
Evans, P. 44, 226
events data 7–8, 17, 18, 26, 35, 40, 42, 141–2
exchange theory 280, 282

Faletto, E. 35, 50
Falkowski, L. 268
Farrands, C. 100, 398
Farrel, R. 341
Farris, L. 232
Faurby, I. 5, 14
Fay, B. 20
Feierabend, I. K. 115
Feigenbaum, E. 224
Ferguson, Y. 32
Fillmore, C. 244
Finkelstein 467
Finlay, D. J. 102, 103
Fischer, C. 268
Fischer, F. 383
Fischer, M. 238
Ford, Gerald 106, 441, 444, 446, 447, 452
foreign policy 1–4, 6, 17, 28–9, 41–2, 105–6, 164, 165, 247–8, 362–3, 413, 415; anomalies of 111–12; as adaptive behavior 119, 120–9; as belief systems 374–81; as distinguished from domestic policy 3–4, 113–14, 129–30; decision units for 333; domestic sources of 44–5, 366–9, 378, 384–404, 456, 458; evaluation of 96–109, 112–14, 119, 128; in dyads 165–8; knowledge about 340, 370–1, 412; opposition to 325–6, 343, 361, 364; processes of 41, 42, 77, 78–9, 98, 358, 410, 413, 425; substitutability for 88–9, 136–40, 142, 151–3

foreign policy, comparative 61, 101–3, 129–30, 131–4; inquiries into 5–8, 13–31, 33–50, 141, 168–76, 221, 409–14, 420–2; pre theory of 23–4, 27, 28, 107–8, 161, 269–70, 414, 416, 434, 455
France 141, 385, 391–4, 400–1, 402, 403, 404
Frankel, J. 102
Fraser, N. 216, 220
Friedrich, C. 341
Frey, B. 37
Friedland, P. 238
Fu, K. 236
Fukui, H. 364, 395, 397

Galtung, J. 17
game theory 204, 214–19
Gamson, W. 48
Gardener, L. 226
General Agreement on Tariffs and Trade (GATT) 463, 464, 465, 470
George, A. 25, 32, 110, 176, 219, 231, 243, 268, 286, 289, 310, 313, 315, 321
George, L. 383
Germany 141, 367, 376, 377, 379
Gilpin, R. 50, 120
Ginsburgs, G. 470
Glass, G. 260
global institutions 378, 379
Gobalet, J. 17
Goblot 392
Gochman, C. 178, 198, 199, 370, 382
Golan, G. 233
Gold, D. 36, 37
Goldberg, R. N. 234
Gorbachev, Mikhail 62, 433
Gottlieb, T. 364
Gottman, J. 79
Gourevitch, P. 456
Graber, D. 208
Granick, D. 393
Gregg, P. M. 112
Griffen, K. 364
Gromyko, A. 70
Gross, E. 103, 109
gross national product (GNP) 459
Group of 77 468
Gurr, T. 117

Haas, E. 250, 455
Hacking, I. 250
Hagan, J. 12, 37, 226, 250, 268, 286, 306, 309–36, 339–65, 404, 426, 431, 432
Hagen, J. D. 364
Hall, P. 234
Halperin, M. 34, 310

Harf, J. 14, 456
Harris, M. 251
Hart, J. 41, 605
Hartmann, F. 102, 103
Hatch, J. 326
Hauslohner, P. 73
Haynes, J. 210
Hays–Roth, F. 226
Hazelwood, L. 174
Helleiner, G. 51
Hellman, D. 364
Henehan, M. 381
Heradstvelt, D. 208
Hermann, C. 4, 7, 8, 9, 13–32, 50, 55, 73,
    109, 154, 221, 243, 268, 280, 284, 306,
    309–36, 340, 364, 404, 409, 410, 412,
    428, 431, 434, 456
Hermann, M. 9, 29, 154, 221, 268, 307,
    309–36, 359, 363, 364, 404, 427, 434,
    456
Herring, R. 50
Herrmann, R. 335
Herz, J. 451
Heuer, R. 208
Hicks, A. 35
Hilsman, R. 349
Hipel, K. W. 220
Hirschberg, D. 238
Hirschmann, A. 35
Hitler, A. 194, 372
Hoaglin, D. 199
Hodnett, G. 74
Hoffman, F. 373
Hoffman, S. 224, 401
Hofstede, G. 385
Hogarth, R. 225
Hoggard, G. 26, 165, 369
Holbraad, C. 459, 462
Holland, H. 394, 395, 396, 397
Hollander, P. 64
Holsti, K. J. 102, 268, 270, 271, 274, 450,
    474
Holsti, O. 17, 289, 310, 362, 381, 425
Honeywell, M. 464
Hoole, F. 108
Hoovler, D. 489
Hopcroft, J. 238
Hopkins, R. 250, 473
Hopmann, P. T. 154, 335, 412, 431, 432
Hosoya, C. 364
Hottel, D. 268
House, E. 109
Hovet, T. 102, 103
Howard, N. 215, 216, 220
Howell, L. 452
Hudson, V. M. 48, 50, 90, 221, 270, 280,
    335

Hungary 237–9, 242
Hunter, J. 260
Hurwitz, L. 346
Hybel, A. 243
Hyde, A. 109
Hynes, N. 405

ideology 45–6
individual variables 34, 275–7, 387, 425
inductionism 19
influence 465–7
information processing 210–13
interdependence 3–4, 434–6, 454, 456,
    457, 469, 471; complex 121–5, 467,
    473
Intergovernmental Maritime
    Consultative Organization (IMCO)
    464
Intergovernmental Organizations (IGOs)
    454–73
International Atomic Energy Agency
    (IAEA) 463, 464
International Court of Justice 468
International Monetary Fund (IMF) 5, 464
Interstate Behavior Analysis (IBA) 27–8,
    340, 343
intuitive heuristics 209–10, 212
Iran 322–4
Iriye, Akira 386
Isaak, R. 268
Israel 321
issue areas 24, 26–7
Italo-Ethiopian War 189–90

Jackson, G. 260
Jackson, Vanik 453
Jacobson, H. 470
Jahrgang 243
James, R. 99, 370
Jameson, K. 35, 39
Janda, K. 354
Janis, I. 208, 268, 290, 310, 315, 321
Japan 11, 111–19, 153, 379, 385, 388–91,
    394–7, 402, 403, 404
Jenkins, G. 198
Jensen, L. 410, 420
Jervis, R. 154, 205, 268, 289, 307, 366,
    375
Job, B. 450
Jodice, D. 41
Johnson, D. 35
Johnson, Lyndon B. 105, 444, 446, 447
Johnson, M. 226, 286
Jones, E. 226
Jonsson, C. 266, 310, 474

Kaagan, L. 452

Kagan D. 5
Kahler, M. 456
Kahneman, D. 20, 225, 307
Kaminsky, E. 399
Kanouse, D. 226
Kaplan, M. 36, 495
Kaplan, S. 232, 495
Karns, M. 10, 48, 429, 432, 454–74
Kasai, T. 238
Katzenstein, P. 51, 459, 462, 463, 465, 466
Kaunda, Kenneth 314, 326–8
Kay, D. A. 457
Kean, J. 34
Keddie, N. 336
Kedes, L. 238
Kegley, C. W. 5, 9, 14, 16, 18, 19, 20, 21,
    22, 30, 33, 35, 47, 95, 133, 154, 221,
    247–68, 286, 362, 364, 378, 383, 431,
    436, 453, 456, 459, 464
Kelley, H. 226
Kennedy, John F. 105, 287, 288, 332, 333,
    441, 446, 447
Keohane, R. 35, 51, 250, 421, 423, 435,
    454, 456, 458, 459, 460, 466, 467, 469
Kernell 451
Khomeini, A. 322, 323
Khrushchev, N. 62, 199
Kick, E. 36
Kieser, A. 387
Kifner, J. 336
Kilgour, M. 215
Kinder, D. 268
Kindleberger, C. 460
King, S. 388, 482
Kirkpatrick, S. 208
Kissinger, H. 105, 110, 432
Kling, R. 226
Kogan, N. 321
Kohl, H. 341
Kohl, W. 286, 341
Koopmans, T. C. 114
Korany, B. 5
Korea 111–19, 302, 305, 368
Krasner, S. 37, 38, 39, 51, 154, 435, 457,
    459, 460, 472
Kratochwil, F. 109, 256
Kravik, R. 465
Kruskal, J. 236
Kuhn, T. 14, 19, 20, 21, 30
Kukui, H. 396
Kumar, A. 91
Kume, T. 389, 390

Lacqueur, W. 188
Lakatos, I. 20, 30
Lakoff, G. 226
Lampert, D. 32

Larson, D. 289
Lave, C. 154
Law of the Sea 469
Lea, G. 227
learning 371–2, 373, 379, 381, 465
Ledeen, M. 336
Lee, K. S. 378, 383, 498–9
legitimacy 38
Lehnert, W. 226
Leng, R. 8, 51, 178–99, 370, 377, 382
Lentner, H. 36, 38
Lenway, S. 267
Lepper, M. 332, 333
Lerche, C. 102
Levenshtein, V. I. 236
Levi, A. 306, 385
Levy, J. 176, 372
Lewin, K. 222
Lewis, W. 336
Liess, A. 232
Lijphart, A. 55, 176, 346
Liker, J. 89, 95
Lindblom, C. 35, 288
Lipset, S. 110
Lipson, C. 470
Lowi, T. 261

Machiavelli, N. 372
MacKuen, M. 351
Macridis, R. 102, 103, 401
Maggiotto, M. 374, 382, 453
Majak, R. 288, 413
Majeski, S. J. 243, 500
Mallory, J. 243
Mann, L. 208
Mannheim, K. 375
Mansbach, R. 32, 377, 464
Maoz, Z. 190, 370
March, J. 154, 261, 264, 286, 299
Martin, A. 38
Marxism 35
mass media 438
Matecki, B. E. 457
Maurice, M. 393
May, E. 226, 375
Mazmanian, D. 105
M'bow, A. M. 466
McArthur, Gen. Douglas 292
McClelland, C. 26, 449
McClosky, H. 249
McDermott, J. 226
McDonald, R. 354
McGaw, B. 260
McGowan, P. 14, 19, 22, 32, 34, 35, 36,
    37, 51, 411, 412, 456
McKeon, T. 307
McLellan, D. S. 226

McSweeney, A. J. 101
Mead, M. 260, 371, 381
Mefford, D. 9, 214, 221–44
Meltzer, R. 457
Merton, R. 110
Metraux, R. 260
Michalski, R. 226, 227
Michels, R. 110
Midlarsky, M. 37
military disputes 182–97
military expenditures 134–5, 138–40,
    143–53
Millar, T. B. 98
Milliband, R. 38, 51
Mingst, K. 10, 48, 428, 454–74
Mitchell, T. 226, 227
Mitterand, F. 401
Mlynar, Z. 233
MNC (MultiNational Corporation) 44
Modigliani, A. 48
Mohr, L. 109
Monsen, R. 340
Montias, J. M. 114
Moon, B. 8, 32, 33–52, 362, 409, 413, 432
Moore, D. 340
Morgenthau, H. 102, 103, 109, 382
Moroccan Crisis 193–4
Morris, C. T. 115
Most, B. 8, 136, 154, 155, 156, 176, 412,
    414, 416, 431
Mtshali, B. 326, 328
Mueller, J. 375, 438, 439, 440, 441, 451
multilateralism 469, 470
Munton, D. 15

Nadler, L. 385
Nadler, M. 385
Nagel, S. 109
Nash, J. 216
national attributes 26, 163, 369, 458–9,
    473
national interest 38
Neo-positivism 18–19, 20
Neustadt, R. E. 310, 364, 451
Newell, A. 217, 241, 302
Nicaragua 468
Nicolson, H. 98
NIEO 266, 267
Nisbett, R. 211, 307
Nitze, P. 266
Norpoth, H. 451
North, R. 17, 32, 366, 370, 381
North Atlantic Treaty Organization
    (NATO) 49, 433
Notarius, C. 83
Novotony, A. 232, 233
Nuclear Test Ban Treaty 332–3

Nye, J. S. 124, 421, 435, 454, 456, 458,
    459, 466, 467

OECD 116, 459, 461, 468
Offe, C. 35, 37, 38
Ogarkov, M. 70
O'Connor, J. 35, 37, 38, 45
O'Leary, M. 26, 27, 41
Olsen, J. 261, 264
Olson, M. 115
Onuf, N. 259
Ore, O. 240
Organski, A. F. K. 102, 103
Ortony, A. 226
Osgood, R. 102
Ostrom, C. 450

Paige, G. 23, 217, 220, 290
Paldam, M. 451
Palmer, G. 73
Papadakis, M. 10, 108, 362, 364, 409–32,
    456, 458
Park, T. W. 112
Parsons, T. 109
Pastor, R. 461, 506
Patterson, T. 226
Patton, M. 99
Payer, C. 464
Payne, J. 210
Peacock, G. 4, 8, 13–32, 34, 95, 154, 221,
    274, 335, 409, 456
Pearl Harbor 367
Pearson, F. 102
Peck, R. 465
Pelikan, J. 233
perception 23
Perlmutter, A. 317
permeability 435–6, 449, 450, 456, 459
Perrow, C. 103, 109
Peterson, T. 238
Petras, J. 35
Phelps, R. 210
Phillips, W. 154
Physical Quality of Life Index (PQLI) 459
political economy 33–50, 456
Popper, K. 20
Potter, W. 364, 464
Poulantzas, N. 37, 38, 51
Powell, C. 9, 14, 33, 203–20, 290, 308,
    364, 456
power 281, 420–3, 426, 431
power politics 369–71, 372–3
Prebisch, R. 466
Price, J. 109
Prisoner's Dilemma 215, 216
Programmed International Computer
    Environment (PRINCE) 26–7

Proust, M. 248
Puchala, D. 102, 103, 250, 268, 364
Purkitt, H. 9, 203–20, 286, 290, 308, 364

Qaddafi, M. 314
quantification 7
Quinlan, J. 227

Radford, K. 215
Rainey, G. 102
Ranney, A. 261
Rapaport, A. 214
Rapkin, D. 36, 460
Rashid, T. 432
rationality 294–5; models of 253–4
Rawls, L. 268
Raymond, G. 8, 96–110, 221, 268, 286,
    378, 383
Reagan, Ronald 440
realism 369–70, 372
receptivity 465, 469
reciprocity 7–8, 179–81
Redner, R. 104
regimes 339–54, 356, 357–64, 454, 457–8,
    473; analysis of 250–1, 255
Regley 109
Remington, R. 233
Reynolds, L. G. 119
Reynolds, P. A. 102
Rhodesia 326–8
Richardson, N. 8, 25, 35, 37, 47, 48, 79,
    95, 161–77, 450
Richter, G. 174
Riggs, R. E. 457, 465, 471
Riker, W. 281
Ringle, M. 226
Roberts, A. 233
Robinson, J. 249, 288, 413
Robinson, W. 233
Rochester, J. M. 102
Roeder, P. 266
Rogers, W. 320
role theory 270–84
Roosevelt, F. 382
Ropp, S. 335, 364
Rosati, J. 33, 154, 268, 311, 313, 362, 364
Rosecrance, R. 102, 153
Rosenau, J. 1–10, 13, 14, 15, 16, 17, 19,
    23, 24, 25, 26, 27, 30, 31, 33, 34, 36,
    53–74, 113, 154, 155, 176, 220, 268,
    286, 361, 362, 364, 369, 409, 411, 412,
    414, 415, 416, 431, 434, 435, 450, 451,
    455, 456, 458
Rosenbloom, P. 227
Ross, L. 211, 307
Rossi, P. 101
Rothe, F. 451

Rothgeb, J. 45
Rothstein, R. 255, 422, 423, 424, 428
Rouleau, E. 336
Rowe, A. 253
Rubenstein, A. Z. 470
Rubin, B. 336
Ruggie, J. 250
Rumelhart, D. 226
Rummel, R. 24, 25, 26, 27, 31, 34, 37, 49,
    176, 177, 370, 410
Russett, B. M. 37, 112, 177, 340, 383, 411,
    421, 431, 467
Rutman, L. 100
Ruttenberg, G. 117

Sabatier, P. 105
Sacerdotti, E. D. 241
Sackett, G. 85
Said, A. 102
Salmore, B. & S. 7, 154, 162, 340, 364,
    365, 410, 428
Sampson, M. 10, 384–405
Sapin, B. 22, 155, 220, 285, 288, 366, 414,
    434
Sarbin, T. 274
Sato, P. 364, 396
Sausnock, J. 268
Sawyer, J. 410
Sayle, M. 74
Schank, R. 208
Schechter, M. 108, 472
Schelling, T. 78, 268
Schlesinger, A. 289
Schmidt, F. 260
Schonfeld 392
Schoultz, L. 105
Schraeder, P. 268
Schreider, J. 236
Schrodt, P. 95, 243
Schuetz, A. 222
Schwartz, M. 364
science 18, 19, 20–1
Scott, R. 109
Scriven, M. 98
Seabury, P. 98
Seashore, S. 109
security dilemma 369
Sellers, P. 234
Selznick, P. 110
Semmel, A. 310, 321
sequence analysis 79–95, 225–42
Shanteau, J. 210
Shapiro, H. 14, 19
Sharp, M. 100
Shaw, T. 326, 328
Shermann, F. 232
Shevechenko, A. 57

Shinkwiler, J. 450
Sick, G. 336
Simes, D. 233
Simis, K. 74
Simon, H. 109, 120, 241, 226, 227, 268, 286, 299, 302
Sinai, J. 188
Singer, J. D. 34, 37, 154, 156, 157, 268, 368, 381, 431, 432
Singer, E. 95, 221, 270, 280, 281, 335, 368, 369, 370, 372, 373, 374, 380, 412, 415, 416
situation analysis 222
Siverson, R. 8, 83, 154, 157
Six-Day War 188–9
Skilling, H. 233
Skinner, R. A. 14
Slovic, P. 220, 307
Small, M. 34, 37, 156, 157, 372
Smelser, N. 171
Smith, S. 5, 15, 336
Smoke, R. 232
Smouts, M. 398
Snyder, D. 36
Snyder, G. 374
Snyder, R. C. 22, 23, 24, 25, 26, 27, 28, 30, 31, 34, 155, 217, 220, 223, 285, 288, 289, 414, 434
social psychology 203–4, 209–11, 214
Soderstrom, E. J. 101
Sorensen, T. 287, 289
Soviet Union 54, 332, 342, 397
Spanier 102, 103
Spiegel, S. 450
Spielman, K. 364
Sprout, H. and M. 24, 155, 414, 415, 416, 456
Stanley, J. 169
Starr, H. 89, 136, 153, 154, 155, 156, 176, 307, 311, 409–32, 456, 458, 467, 473
States 3, 36–40, 162–4, 472; closed 360, 463; hegemonic 459–60, 472; large 459, 461; middle 461, 462; open 360, 434–8, 449, 463; small 420–431, 461, 462, 468, 469
Steers, R. 109
Steinbruner, J. 240, 310
Steiner, J. 206, 306
Steiner, M. 268
Steiner, Z. 387
Stempel, J. D. 336
Stephens, J. 45
Sternberg, R. 226
Stewart, E. 390, 400
Stoessinger, J. 314
Strange, S. 255, 457
Stremlau, J. 73, 102

Stuart, D. 311
Sullivan, M. 37, 154, 420
Sundelius, B. 464
Sutter, R. 364
Swank, D. 35
Swanson, D. 358
Sylvan, David 243
Sylvan, Donald 206, 208, 243, 268, 286, 306
Szanton, P. 310

Taiwan 111–14
Tanaka, E. 238
Tangier 193
Tanter, R. 177
Tatu, M. 233
Taylor, S. 340
Teng, C. C. 112
Tennefoss, M. 141, 157
Terrill, R. 364
Tetlock, P. 306, 310
theories, of foreign policy 21–3, 410; of single countries 53–5, 59–72; structural 37–9
Thies, W. 105
Thomas, A. J. 320
Thomas, A. V. 320
Thompson, K. 102, 103, 247
Thorson, S. 208
Tigrid, P. 233
Ting-Toomey, S. 390
Todaro 41
Tomlin, B. 42, 51
transnational relations 457–8, 466, 473
Truman, Harry 104, 226, 291, 444, 446, 451
Tsuji, K. 389
Tullis, F. L. 39
Turner, J. 405
Tversky, A. 220, 225, 307

Ullman, J. 238
UNCTAD 466, 468, 470
UNESCO 466
Union of Soviet Socialist Republics 55–72, 81–94, 329, 434, 436–8
United States 81–94, 438–50

Valenta, J. 230, 233, 328, 329, 330, 364
Valins, S. 226
Van Lehn, K. 226
Vannicelli, P. 364
Vasquez, J. 9, 366–83, 464
Velleman, P. 199
Verba, S. 171, 176
Vere, S. 227
Vietnam War 301, 302, 305, 341, 342, 362, 368, 379, 401

Vincent, J. 47, 452
Volensky, M. 230, 243
Voslensky, M. 240

Walker, S. 9, 32, 36, 37, 51, 199, 268,
   269–84, 286, 311, 313, 362, 423, 432
Wallace, W. 398, 399
Wallach, M. 321
Wallensteen 108, 372, 381, 382, 383
Wallerstein, I. 35, 36, 46
Walters, R. 35
Waltz, D. 224
Waltz, K. 154, 273, 281, 284, 364
war 367–9, 372, 375–7
Ward,M. 91
Weaver, J. 35, 39, 224
Weber, M. 109
Wedberg, R. 220
Weede, E. 410
Weiner, B. 226
Weinstein, F. 364
Weiss, J. 268
Wendzel, R. 102, 103
Wheeler, H. 51, 198
Wicker, T. 74
Wildavsky, A. 110, 210
Wilkenfeld, J. 17, 27, 31, 37, 48, 286, 340,
   370
Wilks 244

Wilson, P. 211
Windsor, P. 233
Winograd, T. 244
Winston, P. 224, 226
Winters, K. 163
Wish, N. 278
Wittkopf, E. 10, 268, 374, 382, 433–53,
   459
Wittman, A. 217
Wolfers, A. 102, 103
World Health Organization (WHO) 464
world system analysis 35
Wright, E. 38

Yankelovich, D. 452
Yantek, T. 451
Yeaton, W. 104
Young, O. 355
Yost, C. 102, 254
Yuchtman, E. 109
Yugoslavia 229–30

Zagare, F. 215
Zagladin, V. V. 230
Zambia 326–8
Zho En-lai 314
Zimmerman, W. 73, 464
Zinnes, D. 19, 26, 37, 48, 154, 335, 412,
   431, 432